BASIC FINANCIAL MANAGEMENT
Frequently Used Symbols

Dr. Derald Walling
Professor Emeritus of Mathematics
Texas Tech University
Lubbock, TX 79409-1042

α_t	Certainty equivalent coefficient in period t		MCC	Marginal cost of capital
ACF_t	Annual after-tax expected cash flow in time period t		MIRR	Modified internal rate of return
AROR	Accounting rate of return		NPV	Net present value
ß	Beta of an asset, the slope of the regression or characteristic line		PMT	Periodic level payment of an annuity
			P/E	Price/earnings ratio
DCL	Degree of combined leverage		PV	Present value
DFL	Degree of financial leverage		PVIF	Present value interest factor
DOL	Degree of operating leverage		PVIFA	Present value interest factor for an annuity
EAA	Equivalent annual annuity		R	Investor's required and/or expected rate of return
EBIT	Earnings before interest and taxes			
EOQ	Economic order quantity		R_f	Risk free rate of return
EPS	Earnings per share		ROA	Return on assets
FV	Future value		ROE	Return on common equity
FVIF	Future value interest factor		RP	Risk premium
FVIFA	Future value interest factor for an annuity		SML	Security market line
g	Annual growth rate		σ	Standard deviation (lowercase sigma)
IO	the initial cash outlay		σ^2	Variance (standard deviation squared)
IRR	Internal rate of return		TIE	Times interest earned
Kc	Cost of internal common equity (also Kc)		T	Tax rate
Kd	After-tax cost of debt		WCC	Weighted cost of capital
Ko	Weighted cost of capital		W_d, W_c	Percentage (weights) of funds provided by debt and common equity respectively
Kp	Cost of preferred stock			
M/B	Market-to-book ratio		YTM	Yield to maturity

D1545003

If you're as smart as we think you are, the pizza's on HP.

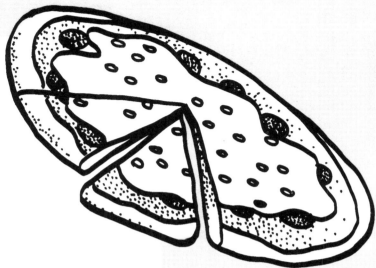

So, you're taking a class in finance. That makes you pretty special in HP's book — because the HP 17BII is part of your book.

This textbook includes keystroke procedures for using the HP 17BII calculator. You'll learn how to calculate basic time and money functions, net present value, internal rate of return, and a multitude of other financial functions on the HP 17BII.

The HP 17BII is a powerful calculator to use and easy to learn. Buying one today is an investment in your education, as well as an investment in your career — a double return on your investment.

And, if you purchase an HP 17BII today, we'll send you $10. Buy yourself a pizza on HP — we'll be there beside you through the all-night study sessions.

The HP 17BII will boost your grades, the pizza will boost your spirits.

Rebate Terms and Limitations

Purchases made before November 1, 1993 or after December 31, 1994 are not eligible for this rebate. Offer good on HP 17BII only. Offer limited to one rebate per product purchased, and one rebate per customer. This coupon may be used for only one rebate claim. Offer is not redeemable at retailer. All purchases must be made in the U.S.A. Rebate will be sent only to U.S.A. addresses. Purchases must be valid only in accordance with terms set forth. If these terms and conditions are not met, rebate checks will not be issued. Offer is not valid in conjunction with any other Hewlett-Packard offer. Hewlett-Packard employee orders are ineligible. Hewlett-Packard is not responsible for requests lost, damaged, or delayed in shipping. Void where prohibited, taxed, or restricted by law. All rebates will be paid in U.S. dollars. Rebate checks are void if not cashed within 90 days of issuance, and cannot be reissued. All incomplete or illegible claims will be returned for resubmission. All resubmitted claims are subject to these same terms and conditions, including postmark and receipt restrictions.

Hewlett-Packard reserves the right to confirm identification. All documentation submitted with this claim becomes the property of HP and cannot be returned. Additional restrictions may apply to government agencies.

Yes! I want $10 back on my purchase of the HP 17BII.

FOUNDATIONS
OF
FINANCE

The Logic and Practice of Financial Management

Arthur J. Keown

Virginia Polytechnic Institute and State University
R.B. Pamplin Professor of Finance

David F. Scott, Jr.

University of Central Florida
Holder, Phillips-Schenck Chair in Amercan Private Enterprise
and Professor of Finance

John D. Martin

University of Texas at Austin
Margaret and Eugene McDermott Professor of Banking
and Finance

J. William Petty

Baylor University
Caruth Professor of Entrepreneurship

Prentice Hall
Englewood Cliffs, New Jersey 07632

Library of Congress Cataloging-in-Publication Data

Foundations of finance: the logic and practice of financial
   management/Arthur J. Keown . . . [et al.].
     p. cm.
   Includes bibliographical references and index.
   ISBN 0-13-211020-2:
    1. Corporations—Finance.   I. Keown, Arthur J.
HG4026.F67   1994
  658.15—dc20   93-4329
                                            CIP

Acquisitions Editor: *Leah Jewell*
Production Service: *Burmar Technical Corporation*
Liaison for Production: *Edith Pullman*
Interior and Cover Designer: *Meryl Poweski*
Manufacturing Buyer: *Patrice Fraccio*
Editorial Assistant: *Eileen Deguzman*

Cover Art: *Ellen Schuster/The Image Bank*

© 1994 by Prentice-Hall, Inc.
A Paramount Communications Company
Englewood Cliffs, New Jersey 07632

Printed in the Untited States of America

10 9 8 7 6 5 4 3

ISBN 0-13-211020-2

Prentice-Hall International (UK) Limited, *London*
Prentice-Hall of Australia Pty. Limited, *Sydney*
Prentice-Hall Canada Inc., *Toronto*
Prentice-Hall Hispanoamericana, *Mexico*
Prentice-Hall of India Private Limited, *New Delhi*
Prentice-Hall of Japan, Inc., *Tokyo*
Simon & Schuster Asia Pte. Ltd., *Singapore*
Editora Prentice-Hall do Brasil, Ltda., *Rio de Janerio*

Foundations of Finance
Dedication

"To my parents, from whom I learned the most."
—Arthur J. Keown

"To my wife, Peggy, and her parents, Dorothy J. and Wilbur D. Pierce."
—David F. Scott, Jr.

"In loving memory of my mother who was ever encouraging and to my father whose life I seek to emulate."
—John D. Martin

"In memory and appreciation of my parents, John and Kate Petty, for their enduring love and constant encouragement."
—J. William Petty

CONTENTS

PREFACE

This book was born in the classroom to provide students with a conceptual understanding of the financial decision-making process, rather than just an introduction to the tools and techniques of finance. It is all too easy for students to lose sight of the logic that drives finance and focus instead on memorizing formulas and procedures. As a result, students have trouble understanding the interrelationships among the topics covered. Moreover, later in life when problems encountered do not match the textbook presentation, students may find themselves unprepared to abstract from what they learned. To overcome this problem, the opening chapter presents nine principles or axioms of finance, which serve as a springboard for the chapters and topics that follow. In essence, the student is presented with a cohesive, interrelated perspective from which future problems can be approached.

Teaching a one-semester introductory finance class while facing an ever-expanding discipline puts added pressures on the instructor. What to cover, what to omit, and how to do this while maintaining a cohesive presentation are inescapable questions. In dealing with these questions and tightening the focus of the text, we found it helpful to trim the content so that most of the material can be covered in one semester. The reduced content helps to maintain a focus on the underlying principles that drive finance rather than attempt to cover concepts and techniques that are better presented in an intermediate finance course. Again, our goal is to provide an enduring understanding of the basic tools and principles on which finance is based.

With a focus on the big picture, we provide an introduction to financial decision making rooted in current financial theory and in the current state of world economic conditions. This focus is perhaps most apparent in the attention given to the capital markets and their influence on corporate financial decisions. What results is an introductory treatment of a discipline rather than the treatment of a series of isolated problems that face the financial manager. The goal of this text is not merely to teach the tools of a discipline or trade but also to enable students to abstract what is learned to new and yet unforeseen problems — in short, to educate the student in finance.

■ DISTINCTIVE FEATURES

Foundations of Finance is not "yet another introductory finance text." Its structure reflects the vitality and expanding nature of the discipline. Finance has grown too comprehensive to continue to teach in a business-as-usual manner, and it has grown too complex to teach without an eye on the big picture, focusing on the interrelationships to be found in what is covered. Listed below are some of the distinctive pedagogical features presented in this book.

NINE AXIOMS OF FINANCE: The principles that drive the practice of corporate finance are presented in nine axioms in Chapter 1. They reappear throughout the text in "Back to the Fundamentals" inserts, which aim to remind students of the underlying principles and to keep students from becoming so immersed in specific calculations that the interrelationships and overall scheme are lost.

PERSPECTIVES IN FINANCE: Inserts entitled *Perspectives in Finance* appear throughout the text to redirect students' attention to the "big picture." Although tools, techniques, and calculations are treated extensively, the use of these Perspectives, as well as the nine axioms, keep the student from losing sight of the interrelationships and motivating factors behind the tools.

FINANCIAL MANAGEMENT IN PRACTICE: Practice is used throughout the text to demonstrate the implementation of theory and is enlivened by "Financial Management in Practice" boxes.

ETHICS IN FINANCIAL MANAGEMENT: We have made a concerted effort to identify some important ethical issues as they relate to financial decision making. In addition to these *Ethics in Financial Management* boxes, which appear in the text, four ethics cases are included in the Instructor's Manual to stimulate constructive classroom dialogue.

INTERNATIONAL FINANCIAL MANAGEMENT: In view of the globalization of world markets, we have integrated international finance into the text through *International Financial Management* boxes. In addition, recognizing that many of us approach the teaching of international finance in different ways, a chapter specifically on international financial management is provided.

SUGGESTED APPLICATIONS FOR DISCLOSURE®: Students frequently have difficulty transferring knowledge to live situations; it is one thing to understand how to work an end-of-chapter problem, but quite another to apply that understanding to an actual company. We are therefore pleased that Prentice Hall has developed an agreement with Disclosure, Incorporated, for the users of Foundations of Finance to have access to the academic edition of Compact DTM/SEC. This database, designed for designed for the personal computer, contains financial and management information on 100 publicly traded firms. Company data is taken from annual and periodic reports filed with the Securities and Exchange Commission. The firms have been selected for their diversity and appropriateness for the classroom. Approximately half the chapters have suggested uses for the database relative to the material in the respective chapter. The use of the database truly takes the student to a higher level of learning.

ABD NEW/PH VIDEO LIBRARY FOR FINANCE: Video cases selected from ABC News are available to all adopters. To enhance the use of the selected ABC News video tapes, a written introduction to each video is presented, followed by a concluding discussion, questions, and suggested readings at the end of the chapter. These introductions and conclusions greatly improve the effectiveness of the videos in the classroom.

FINANCIAL CALCULATORS: The use of financial calculators has been integrated into this text, especially with respect to the presentation of the time value of money. Where appropriate, calculator solutions appear in the margin for the student.

A final, but important, comment to the teacher: We know how frustrating errors in a textbook or instructor's manual can be. Thus, we have worked diligently to provide you with as error-free a book as possible. Not only did we check and recheck the answers ourselves, but Prentice Hall hired faculty members at other universities to check the accuracy of the problem solutions. We therefore make the following offer to users of Foundations of Finance:

Any professor or student identifying an error of substance (for example, an incorrect number in an example or problem) in *Foundations of Finance*, in either the text or the instructor's manual, that has not been previously reported to the authors will receive a $10 reward. If a series of related errors occurs resulting from an original error, the reward will be limited to a maximum of $20 for the group of errors. Please report any errors to Art Keown at the following address:

Art Keown
Department of Finance
Virginia Tech
Blacksburg, VA 24061

■ ACKNOWLEDGEMENTS

We gratefully acknowledge the assistance, support, and encouragement of those individuals who have contributed to *Foundations of Finance*. Specifically, we wish to recognize the very helpful insights provided by many of our colleagues. For their careful comments and helpful reviews of the text, we are indebted to:

Sung C. Bae
Bowling Green State University

Laurey Berk
University of Wisconsin Green Bay

Laurence E. Blose
University of North Carolina Charlotte

Robert Boldin
Indiana University of Pennsylvania

Michael Bond
Cleveland State University

Waldo L. Born
Eastern Illinois University

Paul Bursik
St. Norbert College

Perikolam Raman Chandy
University of North Texas

Santosh Choudhury
Norfolk State University

K. C. Chen
California State University Fresno

Jeffrey S. Christensen
Youngstown State University

M. C. Chung
California State University Sacramento

Steven M. Dawson
University of Hawaii

Yashwant S. Dhatt
University of Southern Colorado

John W. Ellis
Colorado State University

Suzanne Erickson
Seattle University

Slim Feriani
George Washington University

Greg Filbeck
Miami University

Ken Halsey
Wayne State College

James D. Harris
University of North Carolina Wilmington

Dr. Linda C. Hittle
San Diego State University

Steve Johnson
University of Texas at El Paso

Ravi Kamath
Cleveland State University

James D. Keys
Florida International University

Reinhold P. Lamb
University of North Carolina Charlotte

Larry Lang
University of Wisconsin

George B. F. Lanigan
University of North Carolina Greensboro

William R. Lasher
Nichols College

David E. Letourneau
Winthrop University

Judy E. Maese
New Mexico State University

Abbas Mamoozadeh
Slippery Rock University

James E. McNulty
Florida Atlantic University

Emil Meurer
University of New Orleans

Stuart Michelson
Eastern Illinois University

Eric J. Moon
San Francisco State University

Scott Moore
John Carroll University

M.P. Narayanan
University of Michigan

William E. O'Connell Jr.
College of William & Mary

Jeffrey H. Peterson
St. Bonaventure University

Mario Picconi
University of San Diego

Stuart Rosenstein
Clemson University

Ivan C. Roten
Arizona State University

Marjorie A. Rubash
Bradley University

Joseph Stanford
Bridgewater State College

David Suk
Rider College

Elizabeth Sun
San Jose State University

R. Bruce Swensen
Adelphi University

Philip R. Swensen
Utah State University

Lee Tenpao
Niagara University

Paul A. Vanderheiden
*University of Wisconsin
Eau Claire*

K. G. Viswanathan
Hofstra University

Al Webster
Bradley University

Patricia Webster
Bradley University

Herbert Weinraub
Michigan State University

Herbert Weinraub
University of Toledo

Sandra Williams
Moorhead State University

Wold Zemedkun
Norfolk State University

Marc Zenner
Indiana University

We also wish to thank a wonderful group of people at Prentice Hall. To Leah Jewel we owe a debt of gratitude that is immeasurable. Her efforts on this text went well beyond what one might expect from the best of editors. Without her insights, efforts, and prodding this book would have never come to fruition. We also offer our personal expression of appreciation to Eileen Deguzman for her adminstrative deftness; to Patti Arneson for her marketing genius; and to the Prentice Hall field representatives for their input based on interaction with teachers from across the nation. We salute Victoria McWilliams of Arizona State West for her diligent work throughout the text. Her comments and insights added greatly to the value of the book. We thank Clain Anderson at Hewlett Packard for his help in bringing to life the use of calculators in the teaching of financial management. In addition, we owe a debt of thanks to John Byrd of Washington State University for his outstanding work on the accompanying videos.

As a final word, we express our sincere thanks to those using Foundations of Finance in the classroom. We thank you for making us a part of your team. Always feel free to give any of us a call when you have questions or needs.

A.J.K.
D.F.S.
J.W.P.
J.D.M.

CHAPTER 1

AN INTRODUCTION TO THE FOUNDATIONS OF FINANCIAL MANAGEMENT —THE TIES THAT BIND

Goal of the Firm • Legal Forms of Business Organization • Federal Income Taxation • Nine Axioms That Form the Foundations of Financial Management • Overview of the Text

Financial management is concerned with the maintenance and creation of wealth. Consequently, this course focuses on decision making with an eye to creating wealth. In introducing decision-making techniques we will emphasize the logic behind those techniques, thereby ensuring that you don't lose sight of the concepts when dealing with the calculations. To the first-time student of finance this may sound a bit overwhelming, but as we will see, the techniques and tools introduced in this text are all motivated by nine underlying principles, or axioms, that will guide us through the decision-making process.

To lay a foundation for what will follow, we will begin by introducing the goal of the firm—maximization of shareholder wealth—which we will use as a guide in developing rules for decision making. Several alternative business forms, focusing on the corporate form and the tax environment in which the corporation exists, will then be introduced. In discussing the tax environment, we will concentrate only on that portion of the tax code that affects business decisions. Our attention will then turn to the nine axioms that form the foundation of financial management. Although these axioms may seem quite simple or even trivial, they will provide the driving force behind all that follows. They will also provide the threads that tie the concepts and techniques introduced in the chapters together, all driven to create wealth.

1

■ GOAL OF THE FIRM

In this text we designate the goal of the firm to be *maximization of shareholder wealth*, by which we mean maximization of the price of the existing common stock. Not only will this goal directly benefit the shareholders of the company, but it will also provide benefits to society. This will come about as scarce resources are directed to their most productive use by businesses competing to create wealth. With this goal in place, our job as a financial manager becomes to create wealth for the shareholders. To better understand this goal, we will first discuss profit maximization as a possible goal for the firm. Then we will compare it to maximization of shareholder wealth to see why, in financial management, the latter is the more appropriate goal for the firm.

Profit Maximization

In microeconomics courses, profit maximization is frequently given as the goal of the firm. Profit maximization stresses the efficient use of capital resources, but it is not specific with respect to the time frame over which profits are to be measured. Do we maximize profits over the current year, or do we maximize profits over some longer period? A financial manager could easily increase current profits by eliminating research and development expenditures and cutting down on routine maintenance. In the short run, this might result in increased profits, but this clearly is not in the best long-run interests of the firm. If we are to base financial decisions on a goal, that goal must be precise, not allow for misinterpretation, and deal with all the complexities of the real world.

In microeconomics, profit maximization functions largely as a theoretical goal, with economists using it to prove how firms behave rationally to increase profit. Unfortunately, it ignores many real-world complexities that financial managers must address in their decisions. In the more applied discipline of financial management, firms must deal every day with two major factors not considered by the goal of profit maximization: uncertainty and timing.

Microeconomics courses ignore uncertainty and risk to present theory more easily. Projects and investment alternatives are compared by examining their expected values or weighted average profits. Whether one project is riskier than another does not enter into these calculations; economists do discuss risk, but only tangentially.[1] In reality, projects differ a great deal with respect to risk characteristics, and to disregard these differences in the practice of financial management can result in incorrect decisions. As we will discover later in this chapter, there is a very definite relationship between risk and expected return—that is, investors demand a higher expected return for taking on added risk—and to ignore this relationship would lead to improper decisions.

[1]See, for example, Robert S. Pindyck and Daniel Rubenfield, *Microeconomics*, 2d ed. (New York: Macmillan, 1992), pp. 244–46.

Another problem with the goal of profit maximization is that it ignores the timing of the project's returns. If this goal is only concerned with this year's profits, we know it inappropriately ignores profit in future years. If we interpret it to maximize the average of future profits, it is also incorrect. Inasmuch as investment opportunities are available for money in hand, we are not indifferent to the timing of the returns. Given equivalent cash flows from profits, we want those cash flows sooner rather than later. Thus, the real-world factors of uncertainty and timing force us to look beyond a simple goal of profit maximization as a decision criterion. We will turn now to an examination of a more robust goal for the firm: maximization of shareholder wealth.

Maximization of Shareholder Wealth

In formulating the goal of maximization of shareholder wealth we are doing nothing more than modifying the goal of profit maximization to deal with the complexities of the operating environment. We have chosen maximization of shareholder wealth—that is, maximization of the market value of the existing shareholders' common stock—because the effects of all financial decisions are thereby included. Investors react to poor investment or dividend decisions by causing the total value of the firm's stock to fall, and they react to good decisions by pushing up the price of the stock. In effect, under this goal, good decisions are those that create wealth for the shareholder.

Obviously, there are some serious practical problems in direct use of this goal and in using changes in the firm's stock to evaluate financial decisions. Many things affect stock prices; to attempt to identify a reaction to a particular financial decision would simply be impossible. Fortunately, that is not necessary. To employ this goal, we need not consider every stock price change to be a market interpretation of the worth of our decisions. Other factors, such as changes in the economy, also affect stock prices. What we will focus on is the effect that our decision *should* have on the stock price if everything else were held constant. The market price of the firm's stock reflects the value of the firm as seen by its owners and takes into account the complexities and complications of the real-world risk. As we follow this goal throughout our discussions, we must keep in mind one more question: Who exactly are the shareholders? The answer: Shareholders are the legal owners of the firm.

■ LEGAL FORMS OF BUSINESS ORGANIZATION

In the chapters ahead we will focus on financial decisions for corporations. Although the corporation is not the only legal form of business available, it is the most logical choice for a firm that is large or growing. It is also the dominant business form in terms of sales in this country. In this section we will explain why this is so. This will in turn allow us to simplify the remainder of the text, as we will assume that the proper tax code to follow is the corporate tax code, rather than examine different tax codes for different legal forms of businesses. Keep in mind that our primary purpose is to develop an understanding of the logic of financial decision making. Taxes will become important only when they affect our decisions, and our discussion of the choice of the legal form of the business is directed at understanding why we will limit our discussion of taxes to the corporate form.

Legal forms of business organization are diverse and numerous. However, there are three categories: the sole proprietorship, the partnership, and the corporation. To understand the basic differences between each form, we need to define each form and understand its advantages and disadvantages. As we will see, as the firm grows, the advantages of the corporation begin to dominate. As a result, most large firms take on the corporate form.

Sole Proprietorship

The **sole proprietorship** is a business owned by a single individual. The owner maintains title to the assets and is personally responsible, generally without limitation, for the liabilities incurred. The proprietor is entitled to the profits from the business but must also absorb any losses. This form of business is initiated by the mere act of beginning the business operations. Typically, no legal requirement must be met in starting the operation, particularly if the proprietor is conducting the business in his or her own name. If a special name is used, an assumed-name certificate should be filed, requiring a small registration fee. Termination occurs on the owner's death or by the owner's choice. Briefly stated, the sole proprietorship is for all practical purposes the absence of any formal *legal* business structure.

Partnership

The primary difference between a **partnership** and a sole proprietorship is that the partnership has more than one owner. A partnership is an association of two or more persons coming together as co-owners for the purpose of operating a business for profit. Partnerships fall into two types: (1) general partnerships and (2) limited partnerships.

General Partnership

In a general partnership each partner is fully responsible for the liabilities incurred by the partnership. Also, any partner's ill conduct even having the appearance of relating to the firm's business renders the remaining partners liable as well. The relationship among partners is dictated entirely by the partnership agreement, which may be an oral commitment or a formal document.

Limited Partnership

In addition to the general partnership, in which all partners are jointly liable without limitation, many states provide for a limited partnership.

The state statutes permit one or more of the partners to have limited liability, restricted to the amount of capital invested in the partnership. Several conditions must be met to qualify as a limited partner. First, at least one general partner must remain in the association for whom the privilege of limited liability does not apply. Second, the names of the limited partners may not appear in the name of the firm. Third, the limited partners may not participate in the management of the business. If one of these restrictions is violated, all partners forfeit their right to limited liability. In essence, the intent of the statutes creating the limited partnership is to provide limited liability for a person whose interest in the partnership is purely as an investor. That individual may not assume a management function within the organization.

Corporation

The **corporation** has been a significant factor in the economic development of the United States. As early as 1819 Chief Justice John Marshall set forth the legal definition of a corporation as "an artificial being, invisible, intangible, and existing only in the contemplation of law."[2] This entity *legally* functions separate and apart from its owners. As such, the corporation can individually sue and be sued, and purchase, sell, or own property; and its personnel are subject to criminal punishment for crimes. However, despite this legal separation, the corporation is composed of owners who dictate its direction and policies. The owners elect a board of directors, whose members in turn select individuals to serve as corporate officers, including president, vice-president, secretary, and treasurer. Ownership is reflected in common stock certificates, designating the number of shares owned by its holder. The number of shares owned relative to the total number of shares outstanding determines the stockholder's proportionate ownership in the business. Because the shares are transferable, ownership in a corporation may be changed by a shareholder simply remitting the shares to a new shareholder. The investor's liability is confined to the amount of the investment in the company, thereby preventing creditors from confiscating stockholders' personal assets in settlement of unresolved claims. Finally, the life of a corporation is not dependent on the status of the investors. The death or withdrawal of an investor does not affect the continuity of the corporation. The management continues to run the corporation when stock is sold or when it is passed on through inheritance.

Comparison of Organizational Forms

Owners of new businesses have some important decisions to make in choosing an organizational form. Whereas each business form seems to have some advantages over the others, we will see that as the firm grows and needs access to the capital markets to raise funds, the advantages of the corporation begin to dominate.

---

[2]The Trustees of Dartmouth College v. Woodard, 4 Wheaton 636 (1819).

WHY LARGE AND GROWING FIRMS CHOOSE THE CORPORATE FORM: EASE IN RAISING CAPITAL. Because of the limited liability, the ease of transferring ownership through the sale of common shares, and the flexibility in dividing the shares, the corporation is the ideal business entity in terms of attracting new capital. In contrast, the unlimited liabilities of the sole proprietorship and the general partnership are deterrents to raising equity capital. Between the extremes, the limited partnership does provide limited liability for limited partners, which has a tendency to attract wealthy investors. However, the impracticality of having a large number of partners and the restricted marketability of an interest in a partnership prevent this form of organization from competing effectively with the corporation. Therefore, when developing our decision models we will assume we are dealing with the corporate form. The taxes incorporated in these models will deal only with the corporate tax codes. Because our goal is to develop an understanding of the management, measurement, and creation of wealth, and not to become tax experts, we will only focus on those characteristics of the corporate tax code that will affect our financial decisions.

◼ FEDERAL INCOME TAXATION

Before presenting the nine axioms of finance that will provide the conceptual underpinnings for what will follow, we will examine those tax features that will affect our decisions. We will describe the environment and set up the ground rules under which financial decisions are made. As the nations politics change, so does the tax system. The purpose of looking at the current tax structure is not to become tax experts, but rather to gain an understanding of taxes and how they affect business decisions. There is a good chance that corporate tax rates may change significantly before you enter the work force. However, although rates may change, taxes will continue to remain a cash outflow and therefore something to avoid. Thus, we will pay close attention to which expenses are and are not deductible for tax purposes, and in doing so focus on how taxes affect business decisions.

Objectives of Income Taxation

Originally, the sole objective of the federal government in taxing income was to generate financing for government expenditures. Although this purpose continues to be important, social and economic objectives have been added. For instance, a company may receive possible reductions in taxes if (1) it undertakes certain technological research, (2) it pays wages to certain economically disadvantaged groups or (3) if it locates in certain economically depressed areas. Other socially oriented stipulations in the tax laws include exemptions for dependents, old age, and blindness and a reduction in taxes on retirement income. In addition, the government uses tax legislation to stabilize the economy. In recessionary periods taxes may be reduced, giving the public more discretionary income in the hope that this income will be spent to increase the demand for products and thereby generate new jobs.

In short, three objectives may be given for the taxation of revenues: (1) the provision of revenues for government expenditures, (2) the achievement of socially desirable goals, and (3) economic stabilization.

Types of Taxpayers

To understand the tax system, we must first ask, "Who is the taxpayer?" For the most part, there are three basic types of taxable entities: individuals, corporations, and fiduciaries. Individuals include company employees, self-employed persons owning their own businesses, and members of a partnership. Income is reported by these individuals in their personal tax returns.[3] The corporation, as a separate legal entity, reports its income and pays any taxes related to these profits. The owners (stockholders) of the corporation need not report these earnings in their personal tax returns, except when all or a part of the profits are distributed in the form of dividends. Finally, fiduciaries, such as estates and trusts, file a tax return and pay taxes on the income generated by the estate or trust which isn't distributed to (and included in the taxable income of) a beneficiary.

Although taxation of individual and fiduciary income is an important source of income to the government, neither is especially relevant to the financial manager. Since most firms of any size are corporations, we will restrict our discussion to the corporation. A caveat is necessary, however. Tax legislation can be quite complex, with numerous exceptions to most general rules. The laws can also change quickly, and certain details discussed here may no longer apply in the near future. It sometimes is true that "a little knowledge is a dangerous thing."

Computing Taxable Income

The taxable income for a corporation is based on the gross income from all sources, except for allowable exclusions, less any tax-deductible expenses. *Gross income* equals the firm's dollar sales from its product less the cost of producing or acquiring the product. Tax-deductible expenses include any operating expenses, such as marketing expenses and administrative expenses. Also, *interest expense* paid on the firm's outstanding debt is a tax-deductible expense. However, dividends paid to the firm's stockholders, are *not* deductible expenses, but rather distributions of income. Other taxable income includes interest income and dividend income.

To demonstrate how to compute a corporation's taxable income, consider the J and S Corporation, a manufacturer of home accessories. The firm, originally established by Kelly Stites, had sales of $50,000,000 for the year. The cost of producing the accessories totaled $23,000,000. Operating expenses were $10,000,000. The corporation has $12,500,000 in debt outstanding, with an 8 percent interest rate, which resulted in $1,000,000 interest expense ($12,500,000 × .08 = $1,000,000). Management paid $1,000,000 in dividends to the firm's common stockholders. No other income, such as

---

[3]Partnerships report only the income from the partnership. The income is then reported again by each partner, who pays any taxes owed.

TABLE 1–1
J and S Corporation
Taxable Income

Sales		$50,000,000
Cost of goods sold		23,000,000
Gross profit		$27,000,000
Operating expenses		
Administrative expenses	$4,000,000	
Depreciation expenses	1,500,000	
Marketing expenses	4,500,000	
Total operating expenses		10,000,000
Operating income (earnings before interest and taxes)		$17,000,000
Other income		0
Interest expense		1,000,000
Taxable income		$16,000,000

Dividends paid to common stockholders ($1,000,000) are not tax-deductible expenses.

interest or dividend income, was received. The taxable income for the J and S Corporation would be $16,000,000, as shown in Table 1–1.

Once we know the J and S Corporation's taxable income, we can next determine the amount of taxes the firm will owe.

Computing the Taxes Owed

The taxes to be paid by the corporation on its taxable income are based on the corporate tax rate structure. The specific rates effective for the corporation, as of 1994, are given in Table 1–2. Under the Revenue Reconciliation Act of 1993 a new top marginal corporate tax rate of 35 percent was added for taxable income in excess of $10,000,000. Also, a surtax of 3 percent was imposed on taxable income between $15,000,000 and $18,333,333. This, in combination with the previously existing 5 percent surtax on taxable income between $100,000 and $335,000 recaptures the benefits of the lower marginal rates and as a result both the average and marginal tax rate on taxable income above $18,333,333 becomes 35 percent.

For example, the tax liability for the J and S Corporation, which had $16,000,000 in taxable earnings, would be $5,530,000, calculated as follows:

Earnings	×	Marginal Tax Rate	=	Taxes
$ 50,000	×	15%	=	$ 7,500
25,000	×	25%	=	6,250
9,925,000	×	34%	=	3,374,500
6,000,000	×	35%	=	2,100,000
				$5,488,250

Additional Surtaxes:
- Add 5% surtax on income between $100,000 and $335,000
  (5% × [$335,000 – $100,000])   11,750
- Add 3% surtax on income between $15,000,000 and $18,333,333
  (3% × [$16,000,000 – $15,000,000])   30,000

Total Tax Liability	$5,530,000

15%	$	0–$50,000
25%	$	50,001–$75,000
34%		$75,001–$10,000,000
35%		over $10,000,000

Additional surtax:
- 5% on income between $100,000 and $335,000.
- 3% on income between $15,000,000 and $18,333,333.

TABLE 1–2
Corporate Tax Rates

The tax rates shown in Table 1–2 are defined as the *marginal* tax rates, or rates applicable to the next dollar of income. For instance, if a firm has earnings of $60,000 and is contemplating an investment that would yield $10,000 in additional profits, the tax rate to be used in calculating the taxes on this added income is 25 percent; that is, the marginal tax rate is 25 percent. However, if the corporation already expects $20,000,000 without the new investment, the extra $10,000 in earnings would be taxed at 35 percent, the marginal tax rate. In the example, where the J and S Corporation has taxable income of $16,000,000, its marginal tax rate is 38 percent (this is because $16,000,000 falls into the 35% tax bracket *with* a 3% surtax); that is, any additional income from new investments will be taxed at a rate of 38 percent. However, after taxable income exceeds $18,333,333, the marginal tax rate declines to 35 percent, when the 3 percent surtax no longer applies.

For financial decision making, it's the *marginal tax rate* rather than the average tax rate that we will be concerned with. As will become increasingly clear throughout the text, we always want to consider the tax consequences of any financial decision. The appropriate rate to be used in the analysis is the marginal tax rate, because it is this rate that will be applicable for any changes in earnings as a result of the decision being made. Thus, when making financial decisions involving taxes, always use the marginal tax rate in your calculations.[4]

The tax rate structure used in computing the J and S Corporation's taxes assumes that the income occurs in the United States. Given the globalization of the economy, it may well be that some of the income originates in a foreign country. If so, the tax rates, and the method of taxing the firm, frequently vary. Table 1–3 sheds some light on the basic differences in tax rates in several industrialized countries. As financial manager, you would minimize the firm's taxes by reporting as much income as possible in the low-tax-rate countries and as little as possible in the high-tax-rate countries. Of course, other factors, such as political risk, may discourage your efforts to minimize taxes across national borders.

---

[4]On taxable income between $335,000 and $10,000,000, both the marginal and average tax rates equal 34 percent, owing to the imposition of the 5 percent surtax that applies to taxable income between $100,000 and $335,000. After the company's taxable income exceeds $18,333,333, both the marginal and average tax rate equal 35 percent, because the 3 percent surtax on income between $15,000,000 and $18,333,333 eliminates the benefits of having the first $10,000,000 of income taxed at 34 rather than 35 percent.

TABLE 1–3
Comparison of Foreign Taxes

Country	Income Tax Rates	Value-Added Tax	Other Taxes
France	42%	5.5% on food items; up to 33.3% on luxury items	
Japan	42% on income not distributed to stockholders; 32% if distributed		Excise taxes on consumer goods; 13.2% local taxes
Korea	20%–33%	10% on goods and services	
United Kingdom	25%–35%	15% on goods and services	
West Germany	56% on income not distributed to stockholders; 36% if distributed	14% on goods and services	

Source: *International Tax Summaries,* Coopers & Lybrand International Tax Network (New York: Wiley, 1989).

Other Tax Considerations

In addition to the fundamental computation of taxes, several other aspects of the existing tax legislation have relevance for the financial manager. These are (1) the dividend income exclusion for corporations, (2) the effects of depreciation on the firm's taxes, (3) the tax treatment of operating losses, and (4) the recognition of capital gains and losses. We also need to consider any additional taxes that may be imposed on a firm for the "excessive accumulation" of profits within the business in an effort to avoid double taxation. Finally, we should be familiar with the tax provision that allows a corporation to be taxed as a partnership, which became increasingly important with the Tax Reform Act of 1986. Let's look at each of these tax provisions in turn.

Dividend Exclusion

A corporation may normally exclude 70 percent of any dividends received from another corporation. For instance, if corporation A owns common stock in corporation B and receives dividends of $1,000 in a given year, only $300 will be subject to tax, and the remaining $700 (70 percent of $1,000) will be tax exempt. If the corporation receiving the dividend income is in a 34 percent tax bracket, only $102 in taxes (34 percent of $300) will result.[5]

Depreciation

Essentially, there are three methods for computing depreciation expenses: (1) straight-line depreciation, (2) double-declining balance method, and (3) the modified accelerated cost recovery system. Any one of the

---
[5]If corporation A owns at least 20 percent of corporation B, but less than 80 percent, 80 percent of any dividends received may be excluded from taxable income. If 80 percent or more is owned, all the dividends received may be excluded.

three methods results in the same depreciation expense over the life of the asset; however, the last two approaches allow the firm to take the depreciation earlier as opposed to later, which in turn defers taxes until later. Assuming a time value of money, there is an advantage to using the accelerated techniques. (Chapter 5 fully explains the time value of money.) Also, management may use straight-line depreciation for reporting income to the shareholders while still using an accelerated method for calculating taxable income.

Net Operating Loss Deduction

If a corporation has an operating loss (which is simply a loss from operating a business), that loss may be applied against income in other years. The tax laws provide for a **net operating loss carryback and carryforward**. A carryback permits the taxpayer to apply the loss against the profits for the three prior years. If the loss has not been completely absorbed by the profits in these three years, the loss may be carried forward to each of the fifteen following years (carryforward). At that time, any loss still remaining may no longer be used as a tax deduction. To illustrate, a 1994 operating loss may be used to recover, in whole or in part, the taxes paid during 1991, 1992, and 1993. If any part of the loss still remains, this amount may be used to reduce taxable income, if any, during the fifteen-year period of 1995 through 2009. A complete example of the net operating loss deduction is provided in Table 1–4.

Capital Gains and Losses

An important tax consideration prior to 1987 was the preferential tax treatment for capital gains; that is, gains from the sale of assets not bought or sold in the ordinary course of business. The Tax Reform Act of 1986 repealed any special treatment of capital gains and while the Revenue Reconciliation Act of 1993 reinstituted preferential treatment in certain unique circumstances, in general, capital gains are taxed at the same rates as ordinary income. However, if a corporation has capital losses that exceed capital gains in any year, these net capital losses may not be deducted from ordinary income. The net losses may, however, be carried back and applied against net capital gains in each of the three years before the current year. If the loss is not completely used in the three prior years, any remaining loss may be carried forward and applied against any net gains in each of the next five years. For example, if a corporation has an $80,000 net capital loss in 1993, it may apply this loss against any net gains in 1990, 1991, and 1992. If any loss remains, it may be carried forward and applied against any gains through 1998.

EXAMPLE

As an example of the net operating loss carryback and carryforward, assume the Sang Lee Corporation, a trucking operation, has had the following profits and losses reported from 1987 through 1994:

1987	$	52,000
1988		76,000
1989		100,000
1990		(152,000)
1991		100,000
1992		(194,000)
1993		12,000
1994		94,000

In 1990 and 1992 the corporation incurred operating losses, which may be applied to reduce taxable income and taxes in other years. The tax payments and tax refunds for each year are calculated in Table 1–4. ■

Accumulated Earnings Tax

The earnings generated by a corporation are subject to "double taxation," first at the corporate level and then at the stockholder level as the firm's profits are distributed in the form of dividends. If the shareholders have no immediate need for dividend income, the corporation could retain its profits and perhaps even employ the funds for the personal benefit of the company's owners. For example, management could retain the corporate profits but make a personal loan to the stockholders. Also, if the profits were

TABLE 1–4
Sang Lee Corporation Tax
Payments and Refunds

Year	Taxable Income	Tax Consequence
1987	$ 52,000	TAX PAYMENT OF $8,000 15% of $50,000 plus 25% of $2,000.
1988	$ 76,000	TAX PAYMENT OF $14,090 15% of $50,000 plus 25% of $25,000 plus 34% of $1,000.
1989	100,000	TAX PAYMENT OF $22,250 15% of $50,000 plus 25% of $25,000 plus 34% of $25,000.
1990	(152,000)	TAX REFUND OF $30,250 $52,000 of the $152,000 loss is applied against 1987 income for a refund of $8000; $76,000 of the loss is applied against 1988 income for a refund of $14,090, leaving $24,000 to be applied against 1989 income of $100,000 for a refund of $8160—34% of $24,000.
1991	100,000	TAX PAYMENT OF $22,250 Same computation as 1989.
1992	(194,000)	TAX REFUND OF $36,340 AND $18,000 CARRYFORWARD $76,000 of the loss is applied against 1989 income ($24,000 had already been used in 1990) for a refund of $14,090; $100,000 of the loss is applied against 1991 income for a refund of $22,250. The remaining $18,000 loss ($194,000 – $176,000) is to be carried to future years.
1993	12,000	NO TAX PAYMENT OR REFUND; $6000 CARRYFORWARD The $18,000 carryforward from 1992 is used to avoid having to pay any tax, leaving $6000 carryforward ($18,000 – $12,000) for future years.
1994	94,000	TAX PAYMENT OF $18,170 Tax is calculated on $88,000 income ($94,000 income less the $6000 carryforward originating in 1992): 15% of $50,000 plus 25% of $25,000 plus 34% of $13,000.

accumulated within the firm, the price of the common stock should rise. Until the stock is sold, the investor would not be required to pay any tax.

To prevent such stratagems, a 28 percent surtax in addition to the regular income tax is assessed at the corporate level on any accumulation of earnings by a corporation for the purpose of avoiding taxes on its shareholders. The tax does not apply to the retention of profits for *reasonable business* needs. Nor must the money be reinvested immediately as long as there is evidence that future needs require the current accumulation of earnings. Although it is difficult to state exactly when the accumulation of profits is thought to be reasonable, several examples would include (1) providing for the replacement of plant and equipment, (2) retiring debt created in connection with the corporation's business, (3) extending more credit to customers, and (4) financing the acquisition of a new business.

Subchapter S Corporation

In deciding between the sole proprietorship or partnership and the corporation, tax considerations are important. Owners attempt to select the form of business organization that maximizes their after-tax returns. To minimize the tax influence on the decision, Congress established the Subchapter S Corporation, which enables a corporation to be taxed as a partnership. This provision eliminates the "double taxation" effect on the corporation. The Subchapter S Corporation files a tax return for information purposes only and pays no taxes. The taxes from the business are paid by the stockholders, whether or not the earnings are distributed. However, to qualify as a Subchapter S Corporation, the following requirements must be met:

1. The firm must be a domestic corporation.
2. There may be no more than 35 shareholders at the beginning of the corporation's life. These shareholders must be individuals, estates, or certain trusts.
3. The corporation cannot be a member of an affiliated group eligible to file a consolidated tax return with another corporation.
4. There may be only one class of stock.
5. A nonresident alien cannot be a stockholder.

Only small to moderate-sized firms typically can satisfy the Subchapter S Corporation requirements. However, if the qualifications can be met, the company may potentially receive the benefits of a corporation while being taxed as a partnership.

Corporate Taxes: An Example

To illustrate certain portions of the tax laws for a corporation, assume that the Griggs Corporation had sales during the past year of $5 million; its cost of goods sold was $3 million; and it incurred operating expenses of $1 million. In addition, it received $185,000 in interest income and $100,000 in dividend income from another corporation. In turn, it paid $40,000 in interest and $75,000 in dividends. Also, it sold old machinery, which had originally cost $350,000, for $200,000. The equipment, purchased five years ago, was being depreciated (straight-line) over a 10-year life and had a book value of $175,000. Finally, the company sold a piece of land for $100,000 that had cost $50,000 six years ago. Given this information, the firm's taxable income is $1,250,000, as computed in top part of Table 1–5.

Based on the tax rates from Table 1–2, Griggs's tax liability is $425,000, as shown at the bottom of Table 1–5. Note that the $75,000 Griggs paid in dividends is not tax deductible. Also, since the firm's taxable income exceeds $335,000, and the 5 percent surtax no longer applies, the marginal tax rate and the average tax rate both equal 34 percent; that is, we could have computed Griggs's tax liability as 34 percent of $1,250,000, or $425,000.

■ NINE AXIOMS THAT FORM THE FOUNDATIONS OF FINANCIAL MANAGEMENT

To the first-time student of finance, the subject matter may seem like a collection of unrelated decision rules. This could not be further from the truth. In fact, our decision rules, and the logic that underlies them, actually

TABLE 1–5
Griggs Corporation
Tax Computations

Sales			$5,000,000
Cost of goods sold			(3,000,000)
Gross profit			$2,000,000
Operating expenses			(1,000,000)
Operating Income			$1,000,000
Other taxable income and expenses:			
Interest income		$185,000	
Dividend income	$100,000		
Less 70% exclusion	70,000	30,000	
Interest expense		(40,000)	175,000
Gain on sale of equipment:			
Selling price		$200,000	
Book value		175,000	25,000
Gain on land sale:			
Selling price		$100,000	
Cost		(50,000)	$ 50,000
Total taxable income			$1,250,000
Tax computation:			
15% × $ 50,000 = $ 7,500			
25% × 25,000 = 6,250			
34% × 1,175,000 = 399,500			
$1,250,000			
Add 5% surtax for income between $100,000 and $335,000		$ 11,750	
Tax liability		$425,000	

spring from nine simple axioms. *However, although it is not necessary to understand finance in order to understand these axioms, it is necessary to understand these axioms in order to understand finance.* We will use these axioms throughout the text to unify and relate the topics being presented. They will also allow us to focus on the conceptual underpinnings of finance and thereby not lose sight of the concepts as we present the techniques. We will now turn to a presentation of the nine axioms that form the foundations of financial management. Keep in mind that although these axioms may at first appear simple or even trivial, they will provide the driving force behind all that follows. Along with our motivation to create wealth, these axioms will guide us through and weave together the concepts and techniques presented in this text, thereby allowing us to focus on the logic underlying the practice of financial management.

Axiom 1: The Risk-Return Tradeoff—We Won't Take on Additional Risk Unless We Expect To Be Compensated with Additional Return

At some point we have all saved some money. Why have we done this? The answer is simple: to postpone consumption opportunities to the future. We generally invest those savings to expand our future consumption opportunities. We are able to earn a return on our savings dollars because some economic units would rather forgo future consumption opportunities to consume more now. Assuming there are a lot of different economic units out there that would like to have use of our savings, how do we decide where to put our money?

Actually, although the answer is simple, it provides the logic behind much of what is done in finance. First, investors demand a return for delaying consumption. This return must cover the anticipated level of inflation. Why do they demand this? The answer is that if they didn't receive enough to compensate for anticipated inflation they would purchase whatever goods they desired ahead of time or simply invest in assets that were subject to inflation and earn the rate of inflation on those assets. In effect, there isn't much incentive to postpone consumption if your savings are going to decline in terms of purchasing power. Therefore, investors demand a minimum return for delaying consumption, and this return must be greater than the anticipated rate of inflation.

Now that we know what the minimum return is, how do investors decide among all the various investment alternatives? Obviously, some of these investments are safer than others. Why should an investor put his or her money in a risky investment when there are safe investment alternatives offered by our government? The answer is that risky investments are viewed as less desirable than safe investments, and investors simply won't put their money in them unless they are compensated for that additional risk. In other words, investors demand additional expected return for taking on added risk. Notice that we keep referring to expected return rather than actual return. That is because there is risk associated with investing. We may have expectations of what the returns from investing will be, but we can't peer into the future and see what those returns are actually going to be. If investors could see into the future no one would have invested money in the dressmaker Leslie Fay, whose stock dropped 43 percent on April 5, 1993, when it announced it was filing for bankruptcy. Until after the fact, you are never sure what the return on an investment will be. That is why General Motors bonds pay more interest than do U. S. Treasury bonds of the same maturity. It is that added incentive of additional interest that convinces some investors to take on the added risk of a General Motors bond rather than a U. S. Treasury bond. The more risk an investment has, the higher will be its expected return. Graphically, this relationship between risk and expected return is shown in Figure 1–1.

Needless to say, this is a simple relationship that makes a good deal of sense: Investors demand a return for delaying consumption and an additional return for taking on added risk. In this course much of our energy will be directed toward valuing things like stocks, bonds, and proposed new projects. To value something we must first know what kind of return the investment must earn to justify raising funds to finance it. That's where this risk-return relationship comes into play. We simply will not be willing to invest our money in risky projects unless we are compensated for taking on that added risk.

We will also spend some time determining how best to measure risk. Interestingly, much of the work for which the 1990 Nobel Prize for Economics was awarded centered on this graph and how best to measure risk. Both the graph and the risk-return relationship it depicts will reappear often in this text.

Axiom 2: The Time Value of Money — A Dollar Received Today Is Worth More Than a Dollar Received in the Future

One of the most appealing concepts in finance is that money has a time value associated with it: A dollar received today is worth more than a dollar received a year from now. Simply stated, because we can earn

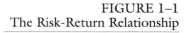

FIGURE 1–1
The Risk-Return Relationship

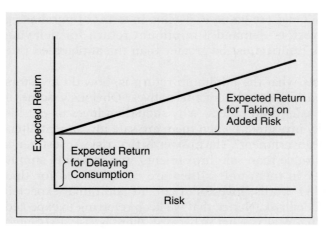

interest on money received today, it is better to receive money earlier rather than later. In your economics courses, this concept of the time value of money is referred to as the *opportunity cost* of passing up the earning potential of a dollar today.

In this text a main focus will be on the creation and measurement of value. To measure value we will use the concept of the time value of money to bring the benefits and costs of a project back to the present. By measuring both the benefits and costs in today's dollars, they will be comparable. Then, if the benefits outweigh the costs, the project creates wealth and should be accepted; if the costs outweigh the benefits, the project does not create wealth and should be rejected. Without recognizing the existence of the time value of money, it is impossible to evaluate projects with benefits and costs occurring in different periods in a meaningful way.

To move money through time and make dollars of different time periods comparable, we must assume a specific opportunity cost of money, or interest rate. Exactly what interest rate should be used in bringing the benefits and costs back to the present to make them comparable is determined by *Axiom 1, The Risk-Return Tradeoff* which states investors demand higher returns for taking on more risky projects. Thus, when we move money through time, we do so taking into account that investors demand a higher return for taking on added risk.

Axiom 3: Cash Is King—Measuring the Timing of Costs and Benefits

In measuring value we will use cash flows, not accounting profits, as our measurement tool. It is only cash flows that the firm receives and is able to reinvest. Accounting profits, on the other hand, are shown when they are earned rather than when the money is actually in hand. Unfortunately, a firm's accounting profits and cash flows may not be timed to occur together. For example, capital expenses, such as the purchase of a new piece of equipment or a new building, are depreciated over several years, with the annual depreciation subtracted from profits. However, the cash flow associated with these expenses generally occurs immediately. It is cash inflows that can be reinvested and cash outflows that involve paying out money. Therefore, cash flows correctly reflect the true timing of the benefits and costs.

Actually, we can use the first three axioms we have presented to determine the value of any asset, be it a business, a new project being considered, or a financial asset like a share of common stock or a bond. So far we know that cash flows measure the true timing of the benefits and costs. From *Axiom 2* we also know that we must incorporate the time value of money into our calculations to compare costs and benefits that occur in different time periods. From *Axiom 1* we know that investors demand an additional return for taking on added risk. Thus, the value of any asset is the current value of the asset's cash flows where the interest rate used to bring those cash flows back to the present reflects the riskiness of the cash flows.

Axiom 4: Incremental Cash Flows—It's Only What Changes That Counts

In making business decisions, we are concerned with the results of those decisions: what happens if we say yes versus what happens if we say no. This makes perfect sense. We also know from *Axiom 3* that we should use cash flows to measure the benefits that accrue from taking on a new project. We are now fine tuning our evaluation process so that we only consider **incremental** cash flows. In effect, we ask ourselves what the cash flows will be if the project is taken on versus what they will be if the project is not taken on.

In making all financial decisions, we will make a conscious effort to think incrementally. As we will see, when evaluating new projects, merely calculating the cash flows from a new project may not be enough. Instead, we as decision makers must ask: What new cash flows will the company as a whole receive if the company takes on a given project? What will the cash flows to the company look like if the project is not taken on? Interestingly, not all the cash flows a firm receives from a new project may be incremental. For example, when Leaf Inc., a manufacturer of sports cards, introduced Donruss Triple Play Baseball Cards in 1992, the product competed directly with the company's Leaf and Donruss baseball cards. There is no doubt that some of the sales dollars that ended up with Donruss Triple Play Cards would have been spent on Leaf or Donruss Cards if Triple Play cards had not been available. Although the Leaf corporation meant to target the low-cost end of the baseball cards market, held by Topps, there was no question that Triple Play sales bit into—actually cannibalized—sales from the company's existing product lines.

What is important is that we *think* incrementally. Our guiding rule in deciding whether a cash flow is incremental is to look at the company with and without the new product. In fact, we will take this incremental concept beyond cash flows and look at all consequences from all decisions on an incremental basis. We will examine what the firm looks like with a positive response versus a negative response to all decisions. It is that difference that reflects the true impact of the decision.

Axiom 5: The Curse of Competitive Markets—Why It's Hard to Find Exceptionally Profitable Projects

Our job as financial managers is to create wealth. Therefore, we will look closely at the mechanics of valuation and decision making. We will focus on estimating cash flows, determining the appropriate required rate of return associated with an investment, and valuing assets and new projects. But it will be easy to get caught up in the mechanics of evaluation and lose sight of the process of creating wealth. Why is it so hard to find projects and investments that are exceptionally profitable? Where do profitable projects come from? The answers to these questions tell us a lot about how competitive markets operate and where we should be looking for profitable projects.

In reality, it is much easier evaluating profitable projects than it is finding them. If, for example, an industry is generating large profits, new entrants are usually attracted. The additional competition and added capacity can result in profits being driven down to the required rate of return. Conversely, if an industry is returning profits below the required rate of return, then some participants in the market drop out, reducing capacity and competition; in turn, prices are driven back up. This is precisely what happened in the VCR video rental market in the mid-1980s. This market developed suddenly with the opportunity for extremely large profits. As a result, because there were no barriers to entry, this market was flooded with new entries in a short time. By 1988 the competition and price cutting produced losses for many firms in the industry, forcing them to flee the market. As the competition lessened with firms moving out of the video rental industry, profits again could rise to the point where the required rate of return could be earned on invested capital.

The point is that in competitive markets, extremely large profits simply cannot exist for very long. Given this somewhat bleak scenario, how can we find good projects—that is, the ones that return more than the required rate of return? The answer is that as long as the markets are competitive they will be difficult to find. What we have to do is look to markets that are not perfectly competitive. The two most common ways of making markets less competitive are to differentiate the product in some key way or to achieve a cost advantage over competitors, which in turn discourages new entrants into the market.

Successful investments involve those that reduce competition by creating barriers to entry either through product differentiation or cost advantages. If products are differentiated, consumer choice is no longer made by price alone. Projects that involve product differentiation open the possibility of extremely large profits.

Product differentiation has long been used as a means of insulating a product from competition, thereby allowing prices to stay sufficiently high to support large profits. For example, in the pharmaceutical industry, patents have traditionally created competitive barriers. Products like SmithKline Beckman's Tagamet, used in the treatment of ulcers, and Hoffman-La Roche's Valium, a tranquilizer, can protect themselves from direct competition.

Patents are one way of differentiating products. Service and quality have also been used successfully. For example, Caterpillar Tractor has long prided itself on the quality of its construction and earth-moving machinery. As a result, it has been able to hold on to its market securely. Similarly, some of the brand loyalty built up in recent years by Toyota and Honda Motors has been based on quality.

Service can also create product differentiation, as shown by McDonald's. McDonald's fast service, cleanliness, and consistency of product bring customers back. Whether product differentiation occurs because of service, advertising, the development of patents through research and development expenditures, or quality, the more the product is differentiated from competing products, the less competition it will face and the greater the possibility of large profits.

Economies of scale and the ability to produce at a cost below competition can effectively deter new entrants to the market and thereby reduce competition. The retail hardware industry is one such case. In the hardware industry, there are several fixed costs that are independent of the store's size or annual sales. For example, inventory costs, advertising expenses, and managerial salaries are essentially the same regardless of annual sales. Therefore, the more that sales can be built up, the lower the per-sale dollar cost of inventory, advertising, and management. Restocking from warehouses also becomes more efficient as delivery trucks can be used to full potential.

Regardless of how the cost advantage is created—by economies of scale, proprietary technology, or monopolistic control of raw materials—the cost advantage deters new market entrants while allowing production at below industry cost. Thus, investment aimed at creating a significant cost advantage has the potential of resulting in large profits.

The key to locating profitable investment projects is first to understand how and where they exist in competitive markets. Then the corporate philosophy must be aimed at creating or taking advantage of some imperfection in these markets, either through product differentiation or creation of a cost advantage, rather than looking to new markets or industries that appear to provide large profits. Any perfectly competitive industry that looks too good to be true won't be for long.

Axiom 6: Efficient Capital Markets—The Markets Are Quick and the Prices Are Right

We have taken as our goal the maximization of shareholder wealth and have defined this as maximizing the price of existing shares of common stock. Thus, decisions that maximize shareholder wealth are those that lead to an increase in the market price of the existing common stock. To understand why good financial decisions are reflected in positive stock price adjustments, as well as how securities are valued or priced in the financial markets, it is necessary to have an understanding of the concept of efficient markets.

Whether a market is efficient has to do with the speed with which information is impounded into security prices. Under the efficient market hypothesis, information is reflected in security prices with such speed that there are no opportunities for investors to profit from publicly available information. An efficient market is one characterized by a large number of profit-driven individuals who act independently of one another. In addition, new information regarding securities arrives in the market in a random manner. Given this setting, investors react to new information immediately and buy and sell the security until they feel the market price correctly reflects the new information. Whether the price adjustment turns out to be correct is not important, but it is important that the price adjustment not be biased (that is, that investors cannot predict whether it is an over or under adjustment).

What types of information are immediately reflected in security prices and how quickly that information is reflected determine how efficient the market actually is. The point is that investors competing for profits ensure that security prices will appropriately reflect the expected earnings and risks involved and thus the true value of the firm.

What are the implications of efficient markets for us? First, the price is right. Stock prices reflect all publicly available information regarding the value of the company. This means we can implement our goal of maximization of shareholder wealth by focusing on the effect each decision *should* have on the stock price if everything else were held constant. That prices reflect value will also be important when we look at stock prices to determine what rate of return investors demand on an investment in our company.

Another implication of efficient markets is that earnings manipulations through accounting changes will not result in price changes. That is, changes in accounting methods that do not affect cash flows are not reflected in prices. Market prices reflect cash flows available to shareholders. Thus, our preoccupation with cash flows to measure the timing of the benefits is justified. As we will see, it is indeed reassuring that prices reflect value. It allows us to look at prices and see value reflected in them. While it may make investing a bit less exciting, it makes corporate finance much less uncertain.

Axiom 7: The Agency Problem — Managers Won't Work for the Owners Unless It's in Their Best Interest

Although the goal of the firm will be maximization of shareholder wealth, in reality an agency problem may interfere with the implementation of this goal. The *agency problem* is the result of a separation of management and the ownership of the firm. For example, a large firm may be run by professional managers who have little or no ownership in the firm. Because of this separation of the decision makers and owners, managers may make decisions that are not in line with the goal of maximization of shareholder wealth. They may approach work less energetically and attempt to benefit themselves in terms of salary and perquisites at the expense of shareholders. The significance of this problem is difficult to measure. However, although it may interfere with the implementation of the goal of maximization of shareholder wealth in some firms, it does not affect the goal's validity.

The costs associated with the agency problem are also difficult to measure, but occasionally we see the problem's effect in the marketplace. For example, if the market feels management of a firm is damaging shareholder wealth, we might see a positive reaction in stock price to the removal of that management. On the day following the death in 1989 of John Dorrance, Jr., chairman of Campbell Soup, Campbell's stock price rose about 15 percent. Some investors felt that Campbell's relatively small growth in earnings might be improved with the departure of Dorrance. There was also speculation that Dorrance was the major obstacle to a possible positive reorganization.

If the management of the firm works for the owners, who are actually the common shareholders, why doesn't the management get fired if they don't do a good job or act in the shareholder's best interest? If management were truly responsive to the wishes of the shareholders, the agency problem wouldn't exist at all. *In theory* the shareholders pick the corporate board of directors and the board of directors in turn picks the management. Unfortunately, *in reality* the system frequently works the other way around. Management selects the board of director nominees and then distributes the ballots. In effect, the shareholders are offered a slate of nominees selected by the management. The end result is management effectively selects the directors, who then may have more allegiance to managers than to shareholders. This in turn sets up the potential for agency problems in which a divergence of interests between managers and shareholders is allowed to exist, with the board of directors not monitoring the managers on behalf of the shareholders as they should.

We will spend considerable time monitoring managers and trying to align the interests of shareholders and managers. Managers can be monitored by auditing financial statements and managers' compensation packages. The interests of managers and shareholders can be aligned by setting up stock options, bonuses, and perquisites that are directly tied to how closely management decisions coincide with the interest of shareholders. The agency problem will persist unless an incentive structure is set up that aligns the interests of managers and shareholders. In other words, what's good for shareholders must also be good for managers. If that is not the case, managers will make decision in their best interest rather than maximizing shareholder wealth.

Axiom 8: Taxes Bias Business Decisions

Taxes play an important role in financial decision making. Hardly a decision is made by the financial manager without considering the impact of taxes. When we introduced *Axiom 4*, we said that only incremental cash flows should be given consideration in the evaluation process. The cash flows we will concern ourselves with will be *after-tax incremental cash flows to the firm as a whole*. In the chapters that follow, we will see taxes playing a major role in investment decisions and in determining the firm's financial structure.

Considering the effect of taxes will sway many of our decisions. When we evaluate new projects, we will see income taxes playing a significant role. When the company is analyzing the possible acquisition of a plant or equipment, the returns from the investment should be measured on an after-tax basis. Otherwise the company will not be evaluating the true incremental cash flows generated by the project.

In computing the taxes resulting from an investment decision, the method of depreciation affects the timing and the amount of the after-tax cash flow. The depreciation method will have an impact on the timing of taxes. Although the *total amount* of taxes is not altered, the use of accelerated depreciation, as opposed to straight-line depreciation, does result in lower taxable profits in the earlier years of the project's life and larger taxable profits in later years. In this manner, lower taxes are paid in the initial years, with counterbalancing higher taxes in later years. When the time value of money is considered, this shift in taxes to later time periods proves beneficial.

The government also realizes taxes can bias business decisions and uses taxes to encourage business spending in certain ways. If, for example, the government wanted to encourage spending on research and development projects it might offer an *investment tax credit* for such investments. This would have the effect of reducing taxes on research and development projects, which would in turn increase the after-tax cash flows from those projects. The end result would be that the increased cash flow from reduced taxes would turn some otherwise unprofitable research and development projects into profitable projects. Thus, by reducing taxes on certain types of investments, those investments are made more attractive, and more of that type of project is taken on by the business sector. In effect, the government can use taxes as a tool to direct business investment to research and development projects, to the inner cities, and to projects that create jobs.

Taxes also play a role in determining the appropriate mix of debt and equity in the firm's financial structure. This area has been the focus of intense controversy for over three decades. However, throughout this controversy, one aspect remains constant: The tax laws give debt financing a definite cost advantage over stock. As we noted when we examined how taxes are computed, *interest payments are a tax-deductible expense, whereas dividend payments to stockholders may not be used as deductions in computing a corporation's taxable profits*. Thus, interest payments lower profits, which are not a cash flow item, and this in turn lowers taxes due, which are a cash flow item. In effect, paying interest as opposed to dividends reduces taxes.

Axiom 9: Ethical Behavior Is Doing the Right Thing, and Ethical Dilemmas Are Everywhere in Finance

Ethics, or rather a lack of ethics in finance, is a recurring theme in the news. During the late 1980s and early 1990s the fall of Ivan Boesky and Drexel, Burnham, Lambert, and the near collapse of Salomon Brothers seemed to make continuous headlines. Meanwhile, the movie Wall Street was a hit at the box office and the book *Liar's Poker*, by Michael Lewis, chronicling unethical behavior in the bond markets, became a best seller. As the lessons of Salomon Brothers and Drexel, Burnham, Lambert so readily illustrate, ethical errors are not forgiven in the business world. Not only is acting in an ethical manner morally correct, it is congruent with our goal of maximization of shareholder wealth.

Ethical behavior means "doing the right thing." A difficulty arises, however, in attempting to define "doing the right thing." The problem is that each of us has his or her own set of values, which forms the basis for our personal judgments about what is the right thing to do. After all, the very essence of personal freedom lies in the individual's right to make choices. But individuals in a society are not completely free. Every society adopts a set of rules or laws that prescribe what it believes to be "doing the right thing." In a sense, we can think of laws as a set of rules that reflect the values of the society as a whole, as they have evolved. There are some who would argue that ethical behavior is more than simply obeying the law. For purposes of this text, we recognize that individuals in a free society have a right to disagree about what constitutes "doing the right thing," and for this reason, we will seldom venture beyond the basic notion that ethical conduct involves abiding by society's rules. However, we will endeavor to point out some of the ethical dilemmas that have arisen in recent years with regard to the practice of financial management. These dilemmas generally arise when some individual behavior is found to be at odds with the wishes of a large portion of the population, even though that behavior is not prohibited by law. Ethical dilemmas can therefore provide a catalyst for debate and discussion, which may eventually lead to a revision in the body of the law. So as we embark on our study of finance and encounter ethical dilemmas, we encourage you to think through the issues and form your own opinion.

At this point you might want to look at the Ethics in Financial Management box, "Is It Wrong to Tell a Lie?" It illustrates that many times ethical questions are not easily answered, but they must be dealt with on a day-to-day basis.

Discussion of ethics in business and finance is a relatively new phenomenon. A question many students ask is, "Is ethics really relevant?" This is a good question and deserves an answer.

First, although business errors can be forgiven, ethical errors tend to end careers and terminate future opportunities. Why? Because *unethical*

ETHICS IN FINANCIAL MANAGEMENT

Is It Wrong to Tell a Lie?

A teacher might not be able to change ethical standards in a college classroom, but he or she can teach students how to analyze questions so that they can bring to bear whatever ethical standards they have when they make decisions.

If you haven't already done so, there is no better time than now to develop a rule or set of rules against which you can measure the "rightness" or "wrongness" of your decisions and actions. It may be nothing more provocative than "Do unto others as you would have them do unto you." Or it may be a question or set of questions that you consistently ask: How would I feel about explaining to my parents or children what I did? How would I feel if the action I took were described, in detail, on the front page of my local newspaper? Have I avoided even the appearance of a conflict of interest in my decision? Would my action infringe on the liberty or constitutional rights of others?

Let's begin our look at ethical dilemmas in finance by asking this question: Is it wrong to tell a lie?

One of the roles of the financial manager is to transmit financial information to people outside the company. Occasionally, the facts that the financial manager must transmit and explain aren't particularly flattering to the firm. This presents the dilemma of whether it is unethical to tell a lie.

For example, at the annual stockholders' meeting a senior financial manager is reviewing her company's financial performance for the previous year. The news is not good. Sales dropped 30 percent, and profits were down 50 percent. A stockholder asks the manager, "What caused this drastic decline and has it been corrected?" The manager knows that the primary cause of the decline was a series of poor top-management decisions made over the past several years, but she also knows that's not what her colleagues want her to say. Furthermore, she personally believes the decline is far from over, but she recognizes that's not what the stockholders want to hear.

Should this financial manager lie? Is lying always wrong, or is it acceptable under certain circumstances? What, if any, would those circumstances be? What do you think?

Adapted by permission from Stephen P. Robbins, *Management*, 3d ed., p. 11. copyright 1991 by Prentice Hall, Inc.

behavior eliminates trust, and without trust businesses cannot interact. Second, *the most damaging event a business can experience is a loss of the public's confidence in its ethical standards.* In finance we have seen several recent examples of such events. It was the ethical scandals involving insider trading at Drexel, Burnham, Lambert that brought down that firm. Then, in 1991 the ethical scandals involving attempts by Salomon Brothers to corner the Treasury bill market led to the removal of its top executives and nearly put the company out of business.

Beyond the question of ethics is the question of social responsibility. In general, corporate social responsibility means that a corporation has responsibilities to society at large beyond the maximization of shareholder wealth. It asserts that a corporation answers to a broader constituency than shareholders alone. As with most debates that center on ethical and moral questions, there is no definitive answer, and strong opinions abound. One opinion is voiced by Milton Friedman in the Ethics in Financial Management box, "Milton Friedman on the Social Responsibility of Corporations." Friedman takes the position that because financial managers are employees of the corporation, and the corporation is owned by the shareholders, the financial managers should run the corporation in such a way that shareholder wealth is maximized and then allow the shareholders to decide if they would like to pass on any of the profits to deserving causes. While Friedman presents a strong case, very few corporations consistently act in this way. For example, in 1992 Bristol-Myers Squibb Co. announced it would start an ambitious program to give away heart medications to those who cannot pay for them. This announcement came in the wake of an American Heart Association report showing that many of the nation's working poor face severe health risks because they cannot afford heart drugs. Clearly, Bristol-Myers Squibb felt it had a social responsibility to provide this medicine to the poor at no cost—a decision with which Friedman would have no doubt disagreed. How do you feel about this decision?

A Final Note on the Axioms

Hopefully, these axioms are as much statements of common sense as they are theoretical statements. These axioms provide the logic behind what is to follow. We will build on them and attempt to draw out their implications for decision making. As we continue, try to keep in mind that while the topics being treated may change from chapter to chapter, the logic driving our treatment of them is constant and finds its roots in these nine axioms.

■ OVERVIEW OF THE TEXT

In this text we will focus on the maintenance and creation of wealth. Although this will involve attention to decision-making techniques, we will emphasize the logic behind those techniques to ensure that you do not lose sight of the concepts driving finance and the creation of wealth.

ETHICS IN FINANCIAL MANAGEMENT

Milton Friedman on the Social Responsibility of Corporations

In a free-enterprise, private-property system, a corporate executive is an employee of the owners of the business. He has direct responsibility to his employers. That responsibility is to conduct the business in accordance with their desires, which generally will be to make as much money as possible while conforming to the basic rules of the society, both those embodied in law and those embodied in ethical custom. Of course, in some cases his employers may have a different objective. A group of persons might establish a corporation for an eleemosynary purpose—for example, a hospital or a school. The manager of such a corporation will not have money profit as his objective but the rendering of certain services.

In either case, the key point is that, in his capacity as a corporate executive, the manager is the agent of the individuals who own the corporation or establish the eleemosynary instruction, and his primary responsibility is to them.

Needless to say, this does not mean that it is easy to judge how well he is performing his task. But at least the criterion of performance is straightforward, and the persons among whom a voluntary contractual arrangement exists are clearly defined.

Of course, the corporate executive is also a person in his own right. As a person, he may have many other responsibilities that he recognizes or assumes voluntarily—to his family, his conscience, his feelings of charity, his church, his clubs, his city, his country. He may feel impelled by these responsibilities to devote part of his income to causes he regards as worthy, to refuse to work for particular corporations, even to leave his job, for example, to join his country's armed forces. If we wish, we may refer to some of these responsibilities as "social responsibilities." But in these respects he is acting as a principal, not an agent; he is spending his own money or time or energy, not the money of his employers or the time or energy he has contracted to devote to their purposes. If these are "social responsibilities," they are the social responsibilities of individuals, not of business.

What does it mean to say that the corporate executive has a "social responsibility" in his capacity as a businessman? If this statement is not pure rhetoric, it must mean that he is to act in some way that is not in the interest of his employers. For example, that he is to refrain from increasing the price of the product in order to contribute to the social objective of preventing inflation, even though a price increase would be in the best interests of the corporation. Or that he is to make expenditures on reducing pollution beyond the amount that is in the best interests of the corporation or that is required by law in order to contribute to the social objective of improving the environment. Or that, at the expense of corporate profits, he is to hire "hard-core" unemployed instead of better-qualified available workmen to contribute to the social objective of reducing poverty.

In each of these cases, the corporate executive would be spending someone else's money for a general social interest. Insofar as his actions with his "social responsibility" reduce returns to stockholders, he is spending their money. Insofar as his actions raise the price to customers, he is spending the customers' money. Insofar as his actions lower the wages of some employees, he is spending their money.

The stockholders or the customers or the employees could separately spend their own money on the particular actions if they wished to do so. The executive is exercising a distinct "social responsibility," rather than serving as an agent of the stockholders or the customers or the employees, only if he spends the money in a different way than they would have spent it.

But if he does this, he is in effect imposing taxes, on the one hand, and deciding how the tax proceeds shall be spent, on the other.

Source: Milton Friedman, "The Social Responsibility of Business Is to Increase Its Profits," *New York Times Magazine* (September 13, 1970), 33, 122–126. Copyright 1970 by The New York Times Company. Reprinted by permission.

The text begins by discussing the goal of the firm, a goal that is to be used in financial decision making. It also presents the legal and tax environment in which these decisions are to be made. Since this environment sets the ground rules, it is necessary to understand it before decision rules can be formulated. The nine guiding axioms that provide the underpinnings for what is to follow are then presented. In Chapter 2, the financial markets and interest rates are examined, looking at both the determinants of interest rates and their effect on business decisions. Chapters 3 and 4 introduce the basic financial tools the financial manager uses to maintain control over the firm and its operations. These tools enable the financial manager to locate potential problem areas and plan for the future.

In Chapter 5 our focus turns to how the firm and its assets are valued. It begins with an examination of the mathematics of finance and the concept of the time value of money. An understanding of this topic allows us to compare benefits and costs that occur in different time periods. Valuation of fixed income securities is then examined in Chapter 6. Valuation models that attempt to explain how different financial decisions affect the firm's stock price are examined in Chapter 7. We move on in Chapter 8 to develop an understanding of the meaning and measurement of risk.

Using the valuation principles just developed our discussion turns to the capital budgeting decision, which involves the financial evaluation of investment proposals in fixed assets. We then examine the measurement of cash flows and introduce methods to incorporate risk in the analysis. Finally, we will examine the financing of a firm's chosen projects, looking at what costs are associated with alternative ways of raising new funds.

Chapter 12 examines the firm's capital structure along with the impact of leverage on returns to the enterprise. It is followed with a discussion of the determination of the dividend-retained earnings decision. Chapters 14 and 15 deal with working-capital management and the management of current assets. We will discuss methods for determining the appropriate investment in cash, marketable securities, inventory, and accounts receivable, as well as the risks associated with these investments and the control of these risks.

Chapter 16 provides an introduction to international financial management, focusing on how financial decisions are affected by the international environment. The final chapter in the text deals with future changes in finance and the dynamic nature of the discipline. It focuses on areas of change in finance: the development of the futures and options markets, recent innovations in corporate restructuring and raising capital, attempts to deal with the agency problem, and recent challenges to the concept of market efficiency and how assets are valued.

SUMMARY

This chapter outlines the framework for the maintenance and creation of wealth. In introducing decision-making techniques aimed at creating wealth, we will emphasize the logic behind those techniques. This chapter begins with an examination of the goal of the firm.

The commonly accepted goal of profit maximization is contrasted with the more complete goal of maximization of shareholder wealth. Because it deals well with uncertainty and time in a real-world environment, the goal of maximization of shareholder wealth is found to be the proper goal for the firm.

The legal forms of business are then examined. The sole proprietorship is a business operation owned and managed by a single individual. Initiating this form of business is simple and generally does not involve any substantial organizational costs. The proprietor has complete control of the firm but must be willing to assume full responsibility for its outcomes.

The general partnership, which is simply a coming together of two or more individuals, is similar to the sole proprietorship. The limited partnership is another form of partnership sanctioned by states to permit all but one of the partners to have limited liability if this is agreeable to all partners.

The corporation increases the flow of capital from public investors to the business community. Although larger organizational costs and regulations are imposed on this legal entity, the corporation is more conducive to raising large amounts of capital. Limited liability, continuity of life, and ease of transfer in ownership, which increase the marketability of the investment, have contributed greatly in attracting large numbers of investors to the corporate environment. The formal control of the corporation is vested in the parties who own the greatest number of shares. However, day-to-day operations are managed by the corporate officers, who theoretically serve on behalf of the common stockholders.

The tax environment is also presented. In introducing taxes we focus on taxes that affect our business decisions. Three taxable entities exist: the individual, including partnerships; the corporation; and the fiduciary. Only information on the corporate tax environment is given here.

For the most part, taxable income for the corporation is equal to the firm's operating income plus capital gains less any interest expense. The corporation is allowed an income exclusion of 70 percent of the dividends received from another corporation. Also, if the Internal Revenue Service considers the corporation to be retaining unreasonable amounts of earnings within the business, an accumulated earnings tax may be imposed. To minimize the tax influence in selecting the form of legal organization, a corporation may choose to be a Subchapter S Corporation and be taxed as a partnership, provided certain qualifications can be satisfied.

Tax consequences have a direct bearing on the decisions of the financial manager. The relationships are grounded in the taxability of investment income and the difference in tax treatment for interest expense and dividend payments. Also, shareholders' tax status may influence their preference between gains from stock sale and dividends, which in turn may influence corporate dividend policy.

This chapter closes with an examination of the nine axioms on which finance is built. The techniques and tools introduced in this text are all motivated by these nine principles or axioms. They are:

Axiom 1: The Risk-Return Tradeoff—We Won't Take on Additional Risk Unless We Expect to Be Compensated with Additional Return

Axiom 2: The Time Value of Money—A Dollar Received Today Is Worth More than a Dollar Received in the Future

Axiom 3: Cash is King—Measuring the Timing of Costs and Benefits

Axiom 4: Incremental Cash Flows—It's Only What Changes That Counts

Axiom 5: The Curse of Competitive Markets—Why It's Hard to Find Exceptionally Profitable Projects

Axiom 6: Efficient Capital Markets—The Markets Are Quick and the Prices Are Right

Axiom 7: The Agency Problem—Managers Won't Work for the Owners Unless It's in Their Best Interest

Axiom 8: Taxes Bias Business Decisions

Axiom 9: Ethical Behavior Is Doing the Right Thing, and Ethical Dilemmas Are Everywhere in Finance

STUDY QUESTIONS

1–1. What are some of the problems involved in the use of profit maximization as the goal of the firm? How does the goal of maximization of shareholder wealth deal with those problems?

1–2. Compare and contrast the goals of profit maximization and maximization of shareholder wealth.

1–3. Firms often involve themselves in projects that do not result directly in profits; for example, IBM and Mobil Oil frequently support public television broadcasts. Do these projects contradict the goal of maximization of shareholder wealth? Why or why not?

1–4. What is the relationship between financial decision making and risk and return? Would all financial managers view risk-return tradeoffs similarly?

1–5. Define (a) sole proprietorship, (b) partnership, and (c) corporation.

1–6. Identify the primary characteristics of each form of legal organization.

1–7. Using the following criteria, specify the legal form of business that is favored: (a) organizational requirements and costs, (b) liability of the owners, (c) continuity of business, (d) transferability of ownership, (e) management control and regulations, (f) ability to raise capital, and (g) income taxes.

1–8. Does a partnership pay taxes on its income? Explain.

1–9. When a corporation receives a dividend from another corporation, how is it taxed?

1–10. What is the purpose of the net operating loss deduction?

1–11. What is the rationale for an accumulated earnings tax?

1–12. What is the purpose of the Subchapter S Corporation? In general, what type of firm would qualify as a Subchapter S Corporation?

SELF-TEST PROBLEMS

ST-1. *(Corporate Income Tax)* The Dana Flatt Corporation had sales of $2 million this past year. Its cost of goods sold was $1.2 million, and its operating expenses were $400,000. Interest expenses on outstanding debts were $100,000, and the company paid $40,000 in preferred stock dividends. The corporation received $10,000 in preferred stock dividends and interest income of $12,000. The firm sold stock that had been owned for two years for $40,000; the original cost of the stock was $30,000. Determine the corporation's taxable income and its tax liability.

ST-2. *(Carryback—Carryforward)* Stocking, Inc., has a chain of fast-food restaurants. The firm has been operating for eight years, during which the profits have fluctuated significantly. The taxable income for the past eight years is shown below. Compute the tax payments and refunds for each year.

1986	$ (50,000)	1990	$ 50,000
1987	25,000	1991	150,000
1988	150,000	1992	200,000
1989	(225,000)	1993	(50,000)

STUDY PROBLEMS

1–1. *(Corporate Income Tax)* The William B. Waugh Corporation is a regional Toyota dealer. The firm sells new and used trucks and is actively involved in the parts business. During the most recent year the company generated sales of $3 million. The combined cost of goods sold and the operating expenses were $2.1 million. Also, $400,000 in interest expense was paid during the year. The firm received $6,000 during the year in dividend income from 1,000 shares of common stock that had been purchased three years previously. However, the stock was sold toward the end of the year for $100 per share; its initial cost was $80 per share. The company also sold land that had been recently purchased and had been held for only four months. The selling price was $50,000; the cost was $45,000. Calculate the corporation's tax liability.

1–2. *(Corporate Income Tax)* Sales for L. B. Menielle, Inc., during the past year amounted to $5 million. The firm provides parts and supplies for oil field service companies. Gross profits for the year were $3 million. Operating expenses totaled $1 million. The interest and dividend income from securities owned were $20,000 and $25,000, respectively. The firm's interest expense was $100,000. The firm sold securities on two occasions during the year, receiving a gain of $40,000 on the first sale but losing $50,000 on thPe second. The stock sold first had been owned for four years; the stock sold second had been purchased three months prior to the sale. Compute the corporation's tax liability.

1–3. *(Corporate Income Tax)* Sandersen, Inc., sells minicomputers. During the past year the company's sales were $3 million. The cost of its merchandise sold came to $2 million, and cash operating expenses were $400,000; depreciation expense was $100,000, and the firm paid $150,000 in interest on bank loans. Also, the corporation received $50,000 in dividend income but paid $25,000 in the form of dividends to its own common stockholders. Calculate the corporation's tax liability.

1–4. *(Corporate Income Tax)* A. Don Drennan, Inc., had sales of $6 million during the past year. The company's cost of goods sold was 70 percent of sales; operating expenses, including depreciation, amounted to $800,000. The firm sold a capital asset (stock) for $75,000, which had been purchased five months earlier at a cost of $80,000. Determine the company's tax liability.

1–5. *(Corporate Income Tax)* The Robbins Corporation is an oil wholesaler. The company's sales last year were $1 million, with the cost of goods sold equal to $600,000. The firm paid interest of $200,000, and its cash operating expenses were $100,000. Also, the firm received $40,000 in dividend income while paying only $10,000 in dividends to its preferred stockholders. Depreciation expense was $150,000. Compute the firm's tax liability. Based on your answer, does management need to take any additional action?

1–6. *(Corporate Income Tax)* The Fair Corporation had sales of $5 million this past year. The cost of goods sold was $4.3 million, and operating expenses were $100,000. Dividend income totaled $5,000. The firm sold land for $150,000 that had cost $100,000 five months ago. The firm received $150 per share from the sale of 1,000 shares of stock. The stock was purchased for $100 per share three years ago. Determine the firm's tax liability.

1–7. *(Corporate Income Tax)* Sales for J. P. Hulett, Inc., during the past year amounted to $4 million. The firm supplies statistical information to engineering companies. Gross profits totaled $1 million, and operating and depreciation expenses were $500,000 and $350,000, respectively. Dividend income for the year was $12,000. Compute the corporation's tax liability.

1–8. *(Corporate Income Tax)* Anderson & Dennis, Inc., sells computer software. The company's past year's sales were $5 million. The cost of its merchandise sold came to $3 million. Operating expenses were $175,000, plus depreciation expenses totaling $125,000. The firm paid $200,000 interest on loans. The firm sold stock during the year, receiving a $40,000 gain on a stock owned six years but losing $60,000 on stock held four months. Calculate the company's tax liability.

1–9. *(Corporate Income Tax)* G. R. Edwin, Inc., had sales of $6 million during the past year. The cost of goods sold amounted to $3 million. Operating expenses totaled $2.6 million and interest expense was $30,000. Determine the firm's tax liability.

1–10. *(Corporate Income Tax)* The Analtoly Corporation is an electronics dealer and distributor. Sales for the last year were $4.5 million, and cost of goods sold and operating expenses totaled $3.2 million. Analtoly also paid $150,000 in interest expense, and depreciation expense totaled $50,000. In addition, the company sold securities for $120,000 that it had purchased four years earlier at a price of $40,000. Compute the tax liability for Analtoly.

1–11. *(Corporate Income Tax)* Utsumi Inc. supplies wholesale industrial chemicals. Last year the company had sales of $6.5 million. Cost of goods sold and operating expenses amounted to 70 percent of sales, and depreciation and interest expenses were $75,000 and $160,000, respectively. Furthermore, the corporation sold 40,000 shares of Sumitono Industries for $10 a share. These shares were purchased a year ago for $8 each. In addition, Utsumi received $60,000 in dividend income. Compute the corporation's tax liability.

1–12. *(Carryback—Carryforward)* The taxable income for Mokita, Inc., for the past seven years is given below. From the information provided, determine the firm's tax payments and tax refunds in each year.

1988	$ 25,000	1992	$(125,000)
1989	(75,000)	1993	(20,000)
1990	100,000	1994	80,000
1991	50,000		

1–13. *(Carryback—Carryforward)* Given the taxable income figures below for the A. O. Faubus Corporation, compute the tax payment or tax refund in each year.

1987	$40,000	1991	$ 60,000
1988	(60,000)	1992	(100,000)
1989	30,000	1993	50,000
1990	80,000	1994	(75,000)

SUGGESTED APPLICATION FOR *DISCLOSURE*®
a. Access the *Disclosure* database and locate information about Pepsico and Coca-Cola. Read the president's letter and the management discussion for each company. Compare what you learn about both companies. Were you able to determine what management has set as each firm's goal?
b. Using the *Disclosure* database, obtain the annual income statement for Pepsico and for Coca-Cola. What is each firm's reported taxable income (income before taxes) and the tax liability (provision for income taxes), as shown by *Disclosure*?
c. Given Pepsi's and Coke's taxable income and using Table 1–2(Corporate Tax Rates), estimate each firm's tax liability.
d. Compare your answers in parts b and c for each company. Why might these numbers be different?

SELF-TEST SOLUTIONS

SS-1.

Sales			$2,000,000
Cost of goods sold			1,200,000
Gross profit			800,000
Tax-deductible expenses:			
Operating expenses		$ 400,000	
Interest expenses		100,000	
			500,000
			$ 300,000
Other income:			
Interest income			12,000
Preferred dividend income		$ 10,000	
Less 70% exclusion		$ 7,000	3,000
Taxable ordinary income			$ 315,000
Gain on sale:			
Selling price		$ 40,000	
Cost		30,000	
Taxable income			10,000
			$ 325,000
Tax liability			
.15 ×	$ 50,000 =	$ 7,500	
.25 ×	25,000 =	6,250	
.34 ×	250,000 =	85,000	
5% surtax		11,250	
		$ 110,000	

SS-2.

Year	Taxable Income	Tax Payments	Carryback	Carryforward	Tax Refunds
1986	$ (50,000)				
1987	25,000			$25,000 from 1986	
1988	150,000	$32,000[a]	$125,000 from 1989	25,000 from 1986	
1989	(225,000)				$32,000[b]
1990	50,000			50,000 from 1989	
1991	150,000	22,250[c]	50,000 from 1993	50,000 from 1989	
1992	200,000	61,250			
1993	(50,000)				14,750[d]

[a] Taxes are based on $125,000 ($150,000 taxable income – $25,000 carryforward from 1986).
[b] The tax refund results from a $125,000 carryback to 1988 to recoup the taxes paid in 1988.
[c] Taxes are based on $100,000 ($150,000 taxable income – $50,000 carryforward).
[d] The tax refund results from a $50,000 carryback to 1991. The taxes in 1991 were originally $22,250, based on $100,000 income. With the $50,000 carryback from 1993, the taxes for 1991 are recomputed on $50,000, or $7,500. The difference between the amount originally paid in 1991, or $22,250, and the recalculated $7,500 in taxes is $14,750.

CHAPTER 2

THE FINANCIAL MARKETS AND INTEREST RATES

The Mix of Corporate Securities Sold in the Capital Market • Why Financial Markets Exist • Financing of Business: The Movement of Funds Through the Economy • Components of the U.S. Financial Market System • The Investment Banker • Private Placements • Flotation Costs • Regulation • More Recent Regulatory Developments • Rates of Return in the Financial Markets • Interest Rate Determinants in a Nutshell • The Term Structure of Interest Rates •

At times internally generated funds will not be sufficient to finance all of the firm's proposed expenditures. In these situations, the corporation may find it necessary to attract large amounts of financial capital externally.[1] This chapter focuses on the market environment in which long-term capital is raised. It also introduces and covers the logic behind the determination of interest rates and required rates of return in the capital markets. We will explore interest rate levels and risk differentials over recent time periods and will study several theories that attempt to explain the shape of the *term structure of interest rates*. Ensuing chapters will discuss the distinguishing features of the instruments by which long-term funds are raised. Long-term funds are raised in the capital market. By the term *capital market*, we mean all institutions and procedures that facilitate transactions in long-term financial instruments (like common stocks and bonds).

---

[1]By *externally generated*, we mean that the funds are obtained by means *other* than through retentions or depreciation. Funds from these latter two sources are commonly called *internally generated* funds.

The Fall of Drexel Burnham Lambert:
Investment Banking *in extremis*
from ABC News, Business World, February 18, 1990

Investment bankers play a crucial role in funneling funds from investors to firms with worthwhile investment opportunities. Until the 1980s the world of investment bankers was one that few people knew about or understood. Increased competition and the rise of Drexel Burnham Lambert, primarily owing to Michael Milken's junk bond business, changed that. Suddenly the high-stakes world of investment banking was front-page news. Billion-dollar takeovers and LBOs became the norm and seemed to occur almost daily. This video describes how Drexel Burnham Lambert, the investment banking firm with the bad-boy image (and proud of it), changed the nature of corporate finance and even the structure of business enterprise in the United States in the 1980s. It also discusses the "deal-doing" attitude that Drexel's aggressive style helped foster on Wall Street and how the fall of Drexel may affect business in the 1990s.

As you read this chapter, think about the role investment bankers play as intermediaries—helping firms that need funds find investors—and how Drexel's junk bonds facilitated that role. What is the role of junk bonds, what motivated the deal making of the 1980s, and what will happen now that Drexel is gone?

Business firms in the nonfinancial corporate sector of the U.S. economy rely heavily on the nation's financial market system to raise cash. Table 2–1 displays the relative internal and external sources of funds for such corporations over the 1981–1990 period. Notice that the percentage of external funds raised in any given year can vary substantially from that of other years. In 1982, for example, the nonfinancial business sector raised only 21.1 percent of its funds by external means (in the financial markets). This was substantially less than the 36.4 percent raised externally only one year earlier, during 1981. In more recent years the same type of significant adjustment made by financial managers is evident. For example, during 1988 nonfinancial firms raised 31.1 percent of new funds in the external markets. By the end of 1990 this proportion dropped to 18.3 percent.

Such adjustments illustrate an important point: The financial executive is perpetually on his or her toes regarding market conditions. Changes in market conditions influence the precise way corporate funds will be raised.

The financial market system must be both organized and resilient. Periods of economic recession, for instance, test the financial markets and those firms that continually use the markets. Economic contractions are especially challenging to financial decision makers because all recessions are *unique*. This forces financing policies to become unique.

During the 1981–82 recession, which lasted 16 months, interest rates remained high during the worst phases of the downturn. This occurred because policy makers at the Federal Reserve System decided to wring a high rate of inflation out of the economy by means of a tight

TABLE 2–1
Nonfinancial Corporate
Business Sources of Funds

Year	Total Sources ($Billions)	Percent Internal Funds	Percent External Funds
1990	$466.7	81.7%	18.3%
1989	548.4	73.9	26.1
1988	586.7	68.9	31.1
1987	545.0	69.0	31.0
1986	521.5	64.6	35.4
1985	464.3	75.8	24.2
1984	491.4	68.5	31.5
1983	431.2	67.8	32.2
1982	313.7	78.9	21.1
1981	375.4	63.6	36.4

Source: *Economic Report of the President*, February 1992, p. 402.

monetary policy. Simultaneously, stock prices were depressed. These business conditions induced firms to forgo raising funds via external means. During 1982 we notice that 78.9 percent of corporate funds were generated internally (see Table 2–1).

The ninth recession since the end of World War II began in July 1990. Realized inflation and inflationary expectations were not the main culprits of contraction this time. As a result of loose monetary policy and low inflation rates, both short- and long-term interest rates moved to low levels. Treasury bills of three- and six-month maturities sold at prices that produced yields of less than 3 percent during early 1993. (By contrast, during the 1981–82 recession, three-month Treasury bills yielded 10.7 percent for all of 1982 and 14 percent for all of 1981.)

Furthermore, common stock prices rose to all-time *highs* during early 1993. Accordingly, corporate financial managers made more trips to the financial markets with new security issues. The cost of corporate capital was *perceived* to be low. In the midst of such business conditions firms turn to the financial markets and raise a greater proportion of their funds externally. As economic policy shapes the environment of the financial markets, managers must understand the meaning of the economic ups and downs and remain **flexible** in their decision-making processes.

The sums involved in tapping the capital markets can be vast. To be able to distribute and absorb security offerings of enormous size, an economy must have a well-developed financial market system. To use that system effectively, the financial officer must have a basic understanding of its structure. Accordingly, this chapter explores the rudiments of raising funds in the capital market.

PERSPECTIVE IN FINANCE

In Chapter 12 we will learn how to assess leverage use—both operating and financial leverage. In addition, we will examine the corporate financing decision in Chapter 12. Portions of those discussions will identify financial managers' confirmed preferences for raising funds through new debt contracts. The next section presents some near-term history of that financing behavior.

THE MIX OF CORPORATE SECURITIES SOLD IN THE CAPITAL MARKET

When corporations decide to raise cash in the capital market, what type of financing vehicle is most favored? Many individual investors think that common stock is the answer to this question. This is understandable, given the coverage of the level of common stock prices by the popular news media. All the major television networks, for instance, quote the closing price of the Dow Jones Industrial Average on their nightly news broadcasts. Common stock, though, is not the financing method relied on most heavily by corporations. The answer to this question is **corporate bonds**. *The corporate debt markets clearly dominate the corporate equity markets when new funds are being raised.* This is a long-term relationship—it occurs year after year. Table 2–2 bears this out.

In Table 2–2 we see the total volume (in millions of dollars) of domestic corporate securities sold for cash over the 1981–1991 period. The percentage breakdown among common stock, preferred stock, and bonds is also displayed. We will learn from our discussions of the cost of capital and planning the firm's financing mix that the U.S. tax system inherently favors debt as a means of raising capital. Quite simply, interest expense is deductible from other income when computing the firm's federal tax liability, whereas the dividends paid on both preferred and common stock are not.

Financial executives responsible for raising corporate cash know this. When they have a choice between marketing new bonds and marketing new preferred stock, the outcome is usually in favor of bonds. The after-tax cost of capital on the debt is less than that incurred on the preferred stock. Likewise, if the firm has unused debt capacity and the general level of equity prices is depressed, financial executives favor the issuance of debt securities over the issuance of new common stock. It is always good to keep some benchmark figures in your head. The average (unweighted) mix of corporate securities sold for cash over the 1981–1991 period follows. This *excludes* private

TABLE 2–2
Corporate Securities Offered for Cash (Domestic Offerings)

Year	Total Volume ($ millions)	Percent Common Stock	Percent Preferred Stock	Percent Bonds and Notes
1991	$352,344	13.6%	4.9%	81.5%
1990	212,712	9.1	1.9	89.0
1989	213,617	12.2	2.9	84.9
1988	244,670	14.7	2.7	82.6
1987	262,725	16.4	3.9	79.7
1986	248,722	23.7	4.9	71.4
1985	133,460	27.5	5.3	67.2
1984	95,287	23.3	4.5	72.2
1983	103,355	43.9	7.7	48.4
1982	73,397	32.3	6.7	61.0
1981	64,500	39.5	2.6	57.9

Source: *Economic Report of the President*, January 1989, p. 415, and *Federal Reserve Bulletin*, February 1993, p. A33.

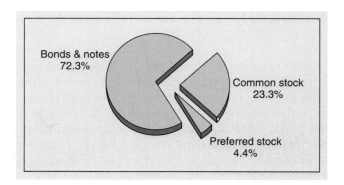

FIGURE 2–1
Corporate External Financing
Patterns 1981–1991

debt placements or the bonds and notes categories would be a bit higher. Figure 2–1 illustrates this financing pattern.

Common stock	23.3%
Preferred stock	4.4
Bonds and notes	72.3
Total	100.0%

PERSPECTIVE IN FINANCE

When you borrow money from a commercial bank to finance a purchase of stereo equipment or take out a mortgage to pay for a new home, you have used this country's financial market system. The average individual (and you are not *that because of your study of financial management) tends to take the reality of the financial markets for granted. But they were not always there, and they have evolved amid much controversy over a long period.*

Recent years have produced heated debates over alterations in our financial system; this just illustrates the dynamic nature of these markets. Much of that debate followed the collapse of the equity markets on Monday, October 19, 1987, when the Dow Jones Industrial Average fell by an unprecedented 508 points. Like banks, the equity markets are another piece of our complex financial market system. One reason underdeveloped countries are underdeveloped is because they lack a financial market system that has the confidence of those who must use it. Without such a system, real assets (like your home) do not get produced at an adequate rate and the populace suffers. We learn next why financial markets exist.

BACK TO THE FUNDAMENTALS

In this chapter we cover material that introduces the financial manager to the processes involved in raising funds in the nation's capital markets and also cover the logic that lies behind the determination of interest rates and required rates of return in those capital markets.

We will see that the United States has a highly developed, complex, and competitive system of financial markets that allows for the quick transfer of savings from those economic units with a surplus of savings to those economic units with a savings deficit. Such a system of highly developed financial markets allows great ideas (like the personal computer) to be financed and increases the overall wealth of the economy. Consider your wealth, for example, compared to that of the average family in Russia. Russia lacks a complex system of financial markets to facilitate transactions in financial claims (securities). As a result, real capital formation there has suffered.

Thus, we return now to **Axiom 6: Efficient Capital Markets— The Markets Are Quick and the Prices Are Right.** Financial managers like our system of capital markets because they trust them. This trust stems from the fact that the markets are "efficient." Managers trust prices in the securities markets because those prices quickly and accurately reflect all available information about the value of the underlying securities. This means that expected risks and expected cash flows matter more to market participants than do simpler things like accounting changes and the sequence of past price changes in a specific security. With security prices and returns (like interest rates) competitively determined, more financial managers (rather than fewer) participate in the markets and help ensure the basic concept of efficiency.

WHY FINANCIAL MARKETS EXIST

Financial markets are institutions and procedures that facilitate transactions in all types of financial claims. The purchase of your home, the common stock you may own, and your life insurance policy all took place in some type of financial market. Why do financial markets exist? What would the economy lose if our complex system of financial markets were not developed? We will address these questions here.

Some *economic units*, such as households, firms, or governments, spend more during a given period than they earn. Other economic units spend *less* on current consumption than they earn. For example, business firms in the aggregate usually spend more during a specific period than they earn. Households in the aggregate spend less on current consumption than they earn. As a result, some mechanism is needed to facilitate the transfer of savings from those economic units with a surplus to those with a deficit. That is precisely the function of financial markets. Financial markets exist in order to allocate the supply of savings in the economy to the demanders of those savings. The central characteristic of a financial market is that it acts as the vehicle through which the forces of demand and supply for a specific type of financial claim (such as a corporate bond) are brought together.

Now, why would the economy suffer without a developed financial market system? The answer is that the wealth of the economy would be less without the financial markets. The rate of capital formation would not be as high if financial markets did not exist. This means that the net additions during a specific period to the stocks of (1) dwellings, (2) productive plant and equipment, (3) inventory, and (4) consumer durables

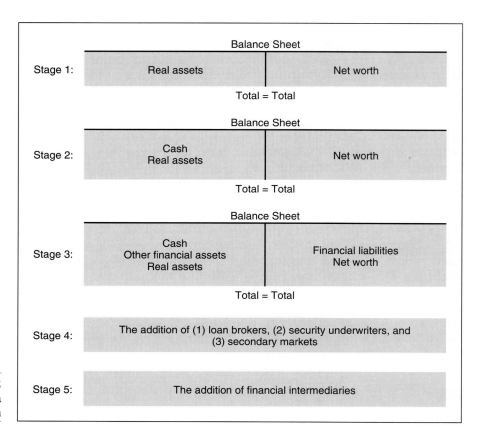

FIGURE 2–2
Development of a
Financial Market System

would occur at lower rates. Figure 2–2 helps clarify the rationale behind this assertion. The abbreviated balance sheets in the figure refer to firms or any other type of economic units that operate in the private as opposed to governmental sectors of the economy. This means that such units cannot issue money to finance their own activities.

At stage 1 in Figure 2–2 only real assets exist in the hypothetical economy. **Real assets** are tangible assets like houses, equipment, and inventories. They are distinguished from **financial assets,** which represent claims for future payment on other economic units. Common and preferred stocks, bonds, bills, and notes all are types of financial assets. If only real assets exist, then savings for a given economic unit, such as a firm, must be accumulated in the form of real assets. If the firm has a great idea for a new product, that new product can be developed, produced, and distributed only out of company savings (retained earnings). Furthermore, all investment in the new product must occur simultaneously as the savings are generated. If you have the idea, and we have the savings, there is no mechanism to transfer our savings to you. This is not a good situation.

At stage 2 paper money (cash) comes into existence in the economy. Here, at least, you can *store* your own savings in the form of money.

Thus, you can finance your great idea by drawing down your cash balances. This is an improvement over stage 1, but there is still no effective mechanism to transfer our savings to you. You see, we will not just hand you our dollar bills. We will want a receipt.

The concept of a receipt that represents the transfer of savings from one economic unit to another is a monumental advancement. The economic unit with excess savings can lend the savings to an economic unit that needs them. To the lending unit these receipts are identified as "other financial assets" in stage 3 of Figure 2–2. To the borrowing unit, the issuance of financial claims (receipts) shows up as "financial liabilities" on the stage 3 balance sheet. The economic unit with surplus savings will earn a rate of return on those funds. The borrowing unit will pay that rate of return, but it has been able to finance its great idea.

In stage 4 the financial market system moves further toward full development. Loan brokers come into existence. These brokers help locate pockets of excess savings and channel such savings to economic units needing the funds. Some economic units will actually purchase the financial claims of borrowing units and sell them at a higher price to other investors; this process is called **underwriting**. Underwriting will be discussed in more detail later in this chapter. In addition, **secondary markets** develop. Secondary markets simply represent trading in already existing financial claims. If you buy your brother's General Motors common stock, you have made a secondary market transaction. Secondary markets reduce the risk of investing in financial claims. Should you need cash, you can liquidate your claims in the secondary market. This induces savers to invest in securities.

The progression toward a developed and complex system of financial markets ends with stage 5. Here, financial intermediaries come into existence. You can think of financial intermediaries as the major financial institutions with which you are used to dealing. These include commercial banks, savings and loan associations, credit unions, life insurance companies, and mutual funds. Financial intermediaries share a common characteristic: They offer their own financial claims, called **indirect securities**, to economic units with excess savings. The proceeds from selling their indirect securities are then used to purchase the financial claims of other economic units. These latter claims can be called **direct securities**. Thus, a mutual fund might sell mutual fund shares (their indirect security) and purchase the common stocks (direct securities) of some major corporations. A life insurance company sells life insurance policies and purchases huge quantities of corporate bonds. Financial intermediaries thereby involve many small savers in the process of capital formation. This means there are more "good things" for everybody to buy.

A developed financial market system provides for a greater level of wealth in the economy. In the absence of financial markets, savings are not transferred to the economic units most in need of those funds. It is difficult, after all, for a household to build its own automobile. The financial market system makes it *easier* for the economy to build automobiles and all the other goods that economic units like to accumulate.

The movement of financial capital (funds) throughout the economy just means the movement of savings to the ultimate user of those savings. Some sectors of the economy save more than other sectors. As a result, these savings are moved to a productive use—say to manufacture that Corvette you want to buy.

The price of using someone else's savings is expressed in terms of interest rates. The financial market system helps to move funds to the most-productive end use. Those economic units with the most promising projects should be willing to bid the highest (in terms of rates) to obtain the savings. The concepts of financing and moving savings from one economic unit to another are now explored.

■ FINANCING OF BUSINESS: THE MOVEMENT OF FUNDS THROUGH THE ECONOMY

The Financing Process

We now understand the crucial role that financial markets play in a capitalist economy. At this point we will take a brief look at how funds flow across some selected sectors of the U.S. economy. In addition, we will focus a little more closely on the process of financial intermediation that was introduced in the preceding section. Some actual data are used to sharpen our knowledge of the financing process. We will see that financial institutions play a major role in bridging the gap between savers and borrowers in the economy. Nonfinancial corporations, we already know, are significant borrowers of financial capital.

Table 2–3 shows how funds were supplied and raised by the major sectors of our economy in 1990. Households were the largest net supplier of funds to the financial markets. This is the case, by the way, year in and year out. In 1990, households made available $160.3 billion in funds to other sectors. That was the excess of their funds supplied over

		[1]	[2]	[2]–[1]
				Net Funds
Sector		*Funds Raised*	*Funds Supplied*	*Supplied*
Households[a]		$259.1	$419.4	$160.3
Nonfinancial corporate business		53.6	100.2	46.6
U.S. government		246.6	29.3	–217.3
State and local governments		20.3	–8.0	–28.3
Foreign		72.9	104.5	31.6

TABLE 2–3
Sector View of Flow of Funds in U.S. Financial Markets for 1990 (Billions of Dollars)

[a]Includes personal trusts and nonprofit organizations.
Source: *Flow of Funds Accounts, Second Quarter 1991,* Flow of Funds Section (Washington, DC: Board of Governors of the Federal Reserve System, September 1991).

their funds raised in the markets. In the jargon of economics, the household sector is a *savings-surplus* sector.

Likewise in 1990, the nonfinancial business sector is a savings-surplus sector. In 1990 we see that nonfinancial corporations supplied $46.6 billion more in funds to the financial markets than they raised. This was due to extensive repurchases of their own common stock by firms in the marketplace. In fact, during the 11-year period of 1980–90 corporations were *net buyers* (rather than issuers) of common stock on eight occasions. However, during longer periods, such as 20 to 30 years, the nonfinancial business sector is typically a *savings-deficit* sector. That is, this sector raises more financial capital in the markets than it supplies.

Next, it can also be seen that the U.S. government sector was a savings-deficit sector for 1990. In 1990 the federal government raised $217.3 billion in excess of the funds it supplied to the financial markets. This highlights a serious problem for the entire economy and for the financial manager. Persistent federal deficits have increased the role of the federal government in the market for borrowed funds. The last time the federal government posted a budget surplus was 1969; the last time prior to that was 1960. The federal government has thus become a "quasi-permanent" savings-deficit sector. Most financial economists agree that this tendency puts upward pressure on interest rates in the financial marketplace and thereby raises the general (overall) cost of capital to corporations. This phenomenon has become known as *crowding-out:* The private borrower is pushed out of the financial markets in favor of the government borrower.

Table 2–3 further highlights how important *foreign* financial investment is to the activity of the U.S. economy. As the federal government has become more of a "confirmed" savings-deficit sector, the need for funds has been increasingly supplied by foreign interests. Thus, in 1990, the foreign sector *supplied* a net $31.6 billion to the domestic capital markets. As recently as 1982, the foreign sector *raised*—rather than supplied—$30.8 billion in the U.S. financial markets! This illustrates the dynamic nature of financial management.

Table 2–3 demonstrates that the financial market system must exist to facilitate the orderly and efficient flow of savings from the surplus sectors to the deficit sectors of the economy. The result during long periods is that the nonfinancial business sector is *typically* dependent on the household sector to finance its investment needs. The governmental sectors—especially the federal government—are quite reliant on foreign financing.

As we noted in the preceding section, the financial market system includes a complex network of intermediaries that assist in the transfer of savings among economic units. Two intermediaries will be highlighted here: life insurance companies and pension funds. They are especially important participants in the capital market of the country.

Because of the nature of their business, life insurance firms can invest heavily in long-term financial instruments. This investment tendency arises for two key reasons: (1) life insurance policies usually include a *savings element* in them, and (2) their liabilities liquidate at a very predictable rate. Thus, life insurance companies invest in the "long end" of the securities markets. This means that they favor (1) mortgages and (2) corporate bonds as investment vehicles rather than shorter-term-to-maturity financial instruments like Treasury bills. To a lesser extent, they acquire corporate stocks for their portfolios.

Over recent years, about 47 percent of the financial assets of life insurance firms are represented by corporate stocks and bonds. We see that life insurance companies are an important financial intermediary. By issuing life insurance policies (indirect securities), they can acquire direct securities (corporate stocks and bonds) for their investment portfolios. Their preference, by far, is for bonds over stocks.

Let us now direct our attention to another financial intermediary, private pension funds. In comparison with life insurance companies, three factors are emphasized. First, since 1960, private pension funds have grown at a *much faster rate* than have the insurance companies. Second, a *greater proportion* of the financial asset mix of the pension funds is devoted to *corporate stocks* and bonds. Third, the pension funds *invest more heavily* in corporate stocks than they do in corporate bonds. Over recent years, about 62 percent of the financial assets of private pension funds have been tied up in corporate stocks and bonds. These financial institutions also are significant *sources* of business financing in this country. The pension funds play the same *intermediary* role as does the life insurance subsector of the economy.

Movement of Savings

Figure 2–3 provides a useful way to summarize our discussion of (1) why financial markets exist and (2) the movement of funds through the economy. It also serves as an introduction to the role of the investment banker—a subject discussed in detail later in this chapter.

We see that savings are ultimately transferred to the business firm in need of cash in three ways:

1. **The direct transfer of funds.** Here the firm seeking cash sells its securities directly to savers (investors) who are willing to purchase them in hopes of earning a reasonable rate of return. New business formation is a good example of this process at work. The new business may go directly to a saver or group of savers called venture capitalists. The venture capitalists will lend funds to the firm or take an equity position in the firm if they feel the product or service the new firm hopes to market will be successful.

2. **Indirect transfer using the investment banker.** In a common arrangement under this system, the managing investment banking house will form a syndicate of several investment bankers. The syndicate will buy the entire issue of securities from the firm that is in need of financial capital. The syndicate will then sell the securities at a higher price than it paid for them to the investing public (the savers). Merrill Lynch Capital Markets and The First Boston Corporation are examples of investment banking firms. They tend to be called "houses" by those who work in the financial community. Notice that under this second method of transferring savings, the securities being issued just pass through the investment banking firm. They are not transformed into a different type of security.

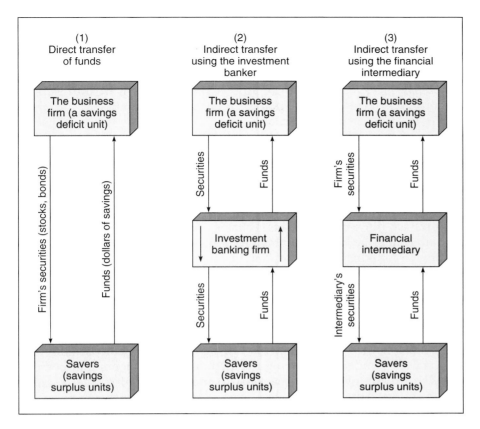

FIGURE 2–3
Three Ways to Transfer
Financial Capital
in the Ecomomy

3. **Indirect transfer using the financial intermediary.** This is the type of system life insurance companies and pension funds operate within. The financial intermediary collects the savings of individuals and issues its own (indirect) securities in exchange for these savings. The intermediary then uses the funds collected from the individual savers to acquire the business firm's (direct) securities, such as stocks and bonds.

We all benefit from the three transfer mechanisms displayed in Figure 2–3. Capital formation and economic wealth are greater than they would be in the absence of this financial market system.

<u>PERSPECTIVE IN FINANCE</u>

Because the United States enjoys such a developed system of financial markets, the terms used to discuss operations in those markets are numerous—some would say limitless. The financial executive, and those who work close to the financial executive, need to master a basic understanding of the commonly used terms and financing situations. There is just no getting around this requirement. But if you can learn the terminology of baseball, basketball, or football, you can do the same relative to the financial markets. It may, in fact, pay off in a much wealthier fashion for you.

THE FINANCIAL MARKETS
AND INTEREST RATES

■ COMPONENTS OF THE U.S. FINANCIAL MARKET SYSTEM

Numerous approaches exist for classifying the securities markets. At times, the array can be confusing. An examination of four sets of dichotomous terms can help provide a basic understanding of the structure of the U.S. financial markets.

Public Offerings and Private Placements

When a corporation decides to raise external capital, those funds can be obtained by making a public offering or a private placement. In a **public offering** both individual and institutional investors have the opportunity to purchase the securities. The securities are usually made available to the public at large by a managing investment banking firm and its underwriting (risk-taking) syndicate. The firm does not meet the ultimate purchasers of the securities in the public offering. The public market is an impersonal market.

In a **private placement,** also called a **direct placement,** the securities are offered and sold to a limited number of investors. The firm will usually hammer out, on a face-to-face basis with the prospective buyers, the details of the offering. In this setting the investment banking firm may act as a finder by bringing together potential lenders and borrowers. The private placement market is a more personal market than its public counterpart.

Primary Markets and Secondary Markets

Primary markets are those in which securities are offered for the *first* time to potential investors. A new issue of common stock by AT&T is a primary market transaction. This type of transaction increases the total stock of financial assets outstanding in the economy.

As mentioned in our discussion of the development of the financial market system, **secondary markets** represent transactions in currently outstanding securities. If the first buyer of the AT&T stock subsequently sells it, he or she does so in the secondary market. All transactions after the initial purchase take place in the secondary market. The sales do *not* affect the total stock of financial assets that exist in the economy. Both the money market and the capital market, described next, have primary and secondary sides.

Money Market and Capital Market

Money Market

The key distinguishing feature between the money and capital markets is the maturity period of the securities traded in them. The **money market** refers to all institutions and procedures that provide for transactions in short-term debt instruments generally issued by borrowers with very high credit ratings. By financial convention, *short term* means maturity periods of one year or less. Notice that equity instruments, either common or preferred, are not traded in the money market. The major instruments issued and traded are U.S. Treasury bills, various federal agency securities, bankers' acceptances, negotiable certificates of deposit, and commercial paper. Keep in mind that the money market is an intangible market. You do not walk into a building on Wall Street that has the words "Money Market" etched in stone over its arches. Rather, the money market is primarily a telephone market.

Capital Market

The **capital market** refers to all institutions and procedures that provide for transactions in long-term financial instruments. *Long-term* here means having maturity periods that extend beyond one year. In the broad sense this encompasses term loans and financial leases, corporate equities, and bonds. The funds that comprise the firm's capital structure are raised in the capital market. Important elements of the capital market are the organized security exchanges and the over-the-counter markets.

Organized Security Exchanges and Over-the-Counter Markets

Organized security exchanges are tangible entities; they physically occupy space (such as a building or part of a building), and financial instruments are traded on their premises. The **over-the-counter markets** include all security markets *except* the organized exchanges. The money market, then, is an over-the-counter market. Because both markets are important to financial officers concerned with raising *long-term capital*, some additional discussion is warranted.

Organized Security Exchanges

For practical purposes there are seven major security exchanges in the United States.[2] These are the (1) New York Stock Exchange, (2) American Stock Exchange, (3) Midwest Stock Exchange, (4) Pacific Stock Exchange, (5) Philadelphia Stock Exchange, (6) Boston Stock Exchange, and (7) Cincinnati Stock Exchange. The New York Stock Exchange (NYSE) and the American Stock Exchange (AMEX) are called *national* exchanges, whereas the others are loosely described as *regionals*. All of these seven active exchanges are registered with the Securities and Exchange Commission (SEC). Firms whose securities are traded on the registered exchanges must comply with reporting requirements of both the specific exchange and the SEC.

An indication of the importance of the NYSE to our financial market system is reflected in something known as "consolidated tape volume." The Consolidated Tape prints all of the transactions on stocks

---

[2]Others include (1) The Honolulu Stock Exchange, which is unregistered; (2) the Board of Trade of the City of Chicago, which does not now trade stocks; and (3) the Chicago Board Options Exchange, Inc., which deals in options rather than stocks. The cities of Colorado Springs, Salt Lake City, and Spokane also have small exchanges. From time to time you may hear of the New York Futures Exchange (NYFE). This subsidiary of the NYSE was incorporated on April 5, 1979. Trading on the NYFE is in futures contracts and options contracts.

that are listed on the NYSE and are traded on other organized markets. These markets include the exchanges mentioned earlier plus over-the-counter markets. In 1991, the NYSE accounted for 82.3 percent of consolidated volume.[3]

The business of an exchange, including securities transactions, is conducted by its **members**. Members are said to occupy "seats." There are 1,366 seats on the NYSE, a number that has remained constant since 1953. Major brokerage firms own seats on the exchanges. An officer of the firm is designated to be the member of the exchange, and this membership permits the brokerage house to use the facilities of the exchange to effect trades. During 1991 the prices of seats that were exchanged for cash ranged from a low of $345,000 to a high of $440,000.[4] The record price, by the way, was $1.15 million paid on September 21, 1987—just prior to the October 19 market debacle.

STOCK EXCHANGE BENEFITS   Both corporations and investors enjoy several benefits provided by the existence of organized security exchanges. These include

1. **Providing a continuous market.** This may be the most important function of an organized security exchange. A continuous market provides a series of continuous security prices. Price changes from trade to trade tend to be smaller than they would be in the absence of organized markets. The reasons are that there is a relatively large sales volume in each security, trading orders are executed quickly, and the range between the price asked for a security and the offered price tends to be narrow. The result is that price volatility is reduced.

2. **Establishing and publicizing fair security prices.** An organized exchange permits security prices to be set by competitive forces. They are not set by negotiations off the floor of the exchange, where one party might have a bargaining advantage. The bidding process flows from the supply and demand underlying each security. This means the specific price of a security is determined in the manner of an auction. In addition, the security prices determined at each exchange are widely publicized.

3. **Helping business raise new capital.** Because a continuous secondary market exists where prices are competitively determined, it is easier for firms to float new security offerings successfully. This continuous pricing mechanism also facilitates the determination of the offering price of a new issue. This means that comparative values are easily observed.

LISTING REQUIREMENTS   To receive the benefits provided by an organized exchange, the firm must seek to have its securities listed on the exchange. An application for listing must be filed and a fee paid. The

[3]New York Stock Exchange, Fact Book (New York, 1992), p. 24.
[4]New York Stock Exchange, Fact Book (New York, 1992), p. 74.

TABLE 2–4
NYSE Listing Requirements

Profitability
Earnings before taxes (EBT) for the most recent year must be at least $2.5 million. For the two years preceding that, EBT must be at least $2.0 million.
Size
Net tangible assets must be at least $18.0 million.
Market Value[a]
The market value of publicly held stock must be at least $18.0 million.
Public Ownership
There must be at least 1.1 million publicly held common shares. There must be at least 2000 holders of 100 shares or more.

[a]The market value is tied to the level of common stock prices prevailing in the marketplace at the time of the listing application. From time to time the $18.0 million requirement noted above may be lessened. Under current regulations of the NYSE, the requirement can never be less than $9.0 million.

requirements for listing vary from exchange to exchange; those of the NYSE are the most stringent. The general criteria for listing fall into these categories: (1) profitability, (2) size, (3) market value, and (4) public ownership. To give you the flavor of an actual set of listing requirements, those set forth by the NYSE are displayed in Table 2–4.[5]

Over-the-Counter Markets

Many publicly held firms do not meet the listing requirements of major stock exchanges. Others may want to avoid the reporting requirements and fees required to maintain listing. As an alternative their securities may trade in the over-the-counter markets. On the basis of sheer numbers (not dollar volume), more stocks are traded over-the-counter than on organized exchanges. As far as secondary trading in corporate bonds is concerned, the over-the-counter markets are where the action is. In a typical year, more than 90 percent of corporate bond business takes place over-the-counter.

Most over-the-counter transactions are done through a loose network of security traders who are known as broker-dealers and brokers. Brokers do not purchase securities for their own account, whereas dealers do. Broker-dealers stand ready to buy and sell specific securities at selected prices. They are said to "make a market" in those securities. Their profit is the spread or difference between the price they will pay for a security (bid price) and the price at which they will sell the security (asked price).

PRICE QUOTES   The availability of prices is not as continuous in the over-the-counter market as it is on an organized exchange. Since February 8, 1971, however, when a computerized network called NASDAQ came into existence, the availability of prices in this market has improved substantially. NASDAQ stands for National Association of Security Dealers Automated Quotation System. It is a telecommunications system that provides a national information link among the bro-

[5]New York Stock Exchange, *Fact Book* (New York, 1992), p. 32.

kers and dealers operating in the over-the-counter markets. Subscribing traders have a terminal that allows them to obtain representative bids and ask prices for thousands of securities traded over-the-counter. NASDAQ is a quotation system, not a transactions system. The final trade is still consummated by direct negotiation between traders.

NASDAQ price quotes for many stocks are published daily in the *Wall Street Journal*. This same financial newspaper also publishes prices on hundreds of other stocks traded over-the-counter. Local papers supply prices on stocks of regional interest. Finally, the National Quotation Bureau publishes daily "pink sheets," which contain prices on about 8,000 securities; these sheets are available in the offices of most security dealers.

<u>PERSPECTIVE IN FINANCE</u>

We touched briefly on the investment banking industry and the investment banker earlier in this chapter when we described various methods for transferring financial capital (see Figure 2–3). The investment banker is to be distinguished from the commercial banker in that the former's organization is not a permanent depository for funds. Later it will be shown, however, that a trend is under way in this country to let commercial banks perform more functions and services that since 1933 have belonged almost exclusively to the investment banking industry. For the moment, it is important for you to learn about the role of the investment banker in the funding of commercial activity.

■ THE INVESTMENT BANKER

Most corporations do not raise long-term capital frequently. The activities of working-capital management go on daily, but attracting long-term capital is, by comparison, episodic. The sums involved can be huge, so these situations are considered of great importance to financial managers. Because most managers are unfamiliar with the subtleties of raising long-term funds, they enlist the help of an expert. That expert is an investment banker.

Definition

The **investment banker** is a financial specialist involved as an intermediary in the merchandising of securities. He or she acts as a "middle person" by facilitating the flow of savings from those economic units that want to invest to those units that want to raise funds. We use the term investment banker to refer both to a given individual and to the organization for which such a person works, variously known as an **investment banking firm** or an **investment banking house**. Although these firms are called investment bankers, they perform no depository or lending functions. The activities of commercial banking and investment banking as we know them today were separated by the Banking Act of 1933 (also known as the Glass-Steagall Act of 1933). Just what does this middleman role involve? That is most easily understood in terms of the basic functions of investment banking.

Functions

The investment banker performs three basic functions: (1) underwriting, (2) distributing, and (3) advising.

Underwriting

The term **underwriting** is borrowed from the field of insurance. It means "assuming a risk." The investment banker assumes the risk of selling a security issue at a satisfactory price. A satisfactory price is one that will generate a profit for the investment banking house.

The procedure goes like this. The managing investment banker and its syndicate will buy the security issue from the corporation in need of funds. The **syndicate** is a group of other investment bankers who are invited to help buy and resell the issue. The managing house is the investment banking firm that originated the business because its corporate client decided to raise external funds. On a specific day, the firm that is raising capital is presented with a check in exchange for the securities being issued. At this point the investment banking syndicate owns the securities. The corporation has its cash and can proceed to use it. The firm is now immune from the possibility that the security markets might turn sour. If the price of the newly issued security falls below that paid to the firm by the syndicate, the syndicate will suffer a loss. The syndicate, of course, hopes that the opposite situation will result. Its objective is to sell the new issue to the investing public at a price per security greater than its cost.

Distributing

Once the syndicate owns the new securities, it must get them into the hands of the ultimate investors. This is the distribution or selling function of investment banking. The investment banker may have branch offices across the United States, or it may have an informal arrangement with several security dealers who regularly buy a portion of each new offering for final sale. It is not unusual to have 300 to 400 dealers involved in the selling effort. The syndicate can properly be viewed as the security wholesaler, and the dealer organization can be viewed as the security retailer.

Advising

The investment banker is an expert in the issuance and marketing of securities. A sound investment banking house will be aware of prevailing market conditions and can relate those conditions to the particular type of security that should be sold at a given time. Business conditions may be pointing to a future increase in interest rates. The investment banker might advise the firm to issue its bonds in a timely fashion to avoid the higher yields that are forthcoming. The banker can analyze the firm's capital structure and make recommendations as to what general source of capital should be issued. In many instances the firm will invite its investment banker to sit on the board of directors. This permits the banker to observe corporate activity and make recommendations on a regular basis.

Distribution Methods

Several methods are available to the corporation for placing new security offerings in the hands of final investors. The investment banker's role is different in each of these. Sometimes, in fact, it is possible to bypass the investment banker. These methods are described in this section. Private placements, because of their importance, are treated separately later in the chapter.

Negotiated Purchase

In a negotiated underwriting, the firm that needs funds makes contact with an investment banker, and deliberations concerning the new issue begin. If all goes well, a *method* is negotiated for determining the price the investment banker and the syndicate will pay for the securities. For example, the agreement might state that the syndicate will pay $2 less than the closing price of the firm's common stock on the day before the offering date of a new stock issue. The negotiated purchase is the most prevalent method of securities distribution in the private sector. It is generally thought to be the most profitable technique as far as investment bankers are concerned.

Competitive Bid Purchase

The method by which the underwriting group is determined distinguishes the competitive bid purchase from the negotiated purchase. In a competitive underwriting, several underwriting groups bid for the right to purchase the new issue from the corporation that is raising funds. The firm does not directly select the investment banker. The investment banker that underwrites and distributes the issue is chosen by an auction process. The syndicate willing to pay the greatest dollar amount per new security will win the competitive bid.

Most competitive bid purchases are confined to three situations, compelled by legal regulations: (1) railroad issues, (2) public utility issues, and (3) state and municipal bond issues. The argument in favor of competitive bids is that any undue influence of the investment banker over the firm is mitigated and the price received by the firm for each security should be higher. Thus, we would intuitively suspect that the cost of capital in a competitive bid situation would be less than in a negotiated purchase situation. Evidence on this question, however, is mixed. One problem with the competitive bid purchase as far as the fundraising firm is concerned is that the benefits gained from the advisory function of the investment banker are lost. It may be necessary to use an investment banker for advisory purposes and then by law exclude the banker from the competitive bid process.

Commission or Best-Efforts Basis

Here, the investment banker acts as an agent rather than as a principal in the distribution process. The securities are *not* underwritten. The investment banker attempts to sell the issue in return for a fixed commission on each security actually sold. Unsold securities are returned to the corporation. This arrangement is typically used for more speculative issues. The issuing firm may be smaller or less established than the investment banker would like. Because the underwriting risk is not passed on to the investment banker, this distribution method is less costly to the issuer than a negotiated or competitive bid purchase. On the other hand the investment banker only has to give it his or her "best effort." A successful sale is not guaranteed.

Privileged Subscription

Occasionally, the firm may feel that a distinct market already exists for its new securities. When a new issue is marketed to a definite and select group of investors, it is called a **privileged subscription**. Three target markets are typically involved: (1) current stockholders, (2) employees, or (3) customers. Of these, distributions directed at current stockholders are the most prevalent. Such offerings are called **rights offerings**. In a privileged subscription the investment banker may act only as a selling agent. It is also possible that the issuing firm and the investment banker might sign a **standby agreement**, which would obligate the investment banker to underwrite the securities that are not accepted by the privileged investors.

Direct Sale

In a **direct sale** the issuing firm sells the securities directly to the investing public without involving an investment banker. Even among established corporate giants this procedure is relatively rare. A variation of the direct sale, though, was used more frequently in the 1970s than in previous decades. This involves the private placement of a new issue by the fundraising corporation *without* the use of an investment banker as an intermediary. Texaco, Mobil Oil, and International Harvester (now Navistar) are examples of large firms that have followed this procedure.[6]

Industry Leaders

All industries have their leaders, and investment banking is no exception. We have discussed investment bankers in general at some length in this chapter. Table 2–5 gives us some idea who the major players are within the investment banking industry. It lists the top 10 houses in 1991 based on the dollar volume of security issues that were managed. The number of issues the house participated in as lead manager is also identified, along with its share of the market.

■ PRIVATE PLACEMENTS

Private placements are an alternative to the sale of securities to the public or to a restricted group of investors through a privileged subscription. Any type of security can be privately placed (directly placed). This mar-

[6]See Wyndham Robertson, "Future Shock at Morgan Stanley," *Fortune* 97 (February 27, 1978), pp. 88, 90.

TABLE 2–5
Leading U.S. Investment
Bankers, 1991

Firm	Underwriting Volume (Billions of Dollars)	Number of Issues	Percent of Market
1. Merrill Lynch	$100.0	1180	17.2%
2. Goldman, Sachs	72.7	1013	12.5
3. Lehman Brothers	67.6	1336	11.7
4. First Boston	56.8	944	9.8
5. Kidder, Peabody	50.0	1705	8.6
6. Morgan Stanley	48.0	564	8.3
7. Salomon Brothers	43.7	626	7.5
8. Bear, Stearns	33.9	1087	5.8
9. Prudential Securities	18.2	613	3.1
10. Donaldson, Lufkin & Jenrette	11.2	324	1.9

Source: IDD Information Services as reported in the *New York Times*, January 2, 1992, p. C6.

ket, however, is clearly dominated by debt issues. Thus, we restrict this discussion to debt securities. From year to year the volume of private placements will vary. Table 2–6 shows, though, that the private placement market is always a significant portion of the U.S. capital market.

The major investors in private placements are large financial institutions. Based on the volume of securities purchased, the three most important investor groups are (1) life insurance companies, (2) state and local retirement funds, and (3) private pension funds.

In arranging a private placement the firm may (1) avoid the use of an investment banker and work directly with the investing institutions or (2) engage the services of an investment banker. If the firm does not use an investment banker, of course, it does not have to pay a fee. Conversely, investment bankers can provide valuable advice in the private placement process. They are usually in contact with several major institutional investors; thus, they will know if a firm is in a position to invest in its proposed offering, and they can help the firm evaluate the terms of the new issue.

Private placements have advantages and disadvantages compared with public offerings. The financial manager must carefully evaluate

TABLE 2–6
Publicly and Privately Placed
Corporate Debt Placed
Domestically (Gross Proceeds
of All New U.S. Corporate
Debt Issues)

Year	Total Volume ($ million)	Percent Publicly Placed	Percent Privately Placed
1991	$362,006	79.3%	20.7%
1990	276,259	68.5	31.5
1989	298,813	60.7	39.3
1988	329,919	61.3	38.7
1987	301,447	69.5	30.5
1986	313,502	74.2	25.8
1985	165,754	72.1	27.9
1984	109,903	66.9	33.1
1983	68,370	69.1	30.9
1982	53,636	81.7	18.3
1981	45,092	84.5	15.5

Source: *Federal Reserve Bulletin*, various issues.

both sides of the question. The advantages associated with private placements are these:

1. **Speed.** The firm usually obtains funds more quickly through a private placement than a public offering. The major reason is that registration of the issue with the SEC is not required.
2. **Reduced flotation costs.** These savings result because the lengthy registration statement for the SEC does not have to be prepared, and the investment banking underwriting and distribution costs do not have to be absorbed.
3. **Financing flexibility.** In a private placement the firm deals on a face-to-face basis with a small number of investors. This means that the terms of the issue can be tailored to meet the specific needs of the company. For example, all of the funds need not be taken by the firm at once. In exchange for a commitment fee the firm can "draw down" against the established amount of credit with the investors. This provides some insurance against capital market uncertainties, and the firm does not have to borrow the funds if the need does not arise. There is also the possibility of renegotiation. The terms of the debt issue can be altered. The term to maturity, the interest rate, or any restrictive covenants can be discussed among the affected parties.

The following disadvantages of private placements must be evaluated:

1. **Interest costs.** It is generally conceded that interest costs on private placements exceed those of public issues. Whether this disadvantage is enough to offset the reduced flotation costs associated with a private placement is a determination the financial manager must make. There is some evidence that on smaller issues, say $500,000 as opposed to $30 million, the private placement alternative would be preferable.
2. **Restrictive covenants.** Dividend policy, working-capital levels, and the raising of additional debt capital may all be affected by provisions in the private-placement debt contract. That is not to say that such restrictions are always absent in public debt contracts. Rather, the financial officer must be alert to the tendency for these covenants to be especially burdensome in private contracts.
3. **The possibility of future SEC registration.** If the lender (investor) should decide to sell the issue to a public buyer before maturity, the issue must be registered with the SEC. Some lenders, then, require that the issuing firm agree to a future registration at their option.

■■ FLOTATION COSTS

The firm raising long-term capital incurs two types of **flotation costs:** (1) the underwriter's spread and (2) issuing costs. Of these two costs, the underwriter's spread is the larger. The **underwriter's spread** is simply the difference between the gross and net proceeds from a given security issue expressed as a percent of the gross proceeds. The **issue costs** include (1) printing and engraving, (2) legal fees, (3) accounting fees, (4) trustee fees, and (5) several other miscellaneous components. The two most significant issue costs are printing and engraving and legal fees.

Data published by the SEC have consistently revealed two relationships about flotation costs. First, the costs associated with issuing common stock are notably greater than the costs associated with preferred stock offerings. In turn, preferred stock costs exceed those of bonds. Second, flotation costs (expressed as a percent of gross proceeds) decrease as the size of the security issue increases.

In the first instance, the stated relationship reflects the fact that issue costs are sensitive to the risks involved in successfully distributing a security issue. Common stock is riskier to own than corporate bonds. Underwriting risk is, therefore, greater with common stock than with bonds. Thus, flotation costs just mirror these risk relationships. In the second case, a portion of the issue costs is fixed. Legal fees and accounting costs are good examples. So, as the size of the security issue rises, the fixed component is spread over a larger gross proceeds base. As a consequence, average flotation costs vary inversely with the size of the issue.

PERSPECTIVE IN FINANCE

Since late 1986, there has been a renewal of public interest in the regulation of the country's financial markets. The key event was a massive insider trading scandal that made the name Ivan F. Boesky one of almost universal recognition—but, unfortunately, in a negative sense. This was followed by the October 19, 1987, crash of the equity markets. More recently, in early 1990, the investing community (both institutional and individual) became increasingly concerned over a weakening in the so-called "junk bond market." The upshot of all of this enhanced awareness is a new appreciation of the crucial role that regulation plays in the financial system. The basics are presented below.

■ REGULATION

Following the severe economic downturn of 1929–32, Congressional action was taken to provide for federal regulation of the securities markets. State statutes (blue sky laws) also govern the securities markets where applicable, but the federal regulations are clearly more pressing and important. The major federal regulations are reviewed here.

Primary Market Regulations

The new issues market is governed by the Securities Act of 1933. The intent of the act is important. It aims to provide potential investors with accurate, truthful disclosure about the firm and the new securities being offered to the public. This does *not* prevent firms from issuing highly speculative securities. The SEC says nothing whatsoever about the possible investment worth of a given offering. It is up to the investor to separate the junk from the jewels. The SEC does have the legal power and responsibility to enforce the 1933 act.

Full public disclosure is achieved by the requirement that the issuing firm file a registration statement with the SEC containing requisite information. The statement details particulars about the firm and the new security being issued. During a minimum 20-day waiting period, the SEC examines the submitted document. In numerous instances the 20-day wait has been extended by several weeks. The SEC can ask for additional information that was omitted in order to clarify the original document. The SEC can also order that the offering be stopped.

During the registration process a preliminary prospectus (the red herring) may be distributed to potential investors. When the registration is approved, the final prospectus must be made available to the prospective investors. The prospectus is actually a condensed version of the full registration statement. If, at a later date, the information in the registration statement and the prospectus is found to be lacking, purchasers of the new issue who incurred a loss can sue for damages. Officers of the issuing firm and others who took part in the registration and marketing of the issue may suffer both civil and criminal penalties.

Generally, the SEC defines public issues as those that are sold to more than 25 investors. Some public issues need not be registered. These include

1. Relatively small issues where the firm sells less than $1.5 million of new securities per year.
2. Issues that are sold entirely intrastate.
3. Issues that are basically short-term instruments. This translates into maturity periods of 270 days or less.
4. Issues that are already regulated or controlled by some other federal agency. Examples here are the Federal Power Commission (public utilities) and the Interstate Commerce Commission (railroads).

Secondary Market Regulations

Secondary market trading is regulated by the **Securities Exchange Act of 1934**. This act created the SEC to enforce federal securities laws. The Federal Trade Commission enforced the 1933 act for one year. The major aspects of the 1934 act can be best presented in outline form:

1. Major security exchanges must register with the SEC. This regulates the exchanges and places reporting requirements on the firms whose securities are listed on them.
2. Insider trading is regulated. Insiders can be officers, directors, employees, relatives, major investors, or anyone having information

The most recognizable inside trader of them all, Mr. Ivan F. Boesky, was scheduled to be set free on April 6, 1990, after a three-year prison sentence. The piece below discusses his opportunities to manage money for others.

How do you feel about an individual who violated the 1934 act being allowed in law to operate as a professional money manager? Once free, Boesky will even be able to resume the life of a money manager—assuming, of course, that people will trust him. Although the Nov. 14, 1986, agreement with the Securities & Exchange Commission barred him for life from the securities business, a loophole in the 1940 statute governing investment advisers allows Boesky to invest for up to 14 people, as long as he doesn't advertise his services. As Boesky lawyer Harvey L. Pitt observes: "If I had 14 people, each with a billion dollars, I could manage $14 billion." An obvious point—but startling nonetheless.

Source: "How Life on the Outside Looks for an Inside Trader," *Business Week*, January 15, 1990, pp. 27–28.

about the operation of the firm that is not public knowledge. If an investor purchases the security of the firm in which the investor is an insider, he or she must hold it for at least six months before disposing of it. Otherwise, profits made from trading the stock within a period of less than six months must be returned to the firm. Furthermore, insiders must file with the SEC a monthly statement of holdings and transactions in the stock of their corporation.[7]

3. Manipulative trading of securities by investors to affect stock prices is prohibited.

4. The SEC is given control over proxy procedures.

5. The Board of Governors of the Federal Reserve System is given responsibility for setting margin requirements. This affects the flow of credit into the securities markets. Buying securities on margin simply means using credit to acquire a portion of the subject financial instruments.

[7]On November 14, 1986, the SEC announced that Ivan F. Boesky had admitted to illegal inside trading after an intensive investigation. Boesky at the time was a very well-known Wall Street investor, speculator, and arbitrageur. Boesky was an owner or part owner in several companies, including an arbitrage fund named Ivan F. Boesky & Co. L. P. Boesky agreed to pay the U.S. government $50 million, which represented a return of illegal profits, another $50 million in civil penalties; to withdraw permanently from the securities industry; and to plead guilty to criminal charges. The far-reaching investigation continued into 1987 and implicated several other prominent investment figures.
The chairman of the SEC during this period was John S. R. Shad. Shad suggested that security trades would be considered illegal if they were based on "material, nonpublic information." As you would expect, this insider trading case garnered a lot of attention in the popular business press and led to renewed discussions of ethics in business schools. See "Who'll Be the Next to Fall?" *Business Week*, December 1, 1986, pp. 28–30; "Wall Street Enters the Age of the Supergrass," *The Economist*, November 22–28, 1986, pp. 77–78; "Going After the Crooks," *Time*, December 1, 1986, pp. 48–51; and "The Decline and Fall of Business Ethics," *Fortune* 114, December 8, 1986, pp. 65–66, 68, 72.

In recent years a number of financial intermediaries, including Drexel Burnham Lambert and Salomon Brothers, have been rocked by ethical scandals. Because financial dealings demand trust, these ethical scandals closed Drexel Burnham Lambert and almost did the same to Salomon Brothers. Once again, this demonstrates the importance of **Axiom 9: Ethical Behavior Is Doing the Right Thing, and Ethical Dilemmas Are Everywhere in Finance.**

■ MORE RECENT REGULATORY DEVELOPMENTS

Securities Acts Amendments of 1975

The Securities Acts Amendments of 1975 touched on three important issues. First, Congress mandated the creation of a national market system (NMS). Only broad goals for this national exchange were identified by Congress. Implementation details were left to the SEC and, to a much lesser extent, the securities industry in general. Congress was really expressing its desire for (1) widespread application of auction market trading principles, (2) a high degree of competition across markets, and (3) the use of modern electronic communication systems to link the fragmented markets in the country into a true NMS. The NMS is still a goal toward which the SEC and the securities industry are moving. Agreement as to its final form and an implementation date have not occurred.

A second major alteration in the habits of the securities industry also took place in 1975. This was the elimination of fixed commissions (fixed brokerage rates) on public transactions in securities. This was closely tied to the desire for an NMS in that fixed brokerage fees provided no incentive for competition among brokers. A third consideration of the 1975 amendments focused on such financial institutions as commercial banks and insurance firms. These financial institutions were prohibited from acquiring membership on stock exchanges in order to reduce or save commissions on their own trades.

Shelf Registration

On March 16, 1982, the SEC began a new procedure for registering new issues of securities. Formally it is called SEC Rule 415; informally the process is known as a **shelf registration**, or a **shelf offering**. The essence of the process is rather simple. Rather than go through the lengthy, full registration process each time the firm plans an offering of securities, it can get a blanket order approved by the SEC. A master registration statement that covers the financing plans of the firm over the coming two years is filed with the SEC. On approval, the firm can market some or all of the securities over this two-year period. The securities are sold in a piecemeal fashion, or "off the shelf." Prior to each specific offering, a short statement about the issue is filed with the SEC.

Corporations raising funds approve of this new procedure. The tedious, full registration process is avoided with each offering pulled off the shelf. This should result in a saving of fees paid to investment bankers. Moreover, an issue can more quickly be brought to the market. Also, if market conditions change, an issue can easily be redesigned to fit the specific conditions of the moment.

As is always the case, there is another side to the story. Recall that the reason for the registration process in the first place is to give investors useful information about the firm and the securities being offered. Under the shelf registration procedure some of the information about the issuing firm becomes old as the two-year horizon unfolds. Some investment bankers feel they do not have the proper amount of time to study the firm when a shelf offering takes place. This is one of those areas of finance where more observations are needed before any final conclusions can be made. Those observations will only come with the passage of time.

▮ RATES OF RETURN IN THE FINANCIAL MARKETS

Earlier in this chapter in discussing "the financing process" we noted that net users of funds (saving-deficit economic units) must compete with one another for the funds supplied by net savers (savings-surplus economic units). Consequently, to obtain financing for projects that will benefit the firm's stockholders, that firm must offer the supplier (savings-surplus unit) a rate of return *competitive* with the next best investment alternative available to that saver (investor). This rate of return on the next best investment alternative to the saver is known as the supplier's **opportunity cost of funds**. The opportunity cost concept is crucial in financial management and will be referred to often.

Next we will review the levels and variability in rates of return that have occurred over the lengthy period of 1926–1990. This review focuses on returns from a wide array of financial instruments. In both Chapters 8 and 11 we will discuss at length the concept of an *overall* cost of capital. Part of that overall cost of capital is attributed to interest rate levels at given points in time. So we will follow this initial broad look at interest rate levels with a discussion of the more recent period of 1981–1992.

PERSPECTIVE IN FINANCE

Opportunity cost is one of the most important concepts in financial management. It matters not that your firm's debt has a cost of 12 percent; the more important issue in making financial decisions is what it would cost the firm to issue the debt today. Put another way, would you loan a firm money at 13 percent if you could earn 15 percent on a similar investment? Not if you have any "smarts."

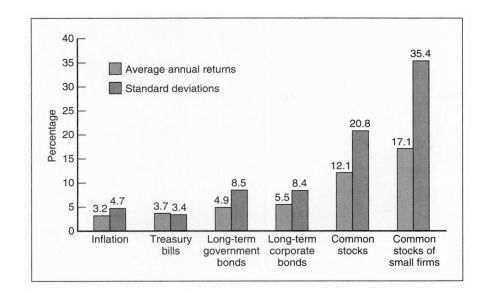

FIGURE 2–4
Average Annual Returns
and Standard Deviations
of Returns

Source: Roger G. Ibbotson and Rex A. Sinquefield, *Stocks, Bonds, Bills, and Inflation: Historical Returns* (Chcago: Dow Jones–Irwin, 1991. © Ibbotson Associates.)

Rates of Return over Long Periods

History can tell us a great deal about the returns that investors earn in the financial markets. A primary source for a historical perspective comes from Ibbotson and Sinquefield's *Stocks, Bonds, Bills, and Inflation*, which examines the realized rates of return for a wide variety of securities spanning the period from 1926 through 1990.[8] As part of their study, Ibbotson and Sinquefield calculated the average annual rates of return investors earned over the preceding 64 years, along with the average inflation rate for the same period. They also calculated the standard deviations of the returns for each type of security. The concept of standard deviation comes from our statistical colleagues, who use this measurement to indicate quantitatively how much dispersion or variability there is around the mean, or average, value of the item being measured–in this case, the rates of return in the financial markets.

Ibbotson and Sinquefield's results are summarized in Figure 2–4. These returns represent the average inflation rate and the average observed rates of return for different types of securities. The average inflation rate was 3.2 percent for the period covered by the study. We will refer to this rate as the "inflation-risk premium." The investor who earns only the rate of inflation has earned no "real return." That is, the *real return* is the return earned above the rate of increase in the general price level for goods and services in the economy, which is the inflation rate. In addition to the danger of not earning above the inflation rate, investors are concerned about the risk of the borrower defaulting or failing to repay the loan when due. Thus, we would expect a default-risk

[8]Roger G. Ibbotson and Rex A. Sinquefield, *Stocks, Bonds, Bills, and Inflation: Historical Returns* (Chicago: Dow Jones–Irwin, 1991).

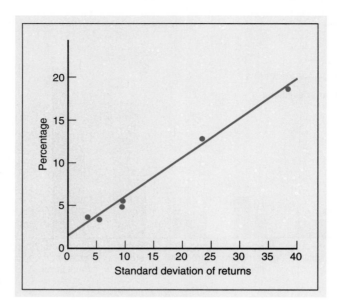

FIGURE 2–5
Rates of Return 1926–90

premium for long-term corporate bonds over long-term government bonds. The premium for 1926 to 1990 as shown in Figure 2–4, was 0.6 percent, or what is called 60 basis points (5.5 percent on long-term corporate bonds minus 4.9 percent on long-term government bonds). We would also expect an even greater risk premium for common stocks vis-a-vis long-term corporate bonds, since the variability in average returns is greater for common stocks. The Ibbotson and Sinquefield study verifies such a risk premium, with common stocks (all firms) earning 6.6 percent more than the rate earned on long-term corporate bonds (12.1 percent for common stocks minus 5.5 percent for long-term corporate bonds). Finally, there is even a greater risk premium associated with the common stock of small firms (5 percent) when compared with all common stocks. This small-firm or "size" risk premium probably reflects the lack of information available for small firms.

Remember that these returns are "averages" across many securities and over an extended period of time. However, these averages reflect the conventional wisdom regarding risk premiums: The greater the risk, the greater will be the expected returns. Such a relationship is shown in Figure 2–5, where the average returns are plotted against their standard deviations; note that higher average returns have historically been associated with higher dispersion in these returns.

Interest Rate Levels over Recent Periods

The *nominal* interest rates on some key fixed-income securities are displayed within both Table 2–7 and Figure 2–6 for the most recent 1981–1992 time frame. The rate of inflation at the consumer level is also presented in those two exhibits. This allows us to observe quite easily several concepts that were mentioned in the section above. Specifically, we can observe (1) the inflation-risk premium, (2) the default-risk premi-

TABLE 2–7.
Interest Rate Levels and
Inflation Rates 1981–1992

Year	3-Month Treasury Bills	30-Year Treasury Bonds	Aaa Rated Corporate Bonds	Inflation Rate
1981	14.08%	13.44%	14.17%	8.9%
1982	10.69	12.76	13.79	3.9
1983	8.63	11.18	12.04	3.8
1984	9.52	12.39	12.71	4.0
1985	7.49	10.79	11.37	3.8
1986	5.98	7.80	9.02	1.1
1987	5.82	8.58	9.38	4.4
1988	6.68	8.96	9.71	4.4
1989	8.12	8.45	9.26	4.6
1990	7.51	8.61	9.32	6.1
1991	5.42	8.14	8.77	3.1
1992	3.45	7.67	8.14	2.9
Mean	7.78%	9.90%	10.64%	4.25%

Source: *Federal Reserve Bulletin,* various issues, and *Federal Reserve Statistical Release* H.15 (519), various issues.

um across the several instruments, and (3) the real return for each instrument. Looking at the mean (average) values for each security and the inflation rate at the bottom of Table 2–7 will facilitate the discussion.

Notice that the average inflation rate over this more recent period is higher than reported in the longer period covered by the Ibbotson and Sinquefield analysis. Over the 11 years from 1981–1992 the consumer price index (December to December change) increased by an average of 4.25 percent each year. According to the logic of the financial markets, investors will *require* a nominal rate of interest that exceeds the inflation rate or else their realized *real* return will be negative. Earning a negative return over long periods of time (like 11 years) is not very smart.

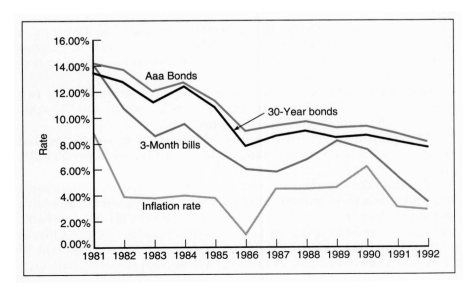

FIGURE 2–6
Interest Rate Levels and
Inflation Rates 1981–1992

Table 2–7 indicates that investor rationality prevailed. For example, the average inflation-risk premium demanded on U.S. Treasury bills with a three-month maturity was 3.53 percent (or 353 basis points). That is, an average 7.78 percent yield on Treasury bills over the period *minus* the average inflation rate of 4.25 percent over the same period produces a premium of 3.53 percent.

The default-risk premium is also evident in Table 2–7 and Figure 2–6. If we array the securities in these two exhibits from low risk to high risk the following tabulation results:

Security	Yield
3–month Treasury bills	7.78%
30–year Treasury bonds	9.90
Aaa Corporate bonds	10.64

Again, the basic rationale of the financial markets prevailed. The default-risk premium on high-rated (Aaa) corporate bonds relative to long-term Treasury bonds of 30-year maturity was 0.74 percent.

The array above can also be used to identify another factor that affects interest rate levels. It is referred to as the "maturity premium." This maturity premium arises even if securities possess equal (or approximately equal) odds of default. This is the case with Treasury bills and Treasury bonds, for instance, since the full faith and credit of the U.S. government stands behind these financial contracts. They are considered risk free (i.e., possessing no chance of default).

Notice that Treasury bonds with a 30-year maturity commanded a 2.12 percent yield differential over the shorter, three-month-to-maturity Treasury bonds. This provides an estimate of the maturity premium demanded by investors over this specific 1981–1992 period. More precisely, the *maturity premium* can be defined as:

The additional return required by investors in longer-term securities (bonds in this case) to compensate them for the greater risk of price fluctuations on those securities caused by interest rate changes.

When you study the basic mathematics of financial decisions in Chapter 5 and the characteristics of fixed-income securities in Chapter 7, you will learn how to quantify this maturity premium that is imbedded in nominal interest rates.

One other type of risk premium that helps determine interest rate levels needs to be identified and defined. It is known as the "liquidity premium." The *liquidity premium* is defined as:

The additional return required by investors in securities that cannot be quickly converted into cash at a reasonably predictable price.

The secondary markets for small-bank stocks, especially community banks, provide a good example of the liquidity premium. A bank holding company that trades on the New York Stock Exchange, like Barnett Bank, will be more liquid to investors than, say, the common stock of Citizens National Bank of Leesburg, Florida. Such a liquidity premium will be reflected across the spectrum of financial assets, from bonds to stocks.

Our first axiom, **Axiom 1: The Risk-Return Tradeoff—We Won't Take on Additional Risk Unless We Expect To Be Compensated with Additional Return**, established the fundamental risk-return trade-offs that govern the financial markets. We are now trying to provide you with an understanding of the kinds of risks that are rewarded in the risk–return tradeoff presented in **Axiom 1**.

◼ INTEREST RATE DETERMINANTS IN A NUTSHELL

Our review of rates of return and interest rate levels in the financial markets permits us to synthesize our introduction to the different types of risks that impact interest rates. We can, thereby, generate a simple equation with the **nominal** (i.e., observed) rate of interest being the output variable from the equation. The nominal interest rate is sometimes called the "quoted" rate. It is the rate that you would read about in the *Wall Street Journal* for a specific fixed-income security. That equation follows:

$$k = k^* + IRP + DRP + MP + LP \qquad (2\text{–}1)$$

where: k = the nominal or observed rate of interest on a specific fixed-income security.

k^* = the real risk-free rate of interest; it is the required rate of interest on a fixed-income security that has no risk and in an economic environment of zero inflation. This can be reasonably thought of as the rate of interest demanded by investors in U.S. Treasury securities during periods of no inflation.

IRP = the inflation-risk premium.

DRP = the default-risk premium.

MP = the maturity premium.

LP = the liquidity premium.

Sometimes in analyzing interest rate relationships over time it is of use to focus on what is called the "nominal risk-free rate of interest." Again, by nominal we mean "observed." So let us designate the nominal risk-free interest rate as k_{rf}. Drawing, then, on our discussions and notation from above we can write this expression for k_{rf}:

$$k_{rf} = k^* + IRP \qquad (2\text{–}2)$$

This equation just says that the nominal risk-free rate of interest is equal to the real risk-free interest rate plus the inflation-risk premium. It also provides a quick and *approximate* way of estimating the risk-free rate of interest, k^*, by solving directly for this rate. This basic relationship in equation (2–2) contains important information for the financial decision maker. It has also for years been the subject of fascinating and lengthy discussions among financial economists. We will look more at the substance of the real rate of interest in the next section. In this following section we will improve on equation (2–2) by making it more *precise*.

The Effects of Inflation on Rates of Return and the Fisher Effect

When a rate of interest is quoted, it is generally the nominal, or observed rate. The **real rate of interest**, on the other hand, represents the rate of increase in actual purchasing power, after adjusting for inflation. For example, if you have $100 today and loan it to someone for a year at a nominal rate of interest of 11.3 percent, you will get back $111.30 in one year. But if during the year prices of goods and services rise by 5 percent, it will take $105 at year end to purchase the same goods and services that $100 purchased at the beginning of the year. What was your increase in purchasing power over the year? The quick and dirty answer is found by subtracting the inflation rate from the nominal rate, 11.3% – 5% = 6.3%, but this is not exactly correct. To be more precise, let the nominal rate of interest be represented by k_{rf}, the anticipated rate of inflation by *IRP*, and the real rate of interest by k^*. Using these notations, we can express the relationship among the nominal interest rate, the rate of inflation, and the real rate of interest as follows:

$$1 + k_{rf} = (1 + k^*)(1 + IRP) \tag{2–3}$$

or

$$k_{rf} = k^* + IRP + (k^* \cdot IRP)$$

Consequently, the nominal rate of interest *(k_{rf})* is equal to the sum of the real rate of interest *(k^*)*, the inflation rate *(IRP)*, and the product of the real rate and the inflation rate. This relationship among nominal rates, real rates, and the rate of inflation has come to be called the **Fisher effect**.[9] It means that the observed nominal rate of interest includes both the real rate and an *inflation premium* as noted in the previous section.

Substituting into equation (2–3) using a nominal rate of 11.3 percent and an inflation rate of 5 percent, we can calculate the real rate of interest, k^*, as follows:

$$k_{rf} = k^* + IRP + (k^* \cdot IRP)$$
$$.113 = k^* + .05 + .05k^*$$
$$k^* = .06 = 6\%$$

Thus, at the new higher prices, your purchasing power will have increased by only 6 percent, although you have $11.30 more than you had at the start of the year. To see why, let's assume that at the outset of the year one unit of the market basket of goods and services costs $1, so you could purchase 100 units with your $100. At the end of the year you have $11.30 more, but each unit now costs 1.05 (remember the 5 percent rate of inflation). How many units can you buy at the end of the year? The answer is $111.30 ÷ $1.05 = 106, which represents a 6 percent increase in real purchasing power.[10]

[9]This relationship was analyzed many years ago by Irving Fisher.
[10]In Chapter 5 we will study more about the time value of money.

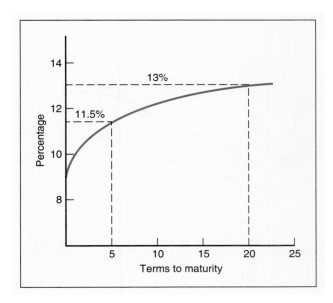

FIGURE 2–7
The Term Structure
of Interest Rates

THE TERM STRUCTURE OF INTEREST RATES

The relationship between a debt security's rate of return and the length of time until the debt matures is known as the **term structure of interest rates** or the **yield to maturity**. For the relationship to be meaningful to us, all the factors other than maturity, meaning factors such as the chance of the bond defaulting, must be held constant. Thus, the term structure reflects observed rates or yields on similar securities, except for the length of time until maturity, at a particular moment in time.

Figure 2–7 shows an example of the term structure of interest rates. The curve is upward sloping, indicating that longer terms to maturity command higher returns, or yields. In this hypothetical term structure, the rate of interest on a 5-year note or bond is 11.5 percent, whereas the comparable rate on a 20-year bond is 13 percent.

Observing Historical Term Structures of Interest Rates

As we might expect, the term structure of interest rates changes over time, depending on the environment. The particular term structure observed today may be quite different from the term structure a month ago and different still from the term structure one month from now. A perfect example of the changing term structure, or yield curve, was witnessed during the early days of the Persian Gulf crisis in August 1990. Figure 2–8 shows the yield curves one day prior to the Iraqi invasion of Kuwait and then again just three weeks later. The change is noticeable, particularly for long-term interest rates. Investors quickly developed new fears about the prospect of increased inflation to be caused by the

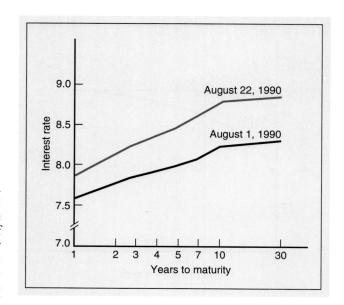

FIGURE 2–8
Changes in the
Term Structure of
Interest Rates for
Government Securites at the
Outbreak of the
Persian Gulf Crisis

crisis and consequently increased their required rates of return.

Although the upward sloping term structure curves in Figures 2–7 and 2–8 are the ones most commonly observed, yield curves can assume several shapes. Sometimes the term structure is downward sloping; at other times it rises and then falls (hump-backed); and at still other times it may be relatively flat. Figure 2–9 shows some yield curves at different points in time.

Trying to Explain the Shape of the Term Structure

A number of theories may explain the shape of the term structure of interest rates at any point. Three possible explanations are prominent:

FIGURE 2–9
Historical Term Structures
of Interest Rates for
Government Securities

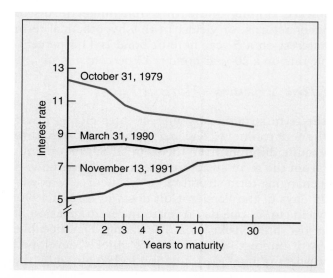

(1) the unbiased expectations theory, (2) the liquidity preference theory, and (3) the market segmentation theory.[11] Let's look at each in turn.

The Unbiased Expectations Theory

The **unbiased expectations theory** says that the term structure is determined by an investor's expectations about future interest rates.[12] To see how this works, consider the following investment problem faced by Mary Maxell. Mary has $10,000 that she wants to invest for two years, at which time she plans to use her savings to make a downpayment on a new home. Wanting not to take any risk of losing her savings, she decides to invest in U.S. government securities. She has two choices. First, she can purchase a government security that matures in two years, which offers her an interest rate of 9 percent per year. If she does this, she will have $11,881 in two years, calculated as follows:[13]

Principal amount	$10,000
Plus: Year 1 interest (.09 × $10,000)	900
Principal plus interest at the end of year 1	$10,900
Plus: Year 2 interest (.09 × $10,900)	981
Principal plus interest at the end of year 2	$11,881

Alternatively, Mary could buy a government security maturing in one year that pays an 8 percent rate of interest. She would then need to purchase another one-year security at the end of the first year. Which alternative Mary will prefer obviously depends in part on the rate of interest she expects to receive on the government security she will purchase a year from now. We cannot tell Mary what the interest rate will be in a year; however, we can at least calculate the rate that will give her the same two-year total savings she would get from her first choice, or $11,881. The interest rate can be calculated as follows:

Savings needed in two years	$11,881
Savings at the end of the first year	
$10,000(1 + .08)	$10,000
Interest needed in year two	$ 1,081

---

[11]See Richard Roll, *The Behavior of Interest Rates: An Application of the Efficient Market Model to U.S. Treasury Bills* (New York: Basic Books, 1970).

[12]Irving Fisher thought of this idea in 1896. The theory was later refined by J. R. Hicks in *Value and Capital* (London: Oxford University Press, 1946) and F. A. Lutz and V. C. Lutz in *The Theory of Investment in the Firm* (Princeton, NJ: Princeton University Press, 1951).

[13]We could also calculate the principal plus interest for Mary's investment using the following compound interest equation: $10,000(1 + .09)^2 = $11,881$. We will study the mathematics of compound interest in Chapter 5.

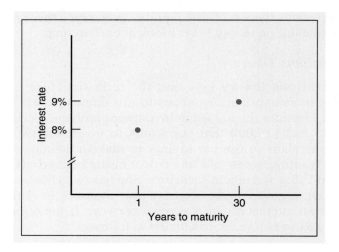

FIGURE 2–10
Term Structure of
Interest Rates

For Mary to receive $1,081 in the second year, she would have to earn about 10 percent on her second-year investment, computed as follows:

$$\frac{\text{interest received in year 2}}{\text{investment made at beginning of year 2}} = \frac{\$1,081}{\$10,800} = 10\%$$

So the term structure of interest rates for our example consists of the one-year interest rate of 8 percent and the two-year rate of 9 percent, which is shown in Figure 2–10. This exercise also gives us information about the *expected* one-year rate for investments made one year hence. In a sense, the term structure contains implications about investor expectations of future interest rates; thus, this explains the unbiased expectations theory of the term structure of interest rates.

Although we can see a relationship between current interest rates with different maturities and the investor's expectations about future interest rates, is this the whole story? Are there influences other than the investor's expectations about future interest rates? Probably, so let's continue to think about Mary's dilemma.

Liquidity Preference Theory

In presenting Mary's choices, we have suggested that she would be indifferent to a choice between the two-year government security offering a 9 percent return and two consecutive one-year investments offering 8 and 10 percent, respectively. However, that would be so only if she is unconcerned about the risk associated with not knowing the rate of interest on the second security as of today. If Mary is risk averse (that is, she dislikes risk), she might not be satisfied with expectations of a 10 percent return on the second one-year government security. She might require some additional expected return to be truly indifferent. Mary might in fact decide that she will expose herself to the uncertainty of future interest rates only if she can reasonably *expect* to earn an additional .5 percent in interest, or 10.5 percent, on the second one-year investment. This *risk premium* (additional required interest rate) to compensate for the risk of changing future interest rates is nothing more than the maturity premium (**MP**) introduced earlier, and this concept underlies the liquidity preference theory of the term structure.[14] In the **liquidity preference theory**, investors require maturity premiums to compensate them for buying securities that expose them to the risks of fluctuating interest rates.

Market Segmentation Theory

The **market segmentation theory** is the third popular theory of the term structure of interest rates. This concept is built on the notion that legal restrictions and personal preferences limit choices for investors to certain ranges of maturities. For example, commercial banks prefer short- to medium-term maturities as a result of the short-term nature of their deposit liabilities. They prefer not to invest in long-term securities. Life insurance companies, on the other hand, have longer-term liabilities, so they prefer longer maturities in investments. At the extreme, the market segmentation theory implies that the rate of interest for a particular maturity is determined solely by demand and supply for a given maturity and that it is independent of the demand and supply for securities having different maturities. A more moderate version of the theory allows investors strong maturity preferences, but it also allows them to modify their feelings and preferences if significant yield inducements occur.

SUMMARY

This chapter centers on the market environment in which corporations raise long-term funds, including the structure of the U.S. financial markets, the institution of investment banking, and the various methods for distributing securities. It also discusses the role of interest rates in allocating savings to ultimate investment.

Mix of Corporate Securities Sold

When corporations go to the capital market for cash, the most favored financing method is debt. The corporate debt markets clearly dominate the equity markets when new funds are raised. The U.S. tax system inherently favors debt capital as a fundraising method. In an average year over the 1981–91 period, bonds and notes made up 72 percent of external cash that was raised.

Why Financial Markets Exist

The function of financial markets is to allocate savings efficiently in the economy to the ultimate demander (user) of the savings. In a financial

---

[14]This theory was first presented by John R. Hicks in *Value and Capital* (London: Oxford University Press, 1946), pp. 141–145, with the risk premium referred to as the liquidity premium. For our purposes we will use the term **maturity premium (MP)** to describe this risk premium, thereby keeping our terminology consistent within this chapter.

BASIC FINANCIAL MANAGEMENT IN PRACTICE

The Federal Reserve and Interest Rates

The following refers to the role of the Federal Reserve System—the nation's central bank—in affecting yields on money market instruments. The two pieces below expand our understanding of the Federal Reserve System. The first discussion deals with the basic organization of the system. The longer discussion focuses on the Fed's role in interest rate determination.

Organization

Many people are not aware that the Federal Reserve System is not part of the executive branch of the federal government, like the U.S. Treasury or Commerce Departments. Rather it is a blend of public and private enterprise. The nation's central bank is an agency created by Congress, but the Fed's decentralized structure of 12 district banks and 25 branches gives each unit some aspects of privately owned businesses. The Fed's operational arms at the various banks and branches, for example, compete with one another—and with private sector organizations—to provide quality financial services.

The Federal Reserve System is also similar to private businesses in that each bank and branch elects a board of directors. Contributing expertise gained from their own professions, the Fed directors play an integral role in the system's ability to formulate monetary policy and provide high-quality financial services to depository institutions and the U.S. Treasury.

The Fed and Interest Rates

It is often suggested that the Federal Reserve tightly controls all interest rates. Actually, the Federal Reserve sets only one interest rate, its discount rate. In addition, the Federal Reserve's open market operations in recent years have been aimed at holding another rate, the federal funds rate, close to levels indicated by the Federal Open Market Committee (FOMC), the Federal Reserve's primary monetary policy-making body.

This article explains how changes in the federal funds rate and the discount rate work through financial markets to affect other short-term interest rates such as those on Treasury bills and certificates of deposit. It also explains why the influence of changes in the funds rate and the discount rate on long-term rates, such as mortgage rates and corporate bond yields, is relatively weak.

Monetary Policy in Brief

The Federal Reserve's monetary policy can be defined as the Fed's use of its influence on reserves in the banking system to influence money and credit and, through them, the economy. The federal funds rate and the discount rate figure importantly in the conduct of monetary policy, and many observers regard these two rates as the principal indicators of the direction of policy. Declines in these rates are taken as signs that the Federal Reserve wants to encourage money and credit growth, or "ease" money and credit conditions, whereas increases in these rates are interpreted as Fed efforts to restrain money and credit growth, or "tighten" money and credit conditions.

Federal funds are reserves lent overnight by depository institutions with excess reserves to depository institutions with insufficient reserves. The **federal funds** rate is a market rate of interest determined by the supply and demand for reserves. The Fed directly affects the funds rate by buying and selling government securities in the "open market" to influence the supply of reserves, and, therefore, federal funds in the banking system. When the Federal Reserve wants to ease money and credit conditions through open market operations, for example, it supplies additional reserves to the banking system by purchasing additional short-term government securities.

When a depository institution is short on the reserves it needs to meet regulatory requirements, it may also borrow reserves from its regional Federal Reserve Bank at the discount rate. The **discount rate** is an "administered" rate, set at a certain level and held there by administrative decision. Changes in the discount rate are initiated by the boards of directors of the individual Reserve Banks, but the Federal Reserve's Board of Governors in Washington must approve all changes. This coordination generally results in roughly simultaneous changes at all Reserve Banks.

Effect of Changes in the Funds Rate on Short-Term Rates

The Federal Reserve exercises a strong influence on other short-term rates through its influence on the federal funds rate, because the funds rate is the base rate to which other money market rates are anchored. To see this, consider the rate on bank certificates of deposit (CDs), which are generally arranged for a few months. Banks can raise funds either through CDs or federal funds and therefore choose whichever option is expected to be cheaper. CD rates are roughly aligned with an average of expected future funds rates over the term of the CD. Hence if bankers see a rise in the federal funds rate, and expect it to persist, they will bid up the rate on CDs. Likewise, corporations considering a Treasury bill purchase have the option of lending their funds daily over the term of the bill at the overnight rate on repurchase agreements, which is closely tied to the federal funds rate. Hence, they will require a higher Treasury bill rate following an increase in the funds rate that they believe to be persistent.

As these examples illustrate, the arbitrage activities of money market participants will generally keep other short-term rates in line with the federal funds rate, abstracting from differences in default risk. Hence, persistent increases in the federal funds rate engineered by the Federal Reserve will generally lead to comparable increases in other short-term interest rates.

Changes in the Discount Rate

As indicated above, banks can borrow reserves at the discount window or they can acquire reserves in the federal funds market. (Of course, individual banks can also acquire reserves by selling off securities.) Under the operating procedures used by the Federal Reserve in the 1980s, increases in the dis-count rate that raise the cost of acquiring borrowed reserves also can lead quickly to an increase in the cost of acquiring reserves in the federal funds market. Hence, under these procedures the discount rate can have a strong direct effect on the funds rate and other market rates.

More generally, if changes in the discount rate are viewed by market participants as signaling a "tighter" monetary policy in the future, then they can influence the current level of market interest rates regardless of the Fed's operating procedures. The reason is that anticipation of a tighter policy will raise the expected future level of the funds rate. A higher expected funds rate will then raise current rates on CDs and Treasury bills as in the examples above. Such effects are usually labeled "announcement effects" by market participants.

Long-Term Rates

The ability of the Federal Reserve to directly influence the level of interest rates diminishes greatly at longer maturities. The reason is that longer-term interest rates, such as mortgage rates and corporate bond yields, are largely determined by the expected rate of inflation. To appreciate the influence of inflation expectations on longer-term rates, suppose that the long-term expected inflation rate were 5 percent. Lenders would be unwilling to lend at 5 percent because the interest income would be completely offset by the inflation loss. Lenders want to cover the expected inflation loss and earn some real rate of return, considered usually to be about

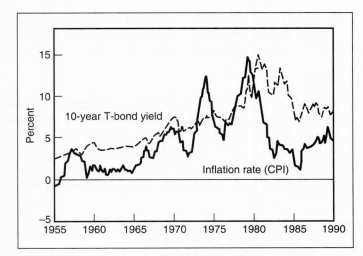

CHART 1
Long-Term Rates Fall After
Inflation Falls

BASIC FINANCIAL MANAGEMENT IN PRACTICE (cont.)

CHART 2
Long-Term Rates
Can Be Stubborn

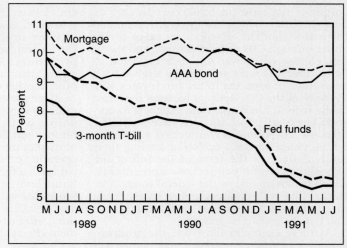

4 percent. Borrowers, for their part, are willing to pay the inflation premium because they expect to repay their debts with cheaper dollars. Therefore, one can reasonably expect long-term interest rates to be about 4 percentage points above the expected inflation rate. It follows that an important way to reduce long-term rates is to lower the expected rate of inflation. The historical data in Chart 1 show that long-term rates have come down only after inflation has declined.

Short- and Long-Term Rates: A Case Study
The relatively weak link between movements in the federal funds rate and movements in

long-term rates can be illustrated by the behavior of rates over two recent years. From June 1989 through June 1991, the federal funds rate fell 4 percentage points, from about 9.75 percent to about 5.75 percent, and other short-term rates also declined about 4 percentage points. Long-term rates, however, fell only about 1 percentage point over this period, as illustrated in Chart 2.

How should these declines be interpreted in light of the previous discussion? Apparently, the public's inflation outlook did not change much from June 1989 through June 1991 because long-term rates did not move much

market the forces of supply and demand for a specific financial instrument are brought together. The wealth of an economy would not be as great as it is without a fully developed financial market system.

Financing of Business

Every year households are a net supplier of funds to the financial markets. The nonfinancial business sector is always a net borrower of funds. Both life insurance companies and private pension funds are important buyers of corporate securities. Savings are ultimately transferred to the business firm seeking cash by means of (1) the direct transfer, (2) the indirect transfer using the investment banker, or (3) the indirect transfer using the financial intermediary.

Components of U.S. Financial Market System

Corporations can raise funds through public offerings or private placements. The public market is impersonal in that the security issuer does not meet the

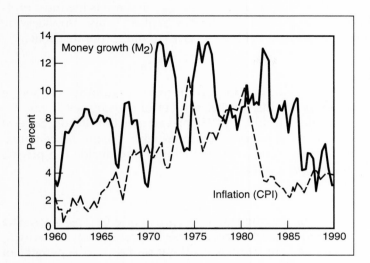

CHART 3
Inflation Follows Excess
Money Growth
Four-Quarter Changes

over this period. Evidently, the public believed that the Fed's downward pressure on short-term rates were anti-recession moves that would not significantly alter the inflation outlook. In July and August of 1991, however, declines in long-term rates suggested perceived progress in reducing expected inflation.

The Fed's Role
The historical data show that long-term interest rates decline when the expected rate of inflation declines. Furthermore, empirical evidence strongly suggests that, over time, inflation results from excessive increases in the money supply (Chart 3). To prevent inflation and to concurrently bring down long-term rates, policymakers must ensure that, over time, the money supply grows only as fast as the economy's potential growth in output.

Sources: "Organization" is from "Board Member Finds Parallels between the Fed and His Own Business," *Financial Update*, Federal Reserve Bank of Atlanta, 3 (Fall 1990), p. 3; "The Fed and Interest Rates" is from Craig Carlock, "How the Federal Reserve Influences Interest Rates," *Cross Sections*, Federal Reserve Bank of Richmond, 8 (Fall 1991), pp. 12–14.

ultimate investors in the financial instruments. In a private placement, the securities are sold directly to a limited number of institutional investors.

The primary market is the market for new issues. The secondary market represents transactions in currently outstanding securities. Both the money and capital markets have primary and secondary sides. The money market refers to transactions in short-term debt instruments. The capital market, on the other hand, refers to transactions in long-term financial instruments. Trading in the money and capital markets can occur in either the organized security exchanges or the over-the-counter market. The money market is exclusively an over-the-counter market.

Investment Banker

The investment banker is a financial specialist involved as an intermediary in the merchandising of securities. He or she performs the functions of (1) underwriting, (2) distributing, and (3) advising. Major methods for the public distribution of securities include (1) the negotiated purchase,

(2) the competitive bid purchase, (3) the commission or best-efforts basis, (4) privileged subscriptions, and (5) direct sales. The direct sale bypasses the use of an investment banker. The negotiated purchase is the most profitable distribution method to the investment banker. It also provides the greatest amount of investment banking services to the corporate client.

Private Placements

Privately placed debt provides an important market outlet for corporate bonds. Major investors in this market are (1) life insurance firms, (2) state and local retirement funds, and (3) private pension funds. Several advantages and disadvantages are associated with private placements. The financial officer must weigh these attributes and decide if a private placement is preferable to a public offering.

Flotation Costs

Flotation costs consist of the underwriter's spread and issuing costs. The flotation costs of common stock exceed those of preferred stock, which, in turn, exceed those of debt. Moreover, flotation costs as a percent of gross proceeds are inversely related to the size of the security issue.

Regulation

The new issues market is regulated at the federal level by the Securities Act of 1933. It provides for the registration of new issues with the SEC. Secondary market trading is regulated by the Securities Exchange Act of 1934. The Securities Acts Amendments of 1975 placed on the SEC the responsibility for devising a national market system. This concept is still being studied. The shelf registration procedure (SEC Rule 415) was initiated in March 1982. Under this regulation and with the proper filing of documents, firms that are selling new issues do not have to go through the old, lengthy registration process each time the firm plans an offering of securities.

The Logic of Rates of Return and Interest Rate Determination

The financial markets give managers an informed indication of investors' opportunity costs. The more efficient the market, the more informed the indication. This information is a useful input about the rates of return that investors require on financial claims. In turn, this will become useful to financial managers as they estimate the overall cost of capital used as a screening rate in the capital budgeting process.

Rates of return on various securities are based on the underlying supply of loanable funds (savings) and demand for those loanable funds. In addition to a risk-free return, investors will want to be compensated for the potential loss of purchasing power resulting from inflation. Moreover, investors require a greater return the greater the default-risk, maturity premium, and liquidity premium are on the securities being analyzed.

STUDY QUESTIONS

2–1. What are financial markets? What function do they perform? How would an economy be worse off without them?

2–2. Define in a technical sense what we mean by *financial intermediary*. Give an example of your definition.

2–3. Distinguish between the money and capital markets.

2–4. What major benefits do corporations and investors enjoy because of the existence of organized security exchanges?

2–5. What are the general categories examined by an organized exchange in determining whether an applicant firm's securities can be listed on it? (Specific numbers are not needed here, but rather areas of investigation.)

2–6. Why do you think most secondary market trading in bonds takes place over-the-counter?

2–7. What is an investment banker, and what major functions does he or she perform?

2–8. What is the major difference between a negotiated purchase and a competitive bid purchase?

2–9. Why is an investment banking syndicate formed?

2–10. Why might a large corporation want to raise long-term capital through a private placement rather than a public offering?

2–11. As a recent business school graduate, you work directly for the corporate treasurer. Your corporation is going to issue a new security and is concerned with the probable flotation costs. What tendencies about flotation costs can you relate to the treasurer?

2–12. When corporations raise funds, what type of financing vehicle (instrument or instruments) is most favored?

2–13. What is the major (most significant) savings-surplus sector in the U.S. economy?

2–14. Identify three distinct ways that savings are ultimately transferred to business firms in need of cash.

2–15. Explain the term opportunity cost with respect to cost of funds to the firm.

2–16. Compare and explain the historical rates of return for different types of securities.

2–17. Explain the impact of inflation on rates of return.

2–18. Define the term structure of interest rates.

2–19. Explain the popular theories for the rationale of the term structure of interest rates.

STUDY PROBLEMS

2–1. (Inflation and Interest Rates) What would you expect the nominal rate of interest to be if the real rate is 4 percent and the expected inflation rate is 7 percent?

2–2. (Inflation and Interest Rates) Assume the expected inflation rate to be 4 percent. If the current real rate of interest is 6 percent, what ought the nominal rate of interest be?

2–3. (Inflation and Interest Rates) Assume the expected inflation rate to be 5 percent. If the current real rate of interest is 7 percent, what would you expect the nominal rate of interest to be?

2–4. (Term Structure of Interest Rates) You want to invest your savings of $20,000 in government securities for the next two years. Currently, you can invest either in a security that pays interest of 8 percent per year for the next two years or in a security that matures in one year but pays only 6 percent interest. If you make the latter choice, you would then reinvest your savings at the end of the first year for another year.

    a. Why might you choose to make the investment in the one-year security that pays an interest rate of only 6 percent, as opposed to investing in the two-year security paying 8 percent? Provide numerical support for your answer. Which theory of term structure have you supported in your answer?

b. Assume your required rate of return on the second-year investment is 11 percent; otherwise, you will choose to go with the two-year security. What rationale could you offer for your preference?

 ## CONCLUSION VIDEO CASE 1

The Fall of Drexel Burnham Lambert: Investment Banking *in extremis*
from ABC News, Business World, February 18, 1990

Junk bonds served a valuable purpose for some firms, especially smaller corporations that did not have access to the public debt markets. Junk bonds, or as they are sometimes called, high-yield securities, allowed riskier companies to raise funds when traditional funding sources such as banks would not consider them. Junk bonds, in and of themselves, are not bad. Sadly, they were put to bad use. Savings-and-loan (S & L) associations invested in junk bonds with little thought about the inherent risk of these securities. The attraction of high yield blinded the S & L executives to the obvious risk. Junk bonds also were used to finance some acquisitions with at best questionable economic value. The ease with which funds could be raised by Milken's junk-bond department made debt the preferred security for acquisitions and going-private transactions. In some cases more debt was piled onto the assets than could be supported.

The deal-doing mentality of the 1980s was summed up by Michael Milken in this video: "There's (are) very few people in the merger and acquisitions department that ever saw a bad deal. Every deal is a great deal; every deal is a good credit. Why? Because they [the investment bankers] usually get their fees up front." And what fees they are. In the RJR-Nabisco buyout the investment banking, attorney, and accountant fees totaled $1.15 billion!

What happens now? As several commentators in the video mentioned, junk bonds will continue to be used, though certainly not to the extent they were in the 1980s. The evaluation of transactions and credit quality will be more conservative, so fewer deals will be done. The biggest effect will likely be in the market for junk bonds. Drexel was the primary market maker; that is, Drexel created much of the liquidity in the junk bond market. Without Drexel acting as the intermediary, holders of junk bonds may find it very difficult to sell those bonds, or they may be able to sell them only at a low price. This has had a profound effect on the S & Ls that were ordered to divest their portfolios of junk bonds. In fact, one economist estimates the cost of not having Drexel as a market maker for junk bonds at $640 million (Wall Street Journal, March 4, 1992, p. A12).

Discussion questions

1. Economists have documented that small firms are increasingly responsible for new product development. How do you think the contraction of the junk-bond market affects this important source of innovation?

2. It has been argued that many firms using junk bonds switched from bank loans. Are junk bonds and bank loans substitutes for one another? How do they differ, and which source is likely to provide the largest amount of funds?

Suggested readings

BRUCK, CONNIE. *The Predator's Ball: The Junk Bond Raiders and the Man Who Staked Them.* New York: Simon & Schuster, 1988.

STONE, DAN. *April Fools: An Insider's Account of the Rise and Collapse of Drexel Burnham.* New York: Donald I. Fine & Co., 1990.

CHAPTER 3

EVALUATING A FIRM'S FINANCIAL PERFORMANCE AND MEASURING CASH FLOW

• Basic Financial Statements • Financial Ratio Analysis

In Chapter 2, we looked at the workings of the financial markets. We found that these markets provide the means for bringing together investors (savers) with the users of capital (businesses that provide products and services to the consumer). There we looked at the world as the economist sees it, with an eye for understanding the marketplace where managers go to acquire capital. It is these financial markets that determine the value of a firm, and given our goal of maximizing shareholder value, no issue is more fundamental to our study. However, we now want to alter our perspective. In this chapter, we ask ourselves, "Does the accountant have anything to say to us that might be productive in our study of finance?" Thus, we will see the world of finance more as the accountant sees it.

Although some might argue that the accountant has less to say to us than the economist, it is an undeniable fact that a significant part of the data used in financial management is provided by the accountant. We also know that this information is used mostly in planning, evaluating, and controlling a firm's financial performance and in measuring its cash flows. These issues are significant for several reasons. Remembering **Axiom 3**, we know that **cash is king.** Although profit is thought to be important by many in finance, we will argue that the investor should assign a greater significance to the firm's cash flows.

Bond Rating Agencies: Using Financial
Analysis to Forecast the Riskiness of Bonds
from ABC News, Business World, June 23, 1991

Chapters 3 and 4 introduce the topics of financial analysis and forecasting. An important use of financial analysis is the evaluation of investments. Bond-rating agencies such as Moody's and Standard and Poor's apply these techniques in evaluating the riskiness of corporate and municipal bonds. Using past financial data and forecasts of economic trends, these agencies give borrowers a letter rating, such as AA (double A) or BBB (triple B), which indicates the overall quality of the bond being sold to investors. The higher the rating (AAA is the highest), the more certain the rating agency is that the interest and principal payments of a bond will be paid in a timely manner. Some investors, such as pension funds, are allowed to invest only in a high-rated (or investment-quality) bonds. Rating agencies periodically review the rating of bonds.

What information would be needed to rate a municipal bond, how is this different/similar to rating a corporation, and why is it such an important process?

The video case describes some of the factors that Moody's and Standard and Poor's consider when assigning or revising a city's bond rating. At the end of this chapter we will return to this video case and discuss some of the issues it raises.

Axiom 7 gives us our second reason for wanting to understand a company's financial position. This axiom tells us there may be a problem resulting from the conflict of interest that can develop between a firm's managers and its common stockholders (owners). Although the management is an agent of the owners, experience suggests that managers do not always act in the best interest of the owners.[1] The incentives for the managers are at times different from those of the owners. Thus, the firm's common stockholders, as well as other providers of capital (such as bankers), have a need for information that can be used to monitor the managers' actions. Because the owners of large companies do not have access to internal information about the firm's operations, they must rely on public information from any and all sources. One of the main sources of such information comes from the company's financial statements provided by the firm's accountants. Although this information is by no means perfect, it is an important source used by outsiders to assess a company's activities.

---

[1]See Janice Castro, "How's Your Pay?" *Time*, April 15, 1991, pp. 40–41, and "Worthy of His Hire." *The Economist*, February 1, 1992, pp. 19–22, for discussions of this potential conflict of interest between managers and stockholders.

Two axioms are especially important in this chapter: **Axiom 3** tells us that **Cash is King.** At times, cash is more important than profits. Thus, in this chapter, considerable time will be devoted to learning how to measure cash flows. **Axiom 7** warns us there may be a conflict between management and owners, especially in large firms where managers and owners have different incentives. That Is, Managers Won't Work For Owners Unless It Is In Their Best Interest To Do So. In this chapter, we will learn how to use data from the firm's public financial statements to monitor management's actions.

In addition to the investors, the managers themselves have a need for financial information to evaluate their decisions. If they are to have any hope of evaluating their own decisions and the decisions of others within their organization, they need to understand the financial consequences of their decisions. Only with this information can a financial decision maker plan and control activities within the firm effectively.[2]

In this chapter, we will undertake several objectives:

- Develop an understanding of the firm's basic financial statements.
- Learn how to measure a firm's cash flows.
- Come to know the important factors that drive a firm's cash flows.
- Gain insights into a company's financial performance through the use of financial ratios.
- Offer a brief caveat about the appropriate use of accounting information.

PERSPECTIVE IN FINANCE

Financial statement analysis has probably been introduced in your basic accounting courses. However, the evaluation of financial performance is so important to the financial manager that a review is appropriate here.

■ BASIC FINANCIAL STATEMENTS

As we set the stage for gaining a better understanding of financial management, it is imperative that we know the "coin of the realm" used in describing a company's financial position. To a large extent, this "coin" is the firm's financial or accounting statements.

We can think of financial statements as consisting of certain pieces of important information about the firm's operations that are reported in the form of (1) an income statement, (2) a balance sheet, and (3) a cash flow statement. We will look at each of these statements in turn.

[2]Chapter 4 develops the use of financial planning and control techniques based on the firm's pro forma or projected financial statements.

The double-entry system of accounting used in this country dates back to about 3600 B.C., with the first published work describing the system by Luca Pacioli of Venice in 1494. Although the details of the double-entry system can be overwhelming to the novice, the mathematical content of these financial statements is straightforward and may be expressed as follows.

> *1. Balance sheet or statement of financial position*
>   *liabilities + owners' equity = assets*
> *2. Income statement or statement of results from operations*
>   *revenues + gains – expenses – losses = income*
> *3. Cash flow statement*
>   *cash inflow – cash outflow = change in cash*

The Income Statement

It is helpful to think of the income statement as comprising four types of activities:

1. Selling the product or service;
2. The cost of producing or acquiring the goods or services sold;
3. The expenses incurred in marketing and distributing the product or service to the customer, along with administrative operating expenses; and
4. The financing costs of doing business, for example, interest paid to creditors and dividend payments to the preferred stockholders.

These "income-statement activities" are represented graphically in Figure 3–1. In this figure, we observe that the top part of the income statement, beginning with sales and continuing down through the **operating income** or **earnings before interest and taxes**, is affected solely by the first three activities, or what is considered the firm's operating activities. No financing costs are included to this point.

Below the line reporting operating income, we see the results of the firm's financing decisions, along with the taxes that are due on the company's income. Here the company's **financing costs** are shown, first in the form of interest expenses and then preferred dividends. The tax rates imposed on the company's **earnings before taxes** determine the amount of the tax liability, or the **tax expenses**.[3] The final number, **net income available to common stockholders** (frequently just called **net income**), is the income that may be distributed to the company's owners or reinvested in the company, provided of course there is cash available to do so. As we shall see later, however, the fact that a firm has a positive net income does not necessarily mean it has any cash—possibly a surprising result to us, but one we shall come to understand.

---

[3]Notice that interest is a tax-deductible expense, while preferred dividends are paid after taxes have been calculated.

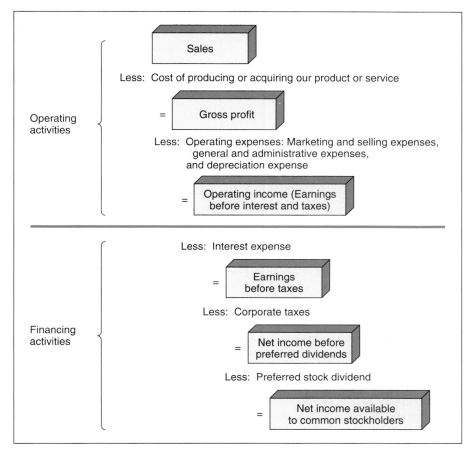

FIGURE 3–1
The Income Statement:
An Overview

An example of an income statement is provided in Table 3–1 for the Jamin Corporation. As shown in the table, the firm had sales of $830,200 for the 12-month period ending December 31, 1993, and the cost of manufacturing the firm's product was $539,750. The result is a gross profit of $290,450. The firm then had $190,750 in operating expenses, which included selling expenses, general and administrative expenses, and depreciation expenses. After deducting operating expenses, the firm's operating profits (earnings before interest and taxes) amount to $99,700. This amount represents the before-tax profits generated as if the Jamin Corporation were an all-equity company. To this point, we have calculated the profits resulting only from operating activities, as opposed to financing decisions, such as how much debt or equity is used to finance the company's operations.

We next deduct Jamin's interest expense (the amount paid for using debt financing) of $20,000 to arrive at the company's earnings before tax of $79,700. Finally, we deduct the income taxes of $17,390 to leave the net income available to common stockholders of $62,310. At the bottom of the income statement, we also see the amount of common dividends paid by the firm to its owners in the amount of $15,000, leaving $47,310, which increases retained earnings in the firm's 1993 balance sheet.

EVALUATING A FIRM'S
FINANCIAL PERFORMANCE
AND MEASURING
CASH FLOW

Sales		$830,200
Cost of goods sold		539,750
Gross profit on sales		$290,450
Operating expenses:		
Marketing expenses	$90,750	
General and administrative expenses	71,800	
Depreciation	28,200	
Total Operating expenses		$190,750
Operating income		$ 99,700
Interest expense		20,000
Earnings before tax		$ 79,700
Income tax		17,390
Net income available to common stockholders		$ 62,310

Net income available to common stockholders	$ 62,310
Common stock dividends	15,000
Change in retained earnings	$ 47,310

The Balance Sheet

Whereas the income statement reports the results from operating the business for a period of time, such as a year, the balance sheet provides a snapshot of the firm's financial position at a specific point in time, presenting its asset holdings, liabilities, and owner-supplied capital. Assets represent the resources owned by the firm, whereas the liabilities and owners' equity indicate how those resources are financed.

The difference between the timing of an income statement and a balance sheet may be represented graphically as follows:

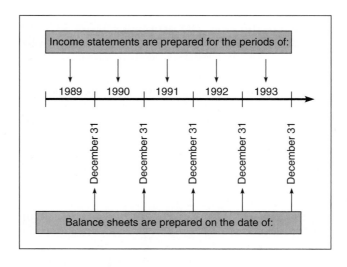

Here we see five periods of operations, 1989 through 1993. There would be an income statement for the period of January 1 through

December 31 for each of the five years' operations and a balance sheet reporting the company's financial position as of December 31 of each year. Thus, the balance sheet on December 31, 1993 is a statement of the company's financial position at that particular date, which is the result of all financial transactions since the company began its operations.

Figure 3–2 gives us the basic ingredients of a balance sheet. In the figure, the assets fall into three categories:

1. **Current assets**—consisting primarily of cash, marketable securities, accounts receivable, inventories, and prepaid expenses;
2. **Fixed or long-term assets**—comprising equipment, buildings, and land; and
3. **Other assets**—all assets not otherwise included in the firm's current assets or fixed assets, such as patents, long-term investments in securities, and goodwill.

In reporting the dollar amounts of these various assets, the conventional practice is to report the value of the assets and liabilities on a historical cost basis. Thus, the balance sheet is not intended to represent the current market value of the company, but rather reports the historical transactions recorded at their cost. Determining a fair value of the business is a different matter.

The remaining part of the balance sheet (the right-hand side of Figure 3–2), headed "Liabilities and Equity," indicates how the firm has financed its investments in assets. The principal sources of financing

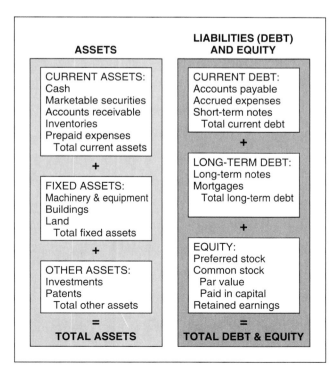

FIGURE 3–2
The Balance Sheet:
An Overview

are debt (liabilities) and equity. The debt consists of such sources as credit extended from suppliers (accounts payable) or a loan from a bank (including notes payable or mortgages). The equity includes the stockholders' investment in the firm (par plus paid in capital) and the cumulative profits retained in the business up to the date of the balance sheet.

Balance sheets for the Jamin Corporation are presented in Table 3–2 for both December 31, 1992 and December 31, 1993, along with the changes in each amount between years. By referring to the two balance sheets, we can see the financial position of the firm both at the beginning and end of 1993. Furthermore, by examining these two balance sheets, along with the income statement for 1993, we will have a more complete picture of the firm's operations. We are then able to see what the firm looked like at the beginning of 1993 (balance sheet on December 31, 1992), what happened during the year (income statement for 1993), and the final outcome at the end of the year (balance sheet on December 31, 1993). Our perspective of 1993 is shown graphically in Figure 3–3.

The balance sheet data for the Jamin Corporation shows the firm having ended the prior year (1992) with $804,000 in total assets and concluded 1993 with total assets of $927,000. Most of the assets are invested

TABLE 3–2
Balance Sheets
The Jamin Corporation
December 31, 1992 and 1993

	1992	1993	Change
ASSETS			
Current Assets			
Cash	$ 39,000	$ 44,000	$ 5,000
Accounts receivable	70,500	78,000	7,500
Inventories	177,000	211,400	34,400
Other current assets	13,500	13,800	300
Total current assets	$300,000	$347,200	$ 47,200
Fixed assets			
Gross plant and equipment	$759,000	$838,000	$ 79,000
Accumulated depreciation	(355,000)	(383,200)	(28,200)
Net plant and equipment	$404,000	$454,800	$ 50,800
Land	70,000	70,000	0
Total fixed assets	$474,000	$524,800	$ 50,800
Patents	30,000	55,000	25,000
Total assets	$804,000	$927,000	$123,000
LIABILITIES AND EQUITY			
Current liabilities			
Accounts Payable	$ 60,810	$ 76,110	$ 15,300
Income tax payable	12,000	17,390	5,390
Accrued wages and salaries	3,400	3,900	500
Interest payable	2,000	2,500	500
Total current liabilities	$ 78,210	$ 99,900	$ 21,690
Long-term notes payable	146,000	200,000	54,000
Total liabilities	$224,210	$299,900	$ 75,690
Common stock (par value and paid in capital)	$300,000	$300,000	$0
Retained earnings	279,790	327,100	47,310
Total stockholders' equity	$579,790	$627,100	$ 47,310
Total liabilities and equity	$804,000	$927,000	$123,000

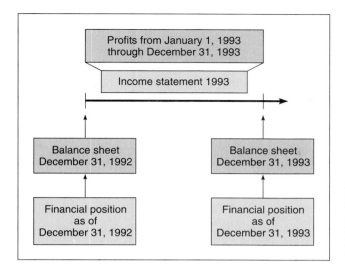

FIGURE 3–3
Visual Perspective of the
Relationship Between the
Balance Sheet and
Income Statement

in plant and equipment, amounting to $404,000 on December 31, 1992 and $454,800 on December 31, 1993. Next, the investments in inventories were $177,000 and $211,400 on December 31, in 1992 and 1993, respectively. Note that it was also in these two accounts (inventories and plant and equipment) that most of the growth in the firm's assets occurred. Finally, the financing of the growth in assets came mostly from additional long-term debt (long-term notes payable) and from the company's 1993 profits, as reflected in the increase in retained earnings.

The Cash Flow Statement

PERSPECTIVE IN FINANCE

In this section, we will learn how to construct a firm's cash flow statement. We could limit our study to interpreting the statement and not get into the computations. However, experience suggests that our understanding of cash flows is limited if we do not know what drives the numbers. Also, without the computations, we will not be able to grasp the relationship between a firm's profits and its cash flows—an item of considerable importance.

The final statement for consideration is the **Cash Flow Statement**, which shows the actual cash flows generated by the firm for the year. The primary categories for this statement are presented in Figure 3–4. Here we see that the cash flows generated are divided into three main areas: (1) cash flow from operations, (2) investments made by the firm, and (3) financing transactions, such as issuing stock and borrowing or repaying debt.

Table 3–3 shows a cash flow statement for the Jamin Corporation. The data needed to construct a cash flow statement come from two sources: (1) balance sheets for the beginning of 1993 (actually December 31, 1992) and the end of 1993, and (2) the income statement for 1993.

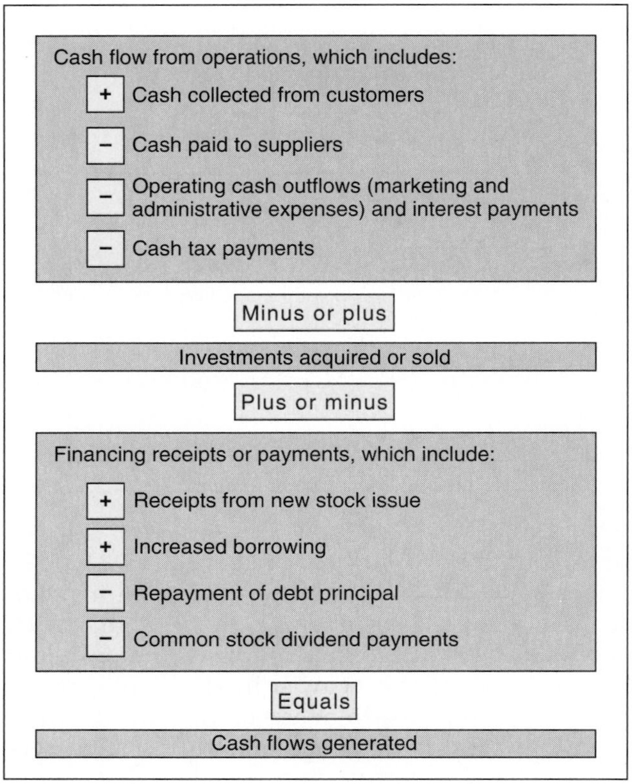

FIGURE 3–4
The Cash Flow Statement:
An Overview

Let's look at the computations required in determining the cash flow for the Jamin Corporation. To do so, we will need to make frequent use of the company's income statement (Table 3–1) and the balance sheets (Table 3–2).

Cash Flow from Operations

As already noted, a firm's cash flow from operations consists of (1) collections from customers, (2) payments to suppliers for the purchase of materials, (3) other operating cash outflows, such as marketing and administrative expenses and interest payments, and (4) cash tax payments.

1. *Collections from customers.* Our beginning point is to determine how much the firm has collected from its customers. We know how much they sold (sales revenue), but we want to know what was actually collected in cash. To find this number, we simply take the firm's sales and subtract the change in accounts receivable. For example, if a firm were to have $200,000 in sales during a year, but its accounts receivable increased from $50,000 to $70,000, or by $20,000, that means that $20,000 of the sales were not collected. Thus, the firm's collections were only $180,000 ($200,000–$20,000).

Cash flows from operations

Cash inflows received from customers

Net sales	$830,200
Less change in accounts receivable	– 7,500
Cash inflows received from customers	$822,700

Cash paid to suppliers

Cost of goods sold	$539,750
Plus change in inventory	34,400
Less change in accounts payable	– 15,300
Cash paid to suppliers	$558,850

Other operating cash outflows and interest payments

Marketing expenses	$ 90,750
General and administrative expenses	71,800
Less change in accrued expenses	– 500
Interest expense	20,000
Less change in interest payable	– 500
Other operating cash outflows and interest payments	$181,550

Cash tax payments

Provision for taxes in the income statement	$ 17,390
Less change in accrued taxes	– 5,390
Cash tax payments	$ 12,000
Total cash flows from operations	$ 70,300

Cash flows—investment activities

Purchase of fixed assets	$ 79,000
Purchase of other current assets	300
Purchase of patents	25,000
Net cash used for investments	$104,300

Cash flows—financing activities

Proceeds from long-term debt	$ 54,000
Common stock dividends	– 15,000
Net cash provided (used) by financing activities	$ 39,000
Total cash flows (change in cash in balance sheets)	$ 5,000

For the Jamin Corporation, sales were $830,200, but accounts receivable increased $7,500, from $70,500 to $78,000. (See the change in receivables in Table 3–2.) Thus, actual collections were $822,700 ($830,200 – $7,500).

2. *Payments to suppliers*. When a firm purchases products from suppliers, the firm's inventories are increased. When the product is sold, the inventory decreases, and cost of goods sold in the income statement increases. Thus, total purchases of products from suppliers are reflected in the cost of goods sold plus any increase in inventories. Then the firm will either pay for the products or rely on additional credit from the supplier, which is shown in accounts payable in the balance sheet. The actual payment to suppliers may therefore be calculated as follows:

$$\begin{pmatrix} \text{Payment} \\ \text{to suppliers} \end{pmatrix} = \begin{pmatrix} \text{cost of} \\ \text{goods sold} \end{pmatrix} + \begin{pmatrix} \text{change in} \\ \text{inventories} \end{pmatrix} - \begin{pmatrix} \text{change in} \\ \text{accounts} \\ \text{payable} \end{pmatrix} \quad \textbf{(3–1)}$$

For the Jamin Corporation, cost of goods sold for 1993 were $539,750; inventories increased from $177,000 to $211,400, or by $34,400; and accounts payable increased $15,300, from $60,810 to $76,110. Thus, payments to suppliers were $558,850, computed as follows:

$$\begin{pmatrix} \text{Payment} \\ \text{to suppliers} \end{pmatrix} = \begin{pmatrix} \text{cost of} \\ \text{goods sold} \end{pmatrix} + \begin{pmatrix} \text{change in} \\ \text{inventories} \end{pmatrix} - \begin{pmatrix} \text{change in} \\ \text{accounts} \\ \text{payable} \end{pmatrix}$$

$$= \$539,750 + \$34,400 - \$15,300$$
$$= \$558,850$$

3. *Other operating cash outflows and interest payments.* We next calculate the actual cash outflows listed as operating expenses and interest expense in the income statement. We only include those operating expenses that are cash outflows and not such items as depreciation expense or other non-cash items. We also adjust for any changes in accrued expenses and interest payable, indications that some of the reported expenses were not really paid but accrued as liabilities. We see in Table 3–3 that the other operating cash outflows for the Jamin Corporation come to $181,550, the combination of marketing expenses, general and administrative expenses (without any depreciation expense), interest expense, and then adjusted for the $500 change in accrued expenses and the $500 change in interest payable to account for expenses recognized under the accrual system of accounting, but not yet paid.[4]

4. *Cash tax payments.* The tax expense shown in a firm's income statement is often times not the actual amount paid at that time. The provision for taxes in the income statement is the amount attributable to the income reported, but the company may be permitted to defer part of the payment. Thus, the cash payment would equal the provision for taxes reported in the income statement less (plus) any increase (decrease) in accrued or deferred taxes in the balance sheet. For the Jamin Corporation, the cash tax payment is $12,000, the $17,390 in the provision for taxes in the income statement less the $5,390 increase in deferred taxes, as reflected from a comparison of the two balance sheets in Table 3–2.

The final cash flow from operations is shown to be $70,300, the net change from the above cash flows ($822,700–$558,850–$181,550 –$12,000.

---

[4]In the income statement, we made a point to compute operating income before deducting interest expenses; that is, operating income or earnings before interest and taxes represents the profits from operations without regard to financing costs, such as interest. Now when calculating cash flows from operations, we deduct interest payments. Why the inconsistency? The answer is that our cash flow statement follows the conventional format used by accountants.

Cash Flows—Investment Activities

Now that we have calculated the cash flows that were generated from the day-to-day operations, we next want to determine the amount of cash used for investments by the Jamin Corporation. As shown in Table 3-3, $104,300 was expended for investments during 1993, including $300 for other current assets (an increase from $13,500 to $13,800); plus $79,000 for fixed assets (an increase from $759,000 to $838,000 in the *gross* fixed assets); and plus $25,000 for patents (increasing from $30,000 to $55,000 in the balance sheet).

Cash Flows—Financing Activities

The last area of cash flows deals with financing activities, including any cash inflows or outflows to or from the firm's investors, both lenders of debt and owners. For the Jamin Corporation, the firm received a net positive cash flow from financing activities in the amount of $39,000. The company borrowed an additional $54,000 in long-term debt and paid $15,000 in common stock dividends.

SUMMARY OF CASH FLOWS We may summarize the cash flows for the Jamin Corporation as follows:

Cash flows from operations		
Collections from customers	$822,700	
Payments to suppliers	(558,850)	
Other operating cash flows	(181,550)	
Cash tax payments	(12,000)	
Total cash flows from operation		$ 70,300
Cash flows—investment activities		(104,300)
Cash flows—financing activities		39,000
Total cash flows		$ 5,000

Thus, the total cash flows generated by the Jamin Corporation from all its activities comes to $5,000 in 1993. We should also note that the firm's change in cash balances shown in the 1992 and 1993 balance sheets increased by that exact amount as well.

Measuring Cash Flows from Operations: An Alternative Approach

The format used in Table 3–3 to measure cash flow from operations is called the **direct method**. It begins with the cash flow collected from the firm's customers and then subtracts the different cash outflows occurring in regular operations of the business, such as the money paid to suppliers and for employee wages, just to mention two examples. We could also measure cash flow from operations by the **indirect method**. This approach, which gives us the same answer as the direct method, is shown in Table 3–4. In this table, we see that the indirect method begins with net income and then adds back all expenses related to the firm's operations that did not result in a cash outflow for the period. So, in a sense, the two methods for arriving at cash flow from operations differ

TABLE 3–4
The Indirect Method for
Measuring Cash Flow
from Operations
The Jamin Corporation
For the Year Ending
December 31, 1993

Net income available to common stockholders (from the income statement)	$62,310
Add (deduct) to reconcile net income to net cash flow	
Depreciation expense	28,200
Less	
Increase in accounts receivable	–7,500
Increase in inventories	–34,400
Plus:	
Increase in accounts payable	15,300
Increase in accrued wages	500
Increase in accrued taxes	5,390
Increase in interest payable	500
Cash flow from operations	$70,300

in terms of whether we start at the top (direct method) or the bottom (indirect method) of the income statement. Both methods simply convert the firm's statement of net income to its cash flow equivalent. Table 3–4 shows how cash flow from operation using the indirect method would be computed for the Jamin Corporation.

As a final thought about measuring cash flow, there is a popular belief that income plus depreciation is a reasonable measure of a company's cash flows. For instance, taking net income available to common stockholders for Jamin Corporation of $62,310 and adding back depreciation of $28,200 gives us $90,510. Given conventional thought, someone might be tempted to use this amount as an estimate of the firm's cash flows. However, from the cash flow statement, we can see that the cash flows were only $5,000. Thus, we can conclude that calculating a firm's cash flow is more complicated than merely adding depreciation expense back to net income. The changes in asset balances resulting from growth are just as important in determining the firm's cash flows as is profits, maybe even more important sometimes. Hence, management, particularly of a growth company, is well advised not to limit its attention to profits, but also focus on cash flows, because they are not the same thing.

■ FINANCIAL RATIO ANALYSIS

We next want to restate the accounting data in relative terms, or what we call **financial ratios**. Financial ratios help us identify some of the financial strengths and weaknesses of a company. The ratios give us two ways of making meaningful comparisons of a firm's financial data: (1) we can examine the ratios across time (say for the last five years) to identify any trends; and (2) we can compare the firm's ratios with those of other firms.

In making a comparison of our firm with other companies, we could select a peer group of companies, or more typically, we could use industry norms published by firms such as Dun & Bradstreet or Robert Morris Associates. Dun and Bradstreet annually publishes a set of 14 key ratios for each of 125 lines of business. Robert Morris Associates, the association of bank loan and credit officers, publishes a set of 16 key ratios for more than 350 lines of business. In both cases, the ratios are classified by industry and by firm size to provide the basis for more meaningful comparisons.

<u>PERSPECTIVE IN FINANCE</u>

Mathematically, a financial ratio is nothing more than a ratio whose numerator and denominator are comprised of financial data. Sound simple? Well, in concept it is. The objective in using a ratio when analyzing financial information is simply to standardize the information being analyzed so that comparisons can be made between ratios of different firms or possibly the same firm at different points in time. So try to keep this in mind as you read through the discussion of financial ratios. All we are doing is trying to standardize financial data so that we can make comparisons with industry norms or other standards.

In learning about ratios, we could simply study the different types or categories of ratios, or we could use ratios to answer some important questions about a firm's operations. We prefer the latter approach and choose the following four questions as a map in using financial ratios:

1. How liquid is the firm?
2. Is management generating adequate *operating* profits on the firm's assets?
3. How is the firm financing its assets?
4. Are the owners (stockholders) receiving an adequate return on *their* investment?

Let's look at each of these questions in turn.

Question 1: How liquid is the firm?

The liquidity of a business is defined as its ability to meet maturing debt obligations. That is, does or will the firm have the resources to pay the creditors when the debt comes due?

There are two ways to approach the liquidity question. First, we can look at the firm's assets that are relatively liquid in nature and compare them to the amount of the debt coming due in the near term.[5] Second, we can look at how quickly the firm's liquid assets are being converted into cash.

Measuring Liquidity: Approach 1

The first approach compares (a) cash and the assets that should be converted into cash within the year with (b) the debt (liabilities) that is

---

[5]This approach has long been used in the finance community; however, it really measures solvency, not liquidity. A firm is solvent when its assets exceed its liabilities, which is in essence what we will be measuring by this approach. For an in-depth discussion of this issue, see Chapter 7 of Terry S. Maness and John T. Zietlow, *Short-Term Financial Management* (New York: West Publishing Company, 1993).

coming due and payable within the year. The assets here are the current assets, and the debt is the current liabilities in the balance sheet. Thus, we could use the following measure, called the **current ratio**, to estimate a company's relative liquidity:

$$\text{current ratio} = \frac{\text{current assets}}{\text{current liabilities}} \tag{3–2}$$

Furthermore, remembering that the three primary current assets include (1) cash, (2) accounts receivable, and (3) inventories, we could make our measure of liquidity more restrictive by excluding inventories, the least liquid of the current assets, in the numerator. This revised ratio is called the **acid-test** (or **quick**) **ratio**, and is calculated as follows:

$$\text{acid-test ratio} = \frac{\text{current assets} - \text{inventories}}{\text{current liabilities}} \tag{3–3}$$

We can demonstrate the computations of the current ratio and the acid-test ratio by using the Jamin Corporation's 1993 balance sheet (Table 3-2). These calculations and the industry norms or averages provided by Robert Morris Associates, are as follows:

	Jamin Corporation	Industry Average
$\text{current ratio} = \dfrac{\text{current assets}}{\text{current liabilities}}$		
$= \dfrac{\$347,200}{\$99,900} = 3.48$		2.70
$\text{acid-test ratio} = \dfrac{\text{current assets} - \text{inventories}}{\text{current liabilities}}$		
$= \dfrac{\$347,200 - \$211,400}{\$99,900} = 1.36$		1.25

Thus, in terms of the current ratio and the acid-test ratio, the Jamin Corporation is more liquid than the average firm in its industry. The Jamin Corporation has $3.48 in current assets for every $1 in current liabilities (debt), compared to $2.70 for a "typical" firm in the industry; and the firm has $1.36 in current assets less inventories per $1 of current debt, compared to $1.25 for the industry norm. Although both ratios suggest the firm is more liquid, the current ratio appears to suggest more liquidity than the acid-test ratio. Why might this be the case? Simply put, Jamin has more inventories relative to current debt than do most other firms. Which ratio should be given greater weight depends on our confidence in the liquidity of the inventories. We will return to this question shortly.

Measuring Liquidity: Approach 2

The second view of liquidity examines the firm's ability to convert accounts receivable and inventory into cash on a timely basis. The conversion of accounts receivable into cash may be measured by computing how long it takes to collect the firm's receivables; that is, how many days of sales are outstanding in the form of accounts receivable? We can answer this question by computing the **average collection period**:

$$\text{average collection period} = \frac{\text{accounts receivable}}{\text{daily credit sales}} \qquad \textbf{(3–4)}$$

If we assume all the Jamin Corporation's sales to be credit sales, as opposed to some cash sales, then the firm's average collection period is 34.3 days, compared to an industry norm of 35 days:[6]

Jamin Corporation	Industry

$$\text{average collection period} = \frac{\text{accounts receivable}}{\text{daily credit sales}}$$

$$= \frac{\$78,000}{\$830,200 \div 365} = 34.3 \qquad\qquad 35$$

Thus, the company collects its receivables in about the same number of days as the average firm in the industry. Accounts receivable, it would at least appear, are reasonably liquid when viewed from the perspective of the length of time required to convert receivables into cash.

We could have reached the same conclusion by measuring how many times accounts receivable are "rolled over" during a year, or the **accounts receivable turnover ratio**. For instance, the Jamin Corporation turns its receivables over 10.64 times a year:[7]

Jamin Corporation	Industry

$$\text{accounts receivable turnover} = \frac{\text{credit sales}}{\text{accounts receivable}} \qquad \textbf{(3–5)}$$

$$= \frac{\$830,200}{\$78,000} = 10.64 \qquad\qquad 10.4$$

Whether we use average collection period or the accounts receivable turnover, the conclusion is the same: The Jamin Corporation is comparable to the average firm in the industry when it comes to the collection of receivables.[8]

---

[6]Information on the proportion of credit sales to total sales is generally unavailable in public financial statements. Thus, we generally use total sales in place of credit sales in computing average collection period. This same assumption is also made when computing accounts receivable turnover, the next ratio we will use. To the extent our assumption is invalid, we are understating the average collection period and overstating the accounts receivable turnover.

[7]We could also measure the accounts receivable turnover by dividing 365 days by the average collection period: 365/34.3 = 10.64.

[8]Although it will not be discussed here, one tool for further assessing the liquidity of a firm's receivables is an aging of accounts receivable schedule. Such a schedule identifies the number and dollar value of accounts outstanding for various periods. For example, accounts that are less than 10 days old, 11 to 20 days, and so forth might be examined. Still another way to construct the schedule would involve analyzing the length of time to eventual collection of accounts over a past period. For example, how many accounts were outstanding less than 10 days when collected, between 10 and 20 days, and so forth.

We now want to know the same thing for inventories that we just determined for accounts receivable: How many times are we turning over inventories during the year? In this manner, we gain some insight into the liquidity of inventories. The **inventory turnover ratio** is calculated as follows:

$$\text{inventory turnover} = \frac{\text{cost of goods sold}}{\text{inventory}} \qquad \textbf{(3–6)}$$

Note that sales in this ratio is replaced by cost of goods sold. Since the inventory (the denominator) is measured at cost, we want to use a cost-based measure of sales in the numerator. Otherwise, our answer would vary from one firm to the next solely due to differences in how each firm marks up its sales over costs.[9]

The inventory turnover for the Jamin Corporation, along with the industry norm, is as follows:

Jamin Corporation	Industry
$\dfrac{\text{inventory}}{\text{turnover}} = \dfrac{\text{cost of goods sold}}{\text{inventory}}$	
$= \dfrac{\$539,750}{\$211,400} = 2.55$	4.00

We may have just discovered a significant problem for the Jamin Corporation. It appears that the firm carries excessive inventory. That is, Jamin generates only $2.55 in sales (at cost) for every $1 of inventory, compared to $4 in sales (at cost) for the average firm. Going back to the current ratio and the acid test-ratio, we remember that the current ratio made the firm look better than did the acid-test ratio, which means that the inventory is a larger component of the current ratio than for other firms. Now we see that we are carrying excessive inventory, maybe even some obsolete inventory. These findings suggest that the inventory may not be of the same quality on average as for other firms in the industry. Thus, the current ratio is probably a bit suspect.

Question 2: Is management generating adequate operating profits on the firm's assets?

We now begin a different line of thinking that will carry us through all the remaining questions. At this point, we want to know if the profits are sufficient relative to the assets being invested. The question is similar to a question one might ask about the interest being earned on a savings account at the bank. When you invest $1,000 in a savings account and receive $60 in interest during the year, you are earning a 6 percent return on your investment ($60 ÷ $1,000 = .06 = 6%). With respect to the Jamin Corporation, we want to know something similar: the rate of return management is earning on the firm's assets.

[9]Whereas our logic may be correct to use cost of goods sold in the numerator, practicality may dictate that we use sales instead. Some suppliers of industry norm data use sales in the numerator. Thus, for consistency in our comparisons, we too may need to use sales.

In answering this question, we have several choices as to how we measure profits: gross profits, operating profits, or net income. Gross profits would not be an acceptable choice because it does not include some important information, such as the cost of marketing and distributing the firm's product. Thus, we should choose between operating profits and net income. For our purposes, we prefer to use operating profits, because this measure of firm profits is calculated before the costs of the company's financing policies have been deducted. Because financing is explicitly considered in our next question, we want to isolate only the operating aspects of the company's profits at this point. In this way, we are able to compare the profitability of firms with different debt-to-equity mixes. Therefore, to examine the level of operating profits relative to the assets, we would use the **operating income return on investment** (OIROI):

$$\frac{\text{operating income}}{\text{return on investment}} = \frac{\text{operating income}}{\text{total assets}} \qquad (3\text{--}7)$$

The operating income return on investment for the Jamin Corporation, and the corresponding industry norm, are shown below:

Jamin Corporation	Industry

$$\frac{\text{operating income}}{\text{return on investment}} = \frac{\text{operating income}}{\text{total assets}}$$

$$= \frac{\$99,700}{\$927,000} = .1076 = 10.76\% \qquad 13.2\%$$

Hence, we see that the Jamin Corporation is not earning an equivalent return on investment relative to the average firm in the industry. For some reason, management is not generating as much income on $1 of assets as are similar firms.[10]

If we were the managers of the Jamin Corporation, we should not be satisfied with merely knowing that we are not earning a competitive return on the firm's assets. We should also want to know *why we are below average*. To understand this issue, we may separate the operating income return on investment, OIROI, into two important pieces: the operating profit margin and the total asset turnover. The firm's OIROI is a multiple of these two ratios and may be shown algebraically as follows:

$$\text{OIROI} = \left(\begin{array}{c}\text{operating}\\\text{profit margin}\end{array}\right) \times \left(\begin{array}{c}\text{total asset}\\\text{turnover}\end{array}\right) \qquad (3\text{--}8a)$$

---

[10]The **return on assets,** ROA, is often used as an indicator of a firm's profitability and is measured as follows:

Return on assets = net income ÷ total assets

We choose not to use this ratio because net income is influenced both by operating decisions and how the firm is financed. We want to restrict our attention only to operating activities; financing is considered in questions 3 and 4. Nevertheless, sometimes the industry norm for operating income return on investment is not available. Instead, return on assets is provided. If so, we have no option but to use the return on assets for measuring the firm's profitability.

or more completely,

$$\text{OIROI} = \frac{\text{operating income}}{\text{sales}} \times \frac{\text{sales}}{\text{total assets}} \qquad \textbf{(3–8b)}$$

The first component of the OIROI, the **operating profit margin**, is an extremely important variable in understanding a company's operating profitability. It is important that we know exactly what drives this ratio. In coming to understand the ratio, think about the makeup of the ratio, which may be expressed as follows

$$\frac{\text{operating income}}{\text{sales}} =$$

$$\frac{\frac{\text{total}}{\text{sales}} - \frac{\text{cost of}}{\text{goods sold}} - \frac{\text{administrative}}{\text{expenses}} - \frac{\text{marketing}}{\text{expenses}}}{\text{sales}}$$

Because total sales equals the number of units sold times the sales price per unit, and the cost of goods sold equals the number of units sold times the cost of goods sold per unit, we may conclude that the driving forces of the operating profit margin are the following:

1. The number of units of product sold;[11]
2. The average selling price for each product unit;
3. The cost of manufacturing or acquiring the firm's product;
4. The ability to control general and administrative expenses; and
5. The ability to control expenses in marketing and distributing the firm's product.

These influences are also apparent simply by looking at the income statement and thinking about what is involved in determining the firm's operating profits or income.[12]

Total asset turnover is the second component of the OIROI. This ratio is a function of how efficiently management is using the firm's assets to generate sales. If Company A can generate $3 in sales with $1 in assets, compared to $2 in sales per asset dollar by Company B, we may say that Company A is using its assets more efficiently in generating sales, which is a major determinant in the return on investment.

Let's turn now to the Jamin Corporation to see what we can learn. We would compute Jamin's operating profit margin and total asset turnover as follows:

---

[11]The number of units affects the operating profit margin only if some of the firm's costs and expenses are fixed. If a company's expenses are all variable in nature, then the ratio would not change as the number of units sold increases or decreases, because the numerator and the denominator would change at the same rate.

[12]We could have used the **net profit margin**, rather than the operating profit margin, which is measured as follows:

net profit margin = net income ÷ sales

However, because net income includes both operating expenses and interest expense, this ratio is influenced both by operating activities and financing activities. We prefer to defer the effect of financing decisions until questions 3 and 4, which follow shortly.

$$\text{Jamin Corporation} \qquad\qquad \text{Industry}$$

$$\frac{\text{operating}}{\text{profit margin}} = \frac{\text{operating income}}{\text{sales}}$$

$$= \frac{\$99,700}{\$830,200} = .1201 = 12.01\% \qquad\qquad 11\%$$

$$\text{Jamin Corporation} \qquad\qquad \text{Industry}$$

$$\frac{\text{total asset}}{\text{turnover}} = \frac{\text{sales}}{\text{total assets}}$$

$$= \frac{\$830,200}{\$927,000} = 0.896 \qquad\qquad 1.20$$

Recalling that:

$$\text{OIROI} = \left(\frac{\text{operating}}{\text{profit margin}}\right) \times \left(\frac{\text{total asset}}{\text{turnover}}\right)$$

we see that for the Jamin Corporation,

$$\text{OIROI}_{\text{Jamin}} = 12.01\% \times 0.896 = .1076 = 10.76\%$$

and for the industry, this same ratio is

$$\text{OIROI}_{\text{Ind}} = 11\% \times 1.20 = .132 = 13.2\%$$

Clearly, the Jamin Corporation is competitive when it comes to keeping costs and expenses in line relative to sales, as is reflected by the operating profit margin. In other words, management is performing satisfactorily in managing the five driving forces of the operating profit margin listed above. However, when we look at the total asset turnover, we can see why management is less than competitive on its operating income return on investment. The firm is not using its assets efficiently. The Jamin Corporation generates about $.90 in sales per dollar of assets, whereas the competition produces $1.20 in sales from every dollar in assets. Here is the company's problem.

We should not stop here with our analysis of Jamin's problem; we should dig deeper. We have concluded that the assets are not being used efficiently, but now we should try to determine which assets are the problem. Are we overinvested in all assets or more so in accounts receivable or inventory or fixed assets? To answer this question, we merely examine the turnover ratios for each respective asset. That is, for

	Jamin Corporation	Industry
Accounts receivable turnover:		
$\dfrac{\text{sales}}{\text{accounts receivable}} = \dfrac{\$830,200}{\$78,000} = 10.64$		10.4
Inventory turnover:		
$\dfrac{\text{cost of goods sold}}{\text{inventory}} = \dfrac{\$539,750}{\$211,400} = 2.55$		4.00
Fixed asset turnover:		
$\dfrac{\text{sales}}{\text{net fixed assets}} = \dfrac{\$830,200}{\$524,800} = 1.58$		2.50

Jamin Corporation's problems are now even clearer. The company has excessive inventories, which we had known from our earlier discussions, and also there is too large an investment in fixed assets for the sales being produced. It would appear that these two asset categories are not being managed well, and the consequence is a lower operating income return on investment.

Question 3: How is the firm financing its assets?

We now turn for the moment to the matter of how the firm is financed. (We shall return to the firm's profitability shortly.) The basic issue is the use of debt versus equity: Do we finance the assets more by debt or equity? In answering this question, we will use two ratios. (Many more could be used.) First, we simply ask what percentage of the firm's assets are financed by debt, including *both* short-term and long-term debt, realizing the remaining percentage must be financed by equity. We would compute the **debt ratio** as follows:[13]

$$\text{debt ratio} = \frac{\text{total debt}}{\text{total assets}} \qquad \textbf{(3-10)}$$

For the Jamin Corporation, debt as a percentage of total assets is 32 percent, compared to an industry norm of 40 percent. The computation is as follows:

	Jamin Corporation	Industry
$\text{debt ratio} = \dfrac{\text{total debt}}{\text{total assets}}$		
	$= \dfrac{\$299,900}{\$927,000} = .32 = 32\%$	40%

Thus, the Jamin Corporation uses somewhat less debt than the average firm in the industry.

Our second perspective regarding the firm's financing decisions comes by looking at the income statement. When we borrow money, there is a minimum requirement that the firm pay the interest on the debt. Thus, it is informative to compare the amount of operating income that is available to service the interest with the amount of interest that is to be paid. Stated as a ratio, we compute the number of times we are earning our interest. Thus, a **times interest earned** ratio is commonly used when examining the firm's debt position and is computed in the following manner:

$$\text{times interest earned} = \frac{\text{operating income}}{\text{interest}} \qquad \textbf{(3-11)}$$

[13]We will often see the relationship stated in terms of debt to equity, rather than debt to total assets. We come to the same conclusion with either ratio.

For the Jamin Corporation,

Jamin Corporation	Industry

$$\begin{matrix} \text{times} \\ \text{interest} \\ \text{earned} \end{matrix} = \frac{\text{operating income}}{\text{interest}}$$

$$= \frac{\$99,700}{\$20,000} = 4.99 \qquad\qquad 4.00$$

Thus, the Jamin Corporation is able to service its interest expense without any great difficulty. In fact, the firm's income could fall by as much as $79,700, or almost 80 percent ($79,700 ÷ $99,700) and still have the income to pay the required interest. We should remember, however, that interest is not paid with income but with cash and that the firm may be required to repay some of the debt principal as well as the interest. Thus, the times interest earned is only a crude measure of the firm's capacity to service its debt. Nevertheless, it does give us a general indication of a company's debt capacity.

Question 4: Are the owners (stockholders) receiving an adequate return on their investment?

Our one remaining question looks at the accounting return on the common stockholders' investment; that is, we want to know if the earnings available to the firm's owners or common equity investors is attractive when compared to the returns of owners of similar companies in the same industry.
    We measure the return to the owners as follows:

$$\textbf{return on equity} = \frac{\text{net income}}{\begin{matrix}\text{common equity (including par, paid in} \\ \text{capital and retained earnings)}\end{matrix}} \qquad \textbf{(3–12)}$$

The return on equity for the Jamin Corporation and the industry are 9.94 percent and 12.5 percent, respectively:

Jamin Corporation	Industry

$$\begin{matrix} \text{return} \\ \text{on equity} \end{matrix} = \frac{\text{net income}}{\text{common equity}}$$

$$= \frac{\$62,310}{\$627,100} = .0994 = 9.94\% \qquad\qquad 12.5\%$$

It would appear that the owners of the Jamin Corporation are not receiving a return on their investment equivalent to what owners involved with competing businesses receive. However, we should also ask, "Why not?" In this case, the answer is twofold: First, the Jamin Corporation is not as profitable in its operation as its competitors. (Remember the operating income return on investment of 10.76 percent for the Jamin Corporation, compared to 13.2 percent for the industry.) Second, the average firm in the industry uses more debt, which causes the return on common equity to be higher, provided of course that a company is earning a return on its investments that exceeds its cost of debt (the interest rate). We should also note, however, that the use of debt increases the firm's risk. An example will help us understand this point.

Firms A and B are identical in size, both having $1,000 in total assets and both having an operating income return on investment of 14 percent. However, they are different in one respect: Firm A uses no debt, but Firm B finances 60 percent of its investments with debt at an interest cost of 10 percent. For the sake of simplicity, we will assume there are no income taxes. The financial statements for the two companies would be as follows:

	Firm A	Firm B
Total assets	$1,000	$1,000
Debt (10% interest rate)	$ 0	$ 600
Equity	1,000	400
Total	$1,000	$1,000
Operating income (OIROI = 14%)	$ 140	$ 140
Interest expense (10%)	0	60
Net profit	$ 140	$ 80

Computing the return on common equity for both companies, we see that Firm B has a much more attractive return to its owners, 20 percent compared to Firm A's 14 percent:

$$\text{return on equity} = \frac{\text{net income}}{\text{common equity}} \qquad (3\text{--}12)$$

Firm A: $\dfrac{\$140}{\$1,000} = .14 = 14\%$ Firm B: $\dfrac{\$80}{\$400} = .20 = 20\%$

Why the difference? The answer is straightforward. Firm B is earning 14 percent on its investments, but is only having to pay 10 percent for its borrowed money. The difference between the return on the firm's investments and the interest rate, 14 percent less the 10 percent, goes to the owners, thus boosting Firm B's return on equity above that of Firm A. We are seeing the results of *favorable* financial leverage at work, where we borrow at 10 percent and invest at 14 percent. The result is an increase in the return on equity.

If debt enhances the owners' returns, why would we not use lots of it all the time? We may continue our example to find the answer. Assume now that the economy falls into a deep recession, business declines sharply, and Firms A and B only earn a 6 percent operating income return on investment. Let's recompute the return on common equity now.

	Firm A	Firm B
Operating Income (OIROI = 6%)	$60	$60
Interest expense	0	60
Net profit	$60	$0

Firm A: $\dfrac{\$60}{\$1,000} = .06 = 6\%$ Firm B: $\dfrac{\$0}{\$400} = .00 = 0\%$

Now the use of leverage has a negative influence on the return on equity, with Firm B earning less than Firm A for its owners. This results from the fact that now Firm B earns less than the interest rate of 10 percent; consequently, the equity investors have to make up the difference. Thus, financial leverage is a two-edged sword; when times are good, financial leverage can make them very, very good, but when times are bad, financial leverage makes them very, very bad. Financial leverage can potentially enhance the returns of the equity investors, but it also increases the uncertainty or risk for the owners. ■

The Determinants of the Return on Equity

From the preceding example, we see that the return on equity is a function of:

1. The difference between the operating income return on investment and the interest rate, and
2. The amount of debt used in the capital structure relative to the size of the firm,

We can even be more specific. Rather than expressing return on equity as net income divided by the common equity, as we did in equation (3–12), we may also measure return on equity as follows:

$$\begin{array}{rl} \text{return} \\ \text{on equity} \end{array} = \left(\begin{array}{c} \text{operating income} \\ \text{return on investment} \end{array} \right) \qquad\qquad \textbf{(3–13)}$$

$$+ \left[\left(\begin{array}{c} \text{operating income} \\ \text{return on investment} \end{array} - \begin{array}{c} \text{interest} \\ \text{rate} \end{array} \right) \times \frac{\text{debt}}{\text{equity}} \right]$$

For the hypothetical example described above, where the operating income return on investment for Company B was 14 percent and the interest rate on the debt was 10 percent, the return on equity may be calculated as follows:[14]

$$\begin{array}{c} \text{Firm B's} \\ \text{return on equity} \end{array} = 14\% + \left[(14\% - 10\%) \times \frac{\$600}{\$400} \right] = 20\%$$

Returning to the Jamin Corporation, we will remember that the operating income return on investment is less for Jamin than for competing firms. Therefore, if the competing firms are paying comparable interest rates, and assuming equal debt ratios, the return on equity for the Jamin Corporation will of necessity be less. Also, we observed that the average firm in the industry uses more debt, which magnifies the return on equity but also exposes the owners to additional risk. So the return on equity for the Jamin Corporation is less than competing firms for two reasons: (1) It has less operating profits, and (2) it uses less debt. The first reason needs to be corrected by improved management of the

---

[14]In this example, we have ignored the effects of taxes. If we had used equation (3–13) in the Jamin Corporation example where there were income taxes, we would have to adjust the returns to their after-tax equivalent. For instance, if Firm B is in a 25-percent tax bracket, then we would have to restate the 14-percent operating return on investment to 10.5 percent [14% × (1–.25)] and the after-tax cost of debt would be 7.5 percent [10% × (1 – .25)].

firm's assets. The second reason may be a conscious decision of management not to assume as much financial risk as other firms do. This latter issue is a matter of "tastes and preferences."

Let's review what we have learned about the use of financial ratios in evaluating a company's financial position. We have presented all the ratios for the Jamin Corporation in Table 3–5. The ratios are grouped by the issue being addressed: liquidity, operating profitability, financing, and profits for the owners. As before, we use some ratios for more than one purpose, namely the turnover ratios for accounts receivable and inventories. These ratios have implications both for the firm's liquidity and its profitability; thus, they are listed in both areas. Also, we have included both average collection period and accounts receivable turnover; typically, we would only use one in our analysis, because they are just different ways of expressing the same thing.

An Integrative Approach to Ratio Analysis: The Du Pont Analysis

In the previous section, we used ratio analysis to answer four questions thought to be important in understanding a company's financial position. The last three of the four questions dealt with a company's earnings capabilities and the common stockholder's return on the equity capital. In our analysis, we measured the return on equity as follows:

$$\textbf{return on equity} = \frac{\text{net income}}{\text{common equity}} \qquad \textbf{(3–12)}$$

Another approach frequently used to evaluate a firm's profitability and the return on equity is the **Du Pont Analysis**. Figure 3–5 shows graphically the Du Pont technique, modified somewhat from the original format developed by the management at the Du Pont Corporation. Beginning at the top of the figure, we see that the return on equity is calculated as follows:

$$\textbf{return on equity} = \left(\begin{array}{c}\text{return} \\ \text{on assets}\end{array}\right) \div \left(1 - \frac{\text{total debt}}{\text{total assets}}\right) \qquad \textbf{(3–14)}$$

where the **return on assets**, or ROA, equals:

$$\text{return on assets} = \frac{\text{net income}}{\text{total assets}} \qquad \textbf{(3–15)}$$

Thus, we see that the return on equity is a function of (1) the firm's overall profitability (net income relative to the amount invested in assets), and (2) the amount of debt used to finance the assets. We also know that the return on assets may be represented as follows:

$$\text{return on assets} = \left(\begin{array}{c}\text{net profit} \\ \text{margin}\end{array}\right) \times \left(\begin{array}{c}\text{total asset} \\ \text{turnover}\end{array}\right) \qquad \textbf{(3–16)}$$

$$= \left(\frac{\text{net income}}{\text{sales}}\right) \times \left(\frac{\text{sales}}{\text{total assets}}\right)$$

Combining equations (3–14) and (3–16) gives us the basic Du Pont equation that shows the firm's return on equity as follows:

TABLE 3–5
Jamin Corporation
Financial Ratio Analysis

Financial Ratios		Jamin Corporation		Industry Average
1. Firm liquidity				
Current ratio =	$\dfrac{\text{current assets}}{\text{current liabilities}}$	$\dfrac{\$347{,}200}{\$99{,}900}$	= 3.48	2.70
Acid-test ratio =	$\dfrac{\text{current assets} - \text{inventories}}{\text{current liabilities}}$	$\dfrac{\$347{,}200 - \$211{,}400}{\$99{,}900}$	= 1.36	1.25
Average collection period =	$\dfrac{\text{accounts receivable}}{\text{daily credit sales}}$	$\dfrac{\$78{,}000}{\$830{,}200 \div 365}$	= 34.30	35 days
Accounts receivable turnover =	$\dfrac{\text{credit sales}}{\text{accounts receivable}}$	$\dfrac{\$830{,}200}{\$78{,}000}$	= 10.64	10.40
Inventory turnover =	$\dfrac{\text{cost of goods sold}}{\text{inventory}}$	$\dfrac{\$539{,}750}{\$211{,}400}$	= 2.55	4.00
2. Operating profitability				
Operating income return on investment =	$\dfrac{\text{operating income}}{\text{total assets}}$	$\dfrac{\$99{,}700}{\$927{,}000}$	= 10.76%	13.2%
Operating profit margin =	$\dfrac{\text{operating income}}{\text{sales}}$	$\dfrac{\$99{,}700}{\$830{,}200}$	= 12.01%	1.0%
Total asset turnover =	$\dfrac{\text{sales}}{\text{total assets}}$	$\dfrac{\$830{,}200}{\$927{,}000}$	= 0.896	1.20
Accounts receivable turnover =	$\dfrac{\text{credit sales}}{\text{accounts receivable}}$	$\dfrac{\$830{,}200}{\$78{,}000}$	= 10.64	10.40
Inventory turnover =	$\dfrac{\text{cost of goods sold}}{\text{inventory}}$	$\dfrac{\$539{,}750}{\$211{,}400}$	= 2.55	4.00
Fixed assets turnover =	$\dfrac{\text{sales}}{\text{fixed assets}}$	$\dfrac{\$830{,}200}{\$524{,}800}$	= 1.58	2.50
3. Financing decisions				
Debt ratio =	$\dfrac{\text{total debt}}{\text{total assets}}$	$\dfrac{\$299{,}900}{\$927{,}000}$	= 32%	40.0%
Times interest earned =	$\dfrac{\text{operating income}}{\text{interest}}$	$\dfrac{\$99{,}700}{\$20{,}000}$	= 4.99	4.00
4. Return on equity				
Return on equity =	$\dfrac{\text{net income}}{\text{common equity}}$	$\dfrac{\$62{,}310}{\$627{,}100}$	= 9.94%	12.5%

FIGURE 3–5
Du Pont Analysis

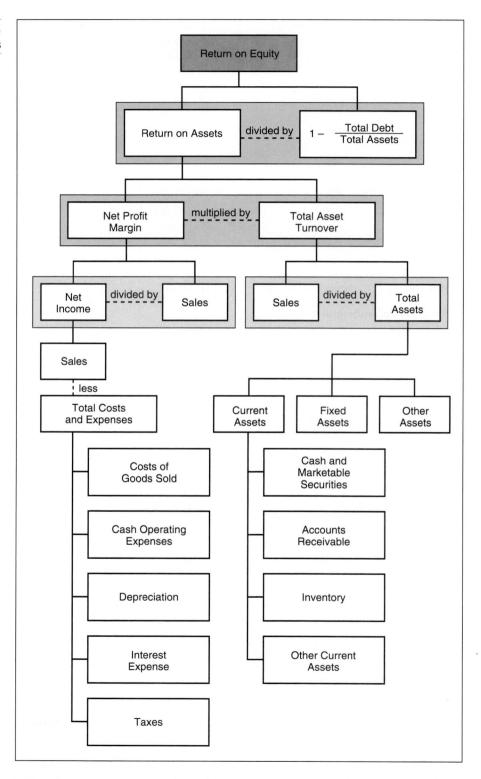

$$\text{return on equity} = \left(\frac{\text{net profit}}{\text{margin}}\right) \times \left(\frac{\text{total asset}}{\text{turnover}}\right) \div \left(1 - \frac{\text{total debt}}{\text{total assets}}\right)$$

$$= \left(\frac{\text{net income}}{\text{sales}}\right) \times \left(\frac{\text{sales}}{\text{total assets}}\right) \div \left(1 - \frac{\text{total debt}}{\text{total assets}}\right)$$

Using the Du Pont equation and the diagram in Figure 3–5 allows management to see more clearly what drives the return on equity and the interrelationships among the net profit margin, the asset turnover, and the debt ratio. Management is provided with a road map to follow in determining their effectiveness in managing the firm's resources to maximize the return earned on the owners' investment. In addition, the manager or owner can determine why that particular return was earned.

Let's return to the Jamin Corporation to demonstrate the use of the Du Pont analysis. Taking the information from the Jamin Corporation's income statement (Table 3–1) and balance sheet as of December 31, 1993 (Table 3–2), we can calculate the company's return on equity as follows:

$$\text{return on equity} = \left(\frac{\text{net income}}{\text{sales}}\right) \times \left(\frac{\text{sales}}{\text{total assets}}\right) \div \left(1 - \frac{\text{total debt}}{\text{total assets}}\right)$$

$$= \left(\frac{\$62,310}{\$830,200}\right) \times \left(\frac{\$830,200}{\$927,000}\right) \div \left(1 - \frac{\$299,900}{\$927,000}\right)$$

$$= \frac{7.51\% \times 0.896}{(1 - 0.3235)}$$

$$= 9.94\%$$

We can also visualize the relationships graphically for the Jamin Corporation, as shown in Figure 3–6.

If the Jamin Corporation's management wants to improve the company's return on equity, they should carefully examine Figure 3–6 for possible avenues. As we study the figure, we quickly see that improvement in the return on equity can come in one or more of four ways:

1. Increase sales without a disproportionate increase in costs and expenses.
2. Reduce the firm's cost of goods sold or operating expenses shown in the left-hand side of Figure 3–6.
3. Increase the sales relative to the asset base, either by increasing sales or by reducing the amounts invested in company assets. From our earlier examination of the Jamin Corporation, we learned that the firm had excessive inventory and fixed assets. Thus, management needs to reduce these assets to the point possible, which would in turn result in an increase in the return on assets and then the return on equity.
4. Increase the use of debt relative to equity, but only to the extent that does not unduly jeopardize the firm's financial position.

The choice between using the four-question approach as described earlier or the Du Pont analysis is largely a matter of personal preference. Both approaches are intended to let us see the variables that determine a

FIGURE 3–6
Du Pont Analysis:
Jamin Corporation

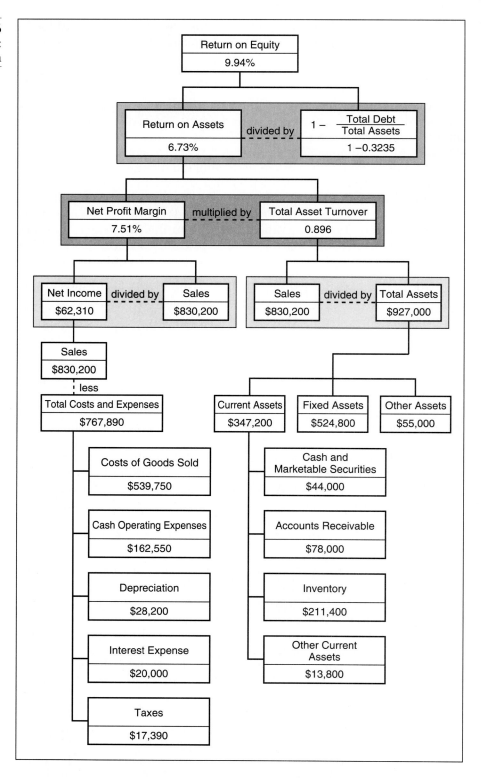

firm's profitability. There are, however, limitations to either technique because of the inherent limitations in using financial ratios—a topic addressed in the next section.

Limitations of Ratio Analysis

We have shown how financial ratios may be used to understand a company's financial position, but anyone who works with these ratios ought to be aware of the limitations involved in their use. The following list includes some of the more important pitfalls that may be encountered in computing and interpreting financial ratios:

1. It is sometimes difficult to identify the industry category to which a firm belongs when the firm engages in multiple lines of business. Thus, we frequently must select our own set of peer firms and construct tailor-made norms.

2. Published industry averages are only approximations and provide the user with general guidelines rather than scientifically determined averages of the ratios of all or even a representative sample of the firms within an industry.

3. Accounting practices differ widely among firms and can lead to differences in computed ratios. For example, the use of last-in, first-out (LIFO) in inventory valuation can, in a period of rising prices, lower the firm's inventory account and increase its inventory turnover ratio as compared with that of a firm that uses first-in, first-out (FIFO). In addition, firms may choose different methods of depreciating their fixed assets.

4. Financial ratios can be too high or too low. For example, a current ratio that exceeds the industry norm may signal the presence of excess liquidity, which results in a lowering of overall profits in relation to the firm's investment in assets. On the other hand, a current ratio that falls below the norm indicates the possibility that the firm has inadequate liquidity and may at some future date be unable to pay its bills on time.

5. An industry average may not provide a desirable target ratio or norm. At best an industry average provides a guide to the financial position of the average firm in the industry. It does not mean it is the ideal or best value for the ratio. Thus, we may choose to compare our firm's ratios with a self-determined peer group or even a single competitor.[15]

6. Many firms experience seasonality in their operations. Thus, balance sheet entries and their corresponding ratios will vary with the

---

[15]Cunningham and Rose (forthcoming in *Journal of Financial Education*) compare the industry financial ratios from Robert Morris and Associates with those of Dun & Bradstreet and find that they differ significantly within the same industry classifications. This finding points out the need to carefully consider the choice of an industry norm. In fact, your analysis may require that you construct your own norm from, say, a list of the four or five firms in a particular industry that might provide the most appropriate standard of comparison for the firm being analyzed.

time of year when the statements are prepared. To avoid this problem, an average account balance should be used (for several months or quarters during the year) rather than the year-end total. For example, an average of month-end inventory balances might be used to compute a firm's inventory turnover ratio when the firm is subject to a significant seasonality in its sales (and correspondingly in its investment in inventories).

In spite of their limitations, financial ratios provide us with a very useful tool for assessing a firm's financial condition. We should, however, be aware of these potential weaknesses when performing a ratio analysis. In many cases the real value derived from analyzing financial ratios is that they tell us what questions to ask.

SUMMARY

Basic Financial Statements

Three basic financial statements are commonly used to describe the financial condition and performance of the firm: the balance sheet, the income statement, and the statement of cash flows. The balance sheet provides a picture of the firm's assets, liabilities, and owners' equity on a particular date, whereas the income statement reflects the net income from the firm's operations over a given period. The statement of cash flows combines information from both the balance sheet and income statement to describe sources and uses of cash for a given period in the firm's history.

Financial Ratios

Financial ratios are the principal tool of financial analysis. Sometimes referred to simply as benchmarks, ratios standardize financial information so that comparisons can be made between firms of varying sizes. Two groups find financial ratios useful. The first is comprised of managers who use them to measure and track company performance through time. The focus of their analysis is frequently related to various measures of profitability used to evaluate the performance of the firm from the perspective of the owners. The second group of users of financial ratios includes analysts external to the firm who, for one reason or another, have an interest in the firm's economic well-being. An example of this group would be a loan officer of a commercial bank who wishes to determine the credit worthiness of a loan applicant. Here the focus of the analysis is on the firm's previous use of financial leverage and its ability to pay the interest and principal associated with the loan request.

Financial ratios may be used to answer at least four questions: (1) How liquid is the company? (2) Is management effective at generating operating profits on the firm's assets? (3) How is the firm financed? (4) Are the returns earned by the common stockholders adequate?

Analysis of Financial Ratios

Two methods may be used in analyzing financial ratios. The first involves trend analysis for the firm over time; the second involves making ratio comparisons with industry norms. In our example, a set of industry norms from Robert Morris Associates was used in analyzing the financial position of the Jamin Corporation.

STUDY QUESTIONS

3–1.   The basic financial statements of an organization consist of the balance sheet, income statement, and cash flow statement. Describe the nature of each and explain how their functions differ.

3–2.   Why is it that the preferred stockholders' equity section of the balance sheet would change only when new shares are sold or repurchased, whereas the common equity section would change from year to year regardless of whether new shares are bought or sold?

3–3.   Discuss the reasons why net income for a particular period does not necessarily reflect a firm's cash flow during that period.

3–4.   Describe the "four-question approach" to using financial ratios.

3–5.   Discuss briefly the two perspectives that can be taken in performing ratio analyses.

3–6.   Where can we obtain industry norms? What are the limitations of industry average ratios? Discuss briefly.

SELF-TEST PROBLEMS

ST-1.   *(Ratio Analysis and Short-term Liquidity)* Ray's Tool and Supply Company of Austin, Texas has been expanding its level of operation for the past two years. The firm's sales have grown rapidly as a result of the expansion in the Austin economy. However, Ray's is a privately held company, and the only source of available funds it has is a line of credit with the firm's bank. The company needs to expand its inventories to meet the needs of its growing customer base but also wishes to maintain a current ratio of at least 3. If Ray's current assets are $6,000,000, and its current ratio is now 4, how much can it expand its inventories (financing the expansion with its line of credit) before the target current ratio is violated?

ST-2.   *(Ratio Analysis)* The statements for M & G Industries are presented below:

M & G Industries Balance Sheet
For December 31, 1993 and 1994

	1993	1994
Cash	$ 9,000	$ 500
Accounts receivable	12,500	16,000
Inventories	29,000	45,500
Total current assets	$ 50,500	$ 62,000
Land	20,000	26,000
Buildings and equipment	70,000	100,000
Less: allowance for depreciation	(28,000)	(38,000)
Total fixed assets	$ 62,000	$ 88,000
Total assets	$112,500	$150,000
Accounts Payable	$ 10,500	$ 22,000
Short-term bank notes	17,000	47,000
Total current liabilities	$ 27,500	$ 69,000
Long-term debt	28,750	22,950
Common stock	31,500	31,500
Retained earnings	24,750	26,550
Total debt and equity	$112,500	$150,000

M & G Industries Income Statement
For the Years Ended December 31, 1993 and 1994

	1993	1994
Sales (all credit)	$125,000	$160,000
Cost of goods sold	75,000	96,000
Gross profit	$ 50,000	$ 64,000
Operating expenses		
Fixed cash operating expenses	$ 21,000	$ 21,000
Variable operating expenses	12,500	16,000
Depreciation	4,500	10,000
Total operating expenses	$ 38,000	$ 47,000
Earnings before interest and taxes	$ 12,000	$ 17,000
Interest expense	3,000	6,100
Earnings before taxes	$ 9,000	$ 10,900
Taxes	4,500	5,450
Net income	$ 4,500	$ 5,450

a. Based on the preceeding statements, complete the following table:

M & G Industries Ratio Analysis

	Industry Averages	Actual 1993	Actual 1994
Current ratio	1.80		
Acid-test ratio	.70		
Average collection period	37.00		
Inventory turnover	2.50		
Debt ratio	58%		
Times interest earned	3.80		
Gross profit margin	38%		
Operating profit margin	10%		
Total asset turnover	1.14		
Fixed asset turnover	1.40		
Operating income return on investment	11.4%		
Return on total assets	4.0%		
Return on common equity	9.5%		

      b. Evaluate the firm's financial position using the "four-question approach" described in the chapter.

ST-3.   *(Cash Flow Statement)*
      a. Using the indirect method, prepare a cash flow statement for M & G Industries for 1994, using information given in Self-Test Problem ST-2.
      b. How does this statement supplement your ratio analysis from Self-Test Problem ST-2? Explain.

STUDY PROBLEMS

3–1.   *(Ratio Analysis)* The Mitchem Marble Company has a target current ratio of 2.0 but has experienced some difficulties financing its expanding sales in the past few months. At present the firm has a current ratio of 2.5 with current assets of $2.5 million. If Mitchem expands its receivables and inventories using its short-term line of credit, how much additional short-term funding can it borrow before its current ratio standard is reached?

3–2.   *(Ratio Analysis)* The balance sheet and income statement for the J. P. Robard Mfg. Company are as follows:

Balance Sheet ($000)	
Cash	$ 500
Accounts receivable	2,000
Inventories	1,000
Current assets	3,500
Net fixed assets	4,500
Total assets	$8,000
Accounts payable	$1,100
Accrued expenses	600
Short-term notes payable	300
Current liabilities	$2,000
Long-term debt	2,000
Owner's equity	4,000
Total liabilities and owners' equity	$8,000

Income Statement ($000)	
Net sales (all credit)	$8,000
Cost of goods sold	(3,300)
Gross profit	4,700
Operating expenses	
(includes $500 depreciation)	(3,000)
Operating income	1,700
Interest expense	(367)
Earnings before taxes	$1,333
Income taxes (40%)	(533)
Net income	$ 800

Calculate the following ratios:

Current ratio	Debt ratio
Times interest earned	Average collection period
Inventory turnover	Fixed asset turnover
Total asset turnover	Gross profit margin
Operating profit margin	Return on equity
Operating income return on investment	

3–3. *(Analyzing Operating Income Return on Investment)* The R. M. Smithers Corporation earned an operating profit margin of 10 percent based on sales of $10 million and total assets of $5 million last year.
   a. What was Smithers' total asset turnover ratio?
   b. During the coming year the company president has set a goal of attaining a total asset turnover of 3.5. How much must firm sales rise, other things being the same, for the goal to be achieved? (State your answer in both dollars and percentage increase in sales.)
   c. What was Smithers' operating income return on investment last year? Assuming the firm's operating profit margin remains the same, what will the operating income return on investment be next year if the total asset turnover goal is achieved?

3–4. *(Using Financial Ratios)* The Brenmar Sales Company had a gross profit margin (gross profits ÷ sales) of 30 percent and sales of $9 million last year. Seventy-five percent of the firm's sales are on credit and the remainder are cash sales. Brenmar's current assets equal $1,500,000, its current liabilities equal $300,000, and it has $100,000 in cash plus marketable securities.
   a. If Brenmar's accounts receivable are $562,500, what is its average collection period?
   b. If Brenmar reduces it average collection period to 20 days, what will be its new level of accounts receivable?
   c. Brenmar's inventory turnover ratio is 9 times. What is the level of Brenmar's inventories?

3–5. *(Ratio Analysis)* Using Pamplin Inc.'s financial statements shown on following pages:
   a. Compute the following ratios for both 1993 and 1994.

	Industry Norm 1994
Current ratio	5.00
Acid-test (quick) ratio	3.00
Inventory turnover	2.20
Average collection period	90.00
Debt ratio	0.33
Times interest earned	7.00
Total asset turnover	0.75
Fixed asset turnover	1.00
Operating profit margin	20%
Return on common equity	9%

b. How liquid is the firm?
c. Is management generating adequate operating profit on the firm's assets?
d. How is the firm financing its assets?
e. Are the common stockholders receiving a good return on their investment?

Pamplin, Inc., Balance Sheet
at 12/31/93 and 12/31/94

Assets

	1993	1994
Cash	$ 200	$ 150
Accounts Receivable	450	425
Inventory	550	625
Current assets	$1,200	$1,200
Plant and equipment	$2,200	$2,600
Less: accumulated depreciation	(1,000)	(1,200)
Net plant and equipment	$1,200	$1,400
Total assets	$2,400	$2,600

Liabilities and Owners' Equity

	1993	1994
Accounts payable	$ 200	$ 150
Notes payable—current (9%)	0	150
Current liabilities	$ 200	$ 300
Bonds (8 1/3% interest)	$ 600	$ 600
Owners' equity		
Common stock	$ 300	$ 300
Paid-in capital	600	600
Retained earnings	700	800
Total owners' equity	$1,600	$1,700
Total liabilities and owners' equity	$2,400	$2,600

Pamplin, Inc., Income Statement
for years ending 12/31/93 and 12/31/94

	1993		1994	
Sales(all credit)		$1,200		$1,450
Cost of goods sold		700		850
Gross profit		$ 500		$ 600
Operating expenses	30		40	
Depreciation	220	250	200	240
Operating income		$ 250		$ 360
Interest expense		50		64
Net income before taxes		$ 200		$ 296
Taxes (40%)		80		118
Net income		$ 120		$ 178

3–6. *(Cash Flow Statement)* Prepare a cash flow statement for Pamplin, Inc., for the year ended December 31, 1994 (problem 3-5). Use both the direct method and the indirect method in calculating cash flow from operations.

3–7. *(Cash Flow Statement)* (a) Prepare a statement of cash flow for the Waterhouse Co. for the year 1994. Use both the direct method and the indirect method in calculating cash flow from operations. (b) What were the firm's primary sources and uses of cash?

	1993	1994
Cash	$ 75,000	$ 82,500
Receivables	102,000	90,000
Inventory	168,000	165,000
Prepaid expenses	12,000	13,500
Total current assets	$357,000	$351,000
Gross fixed assets	325,500	468,000
Accumulated depreciation	(94,500)	(129,000)
Patents	61,500	52,500
Total assets	$649,500	$742,500
Accounts payable	$124,500	$112,500
Taxes payable	97,500	105,000
Total current liabilities	$222,000	$217,500
Mortgage payable	150,000	0
Preferred stock	0	225,000
Additional paid-in capital— preferred	0	6,000
Common stock	225,000	225,000
Retained earnings	52,500	69,000
Total liabilities and equity	$649,500	$742,500

Additional Information
1. The only entry in the acccumulated depreciation account is the depreciation expense for the period.
2. The only entries in the retained earning account are for dividends paid in the amount of $18,000 and for the net income for the year.
3. Expenses include a $9,000 amortization of patents.
4. The income statement for 1994 is as follows:

Sales (all credit)	$187,500
Cost of goods sold	111,000
Gross profit	76,500
Operating expenses	32,000
Provision for taxes	10,000
Net income	$ 34,500

(Cost of goods sold included depreciation expense of $34,500)

3–8. *(Review of Financial Statements)* Prepare a balance sheet and income statement at December 31, 1994, for the Sharpe Mfg. Co. from the scrambled list of items below.

Accounts receivable	$120,000
Machinery and equipment	700,000
Accumulated depreciation	236,000
Notes payable	100,000
Net sales	800,000
Inventory	110,000
Accounts payable	90,000
Long-term debt	160,000
Cost of goods sold	500,000
Operating expenses	280,000
Commmon stock	320,000
Cash	96,000
Retained earnings—prior year	?
Retained earnings—current year	?

3–9. *(Financial Ratios—Investment Analysis)* The annual sales for Salco, Inc., were $4.5 million last year. The firm's end-of-year balance sheet appeared as follows:

Current assets	$ 500,000	Liabilities	$1,000,000
Net fixed assets	1,500,000	Owners' equity	1,000,000
	$2,000,000		$2,000,000

The firm's income statement for the year was as follows:

Sales	$4,500,000
Less: cost of goods sold	(3,500,000)
Gross profit	$1,000,000
Less: operating expenses	(500,000)
Operating income	$ 500,000
Less: interest expense	(100,000)
Earnings before taxes	$ 400,000
Less: taxes (50%)	(200,000)
Net income	$ 200,000

a. Calculate Salco's total asset turnover, operating profit margin, and operating income return on investment.

b. Salco plans to renovate one of its plants, which will require an added investment in plant and equipment of $1 million. The firm will maintain its present debt ratio of .5 when financing the new investment and expects sales to remain constant, while the operating profit margin will rise to 13 percent. What will be the new operating income return on investment for Salco after the plant renovation?

c. Given that the plant renovation in part (b) occurs and Salco's interest expense rises by $50,000 per year, what will be the return earned on the common stockholders' investment? Compare this rate of return with that earned before the renovation.

3–10. *(Statement of Cash Flow)* The consolidated balance sheets of the TMU Processing Company are presented below for May 31, 1993, and May 31, 1994 (millions of dollars). TMU earned $14 million after taxes during the year ended May 31, 1994, and paid common dividends of $10 million.

	May 31 1993	May 31 1994
Cash	$ 10	$ 8
Accounts receivable	12	22
Inventories	8	14
Current assets	$ 30	$ 44
Gross fixed assets	$100	$110
Less: accumulated depreciation	(40)	(50)
Net fixed assets	$ 60	$ 60
Total assets	$ 90	$104
Accounts payable	$ 12	$ 9
Notes payable	7	7
Long-term debt	11	24
Common stock	20	20
Retained earnings	40	44
Total liabilities	$ 90	$104

a. Prepare a statement of cash flow for 1994 for TMU Processing Company. (Hint: You will only be able to use the indirect method.)

b. Summarize your findings.

3–11. *(Comprehensive Financial Analysis Problem)* The T. P. Jarmon Company manufactures and sells a line of exclusive sportswear. The firm's sales were $600,000 for the year just ended, and its total assets exceed $400,000. The company was started by Mr. Jarmon just 10 years ago and has been profitable every year since its inception. The chief financial officer for the firm, Brent Vehlim, has decided to seek a line of credit from the firm's bank totaling $80,000. In the past the company has relied on its suppliers to finance a large part of its needs for inventory. However, in recent months tight money conditions have led the firm's suppliers to offer sizable cash discounts to speed up payments for purchases. Mr. Vehlim wants to use the line of credit to supplant a large portion of the firm's payables during the summer months, which are the firm's peak seasonal sales period.

The firm's two most recent balance sheets were presented to the bank in support of its loan request. In addition, the firm's income statement for the year just ended was provided to support the loan request. These statements are found below:

T. P. Jarmon Company, Balance Sheet
For 12/31/93 and 12/31/94

Assets

	1993	1994
Cash	$ 15,000	$ 14,000
Marketable securites	6,000	6,200
Accounts receivable	42,000	33,000
Inventory	51,000	84,000
Prepaid rent	1,200	1,100
Total current assets	$115,200	$138,300
Net plant and equipment	286,000	270,000
Total assets	$401,200	$408,300

Liabilities and Equity

	1993	1994
Accounts payable	$ 48,000	$ 57,000
Notes payable	15,000	13,000
Accruals	6,000	5,000
Total current liabilities	$ 69,000	$ 75,000
Long-term debt	$160,000	$150,000
Common stockholders' equity	$172,200	$183,300
Total liabilities and equity	$401,200	$408,300

T. P. Jarmon Company, Income Statement
For the Year Ended 12/31/94

Sales (all credit)		$600,000
Less: cost of goods sold		460,000
Gross profits		$140,000
Less: operating and interest expenses		
General and administrative	$30,000	
Interest	10,000	
Depreciation	30,000	
Total		70,000
Earnings before taxes		$ 70,000
Less: taxes		27,100
Net income available to common stockholders		$ 42,900
Less: cash dividends		31,800
Change in retained earnings		$ 11,100

Jan Fama, associate credit analyst for the Merchants National Bank of Midland, Michigan, was assigned the task of analyzing Jarmon's loan request.
a. Calculate the financial ratios for 1994 corresponding to the industry norms provided as follows:

	Ratio Norm
Current ratio	1.8
Acid-test ratio	0.9
Debt ratio	0.5
Times interest earned	10.0
Average collection period	20.0
Inventory turnover (based on cost of goods sold)	7.0
Return on common equity	12.0%
Gross profit margin	25.0%
Operating income return on investment	16.8%
Operating profit margin	14.0%
Total asset turnover	1.20
Fixed asset turnover	1.80

b. Which of the ratios reported above in the industry norms do you feel should be most crucial in determining whether the bank should extend the line of credit?

c. Prepare a cash flow statement for Jarmon covering the year ended December 31, 1994.

d. Use the information provided by the financial ratios and the cash flow statement to decide if you would support making the loan.

e. Use the DuPont analysis to evaluate the firm's financial position.

3–12. *(Preparing the Statement of Cash Flow)* Comparative balance sheets for December 31, 1993, and December 31, 1994, for the Abrams Mfg. Company are found below:

	1993	1994
Cash	$89,000	$100,000
Accounts receivable	64,000	70,000
Inventory	112,000	100,000
Prepaid expenses	10,000	10,000
Total current assets	275,000	280,000
Plant and equipment	238,000	311,000
Accumulated depreciation	(40,000)	(66,000)
Total assets	$473,000	$525,000
Accounts payable	$85,000	$90,000
Accrued liabilities	68,000	63,000
Total current debt	153,000	153,000
Mortgage payable	70,000	0
Preferred stock		100,000
Additional paid-in capital Preferred stock		20,000
Common stock	205,000	205,000
Retained earnings	45,000	47,000
Total debt and equity	$473,000	$525,000

Abram's 1994 income statement is found below:

Sales (all credit)	$184,000
Cost of Sales	150,000
Gross profit	$ 34,000
Operating, interest, and tax expenses	10,000
Net income	$ 24,000

Additional information:

a. The only entry in the accumulated depreciation account is for 1994 depreciation.

b. The firm paid $22,000 in dividends during 1994.

Prepare a 1994 statement of cash flow for Abrams using the indirect method only.

3–13. *(Analyzing the Statement of Cash Flow)* Identify any financial weaknesses revealed in the statement of cash flow for the Westlake Manufacturing Co.

Westlake Manufacturing Co. Statement of Cash Flow for Current Year

Cash flow from operating activities		
Net income	$ 540,000	
Add (deduct) to reconcile net income to net cash flow		
Decrease in accounts receivable	40,000	
Increase in inventories	(240,000)	
Increase in prepaid expenses	(10,000)	
Depreciation expense	60,000	
Decrease in accrued wages	(50,000)	
Net cash flow from operations		$ 340,000
Cash flow from investing activities		
Sale (purchase) of plant and equipment		2,400,000
Cash flow from financing activities		
Issuance of bonds	$1,000,000	
Repayment of short-term debt	(3,000,000)	
Payment of long-term debt	(500,000)	
Payment of dividends	(1,000,000)	
Net cash from financing activities		(3,500,000)
Net increase (decrease) in cash for the period		($760,000)

SUGGESTED APPLICATION FOR *DISCLOSURE*®

a. Access the *Disclosure* database to obtain the last three annual financial statements for the Chrysler Corporation and Ford Motor Company. Calculate the following financial ratios for each firm for each of the last three years:

Current Ratio	Operating profit margin
Quick Ratio	Gross profit margin
Accounts receivable turnover	Total asset turnover
(assuming all reported sales	Debt ratio
are credit sales)	Times interest earned
Inventory turnover	Return on equity
Operating return on investment	

What differences do you see in the two firm's ratios that you consider to be important?

b. Perform an Earning Power analysis for Nike Inc.'s using data from *Disclosure* for the most recent three years. Perform a similar analysis for Reebok. How are the two firms different?

SELF-TEST SOLUTIONS

SS-1.   Note that Ray's current ratio before the inventory expansion is as follows:

current ratio = $6,000,000/current liabilities = 4

Thus, the firm's level of current liabilities is $1,500,000. If the expansion in inventories is financed entirely with borrowed funds, then the change in inventories is equal to the change in current liabilities, and the firm's current ratio after the expansion can be defined as follows:

$$\text{current ratio} = \frac{\$6,000,000 + \text{change in inventory}}{\$1,500,000 + \text{change in inventory}} = 3$$

Note that we set the new current ratio equal to the firm's target of 3. Solving for the change in inventory in the above equation, we determine that the firm can expand its inventories by $750,000 and finance the expansion with current liabilities and still maintain its target current ratio.

SS-2.

a.

M & G Industries Ratio Analysis

	Industry Averages	Actual 1993	Actual 1994
Current ratio	1.80	1.84	0.90
Acid-test ratio	0.70	0.78	0.24
Average collection period (based on a 365-day year and end-of-year figures.)	37.00	36.50	36.50
Inventory turnover	2.50	2.59	2.11
Debt ratio	58%	50%	61.3%
Times interest earned	3.80	4.00	2.79
Gross profit margin	38%	40%	40%
Operating profit margin	10%	9.6%	10.6
Total asset turnover	1.14	1.11	1.07
Fixed asset turnover	1.40	2.02	1.82
Operating income return on investment	11.4%	10.67%	11.3%
Return on common equity	9.5%	8.0%	9.4%

b. M & G's liquidity is poor, as suggested by the low current ratio and acid-test ratio: also, inventories are turning slowly. In 1994, management is doing a satisfactory job at generating profits on the firm's operating assets, as indicated by the operating income return on investment. Note that the operating income return on investment in 1994 is average, owing to a slightly above-average operating profit margin combined with a slightly below-average asset turnover. The problem with the asset turnover ratio comes from a slow inventory turnover.

M & G has increased its use of debt to the point of using slightly more debt than the average company in the industry. As a result, the firm's coverage of interest has decreased to a point well below the industry norm.

As of 1994, M & G's return on equity is average because the operating income return on investment and the debt ratio are average.

SS-3.

a.

M & G Industries Statement of Cash flow
for the Year Ended December 31, 1994

Cash flow from *operating* activities		
Net income (from the income statement)	$ 5,450	
Add (deduct) to reconcile net income to net cash flow		
Increase in accounts payable	11,500	
Increase in inventories	(16,500)	
Depreciation expense	10,000	
Increase in accounts receivable	(3,500)	
Net cash inflow from operating activities		$ 6,950
Cash flows from *investing* activities		
Purchase of land	($6,000)	
Purchase of plant and equipment	(30,000)	
Net cash outflow from investing activities		(36,000)
Cash flows from *financing* activities		
Cash inflows		
Increase in bank notes	$30,000	
Cash outflows		
Decrease in long-term debt	(5,800)	
Common stock dividend	(3,650)	
Net cash inflow from financing activities		20,550
Net increase (decrease) in cash during period		($ 8,500)
Cash balance at the beginning of the period		$ 9,000
Cash balance at the end of the period		$ 500

b. The cash flow statement is an important supplement to ratio analysis. This statement directs analysts' attention to where M & G Industries obtained financing during the period and how those funds were spent. For example, a very large portion of M & G's funds came from an increase in bank notes and from an increase in accounts payable. In addition, the largest uses of funds were additions to buildings and equipment and increases in inventories. Thus, M & G did little in the most recent operating period to alleviate the financial problems we noted earlier in our ratio analysis. In fact, M & G aggravated matters by purchasing fixed assets using short-term sources of financing. It would appear that another short-term loan at this time is *not* warranted.

CONCLUSION VIDEO CASE 2

Bond Rating Agencies: Using Financial Analysis to Forecast the Riskiness of Bonds
from ABC News, Business World, June 23, 1991

The information required for rating a municipal bond is quite different from that needed in rating corporate bonds. In the case of giving a quality rating to a municipal bond, you want to know if the city issuing the bond can pay it back. Moreover, you would like to know how easily the city can make the repayment; that is, how much safety is there in the city's ability to service the debt obligations. If repayment is certain, then you assign the bond a high rating (AAA or AA); however, if there are situations that might threaten repayment, a lower rating is assigned. Similar to analyzing a corporate bond, you want to examine items such as the interest coverage ratio, leverage ratio, and the stability of the revenue stream. Cities and states differ from firms because they raise money through taxation, not the sale of goods. Therefore you need to examine the tax base to determine the revenue stream or the stability of the tax revenues. The tax revenues of states that rely on just a sales tax or just an income tax may be affected differently during economic downturns than states using both types of taxing mechanisms. Other outstanding debt, such as previously issued bonds, also affects a city or state's ability to service its debt.

The bond rating assigned to a city or state government matters very much. When the bond-rating agencies threatened to lower the rating on bonds about to be issued by the state of California from AAA to AA, the state treasurer estimated that it would cost the state of California (actually, taxpayers in California) an extra $8 million per year in higher interest expense over the life of the bonds, about 25 years (New York Times, December 14, 1991, 18, p. 4). Therefore, because the impact of a mistake is significant, bond-rating agencies have to do careful, thorough research.

Discussion question
A strategy that might work well for rating agencies is to underrate all bonds slightly but safely: When in doubt, downgrade. This would help assure that the rating agency is rarely embarrassed by a municipality (or corporation) that defaults after the agency gave the organization a good rating. Who is injured by such a strategy? Why is such a strategy unlikely to exist in the marketplace? As an investor, if you knew that rating agencies used such a strategy, what would you do?

Suggested readings
WAKEMAN, L. MACDONALD. "The Real Function of Bond Rating Agencies," in *The Revolution in Corporate Finance, ed. Stern and Chew*. New York: Blackwell, 1986.

CHAPTER 4
FINANCIAL FORECASTING, PLANNING, AND BUDGETING

Financial Forecasting • Financial Planning and Budgeting
• Computerized Financial Planning

The impact of computers and financial software on the practice of financial forecasting, planning, and budgeting has been dramatic. Financial spreadsheet programs allow the financial analyst to tabulate very large and cumbersome budgets, which, with the aid of a microcomputer, can then be easily modified to reflect any number of possible scenarios. This type of "trial-and-error" analysis can greatly enhance analysts' decision-making capability by allowing them to quickly and easily assess the importance of the projections and assumptions that go into any financial plan.

   This chapter has two primary objectives: First, it will develop an appreciation for the role of forecasting in the firm's financial planning process. Basically, forecasts of future sales revenues and their associated expenses give the firm the information needed to project its future needs for financing. Second, the chapter will provide an overview of the firm's budgetary system, including the cash budget and the pro forma, or planned, income statement and balance sheet. Pro forma financial statements give the financial manager a useful tool for analyzing the effects of the firm's forecasts and planned activities on its financial performance, as well as its needs for financing. In addition, pro forma statements can be used as a benchmark or standard to compare against actual operating results. Used in this way, pro forma statements are an instrument for controlling or monitoring the firm's progress throughout the planning period.

Financial decisions are made today in light of our expectations of an uncertain future. Financial forecasting involves making estimates of the future financing requirements of the firm. **Axiom 3: Cash Is King—Measuring the Timing of Costs and Benefits** speaks directly to this problem. Remember that effective financial management requires that consideration be given to cash flow and when it is received or dispersed.

■ FINANCIAL FORECASTING

Forecasting in financial management is used to estimate a firm's future financial needs. The basic steps involved in predicting those financing needs are the following: **Step 1:** Project the firm's sales revenues and expenses over the planning period. **Step 2:** Estimate the levels of investment in current and fixed assets that are necessary to support the projected sales. **Step 3:** Determine the firm's financing needs throughout the planning period.

Sales Forecast

The key ingredient in the firm's planning process is the **sales forecast**. This projection is generally derived using information from a number of sources. At a minimum, the sales forecast for the coming year would reflect (1) any past trend in sales that is expected to carry through into the new year and (2) the influence of any events that might materially affect that trend.[1] An example of the latter would be the initiation of a major advertising campaign or a change in the firm's pricing policy.

Forecasting Financial Variables

Traditional financial forecasting takes the sales forecast as a given and makes projections of its impact on the firm's various expenses, assets, and liabilities. The most commonly used method for making these projections is the percent of sales method.

Percent of Sales Method of Financial Forecasting

The **percent of sales method** involves estimating the level of an expense, asset, or liability for a future period as a percent of the sales forecast. The percentage used can come from the most recent financial statement item as a percent of current sales, from an average computed

---

[1]A complete discussion of forecast methodologies is outside the scope of this book. The interested reader will find the following references helpful: F. Gerard Adams, *The Business Forecasting Revolution* (Oxford: Oxford University Press, 1986); C.W.J. Granger, *Forecasting in Business and Economics*, 2d ed. (Boston, MA: Academic Press, 1989); and Paul Newbold and Theodore Bos, *Introductory Business Forecasting* (Cincinnati, OH: Southwestern, 1990).

over several years, from the judgment of the analyst, or from some combination of these sources.

Figure 4–1 presents a complete example of the use of the percent of sales method of financial forecasting. In this example each item in the firm's balance sheet that varies with sales is converted to a percentage of 1993 sales. The forecast of the new balance for each item is then calculated by multiplying this percentage times the $12 million in projected sales for the 1994 planning period. This method of forecasting future financing is not as precise or detailed as the method using a cash budget, which is presented later; however, it offers a relatively low-cost and easy-to-use first approximation of the firm's financing needs for a future period.

Note that in the example in Figure 4–1, both current and fixed assets are assumed to vary with the level of firm sales. This means that

Assets	Present (1993)	Percent of Sales (1993 Sales = $10 M)	Projected (Based on 1994 Sales = $12 M)
Current assets	$2.0 M	$\dfrac{\$2\text{ M}}{\$10\text{ M}} = 20\%$	$.2 \times \$12\text{ M} = \$2.4\text{ M}$
Net fixed assets	4.0 M	$\dfrac{\$4\text{ M}}{\$10\text{ M}} = 40\%$	$.4 \times \$12\text{ M} = \underline{4.8\text{ M}}$
Total	$\underline{\$6.0\text{ M}}$		$\underline{\$7.2\text{ M}}$
Liabilities and Owners' Equity			
Accounts payable	$1.0 M	$\dfrac{\$1\text{ M}}{\$10\text{ M}} = 10\%$	$.10 \times \$12\text{ M} = \$1.2\text{ M}$
Accrued expenses	1.0 M	$\dfrac{\$1\text{ M}}{\$10\text{ M}} = 10\%$	$.10 \times \$12\text{ M} = \$1.2\text{ M}$
Notes payable	.5 M	NA[a]	no change .5 M
Long-term debt	$\underline{\$2.0\text{ M}}$	NA[a]	no change $\underline{2.0\text{ M}}$
Total liabilities	$\underline{\$4.5\text{ M}}$		$\underline{\$4.9\text{ M}}$
Common stock	$ .1 M	NA[a]	no change $ .1 M
Paid-in capital	.2 M	NA[a]	no change .2 M
Retained earnings	1.2 M		$1.2\text{ M} + [.05 \times \$12\text{ M} \times (1 - .5)] = \underline{1.5\text{ M}}$[b]
Common equity	$\underline{\$1.5\text{ M}}$		$\underline{\$1.8\text{ M}}$
Total	$\underline{\$6.0\text{ M}}$		Total financing provided $\underline{\$6.7\text{ M}}$
			Discretionary financing needed .5 M[c]
			Total $\underline{\$7.2\text{ M}}$

[a]Not applicable. These account balances are assumed not to vary with sales.
[b]Projected retained earnings equals the beginning level ($1.2 M) plus projected net income less any dividends paid. In this case net income is projected to equal 5 percent of sales, and dividends are projected to equal half of net income: $.05 \times \$12\text{ M} \times (1 - .5) = \$300,000$
[c]Discretionary financing needed equals projected total assets ($7.2 M) less projected total liabilities ($4.9 M) less projected common equity ($1.8), or $7.2 M - 4.9 M - 1.8 M = \$500,000$.

FIGURE 4–1
Using the Percent of Sales Method to Forecast Future Financing Requirements

the firm does not have sufficient productive capacity to absorb a projected increase in sales. Thus, if sales were to rise by $1, fixed assets would rise by $.40, or 40 percent of the projected increase in sales. Note that if the fixed assets the firm currently owns were sufficient to support the projected level of new sales, these assets should not be allowed to vary with sales. If this were the case, then fixed assets would not be converted to a percent of sales and would be projected to remain unchanged for the period being forecast.

Also, we note that accounts payable and accrued expenses are the only liabilities allowed to vary with sales. Both these accounts might reasonably be expected to rise and fall with the level of firm sales; hence the use of the percent of sales forecast. Because these two categories of current liabilities normally vary directly with the level of sales, they are often referred to as **spontaneous sources of financing.** Chapter 14, which discusses working-capital management, has more to say about these forms of financing. Notes payable, long-term debt, common stock, and paid-in capital are not assumed to vary directly with the level of firm sales. These sources of financing are termed **discretionary,** in that the firm's management must make a conscious decision to seek additional financing using any one of them. Finally, we note that the level of retained earnings does vary with estimated sales. The predicted change in the level of retained earnings equals the estimated after-tax profits (projected net income) equal to 5 percent of sales or $600,000 less the common stock dividends of $300,000.

Thus, using the example from Figure 4–1, we estimate that firm sales will increase from $10 million to $12 million, which will cause the firm's needs for total assets to rise to $7.2 million. These assets will then be financed by $4.9 million in existing liabilities plus spontaneous liabilities; $1.8 million in owner funds, including $300,000 in retained earnings from next year's sales; and, finally, $500,000 in discretionary financing, which can be raised by issuing notes payable, selling bonds, offering an issue of stock, or some combination of these sources.

In summary, we can estimate the firm's needs for discretionary financing, using the percent of sales method of financial forecasting, by following a four-step procedure:

Step 1: Convert each asset and liability account that varies directly with firm sales to a percent of current year's sales.

EXAMPLE

$$\frac{\text{current assets}}{\text{sales}} = \frac{\$2\text{ M}}{\$10\text{ M}} = .2 \text{ or } 20\%$$

Step 2: Project the level of each asset and liability account in the balance sheet using its percent of sales multiplied by projected sales or by leaving the account balance unchanged where the account does not vary with the level of sales.

EXAMPLE

projected current assets =

$$\text{projected sales} \times \frac{\text{current assets}}{\text{sales}} = \$12\text{ M} \times .2 = 2.4\text{ M}$$

Step 3: Project the level of new retained earnings available to help finance the firm's operations. This equals projected net income for the period less planned common stock dividends.

EXAMPLE

projected addition to retained earnings =

$$\text{projected sales} \times \frac{\text{net income}}{\text{sales}} \times \left(1 - \frac{\text{cash dividends}}{\text{net income}}\right)$$

$$= \$12\text{ M} \times .05 \times [1 - .5] = \$300,000$$

FINANCIAL FORECASTING,
PLANNING,
AND BUDGETING

Step 4: Project the firm's need for discretionary financing as the projected level of total assets less projected liabilities and owners' equity.

EXAMPLE

discretionary financing needed =
projected total assets – projected total liabilities – projected owners' equity
= $7.2 M – $4.9 M – $1.8 M = $500,000 ∎

PERSPECTIVE IN FINANCE

Are you beginning to wonder exactly where finance comes into financial forecasting? To this point financial forecasting looks for all the world like financial statement forecasting. The reason is that we have adopted the accountant's model of the firm, the balance sheet, as the underlying structure of the financial forecast. The key to financial forecasting is the identification of the firm's anticipated future financing requirements, and these requirements can be identified as the "plug" figure or simply the number that balances a pro forma balance sheet.

The Discretionary Financing Needed (DFN) Model

In the preceding discussion we estimated DFN as the difference in projected total assets and the sum of projected liabilities and owner's equity. We can estimate DFN directly using the predicted change in sales (ΔS) and corresponding changes in assets, liabilities and owner's equity as follows:

$$DFN_{t+1} = \begin{array}{c} \text{projected} \\ \text{change in} \\ \text{assets} \end{array} - \begin{array}{c} \text{projected} \\ \text{change in} \\ \text{liabilities} \end{array} - \begin{array}{c} \text{projected} \\ \text{change in} \\ \text{owner's equity} \end{array}$$

or   **(4–1)**

$$DFN_{t+1} = \left[\frac{assets_t^*}{sales_t} \Delta sales_{t+1}\right] - \left[\frac{liabilities_t^*}{sales_t} \Delta sales_{t+1}\right] - \left[NPM_{t+1} \cdot (1-b)\, sales_{t+1}\right]$$

where

DFN_{t+1} = predicted discretionary financing needed for period $t+1$.

$assets_t^*$ = those assets in period t that are expected to change in proportion to the level of sales. In our example we have assumed that all the firm's assets vary in proportion to sales. We will have more to say about this assumption in the next section where we consider economies of scale and lumpy fixed asset investments.

$sales_t$ = the level of sales for the period just ended.

$\Delta sales_{t+1}$ = the change in sales projected for period $t+1$, i.e., $Sales_{t+1} - Sales_t$. Note that "Δ" is the Greek symbol delta which is used here to represent "change".

liabilities$_t$* = those liabilities in period t that are expected to change in proportion to the level of sales. In our preceding example we assumed that accounts payable and accrued expenses varied with sales but notes payable and long-term debt did not.

NPM_{t+1} = the net profit margin (Net Income ÷ sales) projected for period $t + 1$.

b = dividends as a percent of net income or the dividend payout ratio such that $(1 - b)$ is the proportion of the firm's projected net income that will be retained and reinvested in the firm (i.e., $(1 - b)$ is the retention ratio).

Using the numbers from the preceding example we estimate DFN$_{1994}$ as follows:

$$DFN_{1994} = \left(\frac{\$2M + 4M}{\$10M} \right) \$2M - \left(\frac{\$1M + 1M}{\$10M} \right) \$2\,M - .05 \cdot (1 - .5)\$12\,M$$

$$= \$.5 \text{ million or } \$500,000$$

Analyzing the Effects of Profitability and Dividend Policy on DFN

Using the DFN model we can quickly and easily evaluate the sensitivity of our projected financing requirements to changes in key variables. For example, using the information from the preceding example we evaluate the effect of net profit margins (NPM) ranging from 1 percent, 5 percent, and 10 percent in combination with dividend payout ratios of 30 percent, 50 percent and 70 percent as follows:

Discretionary Financing Needed
for Various Net Profit Margins and Dividend Payout Ratios

Net Profit Margin	Dividend Payout Ratios (Dividends ÷ Net Income)		
	30%	50%	70%
1%	$716,000	$740,000	$764,000
5%	380,000	500,000	620,000
10%	(40,000)	200,000	440,000

If these values for the net profit margin represent reasonable estimates of the possible ranges of values the firm might experience and if the firm is considering dividend payouts ranging from 30 percent to 70 percent, then we estimate that the firm's financing requirements (DFN) will range from ($40,000), which represents a surplus of $40,000, to a situation where it would need to acquire $764,000. Lower net profit margins mean higher funds requirements. Also, higher dividend payout percentages, other things remaining constant, lead to a need for more discretionary financing. This latter observation is a direct result of the fact that a high-dividend-paying firm retains less of its earnings.

The Sustainable Rate of Growth

The **Sustainable Rate of Growth** (g*) represents the rate at which a firm's sales can grow if it wants to maintain its present financial ratios and *does not* want to resort to the sale of new equity shares.[1] We can solve for the Sustainable Rate of Growth directly using the Discretionary Financing Needed formula found in equation 4–1 as we illustrate in the footnote found below.[2] Specifically, the Sustainable Rate of Growth is that rate of sales growth for which Discretionary Financing Needed equals zero. The resulting formula is quite simple and relies on the Return on Equity (ROE) ratio and dividend payout ratio (b).

$$\text{Sustainable Rate of Growth } (g^*) = \text{ROE } (1 - b) \qquad \textbf{(4–2)}$$

and we recall from Chapter 3 that ROE is defined as follows:

$$\text{ROE} = \frac{\text{net income}}{\text{common equity}}$$

Equation 4–2 is deceptively simple. Note that a firm's ROE is determined by a number of factors including the firm's profit margin, asset turnover and its use of financial leverage. Specifically, recall from Chapter 3 that we developed the following relationship for ROE:

$$\text{ROE} = \left(\begin{array}{c} \text{net profit} \\ \text{margin} \end{array} \right) \times \left(\begin{array}{c} \text{total asset} \\ \text{turnover} \end{array} \right) \div \left(1 - \frac{\text{debt}}{\text{ratio}} \right)$$

or

$$\text{ROE} = \left(\frac{\text{net income}}{\text{sales}} \right) \times \left(\frac{\text{sales}}{\text{assets}} \right) \div \left(\frac{\text{total debt}}{1 - \text{total assets}} \right).$$

Hence, the firm's Sustainable Rate of Growth is determined by all the determinants of its return on equity (net profit margin, total asset turnover and financial leverage) and its choice of a dividend payout ratio (b). To illustrate the calculation of the Sustainable Rate of Growth consider the financial information for the Harris Electronics Corporation found in Table 4–1.

Harris experienced reasonably stable Sustainable Rates of Growth ranging from a low of 5.80 percent in 1990 to a high of 6.40 percent in 1992. The reasons for the modest variation are easy to see from the data provided in Table 4–1. The firm's rate of return on common equity (ROCE) varied only slightly over the period, from a low of 9.67 percent

---

[1]Extensive discussion of the Sustainable Rate of Growth concept is found in Robert C. Higgins, "Sustainable Growth with Inflation," *Financial Management* (Autumn 1981): pp. 36–40.

[2]We can evaluate the impact of differing rates of sales growth on DFN by recognizing that the growth in firm sales, g, is simply the ratio of the projected change in sales ($\Delta Sales_{t+1}$) divided by the most recent past level of sales ($Sales_t$). Rearranging terms in equation 4–1 and substituting g for $\dfrac{\Delta sales_{t+1}}{sales_t}$ we get the following result:

$$\text{DFN}_{t+1} = g \cdot \text{assets} - \text{liabilities} \cdot g - \text{NPM} (1 - b) \, sales_{t+1}$$

Note that the Sustainable Rate of Growth is that growth rate in firm sales (g*) which makes $\text{DFN}_{t+1} = 0$. Thus, setting DFN_{t+1} in the above equation equal to zero and solving for g we get the Sustainable Rate of Growth equation:

Sustainable Rate of Growth $(g^*) = \text{ROE}(1 - b)$

where ROE is the return on equity (Net Income ÷ Common Equity) and b is the fraction of firm earnings paid out in dividends or the Dividend Payout Ratio.

in 1990 to a high of 11 percent in 1991, while the retention ratio (1-b) remained steady at 60 percent of earnings. Harris' actual rate of sales growth from 1990 to 1991 was 21.74% which was above its sustainable rate for 1991 which was only 5.80%. The sustainable rate of growth applicable to 1991 is calculated using data from 1990. In this year we calculated the firm's sustainable rate of growth for 1991 to be 5.80 percent [9.67%(1– .40)], but its actual increase in sales for the coming year was 21.74 percent [($1,400 – 1,150)/$1,150]. How did Harris accommodate the financing demands during 1991? The answer can be found by examining the firm's debt-to-assets ratio and changes to the firm's common equity. We see that Harris increased its borrowing from 42.56 percent of assets to 49.48 percent without issuing any new common stock. Thus, Harris has financed its DFN using new debt issues.

Limitations of the Percent of Sales Forecast Method

The **percent of sales method** of financial forecasting provides reasonable estimates of a firm's financing requirements only where asset requirements and financing sources can be accurately forecast as a constant percent of sales. For example, predicting inventories using the percent of sales method involves the following predictive equation:

$$\text{inventories}_t = \%\text{INV} \cdot \text{sales}_t$$

where %INV is the inventories-to-sales ratio.

Figure 4–2a depicts this predictive relationship. Note that the percent-of-sales predictive model is simply a straight line that passes through the origin (i.e., has a zero intercept). There are some fairly common instances in which this type of relationship fails to describe the relationship between an asset category and sales. Two such examples involve assets for which there are scale economies and assets that must be purchased in discrete quantities ("lumpy assets").

	1993	1992	1991	1990	1989
Sales	$1,500	$1,450	$1,400	$1,150	$1,090
Net Income	75	73	70	58	55
Assets	1,350	1,305	1,260	1,035	981
Dividends	30	29	28	23	21.8
Common Equity	725	680	637	595	560
Liabilities	625	625	623	440	421
Liabilities & Owner's Equity	1,350	1,305	1,260	1,035	981
Sustainable Rate of Growth (g*)	6.21%	6.40%	6.60%	5.80%	5.84%
Actual Growth Rate in Sales	NA	3.45%	3.57%	21.74%	5.50%
Return on Equity (ROCE)	10.34%	10.66%	11.00%	9.67%	9.73%
Retention Ratio (1-b)	60.00%	60.00%	60.00%	60.00%	60.00%
Debt to Assets Ratio	46.30%	47.89%	49.48%	42.56%	42.92%
New Common Stock	0	0	0	0	0

NA—Not available or cannot be calculated without 1994 data.

TABLE 4–1
Harris Electronics Corporation: Sustainable Rate of Growth Calculations

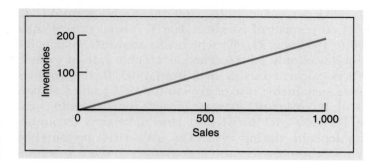

FIGURE 4–2a
Percent of Sales Forecast

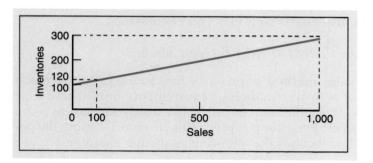

FIGURE 4–2b
Economies of Scale

Economies of scale are sometimes realized from investing in certain types of assets. This means that these assets do not increase in direct proportion to sales. Figure 4–2b reflects one instance in which the firm realizes economies of scale from its investment in inventory. Note that inventories as a percent of sales decline from 120 percent where sales are $100, to 30 percent where sales equal $1,000. This reflects the fact that there is a fixed component of inventories (in this case $100) that the firm must have on hand regardless of the level of sales, plus a variable component (20 percent of sales). In this instance the predictive equation for inventories is as follows:

$$\text{inventories}_t = a + b \text{ sales}_t$$

In this example, a is equal to 100 and b equals .20.[3]

Figure 4–2c is an example of *lumpy assets*, that is, assets that must be purchased in large, non-divisible components. Consequently, when a block of assets is purchased it creates excess capacity until sales grow to the point where the capacity is fully used. The result is a step function like the one depicted in Figure 4–2c. Thus, if the firm does not expect sales to exceed the current capacity of its plant and equipment, there would be no projected need for added plant and equipment capacity.

---

[3]Economies of scale are evidenced here by the nonzero intercept value. However, scale economies can also result in nonlinear relationships between sales and a particular asset category. Later, when we discuss cash management, we will find that one popular cash management model predicts a nonlinear relationship between the optimal cash balance and the level of cash transactions.

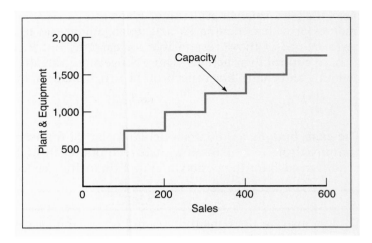

FIGURE 4–2c
Economies of Scale and
Lumpy Investments

FINANCIAL PLANNING AND BUDGETING

As we noted earlier, the principal virtue of the percent of sales method of financial forecasting is its simplicity. To obtain a more precise esti-mate of the amount and timing of the firm's future financing needs, we require a cash budget. The percent of sales method of financial forecast-ing provides a very useful, low-cost forerunner to the development of the more detailed cash budget, which the firm will ultimately use to estimate its financing needs.

BACK TO THE FUNDAMENTALS

Budgets have many important uses; however, their use as a tool of man-agerial control is critically important and often overlooked in the study of financial management. **Axiom 7: The Agency Problem—Managers Won't Work for the Owners Unless It's in Their Best Interest** speaks to the root source of the problem, and budgets provide one tool for attempting to deal with it. Specifically, budgets provide management with a tool for evaluating performance and consequently maintaining a degree of control over employee actions.

Budget Functions

A **budget** is simply a forecast of future events. For example, students preparing for final exams make use of time budgets, which help them allocate their limited preparation time among their courses. Students also must budget their financial resources among competing uses, such as books, tuition, food, rent, clothes, and extracurricular activities.

Budgets perform three basic functions for a firm. First, they indicate the amount and timing of the firm's needs for future financing. Second, they provide the basis for taking corrective action in the event budgeted figures do not match actual or realized figures. Third, budgets provide the basis for performance evaluation. Plans are carried out by people, and budgets provide benchmarks that management can use to evaluate the performance of those responsible for carrying out those plans and, in turn, to control their actions. Thus, budgets are valuable aids in both the planning and controlling aspects of the firm's financial management.

The Cash Budget

The **cash budget** represents a detailed plan of future cash flows and is composed of four elements: cash receipts, cash disbursements, net change in cash for the period, and new financing needed.

EXAMPLE

To demonstrate the construction and use of the cash budget, consider Salco Furniture Company, Inc., a regional distributor of household furniture. Management is in the process of preparing a monthly cash budget for the upcoming six-months (January through June 1994). Salco's sales are highly seasonal, peaking in the months of March through May. Roughly 30 percent of Salco's sales are collected one month after the sale, 50 percent two months after the sale, and the remainder during the third month following the sale.

Salco attempts to pace its purchases with its forecast of future sales. Purchases generally equal 75 percent of sales and are made two months in advance of anticipated sales. Payments are made in the month following purchases. For example, June sales are estimated at $100,000, thus April purchases are $.75 \times \$100,000 = \$75,000$. Correspondingly, payments for purchases in May equal $75,000. Wages, salaries, rent, and other cash expenses are recorded in Table 4–2, which gives Salco's cash budget for the six-month period ended in June 1994. Additional expenditures are recorded in the cash budget related to the purchase of equipment in the amount of $14,000 during February and the repayment of a $12,000 loan in May. In June Salco will pay $7,500 interest on its $150,000 in long-term debt for the period of January-June 1994. Interest on the $12,000 short-term note repaid in May for the period January through May equals $600 and is paid in May.

Salco currently has a cash balance of $20,000 and wants to maintain a minimum balance of $10,000. Additional borrowing necessary to maintain that minimum balance is estimated in the final section of Table 4–2. Borrowing takes place at the beginning of the month in which the funds are needed. Interest on borrowed funds equals 12 percent per annum, or 1 percent per month, and is paid in the month following the one in which funds are borrowed. Thus, interest on funds borrowed in January will be paid in February equal to 1 percent of the loan amount outstanding during January.

The financing-needed line on Salco's cash budget indicates that the firm's cumulative short-term borrowing will be $36,350 in February, $65,874 in March, $86,633 in April, and $97,599 in May. In June the firm will be able to reduce its borrowing to $79,875. Note that the cash budget indicates not only the amount of financing needed during the period but also when the funds will be needed.

Fixed Versus Flexible Budgets

The cash budget given in Table 4–2 for Salco, Inc. is an example of a **fixed budget.** Cash flow estimates are made for a single set of monthly sales estimates. Thus, the estimates of expenses and new financing needed are meaningful only for the level of sales for which they were computed. To avoid this limitation, several budgets corresponding to different sets of sales estimates can be prepared. Such a **flexible budget** fulfills two basic needs: First, it gives information regarding the range of the firm's possible financing needs, and second, it provides a standard against which to measure the performance of subordinates who are responsible for the various cost and revenue items contained in the budget.

This second function deserves some additional comment. The obvious problem that arises relates to the fact that costs vary with the actual level of sales experienced by the firm. Thus, if the budget is to be used as a standard for performance evaluation or control, it must be constructed to match realized sales and production figures. This can involve much more than simply "adjusting cost figures up or down in proportion to the deviation of actual from planned sales"; that is, costs may not vary in strict proportion to sales, just as inventory levels may not vary as a constant percent of sales. Thus, preparation of a flexible budget involves re-estimating all the cash expenses that would be incurred at each of several possible sales levels. This process might utilize a variant of the percent of sales method discussed earlier.

Budget Period

There are no strict rules for determining the length of the budget period. However, as a general rule it should be long enough to show the effect of management policies yet short enough so that estimates can be made

Worksheet	Oct.	Nov.	Dec.
Sales	$55,000	$62,000	$50,000
Collections:			
First month (30%)			
Second month (50%)			
Third month (20%)			
Total			
Purchases (75% of sales in two months)			$56,250
Payments (one-month lag)			
Cash receipts:			
Collections			
Cash disbursements:			
Purchases			
Wages and salaries			
Rent			
Other expenses			
Interest expense on existing debt			
($12,000 note and $150,000 in long-term debt)			
Taxes			
Purchase of equipment			
Loan repayment ($12,000 note due in May)			
Total disbursements:			
Net monthly charge			
Plus: Beginning cash balance			
Less: Interest on short-term borrowing			
Equals: Ending cash balance before short-term no borrowing			
Financing needed[a]			
Ending cash balance			
Cumulative borrowing			

[a]The amount of financing that is required to raise the firm's ending cash balance up to its $10,000 desired cash balance.

with reasonable accuracy. Applying this rule of thumb to the Salco example in Table 4–2, it appears that the six-month budget period is too short. The reason is that we cannot tell whether the planned operations of the firm will be successful over the coming fiscal year. That is, for most of the first six-month period the firm is operating with a cash flow deficit. If this does not reverse in the latter six months of the year, then a reevaluation of the firm's plans and policies is clearly in order.

Longer-range budgets are also prepared in the form of the **capital-expenditure budget.** This budget details the firm's plans for acquiring plant and equipment over a 5-year, 10-year, or even longer period. Furthermore, firms often develop comprehensive long-range plans extending up to 10 years into the future. These plans are generally not as detailed as the annual cash budget, but they do consider such major components as sales, capital expenditures, new-product development, capital funds acquisition, and employment needs.

	Jan.	Feb.	Mar.	Apr.	May	June	July	Aug.
	$60,000	$75,000	$88,000	$100,000	$110,000	$100,000	$80,000	$75,000
	15,000	18,000	22,500	26,400	30,000	33,000		
	31,000	25,000	30,000	37,500	44,000	50,000		
	11,000	12,400	10,000	12,000	15,000	17,600		
	$57,000	55,400	62,500	75,900	89,000	100,600		
	66,000	75,000	82,500	75,000	60,000	56,250		
	56,250	66,000	75,000	82,500	75,000	60,000		
	$57,000	55,400	62,500	75,900	89,000	100,600		
	$56,250	66,000	75,000	82,500	75,000	60,000		
	3,000	10,000	7,000	8,000	6,000	4,000		
	4,000	4,000	4,000	4,000	4,000	4,000		
	1,000	500	1,200	1,500	1,500	1,200		
					600	7,500		
			4,460			5,200		
		14,000						
					12,000			
	$64,250	94,500	91,660	96,000	99,100	81,900		
	$(7,250)	(39,100)	(29,160)	(20,100)	(10,100)	18,700		
	20,000	12,750	10,000	10,000	10,000	10,000		
	—	—	(364)	(659)	(866)	(976)		
	12,750	(26,350)	(19,524)	(10,759)	(966)	27,724		
	—	36,350	29,524	20,759	10,966	(17,724)[b]		
	$12,750	10,000	10,,000	10,000	10,000	10,000		
	—	36,350	65,874	86,633	97,599	79,875		

[b]Negative financing needed simply means the firm has excess cash that can be used to retire a part of its short-term borrowing from prior months.

■ COMPUTERIZED FINANCIAL PLANNING

In recent years a number of developments in both computer hardware (machines) and software (programs) have reduced the tedium of the planning and budgeting process immensely. These include the introduction of "user-friendly" or "easy-to-use" computer programs that are specialized for application to financial planning.

Financial planning software packages (sometimes referred to as electronic spreadsheets) were first made popular on large mainframe computers but quickly spread to personal computers in the early eighties. These packages allow even a computer novice to use a personal computer to construct budgets and forecasts. The real advantage of the computer is realized when there is a need for different scenarios to be evaluated quickly and easily.

FINANCIAL MANAGEMENT IN PRACTICE

Management's Ability to Forecast Accurately

In spite of the importance of forecasting to strategic planning, managers have mixed success in forecasting events and outcomes accurately.* Inaccuracies, when they occur, have more to do with the nature of the environment than with management effort.

There is no shortage of dramatic examples to illustrate carefully designed forecasts that were widely off the mark. In the 1970s school administrators closed elementary schools as enrollments dropped. Forecasting that women's liberation had permanently reduced the birthrate, administrators acted to close schools permanently and, in some cases, even sell them. What happened, however, was that women merely delayed their childbearing years. In the mid-1980s, many of these same administrators found enrollments back at near-record levels.

As another example, the three most important economic outcomes of the Reagan era (1981–88) have been characterized as a high structural fiscal deficit, a chronic balance of payments deficit, and high real interest rates. Yet not one of these was predicted in 1979–80. Finally, most experts thought that the October 1987 stock market crash would bring on a recession in 1988. Managers who strategically positioned their organizations for the 1988 recession found that it didn't come.

Forecasting techniques are most accurate when the environment is static. The more dynamic the environment, the more likely management is to develop inaccurate forecasts. Forecasting has a relatively unimpressive record in predicting nonseasonal turning points such as recessions, unusual events, discontinuities, and the actions or reactions of competitors. The only major consolation for managers is that their competitors are unlikely to be any better than they are at forecasting accurately in a dynamic environment.

Although forecasting has a mixed record, managers continue to engage in the practice. They find that for many factors—such as revenues, demographic trends, new laws, and labor supplies—forecasting's record is quite solid. Moreover, by shortening the length of forecasts, managers improve their accuracy.

---

*This section is based on Essam Mahmoud, "Accuracy in Forecasting: A Survey," *Journal of Forecasting* 3: (1984), 139–59; Reed Moyer, "The Futility of Forecasting," *Long-Range Planning* (February 1983), 65–72; and Ronald Bailey, "Them That Can, Do; Them That Can't, Forecast," *Forbes* (December 26, 1988), 94–100. Used by Permission from Stephen P. Robbins, *Management*, 3d ed., p. 253. © 1991 Prentice Hall Publishing Co.

Another major development that has had a significant impact on the extent to which computers are used in the planning and budgeting process is the advent of the personal computer. For mere hundreds of dollars the financial analyst's desk can contain the computing power it took hundreds of thousands of dollars to buy just a decade ago. The development of financial planning software has paralleled the development of microcomputer technology. The number of spreadsheet packages has mushroomed over the past five years. These packages generally sell for less than $500 and include graphics programs as well as elementary database management capabilities.[4]

---

[4]The number and variety of financial spreadsheet programs has expanded dramatically since the introduction of the original Visi-Calc program. These include Lotus 1-2-3 and Excel, among others. In addition, there is a growing set of products referred to as "expert systems," which attempt to mimic the decisions of experts. To date these efforts have produced a limited number of financial applications software related to such things as the capital budgeting decision, but they offer an opportunity to expand the capabilities of the financial manager of the future.

SUMMARY

This chapter develops the role of forecasting within the context of the firm's financial planning efforts. Forecasts of the firm's sales revenues and related expenses provide the basis for projecting future financing needs. The most popular method for forecasting financial variables is the percent of sales method.

Forecasts of firm sales and expenses are used to develop the cash budget for the planning period, which is then used to estimate the firm's future financing needs. In this chapter all needed financing is supplied through short-term notes. However, in Chapters 12 and 14 we will look more closely at sources of financing. Chapter 12 addresses the choice among long-term sources (bonds, preferred stock, and common stock) while Chapter 14 deals with the choice between current (short-term) financing versus long-term financing.

STUDY QUESTIONS

4–1. Discuss the shortcomings of the percent-of-sales method of financial forecasting.

4–2. Explain how a fixed cash budget differs from a variable or flexible cash budget.

4–3. What two basic needs does a flexible (variable) cash budget serve?

4–4. What would be the probable effect on a firm's cash position of the following events?
   a. Rapidly rising sales
   b. A delay in the payment of payables
   c. A more liberal credit policy on sales (to the firm's customers)
   d. Holding larger inventories

4–5. How long should the budget period be? Why would a firm not set a rule that all budgets be for a 12-month period?

4–6. A cash budget is usually thought of as a means of planning for future financing needs. Why would a cash budget also be important for a firm that had excess cash on hand?

4–7. Explain why a cash budget would be of particular importance to a firm that experiences seasonal fluctuations in its sales.

SELF-TEST PROBLEMS

ST-1. *(Financial Forecasting)* Use the percent of sales method to prepare a pro forma income statement for Calico Sales Co., Inc. Projected sales for next year equal $4 million. Cost of goods sold equals 70 percent of sales, administrative expense equals $500,000, and depreciation expense is $300,000. Interest expense equals $50,000 and income is taxed at a rate of 40 percent. The firm plans to spend $200,000 during the period to renovate its office facility and will retire $150,000 in notes payable. Finally, selling expense equals 5 percent of sales.

ST-2. *(Cash Budget)* Stauffer, Inc., has estimated sales and purchase requirements for the last half of the coming year. Past experience indicates that it will collect 20 percent of its sales in the month of the sale, 50 percent of the remainder one month after the sale, and the balance in the second month following the sale. Stauffer prefers to pay for half its purchases in the month of the purchase and the other half the following month. Labor expense for each month is expected to equal 5 percent of that month's sales, with cash payment being made in the month in which the expense is incurred. Depreciation expense is $5,000 per month; miscellaneous cash expenses are $4,000 per month and are paid in the month incurred. General and administrative expenses of $50,000 are recognized and paid monthly. A $60,000 truck is to be purchased in August and is to be depreciated on a straight-line basis over 10 years with no expected salvage value. The company also plans to pay a $9,000 cash dividend to stockholders in July. The company feels that a minimum cash balance of $30,000 should be maintained. Any borrowing will cost 12 percent annually, with interest paid in the month following the month in which the funds are borrowed. Borrowing takes place at the beginning of the month in which the need for funds arises. For example, if during the month of July the firm should need to borrow $24,000 to maintain its $30,000 desired minimum balance, then $24,000 will be taken out on July 1 with interest owed for the entire month of July. Interest for the month of July would then be paid on August 1. Sales and purchase estimates are shown below. Prepare a cash budget for the months of July and August (cash on hand June 30 was $30,000, while sales for May and June were $100,000 and purchases were $60,000 for each of these months).

Month	Sales	Purchases
July	$120,000	$50,000
August	150,000	40,000
September	110,000	30,000

STUDY PROBLEMS

4–1. *(Financial Forecasting)* Sambonoza Enterprises projects its sales next year to be $4 million and expects to earn 5 percent of that amount after taxes. The firm is currently in the process of projecting its financing needs and has made the following assumptions (projections):
  1. Current assets will equal 20 percent of sales while fixed assets will remain at their current level of $1 million.
  2. Common equity is currently $0.8 million, and the firm pays out half its after-tax earnings in dividends.
  3. The firm has short-term payables and trade credit that normally equal 10 percent of sales and has no long-term debt outstanding.
  What are Sambonoza's financing needs for the coming year?

4–2. *(Financial Forecasting—Percent of Sales)* Tulley Appliances, Inc., projects next year's sales to be $20 million. Current sales are at $15 million based on current assets of $5 million and fixed assets of $5 million. The firm's net profit margin is 5 percent after taxes. Tulley forecasts that current assets will rise in direct proportion to the increase in sales, but fixed assets will increase by only $100,000. Currently, Tulley has $1.5 million in accounts payable plus $2 million in long-term debt (due in 10 years) outstanding and common equity (including $4 million in retained earnings) totaling $6.5 million. Tulley plans to pay $500,000 in common stock dividends next year.

a. What are Tulley's total financing needs (i.e., total assets) for the coming year?

b. Given the firm's projections and dividend payment plans, what are its discretionary financing needs?

c. Based on the projections given and assuming that the $100,000 expansion in fixed assets will occur, what is the largest increase in sales the firm can support without having to resort to the use of discretionary sources of financing?

4-3. *(Pro Forma Balance Sheet Construction)* Use the following industry average ratios to construct a pro forma balance sheet for Carlos Menza Inc.

Total asset turnover	2 times
Average collection period	
(assume a 365-day year)	9 days
Fixed asset turnover	5 times
Inventory turnover	
(based on cost of goods sold)	3 times
Current ratio	2 times
Sales (all on credit)	$4.0 million
Cost of goods sold	75% of sales
Debt ratio	50%

Cash		Current liabilities	
Accounts receivable		Long-term debt	
		Common stock plus	
Net fixed assets	_____	retained earnings	_____
	$ _____		$ _____

4-4. *(Cash Budget)* The Sharpe Corporation's projected sales for the first eight months of 1993 are as follows:

January	$90,000	May	$300,000
February	120,000	June	270,000
March	135,000	July	225,000
April	240,000	August	150,000

Of Sharpe's sales, 10 percent is for cash, another 60 percent is collected in the month following sale, and 30 percent is collected in the second month following sale. November and December sales for 1992 were $220,000 and $175,000, respectively.

Sharpe purchases its raw materials two months in advance of its sales equal to 60 percent of their final sales price. The supplier is paid one month after it makes delivery. For example, purchases for April sales are made in February and payment is made in March.

In addition, Sharpe pays $10,000 per month for rent and $20,000 each month for other expenditures. Tax prepayments of $22,500 are made each quarter, beginning in March.

The company's cash balance at December 31, 1992, was $22,000; a minimum balance of $15,000 must be maintained at all times. Assume that any short-term financing needed to maintain the cash balance would be paid off in the month following the month of financing if sufficient funds are available. Interest on short-term loans (12 percent) is paid monthly. Borrowing to meet estimated monthly cash needs takes place at the beginning of the month. Thus, if in the month of April the firm expects to have a need for an additional $60,500, these funds would be borrowed at the beginning of April with interest of $605 ($.12 \times 1/12 \times $60,500$) owed for April and paid at the beginning of May.

    a. Prepare a cash budget for Sharpe covering the first seven months of 1993.

    b. Sharpe has $200,000 in notes payable due in July that must be repaid or renegotiated for an extension. Will the firm have ample cash to repay the notes?

4–5. *(Percent-of-Sales Forecasting)* Which of the following accounts would most likely vary directly with the level of firm sales? Discuss each briefly.

	Yes	*No*
Cash	——	——
Marketable securities	——	——
Accounts payable	——	——
Notes payable	——	——
Plant and equipment	——	——
Inventories	——	——

4–6. *(Financial Forecasting—Percent of Sales)* The balance sheet of the Thompson Trucking Company (TTC) follows:

Thompson Trucking Company Balance Sheet, December 31, 1993 ($ millions)

Current assets	$10	Accounts payable	$5
Net fixed assets	15	Notes payable	0
Total	$25	Bonds payable	10
		Common equity	10
		Total	$25

TTC had sales for the year ended 12/31/93 of $50 million. The firm follows a policy of paying all net earnings out to its common stockholders in cash dividends. Thus, TTC generates no funds from its earnings that can be used to expand its operations. (Assume that depreciation expense is just equal to the cost of replacing worn-out assets.)

    a. If TTC anticipates sales of $80 million during the coming year, develop a pro forma balance sheet for the firm for 12/31/94. Assume that current assets vary as a percent of sales, net fixed assets remain unchanged, accounts payable vary as a percent of sales, and use notes payable as a balancing entry.

    b. How much "new" financing will TTC need next year?

    c. What limitations does the percent of sales forecast method suffer from? Discuss briefly.

4–7. *(Financial Forecasting—Discretionary Financing Needed)* The most recent balance sheet for the Armadillo Dog Biscuit Co. is shown in the table below. The company is about to embark on an advertising campaign, which is expected to raise sales from the current level of $5 million to $7 million by the end of next year. The firm is currently operating at full capacity and will have to increase its investment in both current and fixed assets to support the projected level of new sales. In fact, the firm estimates that both categories of assets will rise in direct proportion to the projected increase in sales.

The firm's net profits were 6 percent of current year's sales but are expected to rise to 7 percent of next year's sales. To help support its anticipated growth in asset needs next year, the firm has suspended plans to pay cash dividends to its stockholders. In past years a $1.50 per share dividend has been paid annually.

Armadillo Dog Biscuit Co., Inc. ($ millions)

	Present Level	Percent of Sales	Projected Level
Current assets	$2.0		
Net fixed assets	3.0		
Total	$5.0		
Accounts payable	$0.5		
Accrued expenses	0.5		
Notes payable	—		
Current liabilities	$1.0		
Long-term debt	$2.0		
Common stock	0.5		
Retained earnings	1.5		
Common equity	$2.0		
Total	$5.0		

Armadillo's payables and accrued expenses are expected to vary directly with sales. In addition, notes payable will be used to supply the funds that are needed to finance next year's operations and that are not forthcoming from other sources.

a. Fill in the table and project the firm's needs for discretionary financing. Use notes payable as the balancing entry for future discretionary financing needed.

b. Compare Armadillo's current ratio and debt ratio (total liabilities/total assets) before the growth in sales and after. What was the effect of the expanded sales on these two dimensions of Armadillo's financial condition?

c. What difference, if any, would have resulted if Armadillo's sales had risen to $6 million in one year and $7 million only after two years? Discuss only; no calculations required.

4–8. *(Forecasting Discretionary Financing Needs)* Fishing Charter, Inc., estimates that it invests 30 cents in assets for each dollar of new sales. However, 5 cents in profits are produced by each dollar of additional sales, of which 1 cent can be reinvested in the firm. If sales rise from their current level of $5 million by $500,000 next year, and the ratio of spontaneous liabilities to sales is .15, what will be the firm's need for discretionary financing? (*Hint:* In this situation you do not know what the firm's existing level of assets is, nor do you know how those assets have been financed. Thus, you must estimate the change in financing needs and match this change with the expected changes in spontaneous liabilities, retained earnings, and other sources of discretionary financing.)

4–9.   *(Preparation of a Cash Budget)* Harrison Printing has projected its sales for the first eight months of 1993 as follows:

January	$100,000	May	$275,000
February	120,000	June	200,000
March	150,000	July	200,000
April	300,000	August	180,000

Harrison collects 20 percent of its sales in the month of the sale, 50 percent in the month following the sale, and the remaining 30 percent two months following the sale. During November and December of 1992 Harrison's sales were $220,000 and $175,000, respectively.

Harrison purchases raw materials two months in advance of its sales equal to 65 percent of its final sales. The supplier is paid one month after delivery. Thus, purchases for April sales are made in February and payment is made in March.

In addition, Harrison pays $10,000 per month for rent and $20,000 each month for other expenditures. Tax prepayments of $22,500 are made each quarter beginning in March. The company's cash balance as of December 31, 1992, was $22,000; a minimum balance of $20,000 must be maintained at all times to satisfy the firm's bank line of credit agreement. Harrison has arranged with its bank for short-term credit at an interest rate of 12 percent per annum (1 percent per month) to be paid monthly. Borrowing to meet estimated monthly cash needs takes place at the end of the month, and interest is not paid until the end of the following month. Consequently, if the firm were to need to borrow $50,000 during the month of April, then it would pay $500 (= .01 × $50,000) in interest during May. Finally, Harrison follows a policy of repaying any outstanding short-term debt in any month in which its cash balance exceeds the minimum desired balance of $20,000.

a. Harrison needs to know what its cash requirements will be for the next six months so that it can renegotiate the terms of its short-term credit agreement with its bank, if necessary. To evaluate this problem the firm plans to evaluate the impact of a ±20 percent variation in its monthly sales efforts. Prepare a six-month cash budget for Harrison and use it to evaluate the firm's cash needs.

b. Harrison has a $200,000 note due in June. Will the firm have sufficient cash to repay the loan?

4–10.   *(Sustainable Rate of Growth)* ADP, Inc., is a manufacturer of specialty circuit boards used in the personal computer industry. The firm has experienced phenomenal sales growth over its short five-year life. Selected financial statement data are found in the following table:

	19x5	19x4	19x3	19x2	19x1
Sales	$3,000	$2,200	$1,800	$1,400	$1,200
Net Income	150	110	90	70	60
Assets	2,700	1,980	1,620	1,260	1,080
Dividends	60	44	36	28	24
Common Equity	812	722	656	602	560
Liabilities	1,888	1,258	964	658	520
Liabilities & Equity	2,700	1,980	1,620	1,260	1,080

    a. Calculate ADP's Sustainable Rate of Growth for each of the five years of its existence.

    b. Compare the actual rates of growth in sales to the firm's sustainable rates calculated in part a. How has ADP been financing its growing asset needs?

4–11. *(Sustainable Rate of Growth)* The Carrera Game Company has experienced a 100% increase in sales over the last five years. The company president, Jack Cerrera, has become increasingly alarmed by the firm's rising debt level even in the face of continued profitability.

	19x7	19x6	19x5	19x4	19x3
Sales	$60,000	$56,000	$48,000	$36,000	$30,000
Net Income	3,000	2,800	2,400	1,800	1,500
Assets	54,000	50,400	43,200	32,400	27,000
Dividends	1200	1,120	960	720	600
Common Equity	21,000	19,200	17,520	16,080	15,000
Liabilities	33,000	31,200	25,680	16,320	12,000
Liabilities and Equity	54,000	50,400	43,200	32,400	27,000

    a. Calculate the debt to assets ratio, return on common equity, actual rate of growth in firm sales and retention ratio for each of the five years of data provided above.

    b. Calculate the Sustainable Rates of Growth for Carrera for each of the last five years. Why has the firm's borrowing increased so dramatically?

4–12. *(Forecasting Inventories)* Findlay Instruments produces a complete line of medical instruments used by plastic surgeons and has experienced rapid growth over the last five years. In an effort to make more accurate predictions of its financing requirements Findlay is currently attempting to construct a financial planning model based on the percent of sales forecasting method. However, the firm's chief financial analyst (Sarah Macias) is concerned that the projections for inventories will be seriously in error. She recognizes that the firm has begun to accrue substantial economies of scale in its inventory investment and has documented this fact in the following data and calculations:

Year	Sales (000)	Inventory (000)	% of Sales
19X1	$15,000	1,150	7.67%
19X2	18,000	1,180	6.56%
19X3	17,500	1,175	6.71%
19X4	20,000	1,200	6.00%
19X5	25,000	1,250	5.00%
		Average	6.39%

a. Plot Findlay's sales and inventories for the last five years. What is the relationship between these two variables?

b. Estimate firm inventories for 19X6 where firm sales are projected to reach $30,000,000. Use the average percent of sales for the last five years, the most recent percent of sales and your evaluation of the true relationship between the sales and inventories from part a to make three predications.

SELF-TEST SOLUTIONS

SS-1.

Calico Sales Co., Inc., Pro Forma Income Statement

Sales		$4,000,000
Cost of goods sold (70%)		(2,800,000)
Gross profit		1,200,000
Operating expense		
Selling expense (5%)	$200,000	
Administrative expense	500,000	
Depreciation expense	300,000	(1,000,000)
Net operating income		200,000
Interest		(50,000)
Earnings before taxes		150,000
Taxes (40%)		(60,000)
Net income		$ 90,000

Although the office renovation expenditure and debt retirement are surely cash outflows, they do not enter the income statement directly. These expenditures affect expenses for the period's income statement only through their effect on depreciation and interest expense. A cash budget would indicate the full cash impact of the renovation and debt retirement expenditures.

SS-2.

	May	June	July	Aug.
Sales	$100,000	$100,000	$120,000	$150,000
Purchases	60,000	60,000	50,000	40,000

Cash Receipts:

	May	June	July	Aug.
Collections from month of sale (20%)	20,000	20,000	24,000	30,000
1 month later (50% of uncollected amount)		40,000	48,000	48,000
2 months later (balance)			40,000	40,000
Total receipts			$104,000	$118,000

Cash Disbursements:

	July	Aug.
Payments for purchases—		
From 1 month earlier	$30,000	$25,000
From current month	$25,000	20,000
Total	$55,000	$45,000
Miscellaneous cash expenses	4,000	4,000
Labor expense (5% of sales)	6,000	7,500
General and administrative expense		
($50,000 per month)	50,000	50,000
Truch purchase	0	60,000
Cash dividends	9,000	—
Total disbursements	$(124,000)	$(166,500)

	July	Aug.
Net change in cash	(20,000)	(48,500)
Plus: Beginning cash balance	30,000	30,000
Less: Interest on short-term borrowing		
(1% of prior month's borrowing)		(200)
Equals: Ending cash balance—without borrowing	10,000	(18,700)
Financing needed to reach target cash balance	20,000	48,700
Cumulative borrowing	$ 20,000	$ 68,700

CHAPTER 5

THE TIME VALUE OF MONEY

Compound Interest • Compound Interest with Nonannual Periods • Present Value
• Annuities • Amortized Loans • Present Value of an Uneven Stream • Perpetuities

In the next five chapters we will focus on determining the value of the firm and the desirability of investment proposals. A key concept that underlies this material is the *time value of money;* that is, a dollar today is worth more than a dollar received a year from now. Intuitively this idea is easy to understand. We are all familiar with the concept of interest. This concept illustrates what economists call an *opportunity cost* of passing up the earning potential of a dollar today. This opportunity cost is the time value of money.

In evaluating and comparing investment proposals, we need to examine how dollar values might accrue from accepting these proposals. To do this, all dollar values must first be comparable; since a dollar received today is worth more than a dollar received in the future, we must move all dollar flows back to the present or out to a common future date. An understanding of the time value of money is essential, therefore, to an understanding of financial management, whether basic or advanced.

In this chapter we develop the tools to incorporate **Axiom 2: The Time Value of Money—A Dollar Received Today Is Worth More Than a Dollar Received in the Future** into our calculations. In coming chapters we will use this concept to measure value by bringing the benefits and costs from a project back to the present.

■ COMPOUND INTEREST

Most of us encounter the concept of compound interest at an early age. Anyone who has ever had a savings account or purchased a government savings bond has received compound interest. **Compound interest** occurs when interest paid on the investment during the first period is added to the principal and then, during the second period, interest is earned on this new sum.

For example, suppose we place $100 in a savings account that pays 6 percent interest, compounded annually. How will our savings grow? At the end of the first year we have earned 6 percent, or $6 on our initial deposit of $100, giving us a total of $106 in our savings account. The mathematical formula illustrating this phenomenon is

$$FV_1 = PV(1 + i) \tag{5-1}$$

where　　FV_1 = the future value of the investment at the end of one year

　　　　i = the annual interest (or discount) rate

　　　PV = the present value, or original amount invested at the beginning of the first year

In our example

$$FV_1 = PV(1 + i) \tag{5-1}$$

$$= \$100(1 + .06)$$

$$= \$100(1.06)$$

$$= \$106$$

Carrying these calculations one period further, we find that we now earn the 6 percent interest on a principal of $106, which means we earn $6.36 in interest during the second year. Why do we earn more interest during the second year than we did during the first? Simply because we now earn interest on the sum of the original principal, or present value, and the interest we earned in the first year. In effect we are now earning interest on interest; this is the concept of compound interest. Examining the mathematical formula illustrating the earning of interest in the second year, we find

$$FV_2 = FV_1(1 + i) \qquad \textbf{(5–2)}$$

which, for our example, gives

$$FV_2 = \$106(1.06)$$

$$= \$112.36$$

Looking back at equation (5–1), we can see that FV_1, or $106, is actually equal to $PV(1 + i)$, or $100 (1 + .06). If we substitute these values into equation (5–2), we get

$$FV_2 = PV(1 + i)(1 + i)$$

$$= PV(1 + i)^2 \qquad \textbf{(5–3)}$$

Carrying this forward into the third year, we find that we enter the year with $112.36 and we earn 6 percent, or $6.74 in interest, giving us a total of $119.10 in our savings account. Expressing this mathematically:

$$FV_3 = FV_2(1 + i) \qquad \textbf{(5–4)}$$

$$= \$112.36(1.06)$$

$$= \$119.10$$

If we substitute the value in equation (5–3) for FV_2 into equation (5–4), we find

$$FV_3 = PV(1 + i)(1 + i)(1 + i)$$

$$= PV(1 + i)^3 \qquad \textbf{(5–5)}$$

By now a pattern is beginning to be evident. We can generalize this formula to illustrate the value of our investment if it is compounded annually at a rate of i for n years to be

$$FV_n = PV(1 + i)^n \qquad \textbf{(5–6)}$$

where FV_n = the future value of the investment at the
end of n years

TABLE 5–1
Illustration of Compound
Interest Calculations

Year	Beginning Value	Interest Earned	Ending Value
1	$100.00	$ 6.00	$106.00
2	106.00	6.36	112.36
3	112.36	6.74	119.10
4	119.10	7.15	126.25
5	126.25	7.57	133.82
6	133.82	8.03	141.85
7	141.85	8.51	150.36
8	150.36	9.02	159.38
9	159.38	9.57	168.95
10	168.95	10.13	179.08

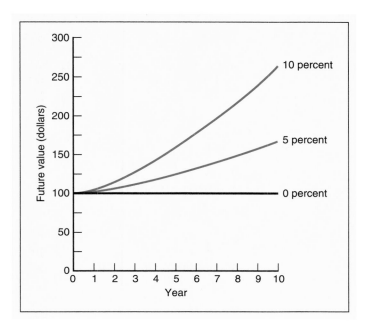

FIGURE 5–1
Future Value of $100 Initially Deposited and Compounded at 0, 5, and 10 percent

n = the number of years during which the compounding occurs

i = the annual interest (or discount) rate

PV = the present value or original amount invested at the beginning of the first year

Table 5–1 illustrates how this investment of $100 would continue to grow for the first 10 years at a compound interest rate of 6 percent. Notice how the amount of interest earned annually increases each year. Again, the reason is that each year interest is received on the sum of the original investment plus any interest earned in the past.

When we examine the relationship between the number of years an initial investment is compounded for and its future value graphically, as shown in Figure 5–1, we see that we can increase the future value of an investment by either increasing the number of years for which we let it compound or by compounding it at a higher interest rate. We can also see this from equation (5–6), since an increase in either i or n while PV is held constant will result in an increase in FV_n.

PERSPECTIVE IN FINANCE

Keep in mind that future cash flows are assumed to occur at the end of the time period during which they accrue. For example, if a cash flow of $100 occurs in time period 5, it is assumed to occur at the end of time period 5, which is also the beginning of time period 6. In addition, cash flows that occur in time t = 0 occur right now; that is, they are already in present dollars.

If we place $1,000 in a savings account paying 5 percent interest compounded annually, how much will our account accrue to in 10 years? Substituting $PV = \$1000$, $i = 5$ percent, and $n = 10$ years into equation (5–6), we get

$$FV_n = PV(1 + i)^n \qquad \textbf{(5–6)}$$

$$= \$1,000(1 + .05)^{10}$$

$$= \$1,000(1.62889)$$

$$= \$1,628.89$$

Thus at the end of 10 years we will have $1,628.89 in our savings account. ∎

As the determination of future value can be quite time consuming when an investment is held for a number of years, the **future-value interest factor** for i and n ($FVIF_{i,n}$), defined as $(1 + i)^n$, has been compiled in the back of the book for various values of i and n. An abbreviated compound interest or future-value interest factor table appears in Table 5–2, with a more comprehensive version of this table appearing in Appendix B at the back of this book. Alternatively, the $FVIF_{i,n}$ values could easily be determined using a calculator. Note that the compounding factors given in these tables represent the value of $1 compounded at rate i at the *end* of the *n*th year. Thus, to calculate the future value of an initial investment we need only determine the $FVIF_{i,n}$ using a calculator or the tables at the end of the text and multiply this times the initial investment. In effect, we can rewrite equation (5–6) as follows:

$$FV_n = PV(FVIF_{i,n}) \qquad \textbf{(5–6a)}$$

TABLE 5–2
$FVIF_{i,n}$ or the Compound Sum of $1

n	1%	2%	3%	4%	5%	6%	7%	8%	9%	10%
1	1.010	1.020	1.030	1.040	1.050	1.060	1.070	1.080	1.090	1.100
2	1.020	1.040	1.061	1.082	1.102	1.124	1.145	1.166	1.188	1.210
3	1.030	1.061	1.093	1.125	1.158	1.191	1.225	1.260	1.295	1.331
4	1.041	1.082	1.126	1.170	1.216	1.262	1.311	1.360	1.412	1.464
5	1.051	1.104	1.159	1.217	1.276	1.338	1.403	1.469	1.539	1.611
6	1.062	1.126	1.194	1.265	1.340	1.419	1.501	1.587	1.677	1.772
7	1.072	1.149	1.230	1.316	1.407	1.504	1.606	1.714	1.828	1.949
8	1.083	1.172	1.267	1.369	1.477	1.594	1.718	1.851	1.993	2.144
9	1.094	1.195	1.305	1.423	1.551	1.689	1.838	1.999	2.172	2.358
10	1.105	1.219	1.344	1.480	1.629	1.791	1.967	2.159	2.367	2.594
11	1.116	1.243	1.384	1.539	1.710	1.898	2.105	2.332	2.580	2.853
12	1.127	1.268	1.426	1.601	1.796	2.012	2.252	2.518	2.813	3.138
13	1.138	1.294	1.469	1.665	1.886	2.133	2.410	2.720	3.066	3.452
14	1.149	1.319	1.513	1.732	1.980	2.261	2.579	2.937	3.342	3.797
15	1.161	1.346	1.558	1.801	2.079	2.397	2.759	3.172	3.642	4.177

If we invest $500 in a bank where it will earn 8 percent compounded annually, how much will it be worth at the end of seven years? Looking at Table 5–2 in the row $n = 7$ and column $i = 8\%$, we find that $FVIF_{8\%,\,7\,\text{yr}}$ has a value of 1.714. Substituting this in equation (5–6a), we find

$$FV_n = PV\,(FVIF_{8\%,\,7\,\text{yr}}) \qquad\qquad \textbf{(5–6a)}$$

$$= \$500(1.714)$$

$$= \$857$$

Thus, we will have $857 at the end of seven years.

In the future we will find several uses for equation (5–6); not only will we find the future value of an investment, but we can also solve for PV, i, or n. In any case, we will be given three of the four variables and will have to solve for the fourth.

PERSPECTIVE IN FINANCE

As you read through the chapter it is a good idea to solve the problems as they are presented. If you just read the problems, the principles behind them often do not sink in. The material presented in this chapter forms the basis for the rest of the course; therefore, a good command of the concepts underlying the time value of money is extremely important.

How many years will it take for an initial investment of $300 to grow to $774 if it is invested at 9 percent compounded annually? In this problem we know the initial investment, $PV = \$300$; the future value, $FV_n = \$774$; the compound growth rate, $i = 9$ percent; and we are solving for the number of years it must compound for, $n = ?$ Substituting the known values in equation (5–6), we find

$$FV_n = PV(1 + i)^n \qquad\qquad \textbf{(5–6)}$$

$$\$774 = \$300(1 + .09)^n$$

$$2.58 = (1 + .09)^n$$

Thus we are looking for a value of 2.58 in the $FVIF_{i,n}$ tables, and we know it must be in the 9% column. Looking down the 9% column for the value closest to 2.58, we find that it occurs in the $n = 11$ row. Thus, it will take 11 years for an initial investment of $300 to grow to $774 if it is invested at 9 percent compounded annually.

At what rate must $100 be compounded annually for it to grow to $179.10 in 10 years? In this case we know the initial investment, $PV = \$100$; the future value of this investment at the end of n years, FV_n = \$179.10; and the number of years that the initial investment will compound for, n = 10 years. Substituting into equation (5–6), we get

$$FV_n = PV(1 + i)^n \qquad\qquad \textbf{(5–6)}$$

$$\$179.10 = \$100(1 + i)^{10}$$

$$1.791 = (1 + i)^{10}$$

We know we are looking in the n = 10 row of the $FVIF_{i,n}$ table for a value of 1.791, and we find this in the i = 6% column. Thus, if we want our initial investment of \$100 to accrue to \$179.10 in 10 years, we must invest it at 6 percent. ■

Moving Money Through Time with the Aid of a Financial Calculator

Time value of money calculations can be made simple with the aid of a **financial calculator.** In general, when solving time value of money problems with a financial calculator you will be given three of four variables and will have to solve for the fourth. Before presenting any solutions using a financial calculator we will introduce the calculator's five most common keys. (In most time value of money problems, only four of these keys are relevant.) These keys are:

Menu Key	Description
$\boxed{N}$	Stores (or calculates) the total number of payments or compounding periods.
$\boxed{I\% \, YR}$	Stores (or calculates) the interest or discount rate.
$\boxed{PV}$	Stores (or calculates) the present value of a cash flow or series of cash flows.
$\boxed{FV}$	Stores (or calculates) the future value, that is, the dollar amount of a final cash flow or the compound value of a single flow or series of cash flows.
$\boxed{PMT}$	Stores (or calculates) the dollar amount of each annuity payment deposited or received at the end of each year.

One thing you must keep in mind when using a financial calculator is that outflows generally have to be entered as negative numbers. In general, each problem will have two cash flows, one an outflow with a negative value and one an inflow with a positive value. The idea is that you deposit money in the bank at some point (an outflow), and at some other point you take money out of the bank (an inflow). Also, every calculator operates a bit differently with respect to entering variables. Needless to say, it is a good idea to familiarize yourself with exactly how your calculator functions.

As stated above, in most problems you will be given three of four variables. These four variables will always include N and I%YR; in addition, two out of the final three variables PV, FV, and PMT will also be included. To solve a time value of money problem using a financial calculator, all you need to do is enter the appropriate numbers for three of the four variables and then press the key of the final variable to calculate its value. It is also a good idea to enter zero for any of the five variables not included in the problem in order to clear that variable.

Now let's solve the previous example using a financial calculator. We were trying to find at what rate must $100 be compounded annually for it to grow to $179.10 in 10 years. The solution using a financial calculator would be as follows:

Step 1: Input Values of Known Variables

Data Input	Function Key	Description
10	N	Stores N = 10 years
−100	PV	Stores PV = −$100
179.10	FV	Stores FV = $179.10
0	PMT	Clears PMT to = 0

Step 2: Calculate the Value of the Unknown Variable

Function Key	Answer	Description
I% YR	6.00%	Calculates $I\%YR$ = 6.00%

Any of the problems in this chapter can easily be solved using a financial calculator; and the solutions to many examples using an HP 17BII financial calculator are provided in the margins. If you are using the HP 17BII, make sure that you have selected both the "END MODE" and "one payment per year" (1 P/YR). This sets the payment conditions to a maximum of one payment per period occurring at the end of the period. Also, to access the time value of money menu from the main menu on the HP 17BII, you must first press the FIN and TVM menu keys. One final point: You will notice that solutions using the present-value tables versus solutions using a calculator may vary slightly—a result of rounding errors in the tables.

For further explanation see Appendix A at the end of the book. It provides a tutorial on the use of other financial calculators, as well.

PERSPECTIVE IN FINANCE

The concepts of compound interest and present value will follow us through the remainder of this book. Not only will they allow us to determine the future value of any investment, but they will allow us to bring the benefits and costs from new investment proposals back to the present and thereby determine the value of the investment in today's dollars.

Andrew Tobias on the Power of Compounding

It was Homer who said that $1,000 invested at a mere 8 percent for 400 years would grow to $23 quadrillion—$5 million for every human on earth. (And you can't see any reason to save?) But, he said, the first 100 years are the hardest. (This was the late Sidney Homer, not Homer Homer—author of the classic *A History of Interest Rates*.)

What invariably happens is that long before the first 100 years are up, someone with access to the cache loses patience. The money burns a hole in his pocket. Or through his nose.

Doubtless that would have been true of the Correa fortune, too, had Domingos Faustino Correa not cut everyone out of his will for 100 years. That was in 1873, in Brazil. You could have gotten very tired waiting, but if you can establish that you are one of that misanthrope's 4,000-odd legitimate heirs, you may now have some money coming to you. Since 1873, Correa's estate has grown, by some estimates, to $12 billion.

Benjamin Franklin had much the same idea, only with higher purpose. Inventive to the end, he left £1,000 each to Boston and Philadelphia. The cities were to lend the money, at interest, to worthy apprentices. Then, after a century, they were to employ part of the fortune Franklin envisioned to construct some public work, while continuing to invest the rest.

One hundred ninety-two years later, when last I checked, Boston's funds exceeded $3 million, even after having been drained to build Franklin Union, and was being lent at interest to medical school students. Philadelphia's fund was smaller, but it, too, had been put to good use. All this from an initial stake of £2,000!

And then there was the king who held a chess tournament among the peasants—I may have this story a little wrong, but the point holds—and asked the winner what he wanted as his prize. The peasant, in apparent humility, asked only that a single kernel of wheat be placed for him on the first square of his chessboard, two kernels on the second, four on the third—and so forth. The king fell for it and had to import grain from Argentina for the next 700 years. Eighteen and a half million trillion kernels, or enough, if each kernel is a quarter-inch long (which it may not be; I've never seen wheat in its pre-English-muffin form), to stretch to the sun and back 391,320 times.

That was nothing more than one kernel's compounding at 100 percent per square for 64 squares. It is vaguely akin to the situation with our national debt.

Source: Andrew Tobias, *Money Angles* (New York: Linden Press, 1984), pp. 35–36. © 1984 by Andrew Tobias. Reprinted by permission of Andrew Tobias.

■ COMPOUND INTEREST WITH NONANNUAL PERIODS

Until now we have assumed that the compounding period is always annual; however, it need not be, as evidenced by savings and loan associations and commercial banks that compound on a quarterly, daily, and in some cases continuous basis. Fortunately, this adjustment of the compounding period follows the same format as that used for annual compounding. If we invest our money for five years at 8 percent interest compounded semiannually, we are really investing our money for 10 six-month periods during which we receive 4 percent interest each period. If it is compounded quarterly, we receive 2 percent interest per period for 20 three-month periods. This process can easily be generalized, giv-

ing us the following formula for finding the future value of an investment for which interest is compounded in nonannual periods:

$$FV_n = PV\left(1+\frac{i}{m}\right)^{mn} \tag{5-7}$$

where FV_n = the future value of the investment at the
end of n years

n = the number of years during which the
compounding occurs

i = annual interest (or discount) rate

PV = the present value or original amount invested
at the beginning of the first year

m = the number of times compounding occurs during
the year

In the case of continuous compounding, the value of m in equation
(5-7) is allowed to approach infinity. In effect, with continuous compounding, interest begins to earn interest immediately. As this happens,
the value of $[1 + (i/m)]^{mn}$ approaches e^{in}, with e being defined as follows
and having a value of approximately 2.71828:

$$e = \lim_{m\to\infty}\left(1+\frac{1}{m}\right)^{m} \tag{5-8}$$

where ∞ indicates infinity. Thus the future value of an investment compounded continuously for n years can be determined from the following
formula:

$$FV_n = PV \cdot e^{in} \tag{5-9}$$

where FV_n = the future value of the investment at the
end of n years

e = 2.71828

n = the number of years during which the
compounding occurs

i = the annual interest (or discount) rate

PV = the present value or original amount invested
at the beginning of the first year

Continuous compounding may appear complicated, but it is used
frequently and is a valuable theoretical concept. Continuous compounding is important because it allows interest to be earned on interest more frequently than any other compounding method does. We can
see the value of intrayear compounding by examining Table 5-3 on
page 160. Since interest is earned on interest more frequently as the
length of the compounding period declines, there is an inverse relationship between the length of the compounding period and the effective
annual interest rate.

TABLE 5–3
The Value of $100
Compounded at Various
Intervals

For One Year at i Percent				
$i =$	2%	5%	10%	15%
Compounded annually	$102.00	$105.00	$110.00	$115.00
Compounded semiannually	102.01	105.06	110.25	115.56
Compounded quarterly	102.02	105.09	110.38	115.87
Compounded monthly	102.02	105.12	110.47	116.08
Compounded weekly (52)	102.02	105.12	110.51	116.16
Compounded daily (365)	102.02	105.13	110.52	116.18
Compounded continuously	102.02	105.13	110.52	116.18

For Ten Years at i Percent				
$i =$	2%	5%	10%	15%
Compounded annually	$121.90	$162.89	$259.37	$404.56
Compounded semiannually	122.02	163.86	265.33	424.79
Compounded quarterly	122.08	164.36	268.51	436.04
Compounded monthly	122.12	164.70	270.70	444.02
Compounded weekly (52)	122.14	164.83	271.57	447.20
Compounded daily (365)	122.14	164.87	271.79	448.03
Compounded continuously	122.14	164.87	271.83	448.17

EXAMPLE

If we place $100 in a savings account that yields 12 percent compounded quarterly, what will our investment grow to at the end of five years? Substituting $n = 5$, $m = 4$, $i = 12$ percent, and $PV = 100 into equation (5–7), we find

$$FV_5 = $100 \left(1 + \frac{.12}{4}\right)^{4 \cdot 5}$$

$$= $100(1 + .03)^{20}$$

$$= $100(1.806)$$

$$= $180.60$$

CALCULATOR SOLUTION

Data Input	Function Key
20	N
3	$I\% \, YR$
100	PV
0	PMT
Function Key	**Answer**
FV	−180.61

Thus, we will have $180.60 at the end of five years. Notice that the calculator solution is slightly different because of rounding errors in the tables, as explained in the previous section, and that it also takes on a negative value. ■

EXAMPLE

How much money will we have at the end of 20 years if we deposit $1,000 in a savings account yielding 10 percent interest continuously compounded? Substituting $n = 20$, $i = 10$ percent, and $PV = 1000 into equation (5–9) yields

$$FV_{10} = \$1{,}000(2.71828)^{.10 \cdot 20}$$

$$= \$1{,}000(2.71828)^2$$

$$= \$1{,}000(7.38905)$$

$$= \$7{,}389.05$$

Thus, we will have \$7,389.05 at the end of 20 years. ■

■ PRESENT VALUE

Up until this point we have been moving money forward in time; that is, we know how much we have to begin with and are trying to determine how much that sum will grow in a certain number of years when compounded at a specific rate. We are now going to look at the reverse question: What is the value in today's dollars of a sum of money to be received in the future? The answer to this question will help us determine the desirability of investment projects in Chapters 9 and 10. In this case we are moving future money back to the present. We will be determining the **present value** of a lump sum, which in simple terms is the current value of a future payment. What we will be doing is, in fact, nothing other than inverse compounding. The differences in these techniques come about merely from the investor's point of view. In compounding we talked about the compound interest rate and the initial investment; in determining the present value we will talk about the discount rate and present value. Determination of the discount rate is the subject of Chapter 11 and can be defined as the rate of return available on an investment of equal risk to what is being discounted. Other than that, the technique and the terminology remain the same, and the mathematics are simply reversed. In equation (5–6) we were attempting to determine the future value of an initial investment. We now want to determine the initial investment or present value. By dividing both sides of equation (5–6) by $(1 + i)^n$, we get

$$PV = FV_n \left[\frac{1}{(1 + i)^n} \right] \qquad \textbf{(5–10)}$$

where FV_n = the future value of the investment at the end of n years

n = the number of years until the payment will be received

i = the annual discount (or interest) rate

PV = the present value of the future sum of money

Because the mathematical procedure for determining the present value is exactly the inverse of determining the future value, we also find that the relationships among n, i, and PV are just the opposite of those

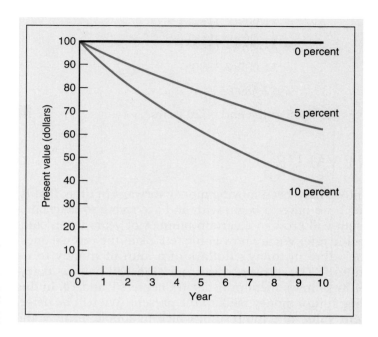

FIGURE 5–2
Present Value of $100 to Be
Received at a Future Date and
Discounted Back to the Present
at 0, 5, and 10 Percent

we observed in future value. The present value of a future sum of money is inversely related to both the number of years until the payment will be received and the discount rate. Graphically, this relationship can be seen in Figure 5–2.

PERSPECTIVE IN FINANCE

Although the present value equation [equation (5–10)] will be used extensively in evaluating new investment proposals, it should be stressed that the present value equation is actually the same as the future value or compounding equation [equation (5–6)], where it is solved for PV.

CALCULATOR SOLUTION	
Data Input	Function Key
10	N
6	$I\%\ YR$
500	FV
0	PMT
Function Key	Answer
PV	−279.20

EXAMPLE

What is the present value of $500 to be received 10 years from today if our discount rate is 6 percent? Substituting $FV_{10} = \$500$, $n = 10$, and $i = 6$ percent into equation (5–10), we find

$$PV = \$500 \left[\frac{1}{(1 + .06)^{10}} \right]$$

$$= \$500 \left(\frac{1}{1.791} \right)$$

$$= \$500(.558)$$

$$= \$279$$

Thus, the present value of the $500 to be received in 10 years is $279. ■

n	1%	2%	3%	4%	5%	6%	7%	8%	9%	10%
1	.990	.980	.971	.962	.952	.943	.935	.926	.917	.909
2	.980	.961	.943	.925	.907	.890	.873	.857	.842	.826
3	.971	.942	.915	.889	.864	.840	.816	.794	.772	.751
4	.961	.924	.888	.855	.823	.792	.763	.735	.708	.683
5	.951	.906	.863	.822	.784	.747	.713	.681	.650	.621
6	.942	.888	.837	.790	.746	.705	.666	.630	.596	.564
7	.933	.871	.813	.760	.711	.655	.623	.583	.547	.513
8	.923	.853	.789	.731	.677	.627	.582	.540	.502	.467
9	.914	.837	.766	.703	.645	.592	.544	.500	.460	.424
10	.905	.820	.744	.676	.614	.558	.508	.463	.422	.386
11	.896	.804	.722	.650	.585	.527	.475	.429	.388	.350
12	.887	.789	.701	.625	.557	.497	.444	.397	.356	.319
13	.879	.773	.681	.601	.530	.469	.415	.368	.326	.290
14	.870	.758	.661	.577	.505	.442	.388	.340	.299	.263
15	.861	.743	.642	.555	.481	.417	.362	.315	.275	.239

TABLE 5–4
$PVIF_{i,n}$ or the
Present Value of $1

To aid in the computation of present values, the **present-value interest factor** for i and n ($PVIF_{i,n}$), defined as $[1/(1 + i)^n]$, has been compiled for various combinations of i and n and appears in Appendix C at the back of this book. An abbreviated version of Appendix C appears in Table 5–4. A close examination shows that the values in Table 5–4 are merely the inverse of those found in Table 5–2 and Appendix B. This, of course, is as it should be, as the values in Appendix B are $(1 + i)^n$ and those in Appendix C are $[1/(1 + i)^n]$. Now, to determine the present value of a sum of money to be received at some future date, we need only determine the value of the appropriate $PVIF_{i,n}$, either by using a calculator or consulting the tables, and multiply it by the future value. In effect we can use our new notation and rewrite equation (5–10) as follows:

$$PV = FV_n(PVIF_{i,n}) \tag{5–10a}$$

Data Input	Function Key
10	N
8	$I\% YR$
1500	FV
0	PMT

Function Key	Answer
FV	−694.79

EXAMPLE

What is the present value of $1,500 to be received at the end of 10 years if our discount rate is 8 percent? By looking at the $n = 10$ row and $i = 8\%$ column of Table 5–4, we find the $PVIF_{8\%, \, 10 \, yr}$ is .463. Substituting this value into equation (5–10), we find

$$PV = \$1,500(.463)$$
$$= \$694.50$$

Thus, the present value of this $1,500 payment is $694.50. ■

Again, we only have one present-value—future-value equation; that is, equations (5–6) and (5–10) are identical. We have introduced them as separate equations to simplify our calculations; in one case we are determining the value in future dollars and in the other case the value in

THE TIME VALUE
OF MONEY

163

today's dollars. In either case the reason is the same: To compare values on alternative investments and to recognize that the value of a dollar received today is not the same as that of a dollar received at some future date. We must measure the dollar values in dollars of the same time period. Because all present values are comparable (they are all measured in dollars of the same time period), we can add and subtract the present value of inflows and outflows to determine the net present value of an investment.

EXAMPLE

What is the present value of an investment that yields $500 to be received in five years and $1,000 to be received in 10 years if the discount rate is 4 percent? Substituting the values of $n = 5$, $i = 4$ percent, and $FV_5 = 500; and $n = 10$, $i = 4$ percent, and $FV_{10} = 1000 into equation (5–10) and adding these values together, we find

$$PV = \$500 \left[\frac{1}{(1 + .04)^5} \right] + \$1,000 \left[\frac{1}{(1 + .04)^{10}} \right]$$

$$= \$500 \, (PVIF_{4\%, \, 5 \, yr}) + \$1,000 \, (PVIF_{4\%, \, 10 \, yr})$$

$$= \$500(.822) + \$1,000(.676)$$

$$= \$411 + \$676$$

$$= \$1,087$$

Again, present values are comparable because they are measured in the same time period's dollars. ■

■ ANNUITIES

An **annuity** is a series of equal dollar payments for a specified number of years. Because annuities occur frequently in finance—for example, as bond interest payments—we will treat them specially. Although compounding and determining the present value of an annuity can be dealt with using the methods we have just described, these processes can be time consuming, especially for larger annuities. Thus, we have modified the formulas to deal directly with annuities.

Compound Annuities

A **compound annuity** involves depositing or investing an equal sum of money at the end of each year for a certain number of years and allowing it to grow. Perhaps we are saving money for education, a new car, or a vacation home. In any case we want to know how much our savings will have grown by some point in the future.

Actually, we can find the answer by using equation (5–6), our compounding equation, and compounding each of the individual deposits to

Year	0	1	2	3	4	5
Dollar deposits at end of year		500	500	500	500	500
						$ 500.00
						530.00
						562.00
						595.50
						631.00
Future value of the annuity						$2,818.50

its future value. For example, if to provide for a college education we are going to deposit $500 at the end of each year for the next five years in a bank where it will earn 6 percent interest, how much will we have at the end of five years? Compounding each of these values using equation (5–6), we find that we will have $2,818.50 at the end of five years.

$$FV_5 = \$500(1 + .06)^4 + \$500(1 + .06)^3 + \$500(1 + .06)^2 + \$500(1 + .06) + \$500$$

$$= \$500(1.262) + \$500(1.191) + \$500(1.124) + \$500(1.060) + \$500$$

$$= \$631.00 + \$595.50 + \$562.00 + \$530.00 + \$500.00$$

$$= \$2818.50$$

From examining the mathematics involved and the graph of the movement of money through time in Table 5–5, we can see that this procedure can be generalized to

$$FV_n = PMT\left[\sum_{t=0}^{n-1} (1 + i)^t\right]$$ (5–11)

where FV_n = the future value of the annuity at the end of the nth year

PMT = the annuity payment deposited or received at the end of each year

i = the annual interest (or discount) rate

n = the number of years for which the annuity will last

To aid in compounding annuities, the **future-value interest factor for an annuity** for i and n ($FVIFA_{i,n}$), defined as $\left[\sum_{t=0}^{n-1} (1 + i)^t\right]$ is provided in Appendix D for various combinations of n and i; an abbreviated version is shown in Table 5–6.[1]

---

[1]Another useful analytical relationship for FV_n is $FV_n = PMT\left[(1 + i)^n - 1\right]/i$.

TABLE 5–6
$FVIFA_{i,n}$ or the Sum of an
Annuity of $1 for n Years

n	1%	2%	3%	4%	5%	6%	7%	8%	9%	10%
1	1.000	1.000	1.000	1.000	1.000	1.000	1.000	1.000	1.000	1.000
2	2.010	2.020	2.030	2.040	2.050	2.060	2.070	2.080	2.090	2.100
3	3.030	3.060	3.091	3.122	3.152	3.184	3.215	3.246	3.278	3.310
4	4.060	4.122	4.184	4.246	4.310	4.375	4.440	4.506	4.573	4.641
5	5.101	5.204	5.309	5.416	5.526	5.637	5.751	5.867	5.985	6.105
6	6.152	6.308	6.468	6.633	6.802	6.975	7.153	7.336	7.523	7.716
7	7.214	7.434	7.662	7.898	8.142	8.394	8.654	8.923	9.200	9.487
8	8.286	8.583	8.892	9.214	9.549	9.897	10.260	10.637	11.028	11.436
9	9.368	9.755	10.159	10.583	11.027	11.491	11.978	12.488	13.021	13.579
10	10.462	10.950	11.464	12.006	12.578	13.181	13.816	14.487	15.193	15.937
11	11.567	12.169	12.808	13.486	14.207	14.972	15.784	16.645	17.560	18.531
12	12.682	13.412	14.192	15.026	15.917	16.870	17.888	18.977	20.141	21.384
13	13.809	14.680	15.618	16.627	17.713	18.882	20.141	21.495	22.953	24.523
14	14.947	15.974	17.086	18.292	19.598	21.015	22.550	24.215	26.019	27.975
15	16.097	17.293	18.599	20.023	21.578	23.276	25.129	27.152	29.361	31.772

CALCULATOR SOLUTION

Data Input	Function Key
5	N
6	$I\%\ YR$
500	PMT
0	PV
Function Key	Answer
FV	–2818.55

CALCULATOR SOLUTION

Data Input	Function Key
8	N
6	$I\%\ YR$
10,000	FV
0	PV
Function Key	Answer
PMT	–1010.36

Using this new notation, we can rewrite equation (5–11) as follows:

$$FV_n = PMT(FVIFA_{i,n}) \qquad \text{(5–11a)}$$

Reexamining the previous example, in which we determined the value after five years of $500 deposited at the end of each of the next five years in the bank at 6 percent, we would look in the $i = 6\%$ column and $n = 5$ year row and find the value of the $FVIFA_{6\%,\ 5\ yr}$ to be 5.637. Substituting this value into equation (5–11a), we get

$$FV_5 = \$500(5.637)$$
$$= \$2,818.50$$

This is the same answer we obtained earlier using equation (5–6)

Rather than asking how much we will accumulate if we deposit an equal sum in a savings account each year, a more common question is how much we must deposit each year to accumulate a certain amount of savings. This problem frequently occurs with respect to saving for large expenditures and pension funding obligations.

For example, we may know that we need $10,000 for education in eight years; how much must we deposit in the bank at the end of each year at 6 percent interest to have the college money ready? In this case we know the values of n, i, and FV_n in equation (5–11); what we do not know is the value of PMT. Substituting these example values in equation (5–11), we find

$$\$10,000 = PMT\left[\sum_{t=0}^{8-1}(1+.06)^t\right]$$

$$\$10,000 = PMT\ (FVIFA_{6\%,\ 8\ yr})$$

$$\$10,000 = PMT\ (9.897)$$

$$\frac{\$10,000}{9.897} = PMT$$

$$PMT = \$1,010.41$$

Thus, we must deposit $1,010.41 in the bank at the end of each year for eight years at 6 percent interest to accumulate $10,000 at the end of eight years.

EXAMPLE

How much must we deposit in an 8 percent savings account at the end of each year to accumulate $5,000 at the end of ten years? Substituting the values $FV_{10} = \$5,000$, $n = 10$, and $i = 8$ percent into equation (5–11), we find

$$\$5,000 = PMT\left[\sum_{t=0}^{10-1}(1 + .08)^t\right] = PMT(FVIFA_{8\%, 10\ yr})$$

$$\$5,000 = PMT(14.487)$$

$$\frac{\$5,000}{14.487} = PMT$$

$$PMT = \$345.14$$

Thus, we must deposit $345.14 per year for 10 years at 8 percent to accumulate $5,000.

PERSPECTIVE IN FINANCE

A timeline often makes it easier to understand time value of money problems. By visually plotting the flow of money you can better determine which formula to use. Arrows placed above the line are inflows, whereas arrows below the line represent outflows. One thing is certain: Timelines reduce errors.

Present Value of an Annuity

Pension funds, insurance obligations, and interest received from bonds all involve annuities. To compare them, we need to know the present value of each. While we can find this by using the present-value table in Appendix C, this can be time consuming, particularly when the annuity lasts for several years. For example, if we wish to know what $500 received at the end of the next five years is worth to us given the appropriate discount rate of 6 percent, we can simply substitute the appropriate values into equation (5–10), such that

$$PV = \$500\left[\frac{1}{(1 + .06)}\right] + \$500\left[\frac{1}{(1 + .06)^2}\right] + \$500\left[\frac{1}{(1 + .06)^3}\right]$$

$$+ \$500\left[\frac{1}{(1 + .06)^4}\right] + \$500\left[\frac{1}{(1 + .06)^5}\right]$$

$$= \$500(.943) + \$500(.890) + \$500(.840) + \$500(.792) + \$500(.747)$$

$$= \$2106$$

TABLE 5–7
Illustration of a Five-Year
$500 Annuity Discounted to
the Present at 6 Percent

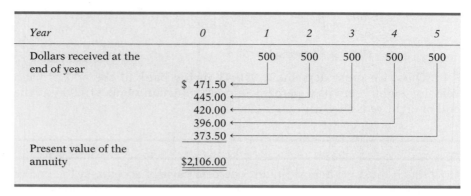

Year	0	1	2	3	4	5
Dollars received at the end of year		500	500	500	500	500
	$ 471.50 ←					
	445.00 ←					
	420.00 ←					
	396.00 ←					
	373.50 ←					
Present value of the annuity	$2,106.00					

Thus, the present value of this annuity is $2,106.00. From examining the mathematics involved and the graph of the movement of these funds through time in Table 5–7, we see that this procedure can be generalized to

$$PV = PMT \left[\sum_{t=0}^{n} \frac{1}{(1+i)^t} \right] \tag{5–12}$$

where PMT = the annuity payment deposited or received at the end of each year

i = the annual discount (or interest) rate

PV = the present value of the future annuity

n = the number of years for which the annuity will last

To simplify the process of determining the present value of an annuity, the **present-value interest factor for an annuity** for i and n

(**$PVIFA_{i,n}$**), defined as $\left[\sum_{t=1}^{n} \frac{1}{(1+i)^t} \right]$ has been compiled for various combinations of i and n in Appendix E with an abbreviated version provided in Table 5–8.[2]

Using this new notation we can rewrite equation (5–12) as follows:

$$PV = PMT (PVIFA_{i,n}) \tag{5–12a}$$

Solving the previous example to find the present value of $500 received at the end of each of the next five years discounted back to the present at 6 percent, we look in the $i = 6\%$ column and $n = 5$ year row and find the $PVIFA_{6\%, 5\ yr}$ to be 4.212. Substituting the appropriate values into equation (5–12a), we find

$$PV = \$500(4.212)$$

$$= \$2,106$$

[2]Another useful analytical relationship for PV is $PV = PMT[1 - 1/(1 + i)^n]/i$.

TABLE 5–8
$PVIFA_{i,n}$ or the Present
Value of an Annuity of $1

n	1%	2%	3%	4%	5%	6%	7%	8%	9%	10%
1	0.990	0.980	0.971	0.962	0.952	0.943	0.935	0.926	0.917	0.909
2	1.970	1.942	1.913	1.886	1.859	1.833	1.808	1.783	1.759	1.736
3	2.941	2.884	2.829	2.775	2.723	2.673	2.624	2.577	2.531	2.487
4	3.902	3.808	3.717	3.630	3.546	3.465	3.387	3.312	3.240	3.170
5	4.853	4.713	4.580	4.452	4.329	4.212	4.100	3.993	3.890	3.791
6	5.795	5.601	5.417	5.242	5.076	4.917	4.767	4.623	4.486	4.355
7	6.728	6.472	6.230	6.002	5.786	5.582	5.389	5.206	5.033	4.868
8	7.652	7.326	7.020	6.733	6.463	6.210	5.971	5.747	5.535	5.335
9	8.566	8.162	7.786	7.435	7.108	6.802	6.515	6.247	5.995	5.759
10	9.471	8.983	8.530	8.111	7.722	7.360	7.024	6.710	6.418	6.145
11	10.368	9.787	9.253	8.760	8.306	7.887	7.499	7.139	6.805	6.495
12	11.255	10.575	9.954	9.385	8.863	8.384	7.943	7.536	7.161	6.814
13	12.134	11.348	10.635	9.986	9.394	8.853	8.358	7.904	7.487	7.103
14	13.004	12.106	11.296	10.563	9.899	9.295	8.746	8.244	7.786	7.367
15	13.865	12.849	11.938	11.118	10.380	9.712	9.108	8.560	8.061	7.606

This, of course, is the same answer we calculated when we individually discounted each cash flow to the present. The reason is that we really only have *one* table; the Table 5–8 value for an *n*-year annuity for any discount rate *i* is merely the sum of the first *n* values in Table 5–4. We can see this by comparing the value in the present-value-of-an-annuity table (Table 5–8) for *i* = 8 percent and *n* = 6 years, which is 4.623, with the sum of the values in the *i* = 8% column and *n* = 1,…, 6 rows of the present-value table (Table 5–4), which is equal to 4.623, as shown in Table 5–9.

EXAMPLE

What is the present value of a 10-year $1,000 annuity discounted back to the present at 5 percent? Substituting *n* = 10 years, *i* = 5 percent, and *PMT* = $1,000 into equation (5–12), we find

$$PV = \$1,000 \left[\sum_{t=1}^{10} \frac{1}{(1+.05)^t} \right] = \$1,000(PVIFA_{5\%,\ 10\ yr})$$

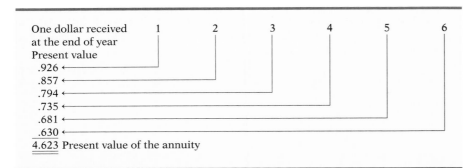

One dollar received at the end of year 1 2 3 4 5 6
Present value
.926 ←
.857 ←
.794 ←
.735 ←
.681 ←
.630 ←
4.623 Present value of the annuity

Determining the value for the $PVIFA_{5\%,\,10\,yr}$ from Table 5–8, row $n = 10$, column $i = 5\%$, and substituting it in, we get

$$PV = \$1,000(7.722)$$
$$= \$7,722$$

Thus, the present value of this annuity is $7,722. ■

As with our other compounding and present-value tables, given any three of the four unknowns in equation (5–12), we can solve for the fourth. In the case of the present-value-of-an-annuity table we may be interested in solving for PMT, if we know i, n, and PV. The financial interpretation of this action would be: How much can be withdrawn, perhaps as a pension or to make loan payments, from account that earns i percent compounded annually for each of the next n years if we wish to have nothing left at the end of n years? For example, if we have $5,000 in an account earning 8 percent interest, how large an annuity can we draw out each year if we want nothing left at the end of five years? In this case the present value, PV, of the annuity is $5,000, $n = 5$ years, $i = 8$ percent, and PMT is unknown. Substituting this into equation (5–12), we find

$$\$5,000 = PMT(3.993)$$
$$\$1,252.19 = PMT$$

Thus, this account will fall to zero at the end of five years if we withdraw $1,252.19 at the end of each year.

■ AMORTIZED LOANS

This procedure of solving for PMT, the annuity payment value when i, n, and PV are known, is also used to determine what payments are associated with paying off a loan in equal installments over time. Loans that are paid off this way, in equal periodic payments, are called *amortized loans*. For example, suppose a firm wants to purchase a piece of machinery. To do this, it borrows $6,000 to be repaid in four equal payments at the end of each of the next four years, and the interest rate that is paid to the lender is 15 percent on the outstanding portion of the loan. To determine what the annual payments associated with the repayment of this debt will be, we simply use equation (5–12) and solve for the value of PMT, the annual annuity. Again we know three of the four values in that equation, PV, i, and n. PV, the present value of the future annuity, is $6,000; i, the annual interest rate, is 15 percent; and n, the number of years for which the annuity will last, is four years. PMT, the annuity payment received (by the lender and paid by the firm) at the end of each year, is unknown. Substituting these values into equation (5–12) we find

$$\$6,000 = PMT\left[\sum_{t=1}^{4}\frac{1}{(1 + .15)^t}\right]$$

Year	Annuity	Interest Portion of the Annuity[a]	Repayment of the Principal Portion of the Annuity[b]	Outstanding Loan Balance after the Annuity Payment
1	$2,101.58	$900.00	$1,201.58	$4,798.42
2	2,101.58	719.76	1,381.82	3,416.60
3	2,101.58	512.49	1,589.09	1,827.51
4	2,101.58	274.07	1,827.51	

[a]The interest portion of the annuity is calculated by multiplying the outstanding loan balance at the beginning of the year by the interest rate of 15 percent. Thus, for year 1 it was $6,000.00 × .15 = $900.00, for year 2 it was $4,798.42 × .15 = $719.76. and so on.

[b]Repayment of the principal portion of the annuity was calculated by subtracting the interest portion of the annuity (column 2) from the annuity (column 1).

$$\$6,000 = PMT\,(PVIFA_{15\%,\ 4\ yr})$$

$$\$6,000 = PMT(2.855)$$

$$\$2,101.58 = PMT$$

To repay the principal and interest on the outstanding loan in four years the annual payments would be $2,101.58. The breakdown of interest and principal payments is given in the *loan amortization schedule* in Table 5–10, with very minor rounding error. As you can see, the interest payment declines each year as the loan outstanding declines.

CALCULATOR SOLUTION

Data Input	Function Key
4	N
15	I% YR
6000	PV
0	FV
Function Key	Answer
PMT	–2101.59

PRESENT VALUE OF AN UNEVEN STREAM

While some projects will involve a single cash flow and some annuities, many projects will involve uneven cash flows over several years. Chapter 9, which examines investments in fixed assets, presents this situation repeatedly. There we will be comparing not only the present value of cash flows between projects but also the cash inflows and outflows within a particular project, trying to determine that project's present value. However, this will not be difficult because the present value of any cash flow is measured in today's dollars and thus can be compared, through addition for inflows and subtraction for outflows, to the present value of any other cash flow also measured in today's dollars. For example, if we wished to find the present value of the following cash flows

Year	Cash Flow	Year	Cash Flow
1	$500	6	500
2	200	7	500
3	–400	8	500
4	500	9	500
5	500	10	500

TABLE 5–11
Illustration of an Example
of Present Value of an
Uneven Stream Involving One
Annuity Discounted to
Present at 6 Percent

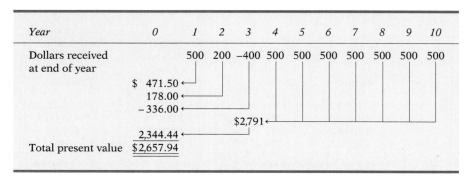

Year	0	1	2	3	4	5	6	7	8	9	10
Dollars received at end of year				500	200	–400	500	500	500	500	500	500	500

$ 471.50
178.00
– 336.00
$2,791
2,344.44

Total present value $2,657.94

given a 6 percent discount rate, we would merely discount the flows back to the present and total them by adding in the positive flows and subtracting the negative ones. However, this problem is complicated by the annuity of $500 that runs from years 4 through 10. To accommodate this, we can first discount the annuity back to the beginning of period 4 (or end of period 3) by multiplying it by the value of $PVIFA_{6\%,\ 7\ yr}$ and get its present value at that point in time. We then multiply this value times the $PVIF_{6\%,\ 3\ yr}$ in order to bring this single cash flow (which is the present value of the 7-year annuity) back to the present. In effect we discount twice, first back to the end of period 3, then back to the present. This is shown graphically in Table 5–11 and numerically in Table 5–12. Thus, the present value of this uneven stream of cash flows is $2,657.94.

EXAMPLE

What is the present value of an investment involving $200 received at the end of years 1 through 5, a $300 cash outflow at the end of year 6, and $500 received at the end of years 7 through 10, given a 5 percent discount rate? Here we have two annuities, one that can be discounted directly back to the present by multiplying it by the value of the $PVIFA_{5\%,\ 5\ yr}$ and one that must be discounted twice to bring it back to the present. This second annuity, which is a four-year annuity, must first be discounted back to the beginning of period 7 (or end of period 6) by multiplying it by the value of the $PVIFA_{5\%,\ 4\ yr}$. Then the present value of this annuity at the end of period 6 (which can be viewed as a single cash flow) must be discounted back to the present by multiplying it by the value of the $PVIF_{5\%,\ 6\ yr}$.

TABLE 5–12
Determination of Present
Value of an Example with
Uneven Stream Involving One
Annuity Discounted to
Present at 6 Percent

1. Present value of $500 received at the end of one year = $500(.943) =	$ 471.50
2. Present value of $200 received at the end of two years = $200(.890) =	178.00
3. Present value of a $400 outflow at the end of three years = –400(.840) =	– 336.00
4. (a) Value at the end of year 3 of a $500 annuity, years 4 through 10 = $500(5.582) = $2,791.00	
(b) Present value of $2,791.00 received at the end of year 3 = $2,791(.840) =	2,344.44
5. Total present value =	$2,657.94

To arrive at the total present value of this investment, we subtract the present value of the $300 cash outflow at the end of year 6 from the sum of the present value of the two annuities. Table 5–13 shows this graphically; Table 5–14 gives the calculations. Thus, the present value of this series of cash flows is $1,964.66. ■

■ PERPETUITIES

A **perpetuity** is an annuity that continues forever; that is, every year from its establishment this investment pays the same dollar amount. An example of a perpetuity is preferred stock that pays a constant dollar

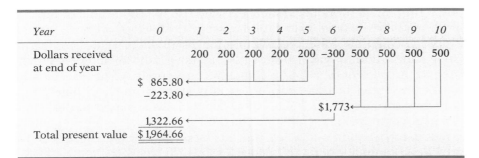

Year	0	1	2	3	4	5	6	7	8	9	10
Dollars received at end of year		200	200	200	200	200	–300	500	500	500	500
	$ 865.80 ←										
	–223.80 ←										
							$1,773←				
	1,322.66 ←										
Total present value	$ 1,964.66										

TABLE 5–13
Illustration of an Example of Present Value of an Uneven Stream Involving Two Annuities Discounted to Present at 5 Percent.

THE TIME VALUE
OF MONEY

173

TABLE 5–14
Determination of Present
Value of an Example with
Uneven Stream Involving Two
Annuities Discounted to
Present at 5 Percent

1. Present value of first annuity, years 1 through 5 = $200(4.329)	$ 865.80
2. Present value of $300 cash outflow = –$300(.746) =	– 223.80
3. (a) Value at end of year 6 of second annuity, years 7 through 10 = $500(3.546) = $1,773.00	
(b) Present value of $1,773.00 received at the end of year 6 = $1,773.00(.746) =	1,322.66
4. Total present value =	$1,964.66

dividend infinitely. Determining the present value of a perpetuity is delightfully simple; we merely need to divide the constant flow by the discount rate. For example, the present value of a $100 perpetuity discounted back to the present at 5 percent is $100/.05 = $2,000. Thus, the equation representing the present value of a perpetuity is

$$PV = \frac{PP}{i} \qquad (5\text{–}13)$$

where PV = the present value of the perpetuity
           PP = the constant dollar amount provided by
                 the perpetuity
            i = the annual interest (or discount) rate

EXAMPLE

What is the present value of a $500 perpetuity discounted back to the present at 8 percent? Substituting PP = $500 and i = .08 into equation (5–13), we find

$$PV = \frac{\$500}{.08} = \$6,250$$

Thus, the present value of this perpetuity is $6,250. ∎

SUMMARY

To make decisions, financial managers must compare the costs and benefits of alternatives that do not occur during the same time period. Whether to make profitable investments or to take advantage of favorable interest rates, financial decision making requires an understanding of the time value of money. Managers who use the time value of money in all of their financial calculations assure themselves of more logical decisions. The time value process first makes all dollar values comparable; because money has a time value, it moves all dollar flows either back to the present or out to a common future date. All time value formulas presented in this chapter actually stem from the single compounding formula $FV_n = PV(1 + i)^n$. The formulas are used to deal simply with common financial situations, for example, discounting single flows, compounding annuities, and discounting annuities. Table 5–15 provides a summary of these calculations.

TABLE 5–15
Summary of Time Value of
Money Equations*

Calculation	Equation
Future value of a single payment	$FV_n = PV(1 + i)^n = PV(FVIF_{i,n})$
Future value of a single payment with nonannual compounding	$FV_n = PV\left(1 + \dfrac{i}{m}\right)^{mn}$
Present value of a single payment	$PV = FV_n\left[\dfrac{1}{(1 + i)^n}\right] = FV_n(PVIF_{i,n})$
Future value of an annuity	$FV_n = PMT\left[\displaystyle\sum_{t=0}^{n-1}(1 + i)^t\right] = PMT\,(FVIFA_{i,n})$
Present value of an annuity	$PV = PMT\left[\displaystyle\sum_{t=1}^{n}\dfrac{1}{(1 + i)^t}\right] = PMT\,(PVIFA_{i,n})$
Present value of a perpetuity	$PV = \dfrac{PP}{i}$

Notation:
FV_n = the future value of the investment at the end of n years
n = the number of years until payment will be received or during which compounding occurs
i = the annual interest or discount rate
PV = the present value of the future sum of money
m = the number of times compounding occurs during the year
PMT = the annuity payment deposited or received at the end of each year
PP = the constant dollar amount provided by the perpetuity

*Related tables appear in Appendixes B through E at the end of the book.

STUDY QUESTIONS

5–1. What is the time value of money? Why is it so important?

5–2. The processes of discounting and compounding are related. Explain this relationship.

5–3. How would an increase in the interest rate (i) or a decrease in the holding period (n) affect the future value (FV_n) of a sum of money? Explain why.

5–4. Suppose you were considering depositing your savings in one of three banks, all of which pay 5 percent interest; bank A compounds annually, bank B compounds semiannually, and bank C compounds continuously. Which bank would you choose? Why?

5–5. What is the relationship between the $PVIF_{i,n}$ (Table 5–4) and the $PVIFA_{i,n}$ (Table 5–8)? What is the $PVIFA_{10\%,\,10\,\text{yr}}$? Add up the values of the $PVIF_{10\%,n}$, for $n = 1, ..., 10$. What is this value? Why do these values have the relationship they do?

5–6. What is an annuity? Give some examples of annuities. Distinguish between an annuity and a perpetuity.

5–7. What does continuous compounding mean?

SELF-TEST PROBLEMS

ST-1. You place $25,000 in a savings account paying annual compound interest of 8 percent for three years and then move it into a savings account that pays 10 percent interest compounded annually. How much will your money have grown at the end of six years?

ST-2. You purchase a boat for $35,000 and pay $5,000 down and agree to pay the rest over the next 10 years in 10 equal annual end of year payments that include principal payments plus 13 percent compound interest on the unpaid balance. What will be the amount of each payment?

ST-3. For an investment to grow eightfold in nine years, at what rate would it have to grow?

STUDY PROBLEMS

5–1. *(Compound Interest)* To what amount will the following investments accumulate?
   a. $5,000 invested for 10 years at 10 percent compounded annually
   b. $8,000 invested for 7 years at 8 percent compounded annually
   c. $775 invested for 12 years at 12 percent compounded annually
   d. $21,000 invested for 5 years at 5 percent compounded annually

5–2. *(Compound Value Solving for n)* How many years will the following take?
   a. $500 to grow to $1,039.50 if invested at 5 percent compounded annually
   b. $35 to grow to $53.87 if invested at 9 percent compounded annually
   c. $100 to grow to $298.60 if invested at 20 percent compounded annually
   d. $53 to grow to $78.76 if invested at 2 percent compounded annually

5–3. *(Compound Value Solving for i)* At what annual rate would the following have to be invested?
   a. $500 to grow to $1,948.00 in 12 years
   b. $300 to grow to $422.10 in 7 years
   c. $50 to grow to $280.20 in 20 years
   d. $200 to grow to $497.60 in 5 years

5–4. *(Present Value)* What is the present value of the following future amounts?
   a. $800 to be received 10 years from now discounted back to present at 10 percent
   b. $300 to be received 5 years from now discounted back to present at 5 percent
   c. $1,000 to be received 8 years from now discounted back to present at 3 percent
   d. $1,000 to be received 8 years from now discounted back to present at 20 percent

5–5. *(Compound Annuity)* What is the accumulated sum of each of the following streams of payments?
   a. $500 a year for 10 years compounded annually at 5 percent
   b. $100 a year for 5 years compounded annually at 10 percent
   c. $35 a year for 7 years compounded annually at 7 percent
   d. $25 a year for 3 years compounded annually at 2 percent

5–6. *(Present Value of an Annuity)* What is the present value of the following annuities?
   a. $2,500 a year for 10 years discounted back to the present at 7 percent
   b. $70 a year for 3 years discounted back to the present at 3 percent
   c. $280 a year for 7 years discounted back to the present at 6 percent
   d. $500 a year for 10 years discounted back to the present at 10 percent

5–7. *(Compound Value)* Brian Mosallam, who recently sold his Porsche, placed $10,000 in a savings account paying annual compound interest of 6 percent.

a. Calculate the amount of money that will have accrued if he leaves the money in the bank for 1, 5, and 15 years.

b. If he moves his money into an account that pays 8 percent or one that pays 10 percent, rework part (a) using these new interest rates.

c. What conclusions can you draw about the relationship between interest rates, time, and future sums from the calculations you have done above?

5–8. *(Compound Interest with Nonannual Periods)* Calculate the amount of money that will be in each of the following accounts at the end of the given deposit period.

Account	Amount Deposited	Annual Interest Rate	Compounding Period (Compounded Every __ Months)	Deposit Period (Years)
Theodore Logan III	$ 1,000	10%	12	10
Vernell Coles	95,000	12	1	1
Thomas Elliott	8,000	12	2	2
Wayne Robinson	120,000	8	3	2
Eugene Chung	30,000	10	6	4
Kelly Cravens	15,000	12	4	3

5–9. *(Compound Interest with Nonannual Periods)*

a. Calculate the future sum of $5,000, given that it will be held in the bank five years at an annual interest rate of 6 percent.

b. Recalculate part (a) using a compounding period that is (1) semiannual and (2) bimonthly.

c. Recalculate parts (a) and (b) for a 12 percent annual interest rate.

d. Recalculate part (a) using a time horizon of 12 years (annual interest rate is still 6 percent).

e. With respect to the effect of changes in the stated interest rate and holding periods on future sums in parts (c) and (d), what conclusions do you draw when you compare these figures with the answers found in parts (a) and (b)?

5–10. *(Solving for i with Annuities)* Nicki Johnson, a sophomore mechanical engineering student, receives a call from an insurance agent, who believes that Nicki is an older woman ready to retire from teaching. He talks to her about several annuities that she could buy that would guarantee her an annual fixed income. The annuities are as follows:

Annuity	Initial Payment into Annuity (at t = 0)	Amount of Money Received per Year	Duration of Annuity (Years)
A	$50,000	$8,500	12
B	$60,000	$7,000	25
C	$70,000	$8,000	20

If Nicki could earn 11 percent on her money by placing it in a savings account, should she place it instead in any of the annuities? Which ones, if any? Why?

5–11. *(Future Value)* Sales of a new finance book were 15,000 copies this year and were expected to increase by 20 percent per year. What are expected sales during each of the next three years? Graph this sales trend and explain.

5–12. *(Future Value)* Reggie Jackson, formerly of the New York Yankees, hit 41 home runs in 1980. If his home-run output grew at a rate of 10 percent per year, what would it have been over the following five years?

5–13. *(Loan Amortization)* Mr. Bill S. Preston, Esq., purchased a new house for $80,000. He paid $20,000 down and agreed to pay the rest over the next 25 years in 25 equal annual end of year payments that include principal payments plus 9 percent compound interest on the unpaid balance. What will these equal payments be?

5–14. *(Solving for PMT of an Annuity)* To pay for your child's education you wish to have accumulated $15,000 at the end of 15 years. To do this you plan on depositing an equal amount into the bank at the end of each year. If the bank is willing to pay 6 percent compounded annually, how much must you deposit each year to obtain your goal?

5–15. *(Solving for i in Compound Interest)* If you were offered $1,079.50 ten years from now in return for an investment of $500 currently, what annual rate of interest would you earn if you took the offer?

5–16. *(Future Value of an Annuity)* In 10 years you are planning on retiring and buying a house in Oviedo, Florida. The house you are looking at currently costs $100,000 and is expected to increase in value each year at a rate of 5 percent. Assuming you can earn 10 percent annually on your investments, how much must you invest at the end of each of the next 10 years to be able to buy your dream home when you retire?

5–17. *(Compound Value)* The Aggarwal Corporation needs to save $10 million to retire a $10 million mortgage that matures on December 31, 2002. To retire this mortgage, the company plans to put a fixed amount into an account at the end of each year for 10 years, with the first payment occurring on December 31, 1993. The Aggarwal Corporation expects to earn 9 percent annually on the money in this account. What equal annual contribution must it make to this account to accumulate the $10 million by December 31, 2002?

5–18. *(Compound Interest with Nonannual Periods)* After examining the various personal loan rates available to you, you find that you can borrow funds from a finance company at 12 percent compounded monthly or from a bank at 13 percent compounded annually. Which alternative is more attractive?

5–19. *(Present Value of an Uneven Stream of Payments)* You are given three investment alternatives to analyze. The cash flows from these three investments are as follows:

End of Year	Investment		
	A	B	C
1	$10,000		$10,000
2	10,000		
3	10,000		
4	10,000		
5	10,000	$10,000	
6		10,000	50,000
7		10,000	
8		10,000	
9		10,000	
10		10,000	10,000

Assuming a 20 percent discount rate, find the present value of each investment.

5–20. *(Present Value)* The Kumar Corporation is planning on issuing bonds that pay no interest but can be converted into $1,000 at maturity, seven years from their purchase. To price these bonds competitively with other bonds of equal risk, it is determined that they should yield 10 percent, compounded annually. At what price should the Kumar Corporation sell these bonds?

5–21. *(Perpetuities)* What is the present value of the following?
   a. A $300 perpetuity discounted back to the present at 8 percent
   b. A $1,000 perpetuity discounted back to the present at 12 percent
   c. A $100 perpetuity discounted back to the present at 9 percent
   d. A $95 perpetuity discounted back to the present at 5 percent

5–22. *(Continuous Compounding)* What is the value of $500 after five years if it is invested at 10 percent compounded continuously? (If you don't have a calculator capable of solving this problem, simply set it up.)

5–23. *(Solving for n with Nonannual Periods)* About how many years would it take for your investment to grow fourfold if it were invested at 16 percent compounded semiannually?

5–24. *(Bond Values)* You are examining three bonds with par value of $1,000 (you receive $1,000 at maturity) and are concerned with what would happen to their market value if interest rates (or the market discount rate) changed. The three bonds are
   Bond A—A bond with 3 years left to maturity that pays 10 percent per year compounded semiannually,
   Bond B—A bond with 7 years left to maturity that pays 10 percent per year compounded semiannually,
   Bond C—A bond with 20 years left to maturity that pays 10 percent per year compounded semiannually.
   What would be the value of these bonds if the market discount rate were
   a. 10 percent per year compounded semiannually?
   b. 4 percent per year compounded semiannually?
   c. 16 percent per year compounded semiannually?
   d. What observations can you make about these results?

5–25. *(Complex Present Value)* How much do you have to deposit today so that beginning 11 years from now you can withdraw $10,000 a year for the next five years (periods 11 through 15) plus an *additional* amount of $20,000 in that last year (period 15)? Assume an interest rate of 6 percent.

5–26. *(Loan Amortization)* On December 31, Beth Klemkosky bought a yacht for $50,000, paying $10,000 down and agreeing to pay the balance in 10 equal annual end of year installments that include both the principal and 10 percent interest on the declining balance. How big would the annual payments be?

5–27. *(Solving for i of an Annuity)* You lend a friend $30,000, which your friend will repay in five equal annual end of year payments of $10,000, with the first payment to be received one year from now. What rate of return does your loan receive?

5–28. *(Solving for i in Compound Interest)* You lend a friend $10,000, for which your friend will repay you $27,027 at the end of five years. What interest rate are you charging your "friend"?

5–29. *(Loan Amortization)* A firm borrows $25,000 from the bank at 12 percent compounded annually to purchase some new machinery. This loan is to be repaid in equal annual installments at the end of each year over the next five years. How much will each annual payment be?

5–30. *(Present Value Comparison)* You are offered $1,000 today, $10,000 in 12 years, or $25,000 in twenty-five years. Assuming that you can earn 11 percent on your money, which should you choose?

5–31. *(Compound Annuity)* You plan on buying some property in Florida five years from today. To do this you estimate that you will need $20,000 at that time for the purchase. You would like to accumulate these funds by making equal annual deposits in your savings account, which pays 12 percent annually. If you make your first deposit at the end of this year and you would like your account to reach $20,000 when the final deposit is made, what will be the amount of your deposits?

5–32. *(Complex Present Value)* You would like to have $50,000 in 15 years. To accumulate this amount you plan to deposit each year an equal sum in the bank, which will earn 7 percent interest compounded annually. Your first payment will be made at the end of the year.
 a. How much must you deposit annually to accumulate this amount?
 b. If you decide to make a large lump-sum deposit today instead of the annual deposits, how large should this lump-sum deposit be? (Assume you can earn 7 percent on this deposit.)
 c. At the end of five years you will receive $10,000 and deposit this in the bank toward your goal of $50,000 at the end of 15 years. In addition to this deposit, how much must you deposit in equal annual deposits to reach your goal? (Again assume you can earn 7 percent on this deposit.)

5–33. *(Comprehensive Present Value)* You are trying to plan for retirement in 10 years, and currently you have $100,000 in a savings account and $300,000 in stocks. In addition you plan on adding to your savings by depositing $10,000 per year in your savings account at the end of each of the next five years and then $20,000 per year at the end of each year for the final five years until retirement.
 a. Assuming your savings account returns 7 percent compounded annually while your investment in stocks will return 12 percent compounded annually, how much will you have at the end of 10 years? (Ignore taxes.)
 b. If you expect to live for 20 years after you retire, and at retirement you deposit all of your savings in a bank account paying 10 percent, how much can you withdraw each year after retirement (20 equal withdrawals beginning one year after you retire) to end up with a zero balance at death?

5–34. *(Loan Amortization)* On December 31, Son-Nan Chen borrowed $100,000, agreeing to repay this sum in 20 equal annual end of year installments that include both the principal and 15 percent interest on the declining balance. How large will the annual payments be?

5–35. *(Loan Amortization)* To buy a new house you must borrow $150,000. To do this you take out a $150,000, 30-year, 10 percent mortgage. Your mortgage payments, which are made at the end of each year (one payment each year), include both principal and 10 percent interest on the declining balance. How large will your annual payments be?

5–36. *(Present Value)* The state lottery's million-dollar payout provides for one million dollars to be paid over 19 years in $50,000 amounts. The first $50,000 payment is made immediately and the 19 remaining $50,000 payments occur at the end of each of the next 19 years. If 10 percent is the appropriate discount rate, what is the present value of this stream of cash flows? If 20 percent is the appropriate discount rate, what is the present value of the cash flows?

5–37. *(Solving for i in Compound Interest—Financial Calculator Needed)* In September 1963 the first issue of the comic book *X-MEN* was issued. The original price for that issue was 12 cents. By September 1992, 29 years later, the value of this comic book had risen to $990. What annual rate of interest would you have earned if you had bought the comic in 1963 and sold it in 1992?

5–38. *(Comprehensive Present Value)* You have just inherited a large sum of money and you are trying to determine how much you should save for retirement and how much you can spend now. For retirement you will deposit today (January 1, 1994) a lump sum in a bank account paying 10 percent compounded annually. You don't plan on touching this deposit until you retire in five years (January 1, 1999), and you plan on living for 20 additional years and then dropping dead on December 31, 2018. During your retirement you would like to receive income of $50,000 per year to be received the first day of each year, with the first payment on January 1, 1999, and the last payment on January 1, 2018. Complicating this objective is your desire to have one final three-year fling during which time you'd like to track down all the original members of "Leave It to Beaver" and "The Brady Bunch" and get their autographs. To finance this you want to receive $250,000 on January 1, 2014, and *nothing* on January 1, 2015 and January 1, 2016, as you will be on the road. In addition, after you pass on (January 1, 2019), you would like to have a total of $100,000 to leave to your children.

  a. How much must you deposit in the bank at 10 percent on January 1, 1994, to achieve your goal? (Use a timeline to answer this question.)

  b. What kinds of problems are associated with this analysis and its assumptions?

SUGGESTED APPLICATION FOR *DISCLOSURE*®
Drawing from *Disclosure*, obtain the annual balance sheet for Marriott. Assume the corporation is able to renegotiate the amount listed as long-term debt as follows: 12 percent annual interest with the amount to be repaid in equal annual installments at the end of each year over the next 20 years. How much will each annual payment be?

SELF-TEST SOLUTIONS

SS-1. This is a compound interest problem in which you must first find the future value of $25,000 growing at 8 percent compounded annually for 3 years and then allow that future value to grow for an additional three years at 10 percent. First, the value of the $25,000 after three years growing at 8 percent is

$$FV_3 = PV(1 + i)^n$$

$$FV_3 = \$25,000(1 + .08)^3$$

$$FV_3 = \$25,000(1.260)$$

$$FV_3 = \$31,500$$

Thus, after three years you have $31,500. Now this amount is allowed to grow for three years at 10 percent. Plugging this into equation (5–6), with $PV = \$31,500$, $i = 10$ percent, $n = 3$ years, we solve for FV_3:

$$FV_3 = \$31,500(1 + .10)^3$$

$$FV_3 = \$31,500(1.331)$$

$$FV_3 = \$41,926.50$$

Thus, after six years the $25,000 will have grown to $41,926.50.

SS-2. This loan amortization problem is actually just a present-value-of-an-annuity problem in which we know the values of i, n, and PV and are solving for PMT. In this case the value of i is 13 percent, n is 10 years, and PV is \$30,000. Substituting these values into equation (5–12) we find

$$\$30,000 = PMT\left[\sum_{t=1}^{10} \frac{1}{(1+.13)^t}\right]$$

$$\$30,000 = PMT(5.426)$$

$$\$5528.93 = PMT$$

SS-3. This is a simple compound interest problem in which FV_9 is eight times larger than PV. Here again three of the four variables are known: $n = 9$ years, $FV_9 = 8$, and $PV = 1$, and we are solving for i. Substituting these values into equation (5–6) we find

$$FV_9 = PV(1+i)^n$$

$$FV_9 = PV\,(FVIF_{i,n})$$

$$8 = 1(FVIF_{i,\,9\,yr})$$

$$8.00 = FVIF_{i,\,9\,yr}$$

Thus we are looking for an $FVIF_{i,\,9\,yr}$ with a value of 8 in Appendix B, which occurs in the 9-year row. If we look in the 9-year row for a value of 8.00, we find it in the 26% column (8.004). Thus, the answer is 26 percent.

CHAPTER 6
VALUATION AND CHARACTERISTICS OF BONDS

• Definitions of Value • Valuation: An Overview • Valuation: The Basic
Process • Terminology and Characteristics of Bonds • Types of Bonds
• Bond Valuation • Bondholders' Expected Rates of Return • Bond
Valuation: Three Important Relationships

What determines the value or price of an asset, such as a bond or stock
or land? Why does the value of an asset change so radically at times?
For example, why did IBM common stock sell for about $100 in 1992
but for only $50 in early 1993? Knowing the fair value or price of an
asset is no easy matter. The *Maxims* of the French writer La
Rouchefoucauld, written over three centuries ago, still speak to us: "The
greatest of all gifts is the power to estimate things at their true worth."

In this chapter we examine the concepts of and procedures for valuing an asset and apply these ideas to valuing bonds, one form of a company's long-term debt. Then in Chapter 7, we continue our study of valuation when we look at valuing both preferred stock and common stock.

Understanding how to value financial securities is essential if managers are to meet the objective of maximizing the value of the firm. If they
are to maximize the investor's value, they must know what drives the
value of an asset. Specifically, they need to understand how bonds and
stocks are valued in the marketplace; otherwise, they cannot act in the
best interest of the firm's investors.

In this chapter, we will undertake to do the following:

1. Examine a variety of definitions given for the term value, including
   book value, liquidation value, market value, and intrinsic value.

2. Explain the basic process for valuing an asset.
3. Develop an understanding of the characteristics of bonds.
4. Describe the different types of bonds.
5. Learn how to value bonds.
6. Examine the concept of the bondholder's *expected* rate of return.
7. Explain three important relationships that exist in bond valuation.

■ DEFINITIONS OF VALUE

The term *value* is often used in different contexts, depending on its application. Examples of different uses of this term include following:

Book value is the value of an asset as shown on a firm's balance sheet. It represents the historical cost of the asset rather than its current worth. For instance, the book value of a company's preferred stock is the amount the investors originally paid for the stock and therefore the amount the firm received when the stock was issued.

Liquidation value is the dollar sum that could be realized if an asset were sold individually and not as part of a going concern. For example, if a firm's operations were discontinued and its assets were divided up and sold, the sales price would represent the asset's liquidation value.

Market value of an asset is the observed value for the asset in the marketplace. This value is determined by supply and demand forces working together in the marketplace, where buyers and sellers negotiate a mutually acceptable price for the asset. For instance, the market price for Ford common stock on March 22, 1993, was $52. This price was reached by a large number of buyers and sellers working through the New York Stock Exchange. In theory, a market price exists for all assets. However, many assets have no readily observable market price because trading seldom occurs. For instance, the market price for the common stock of Blanks Engraving, a Dallas-based family-owned firm, would be more difficult to establish than the market value of J. C. Penney's common stock.

The intrinsic or economic value of an asset can be defined as the present value of the asset's expected future cash flows. This value is the amount the investor considers to be a **fair value,** given the amount, timing, and riskiness of future cash flows. Once the investor has estimated the intrinsic value of a security, this value could be compared with its market value when available. If the intrinsic value is greater than the market value, then the security is undervalued in the eyes of the investor. Should the market value exceed the investor's intrinsic value, then the security is overvalued.

We hasten to add that if the securities market is working efficiently, the market value and the intrinsic value of a security will be equal. Whenever a security's intrinsic value differs from its current market price, the competition among investors seeking opportunities to make a profit will quickly drive the market price back to its intrinsic value. Thus, we may define an **efficient market** as one in which the values of all securities at any instant fully reflect all available public information, which results in the market value and the intrinsic value being the same. If the markets are efficient, it is extremely difficult for an investor to make extra profits from an ability to predict prices.

BACK TO THE FUNDAMENTALS

The fact that investors have difficulty identifying stocks that are undervalued relates to **Axiom 6: Efficient Capital Markets—The Markets Are Quick and the Prices Are Right.** In an efficient market, the price reflects all available public information about the security, and therefore it is priced fairly.

The idea of market efficiency has been the backdrop for an intense battle between professional investors and university professors. The academic community has contended that someone throwing darts at the list of securities in *The Wall Street Journal* could do as well as a professional money manager. Market professionals retort that academicians are grossly mistaken in this view. The war has been intense but also one that the student of finance should find intriguing, and it can be followed each month in *The Wall Street Journal*, where the investment performance of dart throwers and different professional investors are compared. Through March 1993, there had been 34 contests between these rivals. The score: Nineteen for the professional managers and 15 for the dart throwers.

PERSPECTIVE IN FINANCE

Intrinsic value is the present value of expected future cash flows. This statement is true regardless of what type of asset we are valuing. If you remember only one thing from this chapter, remember that intrinsic value is the present value of expected future cash flows.

■ VALUATION: AN OVERVIEW

For our purposes, *the value of an asset is its intrinsic value or the present value of its expected future cash flows*, where these cash flows are discounted back to the present using the investor's required rate of return. This statement is true for valuing all assets and serves as the basis of almost all that we do in finance. Thus, value is affected by three elements:

1. The amount and timing of the asset's expected cash flows
2. The riskiness of these cash flows
3. The investor's required rate of return for undertaking the investment

The first two factors are characteristics of the asset; the third one, the required rate of return, is the minimum rate of return necessary to attract an investor to purchase or hold a security. This rate must be high enough to compensate the investor for the risk perceived in the asset's future cash flows. (The required rate of return is explained more fully in Chapter 8.)

BACK TO THE FUNDAMENTALS

Our discussions should remind us of three of our axioms that help us understand finance:

Axiom 1: The Risk-Return Tradeoff—We Won't Take on Additional Risk Unless We Expect to be Compensated with Additional Return.

Axiom 2: The Time Value of Money—A Dollar Received Today is Worth More than a Dollar Received in the Future.

Axiom 3: Cash Is King—Measuring the Timing of Costs and Benefits.

Determining the economic worth or value of an asset always relies on these three axioms. Without them, we would have no basis for explaining value. With them, we can know that the amount and timing of cash, not earnings, drive value. Also, we must be rewarded for taking risk; otherwise, we will not invest.

Figure 6–1 depicts the basic factors involved in valuation. As the figure shows, finding the value of an asset involves:

1. Assessing the asset's characteristics, which include the amount and timing of the expected cash flows and the riskiness of these cash flows;

2. Determining the investor's required rate of return, which embodies the investor's attitude about assuming risk and perception of the riskiness of the asset; and

FIGURE 6–1
Basic Factors Determining
an Asset's Value

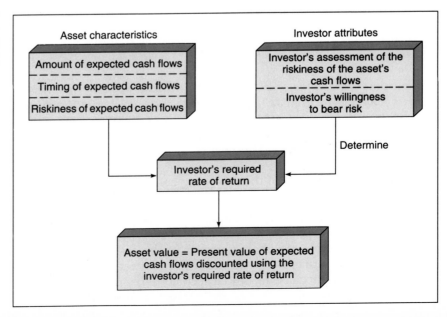

3. Discounting the expected cash flows back to the present, using the investor's required rate of return as the discount rate.

<u>PERSPECTIVE IN FINANCE</u>

Intrinsic value is a function of the cash flows yet to be received, the riskiness of these cash flows, and the investor's required rate of return.

■ VALUATION: THE BASIC PROCESS

The valuation process can be described as follows: It is assigning value to an asset by calculating the present value of its expected future cash flows using the investor's required rate of return as the discount rate. The investor's required rate of return, k, is determined by the level of the risk-free rate of interest and the risk premium that the investor feels is necessary to compensate for the risks assumed in owning the asset. Therefore, a basic security valuation model can be defined mathematically as follows:

$$V = \frac{C_1}{(1 + k)^1} + \frac{C_2}{(1 + k)^2} + \ldots + \frac{C_n}{(1 + k)^n} \qquad (6\text{–}1)$$

or

$$V = \sum_{t=1}^{n} \frac{C_t}{(1 + k)^t}$$

where C_t = cash flow to be received at time t.

V = the intrinsic value or present value of an asset producing expected future cash flows, C_t, in years 1 through n.

k = the investor's required rate of return.

Using equation (6–1), there are three basic steps in the valuation process:

Step 1: Estimate the C_t in equation (6–1), which is the amount and timing of the future cash flows the security is expected to provide.

Step 2: Determine k, the investor's required rate of return.

Step 3: Calculate the intrinsic value, V, as the present value of expected future cash flows discounted at the investor's required rate of return.

Equation (6–1), which measures the present value of future cash flows, is the basis of the valuation process. It is the most important equation in this chapter, because all the remaining equations in this chapter and in Chapter 7 and 8 are merely reformulations of this one equation. If we understand equation (6–1), all the valuation work we do, and a host of other topics as well, will be much clearer in our minds. With the foregoing brief but important principles of valuation as our foundation, let's now look at the nature of bonds and how they are valued.

■ TERMINOLOGY AND CHARACTERISTICS OF BONDS

Before applying our valuation expertise to valuing bonds, we first need to understand the terminology related to bonds. Also, we should be apprised of the different types of bonds that exist. Then we will be better prepared to determine the value of a bond.

When a firm or nonprofit institution needs financing, one source is **bonds.** This type of financing instrument is simply a long-term promissory note, issued by the borrower, promising to pay its holder a predetermined and fixed amount of interest each year. Some of the more important terms and characteristics that you might hear about bonds are as follows:

- Claims on assets and income
- Par value
- Coupon interest rate
- Maturity
- Indenture
- Current yield
- Bond ratings

Let's consider each in turn.

Claims on Assets and Income

In the case of insolvency, claims of debt in general, including bonds, are honored before those of both common stock and preferred stock. However, different types of debt may also have a hierarchy among themselves as to the order of their claim on assets.

Bonds also have a claim on income that comes ahead of common and preferred stock. In general if interest on bonds is not paid, the bond trustees can classify the firm insolvent and force it into bankruptcy. Thus, the bondholder's claim on income is more likely to be honored than that of common and preferred stockholders, whose dividends are paid at the discretion of the firm's management.

Par Value

The **par value** of a bond is its face value that is returned to the bondholder at maturity. In general, corporate bonds are issued in denominations of $1,000, although there are some exceptions to this rule. Also, when bond prices are quoted, either by financial managers or in the financial press, prices are generally expressed as a percentage of the bond's par value. For example, a Detroit Edison bond that pays $90 per year interest and matures in 1999 was recently quoted in *The Wall Street Journal* as selling for 95⅛. That does not mean you can buy the bond for $95.125. It means that this bond is selling for 95⅛ percent of its par value of $1,000. Hence, the market price of this bond is actually $951.25. At maturity in 1999, the bondholder will receive the $1,000.

Coupon Interest Rate

The *coupon interest rate* on a bond indicates the percentage of the par value of the bond that will be paid out annually in the form of interest. Thus, regardless of what happens to the price of a bond with an 8 percent coupon interest rate and a $1,000 par value, it will pay out $80 annually in interest until maturity (.08 × $1,000 = $80).

Maturity

The **maturity** of a bond indicates the length of time until the bond issuer returns the par value to the bondholder and terminates or redeems the bond.

Indenture

An **indenture** is the legal agreement between the firm issuing the bonds and the bond trustee who represents the bondholders. The indenture provides the specific terms of the loan agreement, including a description of the bonds, the rights of the bondholders, the rights of the issuing firm, and the responsibilities of the trustee. This legal document may run 100 pages or more in length, with the majority of it devoted to defining protective provisions for the bondholder. The bond trustee, usually a banking institution or trust company, is then assigned the task of overseeing the relationship between the bondholder and the issuing firm, protecting the bondholder, and seeing that the terms of the indenture are carried out.

Typically, the restrictive provisions included in the indenture attempt to protect the bondholder's financial position relative to that of other outstanding securities. Common provisions involve (1) prohibitions on the sale of accounts receivable, (2) constraints on the issuance of common stock dividends, (3) restrictions on the purchase or sale of fixed assets, and (4) constraints on additional borrowing. Prohibitions on the sale of accounts receivable are specified because such sales would benefit the firm's short-run liquidity position at the expense of its future liquidity position. Constraints on common stock dividends generally mean limiting their issuance when working capital falls below a specified level, or simply limiting the maximum dividend payout to some fraction, say 50 percent or 60 percent of earnings under any circumstance. Fixed-asset restrictions generally require lender permission before the liquidation of any fixed asset or prohibit the use of any existing fixed asset as collateral on new loans. Constraints on additional borrowing are usually in the form of restrictions or limitations on the amount and type of additional long-term debt that can be issued. All these restrictions have one thing in common: They attempt to prohibit action that would improve the status of other securities at the expense of bonds and to protect the status of bonds from being weakened by any managerial action.

Current Yield

The **current yield** on a bond refers to the ratio of the annual interest payment to the bond's current market price. If, for example, we have a bond with an 8 percent coupon interest rate, a par value of $1,000, and a market price of $700, it would have a current yield of

$$\text{current yield} = \frac{\text{annual interest payments}}{\text{market price of the bond}} \qquad (6\text{--}2)$$

$$= \frac{.08 \times \$1000}{\$700} = \frac{\$80}{\$700} = 0.114 = 11.4 \text{ percent}$$

Bond Ratings

John Moody first began to rate bonds in 1909; since that time three rating agencies—Moody's, Standard and Poor's, and Fitch Investor Services—have provided ratings on corporate bonds. These ratings involve a judgment about the future risk potential of the bond. Although they deal with expectations, several historical factors seem to play a significant role in their determination.[1] Bond ratings are favorably affected by (1) a greater reliance on equity then debt in financing the firm, (2) profitable operations, (3) a low variability in past earnings, (4) large firm size, and (5) little use of subordinated debt. (Subordinated debt will be described shortly.) In turn, the rating a bond receives affects the rate of return demanded on the bond by the investors. The poorer the bond rating, the higher the rate of return demanded in the capital markets. Table 6-1 provides an example and description of these ratings. Thus, for the financial manager, bond ratings are extremely important. They provide an indicator of default risk that in turn affects the rate of return that must be paid on borrowed funds.

BACK TO THE FUNDAMENTALS

When we say that a lower bond rating means a higher interest rate charged by the investors (bondholders), we are observing an application of **Axiom 1: The Risk-Return Tradeoff—We Won't Take on Additional Risk Unless We Expect to be Compensated with Additional Return.**

Having an understanding of the basic terms and characteristics of bonds in general, we can now consider the different types of bonds that companies use in funding their debt needs.

[1]See Thomas F. Pogue and Robert M. Soldofsky, "What's in a Bond Rating?" *Journal of Financial and Quantitative Analysis,* 4 (June 1969), pp. 201–28; and George E. Pinches and Kent A. Mingo, "A Multivariate Analysis of Industrial Bond Ratings," *Journal of Finance,* 28 (March 1973), pp. 1–18.

ETHICS IN FINANCE

Bondholders Beware

We have learned that the bond rating attached to a bond when it is issued does not necessarily continue with it until maturity. In fact, with all the debt that corporations piled on in the late 1980s, it seemed that the only direction debt ratings went was down. The ethical question here: Does management have a duty to bondholders to watch out for their interests? Is just living by the letter of the bond covenants—while working hard to evade them—all right?

Let's look at a couple of examples that have infuriated bondholders. In early 1988, Shearson Lehman Hutton helped sell $1 billion of RJR Nabisco bonds. About six months later Shearson helped Kohlberg Kravis Roberts (KKR), an investment banker, buy RJR. The way the purchase was arranged, RJR issued large amounts of new debt, driving the market value of the previously issued bonds down by $100 million. Needless to say, a lot of bondholders were angry.

Texaco is another company that has worked around bond covenants. Several years ago, Pennzoil sued Texaco for $10 billion and won the case. To minimize damage to shareholders as a result of their court battle with Pennzoil, Texaco filed for Chapter 11 bankruptcy protection. The company entered bankruptcy, bond interest payments were passed, and later it emerged from bankruptcy with its credit standing unchanged.

Was what Shearson did unethical—to issue, then destroy? Should Texaco have used bankruptcy to protect its shareholders at the expense of its bondholders? What do you think?

AAA	This is the highest rating assigned by Standard and Poor's for debt obligation and indicates an extremely strong capacity to pay principal and interest.
AA	Bonds rated AA also qualify as high-quality debt obligations. Their capacity to pay principal and interest is very strong, and in the majority of instances they differ from AAA issues only in small degree.
A	Bonds rated A have a strong capacity to pay principal and interest, although they are somewhat more susceptible to the adverse effects of changes in circumstances and economic conditions.
BBB	Bonds rated BBB are regarded as having an adequate capacity to pay principal and interest. Whereas they normally exhibit adequate protection parameters, adverse economic conditions or changing circumstances are more likely to lead to a weakened capacity to pay principal and interest for bonds in this category than for bonds in the A category.
BB **B** **CCC** **CC**	Bonds rated BB, B, CCC, and CC are regarded, on balance, as predominantly speculative with respect to the issuer's capacity to pay interest and repay principal in accordance with the terms of the obligation. BB indicates the lowest degree of speculation and CC the highest. While such bonds will likely have some quality and protective characteristics, these are outweighed by large uncertainties or major risk exposures to adverse conditions.
C	The rating C is reserved for income bonds on which no interest is being paid.
D	Bonds rated D are in default, and payment of principal and/or interest is in arrears.

Plus (+) or Minus (−): To provide more detailed indications of credit quality, the ratings from "AA" to "BB" may be modified by the addition of a plus or minus sign to show relative standing within the major rating categories.

Source: *Standard and Poor's Fixed Income Investor*, Vol. 8 (1980). Reprinted by permission.

TABLE 6–1
Standard and Poor's
Corporate Bond Ratings

■ TYPES OF BONDS

Whereas the term *bond* may be defined simply as long-term debt, there are a variety of such creatures. Just to mention a few, we have

- debentures
- subordinated debentures
- mortgage bonds
- Eurobonds
- zero and very low coupon bonds
- junk bonds

We will briefly explain each of these types of bonds.

Debentures

The term **debenture** applies to any unsecured long-term debt. Because these bonds are unsecured, the earning ability of the issuing corporation is of great concern to the bondholder. They are also viewed as being more risky than secured bonds and as a result must provide investors with a higher yield than secured bonds provide. Often the issuing firm attempts to provide some protection to the holder through the prohibition of any additional encumbrance of assets. This prohibits the future issuance of secured long-term debt that would further tie up the firm's assets and leave the bondholders less protected. To the issuing firm, the major advantage of debentures is that no property has to be secured by them. This allows the firm to issue debt and still preserve some future borrowing power.

Subordinated Debentures

Many firms have more than one issue of debentures outstanding. In this case a hierarchy may be specified, in which some debentures are given subordinated standing in case of insolvency. The claims of the **subordinated debentures** are honored only after the claims of secured debt and unsubordinated debentures have been satisfied.

Mortgage Bonds

A **mortgage bond** is a bond secured by a lien on real property. Typically, the value of the real property is greater than that of the mortgage bonds issued. This provides the mortgage bondholders with a margin of safety in the event the market value of the secured property declines. In the case of foreclosure, the trustees have the power to sell the secured property and use the proceeds to pay the bondholders. In the event that the proceeds from this sale do not cover the bonds, the bondholders become general creditors, similar to debenture bondholders, for the unpaid portion of the debt.

INTERNATIONAL FINANCIAL MANAGEMENT

Wayne Marr and John Trimble on Eurobond Borrowing

Between 1975 and 1988, the volume of U.S. corporate borrowing in the Eurodollar bond market grew at the astonishing rate of 63 percent annually. In 1975 U.S. firms borrowed approximately $30 million overseas, which accounted for less than 1 percent of total U.S. corporate borrowing. In 1987 they borrowed nearly $17 billion overseas, which represented roughly 17 percent of total U.S. corporate borrowing. This amount, moreover, was sharply down from the 1985 high of $42 billion, accounting for 42 percent of total corporate borrowing.

What is behind this huge increase in overseas borrowing? According to the chief financial officers of U.S. companies, it is extraordinarily favorable borrowing rates. Many CFOs, in fact, report interest cost savings between 25 and 100 basis points in the Eurodollar as compared with the domestic market.[a] Though intermittent, such savings have been available often enough to provide a significant advantage. And, harder to believe, the reported savings at times have been much larger than 100 basis points. On September 11, 1984, for example, Coca Cola issued $100 million of seven-year Eurodollar bonds priced at 80 basis points below comparable U.S. Treasury notes.[b] And, while interest cost savings as large as Coca Cola's are clearly an aberration, recent academic research provides support for claims in the financial press of substantial corporate savings in the Eurobond market.[c]

[a]See W. Cooper, "Some Thoughts About Eurobonds," *Institutional Investor* (February 1985), pp. 157–58; S. Lohr, "The Eurobond Market Boom," New York Times, December 31, 1985, p. 31; F. G. Fisher, *The Eurodollar Bond Market* (London: Euromoney Publications Limited, 1979); R. Karp, "How U.S. Companies Are Catching the Eurobond Habit," *Institutional Investor* (August 1982), pp. 208–12; M. S. Mendelson, *Money on the Move* (New York: McGraw-Hill, 1980); Orion Royal Bank Limited, *The Orion Royal Guide to the International Capital Markets* (London: Euromoney Publications Limited, 1982); Securities Industry Association, *The Importance of Access to Capital Markets Outside the United States* (May 1983); and D. W. Starr, "Opportunities of U.S. Corporate Borrowers in the International Bond Markets," *Financial Executive* (June 1979), pp. 50–59.

[b]See Cooper, pp. 157–58.

[c]See Wayne Marr and John Trimble, "Domestic versus Euromarket Bond Sale: A Persistent Borrowing Cost Advantage," University of Tennessee, Department of Finance Working Paper, 1988.

Source: Wayne Marr and John Trimble, "The Persistent Borrowing Advantage of Eurodollar Bonds: A Plausible Explanation," *Journal of Applied Corporate Finance* 1 (Summer 1988), pp. 65–70.

Eurobonds

Eurobonds are not so much a different type of security as they are securities, in this case bonds, issued in a country different from the one in whose currency the bond is denominated. For example, a bond that is issued in Europe or in Asia by an American company and that pays interest and principal to the lender in U.S. dollars would be considered a Eurobond. Thus, even if the bond is not issued in Europe, it merely needs to be sold in a country different from the one in whose currency it is denominated to be considered a Eurobond. The Eurobond market actually had its roots in the 1950s and 1960s as the U.S. dollar became increasingly popular because of its role as the primary international reserve. In recent years as the U.S. dollar has gained a reputation for being one of the most stable currencies, demand for Eurobonds has increased. The primary attractions to borrowers, aside from favorable rates, in the Eurobonds market are the relative lack of regulation (Eurobonds are not registered with the Securities and Exchange Commission, or SEC), less rigorous disclosure requirements than those of the SEC, and the speed with which they can be issued. Interestingly, not only are Eurobonds not registered with the SEC, but U.S. citizens and residents may not be offered them during their initial distribution.

Zero and Very Low Coupon Bonds

Zero and **very low coupon bonds** allow the issuing firm to issue bonds at a substantial discount from their $1,000 face value with a zero or very low coupon rate. The investor receives a large part (or all on the zero coupon bond) of the return from the appreciation of the bond. For example, in April 1983 Homestead Savings issued $60 million of debt maturing in 1995 with a zero coupon rate. These bonds were sold at a 75 percent discount from their par value; that is, investors only paid $250 for a bond with a $1,000 par value. Investors who purchased these bonds for $250 and hold them until they mature in 1995 will receive a 12.25 percent yield to maturity, with all of this yield coming from appreciation of the bond. Homestead Savings, on the other hand, will have no cash outflows until these bonds mature; however, at that time it will have to pay back $60 million even though it only received $15 million when the bonds were first issued.

As with any form of financing, there are both advantages and disadvantages of issuing zero or very low coupon bonds. The disadvantages are, first (as already mentioned), when the bonds mature Homestead Savings will face an extremely large cash outflow, much greater than the cash inflow it experienced when the bonds were first issued. Second, discount bonds are not callable and can only be retired at maturity. Thus, if interest rates fall, Homestead Savings cannot benefit by requiring the investers to sell their bonds back to the company. The advantages of zero and low coupon bonds are, first, that annual cash outflows associated with interest payments do not occur with zero coupon bonds and are at a relatively low level with low coupon bonds. Second, because there is relatively strong investor demand for this type of debt, prices tend to be bid up and yields tend to be bid down. That is to say, Homestead Savings was able to issue zero coupon bonds at about half a percent less than it would have been if they had been traditional coupon bonds. Finally, Homestead Savings is able to deduct the annual amortization of the discount from taxable income, which will provide a positive annual cash flow to Homestead.

Junk Bonds

Junk or **low-rated bonds** are bonds rated BB or below. Originally, the term was used to describe bonds issued by "fallen angels"; that is, firms with sound financial histories that were facing severe financial problems and suffering from poor credit ratings. Today, junk bonds refer to any bond with a low rating. The major participants in this market are new firms that do not have an established record of performance, although junk bonds have been issued to finance corporate buyouts. Still, the backbone of the junk bond market involves young firms without established records of performance. Before the mid-1970s these new firms

TABLE 6–2
New Issues of Junk Bonds
(Billions of Dollars)

Year	(1) Newly Issued Public Straight Junk Bonds[a]	(2) Exchange Offers and Private Issues Going Public[b]	(3) Total Junk Bond Issuance (1) + (2)	(4) Total Public Bond Issues by U.S. Corporations[b]	(5) (1) as % of (4)	(6) (3) as % of (4)
1987	28.9	n.a.	n.a.	219.1	13.2	n.a.
1986	34.3	11.3	45.6	232.5	14.8	19.6
1985	15.4	4.4	19.8	119.6	12.9	16.6
1984	14.8	0.9	15.7	73.6	20.1	21.3
1983	8.0	0.5	8.5	47.6	16.8	17.9
1982	2.7	0.5	3.2	44.3	6.1	7.2
1981	1.4	0.3	1.7	38.1	3.7	4.5
1980	1.4	0.7	2.1	41.6	3.4	5.0
1979	1.4	0.3	1.7	25.8	5.4	6.6
1978	1.5	0.7	2.2	19.8	7.6	11.1
1977	0.6	0.5	1.1	24.1	2.5	4.6

[a]From Drexel, Burnham, Lambert (1987). The 1987 figure from *Investment Dealer's Digest*.
[b]From *Federal Reserve Bulletin*.

Source: Kevin J. Perry and Robert A. Taggart, Jr., "The Growing Role of Junk Bonds," *Journal of Applied Corporate Finance*, 1 (Spring 1988), p. 38.

simply did not have access to the capital markets because of the reluctance of investors to accept speculative grade bonds. However, by the late 1980s, junk bonds grew to the point that they represented between 10 percent and 20 percent of the total public bond issuances by U.S. corporations. As the economy slowed in the late 1980s and early 1990s, junk bonds were issued less frequently. This growth is illustrated in Table 6–2, which shows the proliferation of new issues of junk bonds. Today, with the leveraged buyout movement of the late 1980s over, junk bonds play a smaller role in corporate finance than they had. The bankruptcy of Drexel, Burnham, Lambert; the jailing of the "king of junk bonds," Michael Milken; and the realization that high leverage is dangerous have all contributed to a shrinkage of this market. However, as we look forward to the mid- and late 1990s and the century ahead it appears that although the role of junk bonds may be reduced, they will continue to play an important role for new firms raising capital for the first time.

Because junk bonds are of speculative grade, they carry a coupon interest rate of between 3 percent to 5 percent more than AAA grade long-term debt.

BACK TO THE FUNDAMENTALS

Some have thought junk bonds were fundamentally different from other securities, but they are not. They are bonds with a great amount of risk, and therefore promise high expected returns. Thus, **Axiom 1: The Risk-Return Tradeoff—We Won't Take on Additional Risk Unless We Expect to be Compensated with Additional Return.**

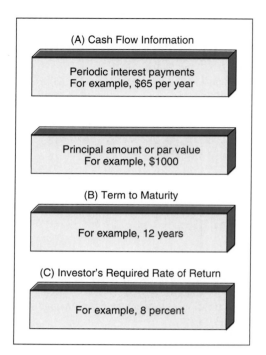

(A) Cash Flow Information

Periodic interest payments
For example, $65 per year

Principal amount or par value
For example, $1000

(B) Term to Maturity

For example, 12 years

(C) Investor's Required Rate of Return

For example, 8 percent

FIGURE 6–2
Data Requirements for
Bond Valuation

Having an understanding of the basic characteristics of bonds, we will now turn our attention to valuing a bond.

■■■ BOND VALUATION

The valuation process for a bond, as depicted in Figure 6–2, requires knowledge of three essential elements: (1) the amount of the cash flows to be received by the investor, (2) the maturity date of the loan, and (3) the investor's required rate of return. The amount of cash flows is dictated by the periodic interest to be received and by the par value to be paid at maturity. Given these elements, we can compute the value of the bond, or the present value.

PERSPECTIVE IN FINANCE

The value of a bond is the present value both of future interest to be received and the par or maturity value of the bond. Simply list these cash flows, use your required rate of return as the discount rate, and find the value.

EXAMPLE

Consider a bond issued by Alaska Airlines in 1984 with a maturity date of 2014 and a stated coupon rate of 6.875 percent.[2] In late 1992, with 22

[2]Alaska Airlines remits the interest to its bondholders on a semiannual basis on January 15 and July 15. However, for the moment assume the interest is to be received annually. The effect of semiannual payments will be examined later.

years left to maturity, investors owning the bonds were requiring an 8.5 percent rate of return. We can calculate the value of the bonds to these investors using the following three-step valuation procedure:

Step 1: Estimate the amount and timing of the expected future cash flows. Two types of cash flows are received by the bondholder:

    a. Annual interest payments equal to the coupon rate of interest times the face value of the bond. In this example the interest payments equal $68.75 = .06875 × $1,000. Assuming that 1992 interest payments have already been made, these cash flows will be received by the bondholder in each of the 22 years before the bond matures (1993 through 2014 = 22 years).

    b. The face value of the bond of $1,000 to be received in 2014. To summarize, the cash flows received by the bondholder are as follows:

Years	1	2	3	4	...	21	22
	$68.75	$68.75	$68.75	$68.75	...	$68.75	$68.75
							+$1,000.00
							$1,068.75

Step 2: Determine the investor's required rate of return by evaluating the riskiness of the bond's future cash flows. An 8.5 percent required rate of return for the bondholders is given. In Chapter 8, we will learn how this rate is determined. For now, simply realize that the investor's required rate of return is equal to a rate earned on a risk-free security plus a risk premium for assuming risk.

Step 3: Calculate the intrinsic value of the bond as the present value of the expected future interest and principal payments discounted at the investor's required rate of return.

The present value of Alaska Airline's bonds is found as follows:

$$\text{bond value} = V_b = \frac{\$ \text{ interest in year 1}}{(1 + \text{required rate of return})^1}$$

$$+ \frac{\$ \text{ interest in year 2}}{(1 + \text{required rate of return})^2}$$

$$+ \dots + \frac{\$ \text{ interest in year 22}}{(1 + \text{required rate of return})^{22}}$$

$$+ \frac{\$ \text{ par value of bond}}{(1 + \text{required rate of return})^{22}}$$

or, summing over the interest payments,

$$V_b = \underbrace{\sum_{t=1}^{22} \frac{\$ \text{ interest in year } t}{(1 + \text{required rate of return})^t}}_{\text{present value of interest}} + \underbrace{\frac{\$ \text{ par value of bond}}{(1 + \text{required rate of return})^{22}}}_{\text{present value of par value}}$$

The forgoing equation is a restatement in a slightly different form of equation (6–1). Recall that equation (6–1) states that the value of an asset is the present value of future cash flows to be received by the investor.

Using I_t to represent the interest payment in year t, M to represent the bond's maturity (or par) value, and k_b to equal the bondholder's required rate of return, we may express the value of a bond maturing in year n as follows:

$$V_b = \sum_{t=1}^{n} \frac{\$I_t}{(1 + k_b)^t} + \frac{\$M}{(1 + k_b)^n} \qquad \text{(6–3a)}$$

Finding the value of the Alaska Airlines bonds may be represented graphically as follows:

Year	0	1	2	3	4	5	6	...	22
Dollars received at end of year		$68.75	$68.75	$68.75	$68.75	$68.75	$68.75	...	$68.75 $1,000.00 $1,068.75
Present Value	$840.59								

However, because the investor's required rate of return is 8.5 percent, we are unable to use the present value tables at the end of the text to solve the problem. We must therefore rely on a calculator solution. Using the HP 17BII, we find the value of the bond to be $840.59, calculated as follows:[3]

Data Input	Function Key
22	N
8.5	I% YR
68.75	PMT
1000	FV

Function Key	Answer
PV	–840.59

Thus, if investors consider 8.5 percent to be an appropriate required rate of return in view of the risk level associated with Alaska Airline's bonds, paying a price of $840.59 would satisfy their return requirement. ■

---

[3]As noted in Chapter 5, we are using the HP 17BII. You may want to return to the Chapter 5 section, *Moving Through Time with the Aid of a Financial Calculator* or Appendix A, to see a more complete explanation of using the HP 17BII. For an explanation of other calculators, see the study guide that accompanies this text.

Semiannual Interest Payments

In the preceding illustration, the interest payments were assumed to be paid annually. However, companies typically pay interest to bondholders semiannually. For example, rather than disbursing $68.75 in interest at the conclusion of each year, Alaska Airlines pays $34.375 (half of $68.75) on January 15 and July 15.

Several steps are involved in adapting equation (6–3a) for semiannual interest payments.[4] First, thinking in terms of *periods* instead of years, a bond with a life of n years paying interest semiannually has a life of $2n$ periods. In other words, a five-year bond ($n = 5$) that remits its interest on a semiannual basis actually makes 10 payments. Yet although the number of periods has doubled, the *dollar* amount of interest being sent to the investors for each period and the bondholders' required rate of return are half of the equivalent annual figures. I_t becomes $I_t/2$ and k_b is changed to $k_b/2$; thus, for semiannual compounding, equation (6–3a) becomes

$$V_b = \sum_{t = 1}^{2n} \frac{\$I_t/2}{\left(1 + \dfrac{k_b}{2}\right)^t} + \frac{\$M}{\left(1 + \dfrac{k_b}{2}\right)^{2n}} \qquad \textbf{(6–3b)}$$

Again using the HP 17BII calcualtor to find the Alaskan Airlines value of the bond, but now assuming semiannual interest payments, we find:

Data Input	Function Key
44	$\boxed{N}$
4.25	$\boxed{I\% \ YR}$
34.375	$\boxed{PMT}$
1000	$\boxed{FV}$

Function Key	Answer
$\boxed{PV}$	–839.45

■ BONDHOLDERS' EXPECTED RATES OF RETURN (YIELD TO MATURITY)

Theoretically, each investor could have a different required rate of return for a particular security. However, the financial manager is only interested in the required rate of return that is implied by the market

---

[4]The logic for calculating the value of a bond that pays interest semiannually is similar to the material presented in Chapter 5, where compound interest with nonannual periods was discussed.

prices of the firm's securities. In other words, the consensus of a firm's investors about the expected rate of return is reflected in the current market price of the stock.

To measure the bondholder's expected rate of return $\hat{k}_b$, we would find the discount rate that equates the present value of the future cash flows (interest and maturity value) with the current market price of the bond.[5] The expected rate of return for a bond is also the rate of return the investor will earn if the bond is held to maturity, or the **yield to maturity**. Thus, when referring to bonds, the terms *expected rate of return* and *yield to maturity* are often used interchangeably.

To illustrate this concept, consider the Brister Corporation's bonds, which are selling for $1,100. The bonds carry a coupon interest rate of 9 percent and mature in 10 years. (Remember the coupon rate determines the interest payment—coupon rate × par value.)

In determining the **expected rate of return** ($\hat{k}_b$), implicit in the current market price, we need to find the rate that discounts the anticipated cash flows back to a present value of $1,100, the existing market price (P_0) for the bond.

Finding the expected rate of return for a bond using the present value tables is done by trial and error. We have to keep trying new rates until we find the discount rate that results in the present value of the future interest and maturity value of the bond just equaling the current market value of the bond. If the expected rate is somewhere between rates in the present value tables, we then must interpolate between the rates.

For our example, if we try 7 percent, the bond's present value is $1,140.16. Since the present value of $1,140.16 is greater than the market price of $1,100, we should next try a higher rate. Increasing the discount rate, say, to 8 percent gives a present value of $1,066.90. (These computations are shown below.) Now the present value is less than the market price; thus, we know that the investor's expected rate of return is between 7 percent and 8 percent.

Years	Cash flow	7 percent Present value factors	7 percent Present value	8 percent Present value factors	8 percent Present value
1–10	$ 90 per year	7.024	$ 632.16	6.710	$ 603.90
10	$1,000 in year 10	0.508	508.00	0.463	$ 463.00
		Present value at 7 percent:	$1,140.16	Present value at 8 percent:	$1,066.90

Because we now know the rate is between 7 percent and 8 percent, we may interpolate to find the expected return. The process is as follows:

[5]When we speak of computing an expected rate of return, we are not describing the situation very accurately. Expected rates of return are ex ante (before the fact) and are based on "expected and unobservable future cash flows" and, therefore, can only be "estimated."

Rate	Value		Differences in Value	
7%	$1,140.16			
$\hat{k}_b$	1,100.00	} $40.16		} $73.26
8%	1,066.90			

Solving for $\hat{k}_b$ by interpolation, we have:

$$\hat{k}_b = 7\% + \left(\frac{\$40.16}{\$73.26}\right)(8\% - 7\%) = 7.55\%$$

Thus, the expected rate of return on the Brister Corporation's bonds for an investor who purchases the bonds for $1,100 is approximately 7.55 percent.

Rather than using the present value tables to compute the expected return for the Brister Corporation's bonds, which is cumbersome, it is much easier to use a calculator. The solution (using an HP 17BII) is shown in the adjacent margin.

◼ BOND VALUATION: THREE IMPORTANT RELATIONSHIPS

We have now learned to find the value of a bond (V_b), given (1) the amount of interest payments (I_t), (2) the maturity value (M), (3) the length of time to maturity (n years), and (4) the investor's required rate of return, k_b. We also know how to compute the expected rate of return ($\hat{k}_b$), which also happens to be the current interest rate on the bond, given (1) the current market value (P_0), (2) the amount of interest payments (I_t), (3) the maturity value (M), and (4) the length of time to maturity (n years). We now have the basics. But let's go further in our understanding of bond valuation by studying several important relationships.

First Relationship

The value of a bond is inversely related to changes in the investor's present required rate of return (the current interest rate). In other words, as interest rates increase (decrease), the value of the bond decreases (increases).

To illustrate, assume that an investor's required rate of return for a given bond is 12 percent. The bond has a par value of $1,000 and annual interest payments of $120, indicating a 12 percent coupon interest rate ($120 ÷ $1,000 = 12%). Assuming a five-year maturity date, the bond would be worth $1,000, computed as follows:

$$V_b = \frac{I_1}{(1 + k_b)^1} + \cdots + \frac{I_n}{(1 + k_b)^n} + \frac{M}{(1 + k_b)^n} \qquad \textbf{(6-3a)}$$

$$= \sum_{t=1}^{n} \frac{I_t}{(1 + k_b)^t} + \frac{M}{(1 + k_b)^n}$$

$$= \sum_{t=1}^{5} \frac{\$120}{(1 + .12)^t} + \frac{\$1,000}{(1 + .12)^5}$$

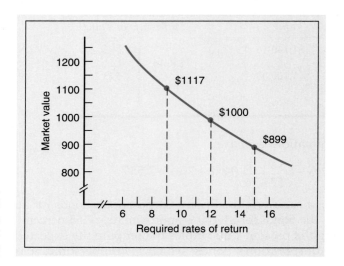

Using present value tables we have:

$$V_b = \$120 \ (PVIFA_{12\%, \ 5 \ yr}) + \$1,000 \ (PVIF_{12\%, \ 5 \ yr})$$

$$V_b = \$120(3.605) + \$1,000(.567)$$

$$= \$432.60 + \$567.00$$

$$= \$999.60 \cong \$1,000.00$$

If, however, the investor's required rate of return increases from 12 percent to 15 percent, the value of the bond would decrease to $899.24, computed as follows:

$$V_b = \$120 \ (PVIFA_{15\%, \ 5 \ yr}) + \$1,000 \ (PVIF_{15\%, \ 5 \ yr})$$

$$V_b = \$120(3.352) + \$1,000(.497)$$

$$= \$402.24 + \$497.00$$

$$= \$899.24$$

On the other hand, if the investor's required rate of return decreases to 9 percent, the bond would increase in value to $1,116.80:

$$V_b = \$120 \ (PVIFA_{9\%, \ 5 \ yr}) + \$1,000 \ (PVIF_{9\%, \ 5 \ yr})$$

$$V_b = \$120(3.890) + \$1,000(.650)$$

$$= \$466.80 + \$650.00$$

$$= \$1,116.80$$

This inverse relationship between the investor's required rate of return and the value of a bond is presented in Figure 6–3. Clearly, as an investor demands a higher rate of return, the value of the bond decreases. The higher rate of return the investor desires can be achieved only by paying less for the bond. Conversely, a lower required rate of return yields a higher market value for the bond.

Changes in bond prices represent an element of uncertainty for the bond investor. If the current interest rate (required rate of return) changes, the price of the bond also fluctuates. An increase in interest rates causes the bondholder to incur a loss in market value. Since future interest rates and the resulting bond value cannot be predicted with certainty, a bond investor is exposed to the risk of changing values as interest rates vary. This risk has come to be known as **interest-rate risk.**

Second Relationship

The market value of a bond will be less than the par value if the investor's required rate is above the coupon interest rate; but it will be valued above par value if the investor's required rate of return is below the coupon interest rate.

Using the previous example, we observed that:

1. The bond has a *market* value of $1,000, equal to the par or maturity value, when the investor's required rate of return equals the 12 percent coupon interest rate. In other words, if

   required rate = coupon rate, then *market value = par value*
       12%   =   12%   , then $1,000   = $1,000

2. When the required rate is 15 percent, which exceeds the 12 percent coupon rate, the market value falls below par value to $899.24; that is, if

   required rate > coupon rate, then *market value < par value*
       15%   >   12%,   , then $899.24   < $1,000

   In this case the bond sells at a discount below par value; thus it is called a **discount bond.**

3. When the required rate is 9 percent, or less than the 12 percent coupon rate, the market value, $1,116.80, exceeds the bond's par value. In this instance, if

   required rate < coupon rate, then *market value > par value*
       9%   <   12%   , then $1,116.80   > $1,000

   The bond is now selling at a premium above par value; thus, it is a **premium bond.**

Third Relationship

Long-term bonds have greater interest-rate risk than do short-term bonds.

As already noted, a change in current interest rates (required rate of return) causes an inverse change in the market value of a bond. However, the impact on value is greater for long-term bonds than it is for short-term bonds.

In Figure 6–3 we observed the effect of interest rate changes on a five-year bond paying a 12 percent coupon interest rate. What if the bond did not mature until 10 years from today instead of 5 years?

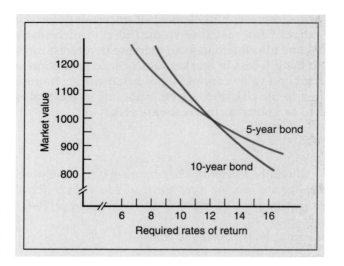

FIGURE 6–4
Market Values of a 5-Year and
a 10-Year Bond at Different
Required Rates

Would the changes in market value be the same? Absolutely not. The changes in value would be more significant for the 10-year bond. For example, if we vary the current interest rates (the bondholder's required rate of return) from 9 percent to 12 percent and then to 15 percent, as we did earlier with the 5-year bond, the values for both the 5-year and the 10-year bonds would be as shown below.

| Required Rate | Market Value for a 12% Coupon-Rate Bond Maturing in | |
	5 Years	10 Years
9%	$1,116.80	$1,192.16
12	1,000.00	1,000.00
15	899.24	849.28

Using these values and the required rates, we can graph the changes in values for the two bonds relative to different interest rates. These comparisons are provided in Figure 6–4. The figure clearly illustrates that the price of a long-term bond (say 10 years) is more responsive or sensitive to interest rate changes than the price of a short-term bond (say 5 years).

The reason long-term bond prices fluctuate more than short-term bond prices in response to interest rate changes is simple. Assume an investor bought a 10-year bond yielding a 12 percent interest rate. If the current interest rate for bonds of similar risk increased to 15 percent, the investor would be locked into the lower rate for 10 years. If, on the other hand, a shorter-term bond had been purchased, say one maturing in 2 years, the investor would have to accept the lower return for only 2 years and not the full 10 years. At the end of year 2, the investor would receive the maturity value of $1,000 and could buy a bond offering the higher 15 percent rate for the remaining 8 years. Thus, interest-rate risk is deter mined, at least in part, by the length of time an investor is required to commit to an investment. However, the holder of a long-term bond may take some comfort from the fact that long-term interest rates are usually not as volatile as short-term rates. If the short-term rate changed one percentage point, for example, it would not be unusual for the long-term rate to change only .3 percentage points.

SUMMARY

Valuation is an important issue if we are to manage the company effectively. An understanding of the concepts and how to compute the value of a security underlie much that we do in finance and in making correct decisions for the firm as a whole. Only if we know what matters to our investors can we maximize the firm's value.

For our purposes, *value is the present value of future cash flows expected to be received from an investment discounted at the investor's required rate of return.* In this context, the value of a security is a function of (1) the *expected cash inflows* from the asset, (2) the *riskiness* of the investment, and (3) the investor's *required rate of return.*

Valuing an asset with a finite stream of cash flows involves computing the present value of the individual cash receipts for each period. A bond that matures on a designated date is an example of such an asset. Here we find both the present value of the interest payments and the present value of the maturity or par value.

The *expected rate of return* on a bond is the required rate of return of the bondholders who are willing to pay the present market price for the bond, but no more. This rate is reached at the point where the present value of future cash flows to be received by the bondholder is just equal to the present market price of the bond. This rate of return is important to the financial manager because it equals the required rate of return of the firm's investors.

Certain key relationships exist in bond valuation, three of these being:

1. A decrease in interest rates (required rates of return) will cause the value of a bond to increase; an interest rate increase will cause a decrease in value. The change in value caused by changing interest rates is called *interest-rate risk*.
2. If the bondholder's required rate of return (current interest rate):
    a. Equals the coupon interest rate, the bond will sell at par, or maturity value.
    b. Exceeds the bond's coupon rate, the bond will sell below par value, or at a *discount.*
    c. Is less than the bond's coupon rate, the bond will sell above par value, or at a *premium.*
3. A bondholder owning a long-term bond is exposed to greater interest-rate risk than one owning a short-term bond.

STUDY QUESTIONS

6–1.   What are the basic differences between book value, liquidation value, market value, and intrinsic value?

6–2.   What is a general definition of the intrinsic value of a security?

6–3.   Explain the three factors that determine the intrinsic or economic value of an asset.

6–4.   Explain the relationship between an investor's required rate of return and the value of a security.

6–5.   **a.** How does a bond's par value differ from its market value?

        b. Explain the difference between a bond's coupon interest rate, the current yield, and a bondholder's required rate of return.

6–6.   Describe the bondholder's claim on the firm's assets and income.

6–7.   What factors determine a bond's rating? Why is the rating important to the firm's manager?

6–8   Distinguish between debentures and mortgage bonds.

6–9.   Define (a) Eurobonds, (b) zero coupon bonds, and (c) junk bonds.

6–10.   Define the bondholder's expected rate of return.

SELF-TEST PROBLEMS

ST-1.   *(Bond Valuation)* Trico bonds have a coupon rate of 8 percent, a par value of $1,000, and will mature in 20 years. If you require a return of 7 percent, what price would you be willing to pay for the bond? What happens if you pay *more* for the bond? What happens if you pay *less* for the bond?

ST-2.   *(Bond Valuation)* Sunn Co.'s bonds, maturing in seven years, pay 8 percent interest on a $1,000 face value. However, interest is paid semiannually. If your required rate of return is 10 percent, what is the value of the bond? How would your answer change if the interest were paid annually?

ST-3.   *(Bondholder's Expected Rate of Return)* Sharp Co. bonds are selling in the market for $1,045. These 15-year bonds pay 7 percent interest annually on a $1,000 par value. If they are purchased at the market price, what is the expected rate of return?

STUDY PROBLEMS

6–1.   *(Bond Valuation)* Calculate the value of a bond that expects to mature in 12 years and has a $1,000 face value. The coupon interest rate is 8 percent and the investors' required rate of return is 12 percent.

6–2.   *(Bond Valuation)* Enterprise, Inc., bonds have a 9 percent coupon rate. The interest is paid semiannually and the bonds mature in eight years. Their par value is $1,000. If your required rate of return is 8 percent, what is the value of the bond? What is its value if the interest is paid annually?

6–3.   *(Bondholder's Expected Rate of Return)* The market price is $900 for a 10-year bond ($1,000 par value) that pays 8 percent interest (4 percent semiannually). What is the bond's expected rate of return?

6–4.   *(Bond Valuation)* Exxon 20-year bonds pay 9 percent interest annually on a $1,000 par value. If bonds sell at $945, what is the bond's expected rate of return?

6–5.   *(Bondholder's Expected Rate of Return)* Zenith Co.'s bonds mature in 12 years and pay 7 percent interest annually. If you purchase the bonds for $1,150, what is your expected rate of return?

6–6.   *(Bond Valuation)* National Steel 15-year, $1,000 par value bonds pay 8 percent interest annually. The market price of the bonds is $1,085, and your required rate of return is 10 percent.

    a. Compute the bond's expected rate of return.

    b. Determine the value of the bond to you, given your required rate of return.

    c. Should you purchase the bond?

6–7.   *(Bond Valuation)* You own a bond that pays $100 in annual interest, with a $1,000 par value. It matures in 15 years. Your required rate of return is 12 percent.

    a. Calculate the value of the bond.

    b. How does the value change if your required rate of return (i) increases to 15 percent or (ii) decreases to 8 percent?

    c. Explain the implications of your answers in part (b) as they relate to interest rate risk, premium bonds, and discount bonds.

    d. Assume that the bond matures in 5 years instead of 15 years. Recompute your answers in part (b).

    e. Explain the implications of your answers in part (d) as they relate to interest rate risk, premium bonds, and discount bonds.

6–8.   *(Bond Valuation)* Arizona Public Utilities issued a bond that pays $80 in annual interest, with a $1,000 par value. It matures in 20 years. Your required rate of return is 7 percent.

    a. Calculate the value of the bond.

    b. How does the value change if your required rate of return (i) increases to 10 percent or (ii) decreases to 6 percent?

    c. Explain the implications of your answers in part (b) as they relate to interest rate risk, premium bonds, and discount bonds.

    d. Assume that the bond matures in 10 years instead of 20 years. Recompute your answers in part (b).

    e. Explain the implications of your answers in part (d) as they relate to interest rate risk, premium bonds, and discount bonds.

SELF-TEST SOLUTIONS

SS-1.

$$\text{Value } (V_b) = \sum_{t=1}^{20} \frac{\$80}{(1.07)^t} + \frac{\$1,000}{(1.07)^{20}}$$

Thus,

$$
\begin{aligned}
\text{Present value of interest:} \quad & \$80(10.594) = \$847.52 \\
\text{Present value of par value:} \quad & \$1,000(0.258) = \underline{258.00} \\
& \text{Value } (V_b) = \underline{\underline{\$1,105.52}}
\end{aligned}
$$

If you pay more for the bond, your required rate of return will not be satisfied. In other words, by paying an amount for the bond that exceeds $1,105.52, the expected rate of return for the bond is less than the required rate of return. If you have the opportunity to pay less for the bond, the expected rate of return exceeds the 7 percent required rate of return.

SS-2.   If interest is paid semiannually:

$$\text{Value } (V_b) = \sum_{t=1}^{14} \frac{\$40}{(1 + 0.05)^t} + \frac{\$1,000}{(1 + 0.05)^{14}}$$

Thus,

$$\$40(9.899) = \$395.96$$
$$\$1,000(0.505) = \underline{505.00}$$
$$\text{Value } (V_b) = \underline{\underline{\$900.96}}$$

If interest is paid annually:

$$\text{Value } (V_b) = \sum_{t=1}^{7} \frac{\$80}{(1.10)^t} + \frac{\$1,000}{(1.10)^7}$$

$$V_b = \$80(4.868) + \$1,000(0.513)$$

$$V_b = \$902.44$$

SS-3.

$$\$1,045 = \sum_{t=1}^{15} \frac{\$70}{(1 + \hat{k}_b)^t} + \frac{\$1,000}{(1 + \hat{k}_b)^{15}}$$

At 6%: $\$70(9.712) + \$1,000(0.417) = \$1,096.84$

At 7%: Value must equal $1,000.

Interpolation:

Expected rate of return: $\hat{k}_b = 6\% + \dfrac{\$51.84}{\$96.84} \ (1\%) = 6.54\%$

FINANCIAL CALCULATOR SOLUTION

Data Input	Function Key
15	N
70	+/– PMT
1000	+/– FV
1045	PV
Function Key	Answer
I% YR	6.52

CHAPTER 7

VALUATION AND CHARACTERISTICS OF STOCK

Preferred Stock • Common Stock • Stockholder's Expected Rate of Return

In Chapter 6, we developed a general concept about valuation, where economic value was defined as the present value of the expected future cash flows generated by the asset. We then applied that concept to valuing bonds, one form of a company's long-term debt.

In this chapter we continue our study of valuation, but our attention is now given to valuing stocks, both preferred stock and common stock. As already noted at the outset of our study of finance, and on several occasions since, the financial manager's objective should be that of maximizing the value of the firm's common stock. Thus, we need to understand what determines stock value. Also, only with an understanding of valuation can we compute the firm's cost of capital, a concept essential to making effective capital investment decisions—an issue to be discussed in Chapter 11.

What we especially seek to accomplish in this chapter is the following:

1. Identify the basic characteristics and features of preferred stock and common stock.

2. Learn how to determine the economic value of preferred stock and common stock.

3. Examine the concept of the *investor's expected rate of return, as it relates to preferred stock and common stock*[1].

---

[1]We have already learned how to measure the expected rate of return on a bond. As we will see, the logic for measuring the expected rate of return for stocks is the same as for bonds; only the procedure is somewhat different.

▪ PREFERRED STOCK

Preferred stock is often referred to as a hybrid security because it has many characteristics of both common stock and bonds. Preferred stock is similar to common stock in that it has no fixed maturity date, the nonpayment of dividends does not bring on bankruptcy, and dividends are not deductible for tax purposes. On the other hand, preferred stock is similar to bonds in that dividends are limited in amount.

The size of the preferred stock dividend is generally fixed either as a dollar amount or as a percentage of the par value. For example, Texas Power and Light has issued $4 preferred stock, while Toledo Edison has some 4.25 percent preferred stock outstanding. The par value on the Toledo Edison preferred stock is $100; hence, each share pays 4.25% × $100, or $4.25 in dividends annually. Because these dividends are fixed, preferred stockholders do not share in the residual earnings of the firm but are limited to their stated annual dividend.

In examining preferred stock we will first discuss several features common to almost all preferred stock. Next we will investigate features less frequently included and take a brief look at methods of retiring preferred stock. We will close by learning how to value preferred stock.

Features of Preferred Stock

Although each issue of preferred stock is unique, a number of characteristics are common to almost all issues. Some of these more frequent traits include:

- Multiple classes of preferred stock
- Preferred stock's claim on assets and income
- Cumulative dividends
- Protective provisions
- Convertibility

Other features that are less common include:

- Adjustable rates
- Participation
- PIK Preferred

In addition, there are provisions frequently used to retire an issue of preferred stock, including the ability of the firm to call its preferred stock or to use a sinking-fund provision. All these features are presented in the discussion that follows.

Multiple Classes

If a company desires, it can issue more than one series or class of preferred stock, and each class can have different characteristics. In fact, it is quite common for firms that issue preferred stock to issue more than one series. For example, Philadelphia Electric has 13 different issues of preferred stock outstanding. These issues can be further differentiated in that some are convertible into common stock and others are not, and they have varying priority status regarding assets in the event of bankruptcy.

Claim on Assets and Income

Preferred stock has priority over common stock with regard to claims on assets in the case of bankruptcy. The preferred stock claim is honored after that of bonds and before that of common stock. Multiple issues of preferred stock may be given an order of priority. Preferred stock also has a claim on income prior to common stock. That is, the firm must pay its preferred stock dividends before it pays common stock dividends. Thus, in terms of risk, preferred stock is safer than common stock because it has a prior claim on assets and income. However, it is riskier than long-term debt because its claims on assets and income come after those of bonds.

Cumulative Feature

Most preferred stocks carry a **cumulative feature** that requires all past unpaid preferred stock dividends be paid before any common stock dividends are declared. The purpose is to provide some degree of protection for the preferred shareholder. Without a cumulative feature there would be no reason why preferred stock dividends would not be omitted or passed when common stock dividends were passed. Because preferred stock does not have the dividend enforcement power of interest from bonds, the cumulative feature is necessary to protect the rights of preferred stockholders.

Protective Provisions

In addition to the cumulative feature, protective provisions are common to preferred stock. These protective provisions generally allow for voting rights in the event of nonpayment of dividends, or they restrict the payment of common stock dividends if sinking-fund payments are not met or if the firm is in financial difficulty. In effect, the protective features included with preferred stock are similar to the restrictive provisions included with long-term debt.

To examine typical protective provisions, consider Tenneco Corporation and Reynolds Metals preferred stocks. The Tenneco preferred stock has a protective provision that provides preferred stockholders with voting rights whenever six quarterly dividends are in arrears. At that point the preferred shareholders are given the power to elect a majority of the board of directors. The Reynolds Metals preferred stock includes a protective provision that precludes the payment of common stock dividends during any period in which the preferred stock sinking fund is in default. Both provisions, which yield protection beyond that provided by the cumulative provision and thereby reduce shareholder risk, are desirable. Given these protective provisions for the investor they reduce the cost of preferred stock to the issuing firm.

Convertibility

Much of the preferred stock that is issued today is **convertible** at the discretion of the holder into a predetermined number of shares of common stock. In fact, today about one-third of all preferred stock issued has a convertibility feature. The convertibility feature is, of course, desirable to the investor and thus reduces the cost of the preferred stock to the issuer.

Adjustable Rate Preferred Stock

In the early 1980s, another new financing alternative was developed aimed at providing investors with some protection against wide swings in principal that occur when interest rates move up and down. This financing vehicle is called **adjustable rate preferred stock**. With adjustable rate preferred stock, quarterly dividends fluctuate with interest rates under a formula that ties the dividend payment at either a premium or discount to the highest of (1) the three-month Treasury bill rate, (2) the 10-year Treasury bond rate, or (3) the 20-year Treasury bond rate. Although adjustable rate preferred stock allows dividend rates to be tied to the rates on Treasury securities, it also provides a maximum and a minimum level to which they can climb or fall, called the *dividend rate band*. The purpose of allowing the interest rate on this preferred stock to fluctuate is, of course, to minimize the fluctuation in the value of the preferred stock. In times of high and fluctuating interest rates, this is a very appealing feature indeed. In Table 7–1 several issues of adjustable rate preferred stock are identified.

In the late 1980s **auction rate preferred stock** began to appear. Auction rate preferred stock is actually variable rate preferred stock in which the dividend rate is set by an auction process. In the case of auction rate preferred, the dividend rate is set every 49 days. At each auction, buyers and sellers place bids for shares, specifying the yield they are willing to accept for the next seven-week period. The yield is then set at the lowest level necessary to match buyers and sellers. As a result, the yield offered on auction rate preferred stock accurately reflects current interest rates, while keeping the market price of these securities at par.

Participation

Although participating features are infrequent in preferred stock, their inclusion can greatly affect its desirability and cost. The **participation feature** allows the preferred stockholder to participate in earnings beyond the payment of the stated dividend. This is usually done in accordance with some set formula. For example, Borden Series A preferred stock currently provides for a dividend of *no less than* 60 cents per share, to be determined by the board of directors. Preferred stock of this sort actually resembles common stock as much as it does normal preferred stock. Although a participating feature is certainly desirable from the point of view of the investor, it is infrequently included in preferred stock.

TABLE 7–1
Adjustable Rate Preferred Stock

Issuer	Amount of Offering ($000)	Dividend Rate at Offering	Dividend Rate Thereafter (Applicable Rate)[a]	Dividend Rate Band	Call Protection
Bank America Corp.	$400,000	9.25%	Adjusted quarterly to 4.00% below the applicable rate	6% – 12%	No call allowed for the first 5 years.
J.P. Morgan & Co., Inc.	250,000	9.25	Adjusted quarterly to 4.875% below the applicable rate	5% – 11½%	No call allowed for the first 5 years.
Integrated Resources, Inc.	100,000	12.50	Adjusted quarterly to 0.75% higher than the applicable rate	8% – 15%	No call allowed for the first 5 years.
Liberty National Corp.	25,000	11.00	Adjusted quarterly to the applicable rate	6½% – 13%	No call allowed for the first 5 years.
Reading & Bates Corp.	37,500	13.00	Adjusted quarterly to 0.75% higher than the applicable rate	7% – 14%	No call allowed for the first 5 years.
Gulf States Utilities Corp.	30,000	11.50	Adjusted quarterly to 0.65% higher than the applicable rate	7% – 13%	No call allowed for the first 5 years.

[a]In all cases the "applicable rate" refers to the highest of (1) the 3-month Treasury bill rate, (2) the 10-year Treasury bond rate, or (3) the 20-year Treasury bond rate.

PIK Preferred

One byproduct of the acquisition boom of the late 1980s was the creation of pay-in-kind (PIK) preferred stock. With **PIK preferred**, investors receive no dividends initially; they merely get more preferred stock, which in turn pays dividends in even more preferred stock. Eventually, usually after five or six years if all goes well for the issuing company, cash dividends should replace the preferred stock dividends. Needless to say, the issuing firm has to offer hefty dividends, generally ranging from 12 percent to 18 percent, to entice investors to purchase PIK preferred.

Retirement Features

Although preferred stock does not have a set maturity associated with it, issuing firms generally provide for some method of retirement. If preferred stock could not be retired, issuing firms could not take advantage of falling interest rates.

CALLABLE PREFERRED   Most preferred stock has some type of call provision associated with it. In fact, the Securities and Exchange Commission discourages the issuance of preferred stock without some call provision. The SEC has taken this stance on the grounds that if a method of retirement is not provided, the issuing firm will not be able to replace its preferred stock if interest rates fall.

TABLE 7–2 Call Provision of Quaker Oats $9.56 Cumulative Preferred	Date		Call Price
	Date of issue	until 7/19/80	Not callable
	7/20/80	until 7/19/85	$109.56
	7/20/85	until 7/19/90	107.17
	7/20/90	until 7/19/95	104.78
	7/20/95	until 7/19/00	102.39
	After 7/19/00		100.00

The call feature on preferred stock usually involves an initial premium above the par value or issuing price of the preferred of approximately 10 percent. Then, over time, the call premium generally falls. For example, Quaker Oats in 1976 issued $9.56 cumulative preferred stock with no par value for $100 per share. This issue was not callable until 1980 and then was callable at $109.56. After that the call price gradually drops to $100 in the year 2000, as shown in Table 7–2.

By setting the initial call price above the initial issue price and allowing it to decline slowly over time, the firm protects the investor from an early call that carries no premium. A call provision also allows the issuing firm to plan the retirement of its preferred stock at predetermined prices.

SINKING-FUND PROVISIONS   A **sinking-fund** provision requires the firm periodically to set aside an amount of money for the retirement of its preferred stock. This money is then used to purchase the preferred stock in the open market or through the use of the call provision, whichever method is cheaper. Although preferred stock does not have a maturity date associated with it, the use of a call provision in addition to a sinking fund can effectively create a maturity date. For example, the Quaker Oats issue we just examined has associated with it an annual sinking fund, operating between the years 1981 and 2005, which requires the annual elimination of a minimum of 20,000 shares and a maximum of 40,000 shares. The minimum payments are designed so that the entire issue will be retired by the year 2005. If any sinking-fund payments are made above the minimum amount, the issue will be retired prior to 2005. Thus, the Quaker Oats issue of preferred stock has a maximum life of 30 years, and the size of the issue outstanding decreases each year after 1981.

Valuing Preferred Stock

As already explained, the owner of preferred stock generally receives a *constant income* from the investment in each period. However, the return from preferred stock comes in the form of *dividends* rather than *interest*. In addition, while bonds generally have a specific maturity date, most preferred stocks are perpetuities (nonmaturing). In this instance, finding the value (present value) of preferred stock, V_{ps}, with a level cash flow stream continuing indefinitely, may best be explained by an example.

Consider AT&T's preferred stock issue. In similar fashion to valuing bonds in Chapter 6, we will use a three-step valuation procedure.

Step 1: Estimate the amount and timing of the receipt of the future cash flows the preferred stock is expected to provide. AT&T's preferred stock pays an annual dividend of $3.64. The shares do not have a maturity date; that is, they go to perpetuity.

Step 2: Evaluate the riskiness of the preferred stock's future dividends and determine the investor's required rate of return. The investor's required rate of return is assumed to equal 7.28 percent[2].

Step 3: Calculate the economic or intrinsic value of the share of preferred stock, which is the present value of the expected dividends discounted at the investor's required rate of return. The valuation model for a share of preferred stock, V_{ps}, is therefore defined as follows:

$$V_{ps} = \frac{\text{dividend in year 1}}{(1 + \text{required rate of return})^1} \qquad \textbf{(7–1)}$$

$$+ \frac{\text{dividend in year 2}}{(1 + \text{required rate of return})^2}$$

$$+ \dots + \frac{\text{dividend in infinity}}{(1 + \text{required rate of return})^\infty}$$

$$= \frac{D_1}{(1 + k_{ps})^1} + \frac{D_2}{(1 + k_{ps})^2} + \dots + \frac{D_\infty}{(1 + k_{ps})^\infty}$$

$$V_{ps} = \sum_{t=1}^{\infty} \frac{D_t}{(1 + k_{ps})^t}$$

PERSPECTIVE IN FINANCE

Equation (7–1) is a restatement in a slightly different form of equation (6–1) in Chapter 6. Recall that equation (6–1) states that the value of an asset is the present value of future cash flows to be received by the investor.

Because the dividends in each period are equal for preferred stock, equation (7–1) can be reduced to the following relationship:[3]

$$V_{ps} = \frac{\text{annual dividend}}{\text{required rate of return}} = \frac{D}{k_{ps}} \qquad \textbf{(7–2)}$$

Equation (7–2) represents the present value of an infinite stream of cash flows, where the cash flows are the same each year. We can determine the value of the AT&T preferred stock, using equation (7–2), as follows:

$$V_{ps} = \frac{D}{k_{ps}} = \frac{\$3.64}{.0728} = \$50$$

■

---

[2]For now the required rate of return is given, but in the next chapter we will learn more about measuring an investor's required rate of return. Trust us for now.

[3]To verify this result, consider the following equation: (continued on next page)

The value of a preferred stock is the present value of all future dividends. But because most preferred stocks are nonmaturing—the dividends continue to infinity—we therefore have to come up with a shortcut for finding value as represented by equation (7–2)

BACK TO THE FUNDAMENTALS

Valuing preferred stock relies on three of our axioms presented in Chapter 1, namely:

Axiom 1: The Risk-Return Tradeoff—We Won't Take on Additional Risk Unless We Expect to be Compensated with Additional Return.

Axiom 2: The Time Value of Money—A Dollar Received Today Is Worth More than a Dollar Received in the Future.

Axiom 3: Cash Is King—Measuring the Timing of Costs and Benefits

Determining the economic worth or value of an asset always relies on these three axioms. Without them, we would have no basis for explaining value. With them, we can know that the amount and timing of cash, not earnings, drives value. Also, we must be rewarded for taking risk; otherwise, we will not invest.

■ COMMON STOCK

Common stock involves ownership in the corporation. In effect, bondholders and preferred stockholders can be viewed as creditors, whereas the common stockholders are the true owners of the firm. Common stock does not have a maturity date, but exists as long as the firm does. Nor does common stock have an upper limit on its dividend payments. Dividend payments must be declared by the firm's board of directors before they are issued. In the event of bankruptcy the common stockholders, as owners of the corporation, cannot exercise claims on assets

---

[3] (cont.)

(i)
$$V_{ps} = \frac{D_1}{(1 + k_{ps})^1} + \frac{D_2}{(1 + k_{ps})^2} + \cdots + \frac{D_n}{(1 + k_{ps})^n}$$

If we multiply both sides of this equation by $(1 + k_{ps})$, we have

(ii)
$$V_{ps}(1 + k_{ps}) = D_1 + \frac{D_2}{(1 + k_{ps})} + \cdots + \frac{D_n}{(1 + k_{ps})^{n-1}}$$

Subtracting (i) from (ii) yields

$$V_{ps}(1 + k_{ps} - 1) = D_1 - \frac{D_n}{(1 + k_{ps})^n}$$

As n approaches infinity, $D_n/(1 + k_{ps})$ approaches zero. Consequently,

$$V_{ps}k_{ps} = D_1 \text{ and } V_{ps} = \frac{D_1}{k_{ps}}$$

Since $D_1 = D_2 = \cdots = D_n$, we need not designate the year. Therefore

(iii)
$$V_{ps} = \frac{D}{k_{ps}}$$

until the firm's creditors, including the bondholders and preferred shareholders, have been satisfied.

In examining common stock, we will look first at several of its features or characteristics. Then we will focus on valuing common stock.

<u>PERSPECTIVE IN FINANCE</u>

Recently, stock repurchases, takeovers, and going-private transactions have severely eaten into the outstanding amount of corporate equity. In fact, between 1983 and 1988, the level of publicly traded corporate equity fell by at least 5 percent per year as a result of these transactions. At the current rate, it has been estimated that in the year 2003 the last individually owned share of publicly traded common stock will be sold. Although the likelihood of this occurring is extremely remote, it does give some perspective on how much corporate equity recently has diminished.

Features or Characteristics of Common Stock

We now examine common stock's claim on income and assets, stockholder voting rights, preemptive rights, and the meaning and importance of its limited-liability feature.

Claim on Income

As the owners of the corporation, the common shareholders have the right to the residual income after bondholders and preferred stockholders have been paid. This income may be paid directly to the shareholders in the form of dividends or retained and reinvested by the firm. Although it is obvious the shareholder benefits immediately from the distribution of income in the form of dividends, the reinvestment of earnings also benefits the shareholder. Plowing back earnings into the firm results in an increase in the value of the firm, in its earning power, and in its future dividends. This action in turn results in an increase in the value of the stock. In effect, residual income is distributed directly to shareholders in the form of dividends or indirectly in the form of capital gains on their common stock.

The right to residual income has both advantages and disadvantages for the common stockholder. The advantage is that the potential return is limitless. Once the claims of the most senior securities (bonds and preferred stock) have been satisfied, the remaining income flows to the common stockholders in the form of dividends or capital gains. The disadvantage: If the bond and preferred stock claims on income totally absorb earnings, common shareholders receive nothing. In years when earnings fall, it is the common shareholder who suffers first.

Claim on Assets

Just as common stock has a residual claim on income, it also has a residual claim on assets in the case of liquidation. Only after the claims of debt holders and preferred stockholders have been satisfied do the claims of common shareholders receive attention. Unfortunately, when bankruptcy does occur, the claims of the common shareholders generally go unsatisfied. This residual claim on assets adds to the risk of common stock. Thus, while common stock has historically provided a large return, averaging 10 percent annually since the late 1920s, it also has large risks associated with it.

Voting Rights

The common stock shareholders are entitled to elect the board of directors and are in general the only security holders given a vote. Early in this century it was not uncommon for a firm to issue two classes of common stock, which were identical except that only one carried voting rights. For example, both the Parker Pen Co. and the Great Atlantic and Pacific Tea Co. (A&P) had two such classes of common stock. This practice was virtually eliminated by (1) the Public Utility Holding Company Act of 1935, which gave the Securities and Exchange Commission the power to require that newly issued common stock carry voting rights, (2) the New York Stock Exchange's refusal to list common stock without voting privileges, and (3) investor demand for the inclusion of voting rights. However, with the merger boom of the eighties, dual classes of common stock with different voting rights again emerged, this time as a defensive tactic used to prevent takeovers. The *Financial Management in Practice* box, "Gregg A. Jarrell on Dual-Class Recapitalizations," speaks to this practice.

Common shareholders not only have the right to elect the board of directors, they also must approve any change in the corporate charter. A typical charter change might involve the authorization to issue new stock or perhaps a merger proposal.

Voting for directors and charter changes occurs at the corporation's annual meeting. While shareholders may vote in person, the majority generally vote by proxy. A **proxy** gives a designated party the temporary power of attorney to vote for the signee at the corporation's annual meeting. The firm's management generally solicits proxy votes and, if the shareholders are satisfied with its performance, has little problem securing them. However, in times of financial distress or when management takeovers are threatened, **proxy fights**—battles between rival groups for proxy votes—occur.

While each share of stock carries the same number of votes, the voting procedure is not always the same from company to company. The two procedures commonly used are majority and cumulative voting. Under **majority voting**, each share of stock allows the shareholder one vote, and each position on the board of directors is voted on separately. Because each member of the board of directors is elected by a simple majority, a majority of shares has the power to elect the entire board of directors.

With **cumulative voting**, each share of stock allows the shareholder a number of votes equal to the number of directors being elected. The shareholder can then cast all of his or her votes for a single candidate or split them among the various candidates. The advantage of a cumulative voting procedure is that it gives minority shareholders the power to elect a director.

PERSPECTIVE IN FINANCE

In theory, the shareholders pick the corporate board of directors, generally through proxy voting, and the board of directors in turn picks the management. Unfortunately, in reality the system frequently works the other way around. Management selects both the issues and the board of director nominees and then distributes the proxy ballots. In effect, shareholders are offered a slate of nominees selected by management from which to choose. The end result is that management effectively selects the directors, who then may have more allegiance to the managers than to the shareholders. This in turn sets up the potential for agency problems in which a divergence of interests between managers and shareholders is allowed to exist, with the board of directors not monitoring the managers on behalf of the shareholders as they should.

Preemptive Rights

The **preemptive right** entitles the common shareholder to maintain a proportionate share of ownership in the firm. When new shares are issued, common shareholders have the first right of refusal. If a shareholder owns 25 percent of the corporation's stock, then he or she is entitled to purchase 25 percent of the new shares. Certificates issued to the shareholders giving them an option to purchase a stated number of new shares of stock at a specified price during a 2- to 10-week period are called **rights.** These rights can be exercised, generally at a price set by manegement below the common stock's current market price, can be allowed to expire, or can be sold in the open market.

Limited Liability

Although the common shareholders are the actual owners of the corporation, their liability in the case of bankruptcy is limited to the amount of their investment. The advantage is that investors who might not otherwise invest their funds in the firm become willing to do so. This limited-liability feature aids the firm in raising funds.

Valuing Common Stock

Like both bonds and preferred stock, a common stock's value is equal to the present value of all future cash flows expected to be received by the stockholder. However, in contrast to bonds, common stock does not promise its owners interest income or a maturity payment at some specified time in the future. Nor does common stock entitle the holder to a predetermined constant dividend, as does preferred stock. For common stock, the dividend is based on the profitability of the firm and on management's decision to pay dividends or to retain the profits for reinvestment purposes. As a consequence, dividend streams tend to increase with the growth in corporate earnings. Thus, the growth of future dividends is a prime distinguishing feature of common stock.

The Growth Factor in Valuing Common Stock

What is meant by the term *growth* when used in the context of valuing common stock? A company can grow in a variety of ways. It can become larger by borrowing money to invest in new projects. Likewise, it can issue new stock for expansion. Management could also acquire another company to merge with the existing firm, which would increase the firm's assets. In all these cases, the firm is growing through the use of new financing, by issuing debt or common stock. Although management could accurately say that the firm has grown, the original stockholders may or may not participate in this growth. Growth is realized through the infusion of new capital. The firm size has clearly increased, but unless the original investors increase their investment in the firm, they will own a smaller portion of the expanded business.

Another means of growing is internal growth, which requires that management retain some or all of the firm's profits for reinvestment in the firm, resulting in the growth of future earnings and hopefully the value of the common stock. This process underlies the essence of potential growth for the firm's current stockholders and what we can call *the only relevant growth, for our purposes in valuing a firm's common shares.*[4]

---

[4]We are not arguing that the existing common stockholders never benefit from the use of external financing; however, such benefit is more evasive when dealing with efficient capital markets.

ETHICS IN FINANCIAL MANAGEMENT

Ethics: Keeping Perspective

Ethical and moral lapses in the business and financial community, academia, politics, and religion fill the daily press. But the rash of insider-trading cases on Wall Street against recent graduates of top business and law schools seems particularly disturbing because the cream of the crop, with six-figure incomes and brilliant careers ahead, is being convicted.

Most appear to have been very bright, highly motivated overachievers, driven by peer rivalries to win a game in which the score had a dollar sign in front of it. While there have been a few big fish, most sold their futures for $20,000 to $50,000 of illicit profits. They missed the point—that life is a marathon, not a sprint.

In fact, most business school graduates become competent executives, managing people and resources for the benefit of society. The rewards-the titles and money-are merely the byproducts of doing a good job.

Source: John S. R. Shad, "Business's Bottom Line: Ethics," *Ethics in American Business: A Special Report, Touche Ross & Co.*, 1988, p. 56.

EXAMPLE

To illustrate the nature of internal growth, assume that the return on equity for PepsiCo is 16 percent.[5] If PepsiCo's management decides to pay all the profits out in dividends to its stockholders, the firm will experience no growth internally. It might become larger by borrowing more money or issuing new stock, but internal growth will come only through the retention of profits. If, on the other hand, PepsiCo retained all the profits, the stockholders' investment in the firm would grow by the amount of profits retained, or by 16 percent. If, however, management kept only 50 percent of the profits for reinvestment, the common shareholders' investment would increase only by half of the 16 percent return on equity, or by 8 percent. Generalizing this relationship, we have

$$g = ROE \times r, \qquad\qquad (7\text{--}3)$$

where g = the growth rate of future earnings and the growth in the common stockholders' investment in the firm.

     ROE = the return on equity (net income/common book value).

     r = the company's percentage of profits retained, called the profit-retention rate.[6]

Therefore, if only 25 percent of the profits were retained by PepsiCo, we

---

[5]The return on equity is the percentage return on the common shareholder's investment in the company and is computed as follows:

$$\text{return on equity} = \frac{\text{net income}}{(\text{par value} + \text{paid in capital} + \text{retained earnings})}$$

[6]The retention rate is also equal to (1 – the percentage of profits paid out in dividends). The percentage of profits paid out in dividends is often called the dividend-payout ratio.

would expect the common stockholders' investment in the firm and the value of the stock price to increase or grow by 4 percent; that is,

$$g = 16\% \times .25 = 4\%$$ ■

In summary, common stockholders frequently rely on an increase in the stock price as a source of return. If the company is retaining a portion of its earnings for reinvestment, future profits and dividends should grow. This growth should be reflected in an increased market price of the common stock in future periods, provided that the return on the funds reinvested exceeds the investor's required rate of return. Therefore, both types of return (dividends and price appreciation) are necessary in the development of a valuation model for common stock.

To explain this process, let us begin by examining how an investor might value a common stock that is to be held for only one year.

Common Stock Valuation—Single Holding Period

For an investor holding a common stock for only one year, the value of the stock should equal the present value of both the expected dividend to be received in one year, D_1, and the anticipated market price of the share at year end, P_1. If k_{cs} represents a common stockholder's required rate of return, the value of the security, V_{cs}, would be

$$V_{cs} = \text{present value of dividend in one year } (D_1)$$

$$+ \text{ present value of market price in one year } (P_1)$$

$$= \frac{D_1}{(1 + k_{cs})} + \frac{P_1}{(1 + k_{cs})}$$

EXAMPLE

Suppose an investor is contemplating the purchase of RMI common stock at the beginning of this year. The dividend at year end is expected to be $1.64, and the market price by the end of the year is projected to be $22. If the investor's required rate of return is 18 percent, the value of the security would be

$$V_{cs} = \frac{\$1.64}{1 + .18} + \frac{\$22}{1 + .18}$$

$$= \$1.39 + \$18.64$$

$$= \$20.03$$ ■

Once again we see that valuation is a three-step process. First, we estimate the expected future cash flows from common stock ownership (a $1.64 dividend and a $22 end-of-year expected share price). Second, we estimate the investor's required rate of return after assessing the riskiness of the expected cash flows (assumed to be 18 percent). Finally, we discount the expected dividend and end-of-year share price back to the present at the investor's required rate of return.

The intrinsic value of a common stock, like preferred stock, is the present value of all future dividends. And we have the same problem we had with preferred stock: It is hard to value cash flows that continue in perpetuity. So we must make some assumptions about the expected growth of future dividends. If, for example, we assume that dividends grow at a constant rate forever, we can then calculate the present value of the stock.

Common Stock Valuation—Multiple Holding Periods

Since common stock has no maturity date and is frequently held for many years, a **multiple-holding-period valuation model** is needed. The general common stock valuation model can be defined as follows:

$$V_{cs} = \frac{D_1}{(1 + k_{cs})^1} + \frac{D_2}{(1 + k_{cs})^2} + ... + \frac{D_n}{(1 + k_{cs})^n} + ... + \frac{D_\infty}{(1 + k_{cs})^\infty} \qquad (7\text{--}4)$$

Turn back to Chapter 6, and compare equation (6–1) with equation (7–4). Equation (7–4) is merely a restatement in a slightly different form of equation (6–1). Recall that equation (6–1), which is the basis for our work in valuing securities, states that the value of an asset is the present value of future cash flows to be received by the investor. Equation (7–4) is simply applying equation (6–1) to valuing common stock.

Equation (7–4) indicates that we are discounting the dividend at the end of the first year, D_1, back one year; the dividend in the second year, D_2, back two years; the dividend in the nth year back n years; and the dividend in infinity back an infinite number of years. The required rate of return is k_{cs}. In using equation (7–4), note that the value of the stock is established at the beginning of the year, say January 1, 1994. The most recent past dividend D_0 would have been paid the previous day, December 31, 1993. Thus, if we purchased the stock on January 1, the first dividend would be received in 12 months, on December 31, 1994, which is represented by D_1.

Fortunately, equation (7–4) can be reduced to a much more manageable form if dividends grow each year at a constant rate, g. The constant growth common stock valuation equation may be presented as follows:[7]

---

[7]Where common stock dividends grow at a constant rate of g every year, we can express the dividend in any year in terms of the dividend paid at the end of the previous year, D_0. For example, the expected dividend one year hence is simply $D_0(1 + g)$. Likewise, the dividend at the end of t years is $D_0(1 + g)^t$. Using this notation, the common stock valuation equation in (7–4) can be rewritten as follows:

$$V_{cs} = \frac{D_0(1 + g)^1}{(1 + k_{cs})^1} + \frac{D_0(1 + g)^2}{(1 + k_{cs})^2} + ... + \frac{D_0(1 + g)^n}{(1 + k_{cs})^n} + ... + \frac{D_0(1 + g)^\infty}{(1 + k_{cs})^\infty} \qquad (7\text{--}5)$$

If both sides of equation (7–5) are multiplied by $(1 + k_{cs})/(1 + g)$ and then equation (7–4) is subtracted from the product, the result is

$$\frac{V_{cs}(1 + k_{cs})}{1 + g} - V_{cs} = D_0 - \frac{D_0(1 + g)^\infty}{(1 + k_{cs})^\infty} \qquad (7\text{--}6)$$

(continued on next page)

$$\text{common stock value} = \frac{\text{dividend in year 1}}{\text{required rate of return} - \text{growth rate}} \quad \textbf{(7–7)}$$

$$V_{cs} = \frac{D_1}{k_{cs} - g}$$

Consequently, the intrinsic value (present value) of a share of common stock whose dividends grow at a constant annual rate can be calculated using equation (7–7). Although the interpretation of this equation may not be intuitively obvious, simply remember that it solves for the present value of the future dividend stream growing at a rate, g, to infinity, assuming that k_{cs} is greater than g.

EXAMPLE

Consider the valuation of a share of common stock that paid a $2 dividend at the end of the last year and is expected to pay a cash dividend every year from now to infinity. Each year the dividends are expected to grow at a rate of 10 percent. Based on an assessment of the riskiness of the common stock, the investor's required rate of return is 15 percent. Using this information, we would compute the value of the common stock as follows:

1. Since the $2 dividend was paid last year (actually yesterday), we must compute the next dividend to be received, that is, D_1, where

$$
\begin{aligned}
D_1 &= D_0(1 + g) \\
&= \$2(1 + .10) \\
&= \$2.20
\end{aligned}
$$

2. Now, using equation (7–7),

$$
\begin{aligned}
V_{cs} &= \frac{D_1}{k_{cs} - g} \\[2mm]
&= \frac{\$2.20}{.15 - .10} \\[2mm]
&= \$44
\end{aligned}
$$

---

[7](con't)

If $k_{cs} > g$, which normally should hold, $[D_0(1 + g)^\infty/(1 + k_{cs})^\infty]$ approaches zero. As a result,

$$\frac{V_{cs}(1 + k_{cs})}{1 + g} - V_{cs} = D_0$$

$$V_{cs}\left(\frac{1 + k_{cs}}{1 + g}\right) - V_{cs}\left(\frac{1 + g}{1 + g}\right) = D_0$$

$$V_{cs}\left[\frac{(1 + k_{cs}) - (1 + g)}{1 + g}\right] = D_0$$

$$V_{cs}(k_{cs} - g) = D_0(1 + g)$$

$$V_{cs} = \frac{D_1}{k_{cs} - g} \quad \textbf{(7–7)}$$

We have argued that the value of a common stock is equal to the present value of all future dividends, which is without question a fundamental premise of finance. In practice, however, managers, along with many security analysts, often talk about the relationship between stock value and earnings, rather than dividends. We would encourage you to be very cautious in using earnings to value a stock. Even though it may be a popular practice, the evidence available suggests that investors look to the cash flows generated by the firm, not the earnings, for value. A firm's value truly is the present value of the cash flows it produces.

We now turn to our last issue in stock valuation, that of the stockholder's expected returns, a matter of key importance to the financial manager.

BACK TO THE FUNDAMENTALS

Valuing common stock is no different from valuing preferred stock; only the pattern of the cash flows changes, but nothing else. Thus, the valuation of common stock relies on the same three axioms developed in Chapter 1 that were used in valuing preferred stock:

Axiom 1: The Risk-Return Tradeoff—We Won't Take on Additional Risk Unless We Expect to be Compensated with Additional Return.

Axiom 2: The Time Value of Money—A Dollar Received Today Is Worth More than a Dollar Received in the Future.

Axiom 3: Cash Is King—Measuring the Timing of Costs and Benefits

Determining the economic worth or value of an asset always relies on these three axioms. Without them, we would have no basis for explaining value. With them, we can know that the amount and timing of cash, not earnings, drives value. Also, we must be rewarded for taking risk; otherwise, we will not invest.

■ STOCKHOLDER'S EXPECTED RATE OF RETURN

As stated in Chapter 6, the expected rate of return on a bond is the return the bondholder expects to receive on the investment by paying the existing market price for the security. This rate of return is of interest to the financial manager because it tells the manager about the investor's expectations. The same can be said for the financial manager needing to know the expected rate of return of the firm's stockholders, which is the topic of this section.

The Preferred Stockholder's Expected Rate of Return

In computing the preferred stockholder's expected rate of return, we use the valuation equation for preferred stock. Earlier, equation (7–2) specified the value of a preferred stock, V_{ps}, as

$$V_{ps} = \frac{\text{annual dividend}}{\text{required rate of return}} = \frac{D}{k_{ps}} \qquad (7\text{–}2)$$

Solving equation (7–2) for k_{ps}, we have:

$$k_{ps} = \frac{\text{annual dividend}}{\text{value}} = \frac{D}{V_{ps}} \qquad \textbf{(7–8)}$$

That is preferred stockholder's *required* rate of return simply equals the stock's annual dividend divided by the intrinsic value. We may also restate equation (7–8) to solve for a preferred stock's *expected* rate of return, $\hat{k}_{ps}$ (pronounced "k-hjat"), as follows:[8]

$$\hat{k}_{ps} = \frac{\text{annual dividend}}{\text{market price}} = \frac{D}{P_0} \qquad \textbf{(7–9)}$$

Note that we have merely substituted the current market price P_0, for the intrinsic value, V_{ps}. The expected rate of return $\hat{k}_{ps}$, therefore equals the annual dividend relative to the price the stock is presently selling for, P_0. Thus, the expected rate of return $\hat{k}_{ps}$, is the rate of return the investor can expect to earn from the investment if bought at the current market price. For example if the present market price of preferred stock is $50 and it pays a $3.64 annual dividend, the expected rate of return implicit in the present market price is

$$\hat{k}_{ps} = \frac{D}{P_0} = \frac{\$3.64}{\$50} = 7.28\%$$

Therefore, investors at the margin (who pay $50 per share for a preferred security that is paying $3.64 in annual dividends) are expecting a 7.28 percent rate of return.

The Common Stockholder's Expected Rate of Return

The valuation equation for common stock was defined earlier in equation (7–4) as

$$\text{value} = \frac{\text{dividend in year 1}}{(1 + \text{required rate of return})^1}$$

$$+ \frac{\text{dividend in year 2}}{(1 + \text{required rate of return})^2}$$

$$+ \ldots + \frac{\text{dividend in year infinity}}{(1 + \text{required rate of return})^\infty} \qquad \textbf{(7–4)}$$

$$V_{cs} = \frac{D_1}{(1 + k_{cs})^1} + \frac{D_2}{(1 + k_{cs})^2} + \ldots + \frac{D_\infty}{(1 + k_{cs})^\infty}$$

$$V_{cs} = \sum_{t=1}^{\infty} \frac{D_t}{(1 + k_{cs})^t}$$

---

[8]We will use $\hat{k}$ ("k-hjat") to represent a security's expected rates of return versus k for the investor's required rate of return.

Owing to the difficulty of discounting to infinity, we made the key assumption that the dividends, D_t, increase at a constant annual compound growth rate of g. If this assumption is valid, equation (7–4) was shown to be equivalent to

$$\text{value} = \frac{\text{dividend in year 1}}{\text{required rate of return} - \text{growth rate}} \qquad \textbf{(7–7)}$$

$$V_{cs} = \frac{D_1}{k_{cs} - g}$$

Thus, V_{cs} represents the maximum value that an investor having a required rate of return of k_{cs} would pay for a security having an anticipated dividend in year 1 of D_1 that is expected to grow in future years at rate g. Solving equation (7–7) for k_{cs}, we can compute the common stockholder's required rate of return as follows:[9]

$$k_{cs} = \underset{\substack{\uparrow \\ \text{dividend} \\ \text{yield}}}{\left(\frac{D_1}{V_{cs}}\right)} + \underset{\substack{\uparrow \\ \text{annual} \\ \text{growth} \\ \text{rate}}}{g} \qquad \textbf{(7–10)}$$

From this equation, the common stockholder's required rate of return is equal to the dividend yield plus a growth factor. Although the growth rate, g, applies to the growth in the company's dividends, given our assumptions the stock's value may also be expected to increase at the same rate. For this reason, g represents the annual percentage growth in the stock value. In other words, the investors' required rate of return is satisfied by receiving dividends and capital gains, as reflected by the expected percentage growth rate in the stock price.

As was done for preferred stock earlier, we may revise equation (7–10) to measure a common stock's *expected* rate of return, $\hat{k}_{cs}$, Replacing the intrinsic value, V_{cs}, in equation (7–10) with the stock's current market price, P_0, we may express the stock's expected rate of return as follows:

$$\hat{k}_{cs} = \frac{\text{dividend in year 1}}{\text{market price}} + \text{growth} = \frac{D_1}{P_0} + g \qquad \textbf{(7–11)}$$

EXAMPLE

As an example of computing the expected rate of return for a common stock where dividends are anticipated to grow at a constant rate to infinity, assume that a firm's common stock has a current market price of $44. If the expected dividend at the conclusion of this year is $2.20

---

[9]At times the expected dividend at year end (D_1) is not given. Instead we might only know the most recent dividend (paid yesterday), that is, D_0. If so, equation (7–7) must be restated as follows:

$$V_{cs} = \frac{D_1}{(k_{cs} - g)} = \frac{D_0(1 + g)}{(k_{cs} - g)}$$

Comparing Values of the World's Businesses

Numerous business magazines, including *Forbes*, *Business Week*, and *Fortune*, publish rankings of firms. They rank the firms according to sales, assets, return on equity, or a host of other measures. *The Economist*, in conjunction with the London Business School, has attempted to measure the quality of the company by what its editors define as "added value." The following is an excerpt from *The Economist* describing this endeavor and a listing of several countries' "best companies" as measured by "added value relative to sales."

Why bother, one could ask: is not profitability good enough, whether that means return on sales or—which may matter more to shareholders—return on equity? No. Comparisons of profit and profitability are affected both by peculiarities of accounting practice and by (unavoidable) differences in the cost of capital and the way it is accounted for. Added value, in the wider-than-usual sense* developed by John Kay and some colleagues at LBS, tries to do better than this.

To see why, take a real example: a comparison of Bethlehem Steel, an American steel maker, with Colgate-Palmolive, a producer of consumer goods. In 1989 the two companies' profit and turnover figures were much alike. A return-on-sales comparison would rank them side by side. But Bethlehem employed $1\frac{1}{2}$ times as much capital as Colgate. A return-on-capital ranking would show the steel maker well behind.

That, as it happens, would be a fair conclusion. Yet it might not have been. Ranking by return on capital favors labor-intensive companies over capital-intensive ones. Instead of using costly machines, Colgate might have been (under) paying thousands of women to fill toothpaste-tubes by hand.

A return-on-capital measure also favors companies with old capital over those with newer capital. This stems from the historic-cost accounts used by nearly all companies. These value capital equipment at what it cost in the past, not what it would cost now, after years of inflation. And they not only thus understate the capital employed, but also overstate the return it earns, because the depreciation deducted from gross profit is artificially (and in fact misleadingly) low. The return-on-capital ratio is doubly falsified.

The LBS version of added value gets round most of these problems. It measures how much more a firm's output is worth than all its inputs of materials, labor and capital. It is thus fair as between capital-intensive and labor-intensive companies. It also gets round differences in the ways companies are financed, by treating all alike, as if all were debt-financed at a standard rate of interest on the real value of their capital.

To find out a firm's added value take its operating profits, adjust for the vagaries of depreciation (the LBS team has a complex formula for this) and then subtract its capital charge. Note that the result, our "added value," is not the same as the "value added" of value-added tax, which is a measure of the company's output, calculated by subtracting all bought-in inputs from turnover. Ours can be thought of as value added for the shareholder...

---

*See Evan Davis, Stephanie Flanders, and Jonathan Star, "Who Are the World's Most Successful Companies?" *Business Strategy Review*, London Business School (Summer 1991).

Source: "The Best Companies: Scrambling to the Top," *Economist* (September 7, 1991), 21–23.

The Top Five[a] Added Value as a Percentage of Sales
1981–90

Country and Company Name	Industry	Percentage
United States		
1. Autodesk	computer services	33.9
2. UST	tobacco	33.7
3. King World	TV, radio	33.0
4. Community Psychiatric	health care	29.5
5. St. Jude Medical equipment	medical	29.3
Japan		
1. Fuji Photo Film	photographics	15.5
2. Murata Manufacturing	electronics	14.4
3. Kyocera	electronics	13.9
4. Matsushita Electric	electronics	7.8
5. Pioneer Electronics	electronics	7.5
Germany		
1. Harpener	conglomerate	20.9
2. Contigas	utilities	19.7
3. Leifheit	household	14.4
4. Boss (Hugo)	clothing	11.9
5. Nordcement	cement	11.5
France		
1. LVMH Moet/Vuitton	luxury goods	18.6
2. Legris	construction materials	12.7
3. Legrand	electricals	12.6
4. CGI Informatique	computer services	11.8
5. Salomon	sports goods	11.7
Britain		
1. Glaxo	pharmaceutical	27.8
2. Alexander Proudfoot	financial services	26.7
3. Tiphook	transport	25.2
4. Cable and Wireless	telecoms	23.1
5. McCarthy and Stone	construction	22.7

[a]Only firms that met certain size criteria were considered.

and dividends and earnings are growing at a 10 percent annual rate (last year's dividend was $2), the expected rate of return implicit in the $44 stock price is as follows:

$$k_{cs} = \frac{\$2.20}{\$44} + 10\% = 15\%$$

■

As a final note, we should understand that the *expected* rate of return implied by a given market price equals the *required* rate of return for investors at the margin. For these investors, the expected rate of return is just equal to their required rate of return, and therefore they are willing to pay the current market price for the security. These investors' required rate of return is of particular significance to the financial manager, because it represents the cost of new financing to the firm.

BACK TO THE FUNDAMENTALS

We have just learned that on average, the expected return will be equal to the investor's required rate of return. This equilibrium condition is achieved by investors paying for an asset only the amount that will exactly satisfy their required rate of return. Thus, finding the expected rate of return based on the current market price for the security relies on two of the axioms given in Chapter 1:

Axiom 1: The Risk-Return Tradeoff—We Won't Take on Additional Risk Unless We Expect to be Compensated with Additional Return.

Axiom 2: The Time Value of Money—A Dollar Received Today is Worth More than a Dollar Received in the Future.

SUMMARY

Valuation is an important process in financial management. An understanding of the concepts and computational procedures in valuing a security underlies sound decision making. Valuation supports the financial officer's objective of maximizing the value of the firm's common stock.

For our purposes, *value is the present value of future cash flows expected to be received from an investment discounted at the investor's required rate of return.* In this context, the value of a security is a function of (1) the *expected cash inflows* from the asset, (2) the *riskiness* of the investment, and (3) the investor's *required rate of return.* In a world of uncertainty returns are measured in terms of the *expected cash flows* anticipated from the security; a derivation of expected value takes into account possible future events and their probability.

Although the valuation of any security entails the same basic principles, the procedures used in each situation vary. For example, valuing a finite stream of cash flows involves computing the present value of the individual cash receipts for each period. An example of this type of valuation problem would be a bond that is scheduled to mature on a designated date as described in Chapter 6. A second category of cash flow patterns involves an *infinite* cash flow stream, such as those from preferred stock and common stock. Although the underlying premise of valuation does not change—that is, value equals the present value of future cash flows—valuing such an asset requires a modification in the procedure. For securities with cash flows that are constant in each year, such as preferred stock, the present value equals the dollar amount of the annual dividend divided by the investor's required rate of return. Furthermore, for common stock where the future dividends are expected to increase at a constant growth rate, value may be given by the following equation:

$$\text{value} = \frac{\text{dividend in year one}}{\text{required rate of return} - \text{growth rate}} \qquad (7\text{--}7)$$

The *expected rate of return* on a security is the required rate of return of investors who are willing to pay the present market price for the security, but no higher price. This rate of return is important to the financial manager because it equals the required rate of return of the firm's investors. This rate is reached at the point where the present value of future cash flows to be received by the investor is just equal to the present market price of the security.

STUDY QUESTIONS

7–1.   Why is preferred stock referred to as a hybrid security? It is often said to combine the worst features of common stock and bonds. What is meant by this statement?

7–2.   Inasmuch as preferred stock dividends in arrears must be paid before common stock dividends, should they be considered a liability and appear on the right-hand side of the balance sheet?

7–3.   Why would a preferred stockholder want the stock to have a cumulative dividend feature and protective provisions?

7–4.   Distinguish between fixed rate preferred stock and adjustable rate preferred stock. What is the rationale for a firm issuing adjustable rate preferred stock?

7–5.   What is PIK preferred stock?

7–6.   Why is preferred stock frequently convertible? Why would it be callable?

7–7.   Compare valuing preferred stock and common stock.

7–8.   Define the investor's *expected* rate of return.

7–9.   State how the investor's required rate of return is computed.

7-10.   The common stockholders receive two types of return from their investment. What are they?

SELF-TEST PROBLEMS

ST-1.   (*Preferred Stock Valuation*) What is the value of a preferred stock where the dividend rate is 16 percent on a $100 par value? The appropriate discount rate for a stock of this risk level is 12 percent.

ST-2.   (*Preferred Stockholder Expected Return*) You own 250 shares of Dalton Resources' preferred stock, which currently sells for $38.50 per share and pays annual dividends of $3.25 per share.
   a. What is your expected return?
   b. If you require an 8 percent return, given the current price, should you sell or buy more stock?

ST-3.   (*Preferred Stock Valuation*) The preferred stock of Armlo pays a $2.75 dividend. What is the value of the stock if your required return is 9 percent?

ST-4. (*Common Stock Valuation*) Crosby Corporation's common stock paid $1.32 in dividends last year and is expected to grow indefinitely at an annual 7 percent rate. What is the value of the stock if you require an 11 percent return?

ST-5. (*Common Stockholder Expected Return*) Blackburn & Smith's common stock currently sells for $23 per share. The company's executives anticipate a constant growth rate of 10.5 percent and an end-of-year dividend of $2.50.
    a. What is your expected rate of return?
    b. If you require a 17 percent return, should you purchase the stock?

STUDY PROBLEMS

7–1. (*Preferred Stock Valuation*) What is the value of a preferred stock where the dividend rate is 14 percent on a $100 par value? The appropriate discount rate for a stock of this risk level is 12 percent.

7–2. (*Preferred Stockholder Expected Return*) Solitron's preferred stock is selling for $42.16 and pays $1.95 in dividends. What is your expected rate of return if you purchase the security at the market price?

7–3. (*Preferred Stockholder Expected Return*) You own 200 shares of Somner Resources' preferred stock, which currently sells for $40 per share and pays annual dividends of $3.40 per share.
    a. What is your expected return?
    b. If you require an 8 percent return, given the current price should you sell or buy more stock?

7–4. (*Common Stock Valuation*) You intend to purchase Marigo common stock at $50 per share, hold it one year, and sell after a dividend of $6 is paid. How much will the stock price have to appreciate for you to satisfy your required rate of return of 15 percent?

7–5. (*Common Stockholder Expected Return*) Made-It's common stock currently sells for $22.50 per share. The company's executives anticipate a constant growth rate of 10 percent and an end-of-year dividend of $2.
    a. What is your expected rate of return if you buy the stock for $22.50?
    b. If you require a 17 percent return, should you purchase the stock?

7–6. (*Common Stock Valuation*) Header Motor, Inc., paid a $3.50 dividend last year. At a constant growth rate of 5 percent, what is the value of the common stock if the investors require a 20 percent rate of return?

7–7. (*Measuring Growth*) Given that a firm's return on equity is 18 percent and management plans to retain 40 percent of earnings for investment purposes, what will be the firm's growth rate?

7–8. (*Common Stockholder Expected Return*) The common stock of Zaldi Co. is selling for $32.84. The stock recently paid dividends of $2.94 per share and has a projected constant growth rate of 9.5 percent. If you purchase the stock at the market price, what is your expected rate of return?

7–9. (*Common Stock Valuation*) Honeywag common stock is expected to pay $1.85 in dividends next year, and the market price is projected to be $42.50 by year end. If the investor's required rate of return is 11 percent, what is the current value of the stock?

7–10. (*Common Stockholder Expected Return*) The market price for Hobart common stock is $43. The price at the end of one year is expected to be $48, and dividends for next year should be $2.84. What is the expected rate of return?

7–11. (*Preferred Stock Valuation*) Pioneer's preferred stock is selling for $33 in the market and pays a $3.60 annual dividend.
    a. What is the expected rate of return on the stock?
    b. If an investor's required rate of return is 10 percent, what is the value of the stock for that investor?
    c. Should the investor acquire the stock?

7–12. (*Common Stock Valuation*) The common stock of NCP paid $1.32 in dividends last year. Dividends are expected to grow at an 8 percent annual rate for an indefinite number of years.

    a. If NCP's current market price is $23.50, what is the stock's expected rate of return?

    b. If your required rate of return is 10.5 percent, what is the value of the stock for you?

    c. Should you make the investment?

7–13. (*A Comprehensive Problem in Valuing Securities*) You are considering three investments. The first is a bond that is selling in the market at $1,100. The bond has a $1,000 par value, pays interest at 13 percent, and is scheduled to mature in 15 years. For bonds of this risk class you believe that a 14 percent rate of return should be required. The second investment that you are analyzing is a preferred stock ($100 par value) that sells for $90 and pays an annual dividend of $13. Your required rate of return for this stock is 15 percent. The last investment is a common stock ($25 par value) that recently paid a $2 dividend. The firm's earnings per share has increased from $3 to $6 in 10 years, which also reflects the expected growth in dividends per share for the indefinite future. The stock is selling for $20, and you think a reasonable required rate of return for the stock is 20 percent.

    a. Calculate the value of each security based on your required rate of return.

    b. Which investment(s) should you accept? Why?

    c. 1. If your required rates of return changed to 12 percent for the bond, 14 percent for the preferred stock, and 18 percent for the common stock, how would your answers change to parts (a) and (b)?

        2. Assuming again that your required rate of return for the common stock is 20 percent, but the anticipated constant growth rate changes to 12 percent, how would your answers to parts (a) and (b) change?

SUGGESTED APPLICATION FOR *DISCLOSURE*®

Using *Disclosure*, obtain the following information for the most recent year available for Johnson & Johnson:

a. Outstanding shares of common stock (Listed at the bottom of the annual income statement.)

b. The dividends and other distributions (See the Cash Flow Provided by Financing Activity section of the Cash Flow Statement.)

c. The firm's total common equity value.

d. The dividend per share.

e. The stock's dividend yield (dividend per share ÷ market price of stock).

f. The expected growth rate in earnings per share over the next five years (Zack's earnings estimates)

g. Assuming the growth rate in earnings per share is a reasonable estimate of the firm's growth rate in share price for the indefinite future, which it may not be, estimate your expected rate of return if you had purchased the stock at the time of the *Disclosure* report.

SS-1.

$$\text{Value } (V_{ps}) = \frac{.16 \times \$100}{.12}$$

$$= \frac{\$16}{12}$$

$$= \$133.33$$

SS-2.

(a) $\text{Expected return} = \dfrac{\text{Dividend}}{\text{Market Price}} = \dfrac{\$3.25}{\$38.50} = 0.0844 = 8.44\%$

(b) Given your 8 percent required rate of return, the stock is worth $40.62 to you:

$$\text{Value} = \frac{\text{Dividend}}{\text{Required Rate of Return}} = \frac{\$3.25}{0.08} = \$40.62$$

Because the expected rate of return (8.44%) is greater than your required rate of return (8%) or because the current market price ($38.50) is less than $40.62, the stock is undervalued and you should buy.

SS-3.

$$\text{Value } (V_{ps}) = \frac{\text{dividend}}{\text{required rate of return}} = \frac{\$2.75}{0.09} = \$30.56$$

SS-4.

$$\text{Value } (V_{cs}) = \left(\frac{\text{last year dividend } (1 + \text{growth rate})}{\text{required rate of return} - \text{growth rate}} \right)$$

$$= \frac{\$1.32(1.07)}{0.11 - 0.07}$$

$$= \$35.31$$

SS-5.

(a) $\begin{array}{l}\text{Expected rate} \\ \text{of return}\end{array} (\hat{k}_{cs}) = \dfrac{\text{Dividend in Year 1}}{\text{Market Price}} + \begin{array}{l}\text{growth} \\ \text{rate}\end{array}$

$$k_{cs} = \frac{\$2.50}{\$23.00} + 0.105 = .2137$$

$$k_{cs} = 21.37\%$$

(b) $V_{cs} = \dfrac{\$2.50}{.17 - .105} = \$38.46$

The expected rate of return exceeds your required rate of return, which means that the value of the security to you is greater than the current market price. Thus, you should buy the stock.

CHAPTER 8

THE MEANING AND MEASUREMENT OF RISK AND RETURN

Expected Return • Risk • The Investor's Required Rate of Return • Fama
and French: What Now? • Rates of Return: The Investor's Experience

Because we live in a world where events are uncertain, the way we see risk
is vitally important in almost all dimensions of our life. The Greek poet
and statesman Solon, writing in the sixth century B.C., put it this way:

> There is risk in everything that one does, and no one knows where
> he will make his landfall when his enterprise is at its beginning.
> One man, trying to act effectively, fails to foresee something and
> falls into great and grim ruination, but to another man, one who is
> acting ineffectively, a god gives good fortune in everything and
> escape from his folly.[1]

Although Solon would have given more of the credit to Zeus than
we might for the outcomes of our ventures, his insight reminds us that
little is new in this world, including the need to acknowledge and compensate as best we can for the risks we encounter.

The need to recognize risk in financial decisions has already become
apparent in earlier chapters. In Chapter 2, we referred to the discount rate
or the interest rate as the opportunity cost of funds, but we did not look at
the reasons that rate might be high or low. For example, we did not
explain why in April 1993 you could buy bonds issued by AT&T that

---

[1]Translated by Arthur W. H. Adkins from the Greek text of Solon's poem "Prosperity,
Justice and the Hazards of Life," in M. L. West, ed., *Iambi et Elegi Gracci ante Alexandrum
Canttati*, vol. 2 (Oxford: Clarendon Press, 1972).

promised to pay a 6.5 percent rate of return; or you could buy Kaiser Aluminum bonds that promised a return of 12.75 percent rate of return, provided both firms make the payments to the investors as promised. Then in Chapters 6 and 7, when valuing bonds, preferred stock and common stock, we suggested there is a relationship between an investor's required rate of return and the riskiness of the investment, but we gave little explanation.

In this chapter, we will examine the factors that determine rates of return (discount rates) in the capital markets and show how risk is integral to these returns. We will answer some important questions about risk and rates of return, including the following:

- What do we mean by expected rates of return? How do we measure the expected return on an investment?
- What is risk? How can it be measured?
- How does diversification of investments affect the risk and expected returns of a portfolio of assets?
- What determines the investor's required rates of return for securities with different levels of risk?
- What can we learn from history about the relationship between risk and investor returns?

BACK TO THE FUNDAMENTALS

This chapter has one primary objective, that of helping us understand **Axiom 1: The Risk-Return Tradeoff—We Won't Take on Additional Risk Unless We Expect to be Compensated with Additional Return**.

■ EXPECTED RETURN

The expected benefits or returns an investment generates come in the form of cash flows. *Cash flows*, not accounting profits, is the relevant variable the financial manager uses to measure returns. This principle holds true regardless of the type of security, whether it is a debt instrument, preferred stock, common stock, or any mixture of these (such as convertible bonds).

Accurately measuring expected future cash flows is not easy in a world of uncertainty. To illustrate: Assume you are considering an investment costing $10,000, where the future cash flows from owning the security depend on the state of the economy, as estimated in Table 8–1.

PERSPECTIVE IN FINANCE

Continue to remember that future cash flows, not the reported earnings figure, determine the investor's rate of return.

TABLE 8–1
Measuring the
Expected Return

State of the Economy	Probability of the States[a]	Cash Flows from the Investment	Percentage Returns (Cash Flow ÷ Investment Cost)
Economic recession	20%	$1,000	10% ($1,000 ÷ $10,000)
Moderate economic growth	30%	1,200	12% ($1,200 ÷ $10,000)
Strong economic growth	50%	1,400	14% ($1 400 ÷ $10,000)

[a]The probabilities assigned to the three possible economic conditions have to be determined subjectively, which requires management to have a thorough understanding of both the investment cash flows and the general economy.

In any given year, the investment could produce any one of three possible cash flows depending on the particular state of the economy. With this information, how should we select the cash flow estimate that means the most for measuring the investment's expected rate of return? One approach is to calculate an *expected* cash flow. The expected cash flow is simply the weighted average of the *possible* cash flow outcomes such that the weights are the probabilities of the occurrence of the various states of the economy. Let X_i designate the ith possible cash flow, n reflect the number of possible states of the economy, and $P(X_i)$ indicate the probability that the ith cash flow or state of economy will occur. The expected cash flow, $\hat{X}$, may then be calculated as follows:

$$\hat{X} = P(X_1)X_1 + P(X_2)X_2 + \ldots + P(X_n)X_n$$

or $$\hat{X} = \sum_{i=1}^{n} P(X_i)X_i \qquad \textbf{(8–1)}$$

For the present illustration

$$\hat{X} = (.2)(\$1,000) + (.3)(\$1,200) + (.5)(\$1,400) = \$1,260$$

In addition to computing an expected dollar return from an investment, we can also calculate an expected rate of return earned on the $10,000 investment. As the last column in Table 8–1 shows, the $1,400 cash inflow, assuming strong economic growth, represents a 14 percent return ($1,400 ÷ $10,000). Similarly, the $1,200 and $1,000 cash flows result in 12 percent and 10 percent returns, respectively. Using these percentage returns in place of the dollar amounts, the expected rate of return, $\hat{k}$, can be expressed as follows:

$$\hat{k} = P(k_1)k_1 + P(k_2)k_2 + \ldots + P(k_n)k_n$$

or $$\hat{k} = \sum_{i=1}^{n} {}_i P(k_i)k_i \qquad \textbf{(8–2)}$$

In our example:

$$\hat{k} = (.2)(10\%) + (.3)(12\%) + (.5)(14\%) = 12.6\%$$

With our concept and measurement of expected returns, let's consider the other side of the investment coin: risk.

■ RISK

In studying risk, we want to consider three questions:

1. What is risk?
2. How do we know the amount of risk associated with a given investment; that is, how do we measure risk?
3. If we choose to diversify our investments by owning more than one asset, as most of us do, will such diversification reduce the riskiness of our combined portfolio of investments?[2]

What Is Risk?

PERSPECTIVE IN FINANCE

Risk is the potential variability in future cash flows. The wider the range of possible events that can occur, the greater the risk. If we think about it, this is a relatively intuitive concept.

Without intending to be trite, risk means different things to different people, depending on the context and on how they feel about taking chances. For the student, risk is the possibility of failing an exam, or the chance of not making his or her best grades. For the coal miner or the oil field worker, risk is the chance of an explosion in the mine or at the well site. For the retired person, risk means perhaps not being able to live comfortably on a fixed income. For the entrepreneur, risk is the chance that a new venture will fail.

While certainly acknowledging these different kinds of risk, we will limit our attention to the risk inherent in an investment. To help us grasp the fundamental meaning of risk within this context, consider two possible investments:

1. The first investment is a U.S. Treasury bill, a government security that matures in 90 days and promises to pay an annual return of 6 percent. If we purchase and hold this security for 90 days, we are virtually assured of receiving no more and no less than 6 percent. For all practical purposes, the risk of loss is nonexistent.

2. The second investment involves the purchase of the stock of a local publishing company. Looking at the past returns of the firm's stock, we have made the following estimate of the annual returns from the investment:

Chance of Occurrence	Rate of Return on Investment
1 chance in 10 (10%)	0%
2 chances in 10 (20%)	5%
4 chances in 10 (40%)	15%
2 chances in 10 (20%)	25%
1 chance in 10 (10%)	30%

[2]The logic in this section is the same as to be used in Chapter 10 for capital budgeting under uncertainty.

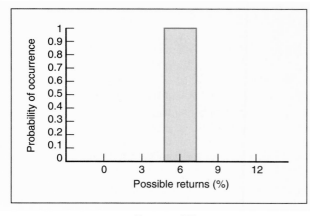

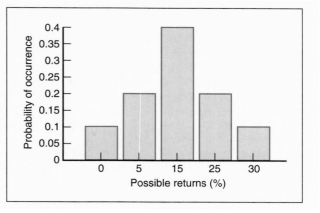

| a. Treasury Bill | b. Publishing Company |

FIGURE 8–1
Probability Distribution of Returns

Investing in the publishing company could conceivably provide a return as high as 30 percent if all goes well, or no return (zero percent) if everything goes against the firm. However, in future years, both good and bad, we could expect a 15 percent return on average.[3]

$$\hat{k} = (.10)(0\%) + (.20)(5\%) + (.40)(15\%) + (.20)(25\%) + (.10)(30\%)$$
$$= 15\%$$

Comparing the Treasury bill investment with the publishing company investment, we see that the Treasury bills offer an expected 6 percent rate of return, whereas the publishing company has an expected rate of return of 15 percent. However, our investment in the publishing firm is clearly more "risky"—that is, there is greater uncertainty about the final outcome. Stated somewhat differently, there is a greater variation or dispersion of possible returns, which in turn implies greater risk.[4] Figure 8–1 shows these differences graphically in the form of discrete probability distributions.

Although the return from investing in the publishing firm is clearly less certain than for Treasury bills, quantitative measures of risk are useful when the difference between two investments is not so evident. The standard deviation (σ) is such a measure. The **standard deviation** is simply the square root of the *average squared deviation of each possible return from the expected return;* that is

---

[3]We assume that the particular outcome or return earned in one year does *not* affect the return earned in the subsequent year. Technically speaking, the distribution of returns in any year is assumed to be independent of the outcome in any prior year.

[4]How can we possibly view variations above the expected return as risk? Should we even be concerned with the positive deviations above the expected return? Some would agree and view risk as only the negative variability in returns from a predetermined minimum acceptable rate of return. However, as long as the distribution of returns is symmetrical, the same conclusions will be reached.

$$\sigma = \sqrt{\sum_{i=1}^{n} (k_i - \hat{k})^2 P(k_i)} \qquad (8\text{--}3)$$

where n = the number of possible outcomes or different rates of return on the investment.

k_i = the value of the ith possible rate of return.

$\hat{k}$ = the expected value of the rates of return.

$P(k_i)$ = the chance or probability that the ith outcome or return will occur.

For the publishing company, the standard deviation would be 9.22 percent, determined as follows:

$$\sigma = \left[\begin{array}{l} (\ 0\% - 15\%)^2\,(.10) + (\ 5\% - 15\%)^2(.20) \\ +\ (15\% - 15\%)^2\,(.40) + (25\% - 15\%)^2(.20) \\ +\ (30\% - 15\%)^2\,(.10) \end{array} \right]$$

$$= \sqrt{85\%} = 9.22\%$$

Although the standard deviation of returns provides us with a quantitative measure of an asset's riskiness, how should we interpret the result? What does it mean? Is the 9.22 percent standard deviation for the publishing company investment good or bad? First, we should remember that statisticians tell us that two-thirds of the time an event will fall within one standard deviation of the expected value (assuming the distribution is normally distributed; that is, it is shaped like a bell). Thus, given a 15 percent expected return and a standard deviation of 9.22 percent for the publishing company investment, we may reasonably anticipate that the actual returns will fall between 5.78 percent and 24.22 percent (15% ± 9.22%) two-thirds of the time—not much certainty with this investment.

A second way of answering the question about the meaning of the standard deviation comes by comparing the investment in the publishing firm against other investments. The attractiveness of a security with respect to its return and risk cannot be determined in isolation. Only by examining other available alternatives can we reach a conclusion about a particular investment's risk. For example, if another investment, say an investment in a firm that owns a local radio station, has the same expected return as the publishing company, 15 percent, but with a standard deviation of 7 percent, we would consider the risk associated with the publishing firm, 9.22 percent, to be excessive. In the technical jargon of modern portfolio theory, the radio company investment is said to "dominate" the publishing firm investment. In common sense terms, this means that the radio company investment has the same expected return as the publishing company investment but is less risky.

What if we compare the investment in the publishing company with one in a quick oil-change franchise, an investment in which the expected rate of return is an attractive 24 percent but where the standard deviation is estimated at 13 percent? Now what should we do? Clearly, the oil-change franchise has a higher expected rate of return, but it also has a larger standard deviation. In this example, we see that the real challenge in selecting the better investment comes when one investment has a higher expected rate of return but also exhibits greater risk. *Here the final choice is determined by our attitude toward risk, and there is no single right answer.* You might select the publishing company, while I might choose the oil-change investment, and neither of us would be wrong. We would simply be expressing our tastes and preferences about risk and return.

<u>PERSPECTIVE IN FINANCE</u>

The first Chinese symbol shown below represents danger, the second stands for opportunity. The Chinese define risk as the combination of danger and

opportunity. Greater risk, according to the Chinese, means we have greater opportunity to do well, but also greater danger of doing badly.

Risk and Diversification

From the preceding discussions, we can define **risk** as the variability of anticipated returns as measured by the standard deviation. However, more can be said about risk, especially as to its nature, when we own more than one asset in our investment portfolio. Let's consider for the moment how risk is affected if we diversify our investment by holding a variety of securities.

To begin our discussion, think about owning Exxon stock. Let's also assume that the date is March 25, 1989. When you awake that morning, you follow your same routine, which includes reading the morning paper. When you open the paper, you cannot help but notice the headlines, "Alaskan Oil Spill Largest Ever!" On reading further, you discover that an Exxon tanker, the Valdez, ran aground off Prince William Sound yesterday and that millions of gallons of crude oil (11 million eventually) will probably be spilled into the sea, potentially causing great damage to the wildlife and the environment. Following this event, Exxon stock declined in price for several months.

Or what if you had been fortunate enough to buy some Pennzoil stock in November 1985, immediately before Pennzoil was awarded $10.5 billion by the courts against Texaco for alleged misconduct in "tortuously" outbidding Pennzoil in Texaco's acquisition of Getty Oil Company? Based on this single event, Pennzoil stock almost doubled, from $46 per share to $90 per share in a matter of days. (Texaco stock, on the other hand, declined from $38 to $25.)

Clearly, what we have described about Exxon and Pennzoil were events unique to these two companies, and as we would expect the investors reacted accordingly. That is, the value of the stock changed in light of the new information. While we might have wished we had owned some Pennzoil stock at the time, most of us would prefer to

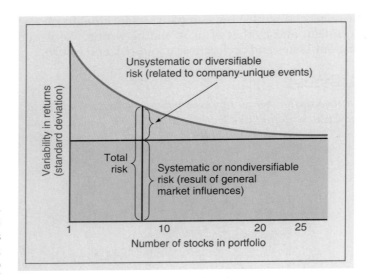

FIGURE 8–2
Variability of Returns
Compared with
Size of Portfolio

avoid such uncertainties; that is, we are risk averse. Instead, we would like to reduce the risk associated with our investment portfolio, without having to accept a lower expected return. Good news: It is possible by diversifying our portfolio!

Diversifying Away the Risk

If we diversify our investments across different securities rather than invest in only one stock, the variability in the returns of our portfolio should decline. The reduction in risk will occur if the stock returns within our portfolio do not move precisely together over time—that is, if they are not perfectly correlated. Figure 8–2 shows graphically what we may expect to happen to the variability of returns as we add additional stocks to the portfolio. The reduction occurs because some of the volatility in returns of a stock are unique to that security. The unique variability of a single stock tends to be countered by the uniqueness of another security. However, we should not expect to eliminate all risk from our portfolio. In practice, it would be rather difficult to cancel all the variations in returns of a portfolio, because stock prices have some tendency to move together. Thus, we can divide the total risk (total variability) of our portfolio into two types of risk: (1) **firm-specific** or **unsystematic risk** and (2) **market-related risk or systematic risk.** Company-unique risk might also be called **diversifiable risk,** in that it can be diversified away. Market risk is **nondiversifiable risk;** it cannot be eliminated, through random diversification. These two types of risk are shown graphically in Figure 8–2. Total risk declines until we have approximately 20 securities, and then the decline becomes very slight.[5] The remaining risk, which would typically be about 40 percent of the total risk, is the portfolio's systematic or market risk. At this

---

[5]A number of studies have noted that portfolios consisting of approximately 20 randomly selected common stocks have virtually no company-unique or diversifiable risk. See Robert C. Klemkosky and John D. Martin, "The Effect of Market Risk on Portfolio Diversification," *Journal of Finance* (March 1975), 147–154.

point, our portfolio is highly correlated with all securities in the market-place. Events that affect our portfolio now are not so much unique events but changes in the general economy, major political events, and sociological changes. Examples include changes in interest rates in the economy, changes in tax legislation that affects all companies, or increasing public concern about the effect of business practices on the environment.

Since we can remove the company-unique, or unsystematic risk, there is no reason to believe the market will reward us with additional returns for assuming risk that could be avoided by simply diversifying. Our measure of risk should therefore measure how responsive a stock or portfolio is to changes in a *market portfolio,* such as the New York Stock Exchange or the S&P 500 Index.[6] This relationship could be estimated by plotting past returns, say on a monthly basis, of a particular stock or a portfolio of stocks against the returns of the *market portfolio* for the same period.

Measuring Market Risk: An Example

To help clarify the idea of systematic risk, let's examine the relationship between the common stock returns of Waste Management and the returns of the S&P 500 Index. The monthly returns for Waste Management and for the S&P 500 Index for the 24 months ending November 1992 are presented in Table 8–2, and in Figure 8–3. These monthly returns, or **holding-period** returns, as they are often called, are calculated as follows:[7]

$$k_t = \frac{P_t}{P_{t-1}} - 1 \tag{8-4}$$

where k_t = the holding-period return in month t for a particular firm like Waste Management or for a portfolio such as the S&P Index.

P_t = a firm's stock price like Waste Management (or the S&P Index) at the end of month t.

For instance, the holding-period return for Waste Management and the S&P Index for December 1990 is computed as follows:

$$\text{Waste Management return} = \frac{\text{stock price end of December 90}}{\text{stock price end of November 90}} - 1$$

$$= \frac{\$35.00}{\$32.75} - 1 = .0687 = 6.87\%$$

$$\text{S\&P 500 Index return} = \frac{\text{index value end of December 90}}{\text{index value end of November 90}} - 1$$

$$= \frac{\$328.72}{\$322.22} - 1 = .0202 = 2.02\%$$

---

[6]The New York Stock Exchange Index is an index that reflects the performance of all stocks listed on the New York Stock Exchange. The Standard & Poor (S&P) 500 Index is similarly an index that measures the combined stock-price performance of the companies that constitute the largest 500 companies in the United States, as designated by Standard & Poor.

[7]For simplicity's sake, we are ignoring the dividend that the investor receives from the stock as part of the total return. In other words, letting D_t equal the dividend received by the investor in month t, the holding-period return would more accurately be measured as:

$$k_t = \frac{P_{t+} D_t}{P_{t-1}} - 1 \tag{8-5}$$

TABLE 8–2
Monthly Holding-Period
Returns, Waste Management,
and the S&P 500 Index
December 1990—
November 1992

Month and Year	Waste Management		S & P 500 Index	
	Prices	Returns	Prices	Returns
1990				
November	$32.75		$322.22	
December	35.00	6.87%	328.72	2.02%
1991				
January	39.38	12.50%	336.07	2.24%
February	42.25	7.30	365.65	8.80
March	39.50	−6.51	367.48	0.50
April	39.00	−1.27	379.02	3.14
May	40.88	4.81	389.83	2.85
June	36.50	−10.70	371.16	−4.79
July	37.75	3.42	380.93	2.63
August	39.50	4.64	395.43	3.81
September	37.13	−6.01	387.86	−1.91
October	37.13	0.00	384.20	−0.94
November	36.63	−1.35	376.55	−1.99
December	45.13	23.21	417.09	10.77
1992				
January	45.63	1.11%	408.79	−1.99%
February	43.75	−4.11	412.70	0.96
March	38.38	−12.29	403.69	−2.18
April	39.38	2.61	414.95	2.79
May	35.75	−9.21	415.35	0.10
June	33.63	−5.94	408.14	−1.74
July	35.63	5.95	424.21	3.94
August	33.13	−7.02	414.03	−2.40
September	36.25	9.43	417.08	0.74
October	37.25	2.76	418.68	0.38
November	40.13	7.72	431.35	3.03
Average monthly return		1.16%		1.28%
Standard deviation		8.22%		3.52%

At the bottom of Table 8–2, we have also computed the averages of the returns for the 24 months, both for Waste Management and for the S&P 500, and the standard deviation for these returns. Because we are using historical return data we assume each observation has an equal probability of occurrence. Thus the average return, $\hat{k}$, is found by summing the returns and dividing by the number of months; that is,

$$\begin{array}{l} \text{average} \\ \text{return} \end{array} = \hat{k} = \frac{\sum\limits_{t=1}^{n} \text{return in month } t}{\text{number of months}} = \frac{\sum\limits_{t=1}^{n} (k_t)}{n} \qquad \textbf{(8–6)}$$

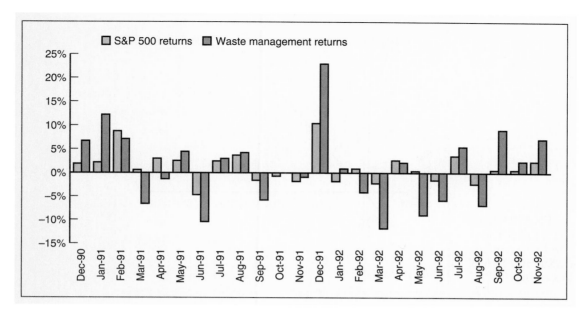

FIGURE 8–3
Monthly Holding Period Returns:
Waste Management and the S&P 500 Index December 1990–November 1992

and the standard deviation σ is computed as:

$$\text{standard deviation} = \sqrt{\frac{\sum_{t=1}^{n} (\text{return in month } t - \text{average return})^2}{\text{number of months} - 1}} \qquad \textbf{(8–7)}$$

$$\sigma = \sqrt{\frac{\sum_{t=1}^{n} (k_t - \hat{k})^2}{n - 1}}$$

The average monthly return for Waste Management and the S&P 500 Index are 1.16 percent and 1.28 percent, respectively. We also see that Waste Management has experienced significantly greater volatility of returns over the two years—a standard deviation of 8.22 percent for Waste Management compared to 3.52 percent for the S&P 500 Index.

It is also helpful to plot Waste Management's returns against the corresponding S&P 500 Index returns, which we have done in Figure 8–4. When we then draw a line of "best fit" through the plotted points, the slope of the line is 1.85.[8] The slope of this line of best fit, which we will call the **characteristic line**, tells us the average movement in the stock price of Waste Management in response to a movement in the

---

[8]Linear regression analysis is the statistical technique used to determine the slope of the line of best fit.

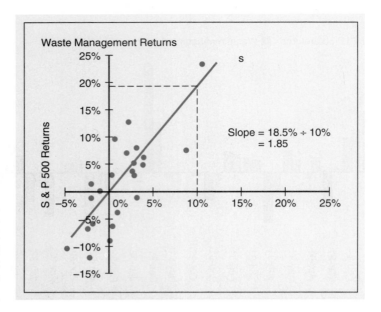

Waste Management Returns

Slope = 18.5% ÷ 10%
= 1.85

FIGURE 8–4
Monthly Holding-Period
Returns: Waste Management
and the S&P 500 Index
December 1990–
November 1992

general market (S&P 500 Index). The slope of the characteristic line, which is also called **beta**, is a measure of a stock's systematic or market risk. As reflected in Figure 8–4, the slope of the line is merely the ratio of the rise of the line relative to the run of the line.[9]

PERSPECTIVE IN FINANCE

Remember: The slope of the characteristic line is called beta, and it is a measure of a stock's systematic or market risk.

Measuring a Portfolio's Beta

From Figure 8–4, we see that the stock price of Waste Management on average changes 1.85 percent, compared to 1 percent for the average stock in the S&P 500 Index—a significantly larger change than for most stocks in the market. However, we also see a lot of fluctuation around the characteristic line. If we were, however, to diversify our holdings and own 20 stocks with betas of 1.85, like that of Waste Management, we could essentially eliminate the variation around the line; that is, we would remove almost all the volatility in returns, except for what is caused by the general market, represented by the slope of the line. If we plotted the returns of our 20-stock portfolio against the S&P 500 Index, the points in our new graph would fit nicely along a straight line with a slope of 1.85. The new graph would look something like the one shown in Figure 8–5.

---

[9]For our purposes we are primarily interested in understanding the concept of beta. However, if you are interested in knowing how to compute a firm's beta, see Chapter 8 of the Study Guide accompanying the text. Also, you should know that an estimate for the beta for many stocks is provided by investment services, such as Value Line or Merrill, Lynch, Pierce, Fenner & Smith.

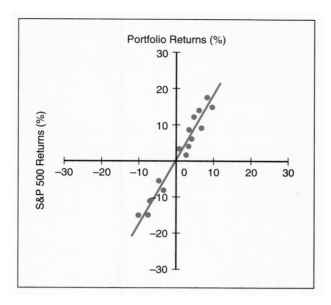

FIGURE 8–5
Holding–Period Returns:
Hypothetical Portfolio and
the S&P 500 Index

What if we were to diversify our portfolio, as we have just suggested, but instead of acquiring stocks with the same beta as Waste Management (1.85) we buy 8 stocks with betas of 1.0 and 12 stocks with betas of 1.5. What would the beta of our portfolio become? As it works out, the **portfolio beta** is merely the average of the individual stock betas. Actually, the portfolio beta is a weighted average of the individual security's betas, with the weights being equal to the proportion of the portfolio invested in each security. Thus, the beta (β) of a portfolio consisting of n stocks is equal to:

$$\beta_{\text{portfolio}} = \sum_{j=1}^{n} (\text{percentage invested in stock } j) \times (\beta \text{ of stock } j) \quad \textbf{(8–8)}$$

So, assuming we bought equal amounts of each stock in our new 20-stock portfolio, the beta would simply be 1.3, calculated as follows:

$$\text{portfolio beta} = \left(\frac{8}{20} \times 1.0 \right) + \left(\frac{12}{20} \times 1.50 \right)$$
$$= 1.3$$

Thus, whenever the general market increases or decreases 1 percent, our new portfolio's returns would change 1.3 percent on average, which says that our new portfolio has more systematic or market risk than the market has as a whole.

We can conclude that the beta of a portfolio is determined by the betas of the individual stocks. If we have a portfolio consisting of stocks with low betas, then our portfolio will have a low beta. The reverse is true as well. Figure 8–6 presents these situations graphically.

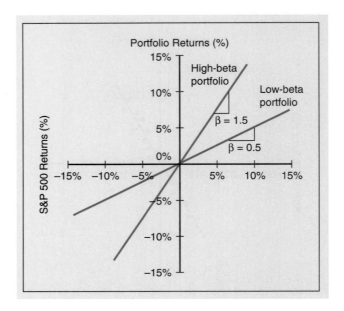

FIGURE 8–6
Holding-Period Returns:
High- and Low-Beta
Portfolios and the
S&P 500 Index

The concept of beta provides a basis for measuring a security's or a portfolio's risk. It also proves useful when we attempt to specify what the relationship should be between an investor's required rate of return and the stock's or portfolio's risk—market risk, that is.

PERSPECTIVE IN FINANCE

We can reduce risk through diversifying our portfolio, but only to a point. What we remove is company-unique or unsystematic risk (also known as diversifiable risk). Systematic risk or market risk (also termed nondiversifiable risk) cannot be eliminated.

■ THE INVESTOR'S REQUIRED RATE OF RETURN

In this section we examine the concept of the investor's required rate of return, especially as it relates to the riskiness of an asset, and then we see how the required rate of return might be measured.

The Required Rate of Return Concept

The **investor's required rate of return** can be defined as the minimum rate of return necessary to attract an investor to purchase or hold a security. This definition considers the investor's opportunity cost of making an investment; that is, if an investment is made, the investor must forgo the return available from the next best investment. This forgone return is an opportunity cost of undertaking the investment and consequently is the investor's required rate of return. In other words, we invest with the intention of achieving a rate of return sufficient to warrant making the investment. The investment will be made only if the purchase price is low enough relative to expected future cash flows to provide a rate of return greater than or equal to our required rate of return.

Investing in Bonds in Different Countries

If you had invested in government bonds in 1991, you would have done quite well, whether you lived in the United States and invested abroad or lived in another country where you invested. The figure to the right shows the rates of return you would have earned by buying government bonds in different countries. (The "dollar-term" returns assume you converted U.S. dollars into the local currency at the beginning of the year, made your investment, and then converted back to dollars at year end. Thus, your return was affected by the currency rates at the time of conversion.)

The high returns, which consisted of the interest received and the price increases in the bonds during the year, were attributable to decreasing interest rates and declining inflation rates. Australia, Japan, and Canada clearly had the highest returns, whereas European countries, with the exception of Spain, produced lower returns.

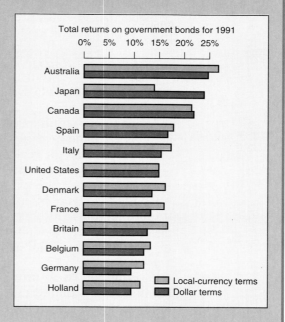

To help us better understand the nature of an investor's required rate of return, we can separate the return into its basic components: the *risk-free rate of return* plus a *risk premium*. Expressed as an equation:

$$k = k_{rf} + k_{rp} \qquad\qquad (8\text{–}9)$$

where
k = the investor's required rate of return.
k_{rf} = the risk-free rate of return.
k_{rp} = the risk premium.

The risk-free rate of return rewards us for deferring consumption, and not for assuming risk; that is, the risk-free return reflects the basic fact that we invest today so that we can consume more later. By itself, the risk-free rate should be used only as the required rate of return, or discount rate, for *riskless* investments. Typically, our measure for the risk-free rate of return is the U.S. Treasury bill rate.

The risk premium, k_{rp}, is the additional return we must expect to receive for assuming risk. As the level of risk increases, we will demand additional expected returns. Even though we may or may not actually receive this incremental return, we must have reason to expect it; otherwise, why expose ourselves to the chance of losing all or part of our money?

Assume you are considering the purchase of a stock that you believe will provide a 14 percent return over the next year. If the expected risk-free rate of return, such as the rate of return for 90-day Treasury bills, is 5 percent, then the risk premium you are demanding to assume the additional risk is 9 percent (14% - 5%).[10] ∎

Measuring the Required Rate of Return

We have seen that (1) systematic risk is the only relevant risk—the rest can be diversified away, and (2) the required rate of return, k, equals the risk-free rate, k_{rf}, plus a risk premium, k_{rp}. We may now examine how we actually estimate investors' required rates of return. Looking at equation (8–9), we see that the really tough task is estimating the risk premium.

The finance profession has had difficulty in developing a practical approach to measure the investor's required rate of return; however, financial managers often use a method called the **capital asset pricing model (CAPM).** Although certainly not without its critics, the **CAPM** provides an intuitive approach for thinking about the return that an investor should require on an investment, given the asset's *systematic* or *market* risk.

Equation (8–9) provides the natural starting point for measuring the investors' required rate of return and sets us up for using the CAPM. Rearranging this equation to solve for the risk premium (k_{rp}), we have

$$k_{rp} = k - k_{rf} \qquad \textbf{(8–10)}$$

which simply says that the risk premium for a security, k_{rp}, equals the required return, k, less the risk-free rate existing in the market, k_{rf}. For example, if the required return is 15 percent and the risk-free rate is 5 percent, the risk premium is 10 percent. Also, if the required return for the market porfolio, k_m, is 12 percent, and the risk-free rate, k_{rf}, is 5 percent, the risk premium, k_{rp}, for the market would be 7 percent. This 7 percent risk premium would apply to any security having systematic (nondiversifiable) risk equivalent to the general market, or a beta of 1.

In this same market, a security with a beta of 2 should provide a risk premium of 14 percent, or twice the 7 percent risk premium existing for the market as a whole. Hence, in general, the appropriate required rate of return for the jth security, k_j, should be determined by

$$k_j = k_{rf} + \beta_j(k_m - k_{rf}) \qquad \textbf{(8–11)}$$

Equation (8–11) is the CAPM. This equation designates the risk-return tradeoff existing in the market, where risk is defined in terms of beta.

---

[10]The risk premium here can be thought of as a composite of a "default risk premium" (reflected in the difference in the bond's rate of return and the rate on a similar maturity government bond) and "term structure" premium (reflected in the difference in the 90-day Treasury bill rate and the long-term government bond rate).

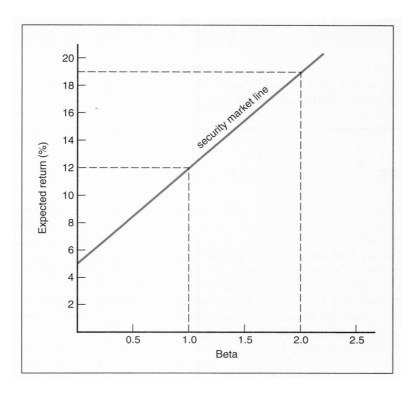

FIGURE 8–7
Security Market Line

Figure 8–7 graphs the CAPM as the **security market line.**[11] As presented in this figure, securities with betas equal to 0, 1, and 2 should have required rates of return as follows:

$$\text{If } \beta_j = 0: k_j = 5\% + 0(12\% - 5\%) = 5\%$$

$$\text{If } \beta_j = 1: k_j = 5\% + 1(12\% - 5\%) = 12\%$$

$$\text{If } \beta_j = 2: k_j = 5\% + 2(12\% - 5\%) = 19\%$$

where the risk-free rate, k_{rf}, is 5 percent and the required return for the market portfolio, k_m, is 12 percent.[12]

[11]Two key assumptions are made in using the security market line. First, we assume that the marketplace where securities are bought and sold is highly efficient. Market efficiency indicates that the price of an asset responds quickly to new information, thereby suggesting that the price of a security reflects all available information. As a result, the current price of a security is considered to represent the best estimate of its future price. Second, the model assumes that a perfect market exists. A perfect market is one in which information is readily available to all investors at a nominal cost. Also, securities are assumed to be infinitely divisible, with any transaction costs incurred in purchasing or selling a security being negligible. Furthermore, investors are assumed to be single-period wealth maximizers who agree on the meaning and the significance of the available information. Finally, within the perfect market, all investors are *price takers,* which simply means that a single investor's actions cannot affect the price of a security. These assumptions are obviously not descriptive of reality. However, from the perspective of positive economics, the mark of a good theory is the accuracy of its predictions, not the validity of the simplifying assumptions that underlie its development.

[12]For a more in-depth explanation of the CAPM, see B. Rosenberg, "The Capital Asset Pricing Model and the Market Model," *Journal of Portfolio Management* (Winter 1981), 5–16.

The conclusion of the matter is that Axiom 1 is alive and well. It tells us, **We won't take on additional risk unless we expect to be compensated with additional return.** That is, there is a risk-return tradeoff in the market.[13]

FAMA AND FRENCH: WHAT NOW?

For several years, the CAPM was touted as the "new investment technology" and received the blessings of the vast majority of professional investors and finance professors. The CAPM was attractive largely because of its ability to present important theoretical insights (which professors loved) in simple and practical terms that could be applied in practice (which professional investors loved). More recently, however, researchers have questioned whether the model really works.

The CAPM, like any abstract theory, creates some unresolved issues. For example, we might question whether the risk of an asset can be totally captured in a single dimension of sensitivity to the market, as the CAPM proposes. There is some evidence that such things as the firm's size and even the time of year may affect risk-return relationships.[13] Also, we could become discouraged in our efforts to measure a security's beta if we find that different computation methods and different periods of measurement (e.g., using three years of data versus five years) give noticeably different results. An even more basic issue is our ability to test the model empirically. Some argue that we cannot verify the accuracy of the model because we cannot know with certainty that we are using the "true market portfolio" in comparing returns and systematic risk.[14]

In 1991, two financial economists, Fama and French, argued that they had developed evidence that the CAPM does not explain why stock returns differ.[15] Thus, beta, at least according to Fama and French, is not a reasonable way to explain the risk-return relationship in the markets. The two economists examined shares traded on the major U.S. stock exchanges between 1963 and 1990. Based on their study, the better predictors of returns were the size of the firm and the ratio of the firm's accounting book value to its market value.

So should we reject the CAPM as a way to explain the relationship between risk and return in the capital markets? Not necessarily. Although Fama and French give us intriguing and controversial findings,

---

[13]See C. Barry and S. Brown, "Differential Information and the Small Firm Effect," *Journal of Financial Economics* (June 1984), 283–94; N. Chen and D. Hsieh, "An Exploratory Investigation of the Firm Size Effect," *Journal of Financial Economics* (September 1985), 451–71; and J. Jaffe and R. Westerfield, "The Week-End Effect in Common Stock Returns: The International Evidence," *Journal of Finance* (June 1985), 433–54.

[14]See, for example, Richard Roll, "A Critique of the Asset Pricing Theory's Tests," *Journal of Financial Economics* (March 1977), 129–76.

[15]Eugene Fama and Kenneth French, "The Cross-Section of Expected Stock Returns," University of Chicago Center for Research in Security Prices, 1991.

Frustrated Investors Press Search for New 'Safe' Stocks

For years, investors have relied on such firms as International Business Machines, Philip Morris and Merck to provide consistently improving profits, attractive dividends and increasing share prices all in one stock, not to mention the comfort received from these stocks performing better than others in market slumps. Such stocks were perceived by most investors as being "safe" investments. But times have changed. In recent times, the "safe" stocks have declined as much or more than any other stock. What had been unthinkable in the past has become the norm today. Some investors are wondering if there are any safe stocks left.

'New Breed' Is Emerging

Given what we have learned in this chapter about risk and rates of return, we may safely conclude that no stock is risk free. Yet some of the professionals on Wall Street believe they see a new group of "safe" stocks emerging. Two candidates, at least according to one group's thinking, are firms with a quasi-monopoly in their industry and banks. American Telephone & Telegraph is an example of the first type because the company controls 61 percent of the nation's long-distance telephone market. Banc One and NationsBank fall into the second type.

Unlike their predecessors, however, the new generation of "safe" stocks could have a much briefer life expectancy. With technological and product innovations occurring so rapidly, few companies can sustain their advantage in the market for as long as Philip Morris and IBM did.Other analysts question the very idea of a "safe" stock. "Remember, there's a difference between a really good company and a safe company," says Edward Kerschner, investment strategist at Paine

Webber. "A safe company is almost immune to external forces." Mr. Kerschner argues that the fundamental changes occurring in the economy today are so powerful that "no company, whether it is cyclical or defensive, is immune to a sea change like disinflation. In the current disinflationary environment, a safe stock is an oxymoron."

STOCK PICKS THEN AND NOW

"Safe" Stocks of 20 Years Ago

	1970 Price	All-time High Price	Recent Price
IBM	$72.90	$175.88	$50.25
General Electric	9.69	92.00	92.00
Exxon	7.72	68.25	68.00
Philip Morris	1.11	86.63	46.25
Merck	3.13	56.57	33.13

Potential 'Safe' Stocks of the 1990s

	Recent Price	52-Week High
AT&T	$58.75	$59.13
NationsBank	55.50	58.00
General Electric	92.00	92.00
Banc One	58.13	58.88
Archer-Daniels-Midland	24.75	29.00

Source: Adapted from Anita Raghavan, "Frustrated Investors Press Search for New 'Safe' Stocks," *The Wall Street Journal*, April 12, 1993, p. C1.

they lack any rationale or basic concept to explain their results. Also, we have already noted the difficulty in measuring beta. Possibly, Fama and French are experiencing data problems, which does not refute the CAPM as a good way of thinking about the problem of risk and return. It simply provides additional evidence that applying beta in practice is at best a difficult, if not hazardous, task. Another possibility: Maybe firm size and book-to-market ratios used by Fama and French to explain stock returns are proxies for other fundamentals related to risk.

For instance, a high book-to-market ratio could suggest that a company is in financial trouble; thus, its earnings prospects might be especially sensitive to economic conditions. For such a firm to attract investors, a higher expected return would be required.[16]

Advocates of CAPM believe the Fama-French results do not call for total rejection of CAPM and beta. Investors, they argue, may simply have a preference for big firms not explained by economic rationality. Or could it be that investors may not have sufficient capital to diversify risk completely, so that systematic risk does not fully explain market returns? Most recently, Chan and Lakonishok extended the Fama-French study by looking at a much longer time frame, 1926 to 1991.[17] They too found little evidence of any relationship between beta and market returns. But when they excluded data after 1982, they found that beta worked relatively well. Thus, according to Chan and Lakonishok, if there is a problem with beta, it may have developed in the 1980s, just when it had become extremely popular with financial analysts. They suggest that the explanation may lie in some of the new investment strategies used in the 1980s by professional money managers. Those strategies appear to have peaked in use, so that conceivably the CAPM could once again be a better predictor of returns, as it was in earlier years. Only time will tell if the CAPM is what it claims to be. The attacks and counterattacks on the effectiveness of the CAPM will, we believe, continue for some time, if for no other reason than there is a lack of attractive alternatives for relating risk and returns.

Only one alternative theory has been offered as a substitute, or as a possible complement, for the CAPM. This newer theory, the **arbitrage pricing model (APM)**, considers multiple economic factors when explaining required rates of return rather than looking at systematic risk or general market returns as the single determinant of an investor's required rate of return.[18]

Despite having some desirable features and potential, the arbitrage pricing model has yet to be put to wide spread use. Thus, we will need not continue beyond the basic concept.

Whatever method is used to assess an appropriate required rate of return for an investment, one key point remains. To formulate a complete concept or understanding of security valuation, we must understand the nature of the investor's required rate of return. The required rate of return, which serves as the discount rate in the valuation processis, the investor's minimum acceptable return that would induce him or her to purchase or hold a security. Despite the problems with establising a link between risk and return, the financial manager is given no choice but to make a good-faith effort to recognize and adapt to the risk-return relationship.

---

[16]The discussion of the Fama-French study comes from "Beta Beaten," *The Economist*, March 7, 1992, p. 87; and *The Economist*, February 6, 1993, p. 81.

[17]Louis Chan and Josef Lakonishok, "Are the Reports of Beta's Death Premature?" University of Illinois, December 1992.

[18]A description of the APM is found in Dorothy H. Bower, Richard S. Bower, and Dennis E. Logue, "A Primer on Arbitrage Pricing Theory," in Joel M. Stern and Donald H. Chew, Jr., eds., *The Revolution in Corporate Finance* (New York: Basil Blackwell, 1986), pp. 69–77.

■ RATES OF RETURN: THE INVESTOR'S EXPERIENCE

In speaking of expected rates of return, we have used a number of hypothetical examples; however, it is also interesting to look at returns that investors have actually received. Such information is readily available. For example, Ibbotson and Sinquefield have provided annual rates of return as far back as 1926.[19] In their results, they summarize, among other things, the annual returns for six portfolios of securities made up of:

1. Common stocks of large companies
2. Common stocks of small firms
3. Long-term corporate bonds
4. Long-term U.S. government bonds
5. Intermediate-term U.S. government bonds
6. U.S. Treasury bills.

Before comparing these returns, we should think about what to expect. First, we would intuitively expect a Treasury bill to be the least risky of the six portfolios. Because a Treasury bill has a short-term maturity date, the price is less volatile (less risky) than the price of an intermediate- or long-term government security. In turn, because there is a chance of default on a corporate bond, which is essentially nonexistent for government securities, a long-term government bond is less risky than a long-term corporate bond. Finally, common stock of large companies is more risky than a corporate bond, with small-company stocks being more risky than the portfolio of large-firm stocks.

With this in mind, we could reasonably expect different rates of return to the holders of these varied securities. If the market rewards an investor for assuming risk, the average annual rates of return should increase as risk increases.

A comparison of the annual rates of return for the six respective portfolios for the years 1926–1991 is provided in Figure 8–8. Four aspects of these returns are included: (1) the *nominal* average annual rate of return; (2) the standard deviation of the returns, which measures the volatility or riskiness of the portfolio returns; (3) the *real* average annual rate of return, which is the nominal return less the inflation rate; and (4) the risk premium, which represents the additional return received beyond the risk-free rate (Treasury bill rate) for assuming risk. Also, a frequency distribution of returns is provided. Looking first at the two columns of average annual returns and standard deviations, we gain a good overview of the risk-return relationships that have existed over the 66 years ending in 1991. For the most part, there has been a positive relationship between risk and return, with Treasury bills being least risky and common stocks being most risky. However, long-term government bonds have been as risky as corporate bonds. This aberration has largely been the result of the

---

[19]Roger G. Ibbotson and Rex A. Sinquefield, *Stocks, Bonds, Bills, and Inflation: Historical Return* (1926–1991) (Chicago: Dow Jones-Irwin, 1992).

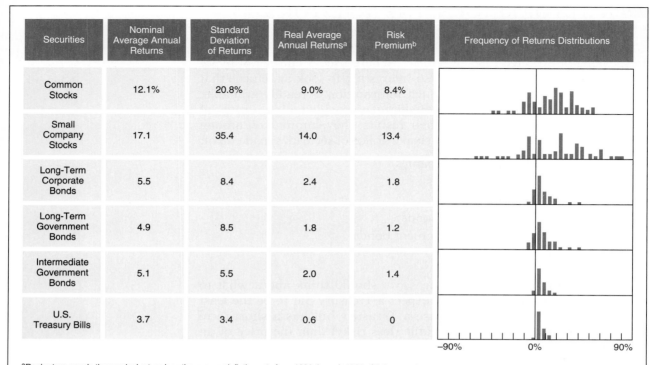

Securities	Nominal Average Annual Returns	Standard Deviation of Returns	Real Average Annual Returns[a]	Risk Premium[b]	Frequency of Returns Distributions
Common Stocks	12.1%	20.8%	9.0%	8.4%	
Small Company Stocks	17.1	35.4	14.0	13.4	
Long-Term Corporate Bonds	5.5	8.4	2.4	1.8	
Long-Term Government Bonds	4.9	8.5	1.8	1.2	
Intermediate Government Bonds	5.1	5.5	2.0	1.4	
U.S. Treasury Bills	3.7	3.4	0.6	0	

[a]Real return equals the nominal return less the average inflation rate from 1926 through 1991 of 3.1 percent.
[b]Risk premium equals the nominal security return less the average risk-free rate (Treasury bills) of 3.7 percent.

FIGURE 8–8
Annual Rates of Return 1926–91
Source: Roger G. Ibbotson and Rex A. Sinquefield, *Stocks, Bonds, Bills and Inflation: Historical Return* (Chicago: Dow Jones-Irwin, 1992), p. 32.

five years from 1977 through 1981, a period when interest rates rose to all-time highs, which had a significantly negative impact on bond prices.

The return information in Figure 8–8 clearly demonstrates that only common stock has in the long run served as an inflation hedge and provided any substantial risk premium. However, it is equally apparent that the common stockholder is exposed to sizable risk, as demonstrated by a 20.8 percent standard deviation for large-company stocks and a 35.4 percent standard deviation for small-company stocks. In fact, in the 1926–1991 time frame, common shareholders received negative returns in 18 of the 66 years, compared with only 1 in 66 for Treasury bills.

SUMMARY

In Chapter 2, the discount rate was defined as the interest rate of the opportunity cost of funds. At that point, we considered a number of important factors that influence interest rates, including (1) the price of deferring consumption, which determines the real rate of interest; (2)

the expected or anticipated inflation rate, which produces an inflation-risk premium; (3) term to maturity, which produces a maturity or liquidity premium; and (4) the variability of future returns, which produces a risk premium.

This chapter returns to the study of rates of return, carefully examining the relationship between risk and rates of return. The variability of returns is the factor that defines risk for investors and financial managers. There is no simple way to measure risk, and attitudes toward risk taking vary. There is an important distinction between nondiversifiable risk and diversifiable risk. The only relevant risk, given an investor's opportunity to diversify a portfolio, is a security's nondiversifiable risk, which is also referred to as systematic or market risk.

The capital asset pricing model (CAPM) is useful in determining an appropriate required rate of return given an asset's systematic risk, as measured by its *beta,* or the way the stock responds to changes in the market's returns. Although the model offers the advantage of being relatively intuitive, it is not definitive. Its assumptions and limitations suggest that critics will continue to look carefully for a more complete explanation for how rates are determined in the capital markets. Nevertheless, our observations do suggest that in general there is a relationship between risk and return in the capital markets. Thus, we can confidently say that as a general rule investors determine an appropriate required rate of return, depending on the amount of systematic risk inherent in a security. This minimum acceptable rate of return is equal to the risk-free rate plus a return premium for assuming the risk associated with the investment.

STUDY QUESTIONS

8–1.   **a**. What is meant by the investor's required rate of return?
       b. How do we measure the riskiness of an asset?
       c. How should the proposed measurement of risk be interpreted?
8–2.   What is (a) unsystematic risk (company-unique or diversifiable risk) and (b) systematic risk (market or nondiversifiable risk)?
8–3.   What is the meaning of beta? How is it used to calculate k, the investor's required rate of return?
8–4.   Define the security market line. What does it represent?
8–5.   How do we measure the beta for a portfolio?
8–6.   If we were to graph the returns of a stock against the returns of the S&P 500 Index, and the points did not follow a very ordered pattern, what could we say about that stock? If the stock's returns tracked the S&P 500 returns very closely, then what could we say?
8–7.   Over the past six decades, we have had the opportunity to observe the rates of return and variability of these returns for different types of securities. Summarize these observations.

SELF-TEST PROBLEMS

ST-1.   *(Expected Return and Risk)* Universal Corporation is planning to invest in a security that has several possible rates of return. Given the following probability distribution of returns, what is the expected rate of return on the investment? Also compute the standard deviation of the returns. What do the resulting numbers represent?

Probability	Return
.10	−10%
.20	5%
.30	10%
.40	25%

ST-2. *(Capital Asset Pricing Model)* Using the CAPM, estimate the appropriate required rate of return for the three stocks listed below, given that the risk-free rate is 5 percent and the expected return for the market is 17 percent.

Stock	Beta
A	.75
B	.90
C	1.40

ST-3. *(Average Expected Return and Risk)* Given the holding-period returns shown below, calculate the average returns and the standard deviations for the Kaifu Corporation and for the market.

Month	Kaifu Corp.	Market
1	4%	2%
2	6	3
3	0	1
4	2	−1

ST-4. *(Holding-Period Returns)* From the price data that follow, compute holding-period returns for periods 2 through 4.

Time	Stock Price
1	$10
2	13
3	11
4	15

ST-5. **a.** *(Security Market Line)* Determine the expected return and beta for the following portfolio:

Stock	Percentage of Portfolio	Beta	Expected Return
1	40%	1.00	12%
2	25	0.75	11
3	35	1.30	15

b. Given the information above, draw the security market line and show where the securities fit on the graph. Assume that the risk-free rate is 8 percent and that the expected return on the market portfolio is 12 percent. How would you interpret these findings?

STUDY PROBLEMS

8–1. *(Expected Rate of Return and Risk)* Pritchard Press, Inc., is evaluating a security. One-year Treasury bills are currently paying 9.1 percent. Calculate the investment's expected return and its standard deviation. Should Pritchard invest in this security?

Probability	Return
.15	5%
.30	7%
.40	10%
.15	15%

8–2. *(Expected Rate of Return and Risk)* Syntex, Inc., is considering an investment in one of two common stocks. Given the information that follows, which investment is better, based on risk (as measured by the standard deviation) and return?

Common Stock A		Common Stock B	
Probability	Return	Probability	Return
		.20	–5%
.30	11%	.30	6%
.40	15%	.30	14%
.30	19%	.20	22%

8–3. *(Expected Rate of Return and Risk)* Friedman Manufacturing, Inc., has prepared the following information regarding two investments under consideration. Which investment should be accepted?

Common Stock A		Common Stock B	
Probability	Return	Probability	Return
.2	–2%	.10	4%
.5	18%	.30	6%
.3	27%	.40	10%
		.20	15%

8–4. *(Required Rate of Return Using CAPM)*
    a. Compute a fair rate of return for Intel common stock, which has a 1.2 beta. The risk-free rate is 6 percent and the market portfolio (New York Stock Exchange stocks) has an expected return of 16 percent.

b. Why is the rate you computed a fair rate?

8–5.　　*(Estimating Beta)* From the graph below relating the holding-period returns for Aram, Inc., to the S&P 500 Index, estimate the firm's beta.

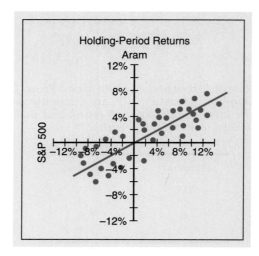

8–6.　　*(Capital Asset Pricing Model)* Johnson Manufacturing, Inc., is considering several investments. The rate on Treasury bills is currently 6.75 percent, and the expected return for the market is 12 percent. What should be the required rates of return for each investment (using the CAPM)?

Security	Beta
A	1.50
B	.82
C	.60
D	1.15

8–7.　　*(Capital Asset Pricing Model)* CSB, Inc., has a beta of .765. If the expected market return is 11.5 percent and the risk-free rate is 7.5 percent, what is the appropriate required return of CSB (using the CAPM)?

8–8.　　*(Capital Asset Pricing Model)* The expected return for the general market is 12.8 percent, and the risk premium in the market is 4.3 percent. Tasaco, LBM, and Exxos have betas of .864, .693, and .575, respectively What are the corresponding required rates of return for the three securities?

8–9.　　*(Computing Holding-Period Returns)* From the price data below, compute the holding-period returns for Asman and Salinas for periods 2 through 4.

Time	Asman	Salinas
1	$10	$30
2	12	28
3	11	32
4	13	35

How would you interpret the meaning of a holding-period return?

8–10. *(Measuring Risk and Rates of Return)*

    a. Given the holding-period returns shown below, compute the average returns and the standard deviations for the Zemin Corporation and for the market.

Month	Zemin Corp.	Market
1	6%	4%
2	3	2
3	−1	1
4	−3	−2
5	5	2
6	0	2

    b. If Zemin's beta is 1.54 and the risk-free rate is 8 percent, what would be an appropriate required return for an investor owning Zemin? (*Note:* Because the above returns are based on monthly data, you will need to annualize the returns to make them compatible with the risk-free rate. For simplicity, you can convert from monthly to yearly returns by multiplying the average monthly returns by 12.)

    c. How does Zemin's historical average return compare with the return you believe to be a fair return, given the firm's systematic risk?

8–11. *(Portfolio Beta and Security Market Line)* You own a portfolio consisting of the following stocks:

Stock	Percentage of Portfolio	Beta	Expected Return
1	20%	1.00	16%
2	30	0.85	14
3	15	1.20	20
4	25	0.60	12
5	10	1.60	24

The risk-free rate is 7 percent. Also, the expected return on the market portfolio is 15.5 percent.

    a. Calculate the expected return of your portfolio. (*Hint:* The expected return of a portfolio equals the weighted average of the individual stock's expected return, where the weights are the percentage invested in each stock.)

    b. Calculate the portfolio beta.

    c. Given the information above, plot the security market line on paper. Plot the stocks from your portfolio on your graph.

    d. From your plot in part (c), which stocks appear to be your winners and which ones appear to be losers?

    e. Why should you consider your conclusion in part (d) to be less than certain?

SELF-TEST SOLUTIONS

SS-1.

(A) Probability $P(k_i)$	(B) Return (k_i)	Expected Return $(\hat{k})$ $(A) \times (B)$	Weighted Deviation $(k_i - \hat{k})^2 P(k_i)$
.10	−10%	− 1%	52.9%
.20	5	1	12.8
.30	10	3	2.7
.40	25	10	57.6
		$\hat{k} = 13\%$	$\sigma^2 = 126.0\%$
			$\sigma = 11.22\%$

From our studies in statistics, we know that if the distribution of returns were normal, then Universal could expect a return of 13 percent with a 67 percent possibility that this return would vary up or down by 11.22 percent between 1.78 percent (13% − 11.22%) and 24.22 percent (13% + 11.22%). However, it is apparent from the probabilities that the distribution is not normal.

SS-2.

Stock A	5% + .75(17% − 5%) = 14.0%
Stock B	5% + .90(17% − 5%) = 15.8
Stock C	5% + 1.40(17% − 5%) = 21.8

SS-3. *Kaifu*
Average return:

$$\frac{4\% + 6\% + 0\% + 2\%}{4} = 3\%$$

Standard deviation:

$$\sqrt{\frac{\begin{array}{l}(4\% - 3\%)^2 \\ + (6\% - 3\%)^2 \\ + (0\% - 3\%)^2 \\ + (2\% - 3\%)^2\end{array}}{4 - 1}} = 2.58\%$$

Market
Average return:

$$\frac{2\% + 3\% + 1\% - 1\%}{4} = 1.25\%$$

Standard deviation:

$$\sqrt{\frac{\begin{array}{l}(\ 2\% - 1.25\%)^2 \\ +(\ 3\% - 1.25\%)^2 \\ +(\ 1\% - 1.25\%)^2 \\ +(-1\% - 1.25\%)^2\end{array}}{4 - 1}} = 1.71\%$$

SS-4.

Time	Stock Price	Holding-Period Return
1	$10	
2	13	($13 ÷ $10) − 1 = 30.0%
3	11	($11 ÷ $13) − 1 = −15.4
4	15	($15 ÷ $11) − 1 = 36.4

SS-5.

a. Portfolio expected return:

$$(.4 \times 12\%) + (.25 \times 11\%) + (.35 \times 15\%) = 12.8\%$$

Portfolio beta:

$$(.4 \times 1) + (.25 \times .75) + (.35 \times 1.3) = 1.04$$

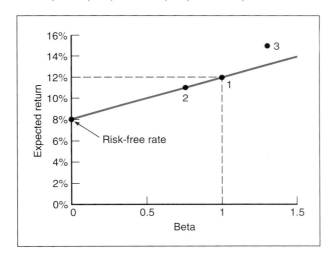

b. Stocks 1 and 2 seem to be right in line with the security market line, which suggests that they are earning a fair return, given their systematic risk. Stock 3, on the other hand, is earning more than a fair return (above the security market line). We might be tempted to conclude that security 3 is undervalued. However, we may be seeing an illusion; it is possible to misspecify the security market line by using bad estimates in our data.

CHAPTER 9

CAPITAL-BUDGETING TECHNIQUES AND PRACTICE

Finding Profitable Projects • Capital-Budgeting Decision Criteria
• Capital Rationing • Ethics in Capital Budgeting • A Glance at Actual
Capital-Budgeting Practices

In Chapter 5 we developed tools for comparing cash flows that occur in different periods. This chapter uses these techniques in conjunction with additional decision rules to determine when to invest money in long-term assets, a process called **capital budgeting.** In evaluating capital investment proposals, we compare the costs and benefits of each in a number of ways. Some of these methods take into account the time value of money, others do not; however, each of these methods is used frequently in the real world. As you will see, our preferred method of analysis will be the net present value (NPV) method that compares the present value of inflows and outflows.

Capital budgeting is a decision-making process for investment in fixed assets; specifically, it involves measuring the incremental cash flows associated with investment proposals and evaluating the attractiveness of these cash flows relative to the project's cost. Typically these investments involve rather large cash outlays at the outset and commit the firm to a particular course of action over a relatively long period. Thus, if a capital-budgeting decision is incorrect, reversing it tends to be costly.

Investing in Employee Productivity: An
Application of Capital Budgeting
from ABC News, Business World, October 14, 1990

This chapter and chapter 10 focus on methods used to evaluate the investment opportunities available to the firm. The capital-budgeting problems included in most financial management texts typically involve analyses of investments in new product lines or the process of replacing an old machine with a new, more efficient machine. It is fairly clear how one might estimate the sales of the new products, the savings from more efficient production, and the costs of acquiring the new machines. However, many situations faced by managers are not so straightforward. In this video case we examine a slightly different type of investment—investing in employee morale and commitment. The managers of Fel-Pro, a small manufacturer of gaskets in the Midwest, have decided that making investments in employee morale is good business. Employees receive cash bonuses on special occasions such as marriage, graduation, and birthdays; the firm provides day care for employee's children, a vacation ranch, and profit sharing.
While investing in employee productivity what does the firm expect as a return, how should costs and benefits be measured, should the NPV technique be applied, and is such an investment appropriate?

For example, about 35 years ago the Ford Motor Company's decision to produce the Edsel entailed an outlay of $250 million to bring the car to market and losses of approximately $200 million during the 2½ years it was produced—in all, a $450 million mistake.[1] This type of decision is costly to reverse. Fortunately for Ford, it was able to convert Edsel production facilities to produce the Mustang, thereby avoiding an even larger loss. In the 1980s General Motors made a major capital-budgeting decision by investing $3.5 billion to construct its Saturn automobile plant. As of 1993 sales looked good, but only time will tell if this decision proves to be profitable in the long run.

In this chapter we look first at the difficulties associated with finding profitable projects. Four capital-budgeting criteria are subsequently provided for evaluating capital investments, followed by a discussion of the problems created when the number of projects that can be accepted or the total budget is limited. Chapter 9 closes with an examination of capital budgeting in practice.

■ FINDING PROFITABLE PROJECTS

Without question it is easier to evaluate profitable projects than it is to find them. In competitive markets, generating ideas for profitable projects is extremely difficult. The competition is brisk for new profitable projects, and once they have been uncovered competitors generally rush

[1]"The Edsel Dies, and Ford Regroups Survivors," *Business Week*, November 28, 1959, p. 27.

in, pushing down prices and profits. For this reason a firm must have a systematic strategy for generating capital-budgeting projects. Without this flow of new projects and ideas, the firm cannot grow or even survive for long, being forced to live off the profits from existing projects with limited lives. So where do these ideas come from for new products, for ways to improve existing products, or for ways to make existing products more profitable? The answer is from inside the firm — from everywhere inside the firm.

BACK TO THE FUNDAMENTALS

The fact that profitable projects are difficult to find relates directly to **Axiom 5: The Curse of Competitive Markets — Why It's Hard to Find Exceptionally Profitable Projects.** When we introduced that axiom we stated that successful investments involve the reduction of competition by creating barriers to entry either through product differentiation or cost advantages. The key to locating profitable projects is to understand how and where they exist.

Typically a firm has a research and development department that searches for ways of improving on existing products or finding new products. These ideas may come from within the R&D department or be based on referral ideas from executives, sales personnel, or anyone in the firm. For example, at Ford Motor Company prior to the 1980s, ideas for product improvement had typically been generated in Ford's research and development department. Unfortunately, this strategy was not enough to keep Ford from losing much of its market share to the Japanese. In an attempt to cut costs and improve product quality, Ford moved from strict reliance on an R&D department to seeking the input of employees at all levels for new ideas. Bonuses are now provided to workers for their cost-cutting suggestions, and assembly line personnel who can see the production process from a hands-on point of view are now brought into the hunt for new projects. The effect on Ford has been positive and significant. Although not all suggested projects prove to be profitable, many new ideas generated from within the firm turn out to be good ones. The best way to evaluate new investment proposals is the topic of the remainder of this chapter.

CAPITAL-BUDGETING DECISION CRITERIA

In deciding whether to accept a new project we will focus on the cash flows. Cash flows represent the benefits generated from accepting a capital-budgeting proposal. In this chapter we will assume a given cash flow is generated by a project and work on determining whether that project should be accepted.

We will consider four commonly used criteria for determining acceptability of investment proposals. The first one is the least sophisticated, in that it does not incorporate the time value of money into its

FINANCIAL MANAGEMENT IN PRACTICE

Finding Profitable Projects in Competitive Markets—Creating Them by Developing a Cost Advantage

Iowa Beef Packers and Federal Express have been able to win strong competitive positions by restructuring the traditional production-cost chains in their industries. In beef packing the traditional production sequence involved raising cattle on scattered farms and ranches, shipping them live to labor-intensive unionized slaughtering plants, and then transporting whole sides of beef to grocery retailers, whose butcher departments cut them into smaller pieces and packaged them for sale to grocery shoppers. Iowa Beef Packers revamped the traditional chain with a radically different strategy: Large automated plants employing nonunion labor were built near economically transportable supplies of cattle, and the meat was partially butchered at the processing plant into smaller high-yield cuts (sometimes sealed in plastic casing ready for purchase), boxed, and shipped to retailers. IBP's inbound cattle transportation expenses, traditionally a major cost item, were cut significantly by avoiding the weight losses that occurred when live animals were shipped long distances. Major outbound shipping cost savings were achieved by not having to ship whole sides of beef, with their high waste factor. Iowa Beef's strategy was so successful that it was, in 1985, the largest U.S. meatpacker, surpassing former industry leaders Swift, Wilson, and Armour.

Federal Express redefined the production-cost chain for rapid delivery of small parcels.

Traditional firms like Emery and Airborne Express operated by collecting freight packages of varying sizes, shipping them to their destination points via air freight and commercial airlines, and then delivering them to the addressee. Federal Express opted to focus only on the market for overnight delivery of small packages and documents. These were collected at local drop points during the late afternoon hours; flown on company-owned planes during early evening hours to a central hub in Memphis, where from 11 p.m. to 3 a.m. each night all parcels were sorted; and then reloaded on company planes and flown during the early morning hours to their destination points, from which they were delivered that morning by company personnel using company trucks. The cost structure thus achieved by Federal Express was low enough to permit guaranteed overnight delivery of a small parcel anywhere in the United States for a price as low as $11. In 1986 Federal Express had a 58 percent market share of the air-express package-delivery market, versus a 15 percent share for UPS, 11 percent for Airborne Express, and 10 percent for Emery/Purolator.

Source: Arthur A. Thompson, Jr., *Economics of the Firm: Theory and Practice* (Englewood Cliffs, NJ: Prentice Hall, 1989), p. 451. Based on information in Michael E. Porter, *Competitive Advantage* (New York: Free Press, 1985), p. 109.

calculations; the other three do take it into account. For the time being, the problem of incorporating risk into the capital-budgeting decision is ignored. This issue will be examined in Chapter 10. In addition, we will assume that the appropriate discount rate, required rate of return, or cost of capital is given. The determination of this rate is the topic of Chapter 11.

Payback Period

The **payback period** is the number of years needed to recover the initial cash outlay. As this criterion measures how quickly the project will return its original investment, it deals with cash flows rather than accounting profits. It also ignores the time value of money and does not discount these cash flows back to the present. The accept-reject criterion involves whether the project's payback period is less than or equal to the firm's maximum desired payback period. For example, if a firm's maximum desired payback period is three years and an investment proposal requires an initial cash outlay of $10,000 and yields the following set of annual cash flows, what is its payback period? Should the project be accepted?

Year	After Tax Cash Flow
1	$2,000
2	4,000
3	3,000
4	3,000
5	1,000

In this case, after three years the firm will have recaptured $9,000 on an initial investment of $10,000, leaving $1,000 of the initial investment to be recouped. During the fourth year a total of $3,000 will be returned from this investment, and, assuming it will flow into the firm at a constant rate over the year, it will take one-third of the year ($1,000/$3,000) to recapture the remaining $1,000. Thus, the payback period on this project is three and a third years, which is more than the desired payback period. Using the payback period criterion, the firm would reject this project.

Although the payback period is used frequently, it does have some rather obvious drawbacks, which can best be demonstrated through the use of an example. Consider two investment projects, A and B, which involve an initial cash outlay of $10,000 each and produce the annual cash flows shown in Table 9–1. Both projects have a payback period of two years; therefore, in terms of the payback period criterion both are equally acceptable. However, if we had our choice, it is clear we would select A over B, for at least two reasons. First, regardless of what happens after the payback period, project A returns our initial investment to us earlier within the payback period. Thus, if there is a time value of money, the cash flows occurring within the payback period should not be weighted equally, as they are. In addition, all cash flows that occur after the payback period are ignored. This violates the principle that investors desire more in the way of benefits rather than less—a principle that is difficult to deny, especially when we are talking about money.

	Projects	
	A	B
Initial cash outlay	–$10,000	–$10,000
Annual net cash inflows:		
Year 1	$ 6,000	$ 5,000
2	4,000	5,000
3	3,000	0
4	2,000	0
5	1,000	0

TABLE 9–1
Payback Period Example

To deal with the criticism that the payback period ignores the time value of money, some firms use the **discounted payback period** approach. The discounted payback period method is similar to the traditional payback period except that it uses discounted net cash flows rather than actual undiscounted net cash flows in calculating the payback period. The discounted payback period is defined as the number of years needed to recover the initial cash outlay from the **discounted net cash flows.** The accept-reject criterion then becomes whether the project's discounted payback period is less than or equal to the firm's maximum desired discounted payback period. Using the assumption that the required rate of return on projects A and B illustrated in Table 9–1 is 17 percent, the discounted cash flows from these projects are given in Table 9–2. The discounted payback period for Project A is 3.07 years, calculated as follows:

$$\text{Discounted Payback Period}_A = 3.0 + \$74/\$1{,}068 = 3.07 \text{ years.}$$

If Project A's discounted payback period was less than the firm's maximum desired discounted payback period, then Project A would be accepted. Project B, on the other hand, does not have a discounted payback period because it never fully recovers the project's initial cash outlay, and thus should be rejected. The major problem with the discounted payback period comes in setting the firm's maximum desired discounted payback period. This is an arbitrary decision that affects which projects are accepted and which ones are rejected. Thus, while the discounted payback period is superior to the traditional payback period, in that it accounts for the time value of money in its calculations, its use is limited

TABLE 9–2
Discounted Payback Period
Example Using a 17 Percent
Required Rate of Return

Project A

Year	Undiscounted Cash Flows	$PVIF_{17\%,\ n}$	Discounted Cash Flows	Cumulative Discounted Cash Flows
0	–$10,000	1.0	–$10,000	–$10,000
1	6,000	.855	5,130	– 4,870
2	4,000	.731	2,924	–1,946
3	3,000	.624	1,872	–74
4	2,000	.534	1,068	994
5	1,000	.456	456	1,450

Project B

Year	Undiscounted Cash Flows	$PVIF_{17\%,\ n}$	Discounted Cash Flows	Cumulative Discounted Cash Flows
0	–$10,000	1.0	–$10,000	–$10,000
1	5,000	.855	4,275	–5,725
2	5,000	.731	3,655	–2,070
3	0	.624	0	–2,070
4	0	.534	0	–2,070
5	0	.456	0	–2,070

by this problem in selecting a maximum desired payback period. Moreover, as we will soon see, the net present value criterion is theoretically superior and no more difficult to calculate.

Although these deficiencies limit the value of the payback period and discounted payback period as tools for investment evaluation, these methods do have several positive features. First, they deal with cash flows, as opposed to accounting profits, and therefore focus on the true timing of the project's benefits and costs, even though the traditional payback period does not adjust the cash flows for the time value of money. Second, they are easy to visualize, quickly understood, and easy to calculate. Finally, although the payback period and discounted payback period methods have serious deficiencies, they are often used as rough screening devices to eliminate projects whose returns do not materialize until later years. These methods emphasize the earliest returns, which in all likelihood are less uncertain, and provide for the liquidity needs of the firm. Although their advantages are certainly significant, their disadvantages severely limit their value as discriminating capital-budgeting criteria.

BACK TO THE FUNDAMENTALS

The final three capital-budgeting criteria all incorporate **Axiom 2: The Time Value of Money—A Dollar Received Today Is Worth More than a Dollar Received in the Future** in their calculations. If we are at all to make rational business decisions we must recognize that money has a time value. In examining the following three capital-budgeting techniques you will notice that this axiom is the driving force behind each of them.

Net Present Value

The **net present value** (NPV) of an investment proposal is equal to the present value of its annual net cash flows after tax less the investment's initial outlay. The net present value can be expressed as follows:

$$NPV = \sum_{t=1}^{n} \frac{ACF_t}{(1 + k)^t} - IO \qquad (9\text{–}1)$$

where ACF_t = the annual after-tax cash flow in time period t (this can take on either positive or negative values)
   k = the appropriate discount rate that is; the required rate of return or cost of capital[2]
   IO = the initial cash outlay
   n = the project's expected life

The project's net present value gives a measurement of the *net value* of an investment proposal in terms of today's dollars. Because all

---

[2]The required rate of return or cost of capital is the rate of return necessary to justify raising funds to finance the project or, alternatively, the rate of return necessary to maintain the firm's current market price per share. These terms will be defined in greater detail in Chapter 11.

cash flows are discounted back to the present, comparing the difference between the present value of the annual cash flows and the investment outlay does not violate the time value of money assumption. The difference between the present value of the annual cash flows and the initial outlay determines the net value of accepting the investment proposal in terms of today's dollars. Whenever the project's NPV is greater than or equal to zero, we will accept the project; and whenever there is a negative value associated with the acceptance of a project, we will reject the project. If the project's net present value is zero, then it returns the required rate of return and should be accepted. This accept-reject criterion is illustrated below:

$$NPV \geq 0.0: \text{ Accept}$$
$$NPV < 0.0: \text{ Reject}$$

The following example illustrates the use of the net present value capital-budgeting criterion.

EXAMPLE

A firm is considering new machinery, for which the after-tax cash flows are shown in Table 9–3. If the firm has a 12 percent required rate of return, the present value of the after-tax cash flows is $47,678, as calculated in Table 9–4. Furthermore, the net present value of the new machinery is $7,678. Because this value is greater than zero, the net present value criterion indicates that the project should be accepted. ∎

Note that the worth of the net present value calculation is a function of the accuracy of cash flow predictions. Before the NPV criterion can reasonably be applied, incremental costs and benefits must first be estimated, including the initial outlay, the differential flows over the project's life, and the terminal cash flow.

The NPV criterion is the capital budgeting decision tool we will find most favorable for several reasons. First of all, it deals with cash flows rather than accounting profits. In this regard it is sensitive to the true timing of the benefits resulting from the project. Moreover, recognizing the time value of money allows comparison of the benefits and costs in a logical manner. Finally, because projects are accepted only if a positive net present value is associated with them, the acceptance of a project using this criterion will increase the value of the firm, which is consistent with the goal of maximizing the shareholders' wealth.

TABLE 9–3 NPV Illustration of Investment in New Machinery		After-Tax Cash Flow
	Initial outlay	–$40,000
	Inflow year 1	15,000
	Inflow year 2	14,000
	Inflow year 3	13,000
	Inflow year 4	12,000
	Inflow year 5	11,000

	After-Tax Cash Flow	Present Value Factor at 12 Percent	Present Value
Inflow year 1	15,000	.893	$13,395
Inflow year 2	14,000	.797	11,158
Inflow year 3	13,000	.712	9,256
Inflow year 4	12,000	.636	7,632
Inflow year 5	11,000	.567	6,237
Present value of cash flows			$47,678
Investment initial outlay			− 40,000
Net present value			$7,678

TABLE 9–4
Calculation for NPV Illustration of Investment in New Machinery

CALCULATOR SOLUTION[3]

Data Input	Function Key
40,000	+/− INPUT
15,000	INPUT
14,000	INPUT
13,000	INPUT
12,000	INPUT
11,000	INPUT
	EXIT CALC
12	I% YR

Function Key	Answer
NPV	7674.63

[3]If you are using an HP 17BII, first get to the CFLO menu and be certain that you have already cleared all prior data entries, selected both the "END MODE" and "one payment per year" (1P/YR), and turned the # times prompting (#T?) off. For further explanation see Appendix A.

The disadvantage of the NPV method stems from the need for detailed, long-term forecasts of the incremental cash flows accruing from the project's acceptance. Despite this drawback, the net present value is the most theoretically correct criterion that we will examine. The following example provides an additional illustration of its application.

EXAMPLE

A firm is considering the purchase of a new computer system, which will cost $30,000 initially, to aid in credit billing and inventory management. The incremental after-tax cash flows resulting from this project are provided in Table 9–5. The required rate of return demanded by the firm is 10 percent. To determine the system's net present value, the three-year $15,000 cash flow annuity is first discounted back to the present at 10 percent. From Appendix E in the back of this book, we find that $PVIFA_{10\%, 3\ yr}$ is 2.487. Thus, the present value of this $15,000 annuity is $37,305.

Because the cash inflows have been discounted back to the present, they can now be compared with the initial outlay. This is because both of the flows are now stated in terms of today's dollars. Subtracting the initial outlay ($30,000) from the present value of the cash inflows ($37,305), we find that the system's net present value is $7,305. Because the NPV on this project is positive, the project should be accepted. ■

	After-Tax Cash Flow
Initial outlay	−$30,000
Inflow Year 1	15,000
Inflow Year 2	15,000
Inflow Year 3	15,000

TABLE 9–5
NPV Example Problem of Computer System

Profitability Index (Benefit/Cost Ratio)

The **profitability index** (PI), or **benefit/cost ratio,** is the ratio of the present value of the future net cash flows to the initial outlay. Although the net present value investment criterion gives a measure of the absolute dollar desirability of a project, the profitability index provides a relative measure of an investment proposal's desirability—that is, the ratio of the present value of its future net benefits to its initial cost. The profitability index can be expressed as follows:

$$PI = \frac{\sum_{t=1}^{n} \frac{ACF_t}{(1 + k)^t}}{IO} \qquad (9\text{–}2)$$

where ACF_t = the annual after-tax cash flow in time period t (this can take on either positive or negative values)

k = the appropriate discount rate; that is, the required rate of return or cost of capital

IO = the initial cash outlay

n = the project's expected life

The decision criterion with respect to the profitability index is to accept the project if the PI is greater than or equal to 1.00, and to reject the project if the PI is less than 1.00.

PI ≥ 1.0: Accept
PI < 1.0: Reject

Looking closely at this criterion, we see that it yields the same accept-reject decision as does the net present value criterion. Whenever the present value of the project's net cash flows is greater than its initial cash outlay, the project's net present value will be positive, signaling a decision to accept. When this is true, then the project's profitability index will also be greater than 1, as the present value of the net cash flows (the PI's numerator) is greater than its initial outlay (the PI's denominator). Although these two decision criteria will always yield the same decision, they will not necessarily rank acceptable projects in the same order. This problem of conflicting ranking will be dealt with at a later point.

Because the net present value and profitability index criteria are essentially the same, they have the same advantages over the other criteria examined. Both employ cash flows, recognize the timing of the cash flows, and are consistent with the goal of maximization of shareholders' wealth. The major disadvantage of this criterion, similar to the net present value criterion, is that it requires long, detailed cash flow forecasts.

EXAMPLE

A firm with a 10 percent required rate of return is considering investing in a new machine with an expected life of six years. The after-tax cash flows resulting from this investment are given in Table 9–6. Discounting the project's future net cash flows back to the present yields a present

TABLE 9–6
PI Illustration of Investment
in New Machinery

	After-Tax Cash Flow
Initial outlay	–$50,000
Inflow year 1	15,000
Inflow year 2	8,000
Inflow year 3	10,000
Inflow year 4	12,000
Inflow year 5	14,000
Inflow year 6	16,000

value of $53,667; dividing this value by the initial outlay of $50,000 gives a profitability index of 1.0733, as shown in Table 9–7. This tells us that the present value of the future benefits accruing from this project is 1.0733 times the level of the initial outlay. Because the profitability index is greater than 1.0, the project should be accepted. ■

Internal Rate of Return

The **internal rate of return (IRR)** attempts to answer this question: What rate of return does this project earn? For computational purposes, the internal rate of return is defined as the discount rate that equates the present value of the project's future net cash flows with the project's initial cash outlay. Mathematically, the internal rate of return is defined as the value *IRR* in the following equation:

	After-Tax Cash Flow	Present Value Factor at 10 Percent	Present Value
Initial outlay	–$50,000	1.000	–$50,000
Inflow year 1	15,000	0.909	13,635
Inflow year 2	8,000	0.826	6,608
Inflow year 3	10,000	0.751	7,510
Inflow year 4	12,000	0.683	8,196
Inflow year 5	14,000	0.621	8,694
Inflow year 6	16,000	0.564	9,024

$$PI = \frac{\sum_{t=1}^{n} \dfrac{ACF_t}{(1 + k)^t}}{IO}$$

$$= \frac{\$13{,}635 + \$6{,}608 + \$7{,}510 + \$8{,}196 + \$8{,}694 + \$9{,}024}{\$50{,}000}$$

$$= \frac{\$53{,}667}{\$50{,}000}$$

$$= 1.0733$$

$$IO = \sum_{t=1}^{n} \frac{ACF_t}{(1 + IRR)^t} \qquad (9\text{–}3)$$

where ACF_t = the annual after-tax cash flow in time period t (this can take on either positive or negative values)
IO = the initial cash outlay
n = the project's expected life
IRR = the project's internal rate of return

In effect, the IRR is analogous to the concept of the yield to maturity for bonds, which was examined in Chapter 6. In other words, a project's internal rate of return is simply the rate of return that the project earns.

The decision criterion associated with the internal rate of return is to accept the project if the internal rate of return is greater than or equal to the required rate of return. We reject the project if its internal rate of return is less than this required rate of return. This accept-reject criterion is illustrated below:

$IRR \geq$ required rate of return: Accept
$IRR <$ required rate of return: Reject

If the internal rate of return on a project is equal to the shareholders' required rate of return, then the project should be accepted. This is because the firm is earning the rate that its shareholders are requiring. However, the acceptance of a project with an internal rate of return below the investors' required rate of return will decrease the firm's stock price.

If the NPV is positive, then the IRR must be greater than the required rate of return, k. Thus, all the discounted cash flow criteria are consistent and will give similar accept-reject decisions. In addition, because the internal rate of return is another discounted cash flow criterion, it exhibits the same general advantages and disadvantages as both the net present value and profitability index, but has an additional disadvantage of being tedious to calculate if a financial calculator is not available.

Computing the IRR with a Financial Calculator

With today's calculators, the determination of an internal rate of return is merely a matter of a few keystrokes. In Chapter 5, whenever we were solving time value of money problems for i, we were really solving for the internal rate of return. For instance, in the example on page 156, when we solved for the rate that $100 must be compounded annually for it to grow to $179.10 in 10 years, we were actually solving for that problem's internal rate of return. Thus, with financial calculators we need only input the initial outlay, the cash flows and their timing, and then input the function key **I% YR** or the **IRR** button to calculate the internal rate of return.

Computing the IRR for Even Cash Flows

In this section we are going to put our calculators aside and examine the mathematical process of calculating internal rates of return for a better understanding of the IRR.

The calculation of a project's internal rate of return can either be very simple or relatively complicated. As an example of a straightforward solution, assume that a firm with a required rate of return of 10 percent is considering a project that involves an initial outlay of $45,555. If the investment is taken, the after-tax cash flows are expected to be $15,000 per annum over the project's four-year life. In this case, the internal rate of return is equal to *IRR* in the following equation:

$$\$45,555 = \frac{\$15,000}{(1 + IRR)^1} + \frac{\$15,000}{(1 + IRR)^2} + \frac{\$15,000}{(1 + IRR)^3} + \frac{\$15,000}{(1 + IRR)^4}$$

From our discussion of the present value of an annuity in Chapter 5, we know that this equation can be reduced to

$$\$45,555 = \$15,000 \left[\sum_{t=1}^{4} \frac{1}{(1 + IRR)^t} \right]$$

Appendix E gives values for the PVIFA$_{i,n}$ for various combinations of i and n, which further reduces this equation to

$$\$45,555 = \$15,000 \; (PVIFA_{i, \, 4 \, yr})$$

Dividing both sides by $15,000, this becomes

$$3.037 = PVIFA_{i, \, 4 \, yr}$$

Hence, we are looking for PVIFA$_{i, \, 4 \, yr}$ of 3.037 in the four-year row of Appendix E. This value occurs when i equals 12 percent, which means that 12 percent is the internal rate of return for the investment. Therefore, since 12 percent is greater than the 10 percent required return, the project should be accepted.

Computing the IRR for Uneven Cash Flows

Unfortunately, although solving for the IRR is quite easy when using a financial calculator or spreadsheet, it can be solved directly in the tables only when the future after-tax net cash flows are in the form of an annuity or a single payment. With a calculator the process is simple: One need only key in the initial cash outlay, the cash flows and theirtiming, and press the **IRR** button. When a financial calculator is not available and these flows are in the form of an uneven series of flows, a trial-and-error approach is necessary. To do this, we first determine the present value of the future after-tax net cash flows using an arbitrary discount rate. If the present value of the future cash flows at this discount rate is larger than the initial outlay, the rate is increased; if it is smaller than the initial outlay, the discount rate is lowered and the process begins again. This search routine is continued until the present value of the future after-tax cash flows is equal to the initial outlay. The interest rate that creates this situation is the internal rate of return. This is the same basic process that a financial calculator uses to calculate an IRR.

CALCULATOR SOLUTION[4]	
Data Input	Function Key
45,555	+/– INPUT
15,000	INPUT
15,000	INPUT
15,000	INPUT
15,000	INPUT
	EXIT CALC
Function Key	Answer
IRR	12.01

[4]If you are using an HP 17BII, first get to the CFLO menu and be certain that you have already cleared all prior data entries, selected both the "END MODE" and "one payment per year" (1P/YR), and turned the # times prompting (#T?) off. For further explanation see Appendix A.

To illustrate the procedure, consider an investment proposal that requires an initial outlay of $3,817 and returns $1,000 at the end of year 1, $2,000 at the end of year 2, and $3,000 at the end of year 3. In this case, the internal rate of return must be determined using trial and error. This process is presented in Table 9–8, in which an arbitrarily selected discount rate of 15 percent was chosen to begin the process. The trial-and-error technique slowly centers in on the project's internal rate of return of 22 percent. The project's internal rate of return is then compared with the firm's required rate of return, and if the *IRR* is the larger, the project is accepted.

TABLE 9–8
Computing IRR for Uneven Cash Flows Without a Financial Calculator

CALCULATOR SOLUTION[5]

Data Input	Function Key
3817	+/– INPUT
1000	INPUT
2000	INPUT
3000	INPUT
	EXIT CALC

Function Key	Answer
IRR%	21.98

[5]If you are using an HP 17BII, first get to the CFLO menu and be certain that you have already cleared all prior data entries, selected both the "END MODE" and "one payment per year" (1P/YR), and turned the # times prompting (#T?) off. For further explanation see Appendix A.

Initial outlay	–$3,817
Inflow year 1	1,000
Inflow year 2	2,000
Inflow year 3	3,000

Solution:

Step 1: Pick an arbitrary discount rate and use it to determine the present value of the inflows.

Step 2: Compare the present value of the inflows with the initial outlay; if they are equal you have determined the IRR.

Step 3: If the present value of the inflows is larger (less than) than the initial outlay, raise (lower) the discount rate.

Step 4: Determine the present value of the inflows and repeat Step 2.

1. Try i = 15 percent:

	Net Cash Flows	Present Value Factor at 15 Percent	Present Value
Inflow year	$1,000	.870	$ 870
Inflow year 2	2,000	.756	1,512
Inflow year 3	3,000	.658	1,974
Present value of inflows			$4,356
Initial outlay			–$3,817

2. Try i = 20 percent:

	Net Cash Flows	Present Value Factor at 20 Percent	Present Value
Inflow year 1	$1,000	.833	$ 833
Inflow year 2	2,000	.694	1,388
Inflow year 3	3,000	.579	1,737
Present value of inflows			$3,958
Initial outlay			–$3,817

3. Try i = 22 percent:

	Net Cash Flows	Present Value Factor at 22 Percent	Present Value
Inflow year 1	$1,000	.820	$ 820
Inflow year 2	2,000	.672	1,344
Inflow year 3	3,000	.551	1,653
Present value of inflows			$3,817
Initial outlay			–$3,817

A firm with a required rate of return of 10 percent is considering three investment proposals. Given the information in Table 9–9, management plans to calculate the internal rate of return for each project and determine which projects should be accepted.

Because project A is an annuity, we can easily calculate its internal rate of return by determining the $PVIFA_{i, 4 \text{ yr}}$ necessary to equate the present value of the future cash flows with the initial outlay. This computation is done as follows:

$$IO = \sum_{t=1}^{n} \frac{ACF_t}{(1 + IRR)^t}$$

$$\$10{,}000 = \sum_{t=1}^{4} \frac{\$3{,}362}{(1 + IRR)^t}$$

$$\$10{,}000 = \$3{,}362 \, (PVIFA_{i, 4 \text{ yr}})$$

$$2.974 = (PVIFA_{i, 4 \text{ yr}})$$

We are looking for a $PVIFA_{i, 4 \text{ yr}}$ of 2.974, in the four-year row of Appendix E, which occurs in the $i = 13$ percent column. Thus, 13 percent is the internal rate of return. Because this rate is greater than the firm's required rate of return of 10 percent, the project should be accepted.

Project B involves a single future cash flow of $13,605, resulting from an initial outlay of $10,000; thus, its internal rate of return can be determined directly from the present-value table in Appendix C as follows:

$$IO = \frac{ACF_t}{(1 + IRR)^t}$$

$$\$10{,}000 = \frac{\$13{,}605}{(1 + IRR)^4}$$

$$\$10{,}000 = \$13{,}605 \, (PVIF_{i, 4 \text{ yr}})$$

$$.735 = (PVIF_{i, 4 \text{ yr}})$$

This tells us that we should look for a $PVIF_{i, 4 \text{ yr}}$ of .735 in the four-year row of Appendix C, which occurs in the $i = 8$ percent column. We may therefore conclude that 8 percent is the internal rate of return. Because this rate is less than the firm's required rate of return of 10 percent, project B should be rejected.

TABLE 9–9
Three IRR Investment Proposal Examples

	A	B	C
Initial outlay	$10,000	$10,000	$10,000
Inflow year 1	3,362	0	1,000
Inflow year 2	3,362	0	3,000
Inflow year 3	3,362	0	6,000
Inflow year 4	3,362	13,605	7,000

TABLE 9–10
Computing IRR for Project C

	Net Cash Flows	Present Value Factor at 15 Percent	Present Value
Try i = 15 percent:			
Inflow year 1	$1,000	.870	$ 870
Inflow year 2	3,000	.756	2,268
Inflow year 3	6,000	.658	3,948
Inflow year 4	7,000	.572	4,004
Present value of inflows			$11,090
Initial outlay			–$10,000

	Net Cash Flows	Present Value Factor at 20 Percent	Present Value
Try i = 20 percent:			
Inflow year 1	$1,000	.833	$ 833
Inflow year 2	3,000	.694	2,082
Inflow year 3	6,000	.579	3,474
Inflow year 4	7,000	.482	3,374
Present value of inflows			$ 9,763
Initial outlay			–$10,000

	Net Cash Flows	Present Value Factor at 19 Percent	Present Value
Try i = 19 percent:			
Inflow year 1	$1,000	.840	$ 840
Inflow year 2	3,000	.706	2,118
Inflow year 3	6,000	.593	3,558
Inflow year 4	7,000	.499	3,493
Present value of inflows			$10,009
Initial outlay			–$10,000

CALCULATOR SOLUTION[6]

Data Input	Function Key
10,000	+/– INPUT
1000	INPUT
3000	INPUT
6000	INPUT
7000	INPUT
	EXIT CALC

Function Key	Answer
IRR%	19.04

[6]If you are using an HP 17BII, first get to the CFLO menu and be certain that you have already cleared all prior data entries, selected both the "END MODE" and "one payment per year" (1P/YR), and turned the # times prompting (#T?) off. For further explanation see Appendix A.

The uneven nature of the future cash flows associated with project C necessitates the use of the trial-and-error method. The internal rate of return for project C is equal to the value of *IRR* in the following equation:

$$\$10,000 = \frac{\$1,000}{(1 + IRR)^1} + \frac{\$3,000}{(1 + IRR)^2} + \frac{\$6,000}{(1 + IRR)^3} + \frac{\$7,000}{(1 + IRR)^4} \quad (9–4)$$

Arbitrarily selecting a discount rate of 15 percent and substituting it into equation (9–4) for IRR reduces the right-hand side of the equation to $11,090, as shown in Table 9–10. Therefore, because the present value of the future cash flows is larger than the initial outlay, we must raise the discount rate to find the project's internal rate of return. Substituting 20 percent for the discount rate, the right-hand side of equation (9–4) now becomes $9,763. As this is less than the initial outlay of $10,000, we must now decrease the discount rate. In other words, we know that the internal rate of return for this project is between 15 and 20 percent. Because the present value of the future flows discounted back to present at 20 percent was only $237 too low, a discount rate of 19 percent is selected. As shown in Table 9–10, a discount rate of 19 percent reduces the present value of the future inflows down to $10,009, which is approximately the same as the initial outlay. Consequently, project C's internal rate of return is approximately 19 percent.[7] Because the internal rate of return is greater than the firm's required rate of return of 10 percent, this investment should be accepted. ◼

Complications with IRR: Multiple Rates of Return

Although any project can have only one NPV and one PI, a single project under certain circumstances can have more than one IRR. The reason for this can be traced to the calculations involved in determining the IRR. Equation (9–3) states that the IRR is the discount rate that equates the present value of the project's future net cash flows with the project's initial outlay:

$$IO = \sum_{t=1}^{n} \frac{ACF_t}{(1 + IRR)^t} \qquad \text{(9–3)}$$

However, because equation (9–3) is a polynomial of a degree n, it has n solutions. Now if the initial outlay (IO) is the only negative cash flow and all the annual after-tax cash flows (ACF_t) are positive, then all but one of these n solutions is either a negative or imaginary number and there is no problem. But problems occur when there are sign reversals in the cash flow stream; in fact there can be as many solutions as there are sign reversals. Thus, a normal pattern with a negative initial outlay and positive annual after-tax cash flows after that (–, +, +, +, ... , +) has only one sign reversal, hence only one positive IRR. However, a pattern with more than one sign reversal can have more than one IRR. Consider, for example, the following pattern of cash flows.[8]

	After-Tax Cash Flow
Initial outlay	–$ 1,600
Year 1	+$ 10,000
Year 2	–$ 10,000

In this pattern of cash flows there are two sign reversals, from –$1,600 to +$10,000 and then from +$10,000 to –$10,000, so there can

---

[7]If desired, the actual rate can be more precisely approximated through interpolation as follows:

Discount Rate	Present Value		
19%	$10,009 } difference $9		
IRR	10,000 }	} difference $246	
20%	9,763		

Thus, IRR = 19% + ($9/246)·1% = 19.04%

[8]This example is taken from James H. Lorie and Leonard J. Savage, "Three Problems in Rationing Capital," *Journal of Business* 28 (October 1955), pp. 229–39.

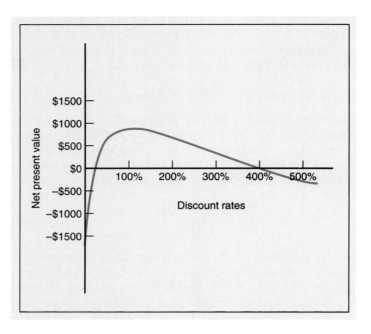

FIGURE 9–1
Multiple IRRs

be as many as two positive IRRs that will make the present value of the future cash flows equal to the initial outlay. In fact two internal rates of return solve this problem, 25 and 400 percent. Graphically what we are solving for is the discount rate that makes the project's NPV equal to zero; as Figure 9–1 illustrates, this occurs twice.

Which solution is correct? The answer is that neither solution is valid. Although each fits the definition of IRR, neither provides any insight into the true project returns. In summary, when there is more than one sign reversal in the cash flow stream, the possibility of multiple IRRs exists, and the normal interpretation of the IRR loses its meaning.

■ CAPITAL RATIONING

The use of our capital-budgeting decision rules developed in this chapter implies that the size of the capital budget is determined by the availability of acceptable investment proposals. However, a firm may place a limit on the dollar size of the capital budget. This situation is called **capital rationing.** As we will see, an examination of capital rationing will not only enable us to deal with complexities of the real world better but will serve to demonstrate the superiority of the NPV method over the IRR method for capital budgeting as well.

Using the internal rate of return as the firm's decision rule, a firm accepts all projects with an internal rate of return greater than the firm's required rate of return. This rule is illustrated in Figure 9–2, where projects A through E would be chosen. However, when capital rationing is imposed, the dollar size of the total investment is limited by the budget constraint. In Figure 9–2 the budget constraint of $X

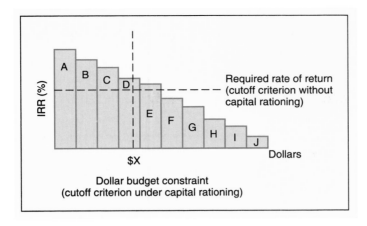

FIGURE 9–2
Projects Ranked by IRR

precludes the acceptance of an attractive investment, project E. This situation obviously contradicts prior decision rules. Moreover, the solution of choosing the projects with the highest internal rate of return is complicated by the fact that some projects may be indivisible; for example, it is meaningless to recommend that half project D be acquired.

PERSPECTIVE IN FINANCE

It is always somewhat uncomfortable to deal with problems associated with capital rationing because, under capital rationing, projects with positive net present values are rejected. This is a situation that violates the firm's goal of shareholder wealth maximization. However, in the real world capital rationing does exist, and managers must deal with it. Often when firms impose capital constraints they are recognizing that they do not have the ability to handle more than a certain number or dollar value of new projects profitably.

Rationale for Capital Rationing

We will first ask why capital rationing exists and whether it is rational. In general, three principal reasons are given for imposing a capital-rationing constraint. First, management may think market conditions are temporarily adverse. In the period surrounding the stock market crash of 1987 this reason was frequently given. At that time interest rates were high, and stock prices were depressed. Second, there may be a shortage of qualified managers to direct new projects; this can happen when projects are of a highly technical nature. Third, there may be intangible considerations. For example, management may simply fear debt, wishing to avoid interest payments at any cost. Or perhaps issuance of common stock may be limited to maintain a stable dividend policy.

Despite strong evidence that capital rationing exists in practice, the question remains as to its effect on the firm. In brief, the effect is negative, and to what degree depends on the severity of the rationing. If the rationing is minor and short-lived, the firm's share price will not suffer

TABLE 9–11
Capital-Rationing Example of
Five Indivisible Projects

Project	Initial Outlay	Profitability Index	Net Present Value
A	$200,000	2.4	$280,000
B	200,000	2.3	260,000
C	800,000	1.7	560,000
D	300,000	1.3	90,000
E	300,000	1.2	60,000

to any great extent. In this case capital rationing can probably be excused, although it should be noted that any capital rationing that rejects projects with positive net present values is contrary to the firm's goal of maximization of shareholders' wealth. If the capital rationing is a result of the firm's decision to limit dramatically the number of new projects or to limit total investment to internally generated funds, then this policy will eventually have a significantly negative effect on the firm's share price. For example, a lower share price will eventually result from lost competitive advantage if, owing to a decision to limit arbitrarily its capital budget, a firm fails to upgrade its products and manufacturing process.

Capital Rationing and Project Selection

If the firm decides to impose a capital constraint on investment projects, the appropriate decision criterion is to select the set of projects with the highest net present value subject to the capital constraint. This guideline may preclude merely taking the highest-ranked projects in terms of the profitability index or the internal rate of return. If the projects shown in Figure 9–2 are divisible, the last project accepted may be only partially accepted. Although partial acceptances may be possible in some cases, the indivisibility of most capital investments prevents it. If a project is a sales outlet or a truck, it may be meaningless to purchase half a sales outlet or half a truck.

To illustrate this procedure, consider a firm with a budget constraint of $1 million and five indivisible projects available to it, as given in Table 9–11. If the highest-ranked projects were taken, projects A and B would be taken first. At that point there would not be enough funds available to take project C; hence, projects D and E would be taken. However, a higher total net present value is provided by the combination of projects A and C. Thus projects A and C should be selected from the set of projects available. This illustrates our guideline: to select the set of projects that maximizes the firm's net present value.

Project Ranking

In the past, we have proposed that all projects with a positive net present value, a profitability index greater than 1.0, or an internal rate of return greater than the required rate of return be accepted, assuming there is no capital rationing. However, this acceptance is not always possible. In some cases, when two projects are judged acceptable by the discounted cash flow criteria, it may be necessary to select only one of them, as they are mutually exclusive. **Mutually exclusive projects** occur when a set of investment proposals perform essentially the same task; acceptance of one will necessarily mean rejection of the others. For example, a company considering the installation of a computer system may evaluate three or four systems, all of which may have positive net present values; however, the acceptance of one system will automatically mean rejection of the others. In general, to deal with mutually exclusive projects, we will simply rank them by means of the discounted cash flow criteria and select the project with the highest ranking. On occasion, however, problems of conflicting ranking may arise. As we will see, in general the net present value method is the preferred decision-making tool because it leads to the selection of the project that increases shareholder wealth the most.

Problems in Project Ranking

There are three general types of ranking problems: the size disparity problem, the time disparity problem, and the unequal lives problem. Each involves the possibility of conflict in the ranks yielded by the various discounted cash flow capital-budgeting criteria. As noted previously, when one discounted cash flow criterion gives an accept signal, they will all give an accept signal, but they will not necessarily rank all projects in the same order. In most cases this disparity is not critical; however, for mutually exclusive projects the ranking order is important.

Size Disparity

The *size disparity problem* occurs when mutually exclusive projects of unequal size are examined. This problem is most easily clarified with an example.

EXAMPLE

Suppose a firm is considering two mutually exclusive projects, A and B, both with required rates of return of 10 percent. Project A involves a $200 initial outlay and cash inflow of $300 at the end of one year, whereas project B involves an initial outlay of $1,500 and a cash inflow of $1,900 at the end of one year. The net present value, profitability index, and internal rate of return for these projects are given in Table 9–12.

In this case, if the net present value criterion is used, project B should be accepted, whereas if the profitability index or the internal rate of return criterion is used, project A should be chosen. The question now becomes: Which project is better? The answer depends on whether capital rationing exists. Without capital rationing, project B is better because it provides the largest increase in shareholders' wealth; that is, it has a larger net present value. If there is a capital constraint, the problem then focuses on what can be done with the additional $1,300 that is freed if project A is chosen (costing $200, as opposed to $1,500). If the firm can earn more on project A plus the project financed with the additional

TABLE 9–12
Size Disparity
Ranking Problem

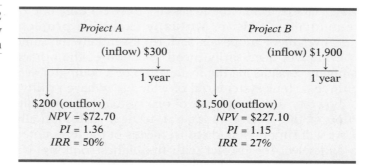

Project A	Project B
(inflow) $300	(inflow) $1,900
1 year	1 year
$200 (outflow)	$1,500 (outflow)
NPV = $72.70	NPV = $227.10
PI = 1.36	PI = 1.15
IRR = 50%	IRR = 27%

$1,300 than it can on project B, then project A and the marginal project should be accepted. In effect, we are attempting to select the set of projects that maximize the firm's NPV. Thus, if the marginal project has a net present value greater than $154.40 ($277.10 – $72.70), selecting it plus project A with a net present value of $72.70 will provide a net present value greater than $227.10, the net present value for project B. ■

In summary, whenever the size disparity problem results in conflicting rankings between mutually exclusive projects, the project with the largest net present value will be selected, provided there is no capital rationing. When capital rationing exists, the firm should select the set of projects with the largest net present value.

Time Disparity

The *time disparity problem* and the conflicting rankings that accompany it result from the differing reinvestment assumptions made by the net present value and internal rate of return decision criteria. The NPV criterion assumes that cash flows over the life of the project can be reinvested at the required rate of return or cost of capital, whereas the IRR criterion implicitly assumes that the cash flows over the life of the project can be reinvested at the internal rate of return. Again, this problem may be illustrated through the use of an example.

EXAMPLE

Suppose a firm with a required rate of return or cost of capital of 10 percent and with no capital constraint is considering the two mutually exclusive projects illustrated in Table 9–13. The net present value and profitability index indicate that project A is the better of the two, whereas the internal rate of return indicates that project B is the better. Project B receives its cash flows earlier than project A, and the different assumptions made as to how these flows can be reinvested result in the difference in rankings. Which criterion should be followed depends on which reinvestment assumption is used. The net present value criterion is preferred in this case because it makes the most acceptable assumption for the wealth-maximizing firm. It is certainly the most conservative assumption that can be made, because the required rate of return is the lowest possible reinvestment rate. Moreover, as we have already

TABLE 9–13
Time Disparity Ranking
Problem

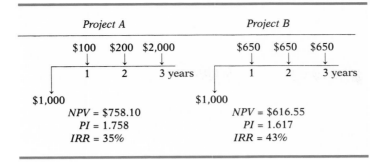

noted, the net present value method maximizes the value of the firm and the shareholders' wealth. ■

Unequal Lives

The final ranking problem to be examined centers on the question of whether it is appropriate to compare mutually exclusive projects with different life spans.

EXAMPLE

Suppose a firm with a 10 percent required rate of return is faced with the problem of replacing an aging machine and is considering two replacement machines, one with a three-year life and one with a six-year life. The relevant cash flow information for these projects is given in Table 9–14.

Examining the discounted cash flow criteria, we find that the net present value and profitability index criteria indicate that project B is the better project, whereas the internal rate of return favors project A. This ranking inconsistency is caused by the different life spans of the projects being compared. In this case the decision is a difficult one because the projects are not comparable.

The problem of incomparability of projects with different lives arises because future profitable investment proposals may be rejected without

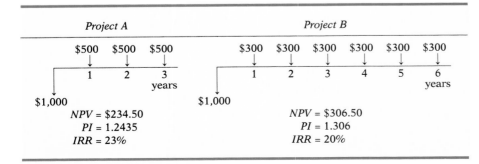

TABLE 9–14
Unequal Lives Ranking
Problem

being included in the analysis. This can easily be seen in a replacement problem such as the present example, in which two mutually exclusive machines with different lives are being considered. In this case a comparison of the net present values alone on each of these projects would be misleading. If the project with the shorter life were taken, at its termination the firm could replace the machine and receive additional benefits, whereas acceptance of the project with the longer life would exclude this possibility, a possibility that is not included in the analysis. The key question thus becomes: Does today's investment decision include all future profitable investment proposals in its analysis? If not, the projects are not comparable. In this case, if project B is taken, then the project that could have been taken after three years when project A terminates is automatically rejected without being included in the analysis. Thus, acceptance of project B not only forces rejection of project A, but also forces rejection of any replacement machine that might have been considered for years 4 through 6 without including this replacement machine in the analysis.

There are several methods to deal with this situation. The first option is to assume that the cash inflows from the shorter-lived investment will be reinvested at the required rate of return until the termination of the longer-lived asset. Although this approach is the simplest, merely calculating the net present value, it actually ignores the problem at hand—that of allowing for participation in another replacement opportunity with a positive net present value. The proper solution thus becomes the projection of reinvestment opportunities into the future—that is, making assumptions about possible future investment opportunities. Unfortunately, while the first method is too simplistic to be of any value, the second is extremely difficult, requiring extensive cash flow forecasts. The final technique for confronting the problem is to assume that reinvestment opportunities in the future will be similar to the current ones. The two most common ways of doing this are by creating a replacement chain to equalize life spans or calculating the project's Equivalent Annual Annuity (EAA). Using a replacement chain, the present example would call for the creation of a two-chain cycle for project A; that is, we assume that project A can be replaced with a similar investment at the end of three years. Thus, project A would be viewed as two A projects occurring back to back, as illustrated in Figure 9–3. The net present value on this replacement chain is $426.50, which is comparable with project B's net present value. Therefore, project A should be accepted because the net present value of its replacement chain is greater than the net present value of project B.

One problem with replacement chains is that depending on the life of each project, it can be quite difficult to come up with equivalent lives. For example, if the two projects had 7- and 13-year lives, a 91-year replacement chain would be needed to establish equivalent lives. In this case it is easier to determine the project's **equivalent annual annuity (EAA)**. A project's EAA is simply an annuity cash flow that yields the same present value as the project's NPV. To calculate a project's EAA we need only calculate a project's NPV and then divide that number by the

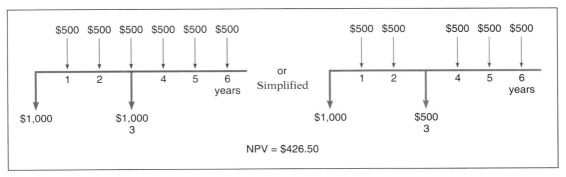

FIGURE 9–3
Replacement Chain Illustration: Two A Project A's Back to Back

PVIFA$_{i,n}$ to determine the dollar value of an n-year annuity that would produce the same NPV as the project. This can be done in two steps as follows:

Step 1: *Calculate the project's NPV.* In Table 9–14 we determined that project A had an NPV of $234.50, whereas project B had an NPV of $306.50.

Step 2: *Calculate the EAA.* The EAA is determined by dividing each project's NPV by the PVIFA$_{i,n}$ where i is the required rate of return and n is the project's life. This determines the level of an annuity cash flow that would produce the same NPV as the project. For project A the PVIFA$_{10\%, 3\ yr}$ is equal to 2.487, whereas the PVIFA$_{10\%, 6\ yr}$ for project B is equal to 4.355. Dividing each project's NPV by the appropriate PVIFA$_{i,n}$ we determine the EAA for each project:

$$EAA_A = NPV/PVIFA_{i,n}$$
$$= \$234.50/2.487$$
$$= \$94.29$$
$$EAA_B = \$306.50/4.355$$
$$= \$70.38$$

How do we interpret the EAA? For a project with an n-year life, it tells us what the dollar value is of an n-year annual annuity that would provide the same NPV as the project. Thus, for project A it means that a three-year annuity of $94.29 given a discount rate of 10 percent would produce a net present value the same as project A's net present value, which is $234.50. We can now compare the equivalent annual annuities directly to determine which project is better. We can do this because we now have found the level of annual annuity that produces an NPV equivalent to the project's NPV. Thus, because they are both annual annuities they are comparable. An easy way to see this is to use the EAAs to create infinite-life replacement chains. To do this we need only calculate the present value of an infinite stream or perpetuity of equivalent annual annuities. This is done by using the present value of an

Bad Apple for Baby

It's a widely held but hard to prove belief that a company gains because it is perceived as more socially responsive than its competitors. Over the years, the three major manufacturers of baby food—Gerber Products, Beech-Nut Nutrition and H. J. Heinz—had, with almost equal success, gone out of their way to build an image of respectability.

Theirs is an almost perfect zero-sum business. They know, at any given time, how many babies are being born. They all pay roughly the same price for their commodities, and their manufacturing and distribution costs are almost identical. So how does one company gain a market share edge over another, especially in a stagnant or declining market?

The answer for Beech-Nut was to sell a cheaper, adulterated product. Beginning in 1977, the company began buying a chemical concoction, made up mostly of sugar and water, and labeling it as apple juice. Sales of that product brought Beech-Nut an estimated $60 million between 1977 and 1982, while reducing material costs about $250,000 annually.

When various investigators tried to do something about it, the company stonewalled. Among other things, they shipped the bogus juice out of a plant in New York to Puerto Rico to put it beyond the jurisdiction of federal investigators, and they even offered the juice as a giveaway to reduce their stocks after they were finally forced to discontinue selling it.

In the end, the company pleaded guilty to 215 counts of introducing adulterated food into commerce and violating the Federal Food Drug and Cosmetic Act. The FDA fined Beech-Nut $2 million.

In addition, Beech-Nut's president, Neils Hoyvald, and its vice president of operations, John Lavery, were found guilty of similar charges. Each was sentenced to a year and one day in jail and fined $100,000. Both are now out on appeal on a jurisdiction technicality.

Why did they do it? The Fort Washington, Pa.-based company will not comment. But perhaps some portion of motive can be inferred from a report Hoyvald wrote to Nestle, the company that had acquired Beech-Nut in the midst of his coverup. "It is our feeling that we can report safely now that the apple juice recall has been completed. If the recall had been effectuated in early June [when the FDA had first ordered it], over 700,000 cases in inventory would have been affected due to our many delays, we were only faced with having to destroy 20,000 cases."

One thing is clear: Two executives of a company with an excellent reputation breached a trust and did their company harm.

Since 1987, when the case was brought to a close, Beech-Nut's share of the overall baby food market has fallen from 19.1% to 15.8%. So what was gained in the past has been lost in the present, and perhaps for the future as well.

Source: Stephen Kindel, "Bad Apple for Baby," *Financial World*, June 27, 1989, p. 48.

infinite annuity formula, that is, simply dividing the equivalent annual annuity by the appropriate discount rate. In this case we find:

$$NPV_{\infty, A} = \$94.29/.10$$
$$= \$942.90$$
$$NPV_{\infty, B} = \$70.38/.10$$
$$= \$703.80$$

Here we have calculated the present value of an infinite-life replacement chain. Because the EAA method provides the same results as the infinite-life replacement chain, it really doesn't matter which method you prefer to use.

ETHICS IN CAPITAL BUDGETING

Although it may not seem obvious, ethics has a role in capital budgeting. Beech-Nut provides an example of how these rules have been violated in the past and what the consequences can be. No doubt this project appeared to have a positive net present value associated with it, but in fact, it cost Beech-Nut tremendously. The *Ethics in Financial Management* insert, "Bad Apple for Baby," tells what occurred.

BACK TO THE FUNDAMENTALS

Ethics and ethical considerations continually crop up when capital-budgeting decisions are being made. This brings us back to **Axiom 9: Ethical Behavior Is Doing the Right Thing, and Ethical Dilemmas Are Everywhere in Finance.** As the *Ethics in Financial Management* insert, "Bad Apple for Baby," points out, the most damaging event a business can experience is a loss of the public's confidence in its ethical standards. In making capital-budgeting decisions we must be aware of this, and that ethical behavior is doing the right thing and is the right thing to do.

A GLANCE AT ACTUAL CAPITAL-BUDGETING PRACTICES

During the past 35 years the popularity of each of the capital-budgeting methods has shifted rather dramatically. In the 1950s the payback period method dominated capital budgeting, but through the 1960s and 1970s the discounted cash flow decision techniques slowly displaced the nondiscounted techniques. This movement from the payback period to net present value and the internal rate of return is shown in Table 9–15, which indicates the growth in popularity of these techniques as reflected in surveys of practices over the years. Interestingly, although most firms use the NPV and IRR as their primary techniques, most firms also use the payback period as a secondary decision method for capital budgeting. In a sense they are using the payback period to control for risk. The logic behind this is that because the payback period dramatically emphasizes early cash flows, which are presumably more certain—that is, have less risk—than cash flows occurring later in a project's life, managers believe its use will lead to projects with more certain cash flows.

A reliance on the payback period came out even more dramatically in a study of the capital-budgeting practices of 12 large manufacturing firms.[9] Information for this study was gathered from interviews over one to three days in addition to an examination of the records of about 400 projects. This study revealed several points of interest. First, firms were typically found to categorize capital investments as mandatory (regulations and contracts, capitalized maintenance, replacement of antiqued

---

[9]Marc Ross, "Capital Budgeting Practices of Twelve Large Manufacturers," *Financial Management*, 15 (Winter 1986), pp. 15–22.

TABLE 9–15
Past Surveys of Capital-Budgeting Practices—Percent of Respondents Using Each Technique

Capital-Budgeting Technique	Klammer, 1959	Klammer, 1964	Klammer, 1970	Petty et al., 1972	Kim and Farragher, 1975	Gitman and Forrester, 1977	Kim and Farragher 1979	Kim, Crick and Kim 1986
Primary method:								
NPV	5%	15%	27%	15%	26%	13%	19%	21%
IRR	8	17	30	41	37	53	49	49
Payback	34	24	12	11	15	9	12	19
Secondary method:								
NPV	2%	3%	7%	14%	7%	28%	8%	24%
IRR	1	2	6	19	7	14	8	15
Payback	18	21	32	37	33	44	39	35

Sources: Thomas Klammer, "Empirical Evidence of the Adoption of Sophisticated Capital Budgeting Techniques," *Journal of Business* (July 1972), pp. 387–397; J. William Petty, David F. Scott, Jr., and Monroe M. Bird, "The Capital Expenditure Decision-Making Process of Large Corporations," *Engineering Economist* (Spring 1975), pp. 159–172; S. H. Kim and E. J. Farragher, "Capital Budgeting Practices in Large Industrial Firms," *Baylor Business Studies* (November 1976), pp. 19–25; Lawrence J. Gitman and John R. Forrester, Jr., "Forecasting and Evaluation Practices and Performance: A Survey of Capital Budgeting," *Financial Management* (Fall 1977), pp. 66–71; S. H. Kim and E. J. Farragher, "Current Capital Budgeting Practices," *Management Accounting* (June 1981), pp. 26–30; and Suk H. Kim, T. Crick, and Sesung H. Kim, "Do Executives Practice What Academics Preach?" *Management Accounting* (November 1986), pp. 49–52.

equipment, product quality) or discretionary (expanded markets, new businesses, cost cutting), with the decision-making process being different for mandatory and discretionary projects. Second, it was found that the decision-making process was different for projects of differing size. In fact, approval authority tended to rest in different locations, depending on the size of the project. Table 9–16 provides the typical levels of approval authority.

The study also showed that while the discounted cash flow methods are used at most firms, the simple payback criterion was the measure relied on primarily in one-third of the firms examined. The use of the payback period seemed to be even more common for smaller projects, with firms severely simplifying the discounted cash flow analysis or relying primarily on the payback period. Thus, although discounted cash flow decision techniques have become more widely accepted, their use depends to an extent on the size of the project and where within the firm the decision is being made.

TABLE 9–16
Project Size and Decision-Making Authority

Project Size	Typical Boundaries	Primary Decision Site
Very small	Up to $100,000	Plant
Small	$100,000 to $1,000,000	Division
Medium	$1 million to $10 million	Corporate investment committee
Large	Over $10 million	CEO & board

SUMMARY

The process of capital budgeting involves decision making with respect to investment in fixed assets. We examine four commonly used criteria for determining the acceptance or rejection of capital-budgeting proposals. The first method, the payback period, does not incorporate the time value of money into its calculations, although a variation of it, the discounted payback period, recognizes the time value of money. The discounted methods, the net present value, profitability index, and internal rate of return, do account for the time value of money. These methods are summarized in Table 9–17.

This chapter introduces several complications into the capital-budgeting process. First, we examine capital rationing and the problems it can create by imposing a limit on the dollar size of the capital budget. Although capital rationing does not, in general, lead to the goal of maximization of shareholders' wealth, it does exist in practice. We also discuss problems associated with the evaluation of mutually exclusive projects. Mutually exclusive projects occur when a set of investment proposals perform essentially the same task. In general, to deal with mutually exclusive projects, we rank them by means of the discounted cash flow criteria and select the project with the highest ranking. Conflicting rankings

TABLE 9–17
Capital-Budgeting Criteria

1. Payback period = number of years required to recapture the initial investment

Accept if payback ≤ maximum acceptable payback period
Reject if payback > maximum acceptable payback period

Advantages:
- Uses cash flows.
- Is easy to calculate and understand.
- May be used as rough screening device.

Disadvantages
- Ignores the time value of money.
- Ignores cash flows occurring after the payback period
- Selection of the maximum acceptable payback period is arbitrary.

2. Discounted Payback period--the number of years needed to recover the initial cash outlay from the *discounted net cash flows*.

Accept if discounted payback ≤ maximum acceptable discounted payback period
Reject if discounted payback > maximum acceptable discounted payback period

Advantages
- Uses cash flows.
- Is easy to calculate and understand.
- Consider time value of money

Disadvantages
- Ignores cash flows occurring after the payback period.
- Selection of the maximum acceptable payback period is arbitrary.

3. Net present value = present value of the annual cash flows after tax less the investment's initial outlay

$$NPV = \sum_{t=1}^{n} \frac{ACF_t}{(1 + k)^t} - IO$$

where ACF_t = the annual after-tax cash flow in time period t (this can take on either positive or negative values)

k = the appropriate discount rate; that is, the required rate of return or the cost of capital

IO = the initial cash outlay

n = the project's expected life

Accept if $NPV \geq 0.0$
Reject if $NPV < 0.0$

Advantages:	Disadvantages:
• Uses cash flows.	• Requires detailed long-term forecasts of the incremental benefits and costs.
• Recognizes the time value of money.	
• Is consistent with the firm goal of shareholder wealth maximization.	

• Profitability index = the ratio of the present value of the future net cash flows to the initial outlay.

$$PI = \frac{\sum_{t=1}^{n} \frac{ACF_t}{(1+k)^t}}{IO}$$

Accept if $PI \geq 1.0$
Reject if $PI < 1.0$

Advantages:	Disadvantages:
• Uses cash flows.	• Requires detailed long-term forecasts of the incremental benefits and costs.
• Recognizes the time value of money.	
• Is consistent with the firm goal of shareholder wealth maximization.	

• Internal rate of return = the discount rate that equates the present value of the project's future net cash flows with the project's initial outlay.

$$IO = \sum_{t=1}^{n} \frac{ACF_t}{(1+IRR)^t}$$

where IRR = the project's internal rate of return

Accept if $IRR \geq$ required rate of return
Reject if $IRR <$ required rate of return

Advantages:	Disadvantages:
• Uses cash flows.	• Requires detailed long-term forecasts of the incremental benefits and costs.
• Recognizes the time value of money.	
• Is in general consistent with the firm goal of shareholder wealth maximization.	• Can involve tedious calculations.
	• Possibility of multiple IRRs.

may arise because of the size disparity problem, the time disparity problem, and unequal lives. The problem of incomparability of projects with different lives is not simply a result of the different lives; rather, it arises because future profitable investment proposals may be rejected without being included in the analysis. Replacement chains and equivalent annual annuities are presented as possible solutions to this problem.

STUDY QUESTIONS

9–1. Why is the capital-budgeting decision such an important process? Why are capital-budgeting errors so costly?

9–2. What are the criticisms of the use of the payback period as a capital-budgeting technique? What are its advantages? Why is it so frequently used?

9–3. In some countries, expropriation of foreign investments is a common practice. If you were considering an investment in one of those countries, would the use of the payback period criterion seem more reasonable than it otherwise might? Why?

9–4. Briefly compare and contrast the NPV, PI and IRR criteria. What are the advantages and disadvantages of using each of these methods?

9–5. What are mutually exclusive projects? Why might the existence of mutually exclusive projects cause problems in the implementation of the discounted cash flow capital-budgeting criteria?

9–6. What are common reasons for capital rationing? Is capital rationing rational?

9–7. How should managers compare two mutually exclusive projects of unequal size? Would your approach change if capital rationing existed?

9–8. What causes the time disparity ranking problem? What reinvestment rate assumptions are associated with the net present value and internal rate of return capital-budgeting criteria?

9–9. When might two mutually exclusive projects having unequal lives be incomparable? How should managers deal with this problem?

SELF-TEST PROBLEMS

ST-1. You are considering a project that will require an initial outlay of $54,200. This project has an expected life of 5 years and will generate after-tax cash flows to the company as a whole of $20,608 at the end of each year over its five-year life. In addition to the $20,608 cash flow from operations during the fifth and final year, there will be an additional cash inflow of $13,200 at the end of the fifth year associated with the salvage value of the machine, making the cash flow in year 5 equal to $33,808. Thus the cash flows associated with this project look like this:

Year	Cash Flow
0	–$54,200
1	20,608
2	20,608
3	20,608
4	20,608
5	33,808

Given a required rate of return of 15 percent, calculate the following:

a. Payback Period
b. Net present value
c. Profitablility index
d. Internal rate of return
Should this project be accepted?

ST-2. The J. Serrano Corporation is considering signing a one-year contract with one of two computer-based marketing firms. Although one is more expensive, it offers a more extensive program and thus will provide higher after-tax net cash flows. Assume these two options are mutually exclusive and that the required rate of return is 12 percent. Given the following after-tax net cash flows:

Year	Option A	Option B
0	−$50,000	−$100,000
1	70,000	130,000

a. Calculate the net present value.
b. Calculate the profitability index.
c. Calculate the internal rate of return.
d. If there is no capital-rationing constraint, which project should be selected? If there is a capital-rationing constraint, how should the decision be made?

STUDY PROBLEMS

9–1. *(IRR Calculation)* Determine the internal rate of return on the following projects:
a. An initial outlay of $10,000 resulting in a single cash flow of $17,182 after 8 years
b. An initial outlay of $10,000 resulting in a single cash flow of $48,077 after 10 years
c. An initial outlay of $10,000 resulting in a single cash flow of $114,943 after 20 years
d. An initial outlay of $10,000 resulting in a single cash flow of $13,680 after 3 years

9–2. *(IRR Calculation)* Determine the internal rate of return on the following projects:
a. An initial outlay of $10,000 resulting in a cash flow of $1,993 at the end of each year for the next 10 years
b. An initial outlay of $10,000 resulting in a cash flow of $2,054 at the end of each year for the next 20 years
c. An initial outlay of $10,000 resulting in a cash flow of $1,193 at the end of each year for the next 12 years
d. An initial outlay of $10,000 resulting in a cash flow of $2,843 at the end of each year for the next 5 years

9–3. *(IRR Calculation)* Determine the internal rate of return to the nearest percent on the following projects:
a. An initial outlay of $10,000 resulting in a cash flow of $2,000 at the end of year 1, $5,000 at the end of year 2, and $8,000 at the end of year 3
b. An initial outlay of $10,000 resulting in a cash flow of $8,000 at the end of year 1, $5,000 at the end of year 2, and $2,000 at the end of year 3
c. An initial outlay of $10,000 resulting in a cash flow of $2,000 at the end of years 1 through 5 and $5,000 at the end of year 6

9–4. *(NPV, PI, and IRR Calculations)* Fijisawa, Inc., is considering a major expansion of its product line and has estimated the following cash flows associated with such an expansion. The initial outlay associated with the expansion would be $1,950,000 and the project would generate incremental after-tax cash flows of $450,000 per year for six years. The appropriate required rate of return is 9 percent.
a. Calculate the net present value.
b. Calculate the profitability index.

c. Calculate the internal rate of return.

d. Should this project be accepted?

9–5. *(Payback Period, Net Present Value, Profitability Index, and Internal Rate of Return Calculations)* You are considering a project with an initial cash outlay of $80,000 and expected after-tax cash flows of $20,000 at the end of each year for 6 years. The required rate of return for this project is 10 percent.

a. What are the project's payback and discounted payback periods?

b. What is the project's NPV?

c. What is the project's PI?

d. What is the project's IRR?

9–6. *(Net Present Value, Profitability Index, and Internal Rate of Return Calculations)* You are considering two independent projects, Project A and Project B. The initial cash outlay associated with Project A is $50,000 and the initial cash outlay associated with Project B is $70,000. The required rate of return on both projects is 12 percent. The expected annual after-tax cash inflows from each project are as follows:

Year	Project A	Project B
0	$12,000	$13,000
1	12,000	13,000
2	12,000	13,000
3	12,000	13,000
4	12,000	13,000
5	12,000	13,000
6	12,000	13,000

Calculate the NPV, PI, and IRR for each project and indicate if the project should be accepted.

9–7. *(Payback Period Calculations)* You are considering three independent projects, Project A, Project B, and Project C. The required rate of return is 10 percent on each. Given the following cash flow information calculate the payback period and discounted payback period for each.

Year	Project A	Project B	Project C
0	–$1,000	–$10,000	–$5,000
1	600	5,000	1,000
2	300	3,000	1,000
3	200	3,000	2,000
4	100	3,000	2,000
5	500	3,000	2,000

If you require a 3-year payback for both the traditional and discounted payback period methods before an investment can be accepted, which projects would be accepted under each criterion?

9–8. *(NPV with Varying Required Rates of Return)* Dowling Sportswear is considering building a new factory to produce aluminum baseball bats. This project would require an initial cash outlay of $5,000,000 and will generate annual after-tax cash inflows of $1,000,000 per year for 8 years. Calculate the project's NPV given:

a. A required rate of return of 9 percent.

b. A required rate of return of 11 percent.

c. A required rate of return of 13 percent.

d. A required rate of return of 15 percent.

9–9. *(Internal Rate of Return Calculations)* Given the following cash flows, determine the internal rate of return for the three independent projects A, B, and C.

	Project A	Project B	Project C
Initial Investment:	−$50,000	−$100,000	−$450,000
Cash Inflows:			
Year 1	$10,000	25,000	200,000
Year 2	15,000	25,000	200,000
Year 3	20,000	25,000	200,000
Year 4	25,000	25,000	–
Year 5	30,000	25,000	–

9–10. *(NPV with Varying Required Rates of Return)* Big Steve's, makers of swizzle sticks, is considering the purchase of a new plastic stamping machine. This investment requires an initial outlay of $100,000 and will generate after-tax cash inflows of $18,000 per year for 10 years. For each of the listed required rates of return, determine the project's net present value.
a. The required rate of return is 10 percent.
b. The required rate of return is 15 percent.
c. Would the project be accepted under part (a) or (b)?
d. What is this project's internal rate of return?

9–11. *(Size Disparity Ranking Problem)* The D. Dorner Farms Corporation is considering purchasing one of two fertilizer-herbicides for the upcoming year. The more expensive of the two is better and will produce a higher yield. Assume these projects are mutually exclusive and that the required rate of return is 10 percent. Given the following after-tax net cash flows:

Year	Project A	Project B
0	−$500	−$5,000
1	700	6,000

a. Calculate the net present value.
b. Calculate the profitability index.
c. Calculate the internal rate of return.
d. If there is no capital-rationing constraint, which project should be selected? If there is a capital-rationing constraint, how should the decision be made?

9–12. *(Time Disparity Ranking Problem)* The State Spartan Corporation is considering two mutually exclusive projects. The cash flows associated with those projects are as follows:

Year	Project A	Project B
0	−$50,000	−$ 50,000
1	15,625	0
2	15,625	0
3	15,625	0
4	15,625	0
5	15,625	$100,000

The required rate of return on these projects is 10 percent.

    a. What is each project's payback period?

    b. What is each project's net present value?

    c. What is each project's internal rate of return?

    d. What has caused the ranking conflict?

    e. Which project should be accepted? Why?

9–13.   *(Unequal Lives Ranking Problem)* The B. T. Knight Corporation is considering two mutually exclusive pieces of machinery that perform the same task. The two alternatives available provide the following set of after-tax net cash flows:

Year	Equipment A	Equipment B
0	–$20,000	–$20,000
1	12,590	6,625
2	12,590	6,625
3	12,590	6,625
4		6,625
5		6,625
6		6,625
7		6,625
8		6,625
9		6,625

Equipment A has an expected life of three years, whereas equipment B has an expected life of nine years. Assume a required rate of return of 15 percent.

    a. Calculate each project's payback period.

    b. Calculate each project's net present value.

    c. Calculate each project's internal rate of return.

    d. Are these projects comparable?

    e. Compare these projects using replacement chains and EAA. Which project should be selected? Support your recommendation.

9–14.   *(EAAs)* The Andrzejewski Corporation is considering two mutually exclusive projects, one with a 3-year life and one with a 7-year life. The after-tax cash flows from the two projects are as follows:

Year	Project A	Project B
0	–$50,000	–$50,000
1	20,000	36,000
2	20,000	36,000
3	20,000	36,000
4	20,000	
5	20,000	
6	20,000	
7	20,000	

    a. Assuming a 10 percent required rate of return on both projects, calculate each project's EAA. Which project should be selected?

    b. Calculate the present value of an infinite-life replacement chain for each project.

9–15.   *(Capital Rationing)* The Cowboy Hat Company of Stillwater, Okla., is considering seven capital investment proposals, for which the funds available are limited to a maximum of $12 million. The projects are independent and have the following costs and profitability indexes associated with them:

Project	Cost	Profitablitity Index
A	$4,000,000	1.18
B	3,000,000	1.08
C	5,000,000	1.33
D	6,000,000	1.31
E	4,000,000	1.19
F	6,000,000	1.20
G	4,000,000	1.18

a. Under strict capital rationing, which projects should be selected?

b. What problems are there with capital rationing?

SELF-TEST SOLUTIONS

SS-1:

a.
$$\text{Payback period} = \frac{\$54,200}{\$20,608} = 2.630 \text{ years}$$

b.
$$NPV = \sum_{t=1}^{n} \frac{ACF_t}{(1+k)^t} - IO$$

$$= \sum_{t=1}^{4} \frac{\$20,608}{(1+.15)^t} + \frac{\$33,808}{(1+.15)^5} - \$54,200$$

$$= \$20,608 \, (2.855) + \$33,808 \, (.497) - \$54,200$$

$$= \$58,836 + \$16,803 - \$54,200$$

$$= \$21,439$$

c.
$$PI = \frac{\sum_{t=1}^{n} \dfrac{ACF_t}{(1+k)^t}}{IO}$$

$$= \frac{\$75,639}{\$54,200}$$

$$= 1.396$$

d.
$$IO = \sum_{t=1}^{n} \frac{ACF_t}{(1+IRR)^t}$$

$$\$54,200 = \$20,608 \, (PVIFA_{IRR\%,\ 4\ yr}) + \$33,808 \, (PVIF_{IRR\%,\ 5\ yr})$$

Try 29 percent

$$\$54,200 = \$20,608 \, (2.203) + \$33,808 \, (.280)$$

$$= \$45,399 + 9,466$$

$$= \$54,865$$

Try 30 percent

$$\$45,200 = \$20,608 \, (2.166) + \$33,808 \, (.269)$$

$$= \$44,637 + 9,094$$

$$= \$53,731$$

Thus, the IRR is just below 30 percent and the project should be accepted because the NPV is positive, the PI is greater than 1.0, and the IRR is greater than the required rate of return of 15 percent.

SS-2.

a.

$$NPV_A = \$70,000 \left[\frac{1}{(1 + .12)^1} \right] - \$50,000$$

$$= \$70,000 \, (.893) - \$50,000$$

$$= \$62,510 - \$50,000$$

$$= \$12,510$$

$$NPV_B = \$130,000 \left[\frac{1}{(1 + .12)^1} \right] - \$100,000$$

$$= \$130,000 \, (.893) - \$100,000$$

$$= \$116,090 - \$100,000$$

$$= \$16,090$$

b.

$$PI_A = \frac{\$62,510}{\$50,000}$$

$$= 1.2502$$

$$PI_B = \frac{\$116,090}{\$100,000}$$

$$= 1.1609$$

c. $\$50,000 = \$70,000 \, (PVIF_{i, \, 1 \, yr})$

$.7143 = PVIF_{i, \, 1 \, yr}$

Looking for a value of $PVIF_{i, \, 1yr}$ in Appendix C, a value of .714 is found in the 40 percent column. Thus, the IRR is 40 percent.

$\$100,000 = \$130,000 \, (FVIF_{i, \, 1 \, yr})$

$.7692 = PVIF_{i, \, 1 \, yr}$

Looking for a value of $PVIF_{i, \, 1 \, yr}$ in Appendix C a value of .769 is found in the 30 percent column. Thus, the IRR is 30 percent.

d. If there is no capital rationing, project B should be accepted because it has a larger net present value. If there is a capital constraint, the problem focuses on what can be done with the additional $50,000 (the additional money that could be invested if project A, with an initial outlay of $50,000, were selected over project B, with an initial outlay of $100,000). In the capital constraint case, if Serrano can earn more on project A plus the marginal project financed with the additional $50,000 than it can on project B, then project A and the marginal project should be accepted.

Investing in Employee Productivity: An Application of Capital Budgeting
from ABC News, Business World, October 14, 1990

In the introduction to this video case we asked a list of pertinent questions. See Video Case 3 Introduction on page 266.

If the programs Fel-Pro implemented increase employee satisfaction, the firm could benefit in many ways. Lower employee turnover, lower absenteeism, and fewer job-related accidents and illnesses (which translate into lower health insurance claims) all reduce costs and thereby increase profits. If the firm ever comes on hard times, the loyalty built by these programs might allow the firm to ask for help from its employees in the form of lower raises, unpaid leaves, and so on.

Program costs are fairly easy to estimate. One problem with cost estimation in programs with volunteer participation is uncertainty about the number of employees who will participate. Once the program is opened to all employees, the firm must either be prepared to make sufficient opportunities available for all interested employees or explain how the resources will be rationed.

Arriving at quantitative estimates for the programs' benefits can be very difficult. One approach would be to estimate how much absenteeism and employee turnover costs the firm, then estimate how absenteeism and turnover are affected by the programs. The value of loyalty and commitment are much more difficult to measure.

In theory NPV analysis could be used to evaluate investments such as this, but the inability to quantify all future benefits makes applying NPV nearly impossible. Because the benefits are more difficult to value than the costs, strict application of NPV analysis may produce results that are biased against acceptance. Managers' primary commitment is to shareholders. If there are no benefits from implementing the employee incentive programs, they should not be implemented. Implementing costly programs that produce no benefits will eventually harm more groups than shareholders alone. If the firm becomes less competitive because of these extra costs, then employees may lose their jobs, and communities may lose factories. Although the objective of maximization of shareholder wealth appears, at first glance, to ignore the many other constituencies associated with a firm— employees, suppliers, customers, and the community—it is the only objective that assures the firm's long-term viability, and thereby the firm's continued support of its various constituents.

Discussion questions

1. Like employee morale, the benefits of adding personal computers to the workplace are difficult to estimate. What are some of the benefits from providing computers to employees and how might these benefits be estimated?

2. One form of employee benefit is training. However, as employees improve their skills or learn new skills, they become more attractive to competitors and may be hired away. Firms that provide training but experience high turnover bear costs but receive no benefits. How would you address this potential problem? Examples to consider are the extensive training programs offered by many banks. After 10 to 16 months of training, during which the employees-in-training have not been particularly productive for the bank, they are attractive to other banks or many corporations.

Suggested readings

FISHER, ANNE. "The Morale Crisis," *Fortune*, November 18, 1991.
KIRKPATRICK, DAVID. "Here Comes the Payoff from PCs," *Fortune*, November 18, 1991.

CHAPTER 10

CASH FLOWS AND OTHER TOPICS IN CAPITAL BUDGETING

Guidelines for Capital Budgeting • Measuring a Project's Benefits and Costs • Risk and the Investment Decision • Methods for Incorporating Risk into Capital Budgeting • Risk-Adjusted Discount Rate and Measurement of a Project's Systematic Risk • Examining a Project's Risk Through Simulation

This chapter continues our discussion of decision rules for deciding when to invest in new projects. First, we will examine what is a relevant cash flow and how to calculate the relevant cash flow. We then turn our attention to the problem of capital budgeting under uncertainty. In discussing capital-budgeting techniques in the preceding chapter, we implicitly assumed the level of risk associated with each investment proposal was the same. In this chapter we lift that assumption and examine various ways in which risk can be incorporated into the capital-budgeting decision.

■ GUIDELINES FOR CAPITAL BUDGETING

To evaluate investment proposals, we must first set guidelines by which we measure the value of each proposal.

Use Cash Flows Rather than Accounting Profits

We will use cash flows, not accounting profits, as our measurement tool. The firm receives and is able to reinvest cash flows, whereas accounting profits are shown when they are earned rather than when the money is actually in hand. Unfortunately, a firm's accounting profits and cash flows may not be timed to occur together. For example, capital expenses, such as vehicles and plant and equipment, are depreciated over several years, with their annual depreciation subtracted from profit. Cash flows correctly reflect the timing of benefits and costs, that is, when the money is received, when it can be reinvested, and when it must be paid out.

BACK TO THE FUNDAMENTALS

If we are to make intelligent capital-budgeting decisions we must accurately measure the timing of the benefits and costs, that is, when we receive money and when it leaves our hands. **Axiom 3: Cash Is King— Measuring the Timing of Costs and Benefits** speaks directly to this. Remember, it is cash inflows that can be reinvested and cash outflows that involve paying out money.

Think Incrementally

Unfortunately, calculating cash flows from a project may not be enough. Decision makers must ask: What new cash flows will the company as a whole receive if the company takes on a given project? What if the company does not take on the project? Interestingly, we may find that not all cash flows a firm expects from an investment proposal are incremental in nature. In measuring cash flows, however, the trick is to *think* incrementally. In doing so, we will see that only *incremental after-tax cash flows* matter. As such, our guiding rule in deciding if a cash flow is incremental will be to look at the company with, versus without, the new product. As you will see in the upcoming sections, this may be easier said than done.

BACK TO THE FUNDAMENTALS

In order to measure the true effects of our decisions we will analyze the benefits and costs of projects on an incremental basis, which relates directly to **Axiom 4: Incremental Cash Flows—It's Only What Changes that Counts.** In effect, we will ask ourselves what the cash flows will be if the project is taken on versus what they will be if the project is not taken on.

Beware of Cash Flows Diverted from Existing Products

Assume for a moment that we are managers of a firm considering a new product line that might compete with one of our existing products and possibly reduce its sales. In determining the cash flows associated with the proposed project, we should consider only the incremental sales brought to the company as a whole. New-product sales achieved at the cost of losing sales of other products in our line are not considered a benefit of adopting the new product. For example, when General Foods' Post Cereal Division introduced its Dino Pebbles in 1991, the product competed directly with the company's Fruity Pebbles. (In fact, the two were the same product with an addition to the former of dinosaur-shaped marshmallows.) Post meant to target the market niche held by Kellogg's Marshmallow Krispies, but there was no question that sales recorded by Dino Pebbles bit into—literally cannibalized—Post's existing product line.

Remember that we are only interested in the sales dollars to the firm if this project is accepted, as opposed to what the sales dollars would be if the project is rejected. Just moving sales from one product line to a new product line does not bring anything new into the company, but if sales are captured from our competitors or if sales that would have been lost to new competing products are retained, then these are relevant incremental cash flows. In each case these are the incremental cash flows to the firm—looking at the firm as a whole with the new product versus without the new product.

Look for Incidental or Synergistic Effects

Although in some cases a new project may take sales away from a firm's current projects, in other cases a new effort may actually bring new sales to the existing line. For example, in September 1991 USAir introduced service to Sioux City, Iowa. The new routes connecting this addition to the USAir system not only brought about new ticket sales on those routes, but also fed passengers to connecting routes. If managers were to look at only the revenue from ticket sales on the Sioux City routes, they would miss the incremental cash flow to USAir as a whole that results from taking on the new route. This is called a *synergistic* effect. The cash flow comes from *any* USAir flight that would not have occurred if service to Sioux City had not been available. The bottom line: Any cash flow to any part of the company that may result from the decision at hand must be considered when making that decision.

Work in Working Capital Requirements

Many times a new project will involve additional investment in working capital. This may take the form of new inventory to stock a sales outlet, additional investment in accounts receivable resulting from additional credit sales, or increased investment in cash to operate cash registers, and more. Working capital requirements are considered a cash flow even though they do not leave the company. How can investment in inventory be considered a cash outflow when the goods are still in the store? Because the firm does not have access to the inventory's cash value, the firm cannot use the money for other investments. Generally, working capital requirements are tied up over the life of the project. When the project terminates there is usually an offsetting cash inflow as the working capital is recovered.

Consider Incremental Expenses

Just as cash inflows from a new project are measured on an incremental basis, expenses should also be measured on an incremental basis. For example, if introducing a new product line necessitates training the sales staff, the after-tax cash flow associated with the training program must be considered a cash outflow and charged against the project. If accepting a new project dictates that a production facility be reengineered, the after-tax cash flows associated with that capital investment should be charged against the project. Again, any incremental after-tax cash flow affecting the company as a whole is a relevant cash flow, whether it is flowing in or flowing out.

Remember That Sunk Costs Are Not Incremental Cash Flows

Only cash flows that are affected by the decision making at the moment are relevant in capital budgeting. The manager asks two questions: (1) Will this cash flow occur if the project is accepted? (2) Will this cash flow occur if the project is rejected? *Yes* to the first question and *no* to the second equals an incremental cash flow. For example, let's assume you are considering introducing a new taste treat called Puddin' in a Shoe. You would like to do some test marketing before production. If you are considering the decision to test market and have not yet done so, the costs associated with the test marketing are relevant cash flows. Conversely, if you have already test marketed, the cash flows involved in test marketing are no longer relevant in project evaluation. It's a matter of timing. Regardless of what you might decide about future production, the cash flows allocated to marketing have already occurred. Cash flows that have already taken place are often referred to as "sunk costs" because they have been sunk into the project and cannot be undone. As a rule, any cash flows that are not affected by the accept-reject decision should not be included in capital-budgeting analysis.

Account for Opportunity Costs

Now we will focus on the cash flows that are lost because a given project consumes scarce resources that would have produced cash flows if that project had been rejected. This is the opportunity cost of doing business. For example, a product may use valuable floor space in a production facility. Although the cash flow is not obvious, the real question remains: What else could be done with this space? The space could have been rented out, or another product could have been stored there. The key point is that opportunity-cost cash flows should reflect net cash flows that would have been received if the project under consideration were rejected. Again, we are analyzing the cash flows to the company as a whole, with or without the project.

Decide if Overhead Costs Are Truly Incremental Cash Flows

Although we certainly want to include any incremental cash flows resulting in changes from overhead expenses such as utilities and salaries, we also want to make sure that these are truly incremental cash flows. Many times, overhead expenses—heat, light, rent—would occur whether a given project were accepted or rejected. There is often not a single specific project to which these expenses can be allocated. Thus, the question is not whether the project benefits from overhead items but whether the overhead costs are incremental cash flows associated with the project—and relevant to capital budgeting.

Ignore Interest Payments and Financing Flows

In evaluating new projects and determining cash flows, we must separate the investment decision from the financing decision. Interest payments and other financing cash flows that might result from raising funds to finance a project should not be considered incremental cash flows. If accepting a project means we have to raise new funds by issuing bonds, the interest charges associated with raising funds are not a relevant cash outflow. When we discount the incremental cash flows back to the present at the required rate of return, we are implicitly accounting for the cost of raising funds to finance the new project. In essence, the required rate of return reflects the cost of the funds needed to support the project. Managers first determine the desirability of the project and then determine how best to finance it.

■ MEASURING A PROJECT'S BENEFITS AND COSTS

In measuring cash flows, we will be interested only in the **incremental,** or differential, **after-tax cash flows** that can be attributed to the proposal being evaluated. That is, we will focus our attention on the difference in the firm's after-tax cash flows *with* versus *without* the project. The worth of our decision depends on the accuracy of our cash flow estimates. For this reason we first examined the question of what cash flows are relevant. Now we will see that, in general, a project's cash flows will fall into one of three categories: (1) the initial outlay, (2) the differential flows over the project's life, and (3) the terminal cash flow.

Initial Outlay

The **initial outlay** involves the immediate cash outflow necessary to purchase the asset and put it in operating order. This amount includes the cost of installing the asset (the asset's purchase price plus any expenses associated with shipping or installation) and any nonexpense cash outlays, such as increased working capital requirements. If we are considering a new sales outlet, there might be additional cash flows associated with investment in working capital in the form of increased inventory and cash necessary to operate the sales outlet. Although these cash flows are not included in the cost of the asset or even expensed on the books, they must be included in our analysis. The after-tax cost of expense items incurred as a result of new investment must also be included as cash outflows—for example, any training expenses or special engineering expenses that would not have been incurred otherwise.

1. Installed cost of asset
2. Additional nonexpense outlays incurred (for example, working capital investments)
3. Additional expenses on an after-tax basis (for example, training expenses)
4. In a replacement decision, the *after-tax* cash flow associated with the sale of the old machine

Finally, if the investment decision is a replacement decision, the cash inflow associated with the selling price of the old asset, in addition to any tax effects resulting from its sale, must be included.

Determining the initial outlay is a complex matter. Table 10–1 summarizes some of the more common calculations involved in determining the initial outlay. This list is by no means exhaustive, but it should help simplify the calculations involved in the example that follows.

PERSPECTIVE IN FINANCE

At this point we should realize that the incremental nature of the cash flow is of great importance. In many cases if the project is not accepted, then "status quo" for the firm will simply not continue. In calculating incremental cash flows we must be realistic in estimating what the cash flows to the company would be if the new project is not accepted. The Financial Management in Practice, "Using the Right Base Case," deals with precisely this question.

Tax Effects—Sale of Old Machine

Potentially one of the most confusing initial outlay calculations is for a replacement project involving the incremental tax payment associated with the sale of an old machine. There are three possible tax situations dealing with the sale of an old asset:

1. The old asset is sold for a price above the depreciated value. Here the difference between the old machine's selling price and its depreciated value is considered a taxable gain and taxed at the marginal corporate tax rate. If, for example, the old machine was originally purchased for $15,000, had a book value of $10,000, and was sold for $17,000, assuming the firm's marginal corporate tax rate is 34 percent, the taxes due from the gain would be ($17,000 – $10,000) × (.34), or $2,380.

2. The old asset is sold for its depreciated value. In this case no taxes result, as there is neither a gain nor a loss in the asset's sale.

3. The old asset is sold for less than its depreciated value. In this case the difference between the depreciated book value and the salvage value of the asset is a taxable loss and may be used to offset ordinary income and thus results in tax savings. For example, if the depreciated book value of the asset is $10,000 and it is sold for $7,000 we have a $3,000 loss. Assuming the firm's marginal corporate tax rate is 34 percent, the cash inflow from tax savings is ($10,000 – $7,000) × (.34), or $1,020.

FINANCIAL MANAGEMENT IN PRACTICE

Using the Right Base Case

Finance theory assumes that a project will be evaluated against its base case, that is, what will happen if the project is not carried out. Managers tend to explore fully the implications of adopting the project but usually spend less time considering the likely outcome of not making the investment. Yet unless the base case is realistic, the incremental cash flows—the difference between the "with" and the "without" scenarios—will mislead.

Often companies implicitly assume that the base case is simply a continuation of the status quo, but this assumption ignores market trends and competitor behavior. It also neglects the impact of changes the company might make anyway, like improving operations management.

Using the wrong base case is typical of product launches in which the new product will likely erode the market for the company's existing product line. Take Apple Computer's introduction of the Macintosh SE. The new PC had obvious implications for sales of earlier generation Macintoshes. To analyze the incremental cash flows arising from the new product, Apple would have needed to count the lost contribution from sales of its existing products as a cost of the launch.

Wrongly applied, however, this approach would equate the "without" case to the status quo: It would assume that without the SE, sales of existing Macintoshes would continue at their current level. In the competitive PC market, however, nothing stands still. Competitors like IBM would likely innovate and take market share away from the earlier generation Macintoshes—which a more realistic base case would have reflected. Sales of existing products would decline even in the base case.

Consider investments in the marketing of existing brands through promotions, media budgets, and the like. They are often sold as if they were likely to lead to ever-increasing market share. But competitors will also be promoting their brands, and market shares across the board still have to add up to 100 percent. Still, such an investment is not necessarily wasted. It may just need a more realistic justification: Although the investment is unlikely to increase sales above existing levels, it may prevent sales from falling. Marketers who like positive thinking may not like this defensive argument, but it is the only argument that makes economic sense in a mature market.

In situations like this, when the investment is needed just to maintain market share, the returns may be high in comparison with the base case, but the company's reported profits may still go down. Senior managers are naturally puzzled at apparently netting only 5 percent on a project that had promised a 35 percent return.[1] Without the investment, however, the profit picture would have looked even worse, especially in the longer term.

Some projects disappoint for other reasons. Sometimes the original proposals are overoptimistic, partly because the base case is implicit or defined incorrectly. That is, if managers are convinced that the investment is sound and are frustrated because the figures fail to confirm their intuition, they may over-inflate projections of sales or earnings. But misstating the base case and then having to make unrealistic projections are unlikely to cancel each other out; they merely cloud the analysis.

---

[1]Joseph L. Bower, *Managing the Resource Allocation Process* (Boston: Harvard Business School Press, 1986), p. 13.

Reprinted by permission of the *Harvard Business Review*. An excerpt from "Must Finance and Strategy Clash?" by Patrick Barwise, Paul R. Marsh, and Robin Wensley (September-October, 1989). Copyright 1989 by the President and Fellows of Harvard College. All rights reserved.

EXAMPLE

To clarify the calculation of the initial outlay, consider an example of a company in the 34 percent marginal tax bracket. This company is considering the purchase of a new machine for $30,000 to be used in manufacturing. It has a five-year life (according to IRS guidelines) and will be depreciated using the *simplified straight-line method*. (This depreciation method will be explained later.) The useful life of this new machine is also five years. The new machine will replace an existing machine, originally purchased for $30,000 10 years ago, which currently has five more years of expected useful life. The existing machine will generate $2,000 of depreciation expenses for each of the next five years, at which time the book value will be equal to zero. To put the new machine in running order, it is necessary to pay shipping charges of $2,000 and installation charges of $3,000. Because the new machine will work faster than the old one, it will require an increase in goods-in-process inventory of $5,000. Finally, the old machine can be sold to a scrap dealer for $15,000.

The installed cost of the new machine would be the $30,000 cost plus $2,000 shipping and $3,000 installation fees, for a total of $35,000. Additional outflows are associated with taxes incurred on the sale of the old machine and with increased investment in inventory. Although the old machine has a book value of $10,000, it could be sold for $15,000. The increased taxes from gain on the sale will be equal to the selling price of the old machine less its depreciated book value times the firm's marginal tax rate, or ($15,000 – $10,000) × (.34), or $1,700. The increase in goods-in-process inventory of $5,000 must also be considered part of the initial outlay, with an offsetting inflow of $5,000 corresponding to the recapture of this inventory occurring at the termination of the project. In effect, the firm invests $5,000 in inventory now, resulting in an initial cash outlay, and liquidates this inventory in five years, resulting in a cash inflow at the end of the project. The total outlays associated with the new machine are $35,000 for its installed cost, $1,700 in increased taxes, and $5,000 in investment in inventory, for a total of $41,700. This is somewhat offset by the sale of the old machine for $15,000. Thus, the net initial outlay associated with this project is $26,700. These calculations are summarized in Table 10–2. ■

Differential Flows over Project's Life

The differential cash flows over the project's life involve the incremental after-tax cash flows resulting from increased revenues, plus labor or

TABLE 10–2
Calculation of Initial Outlay
for Example Problem

Outflows:		
Purchase price	$30,000	
Shipping fee	2,000	
Installation fee	3,000	
Installed cost of machine		$35,000
Increased taxes from sale of old machine		
($15,000 – $10,000)(.34)		1,700
Increased investment in inventory		5,000
Total outflows		$41,700
Inflows:		
Salvage value of old machine		15,000
Net initial outlay		$26,700

1. Added revenue offset by increased expenses
2. Labor and material savings
3. Increases in overhead incurred
4. Tax savings from an increase in depreciation expense if the new project is accepted.
5. Do *not* include interest expenses if the project is financed by issuing debt, as this
   is accounted for in the required rate of return

material savings and reductions in selling expenses. Overhead items, such as utilities, heat, light, and executive salaries, are generally not affected. However, any resultant change in any of these categories must be included. Any increase in interest payments incurred as a result of issuing bonds to finance the project should *not* be included, as the costs of funds needed to support the project are implicitly accounted for by discounting the project back to the present using the required rate of return. Finally, an adjustment for the incremental change in taxes should be made, including any increase in taxes that might result from increased profits or any tax savings from an increase in depreciation expenses. Increased depreciation expenses affect tax-related cash flows by reducing taxable income and thus lowering taxes. Table 10–3 lists some of the factors that might be involved in determining a project's differential cash flows. However, before looking at an example, we will briefly examine the calculation of depreciation.

PERSPECTIVE IN FINANCE

Depreciation plays an important role in the calculation of cash flows. Although it is not a cash flow item, it lowers profits, which in turn lowers taxes. For students developing a foundation in corporate finance, it is the concept of depreciation, not the calculation of it, that is important. The reason the calculation of depreciation is deemphasized is that it is extremely complicated, and its calculation changes every few years as Congress enacts new tax laws. Through all this bear in mind that although depreciation is not a cash flow item, it does affect cash flows by lowering the level of profits on which taxes are calculated.

Depreciation, the Tax Reform Act of 1986, and the Revenue Reconciliation Act of 1993

The Revenue Reconciliation Act of 1993 largely left in tact the modified version of the Accelerated Cost Recovery System introduced in the Tax Reform Act of 1986. Although this was examined in Chapter 1, a review is appropriate here. This modified version of the old Accelerated Cost Recovery System (ACRS) is used for most tangible depreciable property placed in service beginning in 1987. Under this method, the life of the asset is determined according to the asset's class life, which is assigned by the IRS; for example, most computer equipment has a five-year asset life. It also allows for only a half year's deduction in the first year and a half year's deduction in the year after the recovery period. The asset is then depreciated using the 200 percent declining balance method or an optional straight-line method.

Depreciation Calculation—Simplified Straight-Line Depreciation Method

Depreciation is calculated using a simplified straight-line method. This simplified process ignores the half-year convention that allows only a half-year's deduction in the year the project is placed in service and a half-year's deduction in the first year after the recovery period. By ignoring the half-year convention and assuming a zero salvage value we are able to calculate annual depreciation by taking the project's initial depreciable value and dividing by its depreciable life as follows:

$$\text{annual depreciation using the simplified straight-line method} = \frac{\text{initial depreciable value}}{\text{depreciable life}}$$

The initial depreciable value is equal to the cost of the asset plus any expenses necessary to get the new asset into operating order.

This is not how depreciation would actually be calculated. The reason we have simplified the calculation is to allow you to focus directly on what should and should not be included in the cash flow calculations. Moreover, because the tax laws change rather frequently, we are more interested in recognizing the tax implications of depreciation than in understanding the specific depreciation provisions of the current tax laws.

Our concern with depreciation is to highlight its importance in generating cash flow estimates and to indicate that the financial manager must be aware of the current tax provisions when evaluating capital-budgeting proposals.

Differential Flows over Project's Life

Extending the earlier example, which illustrated the calculations of the initial outlay, suppose that purchasing the machine is expected to reduce salaries by $10,000 per year and fringe benefits by $1,000 annually, because it will take only one part-time person to operate, whereas the old machine requires two part-time operators. In addition, the cost of defects will fall from $8,000 per year to $3,000. However, maintenance expenses will increase by $4,000 annually. The annual depreciation on this new machine is $7,000 per year, whereas the depreciation expense lost with the sale of the old machine is $2,000 for each of the next five years. Annual depreciation on the new machine is calculated using the simplified straight-line method just described—that is, taking the cost of the new machine plus any expenses necessary to put it in operating order and dividing by its depreciable life. For the new machine these calculations are reflected in Table 10–4.

Because the depreciation on the old machine is $2,000 per year, the increased depreciation will be from $2,000 per year to $7,000 per year, or an increase of $5,000 per year. Although this increase in depreciation expenses is not a cash flow item, it does affect cash flows by reducing book profits, which in turn reduces taxes.

To determine the annual net cash flows resulting from the acceptance of this project, the net savings *before* taxes using both book profit and cash flows must be found. The additional taxes are then calculated

New machine purchase price	$30,000
Shipping fee	2,000
Installation fee	3,000
Total depreciable value	$35,000
Divided by depreciable life	$35,000/5
Equals: Annual depreciation	$7,000

TABLE 10–5
Calculation of Differential
Cash Flows for
Example Problem

		Book Profit	Cash Flow
Savings:	Reduced salary	$10,000	$10,000
	Reduced fringe benefits	1,000	1,000
	Reduced defects ($8,000 – $3,000)	5,000	5,000
Costs:	Increased maintenance expense	–4,000	–4,000
	Increased depreciation expense ($7,000 – $2,000)	–5,000	
Net savings before taxes		$ 7,000	$12,000
Taxes (34%)		–2,380 →	–2,380
Net cash flow after taxes			$ 9,620

based on the before-tax book profit. For this example, Table 10–5 shows the determination of the differential cash flows on an after-tax basis. Thus, the differential cash flows over the project's life are $9,620.

Terminal Cash Flow

The calculation of the terminal cash flow is in general quite a bit simpler than the preceding two calculations. Flows associated with the project's termination generally include the salvage value of the project plus or minus any taxable gains or losses associated with its sales.

Under the current tax laws, in most cases there will be tax payments associated with the salvage value at termination. This is because the current laws allow all projects to be depreciated to zero, and if a project has a book value of zero at termination and a positive salvage value, then that salvage value will be taxed. The tax effects associated with the salvage value of the project at termination are determined exactly like the tax effects on the sale of the old machine associated with the initial outlay. The salvage value proceeds are compared with the depreciated value, in this case zero, to determine the tax.

In addition to the salvage value, there may be a cash outlay associated with the project termination. For example, at the close of a strip-mining operation, the mine must be refilled in an ecologically acceptable manner. Finally, any working capital outlay required at the initiation of the project—for example, increased inventory needed for the operation of a new plant—will be recaptured at the termination of the project. In effect the increased inventory required by the project can be liquidated when the project expires. Table 10–6 provides a sample list of some of the factors that might affect a project's terminal cash flow.

1. The after-tax salvage value of the project
2. Cash outlays associated with the project's termination
3. Recapture of nonexpense outlays that occurred at the project's initiation
   (for example, working capital investments)

Extending the example to termination, the depreciated book value and salvage value of the machine at the termination date will be equal to zero. However, there will be a cash flow associated with the recapture of the initial outlay of work-in-process inventory of $5,000. This flow is generated from the liquidation of the $5,000 investment in work-in-process inventory. Therefore, the expected total terminal cash flow equals $5,000.

If we were to construct a cash flow diagram from this example (Figure 10–1), it would have an initial outlay of $26,700, differential cash flows during years 1 through 5 of $9,620, and an additional terminal cash flow at the end of year 5 of $5,000. The cash flow occurring in year 5 is $14,620, the sum of the differential cash flow in year 5 of $9,620, and the terminal cash flow of $5,000.

Cash flow diagrams similar to Figure 10–1 will be used through the remainder of this chapter with arrows above the time line indicating cash inflows and arrows below the time line denoting outflows.

Although the preceding calculations for determining the incremental, after-tax, net cash flows do not cover all possible cash flows, they do set up a framework in which almost any situation can be handled. To simplify this framework and to provide an overview of the calculations, Table 10–7 summarizes the rules in Tables 10–1, 10–3, and 10–6.

Discounted Cash Flow Criteria: Comprehensive Example

To demonstrate further the computations for the discounted cash flow techniques, assume that a manufacturing firm in the electronic components field is in the 34 percent marginal tax bracket with a 15 percent required rate of return or cost of capital. Management is considering replacing a hand-operated assembly machine with a fully automated assembly operation. Given the information in Table 10–8, we want to determine the cash flows associated with this proposal, the project's net present value, profitability index, and internal rate of return, and then to apply the appropriate decision criteria.

FIGURE 10–1
Example Cash Flow
Diagram

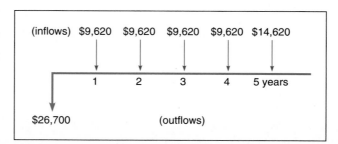

TABLE 10–7
Summary of Calculation
of Incremental After-Tax
Cash Flows

A. Initial Outlay
   1. Installed cost of asset
   2. Additional nonexpense outlays incurred
      (for example, working-capital investments)
   3. Additional expenses, on an after-tax basis (for example, training expenses)
   4. In a replacement decision, the after-tax flow associated with the sale of the
      old machine
B. Differential Cash Flows over the Project's Life
   1. Added revenue offset by increased expenses
   2. Labor and material savings
   3. Increases in overhead incurred
   4. Tax savings from an increase in depreciation if the new project is accepted.
   5. Do not include interest expenses if the project is financed by issuing debt,
      as this is accounted for in the required rate of return
C. Terminal Cash Flow
   1. The after-tax salvage value of the project
   2 .Cash outlays associated with the project's termination
   3. Recapture of nonexpense outlays that occurred at the project's initiation
      (for example, working capital investments)

First, the initial outlay is determined to be $44,680, as reflected in Table 10–9. Next, the differential cash flows over the project's life are calculated as shown in Table 10–10, yielding an estimated $15,008 cash flow per annum. In making these computations, the incremental change in depreciation was determined by first calculating the original depreciable value, which is equal to the cost of the new machine ($50,000) plus any expense charges necessary to get the new machine in operating order (shipping fee of $1,000 plus the installation fee of $5,000). This

TABLE 10–8
Comprehensive Capital
Budgeting Example

Existing situation:	One part-time operator—salary $12,000
	Variable overtime—$1,000 per year
	Fringe benefits—$1,000 per year
	Cost of defects—$6,000 per year
	Current book value—$10,000
	Expected life—15 years
	Expected salvage value—$0
	Age—10 years
	Annual depreciation—$2,000 per year
	Current salvage value of old machine—$12,000
	Annual maintenance—$0
	Marginal tax rate—34 percent
	Required rate of return—15 percent
Proposed situation:	Fully automated operation—no operator necessary
	Cost of machine—$50,000
	Shipping fee—$1,000
	Installation costs—$5,000
	Expected economic life—5 years
	Depreciation method—simplified straight-line over 5 years
	Salvage value after 5 years—$0
	Annual maintenance—$1,000
	Cost of defects—$1,000

TABLE 10–9 Calculation of Initial Outlay for Comprehensive Example		
Outflows:	Cost of new machine	$50,000
	Shipping fee	1,000
	Installation cost	5,000
	Increased taxes on sale of old machine	680
	($12,000 – $10,000) (.34)	
Inflows:	Salvage value—old machine	–12,000
	Net initial outlay	$44,680

depreciable amount was then divided by five years. The annual depreciation lost with the sale of the old machine was then subtracted out ($10,000/5 = $2,000 per year for the old machine's remaining five years of life). Once the change in taxes is determined from the incremental change in book profit, it is subtracted from the net cash flow savings before taxes, yielding the $15,008 net cash flow after taxes.

Finally, the terminal cash flow associated with the project has to be determined. In this case, because the new machine is expected to have a zero salvage value, there will be no terminal cash flow. The cash flow diagram associated with this project is shown in Figure 10–2.

The net present value for this project is calculated as follows:

$$NPV = \sum_{t=1}^{n} \frac{ACF_t}{(1 + k)^t} - IO \qquad (10\text{–}1)$$

$$= \sum_{t=1}^{5} \frac{\$15,008}{(1 + .15)^t} - \$44,680$$

$$= \$15,008 \, (PVIFA_{15\%, \, 5 \, yr}) - \$44,680$$

$$= \$15,008 \, (3.352) - \$44,680$$

$$= \$50,307 - \$44,680$$

$$= \$5627$$

TABLE 10–10 Calculation of Differential Cash Flows for Comprehensive Example		*Book Profit*	*Cash Flow*
Savings:	Reduced salary	$12,000	$12,000
	Reduced variable overtime	1,000	1,000
	Reduced fringe benefits	1,000	1,000
	Reduced defects ($6,000 – $1,000)	5,000	5,000
Costs:	Increased maintenance expense	–1,000	–1,000
	Increased depreciation expense	–9,200	
	($11,200 – $2,000)		
Net savings before taxes		$ 8,800	$18,000
Taxes (34%)		–2,992 →	–2,992
Net cash flow after taxes			$15,008

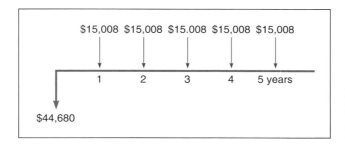

FIGURE 10–2
Cash Flow Diagram for
Comprehensive Example

Because its net present value is greater than zero, the project should be accepted. The profitability index, which gives a measure of relative desirability of a project, is calculated as follows:

$$PI = \frac{\sum_{t=1}^{n} \dfrac{ACF_t}{(1+k)^t}}{IO} \qquad (10\text{--}2)$$

$$= \frac{\$50,307}{\$44,680}$$

$$= 1.13$$

Because the project's PI is greater than 1, the project should be accepted.

The internal rate of return can be determined directly from the PVIFA table, as follows:

$$IO = \sum_{t=1}^{n} \frac{ACF_t}{(1+IRR)^t} \qquad (10\text{--}3)$$

$$\$44,680 = \$15,008 \, (PVIFA_{i, \, 5 \, yr})$$

$$2.977 = PVIFA_{i, \, 5 \, yr}$$

Looking for the value of the $PVIFA_{i, \, 5 \, yr}$ in the 5-year row of the table in Appendix E, we find that the value of 2.977 occurs between the 20 percent column (2.991) and the 21 percent column (2.926). As a result, the project's internal rate of return is between 20 percent and 21 percent, and the project should be accepted.

Applying the decision criteria to this example, we find that each of them indicates the project should be accepted, as the net present value is positive, the profitability index is greater than 1.0, and the internal rate of return is greater than the firm's required rate of return of 15 percent.

■ RISK AND THE INVESTMENT DECISION

Up to this point we have ignored risk in capital budgeting; that is, we have discounted expected cash flows back to the present and ignored any uncertainty that there might be surrounding that estimate. In reality the future cash flows associated with the introduction of a new sales

CALCULATOR SOLUTION[2]	
Data Input	Function Key
44,680	+/-INPUT
15,008	INPUT
15,008	INPUT
15,008	INPUT
15,008	INPUT
15,008	INPUT
Function Key	Answer
IRR%	20.21

[2]If you are using an HP 17BII, first get to the CFLO menu and be certain that you have already cleared all prior data entries, selected both the "END MODE" and "one payment per year" (1P/YR), and turned the # times prompting (#T?) off. For further explanation see Appendix A.

FIGURE 10–3
Cash Flow Diagram Based on
Possible OutcomesExample

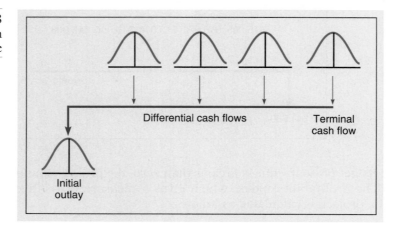

outlet or a new product are estimates of what is expected to happen in the future, not necessarily what will happen in the future. For example, when the Ford Motor Company made its decision to introduce the Edsel, you can bet that the expected cash flows it based its decision on were nothing like the cash flows it realized. The cash flows we have discounted back to the present have only been our best estimate of the expected future cash flows. A cash flow diagram based on the possible outcomes of an investment proposal rather than the expected values of these outcomes appears in Figure 10–3.

In this section we will assume that under conditions of risk we do not know beforehand what cash flows will actually result from a new project. However, we do have expectations concerning the possible outcomes and are able to assign probabilities to these outcomes. Stated another way, although we do not know what the cash flows resulting from the acceptance of a new project will be, we can formulate the probability distributions from which the flows will be drawn.

As we learned in Chapter 8, risk occurs when there is some question as to the future outcome of an event. We will now proceed with an examination of the logic behind this definition. Again, risk is defined as the potential variability in future cash flows.

The fact that variability reflects risk can easily be shown with a coin toss. Consider the possibility of flipping a coin—heads you win, tails you lose—for 25 cents with your finance professor. Most likely you would be willing to take on this game, because the utility gained from winning 25 cents is about equal to the utility lost if you lose 25 cents. Conversely, if the flip is for $1,000, you may be willing to play only if you are offered more than $1,000 if you win—say, you win $1,500 if it turns out heads and lose $1,000 if it turns out tails. In each case the probability of winning and losing is the same; that is, there is an equal chance that the coin will land heads or tails. In each case, however, the width of the dispersion changes, which is why the second coin toss is more risky and why you may not take the chance unless the payoffs are altered. The key here is the fact that only the dispersion changes; the probability of winning or losing is the same in each case. Thus, the potential variability in future returns reflects the risk.

The final question to be addressed is whether individuals are in fact risk averse. Although we do see people gambling where the odds of winning are against them, it should be stressed that monetary return is not the only possible return they may receive. A nonmonetary, psychic reward accrues to some gamblers, allowing them to fantasize that they will break the bank, never have to work again, and retire to some offshore island. Actually, the heart of the question is how wealth is measured. Although gamblers appear to be acting as risk seekers, they actually attach an additional nonmonetary return to gambling; the risk is in effect its own reward. When this is considered, their actions seem totally rational. It should also be noted that although gamblers appear to be pursuing risk on one hand, on the other hand they are eliminating some risk by purchasing insurance and diversifying their investments.

In the remainder of this chapter we assume that although future cash flows are not known with certainty, the probability distribution from which they come is known. Also, because we have illustrated that the dispersion of possible outcomes reflects risk, we are prepared to use a measure of dispersion or variability later in the chapter when we quantify risk.

In the pages that follow, remember that there are only two basic issues that we address: (1) What is risk in terms of capital-budgeting decisions, and how should it be measured? (2) How should risk be incorporated into capital-budgeting analysis?

What Measure of Risk Is Relevant in Capital Budgeting

Before we begin our discussion of how to adjust for risk it is important to determine just what type of risk we are to adjust for. In capital budgeting, a project's risk can be looked at on three levels. First, there is *total project risk*, which is a project's risk ignoring the fact that much of this risk will be diversified away as the project is combined with the firm's other projects and assets. Second, we have the project's *contribution-to-firm risk*, which is the amount of risk that the project contributes to the firm as a whole; this measure considers the fact that some of the project's risk will be diversified away as the project is combined with the firm's other projects and assets, but ignores the effects of diversification of the firm's shareholders. Finally, there is *systematic risk*, which is the risk of the project from the viewpoint of a well-diversified shareholder; this measure takes into account that some of a project's risk will be diversified away as the project is combined with the firm's other projects, and, in addition, some of the remaining risk will be diversified away by shareholders as they combine this stock with other stocks in their portfolio. Graphically, this is shown in Figure 10–4.

Should we be interested in total project risk? The answer is no. Perhaps the easiest way to understand why not is to look at an example. Let's take the case of research and design projects at Johnson & Johnson. Each year Johnson & Johnson takes on hundreds of new R & D projects, knowing that they only have about a 10 percent probability of being successful. If they are successful, the profits can be enormous; if they fail, the investment is lost. If the company has only one project, and it is an R&D project, the company would have a 90 percent chance of failure.

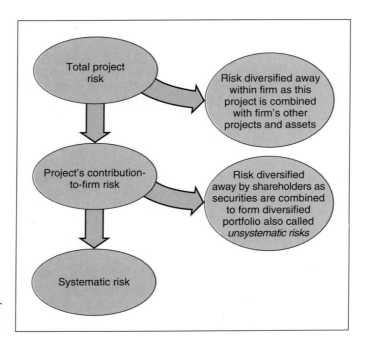

FIGURE 10–4
Looking at Three Measures of
a Project's Risk

Thus, if we look at these R & D projects individually and measure their total project risk, we would have to judge them to be enormously risky. However, if we consider the effect of the diversification that comes about from taking on several hundred independent R & D projects a year, all with a 10 percent chance of success, we can see that these R & D projects do not add much risk to Johnson & Johnson. In short, because much of a project's risk is diversified away within the firm, total project risk is an inappropriate measure of the meaningful level of risk of a capital budgeting project.

Should we be interested in the project's contribution-to-firm risk? Once again, at least in theory the answer is no, provided investors are well diversified and there is no chance of bankruptcy. From our earlier discussion of risk in Chapter 8 we saw that as shareholders, if we combined an individual security with other securities to form a diversified portfolio much of the risk of the individual security would be diversified away. In short, all that affects the shareholders is the systematic risk of the project, and as such is all that is theoretically relevant for capital budgeting.

Measuring Risk for Capital-Budgeting Purposes with a Dose of Reality—Is Systematic Risk All There Is?

According to the CAPM, systematic risk is the only relevant risk for capital-budgeting purposes; however, reality complicates this somewhat. In many instances a firm will have undiversified shareholders including owners of small corporations. Because they are not diversified, for those shareholders the relevant measure of risk is the project's contribution-to-firm risk.

The possibility of bankruptcy also affects our view of what measure of risk is relevant. As you recall in developing the CAPM we made the assumption that bankruptcy costs were zero. Because the project's contribution-to-firm risk can affect the possibility of bankruptcy, this may be an appropriate measure of risk if there are costs associated with bankruptcy. Quite obviously, in the real world there is a cost associated with bankruptcy. First, if a firm fails, its assets, in general, cannot be sold for their true economic value. Moreover, the amount of money actually available for distribution to stockholders is further reduced by liquidation and legal fees that must be paid. Finally, the opportunity cost associated with the delays related to the legal process further reduces the funds available to the shareholder. Therefore, because costs are associated with bankruptcy, reduction of the chance of bankruptcy has a very real value associated with it.

Indirect costs of bankruptcy also affect other areas of the firm, including production, sales, and the quality and efficiency of management. For example, firms with a higher probability of bankruptcy may have a more difficult time recruiting and retaining quality managers because jobs with that firm are viewed as being less secure. Suppliers also may be less willing to sell on credit. Finally, customers may lose confidence and fear that the firm may not be around to honor the warranty or to supply spare parts for the product in the future. As a result, as the probability of bankruptcy increases, the eventual bankruptcy may become self-fulfilling as potential customers and suppliers flee. The end result is that because the project's contribution-to-firm risk affects the probability of bankruptcy for the firm, it is a relevant risk measure for capital budgeting.

Finally, problems in measuring a project's systematic risk make its implementation extremely difficult. It is much easier talking about a project's systematic risk than it is measuring it.

Given all this, what do we use? The answer is that we will give consideration to both measures. We know in theory systematic risk is correct. We also know that bankruptcy costs and undiversified shareholders violate the assumptions of the theory, which brings us back to the concept of a project's contribution-to-firm risk. Still, the concept of systematic risk holds value for capital-budgeting decisions, because that is the risk that shareholders are compensated for assuming. Therefore, we will concern ourselves with both the project's contribution-to-firm risk and the project's systematic risk, and not try to make any specific allocation of importance between the two for capital-budgeting purposes.

▪ METHODS FOR INCORPORATING RISK INTO CAPITAL BUDGETING

In the preceding chapter we ignored any risk differences between projects. This approach is simple but not valid; different investment projects do in fact contain different levels of risk. We will now look at several methods for incorporating risk into the analysis. The first technique, the *certainty equivalent approach*, attempts to incorporate the manager's utility function into the analysis. The second technique, the *risk-adjusted discount rate*, is based on the notion that investors require higher rates of return on more risky projects.

BACK TO THE FUNDAMENTALS

All the methods used to compensate for risk in capital budgeting find their roots in **Axiom 1: The Risk-Return Tradeoff—We Won't Take on Additional Risk Unless We Expect To Be Compensated with Additional Return.** In fact, the risk-adjusted discount method puts this concept directly into play.

Certainty Equivalent Approach

The **certainty equivalent approach** involves a direct attempt to allow the decision maker to incorporate his or her utility function into the analysis. The financial manager is allowed to substitute the certain dollar amount that he or she feels is equivalent to the expected but risky cash flow offered by the investment for that risky cash flow in the capital-budgeting analysis. In effect, a set of riskless cash flows is substituted for the original risky cash flows, between both of which the financial manager is indifferent. To a certain extent this process is like the old television program "Let's Make a Deal." On that show Monty Hall asked contestants to trade certain outcomes for uncertain outcomes. In some cases contestants were willing to make a trade, and in some cases they were not; it all depended on how risk averse they were. The main difference between what we are doing and what was done on "Let's Make a Deal" is that on the TV show contestants were in general not indifferent with respect to the certain outcome and the risky outcome, whereas in the certainty equivalent approach managers are indifferent.

To illustrate the concept of a certainty equivalent, let us look at a simple coin toss. Assume you can play the game only once and if it comes out heads, you win $10,000, and if it comes out tails you win nothing. Obviously, you have a 50 percent chance of winning $10,000 and a 50 percent chance of winning nothing, with an expected value of $5,000. Thus, $5,000 is your uncertain expected value outcome. The certainty equivalent then becomes the amount you would demand for certain to make you indifferent with regard to playing and not playing the game. If you are indifferent with respect to receiving $3,000 for certain and not playing the game, then $3,000 is the certainty equivalent.

To simplify future calculations and problems, let us define certainty equivalent coefficients (α_t) that represent the ratio of the certain outcome to the risky outcome, between which the financial manager is indifferent. In equation form, α_t can be represented as follows:

$$\alpha_t = \frac{\text{certain cash flow}_t}{\text{risky cash flow}_t} \qquad \textbf{(10–4)}$$

Thus, the alphas can vary between 0, in the case of extreme risk, and 1, in the case of certainty. To obtain the value of the equivalent certain cash flow, we need only multiply the risky cash flow and the α_t. When this is done, we are indifferent with respect to this certain cash flow and the risky cash flow. In the preceding example of the simple coin toss, the certain cash flow was $3,000, while the risky cash flow was $5,000, the expected value of the coin toss; thus, the certainty equivalent coefficient is 3000/5000 = .6. In summary, by multiplying the certainty equivalent coefficient (α_t) times the expected but risky cash flow, we can determine an equivalent riskless cash flow.

Once this risk is taken out of the project's cash flows, those cash flows are discounted back to present at the risk-free rate of interest, and the project's net present value or profitability index is determined. If the internal rate of return is calculated, it is then compared with the risk-free rate of interest rather than the firm's required rate of return in determining whether it should be accepted or rejected. The certainty equivalent method can be summarized as follows:

$$NPV = \sum_{t=1}^{n} \frac{\alpha_t ACF_t}{(1 + k_{rf})^t} - IO \qquad (10\text{--}5)$$

where α_t = the certainty equivalent coefficient in period t

ACF_t = the annual after-tax expected cash flow in period t

IO = the initial cash outlay

n = the project's expected life

k_{rf} = the risk-free interest rate

The certainty equivalent approach can be summarized as follows:

Step 1: Risk is removed from the cash flows by substituting equivalent certain cash flows for the risky cash flows. If the certainty equivalent coefficient (α_t) is given, this is done by multiplying each risky cash flow by the appropriate (α_t) value.

Step 2: These riskless cash flows are then discounted back to the present at the riskless rate of interest.

Step 3: The normal capital-budgeting criteria are then applied, except in the case of the internal rate of return criterion, where the project's internal rate of return is compared with the risk-free rate of interest rather than the firm's required rate of return.

EXAMPLE

A firm with a 10 percent required rate of return is considering building new research facilities with an expected life of five years. The initial outlay associated with this project involves a certain cash outflow of $120,000. The expected cash inflows and certainty equivalent coefficients, (α_t), are as follows:

Year	Expected Cash Flow	Certainty Equivalent Coefficient, α_t
1	$10,000	.95
2	20,000	.90
3	40,000	.85
4	80,000	.75
5	80,000	.65

The risk-free rate of interest is 6 percent. What is the project's net present value?

To determine the net present value of this project using the certainty equivalent approach, we must first remove the risk from the future cash flows. We do so by multiplying each expected cash flow by the corresponding certainty equivalent coefficient, α_t.

Expected Cash Flow	Certainty Equivalent Coefficient, α_t	$\alpha_t \times$ (Expected Cash Flow) = Equivalent Riskless Cash Flow
$10,000	.95	$ 9,500
20,000	.90	18,000
40,000	.85	34,000
80,000	.75	60,000
80,000	.65	52,000

The equivalent riskless cash flows are then discounted back to the present at the riskless interest rate, not the firm's required rate of return. The required rate of return would be used if this project had the same level of risk as a typical project for this firm. However, these equivalent cash flows have no risk at all; hence, the appropriate discount rate is the riskless rate of interest. The equivalent riskless cash flows can be discounted back to the present at the riskless rate of interest, 6 percent, as follows:

Year	Equivalent Riskless Cash Flow	Present Value Factor at 6 Percent	Present Value
1	$ 9,500	.943	$ 8,958.50
2	18,000	.890	16,020.00
3	34,000	.840	28,560.00
4	60,000	.792	47,520.00
5	52,000	.747	38,844.00

$$NPV = -\$120,000 + \$8958.50 + \$16,020 + \$28,560 + \$47,520$$
$$+\$38,844$$
$$= \$19,902.50$$

Applying the normal capital-budgeting decision criteria, we find that the project should be accepted, as its net present value is greater than zero. ∎

Risk-Adjusted Discount Rates

The use of **risk-adjusted discount rates** is based on the concept that investors demand higher returns for more risky projects. This is the basic principle behind Axiom 1 and the CAPM, and this relationship between risk and return is illustrated graphically in Figure 10–5.

As we know from Axiom 1, the expected rate of return on any investment should include compensation for delaying consumption equal to the risk-free rate of return, plus compensation for any risk taken on. Under the risk-adjusted discount rate approach, if the risk associated with the investment is greater than the risk involved in a typical endeavor, the discount rate is adjusted upward to compensate for this added risk. Once the firm determines the appropriate required rate of return for a project with a given level of risk, the cash flows are discounted back to the present at the risk-adjusted discount rate. Then the normal capital-budgeting criteria are applied, except in the case of the internal rate of return. For the IRR, the hurdle rate with which the project's internal rate of return is compared now becomes the risk-adjusted discount rate. Expressed mathematically, the net present value using the risk-adjusted discount rate becomes:

$$NPV = \sum_{t=1}^{n} \frac{ACF_t}{(1 + k^*)^t} - IO \qquad \textbf{(10–6)}$$

where ACF_t = the annual after-tax expected cash flow in time period

  IO = the initial cash outlay

  k^* = the risk-adjusted discount rate

  n = The project's expected life

The logic behind the risk-adjusted discount rate stems from the idea that if the level of risk in a project is different from that of the typical firm project, then management must incorporate the shareholders' probable reaction to this new endeavor into the decision-making process. If the project has more risk than a typical project, then a higher required rate of return should apply. Otherwise, marginal projects will

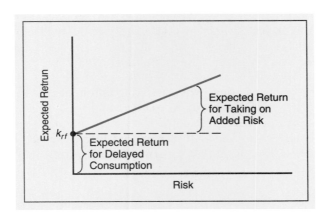

FIGURE 10–5
Risk Return Relationship

lower the firm's share price—that is, reduce shareholders' wealth. This will occur as the market raises its required rate of return on the firm to reflect the addition of a more risky project, whereas the incremental cash flows resulting from the acceptance of the new project are not large enough to offset this change fully. By the same logic, if the project has less than normal risk, a reduction in the required rate of return is appropriate. Thus, the risk-adjusted discount method attempts to apply more stringent standards—that is, require a higher rate of return—to projects that will increase the firm's risk level. This is because these projects will lead shareholders to demand a higher required rate of return to compensate them for the higher risk level of the firm. If this adjustment is not made, the marginal projects containing above-average risk could actually lower the firm's share price.

EXAMPLE

A toy manufacturer is considering the introduction of a line of fishing equipment with an expected life of five years. In the past, this firm has been quite conservative in its investment in new products, sticking primarily to standard toys. In this context, the introduction of a line of fishing equipment is considered an abnormally risky project. Management thinks that the normal required rate of return for the firm of 10 percent is not sufficient. Instead, the minimally acceptable rate of return on this project should be 15 percent. The initial outlay would be $110,000, and the expected cash flows from this project are given below:

Year	Expected Cash Flow
1	$30,000
2	30,000
3	30,000
4	30,000
5	30,000

Discounting this annuity back to the present at 15 percent yields a present value of the future cash flows of $100,560. Because the initial outlay on this project is $110,000, the net present value becomes −$9,440, and the project should be rejected. If the normal required rate of return of 10 percent had been used as the discount rate, the project would have been accepted with a net present value of $3,730. ∎

In practice, when the risk-adjusted discount rate is used, projects are generally grouped according to purpose, or risk class; then the discount rate preassigned to that purpose or risk class is used. For example, a firm with a required rate of return of 12 percent might use the following rate-of-return categorization:

Project	Required Rate of Return
Replacement decision	12%
Modification or expansion of existing product line	15
Project unrelated to current operations	18
Research and development operations	25

The purpose of this categorization of projects is to make their evaluation easier, but it also introduces a sense of the arbitrary into the calculations that makes the evaluation less meaningful. The tradeoffs involved in the classification above are obvious; time and effort are minimized, but only at the cost of precision.

Certainty Equivalent Versus Risk-Adjusted Discount Rate Methods

The primary difference between the certainty equivalent approach and the risk-adjusted discount rate approach involves the point at which the adjustment for risk is incorporated into the calculations. The certainty equivalent penalizes or adjusts downward the value of the expected annual after-tax cash flows, ACF_t, which results in a lower net present value for a risky project. The risk-adjusted discount rate, conversely, leaves the cash flows at their expected value and adjusts the required rate of return, k, upward to compensate for added risk. In either case the project's net present value is being adjusted downward to compensate for additional risk. The computational differences are illustrated in Table 10–11.

TABLE 10–11
Computational Steps in Certainty Equivalent and Risk-Adjusted Discount Rate Methods

Certainty Equivalent	Risk-Adjusted Discount Rate
Step 1: Adjust the expected cash flows, ACF_t, downward for risk by multiplying by the corresponding certainty equivalent risk coefficient, α_t.	Step 1: Adjust the discount rate upward or downward for more or less risk
Step 2: Discount the certainty equivalent riskless cash flows back to the present using the *risk-free rate of interest*.	Step 2: Discount the expected cash flows back to the present using the risk-adjusted discount rate.
Step 3: Apply the normal decision criteria, except in the case of the internal rate of return, where the risk-free rate of interest replaces the required rate of return as the hurdle rate.	Step 3: Apply the normal decision criteria, except in the case of the internal rate of return, where the risk-adjusted discount rate replaces the required rate of return as the hurdle rate.

In addition to the difference in point of adjustment for risk, the risk-adjusted discount rate makes the implicit assumption that risk becomes greater as we move further out in time. Although this is not necessarily a good or bad assumption, we should be aware of it and understand it. In effect, the risk adjustment is compounded over time and, as such, becomes larger in each subsequent year.

Thus, if the risk-adjusted discount rate method is used, we are adjusting downward the value of future cash flows that occur further in the future more severely than earlier cash flows. In summary, the use of the risk-adjusted discount rate assumes that risk increases over time and that cash flows occurring further in the future should be more severely penalized.

<u>PERSPECTIVE IN FINANCE</u>

If performed properly, either of these methods can do a good job of adjusting for risk. However, by far the more popular method of risk adjustment is the risk-adjusted discount rate. The reason for the popularity of the risk-adjusted discount rate over the certainty equivalent approach is purely and simply its ease of implementation.

▩ RISK-ADJUSTED DISCOUNT RATE AND MEASUREMENT OF A PROJECT'S SYSTEMATIC RISK

When we initially talked about systematic risk or the beta, we were talking about measuring it for the entire firm. As you recall, although we could estimate a firm's beta using historical data, we did not have complete confidence in our results. As we will see, estimating the appropriate level of systematic risk for a single project is even more fraught with difficulties. To truly understand what it is we are trying to do and the difficulties we will encounter, let us step back a bit and examine systematic risk and the risk adjustment for a project.

What we are trying to do is use the CAPM to determine the level of risk and the appropriate risk-return tradeoffs for a particular project. We will then take the expected return on this project and compare it to the required return suggested by the CAPM to determine whether the project should be accepted. If the project appears to be a typical one for the firm, using the CAPM to determine the appropriate risk-return tradeoffs and then judging the project against them may be a warranted approach. But if the project is not a typical project, what do we do? Historical data generally do not exist for a new project. In fact, for some capital investments, for example, a truck or a new building, historical data would not have much meaning. What we need to do is make the best of a bad situation. We either (1) fake it—that is, use historical accounting data, if available, to substitute for historical price data in estimating systematic risk—or (2) we attempt to find a substitute firm in the same industry as the capital-budgeting project and use the substitute firm's estimated systematic risk as a proxy for the project's systematic risk.

Beta Estimation Using Accounting Data

When we are dealing with a project that is identical to the firm's other projects, we need only estimate the level of systematic risk for the firm and use that estimate as a proxy for the project's risk. Unfortunately, when projects are not typical of the firm this approach does not work. For example, when R. J. Reynolds introduces a new food through one of its food products divisions, this new product most likely carries with it a different level of systematic risk from what is typical for Reynolds as a whole.

To get a better approximation of the systematic risk level on this project, we will estimate the level of systematic risk for the food division and use that as a proxy for the project's systematic risk. Unfortunately, historical stock price data are available only for the company as a whole, and as you recall historical stock return data are generally used to estimate a firm's beta. Thus, we are forced to use *accounting return data* rather than historical stock return data for the division to estimate the division's systematic risk. To estimate a project's beta using accounting data we need only run a time series regression of the division's return on assets (net income/total assets) on the market index (the S&P 500). The regression coefficient from this equation would be the project's accounting beta and would serve as an approximation for the project's true beta or measure of systematic risk. Alternatively, a multiple regression model based on accounting data could be developed to explain betas. The results of this model could then be applied to firms that are not publicly traded to estimate their betas.

How good is the accounting beta technique? It certainly is not as good as a direct calculation of the beta. In fact, the correlation between the accounting beta and the beta calculated on historical stock return data is only about 0.6; however, better luck has been experienced with multiple regression models used to predict betas. Unfortunately, in many cases there may not be any realistic alternative to the calculation of the accounting beta. Owing to the importance of adjusting for a project's risk, the accounting beta method is much preferred to doing nothing.

The Pure Play Method for Estimating a Project's Beta

Whereas the accounting beta method attempts to directly estimate a project or division's beta, the **pure play method** attempts to identify publicly traded firms that are engaged solely in the same business as the project or division. Once the proxy or pure play firm is identified, its systematic risk is determined and then used as a proxy for the project or division's level of systematic risk. What we are doing is looking for a publicly traded firm on the outside that looks like our project and using that firm's required rate of return to judge our project. In doing so we are presuming that the systematic risk and the capital structure of the proxy firm are identical to those of the project.

In using the pure play method it should be noted that a firm's capital structure is reflected in its beta. When the capital structure of the proxy firm is different from that of the project's firm, some adjustment must be made for this difference. Although not a perfect approach, it does provide some insights as to the level of systematic risk a project might have.

EXAMINING A PROJECT'S RISK THROUGH SIMULATION

Simulation: Explained and Illustrated

Another method for evaluating risk in the investment decision is through the use of **simulation.** The certainty equivalent and risk-adjusted discount rate approaches provided us with a single value for the risk-adjusted net present value, whereas a simulation approach gives us a probability distribution for the investment's net present value or internal rate of return. Simulation imitates the performance of the project under evaluation. This is done by randomly selecting observations from each of the distributions that affect the outcome of the project, combining those observations to determine the final output of the project, and continuing with this process until a representative record of the project's probable outcome is assembled.

The easiest way to develop an understanding of the computer simulation process is to follow through an example simulation for an investment project evaluation. Suppose a chemical producer is considering an extension to its processing plant. The simulation process is portrayed in Figure 10–6. First the probability distributions are determined for all the factors that affect the project's returns; in this case, let us assume there are nine such variables:

1. Market size
2. Selling price
3. Market growth rate
4. Share of market (which results in physical sales volume)
5. Investment required
6. Residual value of investment
7. Operating costs
8. Fixed costs
9. Useful life of facilities

Then the computer randomly selects one observation from each of the probability distributions, according to its chance of actually occurring in the future. These nine observations are combined, and a net present value or internal rate of return figure is calculated. This process is repeated as many times as desired, until a representative distribution of possible future outcomes is assembled. Thus, the inputs to a simulation include all the principal factors affecting the project's profitability, and the simulation output is a probability distribution of net present values or internal rates of return for the project. The decision maker bases the decision on the full range of possible outcomes. The project is accepted if the decision maker feels that enough of the distribution lies above the normal cutoff criteria ($NPV \geq 0$, $IRR \geq$ required rate of return).

Suppose the output from the simulation of a chemical producer's project is as given in Figure 10–7 (page 333). This output provides the decision maker with the probability of different outcomes occurring in addition to the range of possible outcomes. Sometimes called **scenario analysis**, this examination identifies the range of possible outcomes under the worst, best, and most likely case. The firm's management will examine the distribution to determine the project's level of risk and then make the appropriate adjustment.

You'll notice that although the simulation approach helps us to determine the amount of total risk a project has, it does not differentiate between systematic and unsystematic risk. Because systematic risk cannot be diversified away for free, the simulation approach does not provide a complete method of risk assessment. However, it does provide important insights as to the total risk level of a given investment project. Now we will look briefly at how the simulation approach can be used to perform sensitivity analysis.

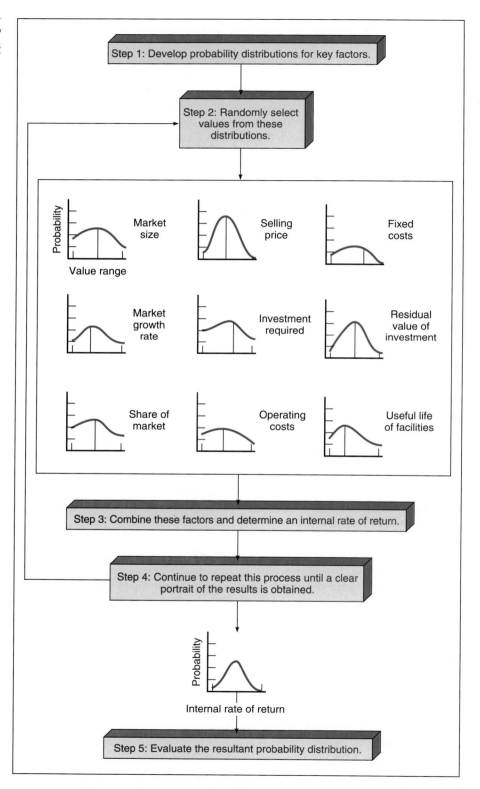

FIGURE 10–6
Capital Budgeting Simulation

Step 1: Develop probability distributions for key factors.

Step 2: Randomly select values from these distributions.

Probability

Market size

Value range

Selling price

Fixed costs

Market growth rate

Investment required

Residual value of investment

Share of market

Operating costs

Useful life of facilities

Step 3: Combine these factors and determine an internal rate of return.

Step 4: Continue to repeat this process until a clear portrait of the results is obtained.

Probability

Internal rate of return

Step 5: Evaluate the resultant probability distribution.

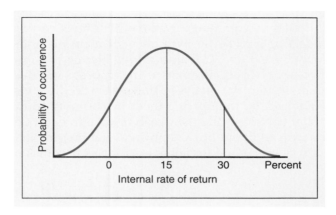

FIGURE 10–7
Output from Simulation

Sensitivity Analysis Through Simulation Approach

Sensitivity analysis involves determining how the distribution of possible net present values or internal rates of return for a particular project is affected by a change in one particular input variable. This is done by changing the value of one input variable while holding all other input variables constant. The distribution of possible net present values or internal rates of return that is generated is then compared with the distribution of possible returns generated before the change was made to determine the effect of the change. For this reason sensitivity analysis is commonly called *"What if?" Analysis.*

For example, the chemical producer that was considering a possible expansion to its plant may wish to determine the effect of a more pessimistic forecast of the anticipated market growth rate. After the more pessimistic forecast replaces the original forecast in the model, the simulation is rerun. The two outputs are then compared to determine how sensitive the results are to the revised estimate of the market growth rate.

SUMMARY

Specifically, we examine the measurement of incremental cash flows associated with a firm's investment proposals and the evaluation of those proposals. In measuring cash flows we focus on the **incremental** or differential **after-tax cash flows** attributed to the investment proposal. In general, a project's cash flows fall into one of three categories: (1) the initial outlay, (2) the differential flows over the project's life, (3) the terminal cash flow. A summary of the typical entries in each of these categories appears in Table 10–7.

We also cover the problem of incorporating risk into the capital-budgeting decision. First we explore just what type of risk to adjust for: total project risk, the project's contribution-to-firm risk, or the project's systematic risk. In theory, systematic risk is the appropriate risk measure, but bankruptcy costs and the issue of undiversified shareholders also give weight to considering a project's contribution-to-firm risk as the appropriate risk measure. Both measures of risk are valid, and we avoid making any specific allocation of importance between the two in capital budgeting.

Several commonly used methods for incorporating risk into capital budgeting are (1) the certainty equivalent method, (2) risk-adjusted discount rates, and (3) simulation. The certainty equivalent approach involves a direct attempt to incorporate the decision maker's utility function into the analysis. Under this method, cash flows are adjusted downward by multiplying them by certainty equivalent coefficients, α_t, which transform the risky cash flows into equivalent riskless cash flows in terms of desirability. A project's net present value using the certainty equivalent method for adjusting for risk becomes

$$NPV = \sum_{t=1}^{n} \frac{\alpha_t ACF_t}{(1 + k_{rf})^t} - IO$$

The risk-adjusted discount rate involves an upward adjustment of the discount rate to compensate for risk. This method is based on the concept that investors demand higher returns for riskier projects.

The simulation method is used to provide information as to the location and shape of the distribution of possible outcomes. Decisions could be based directly on this method, or it could be used to determine input into either certainty equivalent or risk-adjusted discount rate method approaches.

STUDY QUESTIONS

10–1. Why do we focus on cash flows rather than accounting profits in making our capital-budgeting decisions? Why are we interested only in incremental cash flows rather than total cash flows?

10–2. If depreciation is not a cash flow expense, does it affect the level of cash flows from a project in any way? Why?

10–3. If a project requires additional investment in working capital, how should this be treated in calculating cash flows?

10–4. How do sunk costs affect the determination of cash flows associated with an investment proposal?

10–5. In the preceding chapter we examined the payback period capital-budgeting criterion. Often this capital-budgeting criterion is used as a risk-screening device. Explain the rationale behind its use.

10–6. The use of the risk-adjusted discount rate assumes that risk increases over time. Justify this assumption.

10–7. What are the similarities and differences between the risk-adjusted discount rate and certainty equivalent methods for incorporating risk into the capital-budgeting decision?

10–8. Explain how simulation works. What is the value in using a simulation approach?

SELF-TEST PROBLEMS

ST-1. The Scotty Gator Corporation of Meadville, Pa., maker of Scotty's electronic components, is considering replacing one of its current hand-operated assembly machines with a new fully automated machine. This replacement would mean the elimination of one employee, generating salary and benefit savings. Given the following information, determine the cash flows associated with this replacement.

Existing situation:	One full-time machine operator—salary and benefits, $25,000 per year
	Cost of maintenance—$2,000 per year
	Cost of defects—$6,000
	Original depreciable value of old machine—$50,000
	Annual depreciation—$5,000 per year
	Expected life—10 years
	Age—five years old
	Expected salvage value in five years—$0
	Current salvage value—$5,000
	Marginal tax rate—34 percent
Proposed situation:	Fully automated machine
	Cost of machine—$60,000
	Installation fee—$3,000
	Shipping fee—$3,000
	Cost of maintenance—$3,000 per year
	Cost of defects—$3,000 per year
	Expected life—five years
	Salvage value—$20,000
	Depreciation method—simplified straight-line method over five years

ST-2. G. Norohna and Co. is considering two mutually exclusive projects. The expected values for each project's cash flows are given below.

Year	Project A	Project B
0	–$300,000	–$300,000
1	100,000	200,000
2	200,000	200,000
3	200,000	200,000
4	300,000	300,000
5	300,000	400,000

The company has decided to evaluate these projects using the certainty equivalent method. The certainty equivalent coefficients for each project's cash flows are given below.

Year	Project A	Project B
0	1.00	1.00
1	.95	.90
2	.90	.80
3	.85	.70
4	.80	.60
5	.75	.50

Given that this company's normal required rate of return is 15 percent and the after-tax risk-free rate is 8 percent, which project should be selected?

STUDY PROBLEMS

10–1. *(Capital Gains Tax)* The J. Harris Corporation is considering selling one of its old assembly machines. The machine, purchased for $30,000 five years ago, had an expected life of 10 years and an expected salvage value of zero. Assume Harris uses simplified straight-line depreciation, creating depreciation of $3,000 per year, and could sell this old machine for $35,000. Also assume a 34 percent marginal tax rate.
   a. What would be the taxes associated with this sale?
   b. If the old machine were sold for $25,000, what would be the taxes associated with this sale?
   c. If the old machine were sold for $15,000, what would be the taxes associated with this sale?
   d. If the old machine were sold for $12,000, what would be the taxes associated with this sale?

10–2. *(Cash Flow Calculations)* The Winky Corporation, maker of cow grooming equipment, is considering replacing a hand-operated machine used in the manufacture of grooming components with a new fully automated machine. Given the following information, determine the cash flows associated with this replacement.

Existing situation:	Two full-time machine operators— salaries $10,000 each per year
	Cost of maintenance—$5,000 per year
	Cost of defects—$5,000
	Original cost of old machine—$30,000
	Expected life—10 years
	Age—five years old
	Expected salvage value—$0
	Depreciation method—simplified straight-line over 10 years, $3,000 per year
	Current salvage value—$10,000
	Marginal tax rate—34 percent
Proposed situation:	Fully automated machine
	Cost of machine—$55,000
	Installation fee—$5,000
	Cost of maintenance—$6,000 per year
	Cost of defects—$2,000 per year
	Expected life—five years
	Salvage value—$0
	Depreciation method—simplified straight-line method over five years

---

10–3. *(Capital-Budgeting Calculation)* Given the cash flow information in problem 10–2 and a required rate of return of 15 percent, compute the following for the automated machine:
   a. Payback period
   b. Net present value
   c. Profitability index
   d. Internal rate of return
   Should this project be accepted?

10–4. *(Cash Flow and New Project Analysis)* The Chung Chemical Corporation is considering the purchase of a chemical analysis machine. Although the machine being considered will not produce any increase in sales revenues, it will result in a before-tax reduction of labor costs by $35,000 per year. The machine has a purchase price of $100,000, and it would cost an additional $5,000 to install this machine properly. In addition, to operate this machine properly, inventory must be increased by $5,000. This machine has an expected life of 10 years, after which it will have no salvage value. Also, assume simplified straight-line depreciation and that this machine is being depreciated down to zero, a 34 percent marginal tax rate, and a required rate of return of 15 percent.

a. What is the initial outlay associated with this project?

b. What are the annual after-tax cash flows associated with this project for years 1 through 9?

c. What is the terminal cash flow in year 10 (i.e., what is the annual after-tax cash flow in year 10 plus any additional cash flows associated with termination of the project)?

d. Should this machine be purchased?

10–5. *(Cash Flow and New Project Analysis)* Raymobile Motors is considering the purchase of a new production machine for $500,000. Although the purchase of this machine will not produce any increase in sales revenues, it will result in a before-tax reduction of labor costs by $150,000 per year. To operate this machine properly, workers would have to go through a brief training session that would cost $25,000. In addition, it would cost $5,000 to install this machine properly. Also, because this machine is extremely efficient, its purchase would necessitate an increase in inventory of $30,000. This machine has an expected life of 10 years, after which it will have no salvage value. Assume simplified straight-line depreciation and that this machine is being depreciated down to zero, a 34 percent marginal tax rate, and a required rate of return of 15 percent.

a. What is the initial outlay associated with this project?

b. What are the annual after-tax cash flows associated with this project for years 1 through 9?

c. What is the terminal cash flow in year 10 (i.e., what is the annual after-tax cash flow in year 10 plus any additional cash flows associated with termination of the project)?

d. Should this machine be purchased?

10–6. *(Cash Flow and Capital-Budgeting Calculation)* The Jabot Cosmetics Corporation is considering replacing a 10-year-old machine that originally cost $30,000, has a current book value of $10,000 with five years of expected life left, and is being depreciated using the simplified straight-line method over its 15-year expected life down to a terminal value of zero in five years, generating depreciation of $2,000 per year. The replacement machine being considered would cost $80,000 and have a five-year expected life over which it would be depreciated using the simplified straight-line method down to zero. At termination in five years the new machine would have a salvage value of $40,000. Material efficiencies resulting from the replacement would result in savings of $30,000 per year before depreciation and taxes. Currently, the old machine could be sold for $15,000. Assuming simplified straight-line depreciation, a 34 percent marginal tax rate, and a required rate of return of 20 percent, calculate

a. The payback period

b. The net present value

c. The profitability index

d. The internal rate of return

10–7. *(Comprehensive Cash Flow and Capital-Budgeting Calculation)* The L. Knutson Company, a manufacturer of electronic components in the 34 percent marginal tax bracket, is considering the purchase of a new fully automated machine to replace an older, manually operated one. The machine being replaced, now 5 years old, originally had an expected life of 10 years, was being depreciated using the simplified straight-line method from $20,000 down to zero, thus generating $2,000 in depreciation per year, and could be sold for $25,000. The old machine took one operator who earned $15,000 per year in salary and $2,000 per year in fringe benefits. The annual costs of maintenance and defects associated with the old machine were $7,000 and $3,000, respectively. The replacement machine being considered had a purchase price of $50,000, a salvage value after five years of $10,000, and would be depreciated over five years using the simplified straight-line depreciation method down to zero. To get the automated machine in running order, there would be a $3,000 shipping fee and a $2,000 installation charge. In addition, because the new machine would work faster than the old one, investment in raw materials and goods-in-process inventories would need to be increased by a total of $5,000. The annual costs of maintenance and defects on the new machine would be $2,000 and $4,000, respectively. The new machine also requires maintenance workers to be specially trained; fortunately, a similar machine was purchased three months ago, and at that time the maintenance workers went through the $5,000 training program needed to familiarize themselves with the new equipment. The firm's management is uncertain whether to charge half of this $5,000 training fee toward the new project. Finally, to purchase the new machine, it appears the firm would have to borrow an additional $20,000 at 10 percent interest from its local bank, resulting in additional interest payments of $2,000 per year. The required rate of return on projects of this kind is 20 percent.

a. What is the project's initial outlay?
b. What are the differential cash flows over the project's life?
c. What is the terminal cash flow?
d. Draw a cash flow diagram for this project.
e. If the firm requires a minimum payback period on projects of this type of three years, should this project be accepted?
f. What is its net present value?
g. What is its profitability index?
h. What is its internal rate of return?
i. Should the project be accepted? Why or why not?

10–8. *(Risk-Adjusted NPV)* The Hokie Corporation is considering two mutually exclusive projects. Both require an initial outlay of $10,000 and will operate for five years. Project A will produce expected cash flows of $5,000 per year for years 1–5, while Project B will produce expected cash flows of $6,000 per year for years 1–5. Because project B is the riskier of the two projects, the management of Hokie Corporation has decided to apply a required rate of return of 15 percent to its evaluation but only a 12 percent required rate of return to project A. Determine each project's risk-adjusted net present value.

10–9. *(Certainty Equivalents)* The V. Coles Corp. is considering two mutually exclusive projects. The expected values for each project's cash flows are given below:

Year	Project A	Project B
0	–$1,000,000	–$1,000,000
1	500,000	500,000
2	700,000	600,000
3	600,000	700,000
4	500,000	800,000

The management has decided to evaluate these projects using the certainty equivalent method. The certainty equivalent coefficients for each project's cash flows are as follows:

Year	Project A	Project B
0	1.00	1.00
1	.95	.90
2	.90	.70
3	.80	.60
4	.70	.50

Given that this company's normal required rate of return is 15 percent and the after-tax risk-free rate is 5 percent, which project should be selected?

10–10. *(Certainty Equivalents)* Neustal, Inc., has decided to use the certainty equivalent method in determining whether a new investment should be made. The expected cash flows associated with this investment and the estimated certainty equivalent coefficients are as follows:

Year	Expected Values for Cash Flows	Certainty Equivalent Coefficients
0	–$90,000	1.00
1	25,000	0.95
2	30,000	0.90
3	30,000	0.83
4	25,000	0.75
5	20,000	0.65

Given that Neustal's normal required rate of return is 18 percent and that the after-tax risk-free rate is 7 percent, should this project be accepted?

10–11. *(Risk-Adjusted Discount Rates and Risk Classes)* The G. Wolfe Corporation is examining two capital-budgeting projects with five-year lives. The first, project A, is a replacement project; the second, project B, is a project unrelated to current operations. The G. Wolfe Corporation uses the risk-adjusted discount rate method and groups projects according to purpose and then uses a required rate of return or discount rate that has been preassigned to that purpose or risk class. The expected cash flows for these projects are given below:

	Project A	Project B
Initial Investment:	$250,000	$400,000
Cash Inflows:		
Year 1	$ 30,000	$135,000
Year 2	40,000	135,000
Year 3	50,000	135,000
Year 4	90,000	135,000
Year 5	130,000	135,000

The purpose/risk classes and preassigned required rates of return are as follows:

Purpose	Required Rate of Return
Replacement decision	12%
Modification or expansion of existing product line	15
Project unrelated to current operations	18
Research and development operations	20

Determine the project's risk-adjusted net present value.

SELF-TEST SOLUTIONS

SS-1.
Step 1: First calculate the initial outlay.

Initial outlay	
Outflows:	
Cost of machine	$60,000
Installation fee	3,000
Shipping fee	3,000
Inflows:	
Salvage value—old machine	5,000
Tax savings on sale of old machine ($25,000 – $5,000) (.34)	–6,800
	$54,200

Step 2: Calculate the differential cash flows over the project's life.

		Book Profit	Cash Flow
Savings:	Reduced salary	$25,000	$25,000
	Reduced defects	3,000	3,000
Costs:	Increased maintenance	–1,000	–1,000
	Increased depreciation ($13,200 – $5000)[a]	–8,200	
Net savings before taxes		$18,800	$27,000
Taxes (.34)		–6,392	–6,392
Annual net cash flow after taxes			$20,608

[a]Annual depreciation on the new machine is equal to the cost of the new machine ($60,000) plus any expenses necessary to get it in operating order (the shipping fee of $3,000 plus the installation fee of $3,000) divided by the depreciable life (five years).

Step 3: Calculate the terminal cash flow.

Salvage value—new machine	$20,000
Less: Taxes—recapture of depreciation ($20,000 × .34)	6,800
	$13,200

Thus, the cash flow in the final year will be equal to the annual net cash flow in that year of $20,608 plus the terminal cash flow of $13,200 for a total of $33,808.

SS-2.

Project A:

Year	(A) Expected Cash Flow	(B) α_t	(A · B) (Expected Cash Flow) × (α_t)	Present Value Factor at 8%	Present Value
0	−$300,000	1.00	−$300,000	1.000	−$300,000
1	100,000	.95	95,000	0.926	87,970
2	200,000	.90	180,000	0.857	154,260
3	200,000	.85	170,000	0.794	134,980
4	300,000	.80	240,000	0.735	176,400
5	300,000	.75	225,000	0.681	153,225
				NPV_A =	$406,835

Project B:

Year	(A) Expected Cash Flow	(B) α_t	(A · B) (Expected Cash Flow) × (α_t)	Present Value Factor at 8%	Present Value
0	−$300,000	1.00	−$300,000	1.000	−$300,000
1	200,000	.90	180,000	0.926	166,680
2	200,000	.80	160,000	0.857	137,120
3	200,000	.70	140,000	0.794	111,160
4	300,000	.60	180,000	0.735	132,300
5	400,000	.50	200,000	0.681	136,200
				NPV_B =	$383,460

Thus, project A should be selected because it has the higher NPV.

CHAPTER 11

COST OF CAPITAL

The Cost-of-Capital Concept • Factors Determining the Cost-of-Capital Sources • Assumptions of the Weighted Cost-of-Capital Model • Computing the Weighted Cost of Capital • Marginal Cost of Capital: A Comprehensive Example • A Firm's Cost of Capital: Recent Evidence

A firm's cost of capital is simply a weighted average of the rates of return required by investors in the firm's securities. This average rate of return was used earlier in Chapter 9 as the minimum required rate of return, or hurdle rate, for new investments. Thus, the cost of capital serves as the linkage between a firm's investment and financing decisions. In this chapter we take an in-depth look at the cost of capital or hurdle rate for new investments. Specifically, we will discuss the following topics:

1. The cost-of-capital concept
2. The factors that determine investor-required rates of return
3. The assumptions underlying the measurement of a firm's cost of capital
4. The calculation of the weighted average cost of capital
5. An empirical study of large firms' estimates of their cost of capital

■ THE COST-OF-CAPITAL CONCEPT

The cost of capital is the opportunity cost of using funds to invest in new projects. This is appropriate because the cost of capital is that rate of return on the firm's total investment which earns the required rates

343

of return of all the sources of financing. Furthermore, if the firm earns the required rates of return on all its sources of financing, including that of the common shareholders, then the value of its common stock will not be changed by the investment. By the same reasoning, if the firm earns a rate of return higher than the cost of capital then the excess return will lead to an increase in the value of the firm's common stock and consequently, an increase in sh areholder wealth. Thus, the logic of using the cost of capital as the hurdle rate for new capital investment can be summarized as follows:

INVESTMENT RATE OF RETURN			SHAREHOLDER WEALTH
Internal Rate of Return	<	Cost of Capital	Decrease
Internal Rate of Return	=	Cost of Capital	No Change
Internal Rate of Return	>	Cost of Capital	Increase

Figure 11–1 provides an illustration of the use of the cost of capital to determine a firm's capital budget. The internal rates of return on projects A, B and C exceed the firm's cost of capital and should be accepted, whereas projects D and E should be rejected. The result is a capital budget equal to $17 million.

We have made two important assumptions in our analysis thus far, and these should be stated explicitly:

1. We have assumed that all five of the projects in Figure 11–1 are of equivalent risk. That is, the opportunity cost of capital is the same for all five investments. Obviously, we would not have the same opportunity cost of capital for an investment in short-term Treasury bills and for an investment involving drilling for oil in a politically unstable part of the world.

2. We have assumed that the mix of financing sources remains constant for all investments. The reason for this assumption will become clear when we discuss the calculation of the cost of capital.

FIGURE 11–1
Investment and
Financing Schedules

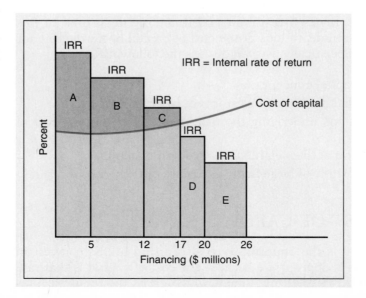

Note that Figure 11–1 holds investment risk constant so that the same required rate of return is appropriate for all investments. This is a direct implication of **Axiom 1: The Risk-Return Tradeoff—We Won't Take on Additional Risk Unless We Expect to be Compensated with Additional Return.** That is, the cost-of-capital concept represents a "risk-appropriate" rate of return. As the riskiness of the project(s) being considered varies, the "risk-appropriate" cost of capital changes accordingly.

To illustrate the calculation of the cost of capital, consider the capital structure of the Salinas Corporation found in Table 11–1. The company has three sources of capital: debt, preferred stock, and common stock. Management is considering a $200,000 investment opportunity with an expected internal rate of return of 14 percent. The current cost of the firm's capital (i.e., its required rates of return) for each source of financing is as follows:

Cost of debt capital	10%
Cost of preferred stock	12
Cost of common stock	16

Given this information, should the firm make the investment? The creditors and preferred stockholders would probably encourage us to undertake the project. However, because the 14 percent internal rate of return on the investment is less than the common stockholders' required rate of return, shareholders might argue that the investment should be forgone. What is the right choice?

To answer this question, we must first determine what percentage of the $200,000 is to be provided by each type of investor. If we intend to maintain the same capital structure mix as reflected in Table 11–1 (30 percent debt, 10 percent preferred stock, and 60 percent common stock), we could compute a **weighted cost of capital**, where the weights equal the percentage of capital to be financed by each source. For our example, the weighted cost of the individual sources of capital as computed in Table 11–2 is 13.8 percent. From this calculation we would conclude that an investment offering at least a 13.8 percent return would be acceptable

	Amount	Percentage of Capital Structure
Bonds	$ 600,000	30%
Preferred stock	200,000	10
Common stock	1,200,000	60
Total liabilities and equity	$2,000,000	100%

TABLE 11–1
Salinas Corporation Capital Structure

TABLE 11–2
Salinas Corporation Weighted
Cost of Capital

	Weights (Percentage of Financing)	Cost of Individual Sources	Weighted Cost
Debt	30%	10%	3.0%
Preferred stock	10	12	1.2
Common stock	60	16	9.6
	100%	Weighted cost of capital:	13.8%

to the company's investors. The investment should be undertaken, because the 14 percent rate of return more than satisfies all investors, as indicated by a 13.8 percent weighted cost of capital. Again, the **weighted cost of capital** is equal to the cost of each source of financing (debt, preferred stock, and common stock) multiplied by the percentage of the financing provided by that source.

In summary, two basic elements are necessary to calculate the cost of capital:

1. Estimates of the required rates of return for each of the firm's sources of capital
2. The proportions of each source of capital used by the firm

In this chapter we will concern ourselves with the determination of the first of these elements and take the second as given. The determination of the proper mix of sources of capital is the subject of Chapter 12 which discusses the firm's financing decisions.

But What If?

The weighted cost of capital may be fine in theory, but what if a company could borrow the entire amount needed for an investment in a new product line? Is it really necessary to use the weighted cost of capital, or would it be all right to make the decision based simply on the cost of the debt which is providing the funding?

Consider the Poling Corporation. Management believes it could earn 14 percent from purchasing $500,000 in new equipment, which would allow it to expand the business. Although the firm works to maintain a capital structure with equal amounts of debt and equity, the bank is willing to loan the firm the entire $500,000 at an interest rate of 12 percent. Without our even having to compute it, we know the firm's earnings per share would increase if the firm earned a rate exceeding the cost of the financing, in this case 12 percent. (We will see later in Chapter 12 that a firm's earnings will increase from using debt, whenever the return on the investment is greater than the cost of the debt financing.)

Poling's financial officer has also estimated the firm's cost of equity (common stock) at 18 percent. Because the firm can finance the purchase fully by debt, however, management has decided to make the investment and finance it by borrowing the money from the bank at 12 percent. The investment is made, and all seems well.

The following year, management finds another investment opportunity costing $500,000 but with an expected internal rate of return this time of 17 percent—better than the previous year's 14 percent. But when management approaches the bankers for financing, they find them unwilling to lend any more money to Poling. In the words of one banker, "Poling has used up all of its debt capacity." The firm must now issue new common stock before the bank will be agreeable to fund any more loans. However, because the investment does not earn the cost of equity of 18 percent, management sees no option other than to reject the investment.

What is the moral of this story? Intuitively, we can see that Poling's management has made a mistake. Making the investment in the first year has denied the firm the opportunity to make a better decision in the second year.

As a more general statement, we can conclude that a firm should never use a single cost of financing as the hurdle rate (discount rate) for making capital-budgeting decisions. Particularly when we use debt, we have implicitly used up some of our *debt capacity* for future investments, and not until we complement the use of debt with equity will we be able to continue to use more debt in the future.[1] Thus, we ought always to use the weighted cost of capital, and not an individual cost of funds, as our discount rate for investment decisions. So, let's look more carefully at the weighted cost of capital.

■ FACTORS DETERMINING THE COSTS-OF-CAPITAL SOURCES

What are the elements in the business environment that cause a company's weighted cost of capital to be high or low? Figure 11–2 identifies four primary factors: general economic conditions, the marketability ofthe firm's securities (market conditions), operating and financing conditions within the company, and the amount of financing needed for new investments. These four variables also relate to our discussion in Chapter 8, where we separated an investor's required rate of return into the riskless or *risk-free rate* of return and the *risk premium*. These two aspects of risk are also key ingredients in the firm's cost of capital.

Factor 1: General Economic Conditions

As briefly noted in Chapter 2, general economic conditions determine the demand for and supply of capital within the economy, as well as the level of expected inflation. This economic variable is reflected in the riskless rate of return. This rate represents the rate of return on risk-free investments, such as the interest rate on short-term U.S. government securities. In principle, as the demand for money in the economy

---

[1]The issue of debt capacity will be discussed more completely in Chapter 12.

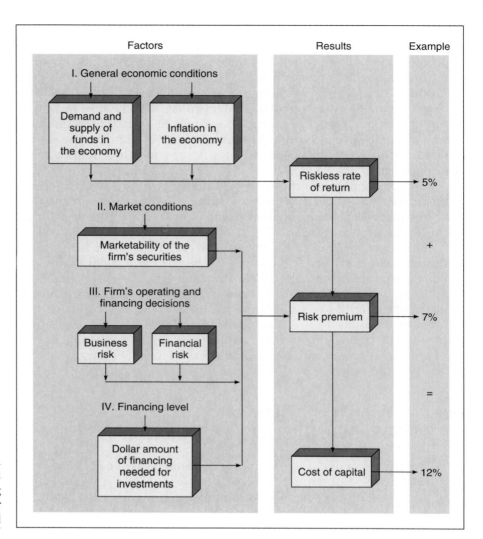

FIGURE 11–2
Primary Factors Influencing
the Cost of Particular
Sources of Capital

changes relative to the supply, investors alter their required rate of return. For example, if the demand for money increases without an equivalent increase in the supply, lenders will raise their required interest rate. At the same time, if inflation is expected to deteriorate the purchasing power of the dollar, investors require a higher rate of return to compensate for this anticipated loss.[2]

Factor 2: Market Conditions

When an investor purchases a security with a significant investment risk, an opportunity for additional returns is necessary to make the investment attractive. Essentially, as risk increases, the investor requires a higher rate of return. This increase is called a **risk premium.** When

[2]This relationship is frequently reffered to as the Fisher Effect.

investors increase their required rate of return, the cost of capital rises simultaneously. Remember we have defined risk as the potential variability of returns. If the security is not readily marketable when the investor wants to sell, or even if a continuous demand for the security exists but the price varies significantly, an investor will require a relatively high rate of return. Conversely, if a security is readily marketable and its price is reasonably stable, the investor will require a lower rate of return and the company's cost of capital will be lower.

Factor 3: Operating and Financing Decisions

Risk, or the variability of returns, also results from decisions made within the company. Risk resulting from these decisions is generally divided into two types: business risk and financial risk. **Business risk** is the variability in returns on assets and is affected by the company's investment decisions. **Financial risk** is the increased variability in returns to common stockholders as a result of financing with debt or preferred stock. As business risk and financial risk increase or decrease, the investor's required rate of return (and the cost of capital) will move in the same direction.[3]

Factor 4: Amount of Financing

The last factor determining the corporation's cost of funds is the level of financing that the firm requires. As the financing requirements of the firm become larger, the weighted cost of capital increases for several reasons. For instance, as more securities are issued, additional **flotation costs,** or the cost incurred by the firm from issuing securities, will affect the percentage cost of the funds to the firm. Also, as management approaches the market for large amounts of capital relative to the firm's size, the investors' required rate of return may rise. Suppliers of capital become hesitant to grant relatively large sums without evidence of management's capability to absorb this capital into the business. This is typically "too much too soon." Also, as the size of the issue increases, there is greater difficulty in placing it in the market without reducing the price of the security, which also increases the firm's cost of capital.

A Summary Illustration

To summarize, the important variables influencing a corporation's cost of capital include the following:

1. **General economic conditions.** This factor determines the risk-free rate or riskless rate of return.
2. **Marketability of a company's securities.** As the marketability of a security increases, investors' required rates of return decrease, lowering the corporation's cost of capital.

---

[3]Both forms of risk, business and financial, are illustrated in Chapter 12.

3. **Operating and financial decisions made by management.** If management accepts investments with high levels of risk or if it uses debt or preferred stock extensively, the firm's risk increases. Investors then require a higher rate of return, which causes a higher cost of capital to the company.

4. **Amount of financing needed.** Requests for larger amounts of capital increase the firm's cost of capital.

The right-hand margin of Figure 11–2 presents an illustration of the cost of capital for a particular source. The risk-free rate, determined by the general economic conditions, is 5 percent. However, owing to the additional risks associated with the security, the firm has to earn an additional 7 percent to satisfy the investors' required rate of return of 12 percent.

■ ASSUMPTIONS OF THE WEIGHTED COST-OF-CAPITAL MODEL

In a complex business world, difficulties quickly arise in computing a corporation's cost of capital. For this reason, we make several simplifying assumptions.

Constant Business Risk

Business risk is defined as the potential variability of returns on an investment, and the level of business risk within a firm is determined by management's investment policies. An investor's required rate of return for a company's securities—and therefore the firm's cost of capital—is a function of the firm's current business risk. If this risk level is altered, the corporation's investors will naturally change their required rates of return, which in turn will modify the cost of capital. However, the amount of change in the cost of capital resulting from a given increase or decrease in business risk is difficult to assess. For this reason, the cost of capital calculation assumes that any investment under consideration will not significantly change the firm's business risk. In other words, *the corporation's cost of capital is an appropriate investment criterion only for an investment having a business risk level similar to that of existing assets.*

Constant Financial Risk

Financial risk has been defined as the increased variability in returns on common stock resulting from the increased use of debt and preferred stock financing.[4] Also, financial risk relates to the threat of bankruptcy. As the percentage of debt in the capital structure increases, the possibility that the firm will be unable to pay interest and the principal balance is also increased. As a result, the level of financial risk in a company has an impact on the investors' required rate of return. As the amount of

[4]This concept is further explained in Chapter 12.

ETHICS IN FINANCIAL MANAGEMENT

How Do Managers Resolve Ethical Decisions?

What makes a managerial choice an ethical one? Brief et al. (1991) suggest that if the decision entails reflection on the moral significance of the choice, then the choice is an ethical one. How do managers resolve ethical dilemmas? There is some evidence suggesting that two factors come to bear on ethical choices: values and accountability.

We will consider two social value systems that are present in Western society, which are particularly relevant to the study of finance. These are the Smithian and Humanitarian value systems. The Smithian system is derived from the writings of the 18th-century moral philosopher and political economist Adam Smith. This value system is reflected in the current-day teachings of economists such as Milton Friedman (1962). Briefly, this system holds that when individuals pursue their own self-interest in the marketplace, they contribute to the good of society. At the firm level this system provides the basis for the market system and is used as the basis for corporate self-interest. In contrast, the Humanitarian system is based on the fundamental premise of the equality of individuals in society. This system seeks to protect individuals from the harshness of the market system and to promote equality of opportunity.

Personal value systems are not all that influence managerial decisions having ethical implications. Managers are influenced by their perception of the value systems of the individuals to whom they are held accountable. That is, ethical choices made by managers are influenced by the values they believe are held by the person to whom they are accountable. Arendt (1951, 1977) provides evidence that suggests that the effects of accountability may be more profound than those of the individual manager's values. Consequently, the potentially overpowering effects of hierarchical accountability may lead individual managers to not construe the moral significance attached to the choices they make. They may see no choice but to comply with the higher authority. Brief et al. (1991) provide empirical evidence bearing on the question of the relative importance of personal values versus accountability in the choices made by individuals. Using a set of experiments involving 135 M.B.A. students, they concluded that personal values may not be related to how an individual chooses to resolve ethical dilemmas when the choices (values) of the higher authority are known explicitly.

Note that we have not addressed the normative issue: How should ethical dilemmas be resolved? Instead we have addressed the positive question: How do managers actually deal with ethical choices? The principal finding of the studies we have reviewed is that the *perceived values of one's superiors* have a profound impact on the way in which a subordinate resolves ethical dilemmas. So choose your superior carefully.

Sources: H. Arendt, *The Origins of Totalitarianism* (New York: Harcourt Brace, 1951); H. Arendt, *Eichmann in Jerusalem* (New York: Penguin Books, 1977); Arthur Brief, Janet M. Dukerich, and Lucinda I. Doran, "Resolving Ethical Dilemmas in Management: Experimental Investigations of Values, Accountability, and Choice," *Journal of Applied Social Psychology* 21 (1991), pp. 380–96; M. Friedman, *Capitalism and Freedom* (Chicago: University of Chicago Press, 1962); C. S. McCoy, *Management of Values: The Ethical Differences in Corporate Policy and Performance* (Boston: Pitman, 1985); P. E. Tetlock, "Accountability and Complexity of Thought," *Journal of Personality and Social Psychology* 45 (1983), pp. 74–83; P. E. Tetlock, "Accountability: The Neglected Social Context of Judgement and Choice," *Research in Organizational Behavior* 7 (1985), pp. 297–332.

debt rises, the common stockholders will increase their required rate of return. *In other words, the costs of individual sources of capital are a function of the current financial structure.* For this reason, the data used in computing the cost of capital are appropriate only if management continues to use the same financial mix. If the present capital structure consists of 40 percent debt, 10 percent preferred stock, and 50 percent common stock, this capital structure is assumed to be maintained in the financing of future investments.

Constant Dividend Policy

A third assumption required in estimating the cost of capital relates to the corporation's dividend policy. For ease of computation, we generally assume that a firm's dividends are increasing at a constant annual growth rate. Also, we assume this growth to be a function of the firm's earning capabilities and not merely the result of paying out a larger percentage of the company's earnings. Thus, it is implicitly assumed that the dividend payout ratio (dividends/net income) is constant.

The forementioned assumptions of the weighted cost of capital model are quite restrictive. In a practical investment analysis, the financial executive may need a range of possible cost of capital values rather than a single-point estimate. For example, it may be more appropriate to talk in terms of a 10 percent to 12 percent range as an estimate of the firm's cost of capital, rather than assuming that a precise number can be determined. In this chapter, however, our principal concern will be with calculating a single cost of capital figure.

PERSPECTIVE IN FINANCE

To compute a firm's weighted cost of capital, we must assume that the firm's financial mix will not change, that we will continue to invest in projects of about the same risk as we have done in the past, and that we will not change the percentage of earnings paid out in dividends to the stockholders.

■ COMPUTING THE WEIGHTED COST OF CAPITAL

A firm's weighted cost of capital is a composite of the individual costs of financing, weighted by the percentage of financing provided by each source. Therefore, a firm's weighted cost of capital is a function of (1) the individual costs of capital and (2) the makeup of the capital structure—the percentage of funds provided by debt, preferred stock, and common stock. Also, as we noted earlier, the amount of funds needed affects the cost of capital. We will discuss this last consideration, the level of financing, later.

As we explain the procedures for computing a company's cost of capital, it is helpful to remember three basic steps outlined in Figure 11–3.

The computations are not difficult if we understand our purpose: We want to calculate the firm's weighted cost of capital. For a simple exercise, calculate the average age of students in a course where 40 percent are 19 years old, 50 percent are 20 years old, and 10 percent are 21 years old. We can easily find the average age to be 19.7 years by weighting each age by the percentage in each age category [(40%)(19) + (50%)(20) + (10%)(21)]. In a similar way, the weighted cost of capital is estimated by weighting the cost of each individual source by the percentage of financing it provides. If we finance an investment by 40 percent debt at a 10 percent cost and 60 percent common equity at a cost of 18 percent, the weighted cost of capital is 14.8 percent (.40 × 10% + .60 × 18% = 14.8%).

> Remember: To compute a firm's weighted cost of capital requires us to do three things:
>
> 1. Compute the cost of capital for each and every source of financing (i.e., each source of debt, preferred stock, and common stock).
> 2. Determine the percentage of debt, preferred stock, and common stock to be used in the financing of future investments.
> 3. Calculate the firm's weighted average cost of capital using the percentage of financing as the weights.

FIGURE 11–3
Computing the Weighted
Cost of Capital: Basic Steps

Thus, although the details become somewhat involved, the basic approach, which is summarized in Figure 11–3, is relatively simple.

Determining Individual Costs of Capital

Companies attempting to attract new investors have created a large variety of financing instruments. However, we will examine only three basic types of securities: debt, preferred stock, and common stock. In calculating their respective costs, the objective is to determine *the rate of return the company must earn on its investments to satisfy investors' required rates of return* after allowing *for any flotation costs incurred in raising new funds.* Also, because the cash flows used in capital-budgeting analysis (net present value, profitability index, and internal rate of return) are on an after-tax basis, the required rates of return should also be expressed on an after-tax basis.

Cost of Debt

The cost of debt may be defined as the rate that must be received from an investment *to achieve the required rate of return for the creditors.* In Chapter 6 the required rate of return for debt capital was found by a trial-and-error process or with the use of a financial calculator, where we solved for R_d in the following equation:

$$P_0 = \sum_{t=1}^{n} \frac{\$I_t}{(1 + \text{bondholder's required rate of return})^t} + \frac{\$M}{(1 + \text{bondholder's required rate of return})^n} \quad \text{(11–1)}$$

where
P_0 = the market price of the debt

$\$I_t$ = the annual dollar interest paid to the investor

$\$M$ = the maturity value of the debt

n = the number of years to maturity

If we use the interest factors in the present value tables, the equation would be restated as follows:

$$P_0 = \$I_t(PVIFA_{\text{required return, } n}) + \$M(PVIF_{\text{required return, } n})$$

When we calculate the bondholder's required rate of return we rely on the observed market price of the firm's bonds to be an accurate reflection of their worth given all available information about the riskiness of those bonds. If the bond price did not fully reflect all available information then our calculated required rate of return would not be an accurate reflection of the bondholder's opportunity cost of funds. When we accept the observed market price of a firm's bonds (or other securities) in calculating required returns, it is founded on the belief that the capital markets are efficient. This notion is captured in **Axiom 6: Efficient Capital Markets—The Markets Are Quick and the Prices Are Right.** What we mean here, very simply, is that investors are ever vigilant and quickly act on information that affects the riskiness and consequently the price of a firm's bonds and other securities.

EXAMPLE

Assume that an investor is willing to pay $908.32 for a bond. The security has a $1,000 par value, pays 8 percent in annual interest, and matures in 20 years. Using either a calculator or table values, the investor's required rate of return is found to be 9 percent, which is the rate that sets the present value of the future interest payments and the maturity value equal to the price of the bond, or

$$\$908.32 = \sum_{t=1}^{20} \frac{\$80}{(1 + .09)^t} + \frac{\$1,000}{(1 + .09)^{20}}$$

$$\$908.32 = \$908.32$$

However, if brokerage commissions and legal and accounting fees are incurred in issuing the security, the company will not receive the full $908.32 market price. As a result, the effective cost of these funds to the firm is larger than the investor's 9 percent required rate of return. To adjust for this difference, we would simply use the *net price* after flotation costs in place of the market price in equation (11–1). Thus, the equation becomes

$$NP_0 = \sum_{t=1}^{n} \frac{\$I_t}{(1 + k_d)^t} + \frac{\$M}{(1 + k_d)^n} \qquad \textbf{(11–2)}$$

where NP_0 represents the net amount received by the company from issuing the debt, k_d equals the *before-tax* cost of debt, and the remaining variables retain their meaning from equation (11–1). If in the present example the company nets $850 after issuance costs, the equation should read

$$\$850 = \sum_{t=1}^{20} \frac{\$80}{(1 + k_d)^t} + \frac{\$1,000}{(1 + k_d)^{20}}$$

$$= \$80(PVIFA_{k_d, 20}) + \$1,000(PVIF_{k_d, 20})$$

Solving for k_d in equation (11–2) may be achieved by trial and error using the present value tables. We know that the rate is above 9 percent because a 9 percent rate had already given us a $908.32 value. We need the discount rate that gives us an $850 value. If *10 percent* is selected as a trial discount rate, a present value of $830.12 results. With this information, we may conclude that the before-tax cost of the debt capital is between 9 percent and 10 percent; therefore, we may approximate it by interpolating between these two rates. The computation is shown as follows:

Rate	Value		Differences in Values	
9%	$908.32			
k_d	850.00 net proceeds	}	58.32	} $78.20
10%	830.12			

Solving for k_d by interpolation,

$$k_d = .09 + \left(\frac{\$58.32}{\$78.20}\right)(.10 - .09) = .0975 = 9.75\%$$

The same answer may be found by using a financial calculator, as shown in the margin. Thus, the company's cost of debt, before recognizing the tax deductibility of interest expense, is 9.75 percent.[5]

We want to know the *after-tax* cost of the debt, however, not the before-tax cost. Because interest is a tax-deductible expense, for every $1 we pay in interest, we lower the firm's tax liability by $1 times the tax rate. If our company has an effective tax rate, including all federal and state taxes, of 40 percent, then a dollar in interest means that we save $.40 in taxes. That is, the after-tax cost is only $.60, or $1(1 − .40 tax rate). Applying the same logic to our cost of debt, we may correctly conclude that the after-tax cost of debt is found by multiplying the before-tax interest rate by (1 − tax rate). If t is the company's marginal tax rate and k_d is the before-tax cost of debt, the after-tax cost of new debt financing, is found as follows:

$$\text{after-tax cost of debt} = k_d(1 - t) \qquad \text{(11–3)}$$

If in the present example the corporation's tax rate is 40 percent, then the after-tax cost of debt is 5.84 percent:

$$9.75\%(1 - .40) = 5.84\%$$

In summary, the firm must earn 5.84 percent on its borrowed capital *after the payment of taxes.* In doing so, the investors will earn a 9 percent rate of return (their required rate) on their $908.32 investment (market price of the bond), and the firm will earn a 9.75 percent before-tax return on the $850 bond proceeds.

CALCULATOR SOLUTION

Data Input	Function Key
20	N
850	+/− PV
80	PMT
1000	FV

Function Key	Answer
I% YR	9.73*

*The difference between 9.75 percent and 9.73 percent is simply the result of rounding.

---

[5]For simplicity, we have ignored the fact that flotation costs may be amortized as a tax-deductible expense over the life of the bond. The difference in the answer is relatively small.

The tax deductibility of interest expense favors the use of debt financing. This is an example of **Axiom 8: Taxes Bias Business Decisions.** The tax deductibility of interest, other things remaining constant, serves to encourage firms to use more debt in their capital structure than they would otherwise.

Cost of Preferred Stock

Determining the cost of preferred stock follows the same logic as the cost of debt computations. *The objective is to find the rate of return that must be earned on money raised through the sale of preferred stock to satisfy their required rate of return.*

In Chapter 7 the value of a preferred stock, P_0, that is nonmaturing and promised a constant dividend per year was defined as follows:

$$P_0 = \frac{\text{dividend}}{\text{required rate of return for a preferred stockholder}} \qquad \text{(11–4)}$$

From this equation, the required rate of return, R_p, is defined as

$$\text{required rate of return} = \frac{\text{dividend}}{\text{market price } (P_0)} \qquad \text{(11–5)}$$

If, for example, a preferred stock pays $1.50 in annual dividends and sells for $15, the investors' required rate of return is 10 percent:

$$\text{required rate of return} = \frac{\$1.50}{\$15.00} = 10\%$$

Yet even if these preferred stockholders have a 10 percent required rate of return, the effective cost of this capital will be greater owing to the flotation costs incurred in issuing the security. If a firm were to net $13.50 per share after issuance costs, rather than the full $15 market price, the cost of preferred stock, k_p, should be calculated using the net price received by the company. Therefore

$$k_p = \frac{\text{dividend}}{\text{net price}} = \frac{D}{NP_0} \qquad \text{(11–6)}$$

For the preceding example, the cost would be

$$k_p = \frac{\$1.50}{\$13.50} = .1111 \text{ or } 11.11\%$$

No adjustment for taxes is required, since preferred stock dividends are not tax deductible. Thus, the firm must earn the cost of preferred capital after taxes have been paid, which for the preceding example was 11.11 percent.

Cost of Common Stock

Although debt and preferred stock must be issued to receive any new money from these sources, common stockholders can provide additional capital in one of two ways. First, new common stock may be issued. Second, the earnings available to common stockholders can be retained, in whole or in part, within the company and used to finance future investments. Retained earnings represent the largest source of capital for most U.S. corporations. On average, as much as 70 percent of a company's financing in any year comes from the profits retained within the business. To distinguish between these two sources, we will use the term **internal common equity** to designate the profits retained within the business for investment purposes, and **external common equity** to represent a new issue of common stock.

COST OF INTERNAL COMMON EQUITY   When managers are considering the retention of earnings as a means for financing an investment, they are serving in a *fiduciary* capacity. That is, the stockholders have entrusted the company assets to management. If the company's objective is to maximize the wealth of its common stockholders, management should retain the profits *only if* the company's investments within the firm are at least as attractive as the stockholders' next best investment opportunity.[6] Otherwise the profits should be paid out in dividends, permitting the investor to invest more profitably elsewhere.

How can management know the stockholders' alternative investment opportunities? Certainly identifying those specific investments is not feasible. However, the investors' required rate of return should be a function of competing investment opportunities. If the only other investment alternative of similar risk has a 12 percent return, one would expect a rational investor to set a minimum acceptable return on investment at 12 percent. In other words, *the investors' required rate of return should be equal to the expected rate of the best competing investment available.* Thus, if the common stockholders' required rate of return is used as a minimum return for investments financed by common stock investors, management may be assured that its investment policies are acceptable to the common stockholder.

To measure the common stockholders' required rate of return, we will suggest three alternative approaches: (1) the dividend-growth model, (2) the capital asset pricing model, and (3) the risk-premium approach.

BACK TO THE FUNDAMENTALS

The dividend-growth model for common stock is based on two of our axioms of finance: **Axiom 2: The Time Value of Money—A Dollar Received Today Is Worth More than a Dollar Received in the Future, and Axiom 3: Cash is King—Measuring the Timing of Costs and Benefits.**

---

[6]Other factors may justify management's not adhering completely to this principle. We will cover these issues in the discussion on dividend policy in Chapter 13.

DIVIDEND-GROWTH MODEL   In Chapter 7, the value of a common stock was defined to equal to the present value of the expected future dividends, discounted at the common stockholders' *required rate of return*. Because the stock has no maturity date, these dividends extend to infinity. Thus, the value of a common stock, P_0, promising dividends of D_t in year t would be

$$P_0 = \frac{\text{Dividend}_1}{(1 + \text{required return})^1} \qquad\qquad\qquad \textbf{(11–7)}$$

$$+ \frac{\text{Dividend}_2}{(1 + \text{required return})^1} + \ldots + \frac{\text{Dividend}_\infty}{(1 + \text{required return})^\infty}$$

Because the market price of the security, P_0, is known, the required rate of return of an investor purchasing the security at this price can be determined by estimating future dividends, D_t, and solving for it using equation (11–7). Furthermore, if the dividends are increasing at a constant annual rate of growth (g), that is, less than the investor's required rate of return, then the required rate of return can be measured as follows:[7]

$$\begin{array}{c} \text{investors} \\ \text{required rate} \\ \text{of return} \end{array} = \left(\frac{\text{dividend in 1 year}}{\text{market place}} \right) + \left(\begin{array}{c} \text{annual growth rate} \\ \text{in dividends} \end{array} \right) \quad \textbf{(11–8)}$$

$$= \frac{D_1}{P_0} + g$$

To convert from the common investor's required rate of return in equation (11–8) to the cost of internal common funds, no adjustment is required for taxes. Dividends paid to the firm's common stockholders are not tax deductible; therefore, the cost is already on an after-tax basis. Also, flotation costs are not involved in computing the cost of internal common equity, because the funds are already within the business. Thus, the investor's required rate of return is the same as the cost of internal common equity, k_c.

EXAMPLE

To demonstrate the computation, the Talbot Corporation's common stockholders recently received a $2 dividend per share, and they expect dividends to grow at an annual rate of 10 percent. If the market price of the security is $50, the investor's required rate of return is

$$k_c = \frac{D_1}{P_0} + g \qquad\qquad\qquad \textbf{(11–8)}$$

$$= \frac{\$2(1 + .10)}{\$50} + .10$$

$$= \frac{\$2.20}{\$50} + .10 = .144$$

$$= 14.4\%$$

[7]For additional explanation, see Chapter 8.

Note that the forthcoming dividend, D_1, is estimated by taking the past dividend, \$2, and increasing it by 10 percent, the expected growth rate. That is, $D_1 = D_0 (1.10) = \$2(1.10) = \$2.20$. ∎

The dividend-growth model has been a relatively popular approach for calculating the cost of equity. The primary difficulty, as you might expect, is estimating the expected growth rate in future dividends. One possible source of such expectations are investment advisory services such as Merrill Lynch and Value Line. There are even services that collect and publish the forecasts of a large number of analysts. For instance, Institutional Broker's Estimate System (IBES) publishes earnings per share forecasts made by about 2,000 analysts on a like number of stocks. Although these forecasts are helpful in reducing the problems of the dividend-growth model, they cannot be considered completely accurate. Growth estimates are generally available only for about five years, and not for the indefinite future, as required by the constant-growth model. Also, analysts usually state their forecasts in terms of earnings rather than dividends, which does not meet the strict requirements of the dividend-growth model. Even so, the earnings information is helpful, because dividend growth in the long run is dependent on earnings. Also, the analysts' forecasts are helpful because they provide direct measures of the expectations that determine prices in the market.

The use of analysts' forecasts in conjunction with the dividend-growth model to compute required rates of return for the Standard and Poor's 500 stocks has been studied by Harris.[8] Computing an average of the analysts' forecasts of five-year growth rates in EPS, Harris used this average as a proxy for the growth rate in dividends. Then, using the dividend-growth model (equation 11–8), he estimated an average cost of equity for the S&P 500 stocks. He next compared these required rates with the yields on U.S. Treasury bonds to see how much risk premium common stockholders were expecting. The analysis was conducted for each quarter from 1982 through 1984. Results of the Harris study are presented in Table 11–3. The findings suggest that common stockholders have required a return of between 17.26 percent and 20.08 percent on average for 1982 through 1984. For the three-year period, the average required rate of return was 18.41 percent. The average risk premiums of common stockholders each year, which are shown in the last column of Table 11–3, ranged from 4.78 percent to 7.16 percent, for an average of 6.16 percent. However, we should remember that these returns apply only for equity investments of average riskiness. As we well know, the risk of individual securities will differ from the average, as will the stockholders' required returns.

Although the results in Table 11–3 look reasonable, the same computations for individual stocks may not be as plausible, largely because of measurement errors that occur when only one or a few stocks are analyzed. Moreover, the constant growth assumption of the model may be inconsistent with reality.

---

[8]Robert Harris, "Using Analysts' Forecasts to Estimate Shareholder Required Returns," *Financial Management* (Spring 1986), pp. 510–67.

TABLE 11–3
Required Rates of Return and
Risk Premiums

	Government Bond Yield	S & P 500	
		Required Return	Risk Premium
1982			
Quarter 1	14.27	20.81	6.54
Quarter 2	13.74	20.68	6.94
Quarter 3	12.94	20.23	7.29
Quarter 4	10.72	18.58	7.86
Average	12.92	20.08	7.16
1983			
Quarter 1	10.87	18.07	7.20
Quarter 2	10.80	17.76	6.96
Quarter 3	11.79	17.90	6.11
Quarter 4	11.90	17.81	5.91
Average	11.34	17.88	6.54
1984			
Quarter 1	12.09	17.22	5.13
Quarter 2	13.21	17.42	4.21
Quarter 3	12.83	17.34	4.51
Quarter 4	11.78	17.05	5.27
Average	12.48	17.26	4.78
Average 1982–1984	12.25	18.41	6.16

Source: Robert Harris, "Using Analysts' Forecasts to Estimate Shareholder Required Returns," *Financial Management* (Spring 1986), p.62. Used by permission.

THE CAPM APPROACH Drawing from Chapter 8, we can estimate the cost of equity using the capital asset pricing model (CAPM). Remember that investors should require a rate of return that at least equals the risk-free rate plus a risk premium appropriate for the level of systematic risk associated with the particular security. Using the CAPM, we may represent the equity-required rate of return (cost of internal equity) as follows:

$$k_c = k_{rf} + \beta(k_m - k_{rf}) \tag{11–9}$$

where k_c = the required rate of return of the equity shareholders, and also the cost of internal equity capital since there are no transactions costs incurred in retaining earnings

k_{rf} = the risk-free rate

β = beta, or the measure of a stock's systematic risk

k_m = the expected rate of return for the market as a whole—that is, the expected return for the "average security"

For example, assume the risk-free rate is 7 percent, the expected return in the market is 16 percent, and the beta for Talbot Corporation's common stock is .82. Then the cost of internal equity would be estimated as follows:

$$k_c = k_{rf} + \beta(k_m - k_{rf})$$
$$= 7\% + .82\,(16\% - 7\%)$$
$$= 14.4\%$$

Although using the CAPM appears relatively easy, its application is not entirely straightforward, particularly in the corporate setting. In estimating the risk-free rate, the market rate, and the security's beta, our goal is to describe the expectations in the minds of the investors, because it is these expectations that determine how assets are valued. Such a task is difficult. However, as indicated earlier, financial service companies now help provide limited information about investor expectations.

BACK TO THE FUNDAMENTALS

The capital asset pricing model (CAPM) is a formal representation of **Axiom 1: The Risk-Return Tradeoff—We Won't Take on Additional Risk Unless We Expect to be Compensated with Additional Return.** By formal we mean that the specific method by which additional returns needed to compensate for additional risk is specified in the form of an equation. The added risk is measured in terms of systematic or nondiversifiable risk, and the additional return is calculated using the beta coefficient and the market risk premium (the difference between the expected rate of return on the market portfolio of all risky securities and the risk-free rate).

RISK-PREMIUM APPROACH   Because we know that common stockholders will demand a return premium above the bondholder's required rate of return, we may state the cost of equity as follows:

$$k_c = k_d + RP_c \qquad\qquad \textbf{(11–10)}$$

where, as before, K_c and K_d represent the cost of common equity and debt, respectively. RP_c is the additional return premium common stockholders expect for assuming greater risk than bondholders. Because we can compute the cost of debt with some degree of confidence, the key to estimating the cost of equity is in knowing RP_c, the risk premium.

We again are in some difficulty, because we have no direct means of computing RP_c. We can only draw from our experience, which tells us that the risk premium of a firm's common stocks relative to its own bonds has for the most part been between 3 percent and 5 percent. In times when interest rates are historically high, the premium is usually low. In years when interest rates are at historical lows, the premium has been higher. Using an average premium of 4 percent, we would approximate the cost of equity capital as follows:

$$k_c = k_d + 4\%$$

For a firm with Aaa-rated bonds that have a cost of 9 percent, the cost of equity would be estimated to be 13 percent (9 percent cost of debt plus the 4 percent average premium); a more risky company, with bonds that are rated Baa with a 13 percent cost, could expect its cost of equity to approximate 17 percent (13 percent + 4 percent).

The risk-premium approach is somewhat similar in concept to CAPM in that both recognize that common stockholders require a risk premium. The differences between the two approaches come from using different beginning points (CAPM uses the risk-free rate and the risk-premium approach uses the firm's cost of debt) and in how the risk premium is estimated. Both estimates of the risk premium involve subjectivity; however, CAPM has a more developed conceptual basis. Even so, the risk-premium approach is at times the best we can do, especially when the dividend-growth model and the CAPM give unreasonable estimates. Even if the dividend-growth and CAPM approaches are thought to fit the situation, the risk-premium technique gives us a good way to verify the reasonableness of our results.

COST OF NEW COMMON STOCK   If internal common equity does not provide all the equity capital needed for new investments, the firm may need to issue new common stock. Again, this capital should not be acquired from the investors unless the expected returns on the prospective investments exceed a rate sufficient to satisfy the stockholders' required rate of return. Returning to the dividend-growth model equation (11–8), the only adjustment necessary is to consider the potential flotation costs incurred from issuing the stock. The effect of the flotation costs on the cost of common stock may be found by reducing the market price of the stock by the amount of these costs.[9] Thus, the cost of new common stock, k_{nc}, is

$$k_{nc} = \frac{D_1}{NP_0} + g \qquad\qquad (11\text{–}11)$$

where NP_0 equals the net proceeds per share received by the company. If, in the preceding example, flotation costs are 15 percent of the market price, the cost of capital for the new common stock, or external common, would be 15.18 percent, calculated as follows:

$$k_{nc} = \frac{\$2.20}{\$50 - .15(\$50)} + .10$$

$$= \frac{\$2.20}{\$42.50} + .10 = .1518$$

$$= 15.18\%$$

In this example, if management achieves a 15.18 percent return on the net capital received from common stockholders, it will satisfy the investors' required rate of return of 14.4 percent, as determined earlier by equation (11–8). ∎

Selection of Capital Structure Weights

The individual costs of capital will be different for each source of capital in the firm's capital structure. To use these costs of capital in our investment analyses, we must compute a composite or overall cost of capital.

[9]For another approach to adjusting for flotation costs, see John R. Ezzell and R. Burr Porter, "Flotation Costs and the Weighted Average Cost of Capital," *Journal of Financial and Quantitative Analysis,* 11 (September 1976), pp. 403–13.

The weights for computing this overall cost should reflect the corporation's financing mix. For instance, if creditors are expected to finance 30 percent of the new investments and common stockholders are to provide the remaining 70 percent, the weighted cost should reflect this mix.

Several choices for selecting the financing weights for a composite cost of capital are available. Theoretically, the actual mix to be used in financing the proposed investments should be used as the weights. This approach, however, presents a problem. The costs of capital for individual sources depend on the firm's financial risk, which in turn is affected by its financial mix. If management alters the present financial structure, the individual costs will change, making it more difficult to compute the cost of capital. Thus, we will assume that the company's financial mix is relatively stable and that these weights will closely approximate future financing. Although this assumption may not be strictly met in any particular year, firms frequently have a **target capital structure** (desired debt—equity mix), which is maintained over the long term. The target financing mix provides the appropriate weights to be used in calculating the firm's weighted cost of capital. Consider the following:

EXAMPLE

The Ash Company's current financing mix is contained in Table 11–4. The firm's chief financial officer, Tony Ash, does not want to alter the firm's financial risk. Instead, he chooses to maintain the same relative mix of capital in financing future investments. Thus, given our assumption of a constant financial mix, we will use these percentages as the weights in computing Ash's weighted cost of capital. ■

Computing the Weighted Cost of Capital

Let's now compute the weighted cost of capital for a firm, which is simply the weighted average of the individual costs, given the firm's financial mix. This calculation is best demonstrated with an example. So let's continue with Ash, Inc. In Table 11–4, we estimated Ash's financial mix for the purpose of computing the firm's weighted or overall cost of capital. Let's further assume that management has computed the individual costs of capital for the firm, shown in Table 11–5. For the time being, we will restrict equity financing to the retained earnings available for reinvestment, or internally generated common equity. We are assuming Ash will

Investor Group	Amount of Funds Raised ($)	Percentage of Total
Bonds	$1,750,000	35%
Preferred stock	250,000	5
Common stock	3,000,000	60
Total new financing	$5,000,000	100%

TABLE 11–4
Ash, Inc., Capital Structure

COST OF CAPITAL

TABLE 11–5
Component Costs of Capital
for Ash, Inc

Investor Group	Component Costs
Bonds (after-tax cost)	7%
Preferred stock	13
Common stock (internal only)	16

not issue any new common stock. Therefore, the cost of new common stock is not relevant. Table 11–6 combines the weights from Table 11–4 and the individual cost for each security from Table 11–5 into a single weighted cost of capital, k_0. Given that the assumptions of the weighted cost of capital concept are met and that common equity requirements can be satisfied internally, the company's weighted cost of capital is 12.7 percent. This rate is the firm's minimum acceptable rate of return for new investments. It therefore is the appropriate discount rate for capital-budgeting analysis for Ash, Inc., and a key number used in the calculation of the net present value of prospective capital investments.

We have now observed the process for measuring a company's weighted cost of capital. We cannot overstate the importance of this calculation; so much of what we do depends on our measuring the firm's weighted cost of capital with some degree of accuracy. Again, however, we must take care not to place too much confidence in our measurement techniques. We cannot say with any real conviction that we can precisely measure a firm's cost of capital. Remember the limiting effects of our assumptions, especially about constant business and financial risk. At best, we will only have an approximation of the firm's weighted cost of capital, but an approximation certainly beats assigning an arbitrary rate. Nevertheless, given the difficulties in measuring the cost, we must test the sensitivity of our results, that is, the value of the net present value, according to a reasonable range of values for the cost of capital rather than using a single-point estimate.

We now need to consider the effects of the level of financing on the firm's cost of capital. That is, as the firm continues to raise more capital for investment purposes, how is the cost of capital affected?

Level of Financing and the Weighted Cost of Capital

Impact of a New Common Stock Issue

In the previous illustration, we assumed that no new common stock was to be issued. If new common stock is issued, the firm's weighted cost of capital will increase, because external equity capital has a higher cost than internal equity owing to flotation costs.

Generally the firm should use its cheapest sources of funds first while maintaining its desired debt-equity mix. In other words, because internally generated common equity costs less than issuing common stock, it should be blended with debt until fully exhausted. Beyond this point, the weighted cost of capital increases, because the firm has to

(1)	(2)	(3)	(4)
Investor Group	Weights[a]	Individual Costs[b]	Weighted Costs (2 × 3)
Bonds	35%	7%	2.45%
Preferred stock	5	13	0.65
Common stock (internal only)	60	16	9.60
		Weighted cost of capital (k_0):	12.70%

[a]Taken from the desired financing mix presented in Table 11–4.
[b]Taken from Table 11–5.

TABLE 11–6
Weighted Cost of Capital for Ash, Inc., If Only Internal Common Is Used

rely on new common stock for its equity financing. This basic concept is best explained through an example.[10]

EXAMPLE

The Crisp Corporation, an independent oil company, is contemplating three major capital investments in 1995. The first proposal is the acquisition of equipment used to examine geological formations. This new equipment should improve the success ratio in discovering productive oil and gas reserves. The second proposal is investing in water flooding equipment. This process would involve injecting large amounts of water into underground oil reserves, which permits a more efficient recovery of the minerals. Third, new and advanced drilling equipment appears to offer significant cost savings in drilling for oil and gas. The costs and expected returns for these three possible investments are shown in Table 11–7. Management must decide which of these projects should be accepted.

If any of the proposed projects are accepted, the financing will consist of 50 percent debt and 50 percent common. Based on the anticipated profits during 1995, the company should have $1,500,000 in profits available for reinvestment (internal common). The costs of capital for each source of financing have been computed and are presented in Table 11–8.

	Investment Cost	Expected Internal Rate of Return
Geological equipment	$1,500,000	14%
Water flooding equipment	2,000,000	18
Drilling equipment	2,500,000	11

TABLE 11–7
Crisp Corporation's Investment Opportunities

---

[10]Although we assume a constant debt equity mix, we have no reason or need to assume a constant mix between internally generated equity and new common stock. Rather, we assume that we first use internal equity funds until exhausted, and then, if more equity is needed, we issue common stock.

TABLE 11–8
Crisp Corporation's Individual
Costs of Capital

Source	Cost
Debt (after-tax cost)	6%
Internally generated common ($1,500,000)	14
New common stock	18

The weighted cost of capital, k_0, would be calculated as follows:

$$k_0 = \left[\left(\begin{array}{c} \text{percentage of} \\ \text{debt financing} \end{array} \right) \times \left(\begin{array}{c} \text{cost of} \\ \text{debt} \end{array} \right) \right] \qquad \textbf{(11–12)}$$

$$+ \left[\left(\begin{array}{c} \text{percentage of} \\ \text{common financing} \end{array} \right) \times \left(\begin{array}{c} \text{cost of} \\ \text{common} \end{array} \right) \right]$$

If only internally generated common is utilized, the weighted cost of capital is 10 percent:

$$k_0 = [50\% \times 6\%] + [50\% \times 14\%] = 10 \text{ percent}$$

When new common stock is used rather than internally generated common, however, the weighted cost of capital is 12 percent:

$$k_0 = [50\% \times 6\%] + [50\% \times 18\%] = 12 \text{ percent}$$

Which weighted cost of capital should be used in evaluating the three investments?

To answer this question, we must first rank the projects in descending order by their respective internal rates of return. Second, we must calculate the level of *total* financing at which point our internal equity is expended. In the Crisp Corporation illustration, $3 million in total new investments may be financed with internal common and debt, without having to change the current financial mix of 50 percent debt and 50 percent common, and without having to issue common stock. The $3 million is determined by solving the following equation:

$$\begin{array}{c} \text{internally generated} \\ \text{common financing} \\ \text{available} \end{array} = \left(\begin{array}{c} \text{percentage of} \\ \text{common financing} \end{array} \right) \times \left(\begin{array}{c} \text{total financing} \\ \text{from all sources} \end{array} \right)$$

$$\textbf{(11–13)}$$

For the Crisp Corporation,

$$\$1,500,000 = (50\%) \times (\text{total financing})$$

which indicates that if Crisp has $1,500,000 in internally generated common and management maintains a 50 percent debt ratio, it will be able to finance $3 million of total investments without issuing new common stock. Equation (11–13) may be changed to solve directly for the amount of total financing; this is

$$\begin{array}{c} \text{total financing} \\ \text{from all sources} \end{array} = \frac{\text{internally generated common}}{\text{percentage of common financing}}$$

$$= \frac{\$1,500,000}{.50} \qquad \textbf{(11–14)}$$

$$= \$3,000,000$$

Therefore, for a total investment level of $3 million or less, the firm's weighted cost of capital is expected to be 10 percent. Beyond this level of total financing our internal common is totally exhausted, and the weighted cost of capital increases to 12 percent. This reflects the increased cost of new common beyond the $3 million in total financing from both debt and common.

The relationship between the weighted costs of capital and the amount of financing being sought is portrayed graphically by Figure 11–4. The graph depicts the firm's **weighted marginal cost of capital.** The term *marginal* is used because the computed cost of capital shows the weighted cost of each additional dollar of financing. This marginal cost of capital represents the appropriate criterion for making investment decisions. Thus, the firm should continue to invest up to the point where the marginal rate of return earned on a new investment (IRR) equals the marginal cost of new capital. This comparison is reflected in Figure 11–5, where the firm's optimal capital budget is found to be $3,500,000. The company should invest in water flooding machinery and the geological equipment. However, because the weighted marginal cost of capital is greater than the expected internal rate of return of the drilling equipment, this investment should be rejected. ■

General Effect of New Financing on the Marginal Cost of Capital

Thus far, we have considered only the effect of increases in the cost of common stock on the firm's weighted marginal cost of capital. Similar effects will occur as the cost of any source of financing increases. If the 6 percent cost of debt capital for Crisp Corporation increased to 8 percent after the firm issued $2 million in bonds, an increase in the weighted marginal cost of capital would have occurred at the $4 million financing level from all sources. This **break** in the marginal cost of capital curve is determined as

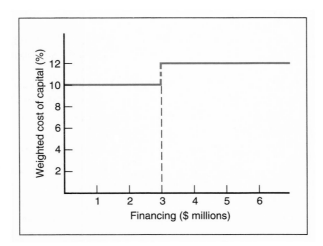

FIGURE 11–4
Crisp Corporation's Weighted
Marginal Cost of Capital

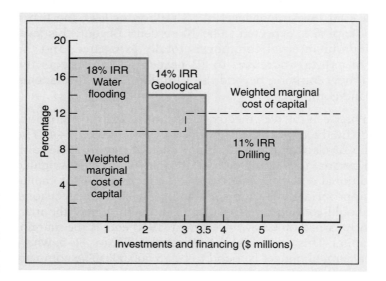

FIGURE 11–5
Crisp Corporation:
Comparison of Investment
Returns and the Weighted
Marginal Cost of Capital

$$\begin{matrix} \text{total financing} \\ \text{from all sources} \end{matrix} = \frac{\text{maximum amount of lower-cost debt}}{\text{percentage of debt financing}} \qquad \textbf{(11–15)}$$

$$= \frac{\$2,000,000}{.50}$$

$$= \$4,000,000$$

As a general rule, *changes in the weighted marginal cost of capital will occur when the cost of an individual source increases.* The break in the marginal cost of capital curve will occur at the dollar financing level where

$$\begin{matrix} \text{total financing} \\ \text{from all sources} \end{matrix} = \frac{\begin{matrix}\text{maximum amount of a}\\ \text{lower-cost source of capital}\end{matrix}}{\begin{matrix}\text{percentage financing}\\ \text{provided by the source}\end{matrix}} \qquad \textbf{(11–16)}$$

Summary of Computations

The steps that have been described in calculating a firm's weighted *marginal* cost of capital may be summarized as follows:

1. Determine the percentage of financing to be used from each source of capital (debt, preferred stock, and common equity).
2. Compute the points on the marginal cost of capital curve where the weighted cost will increase.
3. Calculate the costs of each individual source of capital.
4. Compute the weighted cost of capital for the company, which will be different as the amount of financing increases.
5. Construct a graph that compares the internal rates of return for prospective investment opportunities with the weighted cost of capital, which will indicate which investments should be accepted.

TABLE 11–9
J. M. Williams, Inc.,
December 31, 1994

Total Liabilities and Equity	Financial Structure Equity Mix (%)
Bonds	30.0%
Preferred stock	7.5
Common stock	62.5
Total liabilities and equity	100.0%

MARGINAL COST OF CAPITAL: A COMPREHENSIVE EXAMPLE

To help bring together the principles for computing a firm's weighted cost of capital, consider J. M. Williams, Inc., a manufacturer of medical and surgical instruments. The firm's desired financing mix is presented in Table 11–9. Management attempts to maintain a relatively constant capital structure mix from year to year.

The most recent earnings per share (1994) was $8, which was twice the earnings per share in 1988, and this represents a growth rate of about 12 percent.[11] Dividends and the market price of the firm's common stock have grown at the same rate. The dividend payout ratio, which equals the ratio of common dividends to earnings available to common, has been 50 percent, and J. McDonald Williams, president, intends to hold to this dividend policy in the future.[12] Five investments are being examined by the company for 1995. The costs and the expected internal rates of return for these projects are provided in Table 11–10. To finance these investments, Williams expects to have $500,000 from 1995 retained earnings available for reinvestment, and new security issues can be sold. The firm's current financing mix will be maintained and the firm's business risk should not change. The following information is available regarding the individual costs of capital:

1. **Bonds.** An amount not exceeding $240,000 could be issued in new bonds. The issue, after considering the effect of flotation costs, would have an effective before-tax cost of 13 percent. If additional debt is required, the effective yield would have to be increased to 16 percent. The firm's marginal tax rate is 34 percent.

2. **Preferred stock.** New preferred stock could be issued by Williams with a par value of $50, paying $6 in annual dividends. The market price of the security is $45, but $1.80 per share in flotation costs

---

[11]This growth rate is computed by dividing the 1994 earnings per share by the 1988 earnings per share, $8/$4 = 2, which represents the compound interest factor for 6 years at 12 percent. That is, [EPS 1988 $(1 + g)^6$ = EPS 1994], or 4(1 + g)^6$ = $8; thus, $(1 + g)^6$ = $8/$4 = 2. Looking up a compound interest factor of two for six years in Appendix B, we find it corresponds to a growth rate of about 12 percent. The same solution could be found by using the present value equation.

[12]Dividend policy is discussed in Chapter 13.

TABLE 11–10
J. M. Williams, Inc., 1995
Investment Opportunities

Investment	Estimated Cost	Projected Internal Rates of Return
A	$ 450,000	22%
B	500,000	19
C	300,000	17
D	250,000	14
E	500,000	12
Total proposed budget	$2,000,000	

would be incurred for an issue size of $105,000 or less. Additional preferred stock could be sold at $45; however, the flotation costs would be $3.33 per share.

3. **Common stock.** Common stock can be sold at the existing $75 market price. If the issue size is not greater than $375,000, a 15 percent flotation cost would result. For any additional common stock, the flotation costs would increase to 20 percent of the market price. As already noted, last year's dividend per share was $4 and dividends are expected to grow at 12 percent per year.

With the foregoing information and by using the following five steps, we can construct a weighted marginal cost of capital curve as follows:

Step 1: *Determine the financial mix.* In Table 11–9, the desired financial mix for Williams was shown to be 30 percent in debt, 7.5 percent in preferred stocks, and 62.5 percent in common equity. For Step 1, we assume that future financing will be made in the same proportions.

Step 2: *Compute when costs will increase.* With the preceding weights and knowing the amount of capital available at each cost, we can compute the points at which breaks in the marginal cost curve will occur. Remember that an increase in the weighted cost of capital occurs when one of the individual costs increases. For example, if the cost of debt rises, the weighted cost must also be higher. We need to know where these increases in the weighted cost will occur. For Williams Inc., we know that the cost of the bonds increases if we issue more than $240,000 in new bonds. If debt represents 30 percent of all sources, how much in total financing will be possible before this increase in debt financing (bonds) affects the weighted marginal cost of capital? Using equation (11–16), we see that the weighted cost will increase when $800,000 in total capital has been raised, which is computed as follows:

$$\text{total financing available with the lower-cost debt} = \frac{\text{total debt available at a lower cost}}{\text{percentage of debt financing}}$$

$$= \frac{\$240,000}{.30}$$

$$= \$800,000$$

I. Debt

$$\text{total financing available with the lower-cost debt} = \frac{\text{total debt available at lower cost}}{\text{percentage of debt financing}}$$

$$= \frac{\$240,000}{.30}$$

$$= \$800,000$$

II. Preferred Stock

$$\text{total financing available with cheaper preferred stock} = \frac{\text{total preferred stock available at lower cost}}{\text{percentage of preferred stock financing}}$$

$$= \frac{\$105,000}{.075}$$

$$= \$1,400,000$$

III. Common Stock

$$\text{total financing available with internal common} = \frac{\text{total internal common available}}{\text{percentage of common financing}}$$

$$= \frac{\$500,000}{.625}$$

$$= \$800,000$$

$$\text{total financing available with both internal common and with cheaper new common stock} = \frac{\text{total internal common plus new common stock at lower cost}}{\text{percentage of common financing}}$$

$$= \frac{\$500,000 + \$375,000}{.625}$$

$$= \$1,400,000$$

In other words, when we raise $800,000 in total financing and 30 percent is from debt, we will have used $240,000 in bonds (30 percent of $800,000). This same procedure must be followed for increases in the cost of preferred stock and for common equity, both for internally generated common and new common stock. These calculations are shown in Table 11–11, and the results indicate two breaks in the curve. Increases in the marginal cost of capital occur as the amount of total financing reaches (1) $800,000 (cost of debt and common equity simultaneously increase), and (2) $1,400,000 (cost of preferred stock increases and cost of common equity increases). This result is presented in Figure 11–6.

Step 3: *Calculate the cost of individual sources.* The next step requires computing the individual costs of capital, which is presented in Table 11–12, where the amount of capital and the costs for these funds are provided. For debt the costs need only to be adjusted by

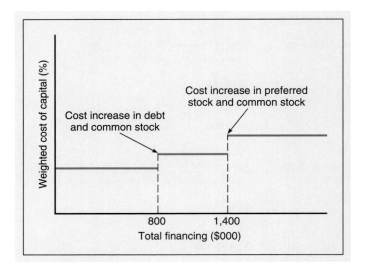

Williams' marginal income tax rate. For a 34 percent income tax rate, the 13 percent and 16 percent costs of debt have an effective after-tax cost of 8.6 percent and 10.6 percent, respectively. The cost of preferred stock, which equals the dollar dividend relative to the net price per share received by the company, equals 13.9 percent for the first $105,000 and 14.4 percent for any greater amounts. The cost of internally generated common equals the dividend yield (the forthcoming dividend per share/ price) plus the expected growth in dividends. The dividend yield is 6 percent ($4.48/$75). An annual compound growth rate of 12 percent is estimated from the past growth in earnings per share. The dividend yield of 6 percent plus the 12 percent growth rate produces an 18 percent cost of internally generated common. The costs of new common stock are easily determined by adjusting the required rate of return of the common stockholders by the flotation costs in issuing the stock. These calculations yield a cost of new common of 19 percent up to $375,000 and 19.5 percent for an amount exceeding $375,000.

Step 4: *Solve for the weighted marginal cost of capital.* With the preceding information, the weighted marginal costs of capital relative to the funds raised may be determined. Because the weighted cost of capital does not change for the first $800,000 in total financing, the weighted marginal cost of capital is determined by using the lowest costs of the individual sources. The weighted costs of financing up to $800,000 are calculated in Table 11–13. The percentage of capital that would be provided by each source is presented in column 2, and the cost of each individual source of capital appears in column 3 (taken from Table 11–12). Multiplying the weights (column 2) times the individual costs (column 3) and summing the results produce a weighted cost of 14.87 percent. This cost applies to any amount of financing (including debt, preferred stock, and common equity) up to but not exceeding $800,000.

TABLE 11–12
J. M. Williams, Inc.
Amount and Costs of Individual Sources

Source	Amount Available	Costs Calculations
I. Debt		
		(after-tax cost of bonds) = (before-tax cost) (1 − tax rate)
	(a) $0 – 240,000	$k_d(1-t) = 13\% (1 - .34) = 8.6\%$
	(b) Over 240,000	$k_d(1-t) = 16\% (1 - .34) = 10.6\%$
II. Perferred stock		
		(cost of preferred) = $\left(\dfrac{\text{dividend per share}}{\text{market price less flotation costs}}\right)$
	(a) $0 – 105,000	$k_p = \left(\dfrac{\$6}{\$45 - \$1.80}\right) = .139$ or 13.9%
	(b) Over $105,000	$k_p = \left(\dfrac{\$6}{\$45 - \$3.33}\right) = .144$ or 14.4%
III. Common financing A. Internal common		
		$\left(\begin{array}{c}\text{cost of}\\ \text{internal common}\end{array}\right) = \left(\dfrac{\text{dividend in year one}}{\text{market price}}\right) + \text{growth}$
	(a) $0 – $500,000	$k_c = \left(\dfrac{\$4 (1 + .12)}{\$75}\right) + .12 = .18$ or 18.0%
B. New common stock		
		$\left(\begin{array}{c}\text{cost of new}\\ \text{common stock}\end{array}\right) = \left(\dfrac{\text{dividend in year one}}{\text{market price less flotation costs}}\right) + \text{growth}$
	(a) $0 – $375,000	$k_{nc} = \dfrac{\$4 (1 + .12)}{\$75 - \$11.25} + .12 = .19$ or 19.0%
	(b) Over $375,000	$k_{nc} = \dfrac{\$4 (1 + .12)}{\$75 - \$15} + .12 = .195$ or 19.5%

After the first $800,000 has been used to finance new investments, the costs of debt and common equity will increase. The costs increase because we will have exceeded $240,000 in debt and $500,000 in common equity. Taking the increased costs from Table 11–12 for these two sources (preferred stock cost has not changed), we calculate a weighted marginal cost of capital for an amount greater than $800,000 but not exceeding $1,400,000. This weighted cost is now 16.10 percent and is given in Table 11–14, where the new costs for debt and common equity are shown in the boxes. Otherwise the calculation is no different from the weighted cost of capital for less than $800,000.

Should the firm finance over $1,400,000, the weighted marginal cost of capital will rise again. Because we now need over $105,000 in preferred stock and $875,000 in common equity to raise more than $1,400,000 in total financing, the costs of preferred stock and common equity will increase. These new costs are presented in Table 11–15. They result in a final weighted cost of capital of 16.45 percent.

In summary, the weighted cost of capital for J. M. Williams, Inc., increases as the amount of money needed becomes larger, with the costs being as follows:

Total Financing	Weighted cost
$0 – $800,000	14.87%
$800,001 – $1,400,000	16.10%
Over $1,400,000	16.45%

Step 5: *Compare investment returns with weighted costs.* The weighted marginal costs of capital are to be used in determining whether to accept any or all of the investment prospects being reviewed by Williams. A ranking of the projects, taken from Table 11–10, and a comparison of the returns against the weighted costs of capital are given in Figure 11–7. As is evident from the figure, Williams' optimal

TABLE 11–13
J. M. Williams Inc., Weighted Marginal Cost of Capital for $0–$800,000 Funds Raised

(1) Source	(2) Proportions	(3) Cost of Capital	(4) Weighted Cost of Capital (2 × 3)
Bonds	30.0%	8.6%	2.58%
Preferred stock	7.5	13.9	1.04
Common equity	62.5	18.0	11.25
	100.0%	Weighted cost of capital:	14.87%

TABLE 11–14
J. M. Williams Inc., Weighted Marginal Cost of Capital for $800,001–$1,400,000 Funds Raised

(1) Source	(2) Proportions	(3) Cost of Capital	(4) Weighted Cost of Capital (2 × 3)
Bonds	30.0%	10.6%	3.18%
Preferred stock	7.5	13.9	1.04
Common equity	62.5	19.0	11.88
	100.0%	Weighted cost of capital:	16.10%

TABLE 11–15
J. M. Williams Inc., Weighted Marginal Cost of Capital for More than $1,400,000 Funds Raised

(2) Source	(2) Proportions	(2) Cost of Capital	(4) Weighted Cost of Capital (2 × 3)
Bonds	30.0%	10.6%	3.18%
Preferred stock	7.5	14.4	1.08
Common equity	62.5	19.5	12.19
	100.0%	Weighted cost of capital:	16.45%

BASIC FINANCIAL MANAGEMENT IN PRACTICE

Management Myopia: Limited Evidence on the Matter

American managers are often accused of short-termism. Corporate nearsightedness, the indictment reads, is the reason American companies invest less than their main foreign competitors and American productivity has grown so slowly in recent years. Is the charge true? Evidence is largely anecdotal. In a study done by James Poterba of MIT and Lawrence Summers of the World Bank, managers were asked their opinion.* The findings are hardly conclusive, but they might lead to a better class of anecdote.

Poterba and Summers sent a questionnaire to the chief executives of Fortune 1,000 firms, with a covering letter from John Young, chairman of Hewlett-Packard, and John MacArthur, dean of Harvard Business School, asking for help. They received 228 replies, 97 of them from identifiable manufacturers—the sort of companies most often said to be short-termist. This fairly unimpressive response, together with the possibility of bias (the chief executives who answered may be untypically concerned about short-termism), means the results have to be handled with care.

The survey asked chief executives what proportion of their investment in R&D was devoted to projects that would generate no income during the next five years. Answers varied widely, but averaged 21 percent overall and 23 percent for manufacturers. The survey then asked what proportion of investment was of that farsighted sort 10 years ago. The answers were 19 percent overall and 22 percent for manufacturers. On this measure, it seems, the firms are slightly less shortsighted than they used to be.

Chief executives were asked to state their "hurdle rates"—the smallest return expected of a project if the company is to go ahead with it. Two-thirds of the answers were given in the form of nominal rates. The authors converted nominal to real by deducting five percentage points, representing long-term expected inflation. The resulting average real rates, shown in the table, are surprisingly high. Since the 1920s the real return on American corporate

bonds has averaged 2 percent; the real return on equities 7 percent. Average hurdle rates of 12 percent seem unduly demanding.

CORPORATE TIME HORIZONS

	All	Manufacturing
Fraction of R&D in long-term projects (%)	21.1	22.6
Real hurdle rate (%)	12.2	11.6
Increase in investment if stock market correctly valued long-term investments (%)	20.7	19.0
Time horizon of the companies relative to: (1 =longer, 5 =shorter)		
U.S. competitors	2.5	2.4
European competitors	3.2	3.1
Asian competitors	3.8	3.8

Source: Poterba and Summers.

Corporate nearsightedness is often blamed on Wall Street. Unsurprisingly, three-quarters of the bosses thought their firms undervalued. Asked how much more they would invest if financial markets valued long-term investment correctly, the average answer was 21 percent.

Next, the survey asked each company to judge its time horizon against (a) other American firms, (b) European firms and (c) Asian firms. Answers were given on a scale of one (less shortsighted) to five (more shortsighted). Interestingly, the chief executives thought themselves less shortsighted than their counterparts at home. But they believed they were more shortsighted than their European competitors, and even more so than Asians.

---

*James Poterba and Lawrence Summers, Time Horizons of American Firms: New Evidence from a Survey of CEOs. Unpublished manuscript.

Source: *The Economist*, December 14, 1991, p. 73. Used by permission.

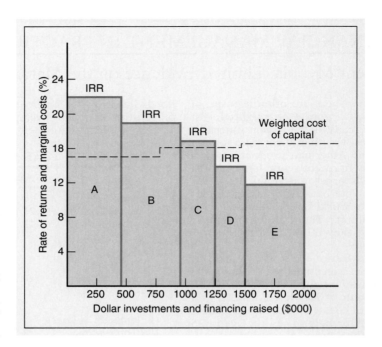

FIGURE 11–7
Investment Returns and
Weighted Cost of Capital for
J. M. Williams Inc.

capital budget for 1995 is $1,250,000. The particular investments that should be included in the budget are projects A, B, and C, with the returns for projects D and E falling short of the weighted cost of capital hurdle rate.

◼ A FIRM'S COST OF CAPITAL: RECENT EVIDENCE

An interesting survey of the 100 largest corporations listed on the New York Stock Exchange was conducted by Blume, Friend, and Westerfield. In this survey, managers were asked to indicate various cost of capital figures.[15] The results are reported in Table 11–16.

Of the 30 companies that responded to the survey, 10 were public utilities and 20 were nonfinancial corporations from a variety of industries. From the results, we can see that higher costs of capital prevailed when public utilities were excluded, which implies that public utilities are less risky. Even more significantly, the results suggest that new common stock is slightly more expensive than internal common (retained earnings) and that internal common is four to five percentage points more costly than the *before-tax* cost of debt. We should also note that the weighted cost of capital, which falls around 12 percent to 13 percent, is at

[15]Marshall E. Blume, Irwin Friend, and Randolph Westerfield, "Impediments to Capital Formation: Summary Report of a Survey of Nonfinancial Corporations," Working Paper (Philadelphia: Wharton School, University of Pennsylvania, 1980), p. 6.

TABLE 11–16
Average Costs of Capital and Investment: Cutoff Rates for Plant and Equipment

| Industries | Before-Tax Cost-of-Debt(%) | After-Tax Cost (%) | | | | After-Tax Cutoff Rate for Plant and Equipment Investments | |
		New Common Equity	Retained Earnings	Debt	Weighted Cost	Least Risky	Most Risky
All industries	12.5%	17.2%	16.6%	6.4%	12.4%	12.9%	19.6%
All industries except public utilities	12.5	17.8	17.0	6.3	13.1	13.1	20.3

Source: Marshall E. Blume, Irwin Friend, and Randolph Westerfield, "Impediments to Capital Formation: Summary Report of a Survey of Nonfinancial Corporations," Working Paper (Philadelphia: Wharton School, University of Pennsylvania, 1980), p.6.

the bottom range of the cutoff or hurdle rate used to evaluate investments in plant and equipment. Thus, either new investments were considered more risky than existing investments or management was imposing capital rationing.

In addition to the results summarized in Table 11–16, the authors found that

1. The dividend-growth model was the most frequently used method for estimating the cost of equity. However, the CAPM is also used.

2. If management perceives the cost of a particular source to be excessive, it will rely more heavily on other sources. That is, how a firm finances its investments is affected by management's perception of the relative costs of each source of capital.

SUMMARY

Cost of capital is an important concept within financial management. In making an investment, the cost of capital is the rate of return that must be achieved on the company's projects in order to satisfy all the investors' required rates of return. If the rate of return from the corporation's investments equals the cost of capital, the price of the stock should remain unchanged. In other words, the firm's cost of capital may be defined as the rate of return from an investment that will leave the company's stock price unchanged. Therefore, the cost of capital, if certain assumptions are met, represents the minimum acceptable rate of return for new corporate investments.

The factors that affect a firm's cost of capital consist of four components. First, general economic conditions (as reflected in the demand and supply of funds in the economy), as well as inflationary pressures, affect the general level of interest rates. Second, the marketability of the firm's securities has an impact on the cost of capital. Any change in the marketability of a firm's stock will affect investors' required rate of return. These changes directly influence the firm's cost of capital. Third, the firm's operating and financial risks are reflected in its cost of capital. Finally, a relationship exists between a firm's cost of capital and the dollar amount of financing needed for future investments.

Cost of Individual Sources of Financing

The cost of debt is equal to the effective interest rate on new debt adjusted for the tax deductibility of the interest expense. The cost of preferred stock is equal to the effective dividend yield on new preferred stock. In making this computation, we should use the net price received by the company from the new issue. Thus,

$$\text{cost of preferred stock} = \frac{\text{annual dividend}}{\text{net price of preferred stock}}$$

In calculating the cost of common equity, we distinguish between the costs of internally generated funds and the costs of new common stock. If historical data reasonably reflect the expectations of investors, the cost of internally generated capital is equal to the dividend yield on the common stock plus the anticipated percentage increase in dividends (and in the price of the stock) during the forthcoming year. If, however, the common equity is to be acquired by issuing new common stock, the cost of common should recognize the effect of flotation costs. This alteration results in the following equation for the cost of new common stock:

$$\binom{\text{cost of new}}{\text{common}} = \left(\frac{\text{dividend in year 1}}{\text{market price} - \text{flotation cost}}\right)$$
$$+ \binom{\text{annual growth rate}}{\text{in dividends}}$$

where (market price – flotation cost) is equivalent to the net market price.

We may also compute the cost of equity by using the CAPM or the risk-premium technique.

Weighted Cost of Capital

A firm's weighted cost of capital is a composite of the individual costs of financing, weighted by the percentage of financing provided by each source. In this chapter we assume that the firm is to finance future investments in the same manner as past investments. The problem of defining the best set of weights is addressed in Chapter 12. Hence, the existing capital structure was used for developing the weighting scheme.

Marginal Cost of Capital

Because the amount of financing has an effect on the firm's weighted cost of capital, the expected return from an investment must be compared with the marginal cost of financing the project. If the cost of capital rises as the level of financing increases, we should use the marginal cost of capital, and not the average cost of all funds raised. Following the basic economic principle of marginal analysis, investments should be made to the point where marginal revenue (internal rate of return) equals the marginal cost of capital.

STUDY QUESTIONS

11–1.   Define the term *cost of capital*.
11–2.   Why do we calculate a firm's cost of capital?
11–3.   In computing the cost of capital, which sources of capital do we consider?
11–4.   In general, what factors determine a firm's cost of capital? In answering this question, identify the factors that are within management's control and those that are not.
11–5.   What limitations exist in using the firm's cost of capital as an investment hurdle rate?
11–6.   How does a firm's tax rate affect its cost of capital? What is the effect of the flotation costs associated with a new security issue?
11–7.   **a.** Distinguish between internal common equity and new common stock.
         b. Why is a cost associated with internal common equity?
         c. Compare approaches that could be used in computing the cost of common equity.
11–8.   Define the expression *marginal cost of capital*. Why is the marginal cost of capital an appropriate investment criterion?
11–9.   How may we avoid the limitation of the weighted cost of capital approach when it requires that we assume business risk is constant?
11–10. What might we expect to see in practice in the relative costs of different sources of capital?

SELF-TEST PROBLEMS

ST-1.   (*Individual Costs of Capital*) Compute the cost for the following sources of financing:
         a. A $1,000 par value bond with a market price of $970 and a coupon interest rate of 10 percent. Flotation costs for a new issue would be approximately 5 percent. The bonds mature in 10 years and the corporate tax rate is 34 percent.
         b. A preferred stock selling for $100 with an annual dividend payment of $8. If the company sells a new issue, the flotation cost will be $9 per share. The company's marginal tax rate is 30 percent.
         c. Internally generated common totaling $4.8 million. The price of the common stock is $75 per share, and the dividend per share was $9.80 last year. The dividend is not expected to increase.
         d. New common stock where the most recent dividend was $2.80. The company's dividends per share should continue to increase at an 8 percent growth rate into the indefinite future. The market price of the stock is currently $53; however, flotation costs of $6 per share are expected if the new stock is issued.

ST-2.   (*Level of Financing*) The Argue Company has the following capital structure mix:

Debt	30%
Preferred stock	15
Common stock	55
	100%

Assuming that management intends to maintain the above financial structure, what amount of total investments may be financed if the firm uses (a) $100,000 of debt, (b) $150,000 of debt, (c) $40,000 of preferred stock, (d) $90,000 of preferred stock, (e) $200,000 of internally generated common equity, (f) $200,000 of internally generated common equity plus $300,000 in new common stock?

ST-3. (*Marginal Cost-of-Capital Curve*) The Zenor Corporation is considering three investments. The costs and expected returns of these projects are shown below:

Investment	Investment Cost	Internal Rate of Return
A	$165,000	17%
B	200,000	13
C	125,000	12

The firm would finance the projects by 40 percent debt and 60 percent common equity. The after-tax cost of debt is 7 percent for the first $120,000, after which the cost will be 11 percent. Internally generated common totaling $180,000 is available, and the common stockholders' required rate of return is 19 percent. If new stock is issued, the cost will be 22 percent.

a. Construct a weighted marginal cost of capital curve.

b. Which projects should be accepted?

ST-4. (*Weighted Cost of Capital*) Todd Owens is the new vice-president-finance for Brister, Inc. He is preparing his recommendations for the firm's capital budget. With the information provided below, prepare a graph comparing the company's weighted cost of capital and the prospective investment returns. Which investments should be made?

Investment	Investment Cost	Internal Rate of Return
A	$200,000	18%
B	125,000	16
C	150,000	12
D	275,000	10

The firm's capital structure consists of $2 million in debt, $500,000 in preferred stock, and $2.5 million in common equity. This capital mix is to be maintained for future investments. The cost of debt (before-tax) is 12 percent for the first $120,000; thereafter, the cost will be 15 percent. The company's preferred stock sells for $95 and pays a 14 percent dividend rate on a par value of $100. A new offering of this stock would entail underwriting costs and a price discount of 8 percent of the current market price. If the issue exceeded $50,000, the flotation costs would increase to 11 percent. The common equity portion of the investments will be financed first by profits retained within the company of $150,000. If additional common financing is needed, new common stock can be issued at the $30 current price less flotation costs of $3 per share. Management expects to pay a dividend at the end of this year of $2.50, and dividends should increase at an annual rate of 9 percent thereafter. The firm's marginal tax rate is 34 percent.

STUDY PROBLEMS

11–1. (*Individual or Component Costs of Capital*) Compute the cost for the following sources of financing:

    a. A bond that has a $1,000 par value (face value) and a contract or coupon interest rate of 11 percent. A new issue would have a flotation cost of 5 percent of the $1,125 market value. The bonds mature in 10 years. The firm's average tax rate is 30 percent and its marginal tax rate is 34 percent.

    b. A new common stock issue that paid a $1.80 dividend last year. The par value of the stock is $15, and earnings per share have grown at a rate of 7 percent per year. This growth rate is expected to continue into the foreseeable future. The company maintains a constant dividend/earnings ratio of 30 percent. The price of this stock is now $27.50, but 5 percent flotation costs are anticipated.

    c. Internal common equity where the current market price of the common stock is $43. The expected dividend this coming year should be $3.50, increasing thereafter at a 7 percent annual growth rate. The corporation's tax rate is 34 percent.

    d. A preferred stock paying a 9 percent dividend on a $150 par value. If a new issue is offered, flotation costs will be 12 percent of the current price of $175.

    e. A bond selling to yield 12 percent after flotation costs, but prior to adjusting for the marginal corporate tax rate of 34 percent. In other words, 12 percent is the rate that equates the net proceeds from the bond with the present value of the future cash flows (principal and interest).

11–2. (*Level of Financing*) The Mathews Company has the following capital structure mix:

Debt	$525,000
Preferred stock	225,000
Common stock	450,000

Using that capital structure mix, compute the total investment amount if the company uses

    a. $700,000 of debt

    b. $67,500 of preferred stock

    c. $300,000 of retained earnings only, or

    d. $100,000 of retained earnings plus $600,000 of new common stock

11–3. (*Individual or Component Costs of Capital*) Compute the cost for the following sources of financing:

    a. A bond selling to yield 8 percent after flotation cost, but prior to adjusting for the marginal corporate tax rate of 34 percent. In other words, 8 percent is the rate that equates the net proceeds from the bond with the present value of the future cash flows (principal and interest).

    b. A new common stock issue that paid a $1.05 dividend last year. The par value of the stock is $2, and the earnings per share have grown at a rate of 5 percent per year. This growth rate is expected to continue into the foreseeable future. The company maintains a constant dividend/earnings ratio of 40 percent. The price of this stock is now $25, but 9 percent flotation costs are anticipated.

    c. A bond that has a $1,000 par value (face value) and a contract or coupon interest rate of 12 percent. A new issue would net the company 90 percent of the $1,150 market value. The bonds mature in 20 years, the firm's average tax rate is 30 percent, and its marginal tax rate is 34 percent.

d. A preferred stock paying a 7 percent dividend on a $100 par value. If a new issue is offered, the company can expect to net $85 per share.

e. Internal common equity where the current market price of the common stock is $38. The expected dividend this forthcoming year should be $3, increasing thereafter at a 4 percent annual growth rate. The corporation's tax rate is 34 percent.

11–4. (*Cost of Equity*) Salte Corporation is issuing new common stock at a market price of $27. Dividends last year were $1.45 and are expected to grow at an annual rate of 6 percent forever. Flotation costs will be 6 percent of market price. What is Salte's cost of equity?

11–5. (*Cost of Debt*) Belton is issuing a $1,000 par value bond that pays 7 percent annual interest and matures in 15 years. Investors are willing to pay $958 for the bond. Flotation costs will be 11 percent of market value. The company is in an 18 percent tax bracket. What will be the firm's after-tax cost of debt on the bond?

11–6. (*Cost of Preferred Stock*) The preferred stock of Walter Industries sells for $36 and pays $2.50 in dividends. The net price of the security after issuance costs is $32.50. What is the cost of capital for the preferred stock?

11–7. (*Cost of Debt*) The Zephyr Corporation is contemplating a new investment to be financed 33 percent from debt. The firm could sell new $1,000 par value bonds at a net price of $945. The coupon interest rate is 12 percent, and the bonds would mature in 15 years. If the company is in a 34 percent tax bracket, what is the after-tax cost of capital to Zephyr for bonds?

11-8. (*Cost of Preferred Stock*) Your firm is planning to issue preferred stock. The stock sells for $115; however, if new stock is issued, the company would receive only $98. The par value of the stock is $100 and the dividend rate is 14 percent. What is the cost of capital for the stock to your firm?

11–9. (*Cost of Internal Equity*) Pathos Co.'s common stock is currently selling for $21.50. Dividends paid last year were $.70. Flotation costs on issuing stock will be 10 percent of market price. The dividends and earnings per share are projected to have an annual growth rate of 15 percent. What is the cost of internal common equity for Pathos?

11–10. (*Cost of Equity*) The common stock for the Bestsold Corporation sells for $58. If a new issue is sold, the flotation cost is estimated to be 8 percent. The company pays 50 percent of its earnings in dividends, and a $4 dividend was recently paid. Earnings per share five years ago were $5. Earnings are expected to continue to grow at the same annual rate in the future as during the past five years. The firm's marginal tax rate is 34 percent. Calculate the cost of (a) internal common and (b) external common.

11–11. (*Cost of Debt*) Sincere Stationery Corporation needs to raise $500,000 to improve its manufacturing plant. It has decided to issue a $1,000 par value bond with a 14 percent annual coupon rate and a 10-year maturity. If the investors require a 9 percent rate of return

a. Compute the market value of the bonds.

b. What will the net price be if flotation costs are 10.5 percent of the market price?

c. How many bonds will the firm have to issue to receive the needed funds?

d. What is the firm's after-tax cost of debt if its average tax rate is 25 percent and its marginal tax rate is 34 percent?

11–12. (*Cost of Debt*)

a. Rework problem 11–11 assuming a 10 percent coupon rate. What effect does changing the coupon rate have on the firm's after-tax cost of capital?

b. Why is there a change?

11–13. (*Weighted Cost of Capital*) The capital structure for the Carion Corporation is provided below. The company plans to maintain its debt structure in the future. If the firm has a 5.5 percent cost of debt, a 13.5 percent cost of preferred stock, and an 18 percent cost of common stock, what is the firm's weighted cost of capital?

Capital Structure ($000)	
Bonds	$1,083
Preferred stock	268
Common stock	3681
	$5,032

11–14. (*Level of Financing*) Using the same capital structure mix as problem 11–13, what would the total investment amount be if the firm used the following?
   a. $200,000 of debt
   b. $40,000 of preferred stock
   c. $100,000 of retained earnings
   d. $100,000 of retained earnings plus $50,000 of new common stock

11–15. (*Weighted Cost of Capital*) The capital structure for Nealon, Inc., is provided below. Flotation costs would be (a) 15 percent of market value for a new bond issue, (b) $1.21 per share for common stock, and (c) $2.01 per share for preferred stock. The dividends for common stock were $2.50 last year and are projected to have an annual growth rate of 6 percent. The firm is in a 34 percent tax bracket. What is the weighted cost of capital if the firm finances in the proportions shown below? Market prices are $1,035 for bonds, $19 for preferred stock, and $35 for common stock. There will be $500,000 of internal common available.

Nealon, Inc., Balance Sheet

Type of Financing	Percentage of Future Financing
Bonds (8%, $1,000 par, 16-year maturity)	38%
Preferred stock (5,000 shares outstanding, $50 par, $1.50 dividend)	15
Common stock	47
Total	100%

11–16. (*Weighted Cost of Capital*) The Bach's Candy Corporation has determined the company's marginal costs of capital for debt, preferred stock, and common equity as follows:

Source	Amount of Capital	Cost
Debt	$0 – $175,000	4.8%
	$175,001 – $300,000	5.5
	over $300,000	6.0
Preferred stock	$0 – $ 50,000	10.0
	$50,001 – $ 75,000	12.0
	over $ 75,000	13.0
Common stock	$0 – $400,000[a]	15.0
	$400,001 – $750,000	18.0
	over $750,000	22.0

[a]$400,000 is available from internally generated common equity.

The firm maintains a capital mix of 45 percent debt, 5 percent preferred stock, and 50 percent common stock. Construct Bach's weighted marginal cost of capital curve.

11–17. (*Marginal Cost of Capital*) Mary Basett, Inc., a national advertising firm, is analyzing the following investment opportunities.

Investment	Investment Cost	Internal Rate of Return
A	$ 50,000	14.5%
B	200,000	17.9
C	325,000	15.6
D	125,000	12.4
E	400,000	10.9
F	75,000	13.8

The information needed to calculate the firm's weighted marginal cost of capital curve is presented below. Construct Basett's weighted marginal cost of capital curve and decide which investments should be accepted.

Source	Percentage	Amount of Capital	After-Tax Cost
Debt	40%	$0 – $300,000	4.5%
		over $300,000	6.0
Preferred stock	8	$0 – $50,000	9.5
		$50,001 – $100,000	10.5
		over $100,000	11.0
Common stock	52	$0 – $520,000	16.0
		over $520,000	18.0

11–18. (*Weighted Cost of Capital*) Blacktop Chemical Co. is considering five investments. The cost of each is shown below. Retained earnings of $650,000 will be available for investment purposes, and management can issue the following securities:

1. **Bonds.** $270,000 can be issued at an after-flotation, before-tax cost of 8.5 percent. Above $270,000 the cost will be 9.75 percent.
2. **Preferred stock.** The stock can be issued at the prevailing market price. Issuance will cost $1.55 per share up to an issue size of $90,000; thereafter costs will be $2.80 per share.
3. **Common stock.** The stock will be issued at the market price. For an issue of $250,000, flotation costs will be $1 per share. For any additional common, the flotation costs should then be $1.75 per share.

The tax rate for the firm is 34 percent. Common dividends last year were $1.80 and are expected to grow at an annual rate of 9 percent. Market prices are $975 for bonds, $39 for preferred stock, and $23 for common stock. Determine which projects should be accepted, based on a comparison of the IRR of the investments and the weighted marginal cost of capital. The firm's capital structure is shown on the following table and the same mix is to be used for future investments.

Investment	Cost	IRR
A	$ 200,000	16%
B	650,000	12
C	115,000	9
D	875,000	10
E	180,000	15
Total	$2,020,000	

Capital Structure	Amount of Capital	Percentages of Financing
Bonds (9%, $1000 par, 18-year maturity)	$3,000,000	43%
Preferred stock (10%, $45 par, 30,000 shares outstanding)	1,350,000	20
Common stock	2,600,000	37
Total	$6,950,000	100%

11–19. (*Weighted Cost of Capital*) Heard Ski, Inc., is a regional manufacturer of ski equipment. The firm's target financing mix appears as follows:

	Percentage
Debt	30%
Preferred stock	10
Common stock	60
Total	100%

The corporation's management is currently involved in evaluating the capital budget. Six investments are under consideration. The costs and the expected internal rates of return for these projects are given as follows:

Investment	Cost	Internal Rate of Return
A	$175,000	16%
B	100,000	14
C	125,000	12
D	200,000	10
E	250,000	9
F	150,000	8

As the accept-reject criterion, Paul Heard, president of the firm, has compiled the necessary data for computing the firm's weighted marginal cost of capital. The cost information indicates the following:

1. Debt can be raised at the following before-tax costs:

Amount	Cost
$0–150,000	8.0%
$150,001–$225,000	9.0
over $225,000	10.5

2. Preferred stock can be issued paying an annual dividend of $8.50. The par value of the stock is $100. Also, the market price of the stock is $100. If new stock were issued, the company would receive a net price of $80 on the first $75,000. Thereafter, the net amount received would be reduced to $75.

3. Common equity is provided first by internally generated funds. Profits for the year that should be available for reinvestment purposes are projected at $150,000. Additional common stock can be issued at the current $72 market price less 15 percent in flotation costs. However, if more than $225,000 in new common stock is required, a 20 percent flotation cost is expected. The dividend per share was $2.75 last year, and the long-term growth rate for dividends is 9 percent.

    a. Given that the firm's marginal tax rate is 34 percent, compute the company's weighted marginal cost of capital at a financing level up to $1 million.

    b. Construct a graph that presents the firm's weighted marginal cost of capital relative to the amount of financing.

    c. What is the appropriate size of the capital budget, and which projects should be accepted?

11–20. (*Individual Project—Required Return*) The Welton Corporation is examining two capital investments. Management wants to analyze the riskiness of the projects in terms of their effect on the riskiness of an investor's diversified portfolio. The beta for project A is 1.05 and .80 for B. The expected return for a diversified portfolio is 16 percent. The risk-free rate is 7 percent. Project A is expected to return 15.7 percent; project B, 17.5 percent. Which investment(s) should the company accept?

SUGGESTED APPLICATION FOR *DISCLOSURE*®
Using *Disclosure*, obtain the following information about AT&T:
1. Latest closing stock price
2. The expected growth rate in earnings per share over the next five years (Zack's earnings estimates).
3. The indicated annual dividend
4. The dividend payout ratio (dividend/earnings)
Assume that (a) the par value of the stock is $15, (b) earnings per share growth rate will continue indefinitely, (c) the company maintains a constant dividend/earnings ratio, and (d) 5 percent flotation costs are anticipated for any new stock issue.
a. Estimate the cost of equity of internally generated common.
b. Estimate the cost of equity for newly issued shares.

SELF-TEST SOLUTIONS

The following notations are used in this group of problems:

k_d = the before-tax cost of debt

k_p = the after-tax cost of preferred stock

k_c = the after-tax cost of internal common stock

k_{nc} = the after-tax cost of new common stock

t = the marginal tax rate

D_t = the dollar dividend per share, where D_0 is the most recently paid dividend and D_1 is the forthcoming dividend

P_0 = the value (present value) of a security

NP_0 = the value of a security less any flotation costs incurred in issuing the security

SS-1.

a.

$$\$921.50 = \sum_{t=1}^{10} \frac{\$100}{(1 + k_d)^t} + \frac{\$1,000}{(1 + k_d)^{10}}$$

Rate	Value
11%	$940.90
k_d%	$921.50
12%	$887.00

$\}$ $19.40 $\}$ $53.90

$$k_d = 0.11 + \left(\frac{\$19.40}{\$53.90}\right) 0.01 = .1136 \text{ or } 11.36\%$$

$$k_{d(1-t)} = 11.36\% (1 - 0.34) = 7.50\%$$

b.
$$k_P = \frac{D}{NP_0}$$

$$k_P = \frac{\$8}{\$100 - \$9} = .0879 \text{ or } 8.79\%$$

c.
$$k_c = \frac{D_1}{P_0} + g$$

$$k_c = \frac{\$9.80}{\$75} + 0\% = .1307 \text{ or } 13.07\%$$

d.
$$k_{nc} = \frac{D_1}{NP_0} + g$$

$$k_{nc} = \frac{\$2.80(1 + 0.08)}{\$53 - \$6} + 0.08 = .1443 \text{ or } 14.43\%$$

SS-2.

$$\text{dollar breaks} = \frac{\text{amount of financing at a given cost}}{\text{percentage of funds provided by the specific source}}$$

a. $\dfrac{\$100,000}{0.30} = \$333,333.33$ **b.** $\dfrac{\$150,000}{0.30} = \$500,000$

c. $\dfrac{\$40,000}{0.15} = \$266,666.67$ **d.** $\dfrac{\$90,000}{0.15} = \$600,000$

e. $\dfrac{\$200,000}{0.55} = \$363,636.36$ **f.** $\dfrac{\$500,000}{0.55} = \$909,090.91$

SS-3.

a. Increases (breaks) in the weighted marginal cost of capital curve will occur as follows:
Increase from the cost of debt:

$$\frac{\$120,000}{.40} = \$300,000$$

Increase from the cost of common:

$$\frac{\$180,000}{.60} = \$300,000$$

	$0–$300,000 Total Financing				Over $300,000 Total Financing		
	Weights	Costs	Weighted Costs		Weights	Costs	Weighted Costs
Debt	40%	7%	2.80%	Debt	40%	11%	4.4%
Common stock	60	19	11.40	Common stock	60	22	13.2
		$k_0 =$	14.20%			$k_0 =$	17.6%

b. Only project A should be accepted.

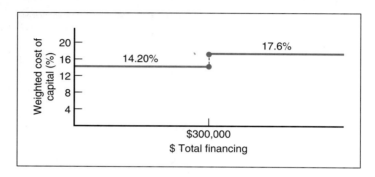

SS-4.

(1) Compute weights

	Capital Structure	Capital Mix (Weights)
Debt	$2,000,000	40%
Preferred stock	500,000	10
Common stock	2,500,000	50
	$5,000,000	100%

(2) Compute individual costs

Debt

$0–$120,000: 12% (1 – .34) = 7.92%
over $120,000: 15% (1 – .34) = 9.90%

Preferred stock

$0–$50,000: $\dfrac{\$14}{\$95(1-.08)} = \dfrac{\$14}{\$87.40} = .1602$ or 16.02%

over $50,000: $\dfrac{\$14}{\$95(1-.11)} = \dfrac{\$14}{\$84.55} = .1656$ or 16.56%

Common stock

$0–$150,000: $\left(\dfrac{\$2.50}{\$30}\right) + .09 = .1733$ or 17.33%

over $150,000: $\left(\dfrac{\$2.50}{\$27}\right) + .09 = .1826$ or 18.26%

(3) Calculate increases (breaks) in the weighted marginal cost of capital curve caused by increases in the cost of

Debt	Preferred Stock	Common Stock
$\dfrac{\$120,000}{.40} = \$300,000$	$\dfrac{\$50,000}{.10} = \$500,000$	$\dfrac{\$150,000}{.50} = \$300,000$

(4) Construct the weighted cost of capital curve

$0–$300,000 Total Financing

	Weights	Individual Costs	Weighted Costs
Debt	40%	7.92%	3.17
Preferred stock	10	16.02	1.60
Common stock	50	17.33	8.67
			$k_0 = 13.44\%$

At Least $300,001 but Not More Than $500,000

	Weights	Individual Costs	Weighted Costs
Debt	40%	9.90%	3.96%
Preferred stock	10	16.02	1.60
Common stock	50	18.26	9.13
			$k_0 = 14.69\%$

Over $500,000

	Weights	Individual Costs	Weighted Costs
Debt	40%	9.90%	3.96%
Preferred stock	10	16.56	1.66
Common stock	50	18.26	9.13
			$k_0 = 14.75\%$

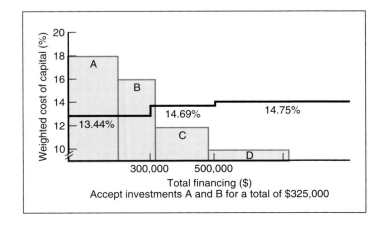

Accept investments A and B for a total of $325,000

CHAPTER 12

DETERMINING THE FINANCING MIX

Business and Financial Risk • Breakeven Analysis • Operating Leverage • Financial Leverage • Combination of Operating and Financial Leverage • Planning the Financing Mix • A Quick Look at Capital Structure Theory • Basic Tools of Capital Structure Management • A Glance at Actual Capital Structure Management

Our work in Chapters 6, 7, 8 and 11 allowed us to develop an understanding of how financial assets are valued in the marketplace. Drawing on the tenets of valuation theory, we presented various approaches to measuring the cost of funds to the business organization. This chapter presents concepts that relate to the valuation process and the cost of capital; it also discusses the crucial problem of planning the firm's financing mix.

The cost of capital provides a direct link between the formulation of the firm's asset structure and its financial structure. This is illustrated in Figure 12–1. Recall that the cost of capital is a basic input to the time-adjusted capital-budgeting models. It therefore affects the capital-budgeting, or asset-selection, process. The cost of capital is affected, in turn, by the composition of the right-hand side of the firm's balance sheet—that is, its financial structure.

This chapter examines tools that can be useful aids to the financial manager in determining the firm's proper financial structure. First, we review the technique of breakeven analysis. This provides the foundation for the relationships to be highlighted in the remainder of the chapter. We then examine the concept of operating leverage, some consequences of the firm's use of financial leverage, and the impact on the firm's earnings stream when operating and financial leverage are combined in various patterns. With the foundation in place whereby we

RJR Nabisco Bondholder Lawsuits:
A Leverage Related Agency Problem
from ABC News, Business World, November 20, 1988

Chapter 12 of the text introduces the concept of financial leverage, describes the costs and benefits associated with debt financing, and discusses how firms might choose an optimal mix of debt and equity. The accompanying video case provides a real-world example of some of the factors involved in leverage increases.

The video case describes how the announcement of the RJR management buyout proposal has sparked the wrath of several investors who own RJR Nabisco bonds. These bondholders suddenly own bonds worth 20 percent less than they were yesterday. For some bondholders that amounts to a lot of money. For example, Metropolitan Life Insurance suffered a $40 million loss on the value of their investment in RJR bonds.

For the management buyout to proceed, RJR will have to borrow an enormous amount of money—possible $12 to $16 billion. The borrowed funds will be used to repurchase all the firm's outstanding stock and take the firm private. By adding this new debt to the existing bonds, such as those owned by MetLife and other insurance companies, the risk of the existing bonds increases dramatically. As you know from earlier chapters, as risk increases security prices fall. Risk has increased with the proposed buyout, but bondholders are stuck with the agreed-on coupon rate—a coupon rate that no longer reflects the risk of the firm.

If going private reduces the total market value of the firm is it a good move from the shareholders perspective, why are bondholders treated so poorly, and what can bondholders do to protect themselves?

---

can effectively analyze the variability in the firm's earnings streams, we move on to a discussion of capital structure theory and the basic tools of capital structure management. Actual capital structure practices are also placed in perspective. Our immediate tasks are to distinguish two types of risk that confront the firm and to clarify some key terminology that will be used throughout this chapter.

PERSPECTIVE IN FINANCE

In this chapter we become more precise in assessing the causes of variability in the firm's expected revenue streams. It is useful to think of business risk as induced by the firm's investment decisions. That is, the composition of the firm's assets determines its exposure to business risk. In this way, business risk is a direct function of what appears on the left-hand side of the company's balance sheet. Financial risk is properly attributed to the manner in which the firm's managers have decided to arrange the right-hand side of the company's balance sheet. The choice to use more financial leverage means that the firm will experience greater exposure to financial risk. The tools developed here will help you quantify the firm's business and financial risk. A solid understanding of these tools will make you a better financial manager.

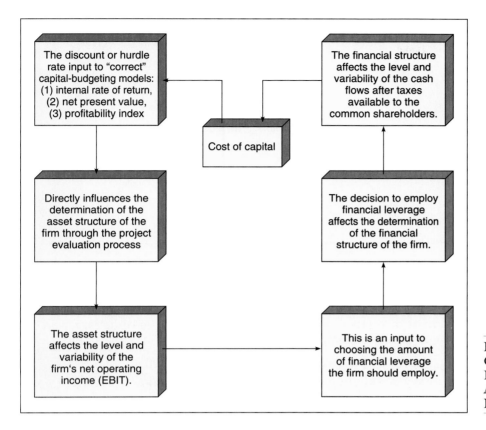

FIGURE 12–1
Cost of Capital as a
Link between Firm's
Asset Structure and
Financial Structure

■■■ BUSINESS AND FINANCIAL RISK

In studying capital-budgeting techniques we referred to **risk** as the likely variability associated with expected revenue or income streams. As our attention is now focused on the firm's financing decision rather than its investment decision, it is useful to separate the income stream variations attributable to (1) the company's exposure to business risk and (2) its decision to incur financial risk.

Business risk refers to the relative dispersion (variability) in the firm's expected earnings before interest and taxes (EBIT).[1] Figure 12–2 shows a subjectively estimated probability distribution of next year's EBIT for the Pierce Grain Company and the same type of projection for Pierce's larger competitor, the Blackburn Seed Company. The expected value of EBIT for Pierce is $100,000, with an associated standard deviation of $20,000. If next year's EBIT for Pierce fell one standard deviation short of the expected $100,000, the actual EBIT would equal $80,000. Blackburn's expected EBIT is $200,000, and the size of the associated standard deviation is $20,000. The standard deviation for the expected level of EBIT is the same for both firms. We would say that Pierce's

---

[1] If what accountants call "other income" and "other expenses" are equal to zero, then EBIT is equal to net operating income. These terms will be used interchangeably.

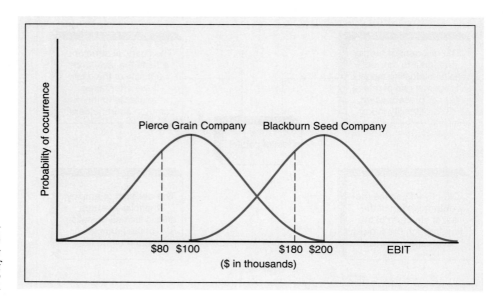

FIGURE 12–2
Subjective Probability
Distribution of
Next Year's EBIT

degree of business risk exceeds Blackburn's because of its larger coefficient of variation of expected EBIT, as follows:

$$\text{Pierce's coefficient of variation of expected EBIT} = \frac{\$20,000}{\$100,000} = .20$$

$$\text{Blackburn's coefficient of variation of expected EBIT} = \frac{\$20,000}{\$200,000} = .10$$

The relative dispersion in the firm's EBIT stream, measured here by its expected coefficient of variation, is the *residual* effect of several causal influences. Dispersion in operating income does not *cause* business risk; rather, this dispersion, which we call business risk, is the *result* of several influences. The company's cost structure, product demand characteristics, and intraindustry competitive position all affect its business risk exposure. Such business risk is a direct result of the firm's investment decision. It is the firm's asset structure, after all, that gives rise to both the level and variability of its operating profits.

Financial risk, conversely, is a direct result of the firm's financing decision. In the context of selecting a proper financing mix, this risk applies to (1) the additional variability in earnings available to the firm's common shareholders and (2) the additional chance of insolvency borne by the common shareholder caused by the use of financial leverage.[2] **Financial leverage** means financing a portion of the firm's assets with securities bearing a fixed (limited) rate of return in hopes of increasing the ultimate return to the common stockholders. The decision to use debt or preferred stock in the financial structure of the corporation means that those who own the common shares of the firm are exposed to financial risk. Any given level of variability in EBIT will be *magnified*

[2]Note that the concept of financial risk used here differs from that used in our examination of cash and marketable securities management in Chapter 15.

by the firm's use of financial leverage, and such additional variability will be embodied in the variability of earnings available to the common stockholder and earnings per share. If these magnifications are negative, the common stockholder has a higher chance of insolvency than would have existed had the use of fixed-charge securities (debt and preferred stock) been avoided.

In the rest of this chapter we study techniques that permit a precise assessment of the earnings stream variability caused by (1) operating leverage and (2) financial leverage. **Operating leverage** refers to the incurrence of fixed operating costs in the firm's income stream. To understand the nature and importance of operating leverage, we need to draw on the basics of cost-volume-profit analysis, or *breakeven analysis*.

PERSPECTIVE IN FINANCE

The breakeven analysis concepts presented in the next section are often covered in many of your other classes, such as basic accounting principles and managerial economics. This just shows you how important and accepted this tool is within the realm of business decision making. Hotels and motels, for instance, know exactly what their breakeven occupancy rate is. This breakeven occupancy rate gives them an operating target. This operating target, in turn, often becomes a crucial input to the hotel's advertising strategy. You may not want to become a financial manager— but you do want to understand how to compute breakeven points.

■ BREAKEVEN ANALYSIS

The technique of breakeven analysis is familiar to legions of businesspeople. It is usefully applied in a wide array of business settings, including both small and large organizations. This tool is widely accepted by the business community for two reasons: It is based on straightforward assumptions, and companies have found that the information gained from the breakeven model is beneficial in decision-making situations.

Objective and Uses

The objective of *breakeven analysis* is to determine the *breakeven quantity of output* by studying the relationships among the firm's cost structure, volume of output, and profit. Alternatively, the firm ascertains the breakeven level of sales dollars that corresponds to the breakeven quantity of output. We will develop the fundamental relationships by concentrating on units of output and then extend the procedure to permit direct calculation of the breakeven sales level.

What is meant by the breakeven quantity of output? It is that quantity of output, denominated in units, that results in an EBIT level equal to zero. Use of the breakeven model, therefore, enables the financial officer (1) to determine the quantity of output that must be sold to cover all operating costs, as distinct from financial costs, and (2) to calculate the EBIT that will be achieved at various output levels.

Essential Elements of the Breakeven Model

To implement the breakeven model, we must separate the production costs of the company into two mutually exclusive categories: fixed costs and variable costs. You will recall from your study of basic economics that in the long run all costs are variable. Breakeven analysis, therefore, is a short-run concept.

Assumed Behavior of Costs

FIXED COSTS Fixed costs, also referred to as **indirect costs,** do not vary in total amount as sales volume or the quantity of output changes over some *relevant* range of output. Total fixed costs are independent of the quantity of product produced and equal some constant dollar amount. As production volume increases, fixed cost per unit of product falls, as fixed costs are spread over larger and larger quantities of output. Figure 12–3 graphs the behavior of total fixed costs with respect to the company's relevant range of output. This total is shown to be unaffected by the quantity of product that is manufactured and sold. Over some other relevant output range, the amount of total fixed costs might be higher or lower for the same company.

In a manufacturing setting, some specific examples of fixed costs are

1. Administrative salaries
2. Depreciation
3. Insurance
4. Lump sums spent on intermittent advertising programs
5. Property taxes
6. Rent

VARIABLE COSTS Variable costs are sometimes referred to as **direct costs.** Variable costs are fixed per unit of output but vary in total as output changes. Total variable costs are computed by taking the variable cost per unit and multiplying it by the quantity produced and sold. The breakeven model assumes proportionality between total variable costs

FIGURE 12–3
Fixed-Cost Behavior over
Relevant Range of Output

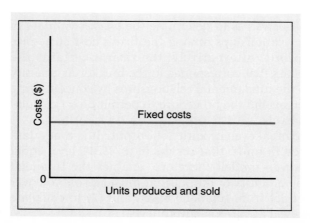

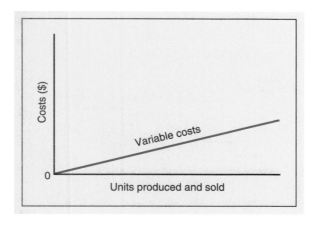

FIGURE 12–4
Variable-Cost Behavior over
Relevant Range of Output

and sales. Thus, if sales rise by 10 percent, it is assumed that variable costs will rise by 10 percent. Figure 12–4 graphs the behavior of total variable costs with respect to the company's relevant range of output. Total variable costs are seen to depend on the quantity of product that is manufactured and sold. Notice that if zero units of the product are manufactured, then variable costs are zero, but fixed costs are greater than zero. This implies that some contribution to the coverage of fixed costs occurs as long as the selling price per unit exceeds the variable cost per unit. This helps explain why some firms will operate a plant even when sales are *temporarily* depressed—that is, to provide some increment of revenue toward the coverage of fixed costs.

For a manufacturing operation, some examples of variable costs include

1. Direct labor
2. Direct materials
3. Energy costs (fuel, electricity, natural gas) associated with the production area
4. Freight costs for products leaving the plant
5. Packaging
6. Sales commissions

MORE ON BEHAVIOR OF COSTS   No one really believes that *all* costs behave as neatly as we have illustrated the fixed and variable costs in Figures 12–3 and 12–4. Nor does any law or accounting principle dictate that a certain element of the firm's total costs always be classified as fixed or variable. This will depend on each firm's specific circumstances. In one firm energy costs may be predominantly fixed, whereas in another they may vary with output.[3]

---

[3]In a greenhouse operation, where plants are grown (manufactured) under strictly controlled temperatures, heat costs will tend to be fixed whether the building is full or only half full of seedlings. In a metal stamping operation, where levers are being produced, there is no need to heat the plant to as high a temperature when the machines are stopped and the workers are not there. In this latter case, the heat costs will tend to be variable.

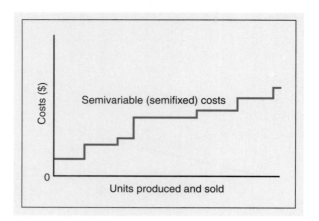

Furthermore, some costs may be fixed for a while, then rise sharply to a higher level as a higher output is reached, remain fixed, and then rise again with further increases in production. Such costs may be termed either (1) **semivariable** or (2) **semifixed.** The label is your choice, because both are used in industrial practice. An example might be the salaries paid production supervisors. Should output be cut back by 15 percent for a short period, the management of the organization is not likely to lay off 15 percent of the supervisors. Similarly, commissions paid to salespeople often follow a stepwise pattern over wide ranges of success. This sort of cost behavior is shown in Figure 12–5.

To implement the breakeven model and deal with such a complex cost structure, the financial manager must (1) identify the most relevant output range for planning purposes and then (2) approximate the cost effect of semivariable items over this range by segregating a portion of them to fixed costs and a portion to variable costs. In the actual business setting this procedure is not fun. It is not unusual for the analyst who deals with the figures to spend considerably more time allocating costs to fixed and variable categories than in carrying out the actual breakeven calculations.

Total Revenue and Volume of Output

Besides fixed and variable costs, the essential elements of the breakeven model include total revenue from sales and volume of output. **Total revenue** means sales dollars and is equal to the selling price per unit multiplied by the quantity sold. The **volume of output** refers to the firm's level of operations and may be indicated either as a unit quantity or as sales dollars.

Finding the Breakeven Point

Finding the breakeven point in terms of units of production can be accomplished in several ways. All approaches require the essential elements of the breakeven model just described. The breakeven model is a simple adaptation of the firm's income statement expressed in the following analytical format:

$$\text{sales} - (\text{total variable cost} + \text{total fixed cost}) = \text{profit} \quad \textbf{(12–1)}$$

On a units of production basis, it is necessary to introduce (1) the price at which each unit is sold and (2) the variable cost per unit of output. Because the profit item studied in breakeven analysis is EBIT, we will use that acronym instead of the word "profit." In terms of units, the income statement shown in equation (12–1) becomes the breakeven model by setting EBIT equal to zero:

$$\binom{\text{sales price}}{\text{per unit}}\binom{\text{units}}{\text{sold}} - \left[\binom{\text{variable cost}}{\text{per unit}}\binom{\text{units}}{\text{sold}}\right. \quad \textbf{(12–2)}$$
$$\left. + \binom{\text{total fixed}}{\text{cost}}\right] = \text{EBIT} = \$0$$

Our task now becomes finding the number of units that must be produced and sold in order to satisfy equation (12–2) — that is, to arrive at an EBIT = \$0. This can be done by (1) contribution-margin analysis or (2) algebraic analysis. Each approach will be illustrated using the same set of circumstances.

Problem Situation

Even though the Pierce Grain Company manufactures several different products, it has observed over a lengthy period that its product mix is rather constant. This allows management to conduct its financial planning by use of a "normal" sales price per unit and "normal" variable cost per unit. The "normal" sales price and variable cost per unit are calculated from the constant product mix. It is like assuming that the product mix is one big product. The selling price is \$10 and the variable cost is \$6. Total fixed costs for the firm are \$100,000 per year. What is the breakeven point in units produced and sold for the company during the coming year?

Contribution-Margin Analysis

The contribution-margin technique permits direct computation of the breakeven quantity of output. The **contribution margin** is the difference between the unit selling price and unit variable costs, as follows:

$$\begin{array}{l}\text{Unit sales price} \\ -\ \underline{\text{Unit variable cost}} \\ =\ \underline{\underline{\text{Unit contribution margin}}}\end{array}$$

The use of the word "contribution" in the present context means contribution to the coverage of fixed operating costs. For the Pierce Grain Company, the unit contribution margin is

Unit sales price	\$10
Unit variable cost	− 6
Unit contribution margin	\$ 4

If the annual fixed costs of \$100,000 are divided by the unit contribution margin of \$4, we find the breakeven quantity of output for Pierce

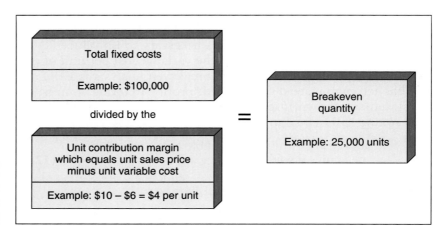

FIGURE 12–6
Contribution-Margin
Approach to Breakeven
Analysis

Grain is 25,000 units. Figure 12–6 portrays the contribution-margin technique for finding the breakeven point.

Algebraic Analysis

To explain the algebraic method for finding the breakeven output level, we need to adopt some notation. Let

Q = the number of units sold
Q_B = the breakeven level of Q
P = the unit sales price
F = total fixed costs anticipated over the planning period
V = the unit variable cost

Equation (12–2), the breakeven model, is repeated below as equation (12–2a) with the model symbols used in place of words. The breakeven model is then solved for Q, the number of units that must be sold in order that EBIT will equal $0. We label the breakeven point quantity Q_B.

$$(P \cdot Q) - [(V \cdot Q) + (F)] = \text{EBIT} = \$0 \qquad \textbf{(12–2a)}$$
$$(P \cdot Q) - (V \cdot Q) - F = \$0$$
$$Q(P - V) = F$$

$$Q_B = \frac{F}{P - V} \qquad \textbf{(12–3)}$$

Observe that equation (12–3) says: Divide total fixed operating costs, F, by the unit contribution margin, $P - V$, and the breakeven level of output, Q_B, will be obtained. The contribution margin analysis is nothing more than equation (12–3) in different garb.

Application of equation (12–3) permits direct calculation of Pierce Grain's breakeven point, as follows:

$$Q_B = \frac{F}{P - V} = \frac{\$100,000}{\$10 - \$6} = 25,000 \text{ units}$$

TABLE 12–1
Pierce Grain Company
Analytical Income Statement

Sales	$300,000
Less: Total variable costs	180,000
Revenue before fixed costs	$120,000
Less: Total fixed costs	100,000
EBIT	$ 20,000

Breakeven Point in Sales Dollars

In dealing with the multiproduct firm, it is convenient to compute the breakeven point in terms of sales dollars rather than units of output. Sales, in effect, become a common denominator associated with a particular product mix. Furthermore, an outside analyst may not have access to internal unit cost data. He or she may, however, be able to obtain annual reports for the firm. If the analyst can separate the firm's total costs as identified from its annual reports into their fixed and variable components, he or she can calculate a general breakeven point in sales dollars.

We will illustrate the procedure using the Pierce Grain Company's cost structure. Suppose that the reported financial information is arranged in the format shown in Table 12–1. We will refer to this type of financial statement as an **analytical income statement.** This distinguishes it from audited income statements published, for example, in the annual reports of public corporations. If we are aware of the simple mathematical relationships on which cost-volume-profit analysis is based, we can use Table 12–1 to find the breakeven point in sales dollars for the Pierce Grain Company.

First, let us explore the logic of the process. Recall from equation (12–1) that

$$\text{sales} - (\text{total variable cost} + \text{total fixed cost}) = \text{EBIT}$$

If we let total sales = S, total variable cost = VC, and total fixed cost = F, the preceding relationship becomes

$$S - (VC + F) = \text{EBIT}$$

Because variable cost per unit of output and selling price per unit are *assumed* constant over the relevant output range in breakeven analysis, the ratio of total variable costs to sales, VC/S, is a constant for any level of sales. This permits us to rewrite the previous expression as

$$S - \left[\left(\frac{VC}{S} \right) S \right] - F = \text{EBIT}$$

and

$$S \left(1 - \frac{VC}{S} \right) - F = \text{EBIT}$$

At the breakeven point, however, EBIT = 0, and the corresponding breakeven level of sales can be represented as S^*. At the breakeven level of sales, we have

$$S^* \left(1 - \frac{VC}{S} \right) - F = 0$$

or

$$S^* \left(1 - \frac{VC}{S} \right) = F$$

Therefore,

$$S^* = \frac{F}{1 - \dfrac{VC}{S}} \qquad\qquad \textbf{(12–4)}$$

The application of equation (12–4) to Pierce Grain's analytical income statement in Table 12–1 permits the breakeven sales level for the firm to be directly computed, as follows:

$$S^* = \frac{\$100,000}{1 - \dfrac{\$180,000}{\$300,000}}$$

$$= \frac{\$100,000}{1 - .60} = \$250,000$$

■ OPERATING LEVERAGE

If *fixed* operating costs are present in the firm's cost structure, so is *operating leverage*. Fixed operating costs do *not* include interest charges incurred from the firm's use of debt financing. Those costs will be incorporated into the analysis when financial leverage is discussed.

So operating leverage *arises* from the firm's use of fixed operating costs. But what is operating leverage? **Operating leverage** is the responsiveness of the firm's EBIT to fluctuations in sales. By continuing to draw on our data for the Pierce Grain Company, we can illustrate the concept of operating leverage. Table 12–2 contains data for a study of a possible fluctuation in the firm's sales level. It is assumed that Pierce Grain is currently operating at an annual sales level of $300,000. This is referred to in the tabulation as the base sales level at t (time period zero). The question is: How will Pierce Grain's EBIT level respond to a positive 20 percent change in sales? A sales volume of $360,000, referred

TABLE 12–2
Concept of Operating
Leverage: Increase
in Pierce Grain Company Sales

Item	Base Sales Level, t	Forecast Sales Level, t + 1
Sales	$300,000	$360,000
Less: Total variable costs	180,000	216,000
Revenue before fixed costs	$120,000	$144,000
Less: Total fixed costs	100,000	100,000
EBIT	$ 20,000	$ 44,000

to as the forecast sales level at $t + 1$, reflects the 20 percent sales rise anticipated over the planning period. Assume that the planning period is one year.

Operating leverage relationships are derived within the mathematical assumptions of cost-volume-profit analysis. In the present example, this means that Pierce Grain's variable cost-to-sales ratio of .6 will continue to hold during time period $t + 1$, and the fixed costs will hold steady at $100,000.

Given the forecasted sales level for Pierce Grain and its cost structure, we can measure the responsiveness of EBIT to the upswing in volume. Notice in Table 12–2 that EBIT is expected to be $44,000 at the end of the planning period. The percentage change in EBIT from t to $t + 1$ can be measured as follows:

$$\text{percentage change in EBIT} = \frac{\$44,000_{t+1} - \$20,000_t}{\$20,000_t}$$

$$= \frac{\$24,000}{\$20,000}$$

$$= 120\%$$

We know that the projected fluctuation in sales amounts to 20 percent of the base period, t, sales level. This is verified below:

$$\text{percentage change in sales} = \frac{\$360,000_{t+1} - \$300,000_t}{\$300,000_t}$$

$$= \frac{\$60,000}{\$300,000}$$

$$= 20\%$$

By relating the percentage fluctuation in EBIT to the percentage fluctuation in sales, we can calculate a specific measure of operating leverage. Thus, we have

$$\begin{matrix} \text{degree of operating leverage} \\ \text{from the base sales level(s)} \end{matrix} = \text{DOL}_s = \frac{\text{percentage change in EBIT}}{\text{percentage change in sales}} \quad \textbf{(12–5)}$$

Applying equation (12–5) to our Pierce Grain data gives

$$\text{DOL}_{\$300,000} = \frac{120\%}{20\%} = 6 \text{ times}$$

Unless we understand what the specific measure of operating leverage tells us, the fact that we may know it is equal to 6 times is nothing more than sterile information. For Pierce Grain, the inference is that for *any* percentage fluctuation in sales from the base level, the percentage fluctuation in EBIT will be six times as great. If Pierce Grain expected only a 5 percent rise in sales over the coming period, a 30 percent rise in EBIT would be anticipated as follows:

$$(\text{percentage change in sales}) \times (\text{DOL}_s) = \text{percentage change in EBIT}$$
$$(5\%) \times (6) = 30\%$$

Item	Base Sales Level, t	Forecast Sales Level, t + 1
Sales	$300,000	$240,000
Less: Total variable costs	180,000	144,000
Revenue before fixed costs	$120,000	$ 96,000
Less: Total fixed costs	100,000	100,000
EBIT	$ 20,000	$ –4,000

We will now return to the postulated 20 percent change in sales. What if the direction of the fluctuation is expected to be negative rather than positive? What is in store for Pierce Grain? Unfortunately for Pierce Grain, but fortunately for the analytical process, we will see that the operating leverage measure holds in the negative direction as well. This situation is displayed in Table 12–3.

At the $240,000 sales level, which represents the 20 percent decrease from the base period, Pierce Grain's EBIT is expected to be –$4,000. How sensitive is EBIT to this sales change? The magnitude of the EBIT fluctuation is calculated as

$$\text{percentage change in EBIT} = \frac{-\$4,000_{t+1} - \$20,000_t}{\$20,000_t}$$

$$= \frac{-\$24,000}{\$20,000}$$

$$= -120\%$$

Making use of our knowledge that the sales change was equal to –20 percent permits us to compute the specific measure of operating leverage as

$$\text{DOL}_{\$300,000} = \frac{-120\%}{-20\%} = 6 \text{ times}$$

What we have seen, then, is that the degree of operating leverage measure works in the positive or negative direction. A negative change in production volume and sales can be magnified severalfold when the effect on EBIT is calculated.

To this point our calculations of the degree of operating leverage have required two analytical income statements: one for the base period and a second for the subsequent period that incorporates the possible sales alteration. This cumbersome process can be simplified. If unit cost data are available to the financial manager, the relationship can be expressed directly in the following manner:

$$\text{DOL}_s = \frac{Q(P - V)}{Q(P - V) - F} \tag{12–6}$$

Observe in equation (12–6) that the variables were all previously defined in our algebraic analysis of the breakeven model. Recall that

Pierce sells its product at $10 per unit, the unit variable cost is $6, and total fixed costs over the planning horizon are $100,000. Still assuming that Pierce is operating at a $300,000 sales volume, which means output (Q) is 30,000 units, we can find the degree of operating leverage by application of equation (12–6):

$$\text{DOL}_{\$300,000} = \frac{30,000(\$10 - \$6)}{30,000(\$10 - \$6) - \$100,000} = \frac{\$120,000}{\$20,000} = 6 \text{ times}$$

Whereas equation (12–6) requires us to know unit cost data to carry out the computations, the next formulation we examine does not. If we have an analytical income statement for the base period, then equation (12–7) can be employed to find the firm's degree of operating leverage:

$$\text{DOL}_s = \frac{\text{revenue before fixed costs}}{\text{EBIT}} = \frac{S - VC}{S - VC - F} \qquad \textbf{(12–7)}$$

Use of equation (12–7) in conjunction with the base period data for Pierce Grain shown in Table 12–3 gives

$$\text{DOL}_{\$300,000} = \frac{\$120,000}{\$20,000} = 6 \text{ times}$$

The three versions of the operating leverage measure all produce the same result. Data availability will sometimes dictate which formulation can be applied. The crucial consideration, though, is that you grasp what the measurement tells you. For Pierce Grain, a 1 percent change in sales will produce a 6 percent change in EBIT.

PERSPECTIVE IN FINANCE

Before we complete our discussion of operating leverage and move on to the subject of financial leverage, ask yourself, "which type of leverage is more under the control of management?" You will probably (and correctly) come to the conclusion that the firm's managers have less control over its operating cost structure and almost complete control over its financial structure. What the firm actually produces, for example, will determine to a significant degree the division between fixed and variable costs. There is more room for substitution among the various sources of financial capital than there is among the labor and real capital inputs that enable the firm to meet its production requirements. Thus, you can anticipate more arguments over the choice to use a given degree of financial leverage than the corresponding choice over operating leverage use.

Implications

As the firm's scale of operations moves in a favorable manner above the breakeven point, the degree of operating leverage at each subsequent (higher) sales base will decline. In short, the greater the sales level, the lower the degree of operating leverage. As long as some fixed operating costs are present in the firm's cost structure, however, operating leverage exists, and the degree of operating leverage (DOL_s) will exceed 1.00. Operating leverage is present, then, whenever the firm faces the following situation:

$$\frac{\text{percentage change in EBIT}}{\text{percentage change in sales}} > 1.00$$

The greater the firm's degree of operating leverage, the more its profits will vary with a given percentage change in sales. Thus, operating leverage is definitely an attribute of the business risk that confronts the company. We know that the degree of operating leverage falls as sales increase past the firm's breakeven point. The sheer size and operating profitability of the firm, therefore, affect and can lessen its business-risk exposure.

The manager considering an alteration in the firm's cost structure will benefit from an understanding of the operating leverage concept. It might be possible to replace part of the labor force with capital equipment (machinery). A possible result is an increase in fixed costs associated with the new machinery and a reduction in variable costs attributable to a lower labor bill. This conceivably could raise the firm's degree of operating leverage at a specific sales base. If the prospects for future sales increases are high, then increasing the degree of operating leverage might be a prudent decision. The opposite conclusion will be reached if sales prospects are unattractive.

PERSPECTIVE IN FINANCE

As you are introduced to the topic of financial leverage remember that this is one of the most crucial policy areas on which a financial executive spends his or her time. We describe and measure here what happens to the firm's earnings per share when financial risk is assumed. Try to understand this effect. We demonstrate how actually to measure this effect in the next section. By now you should be realizing that variability of all types—be it in an earnings stream or in stock returns—is a central element of financial thought and the practice of financial management.

■ FINANCIAL LEVERAGE

We have defined *financial leverage* as the practice of financing a portion of the firm's assets with securities bearing a fixed rate of return in hope of increasing the ultimate return to the common shareholders. In the present discussion we focus on the responsiveness of the company's earnings per share to changes in its EBIT. For the time being, then, the return to the common stockholder being concentrated on is earnings per share. We are *not* saying that earnings per share is the appropriate criterion for all financing decisions. In fact, the weakness of such a contention will be examined later. Rather, the use of financial leverage produces a certain type of *effect*. This effect can be illustrated clearly by concentrating on an earnings-per-share criterion.

TABLE 12–4
Pierce Grain Company
Possible Financial Structures

Plan A: 0% debt

		Total debt	$ 0
		Common equity	200,000[a]
Total assets	$200,000	Total liabilities and equity	$200,000

Plan B: 25% debt at 8% interest rate

		Total debt	$ 50,000
		Common equity	150,000[b]
Total assets	$200,000	Total liabilities and equity	$200,000

Plan C: 40% debt at 8% interest rate

		Total debt	$ 80,000
		Common equity	120,000[c]
Total assets	$200,000	Total liabilities and equity	$200,000

[a]2,000 common shares outstanding
[b]1,500 common shares outstanding
[c]1,200 common shares outstanding

Let us assume that the Pierce Grain Company is in the process of getting started as a going concern. The firm's potential owners have calculated that $200,000 is needed to purchase the necessary assets to conduct the business. Three possible financing plans have been identified for raising the $200,000; they are presented in Table 12–4. In plan A no financial risk is assumed: The entire $200,000 is raised by selling 2,000 common shares, each with a $100 par value. In plan B a moderate amount of financial risk is assumed: 25 percent of the assets are financed with a debt issue that carries an 8 percent annual interest rate. Plan C would use the most financial leverage: 40 percent of the assets would be financed with a debt issue costing 8 percent.

Table 12–5 presents the impact of financial leverage on earnings per share associated with each fund-raising alternative. If EBIT should increase from $20,000 to $40,000, then earnings per share would rise by 100 percent under plan A. The same positive fluctuation in EBIT would occasion an earnings per share rise of 125 percent under plan B, and 147 percent under plan C. In plans B and C the 100 percent increase in EBIT (from $20,000 to $40,000) is magnified to a greater than 100 percent increase in earnings per share. The firm is employing financial leverage and exposing its owners to financial risk when the following situation exists:

$$\frac{\text{percentage change in earnings per share}}{\text{percentage change in EBIT}} > 1.00$$

By following the same general procedures that allowed us to analyze the firm's use of operating leverage, we can lay out a precise measure of financial leverage. Such a measure deals with the sensitivity of earnings per share to EBIT fluctuations. The relationship can be expressed as

$$\begin{matrix} \text{degree of financial} \\ \text{leverage (DFL) from} = \text{DFL}_{EBIT} = \dfrac{\text{percentage change in earnings per share}}{\text{percentage change in EBIT}} \end{matrix} \quad \text{(12–8)}$$
base EBIT level

(1)	(2)	(3)=(1)−(2)	(4)=(3) ¥.5	(5)=(3)−(4) Net Income to Common	(6) Earnings per Share
EBIT	Interest	EBT	Taxes		
Plan A: 0% debt; $200,000 common equity; 2000 shares					
$ 0	$ 0	$ 0	$ 0	$ 0	$ 0
20,000	0	20,000	10,000	10,000	5.00
40,000	0	40,000	20,000	20,000	10.00
60,000	0	60,000	30,000	30,000	15.00
80,000	0	80,000	40,000	40,000	20.00
Plan B: 25% debt; 8% interest rate; $150,000 common equity; 1500 shares					
$ 0	$ 4,000	$ (4,000)	$(2,000)ᵃ	$(2,000)	$ (1.33)
20,000	4,000	16,000	8,000	8,000	5.33
40,000	4,000	36,000	18,000	18,000	12.00
60,000	4,000	56,000	28,000	28,000	18.67
80,000	4,000	76,000	38,000	38,000	25.33
Plan C: 40% debt; 8% interest rate; $120,000 common equity; 1200 shares					
$ 0	$ 6,400	$ (6,400)	$(3,200)ᵃ	$(3,200)	$ (2.67)
20,000	6,400	13,600	6,800	6,800	5.67
40,000	6,400	33,600	16,800	16,800	14.00
60,000	6,400	53,600	26,800	26,800	22.33
80,000	6,400	73,600	36,800	36,800	30.67

Plan A: 100%
Plan B: 125%
Plan C: 147%

ᵃThe negative tax bill recognizes the credit arising from the carryback and carryforward provision of the tax code.

Use of equation (12–8) with each of the financing choices outlined for Pierce Grain is shown subsequently. The base EBIT level is $20,000 in each case.

$$\text{Plan A:} \quad \text{DFL}_{\$20,000} = \frac{100\%}{100\%} = 1.00 \text{ time}$$

$$\text{Plan A:} \quad \text{DFL}_{\$20,000} = \frac{125\%}{100\%} = 1.25 \text{ times}$$

$$\text{Plan C:} \quad \text{DFL}_{\$20,000} = \frac{147\%}{100\%} = 1.47 \text{ times}$$

Like operating leverage, the *degree of financial leverage* concept performs in the negative direction as well as the positive. Should EBIT fall by 10 percent, the Pierce Grain Company would suffer a 12.5 percent decline in earnings per share under plan B. If plan C were chosen to raise the necessary financial capital, the decline in earnings would be 14.7 percent. Observe that the greater the DFL, the greater the fluctuations (positive or negative) in earnings per share. The common stockholder is required to endure greater variations in returns when the firm's management chooses to use more financial leverage rather than less. The DFL measure allows the variation to be quantified.

Rather than taking the time to compute percentage changes in EBIT and earnings per share, the DFL can be found directly, as follows:

$$\text{DFL}_{EBIT} = \frac{\text{EBIT}}{\text{EBIT} - I} \qquad (12\text{–}9)$$

BASIC FINANCIAL MANAGEMENT IN PRACTICE

Corporate Financial Policies

The fact that financial leverage effects can be measured provides management with the opportunity to shape corporate policy formally around the decision to use or avoid the use of leverage-inducing financial instruments (primarily debt issues). One company with very specific policies on the use of financial leverage is the Coca-Cola Company. The following discussion is from that firm's 1990 *Annual Report*.

Note how several of the key concepts and techniques presented throughout this book are mentioned in this excerpt. For example, mention is made of (1) the firm's primary objective, (2) its weighted average cost of capital, (3) investment risk characteristics, (4) the prudent use of debt capital, and (5) borrowing capacity.

Management's primary objective is to increase shareholder value over time. To accomplish this objective, the Coca-Cola Company and subsidiaries (the Company) have developed a comprehensive business strategy that emphasizes maximizing long-term cash flow by expanding its global business systems, increasing gallon sales, improving margins, investing in areas offering attractive returns and maintaining an appropriate capital structure.

Management seeks investments that strategically enhance existing operations and offer long-term cash returns that exceed the Company's weighted average cost of capital. For investments with risk characteristics similar to the soft drink industry and assuming a net-debt-to-net-capital ratio ceiling of 35 percent, that cost of capital is estimated by management to be approximately 12 percent after taxes.

The Company utilizes prudent amounts of debt to lower its overall cost of capital and increase its total return to shareholders. The Company has established a net-debt-to-net-capital ratio ceiling of 35 percent. Net debt is defined as total debt less excess cash, cash equivalents and current marketable securities. Excluding the Company's finance subsidiary, net debt represented 22.8 percent of net capital at December 31, 1990.

Additional borrowing capacity within the 35 percent debt ceiling was approximately $940 million at December 31, 1990, excluding the Company's finance subsidiary. The Company anticipates using this additional borrowing capacity principally to fund investment opportunities that meet its strategic and financial objectives and, as a second priority, to fund the share repurchase program.

Source: The Coca-Cola Company, *Annual Report*, 1990, pp. 32–34.

In equation (12–9) the variable, I, represents the total interest expense incurred on *all* the firm's contractual debt obligations. If six bonds are outstanding, I is the sum of the interest expense on all six bonds. If the firm has preferred stock in its financial structure, the dividend on such issues must be inflated to a before-tax basis and included in the computation of I.[4] In this latter instance, I is in reality the sum of all fixed financing costs.

Equation (12–9) has been applied to each of Pierce Grain's financing plans (Table 12–5) at a base EBIT level of $20,000. The results are as follows:

---

[4]Suppose (1) preferred dividends of $4,000 are paid annually by the firm and (2) it faces a 40 percent marginal tax rate. How much must the firm earn *before taxes* to make the $4,000 payment out of after-tax earnings? Because preferred dividends are not tax deductible to the paying company, we have $4000/(1 − .40) = $6666.67.

$$\text{Plan A:} \qquad \text{DFL}_{\$20,000} = \frac{\$20,000}{\$20,000 - 0} = 1.00 \text{ time}$$

$$\text{Plan B:} \qquad \text{DFL}_{\$20,000} = \frac{\$20,000}{\$20,000 - \$4000} = 1.25 \text{ times}$$

$$\text{Plan C:} \qquad \text{DFL}_{\$20,000} = \frac{\$20,000}{\$20,000 - \$6400} = 1.47 \text{ times}$$

As you probably suspected, the measures of financial leverage shown previously are identical to those obtained by use of equation (12–8). This will always be the case.

PERSPECTIVE IN FINANCE

The effect on the earnings stream available to the firm's common stockholders from combining operating and financial leverage in large degrees is dramatic. When the use of both leverage types is indeed heavy, a large sales increase will result in a very large rise in earnings per share. Be aware, though, that the very same thing happens in the opposite direction should the sales change be negative! Piling heavy financial leverage use on a high degree of operating leverage, then, is a very risky way to do business. This is why you will find leveraged buyouts are not concentrated in heavy, durable goods industries. The firms in such industries have major (real) capital spending requirements. Rather, the firms favored in leveraged buyouts will be those with comparatively low levels of operating leverage; retail operations are good examples. As a result, many national retail chains and department stores have been involved in leveraged buyouts during the past few years. The leveraged buyout, by its very nature, translates into a high degree of financial leverage use.

■ COMBINATION OF OPERATING AND FINANCIAL LEVERAGE

Changes in sales revenues cause greater changes in EBIT. Additionally, changes in EBIT translate into larger variations in both earnings per share (EPS) and total earnings available to the common shareholders (EAC), if the firm chooses to use financial leverage. It should be no surprise, then, to find out that combining operating and financial leverage causes rather

FIGURE 12–7
Leverage and Earnings
Fluctuations

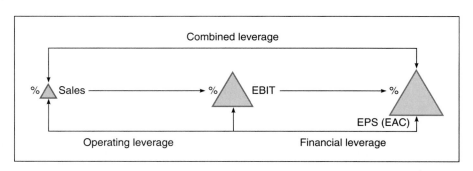

TABLE 12–6
Pierce Grain Company
Combined Leverage Analysis

Item	Base Sales Level, t	Forecast Sales Level, t + 1	Selected Percentage Changes
Sales	$300,000	$360,000	+20
Less: Total variable costs	180,000	216,000	
Revenue before fixed costs	$120,000	$144,000	
Less: Total fixed costs	100,000	100,000	
EBIT	$ 20,000	$ 44,000	+120
Less: Interest expense	4,000	4,000	
Earnings before taxes (EBT)	$ 16,000	$ 40,000	
Less: Taxes at 50%	8,000	20,000	
Net income	$ 8,000	$ 20,000	+150
Less: Preferred dividends	0	0	
Earnings available to common (EAC)	$ 8,000	$ 20,000	+150
Number of common shares	1,500	1,500	
Earnigs per share (EPS)	$ 5.33	$ 13.33	+150

$$\text{Degree of operating leverage } = \text{DOL}_{\$300,000} = \frac{120\%}{20\%} = 6 \text{ times}$$

$$\text{Degree of financial leverage } = \text{DFL}_{\$20,000} = \frac{150\%}{120\%} = 1.25 \text{ times}$$

$$\text{Degree of combined leverage } = \text{DCL}_{\$300,000} = \frac{150\%}{20\%} = 7.50 \text{ times}$$

large variations in earnings per share. This entire process is visually displayed in Figure 12–7.

Because the risk associated with possible earnings per share is affected by the use of combined or total leverage, it is useful to quantify the effect. For an illustration, we refer once more to the Pierce Grain Company. The cost structure identified for Pierce Grain in our discussion of breakeven analysis still holds. Furthermore, assume that plan B, which carried a 25 percent debt ratio, was chosen to finance the company's assets. Turn your attention to Table 12–6.

In Table 12–6 an increase in output for Pierce Grain from 30,000 to 36,000 units is analyzed. This increase represents a 20 percent rise in sales revenues. From our earlier discussion of operating leverage and the data in Table 12–6, we can see that this 20 percent increase in sales is magnified into a 120 percent rise in EBIT. From this base sales level of $300,000 the degree of operating leverage is 6 times.

The 120 percent rise in EBIT induces a change in earnings per share and earnings available to the common shareholders of 150 percent. The degree of financial leverage is therefore 1.25 times.

The upshot of the analysis is that the 20 percent rise in sales has been magnified to 150 percent, as reflected by the percentage change in earnings per share. The formal measure of combined leverage can be expressed as follows:

$$\begin{pmatrix} \text{degree of combined} \\ \text{leverage from the} \\ \text{base sales level} \end{pmatrix} = \text{DCL}_s = \begin{pmatrix} \dfrac{\text{percentage change in}}{\text{earnings per share}} \\ \overline{\text{percentage change in sales}} \end{pmatrix} \quad \textbf{(12–10)}$$

This equation was used in the bottom portion of Table 12–6 to determine that the degree of combined leverage from the base sales level of $300,000 is 7.50 times. Pierce Grain's use of both operating and financial leverage will cause any percentage change in sales (from the specific base level) to be magnified by a factor of 7.50 when the effect on earnings per share is computed. A 1 percent change in sales, for example, will result in a 7.50 percent change in earnings per share.

Notice that the degree of combined leverage is actually the *product* (not the simple sum) of the two independent leverage measures. Thus, we have

$$(\text{DOL}_s) \times (\text{DFL}_{EBIT}) = \text{DCL}_s \quad \textbf{(12–11)}$$

or $\qquad (6) \times (1.25) = 7.50$ times

It is possible to ascertain the degree of combined leverage in a direct fashion, without determining any percentage fluctuations or the separate leverage values. We need only substitute the appropriate values into equation (12–12):[5]

The variable definitions in equation (12–12) are the same ones that have been employed throughout this chapter. Use of equation (12–12) with the information in Table 12–6 gives

$$\begin{aligned} \text{DCL}_{\$300,000} &= \frac{\$30,000(10 - \$6)}{\$30,000(10 - \$6) - \$100,000 - \$4,000} \\ &= \frac{\$120,000}{\$16,000} \\ &= 7.5 \text{ times} \end{aligned}$$

Implications

The total risk exposure the firm assumes can be managed by combining operating and financial leverage in different degrees. Knowledge of the various leverage measures aids the financial officer in determining the proper level of overall risk that should be accepted. If a high degree of business risk is inherent in the specific line of commercial activity, then a low posture regarding financial risk would minimize *additional* earnings fluctuations stemming from sales changes. Conversely, the firm that by its very nature incurs a low level of fixed operating costs might choose to use a high degree of financial leverage in the hope of increasing

---

[5]As was the case with the degree of financial leverage metric, the variable, I in the combined leverage measure must include the before-tax equivalent of any preferred dividend payments when preferred stock is in the financial structure.

$$DLC_s = \frac{Q(P - V)}{Q(P - V) - F - I} \quad \textbf{(12–12)}$$

TABLE 12–7
Summary of Leverage Concepts and Calculations

Technique	Description or Concept	Calculation	Text Reference
Breakeven Analysis			
1. Breakeven point quantity	Total fixed costs divided by the unit contribution margin	$Q_B = \dfrac{F}{P-V}$	(12–3)
2. Breakeven sales level	Total fixed costs divided by 1 minus the ratio of total variable costs to the associated level of sales	$S^* = \dfrac{F}{1 - \dfrac{VC}{S}}$	(12–4)
Operating Leverage			
3. Degree of operating leverage	Percentage change in EBIT divided by the percentage change in sales; or revenue before fixed costs divided by revenue after fixed costs	$DOL_S = \dfrac{Q(P-V)}{Q(P-V)-F}$	(12–6)
Financial Leverage			
4. Degree of financial leverage	Percentage change in earnings per share divided by the percentage change in EBIT; or EBIT divided by EBT.[a]	$DFL_{EBIT} = \dfrac{EBIT}{EBIT - I}$	(12–9)
Combined Leverage			
5. Degree of combined leverage	Percentage change in earnings per share divided by the percentage change in sales; or revenue before fixed costs divided by EBT.[a]	$DCL_S = \dfrac{Q(P-V)}{Q(P-V)-F-I}$	(12–12)

[a]The use of EBT here presumes no preferred dividend payments. In the presence of preferred dividend payments replace EBT with earnings available to common stock (EAC).

earnings per share and the rate of return on the common equity investment. Table 12–7 summarizes the salient concepts and calculation formats discussed thus far in this chapter.

■ PLANNING THE FINANCING MIX

Given our understanding of both operating and financial leverage we now direct our attention to the determination of an appropriate financing mix for the firm. First, we must distinguish between financial structure and capital structure. **Financial structure** is the mix of all items that appear on the right-hand side of the company's balance sheet. **Capital structure** is the mix of the *long-term* sources of funds used by the firm. The relationship between financial and capital structure can be expressed in equation form:

(financial structure) − (current liabilities) = capital structure **(12–13)**

Prudent *financial structure design* requires answers to the following two questions:

1. What should be the maturity composition of the firm's sources of funds; in other words, how should a firm best divide its total fundsources between short- and long-term components?

Taxes and Debt

In the next section we will explore in more detail the theory and practice of financial structure determination. All this means, really, is deciding how to arrange the funds sources that accountants place on the right-hand side of the balance sheet. This is both a controversial and fascinating area of research and financial policy making. Of course, arranging those sources of financial capital should be done with the best interests of the firm's shareholders in mind.

Mr. Frederick T. Furlong, a research officer with the Federal Reserve Bank of San Francisco, discusses the tendency present in our financial system for firms to favor debt financing over common equity financing. Notice his emphasis on the U.S. tax system.

In recent years, nonfinancial corporations have expanded debt and retired equity. This trend towards increased debt has raised concerns that U.S. firms are becoming more vulnerable to an economic downturn. The well-publicized problems of specific high-leveraged corporations have added to this concern, and have led to increases in interest rates on speculative-grade, or junk bonds, which should limit issuance of this type of debt. For most corporations, however, the trend in debt issuance could continue, given the way U.S. tax laws favor debt over equity.

U.S. tax policy generally favors the use of debt over equity financing by corporations. Owners of corporate stock in effect pay taxes on profits twice, once when the corporation pays taxes on its earnings and again when individuals pay taxes on dividends or capital gains. In contrast, interest on debt is a tax-deductible expense for businesses, and so, is taxed only once, as ordinary income to debt holders.

Tax considerations are not the only factors affecting a firm's leverage, or debt/equity mix. For example, the higher risk associated with heavy reliance on debt (relative to equity) tends to limit corporate leverage. By increasing the probability that a firm will not be able to meet promised payments, increased reliance on debt raises expected bankruptcy costs. Because debt holders require compensation for this increased risk, the cost of issuing debt should rise and offset tax benefits (and other factors) favoring debt financing.

In the long run, corporations can be expected to operate with a debt/equity mix that balances these and many other influences. Changes in the tax code that increase the tax advantage of debt financing, then, alter this balance and encourage corporations to increase leverage and realign their debt/equity mix.

It is clear that U.S. tax policy has contributed to higher corporate leverage. It is equally clear that changes in tax policy aimed at reducing the bias toward debt could greatly reduce leverage. Significant changes in the tax laws that would eliminate or reduce taxes on dividends and/or capital gains, however, are not likely in the near future. Without such measures, U.S. tax policy will continue to foster a market environment that is favorable to high corporate leverage.

Source: "Corporate Debt," *Federal Reserve Bank of San Francisco Weekly Letter*, November 24, 1989, pp. 1, 3.

2. In what proportions relative to the total should the various forms of *permanent* financing be utilized?

The major influence on the maturity structure of the financing plan is the nature of the assets owned by the firm. A company heavily committed to real capital investment, represented primarily by fixed assets on its balance sheet, *should* finance those assets with permanent (long-term) types of financial capital. Furthermore, the permanent portion of the firm's investment in current assets should likewise be financed with permanent capital. Alternatively, assets held on a temporary basis are to be

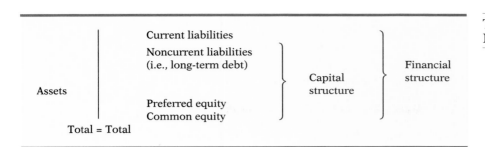

TABLE 12–8
Balance Sheet

financed with temporary sources. The present discussion assumes that the bulk of the company's current liabilities are comprised of temporary capital.

This **hedging concept** is discussed in Chapters 14. Accordingly, our focus in this chapter is on answering the second of the two questions noted previously—this process is usually called *capital-structure management.*

The *objective* of capital-structure management is to mix the permanent sources of funds used by the firm in a manner that will maximize the company's common stock price. Alternatively, this objective may be viewed as a search for the funds mix that will minimize the firm's composite cost of capital. We can call this proper mix of funds sources the **optimal capital structure.**

Table 12–8 looks at equation (12–13) in terms of a simplified balance sheet format. It helps us visualize the overriding problem of capital structure management. The sources of funds that give rise to financing fixed costs (long-term debt and preferred equity) must be combined with common equity in the proportions most suitable to the investing marketplace. If that mix can be found, then holding all other factors constant, the firm's common stock price will be maximized.

Although equation (12–13) quite accurately indicates that the corporate capital structure may be viewed as an absolute dollar *amount,* the *real* capital structure problem is one of balancing the array of funds sources in a proper manner. Our use of the term *capital structure* emphasizes this latter problem of relative magnitude, or proportions.

The rest of this chapter will cover three main areas. First, we briefly discuss the theory of capital structure to provide a perspective. Second, we examine the basic tools of capital structure management. We conclude with a real-world look at actual capital structure management.

PERSPECTIVE IN FINANCE

It pays to understand the essential components of capital structure theory. The assumption of excessive financial risk can put the firm into bankruptcy proceedings. Some argue that the decision to use little financial leverage results in an undervaluation of the firm's shares in the marketplace. The effective financial manager must know how to find the area of optimum financial leverage use—this will enhance share value, all other considerations held constant. Thus, grasping the theory will make you better able to formulate a sound financial structure policy.

BASIC FINANCIAL MANAGEMENT IN PRACTICE

Financing Mix and Corporate Strategy

It is important to understand the basics of capital structure theory because the choice of an appropriate *financing mix* is a central component of overall business strategy. The theory, then, affects strategy.

This is illustrated in the following excerpt from the 1985 annual report published by the Coca-Cola Company. Notice how the concepts of *financial leverage* and *debt capacity* are woven into the discussion.

In the financial arena, the Coca-Cola Company is pursuing a more aggressive policy. We are using greater financial leverage whenever strategic investment opportunities are available. We are reinvesting a larger portion of our earnings by increasing dividends at a lesser rate than earnings per share growth. We

are maintaining our effective income tax rate at a level well below our historical rate. And, we are continuing to repurchase our common shares when excess cash or debt capacity exceed near-term investment requirements.

Another principle in our strategy requires us to consider divesting assets when they no longer generate acceptable returns and earnings growth or are inconsistent with our focus on consumer products. Accordingly, over the last five years we have sold a wine business, a private-label instant coffee and tea unit, a boiler and industrial water purification subsidiary, a regional pasta operation and private-label plastic products businesses.

Source: The Coca-Cola Company, *Annual Report*, 1985, p. 6.

◼◼ A QUICK LOOK AT CAPITAL STRUCTURE THEORY

An enduring controversy within financial theory concerns the effect of financial leverage on the overall cost of capital to the enterprise. The heart of the argument may be stated in the form of a question:

> Can the firm affect its overall cost of funds, either favorably or unfavorably, by varying the mixture of financing sources used?

This controversy has taken many elegant forms in the finance literature. Most of these presentations appeal more to academics than financial management practitioners. To emphasize the ingredients of capital structure theory that have practical applications for business financial management, we will pursue an intuitive, or nonmathematical, approach to reach a better understanding of the underpinnings of this *cost of capital-capital structure argument*.

The Importance of Capital Structure

It makes economic sense for the firm to strive to minimize the cost of using financial capital. Both capital costs and other costs, such as manufacturing costs, share a common characteristic in that they potentially reduce the size of the cash dividend that could be paid to common stockholders.

We saw in Chapters 7 and 8 that the ultimate value of a share of common stock depends in part on the returns investors expect to receive from holding the stock. Cash dividends comprise all (in the case of an infinite holding period) or part (in the case of a holding period less than infinity) of these expected returns. Now, hold constant all factors that could affect share price except capital costs. If these capital costs could be kept at a minimum, the dividend stream flowing to the common stockholders would be maximized. This, in turn, would maximize the firm's common stock price.

If the firm's cost of capital can be affected by its capital structure, then capital structure management is clearly an important subset of business financial management.

Analytical Setting

The essentials of the capital structure controversy are best highlighted within a framework that economists would call a "partial equilibrium analysis." In a partial equilibrium analysis changes that *do* occur in several factors and have an impact on a certain key item are ignored to study the effect of changes in a main factor on that same item of interest. Here, two items are simultaneously of interest: (1) K_o, the firm's composite cost of capital, and (2) P_0, the market price of the firm's common stock. The firm's use of financial leverage is the main factor that is allowed to vary in the analysis. This means that important financial decisions, such as investing policy and dividend policy, are held constant throughout the discussion. We are only concerned with the effect of changes in the financing mix on share price and capital costs.

Consider a rarified economic world where:

1. Corporate income is not subject to taxation
2. Capital structures consist only of stock and bonds
3. Investors make homogeneous forecasts of net operating income (what we earlier called "EBIT")
4. Securities are traded in perfect or efficient markets

In this market setting the direct answer to our question, "Can the firm affect its overall cost of funds, either favorably or unfavorably, by varying the mixture of financing sources used?" would be **no.** This view of capital structure importance was put into rather elegant form back in 1958 by two well-known financial economists, Franco Modigliani and Merton Miller, both of whom have been awarded the Nobel Prize in economics.

The Modigliani and Miller hypothesis, or the MM view, puts forth that within the perfect economic world described above, the total market value of the firm's outstanding securities will be *unaffected* by the manner in which the right-hand side of the balance sheet is arranged. This means the sum of the market value of outstanding common stock will always be the same regardless of how much or little debt is actually used by the company. This MM view is sometimes called the **independence hypothesis,** as firm value is independent of capital structure design.[6]

---

[6]See Franco Modigliani and Merton H. Miller, "The Cost of Capital, Corporation Finance and the Theory of Investment," *American Economic Review* 48 (June 1958), pp. 261–97; Modigliani and Miller, "Corporate Income Taxes and the Cost of Capital: A Correction," *American Economic Review* 53 (June 1963), pp. 433–43; and Merton H. Miller, "Debt and Taxes," *Journal of Finance* 32 (May 1977), pp. 261–75.

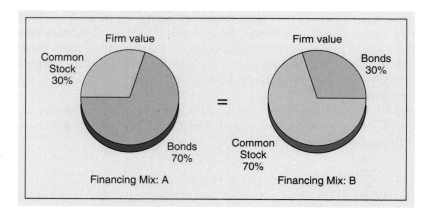

FIGURE 12–8
Firm Value and Capital
Structure Design

The crux of this position on financing choice is illustrated in Figure 12–8. Here the firm's asset mix (i.e., the left-hand side of the balance sheet) is held constant. All that is different is the way the assets are financed. Under Financing Mix A, the firm funds 30 percent of its assets with common stock and the other 70 percent with bonds. Under Financing Mix B, the firm reverses this mix and funds 70 percent of the assets with common stock and only 30 percent with bonds. From our earlier discussions we know that Financing Mix A is the more heavily levered plan.

Notice, however, that the size of each "pie" in Figure 12–8 is exactly the same. The pie represents firm value—the total market value of the firm's outstanding securities. Thus, total firm value associated with Financing Mix A equals that associated with Financing Mix B. Firm value is *independent* of the actual financing mix that has been chosen.

This implication is taken further in Figures 12–9 and 12–10. They display how (1) the firm's cost of funds and (2) common stock price, P_o, relate to the firm's financing mix. In Figure 12–9 we see that the firm's overall cost of capital, K_o, is unaffected by an increased use of financial

FIGURE 12–9
Capital Costs and Financial
Leverage: No Taxes —
Independence Hypothesis

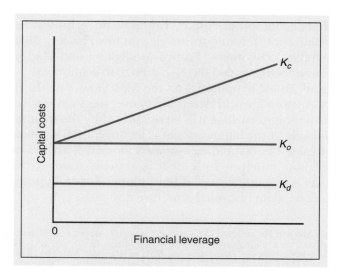

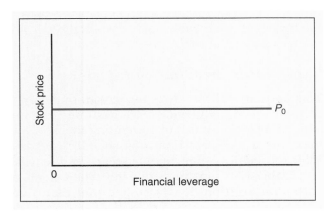

FIGURE 12–10
Stock Price and Financial
Leverage: No Taxes —
Independence Hypothesis

leverage. If more debt is used with a cost of K_d in the capital structure, the cost of common equity, k_c, will rise at the same rate additional earnings are generated. This will keep the composite cost of capital to the corporation unchanged. Figure 12–10 shows that because the overall cost of capital will not change with the leverage use, neither will the firm's common stock price.

The lesson of this view on financing choices is that debt financing is not as cheap as it first appears to be. This will keep the composite cost of funds constant over the full range of financial leverage use. The stark implication for financial officers is that one capital structure is just as good as any other.

Recall, though, the strict economic world in which this viewpoint was developed. We will turn next to a market and legal environment that relaxes the extreme assumptions.

BACK TO THE FUNDAMENTALS

The suggestion from capital structure theory that one capital structure is just as good as any other within a perfect ("pure") market framework relies directly on **Axiom 1: The Risk-Return Tradeoff—We Won't Take on Added Risk Unless We Expect to Be Compensated with Additional Return.** This means that using more debt in the capital structure will not be ignored by investors in the financial markets. These rational investors will require a higher return on common stock investments in the firm that uses more leverage (rather than less), to compensate for the increased uncertainty stemming from the addition of the debt securities in the capital structure.

Moderate Position: Corporate Income Is Taxed and Firms May Fail

We turn now to a description of the cost of capital-capital structure relationship that has rather wide appeal to both business practitioners and academics. This moderate view (1) admits to the fact that interest expense is tax deductible and (2) acknowledges that the probability of the firm's suffering bankruptcy costs is directly related to the company's use of financial leverage.

Tax Deductibility of Interest Expense

This portion of the analysis recognizes that corporate income is subject to taxation. Furthermore, we assume that interest expense is tax deductible for purposes of computing the firm's tax bill. In this environment the use of debt financing should result in a higher total market value for the firm's outstanding securities. We will see why subsequently.

Table 12–9 illustrates this important element of the U.S. system of corporate taxation. It is assumed that Skip's Camper Manufacturing Company has an expected level of net operating income (EBIT) of $2,000,000 and faces a corporate tax rate (made simple for example purposes) of 50 percent. Two financing plans are analyzed. The first is an unlevered capital structure. The other assumes that Skip's Camper has $8 million of bonds outstanding that carry an interest rate of 6 percent per year.

Notice that if corporate income is *not* taxed then earnings before taxes of $2,000,000 per year could be paid to shareholders in the form of cash dividends or to bond investors in the form of interest payments, or any combination of the two. This means that the *sum* of the cash flows that Skip's Camper could pay to its contributors of debt or equity is *not* affected by its financing mix.

When corporate income is taxed by the government, however, the sum of the cash flows made to all contributors of financial capital *is affected* by the firm's financing mix. Table 12–9 illustrates this point.

If Skip's Camper chooses the levered capital structure, the total payments to equity and debt holders will be $240,000 *greater* than under the all-common-equity capitalization. Where does this $240,000 come from? The government's take, through taxes collected, is lower by that amount. This difference, which flows to the Skip's Camper security holders, is called the **tax shield** on interest. In general, it may be calculated by equation (12–14), where r_d is the interest rate paid on the debt, M is the principal amount of the debt, and t is the firm's marginal tax rate:

$$\text{tax shield} = r_d\,(M)(t) \qquad\qquad \textbf{(12–14)}$$

TABLE 12–9
Skip's Camper Company Cash Flows to All Investors — The Case of Taxes

	Unlevered Capital Structure	Levered Capital Structure
Expected level of net operating income	$2,000,000	$2,000,000
Less: Interest expense	0	480,000
Earnings before taxes	$2,000,000	$1,520,000
Less: Taxes at 50%	1,000,000	760,000
Earnings available to common stockholders	$1,000,000	$ 760,000
Expected payments to *all* security holders	$1,000,000	$1,240,000

The moderate position on the importance of capital structure presumes that the tax shield must have value in the marketplace. Accordingly, this tax benefit will increase the total market value of the firm's outstanding securities relative to the all-equity capitalization. Financial leverage does affect firm value. Because the cost of capital is just the other side of the valuation coin, financial leverage also affects the firm's composite cost of capital. Can the firm increase firm value indefinitely and lower its cost of capital continuously by using more and more financial leverage? Common sense would tell us "No"! So would most financial managers and academicians. The acknowledgment of bankruptcy costs provides one possible rationale.

BACK TO THE FUNDAMENTALS

The section above on the "Tax Deductibility of Interest Expense" is a compelling example of **Axiom 8: Taxes Bias Business Decisions.** We have just seen that corporations have an important incentive provided by the tax code to finance projects with debt securities rather than new issues of common stock. The interest expense on the debt issue will be tax deductible. The common stock dividends will not be tax deductible. So firms can indeed increase their total after-tax cash flows available to all investors in their securities by using financial leverage. This element of the U.S. tax code should also remind you of **Axiom 3: Cash is King.**

The Likelihood of Firm Failure

The probability that the firm will be unable to meet the financial obligations identified in its debt contracts increases as more debt is employed. The highest costs would be incurred if the firm actually went into bankruptcy proceedings. Here, assets would be liquidated. If we admit that these assets might sell for something less than their perceived market values, both equity investors and debt holders could suffer losses. Other problems accompany bankruptcy proceedings. Lawyers and accountants have to be hired and paid. Managers must spend time preparing lengthy reports for those involved in the legal action.

Milder forms of financial distress also have their costs. As their firm's financial condition weakens, creditors may take action to restrict normal business activity. Suppliers may not deliver materials on credit. Profitable capital investments may have to be forgone, and dividend payments may even be interrupted. At some point the expected cost of default will be large enough to outweigh the tax shield advantage of debt financing. The firm will turn to other sources of financing, mainly common equity. At this point the real cost of debt is thought to be higher than the real cost of common equity.

Moderate View: Saucer-Shaped Cost of Capital Curve

This moderate view of the relationship between financing mix and the firm's cost of capital is depicted in Figure 12–11. The result is a saucer-shaped (or U-shaped) average cost of capital curve, K_o. The firm's aver-

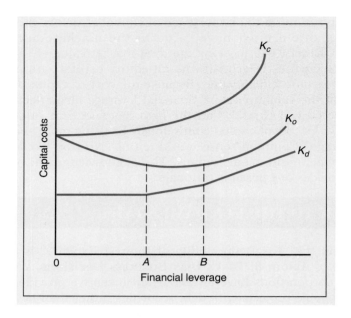

FIGURE 12–11
Capital Costs and Financial
Leverage: The Moderate View,
Considering Taxes and
Financial Distress

age cost of equity, K_c, is seen to rise over all positive degrees of financial leverage use. For a while the firm can borrow funds at a relatively low after-tax cost of debt, K_d. Even though the cost of equity is rising, it does not rise at a fast enough rate to offset the use of the less expensive debt financing. Thus, between points 0 and A on the financial-leverage axis, the average cost of capital declines and stock price rises.

Eventually, the threat of financial distress causes the cost of debt to rise. In Figure 12–11 this increase in the cost of debt shows up in the after-tax average cost of debt curve, K_d, at point A. Between points A and B, mixing debt and equity funds produces an average cost of capital that is (relatively) flat. The firm's **optimal range of financial leverage** lies between points A and B. All capital structures between these two points are *optimal* because they produce the lowest composite cost of capital. As we said earlier in this chapter, finding this optimal range of financing mixes is the *objective of capital structure management.*

Point B signifies the firm's debt capacity. **Debt capacity** is the maximum proportion of debt the firm can include in its capital structure and still maintain its lowest composite cost of capital. Beyond point B, additional fixed-charge capital can be attracted only at very costly interest rates. At the same time, this excessive use of financial leverage would cause the firm's cost of equity to rise at a faster rate than previously. The composite cost of capital would then rise quite rapidly, and the firm's stock price would decline.

PERSPECTIVE IN FINANCE

Given the same task or assignment, it is quite likely that you will do it better for yourself than for someone else. If you are paid well enough, you might do the job about as effectively for that other person. Once you receive compensation, your work will be evaluated by someone. This process of evaluation is called "monitoring" within most discussions on agency costs.

This describes the heart of what is called the "agency problem." As American businesses have grown, the owners and managers have become (for the most part) separate groups of individuals. An inherent conflict exists, therefore, between managers and shareholders for whom managers act as agents in carrying out their objectives (for example, corporate goals). The following discussion relates the agency problem to the financial decision-making process of the firm.

Firm Value and Agency Costs

In Chapter 1 of this text we mentioned *the agency problem.* Recall that the agency problem gives rise to *agency costs*, which tend to occur in business organizations because ownership and management control are often separate. Thus, the firm's managers can be properly thought of as agents for the firm's stockholders.[7] To ensure that agent-managers act in the stockholders' best interests requires that they have (1) proper incentives to do so and (2) their decisions are monitored. The incentives usually take the form of executive compensation plans and perquisites. The perquisites, though, might be a bloated support staff, country club memberships, luxurious corporate planes, or other amenities. Monitoring requires that certain costs be borne by the stockholders, such as (1) bonding the managers, (2) auditing financial statements, (3) structuring the organization in unique ways that limit useful managerial decisions, and (4) reviewing the costs and benefits of management perquisites. This list is indicative, not exhaustive. The main point is that monitoring costs are ultimately covered by the owners of the company—its common stockholders.

Capital structure management *also* gives rise to agency costs. Agency problems stem from conflicts of interest, and capital structure management encompasses a natural conflict between stockholders and bondholders. Acting in the stockholders' best interests might cause management to invest in extremely risky projects. Existing investors in the firm's bonds could logically take a dim view of such an investment policy. A change in the risk structure of the firm's assets would change the business risk exposure of the firm. This could lead to a downward revision of the bond rating the firm currently enjoys. A lowered bond rating in turn would lower the current market value of the firm's bonds. Clearly, bondholders would be unhappy with this result.

To reduce this conflict of interest, the creditors (bond investors) and stockholders may agree to include several protective covenants in the bond contract. These bond covenants are discussed in more detail in

---

[7]Economists have studied the problems associated with control of the corporation for decades. An early, classic work on this topic was A. A. Berle, Jr., and G. C. Means, *The Modern Corporation and Private Property* (New York: Macmillan, 1932). The recent emphasis in corporate finance and financial economics stems from the important contribution of Michael C. Jensen and William H. Meckling, "Theory of the Firm: Managerial Behavior, Agency Costs and Ownership Structure," *Journal of Financial Economics* 3 (October 1976), pp. 305–60. Professors Jensen and Clifford Smith have analyzed the bondholder—stockholder conflict in a very clear style. See Michael C. Jensen and Clifford W. Smith, Jr., "Stockholder, Manager, and Creditor Interests: Applications of Agency Theory," in Edward I. Altman and Marti G. Subrahmanyam, eds., *Recent Advances in Corporate Finance* (Homewood, IL: Richard D. Irwin, 1985), pp. 93–131.

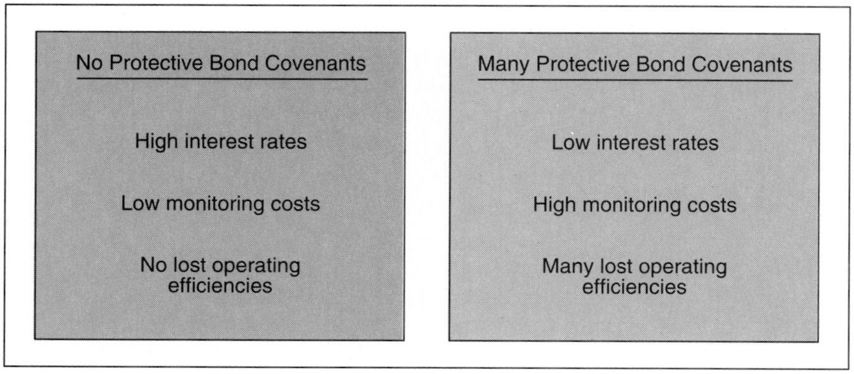

No Protective Bond Covenants	Many Protective Bond Covenants
High interest rates	Low interest rates
Low monitoring costs	High monitoring costs
No lost operating efficiencies	Many lost operating efficiencies

FIGURE 12–12
Agency Costs of Debt:
Tradeoffs

Chapter 6, but essentially they may be thought of as restrictions on managerial decision making. Typical covenants restrict payment of cash dividends on common stock, limit the acquisition or sale of assets, or limit further debt financing. To make sure management complies with the protective covenants means that monitoring costs are incurred. Like all monitoring costs, they are borne by common stockholders. Furthermore, like many costs, they involve the analysis of an important tradeoff.

Figure 12–12 displays some of the tradeoffs involved with the use of protective bond covenants. Note (in the left panel of Figure 12–12) that the firm might be able to sell bonds that carry no protective covenants only by incurring very high interest rates. With no protective covenants, there are no associated monitoring costs. Also, there are no lost operating efficiencies, such as being able to move quickly to acquire a particular company in the acquisitions market. Conversely, the willingness to submit to several covenants could reduce the explicit cost of the debt contract, but would involve incurring significant monitoring costs and losing some operating efficiencies (which also translates into higher costs). When the debt issue is first sold, then, a tradeoff will be arrived at among incurring monitoring costs, losing operating efficiencies, and enjoying a lower explicit interest cost.

Next, we have to consider the presence of monitoring costs at low and higher levels of leverage. When the firm operates at a low debt-to-equity ratio, there is little need for creditors to insist on a long list of bond covenants. The financial risk is just not there to require that type of activity. The firm will likewise benefit from low explicit interest rates when leverage is low. When the debt-to-equity ratio is high, however, it is logical for creditors to demand a great deal of monitoring. This increase in agency costs will raise the implicit cost (the true total cost) of debt financing. It seems logical, then, to suggest that monitoring costs will rise as the firm's use of financial leverage increases. Just as the likelihood of firm failure (financial distress) raises a company's overall cost of capital (K_o), so do agency costs. On the other side of the coin, this means that total firm value (the total market value of the firm's securities) will be *lower* owing to the presence of agency costs. Taken together, the presence of agency costs and the costs associated

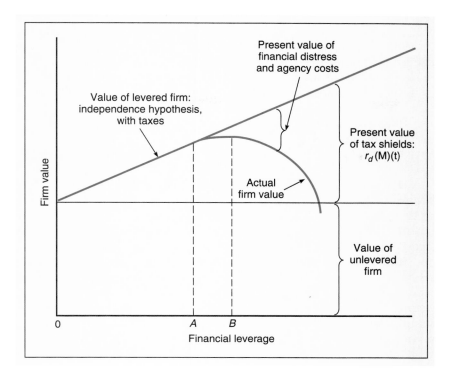

FIGURE 12–13
Firm Value Considering
Taxes, Agency Costs, and
Financial Distress Costs

with financial distress argue in favor of the concept of an *optimal* capital structure for the individual firm.

This discussion can be summarized by introducing equation (12–15) for the market value of the levered firm.

$$
\begin{aligned}
\text{market value of} \atop \text{levered firm} &= \text{market value of} \atop \text{unlevered firm} + \text{present value} \atop \text{of tax shields} \\
&- \left(\text{present value} \atop \text{of financial} \atop \text{distress costs} + \text{present value} \atop \text{of agency} \atop \text{costs} \right)
\end{aligned}
\qquad \textbf{(12–15)}
$$

The relationship expressed in equation (12–15) is presented graphically in Figure 12–13. There we see that the tax shield effect is dominant until point *A* is reached. After point *A*, the rising costs of the likelihood of firm failure (financial distress) and agency costs cause the market value of the levered firm to decline. The *objective* for the financial manager here is to find point *B* by using all of his or her analytical skill; this must also include a good dose of seasoned judgment. At point *B* the actual market value of the levered firm is maximized, and its composite cost of capital (K_o) is at a minimum. The implementation problem is that the precise costs of financial distress and monitoring can only be estimated by subjective means; a definite mathematical solution is not available. Thus, planning the firm's financing mix always requires good decision-making and management judgment.

In 1986, Professor Michael C. Jensen further extended the concept of agency costs into the area of capital structure management. The contribution revolves around a concept that Jensen labels "free cash flow."

Jensen defines free cash flow as follows:[8]

> Free cash flow is cash flow in excess of that required to fund all projects that have positive net present values when discounted at the relevant cost of capital.

Jensen then proposes that substantial free cash flow can lead to misbehavior by managers and poor decisions that are *not* in the best interests of the firm's common stockholders. In other words, managers have an incentive to hold on to the free cash flow and have "fun" with it, rather than "disgorging" it, say, in the form of higher cash dividend payments.

But all is not lost. This leads to what Jensen calls his "control hypothesis" for debt creation. This means that by levering up, the firm's shareholders will enjoy increased control over their management team. For example, if the firm issues new debt and uses the proceeds to retire outstanding common stock, then management is obligated to pay out cash to service the debt—this simultaneously reduces the amount of free cash flow available to management with which to have fun.

We can also refer to this motive for financial leverage use as the "threat hypothesis." Management works under the threat of financial failure, therefore, according to the "free cash flow theory of capital structure," it works more efficiently. This is supposed to reduce the agency costs of free cash flow, which will in turn be recognized by the marketplace in the form of greater returns on the common stock.

BACK TO THE FUNDAMENTALS

The discussions on agency costs, free cash flow and the control hypothesis for debt creation return us to **Axiom 7: The Agency Problem— Managers Won't Work for the Owners Unless It's in Their Best Interest.** The control hypothesis put forth by Jensen suggests that managers will work harder for shareholder interests when they have to "sweat it out" to meet contractual interest payments on debt securities. But we also learned that managers and bond investors can have a conflict that leads to agency costs associated with using debt capital. Thus, the theoretical benefits that flow from minimizing the agency costs of free cash flow by using more debt will cease when the rising agency costs of debt exactly offset those benefits. You can see how very difficult it is, then, for financial managers to identify precisely their true optimal capital structure.

[8]Michael C. Jensen, "Agency Costs of Free Cash Flow, Corporate Finance, and Takeovers," *American Economic Review* 76 (May 1986), pp. 323–29.

Note that the *free cash flow theory of capital structure* does not give a theoretical solution to the question of just how much financial leverage is enough. Nor does it suggest how much leverage is too much leverage. It is a way of thinking about why shareholders and their boards of directors might use more debt to control management behavior and decisions. The basic decision tools of capital structure management still have to be utilized. They will be presented later in this chapter.

Managerial Implications

Where does our examination of capital structure theory leave us? The upshot is that the determination of the firm's financing mix is centrally important to the financial manager. The firm's stockholders are affected by capital structure decisions.

At the very least, and before bankruptcy costs and agency costs become detrimental, the tax shield effect will cause the shares of a levered firm to sell at a higher price than they would if the company had avoided debt financing. Owing to both the risk of failure and agency costs that accompany the excessive use of leverage, the financial manager must exercise caution in the use of fixed-charge capital. This problem of searching for the optimal range of use of financial leverage is our next task.[9]

PERSPECTIVE IN FINANCE

You have now developed a workable knowledge of capital structure theory. This makes you better equipped to search for your firm's optimal capital structure. Several tools are available to help you in this search process and simultaneously help you make prudent financing choices. These tools are decision oriented. They assist us in answering this question: "The next time we need $20 million, should we issue common stock or sell long-term bonds?"

■ BASIC TOOLS OF CAPITAL STRUCTURE MANAGEMENT

Recall from our earlier work that the use of financial leverage has two effects on the earnings stream flowing to the firm's common stockholders. For clarity of exposition Tables 12–4 and 12–5 are repeated here as Tables 12–10 and 12–11. Three possible financing mixes for the Pierce Grain Company are contained in Table 12–10, and an analysis of the corresponding financial leverage effects is displayed in Table 12–11.

The *first financial leverage effect* is the added variability in the earnings-per-share stream that accompanies the use of fixed-charge securities in the company's capital structure. By means of the degree-of-financial-leverage measure (DFL_{EBIT}) we explained how this variability can be

---

[9]The relationship between capital structure and enterprise valuation by the marketplace continues to stimulate considerable research output. The complexity of the topic is reviewed in Stewart C. Myers, "The Capital Structure Puzzle," *Journal of Finance* 39 (July 1984), pp. 575–92. Ten useful papers are contained in Benjamin M. Friedman, ed., *Corporate Capital Structures in the United States* (Chicago: National Bureau of Economic Research and The University of Chicago Press, 1985).

TABLE 12–10
Pierce Grain Company
Possible Capital Structures

Plan A: 0% debt

		Total debt	$ 0
		Common equity	200,000[a]
Total assets	$200,000	Total liabilities and equity	$200,000

Plan B: 25% debt at 8% interest rate

		Total debt	$ 50,000
		Common equity	150,000[b]
Total assets	$200,000	Total liabilities and equity	$200,000

Plan C: 40% debt at 8% interest rate

		Total debt	$ 80,000
		Common equity	120,000[c]
Total assets	$200,000	Total liabilities and equity	$200,000

[a]2,000 common shares outstanding
[b]1,500 common shares outstanding
[c]1,200 common shares outstanding

quantified. The firm that uses more financial leverage (rather than less) will experience larger relative changes in its earnings per share (rather than smaller) following EBIT fluctuations. Assume that Pierce Grain elected financing plan C rather than plan A. Plan C is highly levered and plan A is unlevered. A 100 percent increase in EBIT from $20,000 to

(1)	(2)	(3)=(1) – (2)	(4)=(3) × .5	(5)=(3) – (4)	(6)
				Net Income	Earnings
EBIT	Interest	EBT	Taxes	to Common	per Share
Plan A: 0% debt; $200,000 common equity; 2000 shares					
$ 0	$ 0	$ 0	$ 0	$ 0	$ 0
20,000	0	20,000	10,000	10,000	5.00
40,000	0	40,000	20,000	20,000	10.00
60,000	0	60,000	30,000	30,000	15.00
80,000	0	80,000	40,000	40,000	20.00
Plan B: 25% debt; 8% interest rate; $150,000 common equity; 1500 shares					
$ 0	$4,000	$(4,000)	$(2,000)[a]	$(2,000)	$ (1.33)
20,000	4,000	16,000	8,000	8,000	5.33
40,000	4,000	36,000	18,000	18,000	12.00
60,000	4,000	56,000	28,000	28,000	18.67
80,000	4,000	76,000	38,000	38,000	25.33
Plan C: 40% debt; 8% interest rate; $120,000 common equity; 1200 shares					
$ 0	$6,400	$(6,400)	$(3,200)[a]	$(3,200)	$ (2.67)
20,000	6,400	13,600	6,800	6,800	5.67
40,000	6,400	33,600	16,800	16,800	14.00
60,000	6,400	53,600	26,800	26,800	22.33
80,000	6,400	73,600	36,800	36,800	30.67

Plan A: } 100%

Plan B: } 125%

Plan C: } 147%

[a]The negative tax bill recognizes the credit arising from the carryback and carryforward provision of the tax code.

$40,000 would cause earnings per share to rise by 147 percent under plan C, but only 100 percent under plan A. Unfortunately, the effect would operate in the negative direction as well. A given change in EBIT is *magnified* by the use of financial leverage. This magnification is reflected in the variability of the firm's earnings per share.

The *second financial leverage effect* concerns the level of earnings per share at a given EBIT under a given capital structure. Refer to Table 12–11. At the EBIT level of $20,000, earnings per share would be $5, $5.33, and $5.67 under financing arrangements A, B, and C, respectively. Above a critical level of EBIT, the firm's earnings per share will be higher if greater degrees of financial leverage are employed. Conversely, below some critical level of EBIT, earnings per share will suffer at greater degrees of financial leverage. Whereas the first financial-leverage effect is quantified by the degree-of-financial-leverage measure (DFL_{EBIT}), the second is quantified by what is generally referred to as EBIT-EPS analysis. EPS refers, of course, to earnings per share. The rationale underlying this sort of analysis is simple. Earnings is one of the key variables that influences the market value of the firm's common stock. The effect of a financing decision on EPS, then, should be understood because the decision will probably affect the value of the stockholders' investment.

EBIT-EPS Analysis

Example Assume that plan B in Table 12–11 is the existing capital structure for the Pierce Grain Company. Furthermore, the asset structure of the firm is such that EBIT is expected to be $20,000 per year for a very long time. A capital investment is available to Pierce Grain that will cost $50,000. Acquisition of this asset is expected to raise the projected EBIT level to $30,000, permanently. The firm can raise the needed cash by (1) selling 500 shares of common stock at $100 each or (2) selling new bonds that will net the firm $50,000 and carry an interest rate of 8.5 percent. These capital structures and corresponding EPS amounts are summarized in Table 12–12.

At the projected EBIT level of $30,000, the EPS for the common stock and debt alternatives are $6.50 and $7.25, respectively. Both are considerably above the $5.33 that would occur if the new project were rejected and the additional financial capital were not raised. Based on a criterion of selecting the financing plan that will provide the highest EPS, the bond alternative is favored. But what if the basic business risk to which the firm is exposed causes the EBIT level to vary over a considerable range? Can we be sure that the bond alternative will *always* have the higher EPS associated with it? The answer, of course, is "No." When the EBIT level is subject to uncertainty, a graphic analysis of the proposed financing plans can provide useful information to the financial manager.

Graphic Analysis

The EBIT-EPS analysis chart allows the decision maker to visualize the impact of different financing plans on EPS over a range of EBIT levels. The relationship between EPS and EBIT is linear. All we need, therefore, to construct the chart is two points for each alternative. Part B of

TABLE 12–12
Pierce Grain Company Analysis of Financing Choices

Part A: Capital Structures

Existing Capital Structure		With New Common Stock Financing		With New Debt Financing	
Long-term debt at 8%	$ 50,000	Long-term debt at 8%	$ 50,000	Long-term debt at 8%	$ 50,000
Common stock	150,000	Common stock	200,000	Long-term debt at 8.5%	50,000
				Common stock	150,000
Total liabilities and equity	$200,000	Total liabilities and equity	$250,000	Total liabilities and equity	$250,000
Common shares outstanding	1,500	Common shares outstanding	2,000	Common shares outstanding	1,500

Part B: Projected EPS Levels

	Existing Capital Structure	With New Common Stock Financing	With New Debt Financing
EBIT	$20,000	$30,000	$30,000
Less: Interest expense	4,000	4,000	8,250
Earnings before taxes (EBT)	$16,000	$26,000	$21,750
Less: Taxes at 50%	8,000	13,000	10,875
Net Income	$ 8,000	$13,000	$10,875
Less: Preferred dividends	0	0	0
Earnings available to common	$ 8,000	$13,000	$10,875
EPS	$ 5.33	$ 6.50	$ 7.25

Table 12–12 already provides us with one of these points. The answer to the following question for each choice gives us the second point: At what EBIT level will the EPS for the plan be exactly zero? If the EBIT level *just covers* the plan's financing costs (on a before-tax basis), then EPS will be zero. For the stock plan, an EPS of zero is associated with an EBIT of $4,000. The $4,000 is the interest expense incurred under the existing capital structure. If the bond plan is elected, the interest costs will be the present $4,000 plus $4,250 per year arising from the new debt issue. An EBIT level of $8,250, then, is necessary to provide a zero EPS with the bond plan.

The EBIT-EPS analysis chart representing the financing choices available to the Pierce Grain Company is shown as Figure 12–14. EBIT is charted on the horizontal axis and EPS on the vertical axis. The intercepts on the horizontal axis represent the before-tax equivalent financing charges related to each plan. The straight lines for each plan tell us the EPS amounts that will occur at different EBIT amounts.

Notice that the bond-plan line has a *steeper slope* than the stock-plan line. This ensures that the lines for each financing choice will *intersect*. Above the intersection point, EPS for the plan with greater leverage will exceed that for the plan with lesser leverage. The intersection point, encircled in Figure 12–14, occurs at an EBIT level of $21,000 and produces EPS of $4.25 for each plan. When EBIT is $30,000, notice that the bond plan produces EPS of $7.25 and the stock plan, $6.50. Below the

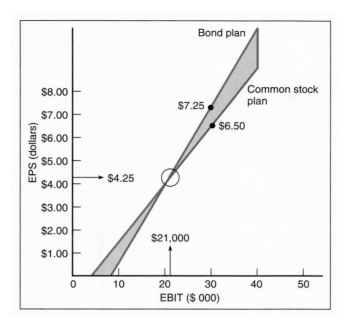

FIGURE 12–14
EBIT—EPS Analysis Chart

intersection point, EPS with the stock plan will *exceed* that with the more highly levered bond plan. The steeper slope of the bond-plan line indicates that with greater leverage, EPS is more sensitive to EBIT changes.

Computing Indifference Points

The point of intersection in Figure 12–14 is called the **EBIT-EPS indifference point.** It identifies the EBIT level at which the EPS will be the same regardless of the financing plan chosen by the financial manager. This indifference point, sometimes called the breakeven point, has major implications for financial planning. At EBIT amounts in excess of the EBIT indifference level, the more heavily levered financing plan will generate a higher EPS. At EBIT amounts below the EBIT indifference level, the financing plan involving less leverage will generate a higher EPS. It is important, then, to know the EBIT indifference level.

We can find it graphically, as in Figure 12–14. At times it may be more efficient, though, to calculate the indifference point directly. This can be done by using the following equation:

$$\overset{\text{EPS: Stock Plan}}{\frac{(\text{EBIT} - I)(1 - t) - P}{S_s}} = \overset{\text{EPS: Bond Plan}}{\frac{(\text{EBIT} - I)(1 - t) - P}{S_b}} \qquad \textbf{(12–16)}$$

where S_s and S_b are the number of common shares outstanding under the stock and bond plans, respectively, I is interest expense, t is the firm's income tax rate, and P is preferred dividends paid. In the present case P is zero, because there is no preferred stock outstanding. If preferred stock is associated with one of the financing alternatives, keep in mind that the preferred dividends, P, are not tax deductible. Equation (12–16) *does* take this fact into consideration.

For the present example, we calculate the indifference level of EBIT as

$$\frac{(\text{EBIT} - \$4000)(1 - 0.5) - 0}{2000} = \frac{(\text{EBIT} - \$8250)(1 - 0.5) - 0}{1500}$$

When the expression above is solved for EBIT, we obtain $21,000. If EBIT turns out to be $21,000, then EPS will be $4.25 under both plans.

Word of Caution

Above the EBIT-EPS indifference point, a more heavily levered financial plan promises to deliver a larger EPS. Strict application of the criterion of selecting the financing plan that produces the highest EPS might have the firm issuing debt most of the time it raised external capital. Our discussion of capital-structure theory taught us the dangers of that sort of action.

The primary weakness of EBIT-EPS analysis is that it disregards the implicit costs of debt financing. The effect of the specific financing decision on the firm's cost of common equity capital is totally ignored. Investors should be concerned with both the *level* and *variability* of the firm's expected earnings stream. EBIT-EPS analysis considers only the level of the earnings stream and ignores the variability (riskiness) inherent in it. Thus, this type of analysis must be used in conjunction with other basic tools in reaching the objective of capital-structure management.

Comparative Leverage Ratios

In Chapter 3 we explored the overall usefulness of financial ratio analysis. Leverage ratios are one of the categories of financial ratios identified in that chapter. We emphasize here that the computation of leverage ratios is one of the basic tools of capital structure management.

Two types of leverage ratios must be computed when a financing decision faces the firm. We call these *balance sheet leverage ratios* and *coverage ratios*. The firm's balance sheet supplies inputs for computing the balance sheet leverage ratios. In various forms these balance sheet metrics compare the firm's use of funds supplied by creditors with those supplied by owners.

Inputs to the coverage ratios *generally* come from the firm's income statement. At times the external analyst may have to consult balance sheet information to construct some of these needed estimates. On a privately placed debt issue, for example, some fraction of the current portion of the firm's long-term debt might have to be used as an estimate of that issue's sinking fund. Coverage ratios provide estimates of the firm's ability to service its financing contracts. High coverage ratios, compared with a standard, imply unused debt capacity.

In reality we know that EBIT might be expected to vary over a considerable range of outcomes. For this reason the coverage ratios should be calculated several times, each at a different level of EBIT. If this is accomplished over all possible values of EBIT, a probability distribution for each coverage ratio can be constructed. This provides the financial manager with much more information than simply calculating the coverage ratios based on the expected value of EBIT.

Industry Norms

The comparative leverage ratios that are calculated have additional utility to the decision maker if they can be compared with some standard. Generally, corporate financial analysts, investment bankers, commercial bank loan officers, and bond-rating agencies rely on industry classes from which to compute "normal" ratios. Although industry groupings may actually contain firms whose basic business risk exposure differs widely, the practice is entrenched in American business behavior. At the very least, then, the financial officer must be interested in *industry standards* because almost everybody else is.

Several published studies indicate that capital structure ratios vary in a significant manner among industry classes.[10] For example, random samplings of the common equity ratios of large retail firms seem to differ statistically from those of major steel producers. The major steel producers use financial leverage to a lesser degree than do the large retail organizations. On the whole, firms operating in the *same* industry tend to exhibit capital structure ratios that cluster around a central value, which we call a norm. Business risk will vary from industry to industry. As a consequence, the capital structure norms will vary from industry to industry.

This is not to say that all companies in the industry will maintain leverage ratios "close" to the norm. For instance, firms that are very profitable may display *high* coverage ratios and *high* balance sheet leverage ratios. The moderately profitable firm, though, might find such a posture unduly risky. Here the usefulness of industry normal leverage ratios is clear. If the firm chooses to deviate in a material manner from the accepted values for the key ratios, it must have a sound reason.

■ A GLANCE AT ACTUAL CAPITAL STRUCTURE MANAGEMENT

We now examine some opinions and practices of financial executives that support our emphasis on the importance of capital structure management.

The Conference Board has surveyed 170 senior financial officers with respect to their capital structure practices.[11] Of these 170 executives, 102, or 60 percent, stated that they *do* believe there is an optimum capital structure for the corporation. Sixty-five percent of the responding practitioners worked for firms with annual sales in excess of $200 million. One executive who subscribed to the optimal capital structure concept stated:

---

[10]See, for example, Eli Schwartz and J. Richard Aronson, "Some Surrogate Evidence in Support of the Concept of Optimal Financial Structure," *Journal of Finance* 22 (March 1967), pp. 10–18; David F. Scott, Jr., "Evidence on the Importance of Financial Structure," *Financial Management* 1 (Summer 1972), pp. 45–50; and David F. Scott, Jr., and John D. Martin, "Industry Influence on Financial Structure," *Financial Management* 4 (Spring 1975), pp. 67–73.

[11]Francis J. Walsh, Jr., *Planning Corporate Capital Structures* (New York: The Conference Board, 1972).

In my opinion, there is an optimum capital structure for companies. However, this optimum capital structure will vary by individual companies, industries, and then is subject to changing economies, by money markets, earnings trends, and prospects....the circumstances and the lenders will determine an optimum at different points in time.[12]

This survey and others consistently point out that (1) financial officers set target debt ratios for their companies, and (2) the values for those ratios are influenced by a conscious evaluation of the basic business risk to which the firm is exposed.

Target Debt Ratios

Selected comments from financial executives point to the widespread use of target debt ratios. A vice-president and treasurer of the American Telephone and Telegraph Company (AT&T) described his firm's debt ratio policy in terms of a range:

> All of the foregoing considerations led us to conclude, and reaffirm for a period of many years, that the proper range of our debt was 30% to 40% of total capital. Reasonable success in meeting financial needs under the diverse market and economic conditions that we have faced attests to the appropriateness of this conclusion.[13]

In a similar fashion the president of Fibreboard Corporation identified his firm's target debt ratio and noted how it is related to the uncertain nature of the company's business:

> Our objective is a 30% ratio of debt to capitalization. We need that kind of flexibility to operate in the cyclical business we are in.[14]

In the Conference Board survey mentioned earlier, 84 of the 102 financial officers who subscribed to the optimal capital structure concept stated that their firm *has* a target debt ratio. The most frequently mentioned influence on the level of the target debt ratio was ability to meet financing charges. Other factors identified as affecting the target were (1) maintaining a desired bond rating, (2) providing an adequate borrowing reserve, and (3) exploiting the advantages of financial leverage.

Who Sets Target Debt Ratios?

From the preceding discussion, we know that firms *do* use target debt ratios in arriving at financing decisions. But who sets or influences these target ratios? This and other questions concerning corporate financing policy were investigated in one study published in 1982.[15] This survey of

---

[12]Ibid., p. 14.

[13]John J. Scanlon, "Bell System Financial Policies," *Financial Management* 1 (Summer 1972), pp. 16–26.

[14]*Business Week*, December 6, 1976, p. 30.

[15]David F. Scott, Jr., and Dana J. Johnson, "Financing Policies and Practices in Large Corporations," *Financial Management* 11 (Summer 1982), pp. 51–59.

TABLE 12–13
Setting Target Financial
Structure Ratios

Type of Influence	Rank	
	1	*2*
Internal management and staff analysts	85%	7%
Investment bankers	3	39
Commercial bankers	0	9
Trade creditors	1	0
Security analysts	1	4
Comparative industry ratios	3	23
Other	7	18
Total	100%	100%

Source: David F. Scott, Jr., and Dana J. Johnson, "Financing Policies and Practices in Large Corporations," *Financial Management* 11 (Summer 1982), p. 53.

the 1,000 largest industrial firms in the United States (as ranked by total sales dollars) involved responses from 212 financial executives.

In one portion of this study the participants were asked to rank several possible influences on their target leverage (debt) ratios. Table 12–13 displays the percentage of responses ranked either number one or number two in importance. Ranks past the second are omitted in that they were not very significant. Notice that the most important influence is the firm's own management group and staff of analysts. This item accounted for 85 percent of the responses ranked number one. Of the responses ranked number two in importance, investment bankers dominated the outcomes and accounted for 39 percent of such replies. The role of investment bankers in the country's capital market system is explored in some detail in Chapter 2. Also notice that comparisons with ratios of industry competitors and commercial bankers have some impact on the determination of leverage targets.

Debt Capacity

Previously in this chapter we noted that the firm's debt capacity is the maximum proportion of debt that it can include in its capital structure- and still maintain its lowest composite cost of capital. But how do financial executives make the concept of debt capacity operational? Table 12–14 is derived from the same 1982 survey, involving 212 executives, mentioned above. These executives defined debt capacity in a wide variety of ways. The most popular approach was as a target percentage of total capitalization. Twenty-seven percent of the respondents thought of debt capacity in this manner. Forty-three percent of the participating executives remarked that debt capacity is defined in terms of some balance-sheet-based financial ratio (see the first three items in Table 12–14). Maintaining a specific bond rating was also indicated to be a popular approach to implementing the debt capacity concept.

Business Risk

The single most important factor that should affect the firm's financing mix is the underlying nature of the business in which it operates. In this

TABLE 12–14
Definitions of Debt Capacity
in Practice

Standard or Method	1,000 Largest Corporations (Percent Using)
Target percent of total capitalization (long-term debt to total capitalization)	27%
Long-term debt to net worth ratio (or its inverse)	14
Long-term debt to total assets	2
Interest (or fixed charge) coverage ratio	6
Maintain bond ratings	14
Restrictive debt covenants	4
Most adverse cash flow	4
Industry standard	3
Other	10
No response	16
Total	100%

Source: Derived from David F. Scott, Jr., and Dana J. Johnson, "Financing Polices and Practices in Large Corporations," *Financial Management* 11 (Summer 1982), pp. 51–59.

chapter we defined business risk as the relative dispersion in the firm's expected stream of EBIT. If the nature of the firm's business is such that the variability inherent in its EBIT stream is high, then it would be unwise to impose a high degree of financial risk on top of this already uncertain earnings stream.

Corporate executives are likely to point this out in discussions of capital-structure management. A financial officer in a large steel firm related:

> The nature of the industry, the marketplace, and the firm tend to establish debt limits that any prudent management would prefer not to exceed. Our industry is capital intensive and our markets tend to be cyclical....The capability to service debt while operating in the environment described dictates a conservative financial structure.[16]

Notice how that executive was concerned with both his firm's business risk exposure and its cash flow capability for meeting any financing costs. The AT&T financial officer referred to earlier also has commented on the relationship between business and financial risk:

> In determining how much debt a firm can safely carry, it is necessary to consider the basic risks inherent in that business. This varies considerably among industries and is related essentially to the nature and demand for an industry's product, the operating characteristics of the industry, and its ability to earn an adequate return in an unknown future.[17]

It appears clear that the firm's capital structure cannot be properly designed without a thorough understanding of its commercial strategy.

[16]Walsh, *Planning Corporate Capital Structures*, p. 18.
[17]Scanlon, "Bell System Financial Policies," p. 19.

SUMMARY

In this chapter we study the process of arriving at an appropriate financial structure for the firm and examine tools that can assist the financial manager in this task. We are concerned with assessing the variability in the firm's residual earnings stream (either earnings per share or earnings available to the common shareholders) induced by the use of operating and financial leverage. This assessment builds on the tenets of breakeven analysis.

We then deal with the design of the firm's financing mix, particularly emphasizing management of the firm's permanent sources of funds—that is, its capital structure. The objective of capital structure management is to arrange the company's sources of funds so that its common stock price will be maximized, all other factors held constant.

Breakeven Analysis

Breakeven analysis permits the financial manager to determine the quantity of output or the level of sales that will result in an EBIT level of zero. This means the firm has neither a profit nor a loss before any tax considerations. The effect of price changes, cost structure changes, or volume changes on profits (EBIT) can be studied. To make the technique operational, it is necessary that the firm's costs be classified as fixed or variable. Not all costs fit neatly into one of these two categories. Over short planning horizons, though, the preponderance of costs can be assigned to either the fixed or variable classification. Once the cost structure has been identified, the breakeven point can be found by use of contribution-margin analysis or algebraic analysis.

Operating Leverage

Operating leverage is the responsiveness of the firm's EBIT to changes in sales revenues. It arises from the firm's use of fixed operating costs. When fixed operating costs are present in the company's cost structure, changes in sales are magnified into even greater changes in EBIT. The firm's degree of operating leverage from a base sales level is the percentage change in EBIT divided by the percentage change in sales. All types of leverage are two-edged swords. When sales decrease by some percentage, the negative impact on EBIT will be even larger.

Financial Leverage

A firm employs financial leverage when it finances a portion of its assets with securities bearing a fixed rate of return. The presence of debt and/or preferred stock in the company's financial structure means that it is using financial leverage. When financial leverage is used, changes in EBIT translate into larger changes in earnings per share. The concept of the degree of financial leverage dwells on the sensitivity of earnings per share to changes in EBIT. The DFL from a base EBIT level is defined as the percentage change in earnings per share divided by the percentage change in EBIT. All other things equal, the more fixed-charge securities the firm employs in its financial structure, the greater its degree of financial leverage. Clearly, EBIT can rise or fall. If it falls, and financial leverage is used, the firm's shareholders endure negative changes in earnings per share that are larger than the relative decline in EBIT. Again, leverage is a two-edged sword.

Combining Operating and Financial Leverage

Firms use operating and financial leverage in various degrees. The joint use of operating and financial leverage can be measured by computing the degree of combined leverage, defined as the percentage change in earnings per share divided by the percentage change in sales. This measure allows the financial manager to ascertain the effect on total leverage caused by adding financial leverage on top of operating leverage. Effects can be dramatic, because the degree of combined leverage is the product of the degrees of operating and financial leverage.

Capital Structure Theory

Can the firm affect its composite cost of capital by altering its financing mix? Attempts to answer this question have comprised a significant portion of capital structure theory for over three decades. Extreme positions show that the firm's stock price is either unaffected or continually affected as the firm increases its reliance on leverage-inducing funds. In the real world, an operating environment where interest expense is tax deductible and market imperfections operate to restrict the amount of fixed-income obligations a firm can issue, most financial officers and financial academics subscribe to the concept of an optimal capital structure. The optimal capital structure minimizes the firm's composite cost of capital. Searching for a proper range of financial leverage, then, is an important financial management activity.

Complicating the manager's search for an optimal capital structure are conflicts that lead to agency costs. A natural conflict exists between stockholders and bondholders (the agency costs of debt). To reduce excessive risk-taking by management on behalf of stockholders, it may be necessary to include several protective covenants in bond contracts that serve to restrict managerial decision making.

Another type of agency cost is related to "free cash flow." Managers, for example, have an incentive to hold on to free cash flow and enjoy it, rather than paying it out in the form of higher cash-dividend payments. This conflict between managers and stockholders leads to the concept of the *free cash flow theory of capital structure*. This same theory is also known as the *control hypothesis* and the *threat hypothesis*. The ultimate resolution of these agency costs affects the specific form of the firm's capital structure.

Tools of Capital Structure Management

The decision to use senior securities in the firm's capitalization causes two types of financial leverage effects. The first is the added variability in the earnings per share stream that accompanies the use of fixed-charge securities. We explain how this can be quantified by use of the degree of financial leverage metric. The second financial leverage effect relates to the level of earnings per share (EPS) at a given EBIT under a specific capital structure. We rely on EBIT-EPS analysis to measure this second effect. Through EBIT-EPS analysis the decision maker can inspect the impact of alternative financing plans on EPS over a full range of EBIT levels.

A second tool of capital structure management is the calculation of comparative leverage ratios. Balance sheet leverage ratios and coverage ratios can be computed according to the contractual stipulations of the proposed financing plans. Comparison of these ratios with industry standards enables the financial officer to determine if the firm's key ratios are materially out of line with accepted practice.

Capital Structure Practices

Surveys indicate that most financial officers in large firms believe in the concept of an optimal capital structure. The optimal capital structure is approximated by the identification of target debt ratios. The targets reflect the firm's ability to service fixed financing costs and also consider the business risk to which the firm is exposed.

Survey studies have provided information on who sets or influences the firm's target leverage ratios. The firm's own management group and staff of analysts are the major influence, followed in importance by investment bankers. Studies also show that executives put the concept of debt capacity in operation in many ways. The most popular approach is to define debt capacity in terms of a target long-term debt to total capitalization ratio. Maintaining a specific bond rating (such as Aa or A) is also a popular approach to implementing the debt capacity concept.

STUDY QUESTIONS

12–1. Distinguish between business risk and financial risk. What gives rise to, or causes, each type of risk?

12–2. Define the term *financial leverage*. Does the firm use financial leverage if preferred stock is present in the capital structure?

12–3. Define the term *operating leverage*. What type of effect occurs when the firm uses operating leverage?

12–4. A manager in your firm decides to employ breakeven analysis. Of what shortcomings should this manager be aware?

12–5. If a firm has a degree of combined leverage of 3.0 times, what does a negative sales fluctuation of 15 percent portend for the earnings available to the firm's common stock investors?

12–6. Breakeven analysis assumes linear revenue and cost functions. In reality these linear functions over large output and sales levels are highly improbable. Why?

12–7. Define the following terms:
a. Financial structure
b. Capital structure
c. Optimal capital structure
d. Debt capacity

12–8. What is the primary weakness of EBIT-EPS analysis as a financing decision tool?

12–9. What is the objective of capital structure management?

12–10. Distinguish between (a) balance sheet leverage ratios and (b) coverage ratios. Give two examples of each and indicate how they would be computed.

12–11. Why might firms whose sales levels change drastically over time choose to use debt only sparingly in their capital structures?

12–12. What condition would cause capital structure management to be a meaningless activity?

12–13. What does the term *independence hypothesis* mean as it applies to capital structure theory?

12–14. Who have been the foremost advocates of the independence hypothesis?

12–15. A financial manager might say that the firm's composite cost of capital is saucer-shaped or U-shaped. What does this mean?

12–16. Define the EBIT-EPS indifference point.

12–17. Explain how industry norms might be used by the financial manager in the design of the company's financing mix.

12–18. Define the term *free cash flow*.

12–19. What is meant by the *free cash flow theory of capital structure?*

12–20. In almost every instance, what funds source do managers use first in the financing of their capital budgets?

SELF-TEST PROBLEM

ST-1. (*Fixed Costs and the Breakeven Point*) Bonaventure Manufacturing expects to earn $210,000 next year after taxes. Sales will be $4 million. The firm's single plant is located on the outskirts of Olean, N.Y. The firm manufactures a combined bookshelf and desk unit used extensively in college dormitories. These units sell for $200 each and have a variable cost per unit of $150. Bonaventure experiences a 30 percent tax rate.
   a. What are the firm's fixed costs expected to be next year?
   b. Calculate the firm's breakeven point in both units and dollars.

STUDY PROBLEMS

12–1. (*Leverage Analysis*) You have developed the following analytical income statement for your corporation. It represents the most recent year's operations, which ended yesterday.

Sales	$45,750,000
Variable costs	22,800,000
Revenue before fixed costs	$22,950,000
Fixed costs	9,200,000
EBIT	$13,750,000
Interest expense	1,350,000
Earnings before taxes	$12,400,000
Taxes (.50)	6,200,000
Net income	$ 6,200,000

Your supervisor in the controller's office has just handed you a memorandum asking for written responses to the following questions:
   a. At this level of output, what is the degree of operating leverage?
   b. What is the degree of financial leverage?

c. What is the degree of combined leverage?

d. What is the firm's breakeven point in sales dollars?

e. If sales should increase by 25 percent, by what percent would earnings before taxes (and net income) increase?

12–2. (*Breakeven Point and Operating Leverage*) Footwear, Inc., manufactures a complete line of men's and women's dress shoes for independent merchants. The average selling price of its finished product is $85 per pair. The variable cost for this same pair of shoes is $58. Footwear, Inc., incurs fixed costs of $170,000 per year.

a. What is the breakeven point in pairs of shoes for the company?

b. What is the dollar sales volume the firm must achieve to reach the breakeven point?

c. What would be the firm's profit or loss at the following units of production sold: 7,000 pairs of shoes? 9,000 pairs of shoes? 15,000 pairs of shoes?

d. Find the degree of operating leverage for the production and sales levels given in part (c) above.

12–3. (*Breakeven Point and Profit Margin*) Mary Clark, a recent graduate of Clarion South University, is planning to open a new wholesaling operation. Her target operating profit margin is 26 percent. Her unit contribution margin will be 50 percent of sales. Average annual sales are forecast to be $3,250,000.

a. How large can fixed costs be for the wholesaling operation and still allow the 26 percent operating profit margin to be achieved?

b. What is the breakeven point in dollars for the firm?

12–4. (*Leverage Analysis*) You have developed the following analytical income statement for your corporation. It represents the most recent year's operations, which ended yesterday. Your supervisor in the controller's office has just handed you a memorandum asking for written responses to the following questions:

a. At this level of output, what is the degree of operating leverage?

b. What is the degree of financial leverage?

Sales	$30,000,000
Variable costs	13,500,000
Revenue before fixed costs	$16,500,000
Fixed costs	8,000,000
EBIT	$8,500,000
Interest expense	1,000,000
Earnings before taxes	$7,500,000
Taxes (.50)	3,750,000
Net income	$3,750,000

c. What is the degree of combined leverage?

d. What is the firm's breakeven point in sales dollars?

e. If sales should increase by 25 percent, by what percent would earnings before taxes (and net income) increase?

12–5. (*Breakeven Point and Selling Price*) Parks Castings, Inc., will manufacture and sell 200,000 units next year. Fixed costs will total $300,000, and variable costs will be 60 percent of sales.

a. The firm wants to achieve an earnings before interest and taxes level of $250,000. What selling price per unit is necessary to achieve this result?

b. Set up an analytical income statement to verify your solution to part (a).

12–6. *(Operating Leverage)* Rocky Mount Metals Company manufactures an assortment of woodburning stoves. The average selling price for the various units is $500. The associated variable cost is $350 per unit. Fixed costs for the firm average $180,000 annually.

  a. What is the breakeven point in units for the company?
  b. What is the dollar sales volume the firm must achieve to reach the breakeven point?
  c. What is the degree of operating leverage for a production and sales level of 5,000 units for the firm? (Calculate to three decimal places.)
  d. What will be the projected effect on earnings before interest and taxes if the firm's sales level should increase by 20 percent from the volume noted in part (c) above?

12–7. *(Sales Mix and Breakeven Point)* Toledo Components produces four lines of auto accessories for the major Detroit automobile manufacturers. The lines are known by the code letters A, B, C, and D. The current sales mix for Toledo and the contribution margin ratio (unit contribution margin divided by unit sales price) for these product lines are as follows:

Product Line	Percent of Total Sales	Contribution Margin Ratio
A	33⅓%	40%
B	41⅔	32
C	16⅔	20
D	8⅓	60

Total sales for next year are forecast to be $120,000. Total fixed costs will be $29,400.

  a. Prepare a table showing (1) sales, (2) total variable costs, and (3) the total contribution margin associated with each product line.
  b. What is the aggregate contribution margin ratio indicative of this sales mix?
  c. At this sales mix, what is the breakeven point in dollars?

12–8. *(Sales Mix and Breakeven Point)* Because of production constraints, Toledo Components (see problem 12–7) may have to adhere to a different sales mix for next year. The alternative plan is outlined below:

Product Line	Percent of Total Sales
A	25%
B	36 ⅔
C	33 ⅓
D	5

  a. Assuming all other facts in problem 12–7 remain the same, what effect will this different sales mix have on Toledo's breakeven point in dollars?
  b. Which sales mix will Toledo's management prefer?

12–9. *(EBIT-EPS Analysis)* A group of retired college professors has decided to form a small manufacturing corporation. The company will produce a full line of traditional office furniture. Two financing plans have been proposed by the investors. Plan A is an all-common-equity alternative.

Under this agreement, 1 million common shares will be sold to net the firm $20 per share. Plan B involves the use of financial leverage. A debt issue with a 20-year maturity period will be privately placed. The debt issue will carry an interest rate of 10 percent, and the principal borrowed will amount to $6 million. The corporate tax rate is 50 percent.

a. Find the EBIT indifference level associated with the two financing proposals.

b. Prepare an analytical income statement that proves EPS will be the same regardless of the plan chosen at the EBIT level found in part (a).

c. Prepare an EBIT-EPS analysis chart for this situation.

d. If a detailed financial analysis projects that long-term EBIT will always be close to $2.4 million annually, which plan will provide for the higher EPS?

12–10. *(EBIT-EPS Analysis)* Four recent liberal arts graduates have interested a group of venture capitalists in backing a new business enterprise. The proposed operation would consist of a series of retail outlets to distribute and service a full line of vacuum cleaners and accessories. These stores would be located in Dallas, Houston, and San Antonio. Two financing plans have been proposed by the graduates. Plan A is an all-common-equity structure. Two million dollars would be raised by selling 80,000 shares of common stock. Plan B would involve the use of long-term debt financing. One million dollars would be raised by marketing bonds with an effective interest rate of 12 percent. Under this alternative, another million dollars would be raised by selling 40,000 shares of common stock. With both plans, then, $2 million is needed to launch the new firm's operations. The debt funds raised under Plan B are considered to have no fixed maturity date, in that this portion of financial leverage is thought to be a permanent part of the company's capital structure. The fledgling executives have decided to use a 40 percent tax rate in their analysis, and they have hired you on a consulting basis to do the following:

a. Find the EBIT indifference level associated with the two financing proposals.

b. Prepare an analytical income statement that proves EPS will be the same regardless of the plan chosen at the EBIT level found in part (a) above.

12-11. *(Assessing Leverage Use)* Some financial data for three corporations are displayed below:

Measure	Firm A	Firm B	Firm C	Industry Norm
Debt ratio	20%	25%	40%	20%
Times burden covered	8 times	10 times	7 times	9 times
Price/earnings ratio	9 times	11 times	6 times	10 times

a. Which firm appears to be excessively levered?

b. Which firm appears to be employing financial leverage to the most appropriate degree?

c. What explanation can you provide for the higher price/earnings ratio enjoyed by firm B as compared with firm A?

a. Using *Disclosure,* find the following information for the Proctor & Gamble Company for the most recent year: (1) number of shares of common stock outstanding, (2) common stock share price, (3) earnings before interest and taxes (income before tax + interest expense), (4) the company's total debt, and (5) the firm's debt-to-equity mix

b. What is the total equity value of the company?

c. Assume that the company's dividend payout ratio is 100 percent; that corporate income is not taxed; and that the required rate of return for the firm if it were all equity is 12 percent. Then: (1) Use the net operating income approach to estimate the firm's total equity value. (2) Use the net income approach to value the company's equity value. (3) Explain why there are differences in the values found above.

SELF-TEST SOLUTION

SS-1. **a.**

$$[(P \cdot Q) - [(V \cdot Q) + (F)]] \, (1 - T) = \$210{,}000$$
$$[(\$4{,}000{,}000) - (\$3{,}000{,}000) - F] \, (.7) = \$210{,}000$$
$$(\$1{,}000{,}000 - F) \, (.7) = \$210{,}000$$
$$\$700{,}000 - .7F = \$210{,}000$$
$$.7F = \$490{,}000$$
$$F = \underline{\underline{\$700{,}000}}$$

Fixed costs next year, then, are expected to be $700,000.

b.

$$Q_B = \frac{F}{P - V} = \frac{\$700{,}000}{\$50} = \underline{\underline{14{,}000}} \text{ units}$$

$$S^* = \frac{F}{1 - \dfrac{VC}{S}} = \frac{\$700{,}000}{1 - .75} = \frac{\$700{,}000}{.25} = \underline{\underline{\$2{,}800{,}000}}$$

The firm will break even (**EBIT** = 0) when it sells 14,000 units. With a selling price of $200 per unit, the breakeven sales level is $2,800,000.

RJR Nabisco Bondholder Lawsuits:
A Leverage Related Agency Program
from ABC News, Business World, November 20, 1988

In the introduction to Video Case 4 on page 392 we asked several important questions that you should now refer to.

Although the announcement of the RJR Nabisco management buyout proposal caused the market value of RJR bonds to fall by 20 percent, the transaction could be valuable to shareholders. If the transaction shifts value from bondholders to shareholders then the transaction might be very attractive to shareholders, despite (or possibly because of) the losses suffered by bondholders. The static tradeoff theory suggests that managers should search for the amount of leverage that maximizes firm value, but the theory does not recognize that the interests of shareholders and bondholders may differ. Once bondholders commit funds and agree to a coupon rate, they are at the mercy of shareholders. Shareholders have an incentive, once bonds have been issued, to change the riskiness of the firm. Increased risk provides shareholders with an opportunity for high returns. Moreover, they won't have to share those returns with bondholders because the bondholders have agreed to accept a fixed coupon rate as payment for the use of their funds. This is where the agency conflict between bondholders and shareholders arises. Because managers work for shareholders, we would expect managers to make decisions that maximize share value with little concern about bondholders. In the RJR case, shareholders will be offered a large premium for their shares, so they will benefit; whereas bondholders suffer the affects of increased risk.

Bondholders are not stupid and do recognize the incentives shareholders have to pull such bait-and-switch tricks on them. How can they avoid such problems? Bond covenants provide some protection by restricting the ways managers, on behalf of shareholders can enhance share value by reducing the value of the bondholders' claim on the firm. Before the early 1980s bondholders could not have foreseen the emergence of leveraged buyouts, so they did not include protective covenants for such transactions. Since then, however, rating agencies evaluate bonds for event risk, the possibility of a takeover or other type of restructuring.

This video has introduced just one dimension of a complex transaction that although fraught with potential conflicts of interest may also produce enormous benefits for shareholders and the buyout teams.

Discussion questions

1. What is the opposite of event risk? This situation occurs when a firm becomes safer than it was when bonds were originally used. As a manager would this concern you? If so, what would you do? (Hint: See Frank Easterbrook, "Two Agency Cost Explanations for Dividends," American Economic Review, 1984.)

2. Why do you think that bondholders did not demand more complex contractual protection? Can you imagine a contract that protects one of the contracting parties from every eventuality? Why are such contracts unlikely to exist?

Suggested reading

CRABBE, LELAND. "Event Risk: An Analysis of Losses to Bondholders," and "Super Poison Put," Bond Covenants, Federal Reserve Board Discussion Paper #111, February 1990.

CHAPTER 13

DIVIDEND POLICY AND INTERNAL FINANCING

Key Terms • Does Dividend Policy Affect Stock Price? • The Dividend Decision in Practice • Dividend Payment Procedures • Stock Dividends and Stock Splits • Stock Repurchases

The primary task given the financial manager is to maximize the value, or price, of the firm's common stock. The success or failure of a management decision is determined by its effect on the common stock price. In the previous chapters, both the company's investment decisions and financing decisions were viewed within the context of increasing shareholder value. As we now look at the firm's *dividend* and *internal financing* policies, we return to the same basic question: Can management influence the price of the firm's stock, in this case through its dividend policies? Toward that end, we have six specific objectives for this chapter.

1. Study the relationship between a corporation's dividend policy and the market price of its common stock.

2. Present practical considerations that may be important to the firm's dividend policy.

3. Review the types of dividend policy corporations frequently use.

4. Study the procedures a company follows in administering the dividend payment.

5. Examine the use of noncash dividends (stock dividends and stock splits).

6. Explain the use of stock repurchases.

Given what we have studied in earlier chapters, we would certainly expect that dividends, and therefore the firm's dividend policy, would be important to stockholders. However, when we consider the whole scheme of things, whether a firm pays a dividend may not matter much to investors, in terms of affecting the firm's stock price. In fact, we have difficulty explaining a firm's actions in regard to paying dividends. Yet chief financial officers, from time immemorial, have acted as if dividend policy is important. In this chapter, we will try to resolve this question, but not as completely as we would honestly like.

▦ KEY TERMS

Before taking up the particular issues relating to dividend policy, we must understand several key terms and interrelationships.

A firm's dividend policy includes two basic components. First, the **dividend payout ratio** indicates the amount of dividends paid relative to the company's earnings. For instance, if the dividend per share is $2 and the earnings per share is $4, the payout ratio is 50 percent ($2/$4). The second component is the *stability* of the dividends over time. As will be observed later in the chapter, dividend stability may be almost as important to the investor as the amount of dividends received.

In formulating a dividend policy, the financial manager faces trade-offs. Assuming that management has already decided how much to invest and chosen its debt-equity mix for financing these investments, the decision to pay a large dividend means simultaneously deciding to retain little, if any, profits; this in turn results in a greater reliance on external equity financing. Conversely, given the firm's investment and financing decisions, a small dividend payment corresponds to high profit retention with less need for externally generated equity funds. These tradeoffs, which are fundamental to our discussion, are illustrated in Figure 13–1.

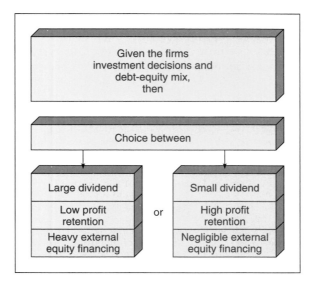

FIGURE 13–1
Dividend-Retention-Financing
Tradeoffs

■ DOES DIVIDEND POLICY AFFECT STOCK PRICE?[1]

The fundamental question to be resolved in our study of the firm's dividend policy may be stated simply: What is a sound rationale or motivation for dividend payments? If we believe our objective should be to maximize the value of the common stock, we may restate the question as follows: Given the firm's capital-budgeting and borrowing decisions, what is the effect of the firm's dividend policies on the stock price? *Does a high dividend payment decrease stock value, increase it, or make no real difference?*

At first glance, we might reasonably conclude that a firm's dividend policy is important. We have already (Chapter 7) defined the value of a stock to be equal to the present value of future dividends. How can we now suggest that dividends are not important? Why do so many companies pay dividends, and why is a page in *The Wall Street Journal* devoted to dividend announcements? Based on intuition, we could quickly conclude that dividend policy is important. However, we might be surprised to learn that the dividend question has been a controversial issue for well over three decades. It has even been called the "dividend puzzle."[2]

Three Basic Views

Some would argue that the amount of the dividend is irrelevant and any time spent on the decision is a waste of energy. Others contend that a high dividend will result in a high stock price. Still others take the view that dividends actually hurt the stock value. Let us look at these three views in turn.

View 1: Dividend Policy Is Irrelevant

Much of the controversy about the dividend issue is based in the time-honored disagreements between the academic and professional communities. Experienced practitioners perceive stock price changes as resulting from dividend announcements and therefore see dividends as important. Professors who argue that dividends are irrelevant see a failure to carefully define dividend policy and argue that the relationship between dividends and stock price may be an illusion.[3]

---

[1]The concepts of this section draw heavily from Donald H. Chew, Jr., ed., "Do Dividends Matter? A Discussion of Corporate Dividend Policy," in *Six Roundtable Discussions of Corporate Finance with Joel Stern* (New York: Quorum Books, 1986), pp. 67–101; and a book of readings edited by Joel M. Stern and Donald H. Chew, Jr., *The Revolution in Corporate Finance* (New York: Basil Blackwell, 1986). Specific readings included Merton Miller, "Can Management Use Dividends to Influence the Value of the Firm?" pp. 299–303; Richard Brealey, "Does Dividend Policy Matter?" pp. 304–9; and Michael Rozeff, "How Companies Set Their Dividend Payout Ratios," pp. 320–26.

[2]See Fischer Black, "The Dividend Puzzle," *Journal of Portfolio Management*, 2 (Winter 1976), pp. 5–8.

[3]For an excellent presentation of this issue, see Merton Miller, "Can Management Use Dividends to Influence the Value of the Firm?" in Joel M. Stern and Donald H. Chew, Jr., eds., *The Revolution in Corporate Finance* (New York: Basil Blackwell, 1986), pp. 299–305.

The position that dividends are not important rests on two preconditions. First, we assume that investment and borrowing decisions have already been made and that these decisions will not be altered by the amount of any dividend payments. Second, "perfect" capital markets are assumed to exist, which means that (1) investors can buy and sell stocks without incurring any transaction costs, such as brokerage commissions; (2) companies can issue stocks without any cost of doing so; (3) there are no corporate or personal taxes; (4) complete information about the firm is readily available; and (5) there are no conflicts of interest between managements and stockholders.

The first assumption—that we have already made the investment and financing decisions—simply keeps us from confusing the issues. We want to know the effect of dividend decisions on a stand-alone basis, without mixing in other decisions. The second assumption, that of perfect markets, also allows us to study the effect of dividend decisions in isolation, much like a physicist studies motion in a vacuum to avoid the influence of friction.

Given these assumptions, the effect of a dividend decision on share price may be stated unequivocally: *There is no relationship between dividend policy and stock value.* One dividend policy is as good as another one. In the aggregate, investors are concerned only with *total* returns from investment decisions; they are indifferent whether these returns come from capital gains or dividend income. They also recognize that the dividend decision, given the investment policy, is really a choice of financing strategy. That is, to finance growth, the firm (a) may choose to issue stock, allowing internally generated funds (profits) to be used to pay dividends; or (b) it may use internally generated funds to finance its growth, while paying less in dividends but not having to issue stock. In the first case, shareholders receive dividend income; in the second case, the value of their stock should increase, providing capital gains. The nature of the return is the only difference; total returns should be about the same. Thus, to argue that paying dividends can make shareholders better off is to argue that paying out cash with one hand and taking it back with the other hand is a worthwhile activity for management.

The firm's dividend payout could affect stock price if the shareholder has no other way to receive income from the investment. However, assuming the capital markets are relatively efficient, a stockholder who needs current income could always sell shares. If the firm pays a dividend, the investor could eliminate any dividend received, in whole or in part, by using the dividend to purchase stock. The investor can thus personally create any desired dividend stream, no matter what dividend policy is in effect.

View 2: High Dividends Increase Stock Value

The belief that a firm's dividend policy is unimportant implicitly assumes that an investor should use the same required rate of return whether income comes through capital gains or through dividends. However, dividends are more predictable than capital gains; management can control dividends, but it cannot dictate the price of the stock. Investors are less certain of receiving income from capital gains than from dividends. The incremental risk associated with capital gains relative to dividend income implies a higher required rate for discounting a dollar of capital gains than for discounting a dollar of dividends. In other words, we would value a dollar of expected dividends more highly than a dollar of expected capital gains. We might, for example, require a 14 percent rate of return for a stock that pays its entire return from dividends, but a 20 percent return for a high-growth stock that pays no dividend. In so doing, we would give a higher value to the dividend income than we would to the capital gains. This view, which says dividends are more certain than capital gains, has been called the "bird-in-the-hand" theory.

The position that dividends are less risky than capital gains, and should therefore be valued differently, is not without its critics. If we hold to our basic decision not to let the firm's dividend policy influence its investment and capital-mix decisions, the company's operating cash flows, both in expected amount and variability, are unaffected by its dividend policy. Because the dividend policy has no impact on the volatility of the company's overall cash flows, it has no impact on the riskiness of the firm.

Increasing a firm's dividend does not reduce the basic riskiness of the stock; rather, if a dividend payment requires management to issue new stock, it only transfers risk *and* ownership from the current owners to new owners. We would have to acknowledge that the current investors who receive the dividend trade an uncertain capital gain for a "safe" asset (the cash dividend). However, if risk reduction is the only goal, the investor could have kept the money in the bank and not bought the stock in the first place.

We might find fault with this "bird-in-the-hand" theory, but there is still a strong perception among many investors and professional investment advisers that dividends are important. They frequently argue their case based on their own personal experience. As expressed by one investment adviser:

> In advising companies on dividend policy, we're absolutely sure on one side that the investors in companies like the utilities and the suburban banks want dividends. We're absolutely sure on the other side that...the high-technology companies should have no dividends. For the high earners—the ones that have a high rate of return like 20 percent, or more than their cost of capital—we think they should have a low payout ratio. We think a typical industrial company which earns its cost of capital—just earns its cost of capital—probably should be in the average [dividend payout] range of 40 to 50 percent.[4]

View 3: Low Dividends Increase Stock Value

The third view of how dividends affect stock price argues that dividends actually hurt the investor. This belief has largely been based on the difference in tax treatment for dividend income and capital gains. Contrary

---

[4]From a discussion by John Childs, an investment adviser at Kidder Peabody, in Donald H. Chew, Jr., ed., "Do Dividends Matter? A Discussion of Corporate Dividend Policy," in *Six Roundtable Discussions of Corporate Finance with Joel Stern* (New York: Quorum Books, 1986), pp. 83–84.

to the perfect-markets assumption of no taxes, most investors do pay income taxes. For these taxpayers, the objective is to maximize the *after-tax* return on investment relative to the risk assumed. This objective is realized by *minimizing* the effective tax rate on the income and, whenever possible, by *deferring* the payment of taxes.

Until 1987, the effective tax rate on the gain from the sale of stock was usually only 40 percent of the tax on dividend income, assuming the investor was subject to taxes. Effective January 1, 1987, federal tax law eliminated the special tax treatment given capital gains so that such gains are now taxed at the same rates as dividend income.

Although the relative tax rate advantage available for capital gains no longer exists, a distinct benefit still remains for capital gains vis-a'-vis dividend income. Taxes on dividend income are paid when the dividend is received, while taxes on price appreciation (capital gains) are deferred until the stock is actually sold. Thus, when it comes to tax considerations, most investors still prefer the retention of a firm's earnings as opposed to the payment of cash dividends. If earnings are retained within the firm, the stock price increases, but the increase is not taxed until the stock is sold.

Although the majority of investors are subject to taxes, certain investment companies, trusts, and pension plans are exempt on their dividend income. Also, for tax purposes a corporation may exclude 70 percent of the dividend income received from another corporation. In these cases, investors may prefer dividends over capital gains.

To summarize, when it comes to taxes, we want to maximize our *after*-tax return, as opposed to the *before*-tax return. Investors try to defer taxes whenever possible. Stocks that allow tax deferral (low dividends—high capital gains) will possibly sell at a premium relative to stocks that require current taxation (high dividends—low capital gains). In this way, the two stocks may provide comparable *after-tax* returns. This suggests that a policy of paying low dividends will result in a higher stock price. Again, we are reminded of the fundamental **Axiom 8: Taxes Bias Business Decisions** with the tax benefits associated with capital gains as opposed to dividend income supporting a low-dividend policy.

Improving Our Thinking

We have now looked at three views on dividend policy. Which is right? The argument that dividends are irrelevant is difficult to refute, given the perfect-market assumptions. However, in the real world, it is not always easy to feel comfortable with such an argument. Conversely, the high-dividend philosophy, which measures risk by how we split the firm's cash flows between dividends and retention, is not particularly appealing when studied carefully. The third view, which is essentially a tax argument against high dividends, is persuasive. Even today, although the preferential tax rate for capital gains no longer exists, its "deferral advantage" is still alive and well. However, if low dividends are so advantageous and generous dividends are so hurtful, why do companies continue to pay dividends? It is difficult to believe that managers would forgo such an easy opportunity to benefit their stockholders. What are we missing?

BASIC FINANCIAL MANAGEMENT IN PRACTICE

Excerpts from "Do Dividends Matter? A Discussion of Corporate Dividend Policy"

Joseph T. Willett, Moderator: I would like to welcome the participants and guests to this discussion, the subject of which is Corporate Dividend Policy. The general questions we want to address are these: Does dividend policy matter? And if so, why and how does it matter? Certain people argue that the theory of finance, combined with the treatment of dividends under U.S. tax law, would suggest that low dividends benefit investors. Others argue that because of the demand by some investors for current income, high dividends benefit investors. In the presence of these widely held views, I think it is fair to say that most carefully executed research has revealed no consistent relationship between dividends and share prices. From these studies, the market collectively appears to be "dividend neutral." That is, while individual investors may have preferences between dividends and capital gains, the results suggest neither a preference for nor an aversion to dividends. Which, of course, doesn't satisfy either the pro-dividend or anti-dividend group. Amid all this confusion, one observation stands out: nearly all successful firms pay dividends. And, furthermore, dividend policy is an important concern of most chief financial officers and financial managers generally. These facts of corporate practice, in light of all the evidence on the subject, present us with a puzzle—one which has continued to baffle the academic finance profession. In a paper written in 1976, entitled "The Dividend Puzzle," Fischer Black of MIT—one of the most widely respected researchers in the field—posed the question: "What should the individual investor do about dividends in his portfolio? What should the corporation do about dividend policy?"

Joel Stern: I'd like to point out that the major reason why people like Fischer Black believe they don't know the answer to the question of the appropriate dividend policy is this: the evidence that has been accumulated in the academic community by serious researchers—by people that we have a lot of respect for, who are on the faculties of the premiere business schools—almost without exception, these academics find that there is no evidence to suggest that investors at the margin, where prices are set, have any preference for dividends over capitagains. This supports the point of view that the price-setting, marginal investor is "dividend-neutral," which means that a dollar of dividends gained is equal to a dollar of capital

The need to find the missing elements in our "dividend puzzle" has not been ignored. When we need to understand better an issue or phenomenon, we have two options: improving our thinking or gathering more evidence about the topic. Scholars and practitioners have taken both approaches. Although no single definitive answer has yet been found that is acceptable to all, several plausible extensions have been developed. Some of the more popular additions include (1) the residual dividend theory, (2) the clientele effect, (3) information effects, (4) agency costs, and (5) expectations theory.

The Residual Dividend Theory

In perfect markets, we assume there is no cost to the firm when it issues new securities. However, in reality the process is quite expensive, and the flotation costs associated with a new offering may be as much as 20 percent of the dollar issue size. Thus, if management chooses to issue stock rather than retain profits to finance new investments, a larger amount of securities is required to receive the amount needed for the gains returned, while being indifferent how that return was divided between dividends and price appreciation. There is a second point of view, that has been expressed recently in research, which shows that investors who receive dividends cannot undo the harmful tax consequences of receiving that dividend. And, as a result, the market is actually "dividend averse," marking down prices of shares that pay cash dividends, so that the pretax returns that investors earn are high enough such that, post-tax, the returns are what they would have been had the company not paid cash dividends in the first place. But there is no creditable evidence that I am aware of—none that has been accepted by the academic finance community—that shows that investors prefer dividends over capital gains.

If the evidence that has been published to date says that investors are dividend neutral or dividend averse, then how is it that somebody with the esteem of Fischer Black can come along and say: "We don't know what the right dividend policy is." The problem is that he is what we call a "positive economist." That doesn't mean that he is an economist who is positive about things. It means that he says the job of the economist is to account for what we see around us. He believes that markets behave in a sensible fashion at the margin; that under the guidance of the dominant price-setting investors, the market behaves in a rational manner, making the right choices for itself. Therefore, he is saying that there must be a reason why almost all companies for all time have been paying cash dividends. If a few companies paid dividends for all time, or almost all companies paid dividends only occasionally, then one could make the case that it is possible dividends are really not important. But, if we find that almost all companies pay dividends for almost all time, there must be a good reason why they are paying the dividends. Therefore, who are we, as financial advisers, to say to a company, "No, don't pay cash dividends. After all, it won't harm you very much despite the fact that almost all companies are paying cash dividends"? That wouldn't make very much sense.

Source: Donald H. Chew, Jr., ed., "Do Dividends Matter? A Discussion of Corporate Dividend Policy," in *Six Roundtable Discussions of Corporate Finance with Joel Stern* (New York: Quorum Books, 1986), pp. 67–101.

investment. For example, if $300,000 is needed to finance proposed investments, an amount exceeding the $300,000 will have to be issued to offset flotation costs incurred in the sale of the new stock issue. This means, very simply, that new equity capital raised through the sale of common stock will be more expensive than capital raised through the retention of earnings.

In effect, flotation costs eliminate our indifference between financing by internal capital and by new common stock. Given these costs, dividends would be paid only if profits are not completely used for investment purposes; that is, only when there are "residual earnings" after the financing of new investments. This policy is called the **residual dividend theory.**[5]

---

[5]The residual dividend theory is consistent with the "pecking order" theory of finance as described by Stewart Myers, "The Capital Structure Puzzle," *The Journal of Finance* (July 1984), pp. 575–92.

Given the existence of flotation costs, the firm's dividend policy should now be as follows:

1. Accept an investment if the net present value is positive; that is, the expected rate of return exceeds the cost of capital.

2. Finance the equity portion of new investments *first* by internally generated funds. Only after this capital is fully utilized should the firm issue new common shares.

3. If any internally generated funds still remain after making all investments, pay dividends to the investors. However, if all internal capital is needed for financing the equity portion of proposed investments, pay no dividend.

Thus, dividend policy is influenced by (1) the company's investment opportunities, and (2) the availability of internally generated capital, where dividends are paid *only* after all acceptable investments have been financed. According to this concept, dividend policy is totally passive in nature, having by itself no direct influence on the market price of the common stock.

The Clientele Effect

What if the investors do not like the dividend policy chosen by management? In perfect markets, where we have no costs in buying or selling stock, there is no problem. The investors may simply satisfy their personal income preferences by purchasing or selling securities when the dividends received do not satisfy their current needs for income. If an investor does not view the dividends received in any given year to be sufficient, he or she can simply sell a portion of stock, thereby "creating a dividend." In addition, if the dividend is larger than the investor desired, he or she will purchase stock with the "excess cash" created by the dividend. However, once we remove the assumption of perfect markets, we find that buying or selling stock is not cost free. Brokerage fees are incurred, ranging from approximately 1 percent to 10 percent. Even more costly is that the investor who buys the stock with cash received from a dividend will have to pay taxes before reinvesting the cash. And when a stock is bought or sold, it must first be reevaluated. Acquisition of the information for decision making also may be time consuming and costly. Finally, aside from the cost of buying or selling part of the stock, some institutional investors, such as university endowment funds, are precluded from selling stock and "spending" the proceeds.

As a result of these considerations, investors may not be too inclined to buy stocks that require them to "create" a dividend stream more suitable to their purposes. Rather, if investors do in fact have a preference between dividends and capital gains, we could expect them to seek firms that have a dividend policy consistent with these preferences. They would, in essence, "sort themselves out" by buying stocks that satisfy their preferences for dividends and capital gains. Individuals and institutions that need current income would be drawn to companies that have high dividend payouts. Other investors, such as wealthy individuals, would much prefer to avoid taxes by holding securities that offer no or small dividend income but large capital gains. In other words, there would be a **clientele effect:** Firms draw a given clientele, given their stated dividend policy.

The possibility that clienteles of investors exist might lead us to believe that the firm's dividend policy matters. However, unless there is a greater aggregate demand for a particular policy than the market can satisfy, dividend policy is still unimportant; one policy is as good as the other. The clientele effect only warns firms to avoid making capricious changes in their dividend policy. Given that the firm's investment decisions are already made, the level of the dividend is still unimportant. The change in the policy matters only when it requires clientele to shift to another company.

The Information Effect

The investor in the world of perfect markets would argue with considerable persuasion that a firm's value is determined strictly by its investment and financing decisions and that the dividend policy has no impact on value. Yet we know from experience that a large, unexpected change in dividends can have a significant impact on the stock price. For instance, in November 1990 Occidental Petroleum cut its dividend from $2 to $1. In response, the firm's stock price went from about $32 to $17. How can we suggest that dividend policy matters little, when we can cite numerous such examples of a change in dividend affecting the stock price, especially when the change is negative?

Despite such "evidence," we are not looking at the real cause and effect. It may be that investors use a change in dividend policy as a *signal* about the firm's financial condition, especially its earning power. Thus, a dividend increase that is larger than expected might signal to investors that management expects significantly higher earnings in the future. Conversely, a dividend decrease, or even a less than expected increase, might signal that management is forecasting less favorable future earnings.

Some would claim that management frequently has inside information about the firm that it cannot make available to investors. This difference in accessibility to information between management and investors, called **information asymmetry,** may result in a lower stock price than would occur under conditions of certainty. This reasoning says that, by regularly increasing dividends, management is making a commitment to continue these cash flows to the stockholders for the foreseeable future. So in a risky marketplace, dividends become a means to minimize any "drag" on the stock price that might come from differences in the level of information available to managers and investors.

Dividends may therefore be important only as a communication tool; management may have no other credible way to inform investors about future earnings, or at least no convincing way that is less costly.

Agency Costs

Up to this point, we have not allowed for separation between management and owners. However, with only a superficial look at the real world, we know that managers and investors are typically not the same people. Moreover, they do not have access to the same information about the firm; nor at times do they even have the same incentives.

If the two groups are not the same, we must then assume that management is dedicated to the same goals as its owners. That is, we are making a presupposition that the behavior of companies with separate owners and managers will not differ from the behavior of owner-managed firms.

BACK TO THE FUNDAMENTALS

Axiom 7 warned us there may be a conflict between management and owners, especially in large firms where managers and owners have different incentives. That is, **Managers Won't Work for Owners Unless It Is in Their Best Interest to Do So.** As we shall see in this section, the dividend policy may be one way to reduce this problem.

In reality, however, conflicts may still exist, and the stock price of a company owned by investors who are separate from management may be less than the stock value of a closely held firm. This potential difference in price is the cost of the conflict to the owners, which has come to be called **agency costs.**[6]

Recognizing the possible problem, management, acting independently or at the insistence of the board of directors, frequently takes action to minimize the cost associated with the separation of ownership and management control. Such action, which in itself is costly, includes auditing by independent accountants, assigning supervisory functions to the company's board of directors, creating covenants in lending agreements that restrict management's powers, and providing incentive compensation plans for management that help "bond" management with the owners.

A firm's dividend policy may be perceived by owners as a tool to minimize agency costs. Assuming that the payment of a dividend requires management to issue stock to finance new investments, new investors may be attracted to the company only if management provides convincing information that the capital will be used profitably. Thus, the payment of dividends indirectly results in a closer monitoring of management's investment activities. In this case, dividends may make a meaningful contribution to the value of the firm.

Expectations Theory[7]

A common thread through much of our discussion of dividend policy, particularly as it relates to information effects, is the word *expected*. We should not overlook the significance of this word when we are making

---

[6]See M. C. Jenson, and W. H. Meckling, "Theory of the Firm: Managerial Behavior, Agency Costs, and Ownership Structure," *Journal of Financial Economics* (October 1976), pp. 305–60.

[7]Much of the thinking in this section came from Merton Miller, "Can Management Use Dividends to Influence the Value of the Firm?" in *The Revolution in Corporate Finance*, ed., Joel M. Stern, and Donald H. Chew, Jr. (New York: Basil Blackwell, 1986), pp. 299–303.

any financial decision within the firm. No matter what the decision area, how the market price responds to management's actions is not determined entirely by the action itself; it is also affected by investors' expectations about the ultimate decision to be made by management.

As the time approaches for management to announce the amount of the next dividend, investors form expectations as to how much that dividend will be. These expectations are based on several factors internal to the firm, such as past dividend decisions, current and expected earnings, investment strategies, and financing decisions. They also consider such things as the condition of the general economy, the strength or weakness of the industry at the time, and possible changes in government policies.

When the actual dividend decision is announced, the investor compares the actual decision with the expected decision. If the amount of the dividend is as expected, even if it represents an increase from prior years, the market price of the stock will remain unchanged. However, if the dividend is higher or lower than expected, investors will reassess their perceptions of the firm. They will question the meaning of the *unexpected* change in the dividend. They may use the unexpected dividend decision as a clue about unexpected changes in earnings; that is, the unexpected dividend change has information content about the firm's earnings and other important factors. In short, management's actual decision about the firm's dividend policy may not be terribly significant, unless it departs from investors' expectations. If there is a difference between actual and expected dividends, we will more than likely see a movement in the stock price.

The Empirical Evidence

Our search for an answer to the question of dividend relevance has been less than successful. We have given it our best thinking, but still no single definitive position has emerged. Maybe we could gather evidence to show the relationship between dividend practices and security prices. We might also inquire into the perceptions of financial managers who make decisions about dividend policies, with the idea that their beliefs affect their decision making. Then we could truly know that dividend policy is important or that it does not matter.

To test the relationship between dividend payments and security prices, we could compare a firm's dividend yield (dividend/stock price) and the stock's total return. The question is: Do stocks that pay high dividends provide higher or lower returns to investors? Such tests have been conducted with the use of highly sophisticated statistical techniques. Despite the use of these extremely powerful analytical tools, which involve intricate and complicated procedures, the results have been mixed.[8] However, over long periods, the results have given a slight advantage to the low-dividend stocks; that is, stocks that pay lower

---

[8]See F. Black and M. Scholes, "The Effects of Dividend Yield and Dividend Policy on Common Stock Prices and Returns," *Journal of Financial Economics*, 1 (May 1974), pp. 1–22; and M. H. Miller and M. Scholes, "Dividends and Taxes: Some Empirical Evidence," *Journal of Political Economy*, 90 (1982), pp. 1118–41.

dividends appear to have higher prices. The findings are far from conclusive, however, owing to the relatively large standard errors of the estimates. (The apparent differences may be the result of random sampling error and not real differences.) We simply have been unable to disentangle the effect of dividend policy from other influences.

Several reasons may be given for our inability to arrive at conclusive results. First, to be accurate, we would need to know the amount of dividends investors *expected* to receive. Because these expectations cannot be observed, we can only use historical data, which may or may not relate to current expectations. Second, most empirical studies have assumed a linear relationship between dividend payments and stock prices. The actual relationship may be nonlinear, possibly even discontinuous. Whatever the reasons, the evidence to date is inconclusive and the vote is still out.

Because our statistical prowess does not provide any conclusive evidence, let's turn to our last hope. What do the financial managers of the world believe about the relevance of dividend policy? Although we may not conclude that a manager's opinion is necessarily the "final word on the matter," having these insights is helpful. If financial managers believe that dividends matter and act consistently in accordance with that conviction, they could influence the relationship between stock value and dividend policy.

To help us gain some understanding of managements' perceptions, let's turn to a study by Baker, Farrelly, and Edelman, which surveyed financial executives at 318 firms listed on the New York Stock Exchange.[9] The study, conducted in 1983, favors the relevance of dividend policy, but not overwhelmingly so. For the most part, managers are divided between (a) believing that dividends are important or (b) having no opinion about the matter.

Regarding the question about the price-dividend relationship, Baker et al. asked the financial managers straight up, "Does the firm's dividend policy affect the price of the common stock?" Slightly more than 60 percent of the responses were affirmative, which is significant, but there were still almost 40 percent who had no opinion or disagreed. Thus, we could conclude that most managers think that dividends matter, but they have no mandate. Similarly, when asked if dividends provide informational content about the firm's future, the managers are basically split between "no opinion" and "agreement." When asked about the tradeoff between dividends and capital gains, almost two-thirds of the managers thought stockholders have a preference either for dividend or capital gains, with a lesser number (56 percent) believing that investors perceive the relative riskiness of capital gains and dividends to be different. Interestingly enough, though, almost half of the managers felt no clear responsibility to be responsive to stockholders' preferences.

---

[9]H. Kent Baker, Gail E. Farrelly, and Richard B. Edelman, "A Survey of Management Views on Dividend Policy," *Financial Management*, Autumn 1985, pp. 78–84.

What Are We to Conclude?

We have now looked carefully at the importance of a firm's dividend policy as management seeks to increase the shareholders' wealth. We have gone to great lengths to gain insight and understanding from our best thinking. We have even drawn from the empirical evidence on hand to see what the findings suggest.

A reasonable person cannot reach a definitive conclusion; nevertheless, management is left with no choice. A firm must develop a dividend policy, it is hoped, based on the best available knowledge. Although we can give advice only with some reservation, the following conclusions would appear reasonable:

1. As a firm's investment opportunities increase, the dividend payout ratio should decrease. In other words, an inverse relationship should exist between the amount of investments with an expected rate of return that exceeds the cost of capital (positive *NPVs)* and the dividends remitted to investors. Because of flotation costs associated with raising external capital, the retention of internally generated equity financing is preferable to selling stock (in terms of the wealth of the current common shareholders).

2. The firm's dividend policy appears to be important; however, appearances may be deceptive. The real issue may be the firm's *expected* learning power and the riskiness of these earnings. Investors may be using the dividend payment as a source of information about the company's *expected* earnings. Management's actions regarding dividends may carry greater weight than a statement by management that earnings will be increasing.

3. If dividends influence stock price, this is probably based on the investor's desire to minimize and defer taxes, and from the role of dividends in minimizing agency costs.

4. If the expectations theory has merit, which we believe it does, management should avoid surprising investors when it comes to the firm's dividend decision. The firm's dividend policy might effectively be treated as a *long-term residual.* Rather than projecting investment requirements for a single year, management could anticipate financing needs for several years. Based on the expected investment opportunities during the planning horizon, the firm's debt-equity mix, and the funds generated from operations, a *target* dividend payout ratio could be established. If internal funds remained after projection of the necessary equity financing, dividends would be paid. However, the planned dividend stream should distribute residual capital evenly to investors over the planning period. Conversely, if over the long term the entire amount of internally generated capital is needed for reinvestment in the company, then no dividend should be paid.

THE DIVIDEND DECISION IN PRACTICE

In setting a firm's dividend policy, financial managers must work in the world of reality with the concepts we have set forth so far in this chapter. Again, although these concepts do not provide an equation that explains the key relationships, they certainly give us a more complete view of the finance world, which can only help us make better decisions. Other considerations of a more practical nature also appear as part of the firm's decision making about its dividend policy.

Other Practical Considerations

Many considerations may influence a firm's decision about its dividends, some of them unique to that company. Some of the more general considerations are given subsequently.

Legal Restrictions

Certain legal restrictions may limit the amount of dividends a firm may pay. These legal constraints fall into two categories. First, *statutory restrictions* may prevent a company from paying dividends. While specific limitations vary by state, generally a corporation may not pay a dividend (1) if the firm's liabilities exceed its assets, (2) if the amount of the dividend exceeds the accumulated profits (retained earnings), and (3) if the dividend is being paid from capital invested in the firm.

The second type of legal restriction is unique to each firm and results from restrictions in debt and preferred stock contracts. To minimize their risk, investors frequently impose restrictive provisions on management as a condition to their investment in the company. These constraints may include the provision that dividends may not be declared prior to the debt being repaid. Also, the corporation may be required to maintain a given amount of working capital. Preferred stockholders may stipulate that common dividends may not be paid when any preferred dividends are delinquent.

Liquidity Position

Contrary to common opinion, the mere fact that a company shows a large amount of retained earnings in the balance sheet does not indicate that cash is available for the payment of dividends. The firm's current position in liquid assets, including cash, is basically independent of the retained earnings account. Historically, a company with sizable retained earnings has been successful in generating cash from operations. Yet these funds are typically either reinvested in the company within a short period or used to pay maturing debt. Thus, a firm may be extremely profitable and still be *cash poor*. Because dividends are paid with cash, *and not with retained earnings*, the firm must have cash available for dividends to be paid. Hence, the firm's liquidity position has a direct bearing on its ability to pay dividends.

By the Throat

An Irishman raised in England and educated at Oxford and Harvard Business School is going to end up a firm favourite with management academics. Dermot Dunphy, who runs Sealed Air, America's leading specialty packaging company, has made a high-debt strategy work where so many others ... have failed.

Sealed Air produces the sheets of plastic bubble wrap that are so tempting to pop. By the mid-1980s the 25-year-old firm had changed packaging worldwide with proprietary light-weight materials such as padded "Jiffy" envelopes and the polystyrene foam that encloses most things packed in boxes. The company dominated its domestic market and was successful abroad, even in such tough markets as Japan. But it had also become complacent. The business was such a cash-cow that Sealed Air's managers just milked its sales and grew lazy at manufacturing.

This was dangerous. Its bubble-wrap patents were starting to run out, and rivals were appearing on the horizon. After buying several other packaging firms to expand its product line, there were few companies in the industry left to buy. In 1989 Mr. Dunphy decided to shake his colleagues' complacency by abruptly handing $328m back to shareholders in the form of a $40-a-share special dividend, at a time when the shares were trading at $45.

This was, indeed, quite a jolt. The biggest annual dividend Sealed Air had ever paid shareholders was 58 cents. The payout was equivalent to 87% of the company's market capitalisation—and 94% of the cash had to be borrowed. Mr Dunphy borrowed 70% of the dividend-money from his banks, after some arm-twisting. He raised the rest by selling junk bonds. The dividend transformed Sealed Air into a company with negative net worth of $177.5m.

This created what Mr. Dunphy calls a "controlled crisis." But high debt-repayments have concentrated managers' minds wonderfully. Delivery lead times have been halved and operating margins improved by one-third compared with levels before the debt was taken on. Earnings per share (calculated after tax) soared 56% last year and are likely to rise 27% this year. Pre-tax profits are set to rise 20%, to around $30m, on sales up 4% to about $430m compared with a year earlier. This is despite the fact that many of the company's customers, especially in America, are suffering from recession.

Source: "Sealed Air," *The Economist*, September 14, 1991. Used by permission.

Absence or Lack of Other Sources of Financing

As already noted, a firm may (1) retain profits for investment purposes, or (2) pay dividends and issue new debt or equity securities to finance investments. For many small or new companies, this second option is not realistic. These firms do not have access to the capital markets, so they must rely more heavily on internally generated funds. As a consequence, the dividend payout ratio is generally much lower for a small or newly established firm than for a large, publicly owned corporation.

Earnings Predictability

A company's dividend payout ratio depends to some extent on the predictability of a firm's profits over time. If earnings fluctuate significantly, management cannot rely on internally generated funds to meet future needs. When profits are realized, the firm may retain larger amounts to ensure that money is available when needed. Conversely, a firm with a stable earnings trend will typically pay a larger portion of its earnings out in dividends. This company has less concern about the availability of profits to meet future capital requirements.

Ownership Control

For many large corporations, control through the ownership of common stock is not an issue. However, for many small and medium-sized companies, maintaining voting control takes a high priority. If the current common shareholders are unable to participate in a new offering, issuing new stock is unattractive, in that the control of the current stockholders is diluted. The owners might prefer that management finance new investments with debt and through profits rather than by issuing new common stock. This firm's growth is then constrained by the amount of debt capital available and by the company's ability to generate profits.

Inflation

Before the late 1970s, inflationary pressures had not been a significant problem for either consumers or businesses. However during much of the 1980s, the deterioration of the dollar's purchasing power had a direct impact on the replacement of fixed assets. In a period of inflation, ideally, as fixed assets become worn and obsolete, the funds generated from depreciation are used to finance the replacements. As the cost of equivalent equipment continues to increase, the depreciation funds become insufficient. This requires a greater retention of profits, which implies that dividends have to be adversely affected. In the 1990s, however, inflation has not been a primary concern for most companies.

Alternate Dividend Policies

Regardless of a firm's long-term dividend policy, most firms choose one of several year-to-year dividend payment patterns:

1. **Constant dividend payout ratio.** In this policy, the percentage of earnings paid out in dividends is held constant. Although the dividend-to-earnings ratio is stable, the dollar amount of the dividend naturally fluctuates from year to year as profits vary.

2. **Stable dollar dividend per share.** This policy maintains a relatively stable dollar dividend over time. An increase in the dollar dividend usually does not occur until management is convinced that the higher dividend level can be maintained in the future. Management also will not reduce the dollar dividend until the evidence clearly indicates that a continuation of the current dividend cannot be supported.

3. **Small, regular dividend plus a year-end extra.** A corporation following this policy pays a small regular dollar dividend plus a year-end *extra dividend* in prosperous years. The extra dividend is declared toward the end of the fiscal year, when the company's profits for the period can be estimated. Management's objective is to avoid the connotation of a permanent dividend. However, this purpose may be defeated if *recurring* extra dividends come to be expected by investors.

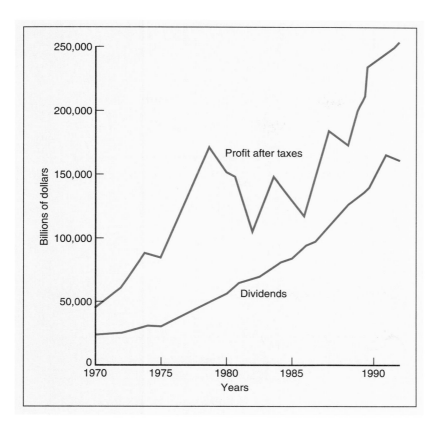

FIGURE 13–2
Corporate Earnings and
Dividends

Of the three dividend policies, the stable dollar dividend is by far the most common. Figure 13–2 graphs the general tendency of companies to pay stable, but increasing, dividends, even though the profits fluctuate significantly. In one study, corporate managers were found to be reluctant to change the dollar amount of the dividend in response to temporary fluctuations in earnings from year to year. This aversion was particularly evident when it came to decreasing the amount of the dividend from the previous level.[10] One explanation for the stable dividend is the "increasing-stream hypothesis of dividend policy," which suggests that dividend stability is essentially a smoothing of the dividend stream to minimize the effect of other types of company reversals.[11] Thus, corporate managers make every effort to avoid a dividend cut, attempting instead to develop a gradually increasing dividend series over the long-term future. However, if a dividend reduction is absolutely necessary, the cut should be large enough to reduce the probability of future cuts.

As an example of a stable dividend policy, Figure 13–3 compares W. R. Grace & Co.'s earnings per share and dividends per share for 1980 through 1993. Ignoring some of the less typical years, the firm has paid

[10]John Lintner, "Distribution of Income of Corporations Among Dividends, Retained Earnings, and Taxes," *American Economic Review*, 46 (May 1956), pp. 97–113.
[11]Keith V. Smith, "Increasing-Stream Hypothesis of Corporate Dividend Policy," *California Management Review*, 15 (Fall 1971), pp. 56–64.

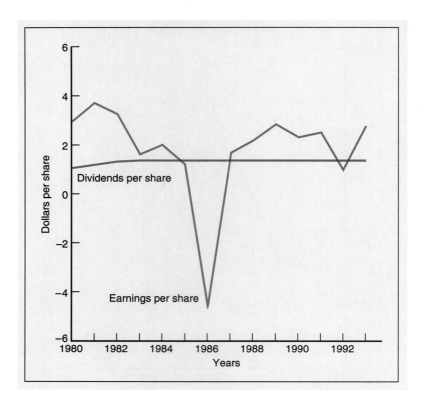

FIGURE 13–3
Earnings per Share and
Dividends per Share:
W. R. Grace & Company

around 50 percent to 60 percent of its earnings out in dividends. This percentage, however, has varied from 33 percent in 1981 to 140 percent in 1992. Thus, the historical dividends and earnings patterns for the firm clearly demonstrate management's hesitancy to change dividends in response to short-term fluctuations in earnings. Profits have been highly volatile since 1981; however, the dollar dividends have been held constant or even increased. On the other hand, when profits rose sharply in 1981 and again in 1993, dividends were increased only slightly if at all.

PERSPECTIVE IN FINANCE

We don't know much with certitude about dividend policy and its effect on the firm's stock price, but we do know quite a lot about dividend practices, including that managers fear the thought of cutting the dividend. It usually will be done only as a last resort. Count on it.

■ DIVIDEND PAYMENT PROCEDURES

After the firm's dividend policy has been structured, several procedural details must be arranged. For instance, how frequently are dividend payments to be made? If a stockholder sells the shares during the year, who is entitled to the dividend? To answer these questions, we need to understand dividend payment procedures.

Dividend Payouts: Different Practices in Different Countries

How much of earnings do most firms pay out in dividends? It depends on the country. As shown in the accompanying graph, British firms pay out a lot more than German and Japanese companies.

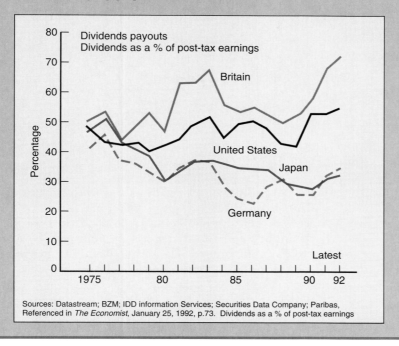

Dividends payouts
Dividends as a % of post-tax earnings

Sources: Datastream; BZM; IDD information Services; Securities Data Company; Paribas, Referenced in *The Economist*, January 25, 1992, p.73. Dividends as a % of post-tax earnings

Generally, companies pay dividends on a quarterly basis. To illustrate, General Electric pays $2.52 per share in annual dividends. However, the firm actually issues a $.63 quarterly dividend for a total yearly dividend of $2.52 ($.63 × 4 quarters).

The final approval of a dividend payment comes from the board of directors. As an example, Delta Airlines, on January 26, 1993, announced that holders of record as of February 5 would receive a $.30 dividend. The dividend payment was to be made on March 1. January 26 is the **declaration date**—the date when the dividend is formally declared by the board of directors. The **date of record,** February 5, designates when the stock transfer books are to be closed. Investors shown to own the stock on this date receive the dividend. If a notification of a transfer is recorded subsequent to February 5, the new owner is not entitled to the dividend. However, a problem could develop if the stock were sold on February 4, one day prior to the record date. Time would not permit the sale to be reflected on the stockholder list by the February 5 date of record. To avoid this problem, stock brokerage companies have uniformly decided to terminate the right of ownership to the dividend four working days prior to the record date.

DIVIDEND POLICY AND
INTERNAL FINANCING

This prior date is the **ex-dividend date.** Therefore, any acquirer of Delta stock on February 2 or thereafter does not receive the dividend. Finally, the company mails the dividend check to each investor on March 1, the **payment date.** These events may be diagrammed as follows:

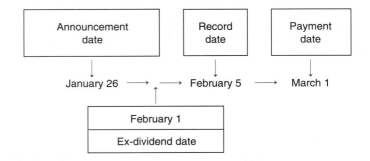

■ STOCK DIVIDENDS AND STOCK SPLITS

An integral part of dividend policy is the use of **stock dividends** and **stock splits.** Both involve issuing new shares of stock on a pro rata basis to the current shareholders, while the firm's assets, its earnings, the risk assumed, and the investor's percentage of ownership in the company remain unchanged. The only *definite* result from either a stock dividend or stock split is the increase in the number of shares of stock outstanding.

To illustrate the effect of a stock dividend, assume that the Katie Corporation has 100,000 shares outstanding.[12] The firm's after-tax profits are $500,000, or $5 in earnings per share. Currently, the company's stock is selling at a price/earnings multiple of 10, or $50 per share. Management is planning to issue a 20 percent stock dividend, so that a stockholder owning 10 shares would receive two additional shares. We might immediately conclude that this investor is being given an asset (two shares of stock) worth $100; consequently, his or her personal worth should increase by $100. This conclusion is erroneous. The firm will be issuing 20,000 new shares (100,000 shares × 20 percent). Since the $500,000 in after-tax profits does not change, the new earnings per share will be $4.167 ($500,000/120,000 shares). If the price/earnings multiple remains at 10, the market price of the stock after the dividend should fall to $41.67 ($4.167 earnings per share × 10). The investor now owns 12 shares worth $41.67, which provides a $500 total value; thus he or she is neither better nor worse off than before the stock dividend.

This example may make us wonder why a corporation would even bother with a stock dividend or stock split if no one benefits. However, before we study the rationale for such distributions, we should understand the differences between a stock split and a stock dividend.

---

[12]The logic of this illustration is equally applicable to a *stock split.*

Common stock		
Par value (1,000,000 shares outstanding; $2 par value)	$ 2,000,000	
Paid-in capital	8,000,000	
Retained earnings	15,000,000	
Total equity	$25,000,000	

TABLE 13–1
L. Bernard Corporation
Balance Sheet
Before Stock Dividend

Common stock		
Par value (1,150,000 shares outstanding; $2 par value)	$ 2,300,000	
Paid-in capital	9,800,000	
Retained earnings	12,900,000	
Total equity	$25,000,000	

TABLE 13–2
L. Bernard Corporation
Balance Sheet
After Stock Dividend

Common stock		
Par value (2,000,000 shares outstanding; $1 par value)	$ 2,000,000	
Paid-in capital	8,000,000	
Retained earnings	15,000,000	
Total equity	$25,000,000	

TABLE 13–3
L. Bernard Corporation
Balance Sheet
After Stock Split

Stock Dividend versus Split

The only difference between a stock dividend and a stock split relates to their respective accounting treatment. Stated differently, *there is absolutely no difference on an economic basis between a stock dividend and a stock split.* Both represent a proportionate distribution of additional shares to the current stockholders. However, *for accounting purposes* the stock split has been defined as a stock dividend exceeding 25 percent.[13] Thus, a stock dividend is conventionally defined as a distribution of shares up to 20 percent of the number of shares currently outstanding.

The accounting treatment for a stock dividend requires the issuing firm to capitalize the "market value" of the dividend. In other words, the dollar amount of the dividend is transferred from retained earnings to the capital accounts (par and paid-in capital). This procedure may best be explained by an example. Assume that the L. Bernard Corporation is preparing to issue a 15 percent stock dividend. Table 13–1 presents the equity portion of the firm's balance sheet prior to the distribution. The market price for the stock has been $14. Thus, the 15 percent stock dividend increases the number of shares by 150,000 (1,000,000 shares × 15 percent). The "market value" of this increase is $2,100,000 (150,000 shares × $14 market price). To record this transaction, $2,100,000 would be transferred from retained earnings, resulting in a $300,000 increase in total par value (150,000 shares × $2 par value) and a $1,800,000 increment

[13]A 25 percent standard applies to corporations listed on the New York Stock Exchange.

to paid-in capital. The $1,800,000 is the residual difference between $2,100,000 and $300,000. Table 13–2 shows the revised balance sheet.

What if the management of L. Bernard Corporation changed the plan and decided to split the stock two for one? In other words, a *100 percent increase* in the number of shares would result. In accounting for the split, the changes to be recorded are (1) an increase in the number of shares and (2) a decrease in the per-share par value from $2 to $1. The dollar amounts of each account do not change. Table 13–3 reveals the new balance sheet.

Thus, for a stock dividend, an amount equal to the market value of the stock dividend is transferred from retained earnings to the capital stock accounts. When stock is split, only the number of shares changes, and the par value of each share is decreased proportionately. Despite this dissimilarity in accounting treatment, remember that no real economic difference exists between a split and a dividend.

Rationale for a Stock Dividend or Split

Although *stock* dividends and splits occur far less frequently than *cash* dividends, a significant number of companies choose to use these share distributions either with or in lieu of cash dividends. Since no economic benefit results, how do corporations justify these distributions?

Proponents of stock dividends and splits frequently maintain that stockholders receive a key benefit because the price of the stock will not fall precisely in proportion to the share increase. For a two-for-one split, the price of the stock might not decrease a full 50 percent, and the stockholder is left with a higher total value. There are two reasons for this disequilibrium. First, many financial executives believe that an optimal price range exists. Within this range the total market value of the common stockholders is thought to be maximized. As the price exceeds this range, fewer investors can purchase the stock, thereby restraining the demand. Consequently, downward pressure is placed on its price. The second explanation relates to the *informational content* of the dividend-split announcement. Stock dividends and splits have generally been associated with companies with growing earnings. The announcement of a stock dividend or split has therefore been perceived as favorable news. The empirical evidence, however, fails to verify these conclusions. Most studies indicate that investors are perceptive in identifying the true meaning of a share distribution. If the stock dividend or split is not accompanied by a positive trend in earnings and increases in cash dividends, price increases surrounding the stock dividend or split are insignificant.[14] Therefore, we should be suspicious of the assertion that a stock dividend or split can help increase investors' worth.

A second reason for stock dividends or splits is the conservation of corporate cash. If a company is encountering cash problems, it may substitute a stock dividend for a cash dividend. However, as before,

---

[14]See James A. Millar and Bruce D. Fielitz, "Stock Split and Stock-Dividend Decisions," *Financial Management*, Winter 1973, pp. 35–45; and Eugene Fama, Lawrence Fisher, Michael Jensen, and Richard Roll, "The Adjustment of Stock Prices to New Information," *International Economic Review*, February 1969, pp. 1–21.

investors will probably look beyond the dividend to ascertain the underlying reason for conserving cash. If the stock dividend is an effort to conserve cash for attractive investment opportunities, the shareholder may bid up the stock price. If the move to conserve cash relates to financial difficulties within the firm, the market price will most likely react adversely.

■ STOCK REPURCHASES

For well over three decades, corporate managements have been active in repurchasing their own equity securities. Several reasons have been given for repurchasing stock. Examples of such benefits include

1. Means for providing an internal investment opportunity
2. Approach for modifying the firm's capital structure
3. Favorable impact on earnings per share
4. Elimination of a minority ownership group of stockholders
5. Minimize the dilution in earnings per share associated with mergers
6. Reduction in the firm's costs associated with servicing small stockholders

Also, from the shareholders' perspective, a stock repurchase, as opposed to a cash dividend, has a potential tax advantage.

Share Repurchase as a Dividend Decision

Clearly, the payment of a common stock dividend is the conventional method for distributing a firm's profits to its owners. However, it need not be the only way. Another approach is to repurchase the firm's stock. The concept may best be explained by an example.

EXAMPLE

Telink, Inc., is planning to pay $4 million ($4 per share) in dividends to its common stockholders. The following earnings and market price information is provided for Telink:

Net income	$7,500,000
Number of shares	1,000,000
Earnings per share	$7.50
Price/earnings ratio	8
Expected market price per share after dividend payment	$60

In a recent meeting several board members, who are also major stockholders, question the need for a dividend payment. They maintain that they do not need the income, so why not allow the firm to retain the funds for future investments? In response, management contends that the available investments are not sufficiently profitable to justify retention of the income. That is, the investors' required rates of return exceed the expected rates of return that could be earned with the additional $4 million in investments.

Because management opposes the idea of retaining the profits for investment purposes, one of the firm's directors has suggested that the $4 million be used to repurchase the company's stock. In this way, the value of the stock should increase. This result may be demonstrated as follows:

1. Assume that shares are repurchased by the firm at the $60 market price (ex-dividend price) plus the contemplated $4 dividend per share, or for $64 per share.

2. Given a $64 price, 62,500 shares would be repurchased ($4 million ÷ $64 price).

3. If net income is not reduced, but the number of shares declines as a result of the share repurchase, earnings per share would increase from $7.50 to $8, computed as follows:

$$\text{earnings per share} = \text{net income/outstanding shares}$$
$$(\text{before repurchase}) = \$7,500,000/1,000,000$$
$$= \$7.50$$
$$(\text{after repurchase}) = \$7,500,000/(1,000,000 - 62,500)$$
$$= \$8$$

4. Assuming that the price/earnings ratio remains at 8, the new price after the repurchase would be $64, up from $60, where the increase exactly equals the amount of the dividend forgone. ■

In this example, Telink's stockholders are essentially provided the same value, whether a dividend is paid or stock is repurchased. If management pays a dividend, the investor will have a stock valued at $60 plus $4 received from the dividend. Conversely, if stock is repurchased in lieu of the dividend, the stock will be worth $64. These results were based on assuming (1) the stock is being repurchased at the exact $64 price, (2) the $7,500,000 net income is unaffected by the repurchase, and (3) the price/earnings ratio of 8 does not change after the repurchase. Given these assumptions, however, the stock repurchase serves as a perfect substitute for the dividend payment to the stockholders.

The Investor's Choice

Given the choice between a stock repurchase and a dividend payment, which would an investor prefer? In perfect markets, where there are no taxes, no commissions when buying and selling stock, and no informational content assigned to a dividend, the investor would be indifferent with regard to the choices. The investor could create a dividend stream by selling stock when income is needed.

If market imperfections exist, the investor may have a preference for one of the two methods of distributing the corporate income. First, the firm may have to pay too high a price for the repurchased stock, which is to the detriment of the remaining stockholders. If a relatively large number of shares are being bought, the price may be bid up too high, only to fall after the repurchase operation. Second, as a result of the repurchase the market may perceive the riskiness of the corporation as increasing, which would lower the price/earnings ratio and the value of the stock.

Financing or Investment Decision

Repurchasing stock when the firm has excess cash may be regarded as a dividend decision. However, a stock repurchase may also be viewed as a financing decision. By issuing debt and then repurchasing stock, a firm can immediately alter its debt-equity mix toward a higher proportion of debt. Rather than choosing how to distribute cash to the stockholders, management is using a stock repurchase as a means to change the corporation's capital structure.

In addition to dividend and financing decisions, many managers consider a stock repurchase an investment decision. When equity prices are depressed in the marketplace, management may view the firm's own stock as being materially undervalued and representing a good investment opportunity. While the firm's management may be wise to repurchase stock at unusually low prices, this decision cannot and should not be viewed in the context of an investment decision. Buying its own stock cannot provide expected returns as other investments do. No company can survive, much less prosper, by investing only in its own stock.

The Repurchase Procedure

If management intends to repurchase a block of the firm's outstanding shares, it should make this information public. All investors should be given the opportunity to work with complete information. They should be told the purpose of the repurchase, as well as the method to be used to acquire the stock.

Three methods for stock repurchase are available. First, the shares could be bought in the *open market*. Here the firm acquires the stock through a stockbroker at the going market price. This approach may place an upward pressure on the stock price until the stock is acquired. Also, commissions must be paid to the stockbrokers as a fee for their services.

The second method is to make a tender offer to the firm's shareholders. A **tender offer** is a formal offer by the company to buy a specified number of shares at a predetermined and stated price. The tender price is set above the current market price in order to attract sellers. A tender offer is best when a relatively large number of shares are to be bought, since the company's intentions are clearly known and each shareholder has the opportunity to sell the stock at the tendered price.

The third and final method for repurchasing stock entails the purchase of the stock from one or more major stockholders. These purchases are made on a *negotiated basis*. Care should be taken to ensure a fair and equitable price. Otherwise the remaining stockholders may be hurt as a result of the sale.

SUMMARY

In determining the firm's dividend policy, the key issue is the dividend payout ratio (the percentage of the earnings paid out in dividends). This decision has an immediate impact on the firm's financial mix. As the dividend payment is increased, fewer funds are available internally for financing investments. Consequently, if additional equity capital is needed, the company has to issue new common stock. Keeping this interaction between the level of dividends and financing in mind, management has to determine the *best* dividend policy for the company's investors. However, selection of the most beneficial dividend payment is not easily accomplished. Management cannot apply an equation to resolve the question. We simply have been unable to disentangle the relationship between dividend policy and share price.

In its simplest form, the dividend payment is a *residual* factor. In this context, the dividend equals the remaining internal capital after financing the equity portion of investments. However, this single criterion fails to recognize (1) the tax benefit of capital gains, (2) agency costs, (3) the clientele effect, and (4) the informational content of a given policy. Furthermore, other considerable factors include the firm's liquidity position, the accessibility to capital markets, inflation, legal restrictions, the stability of earnings, and the desire of investors to maintain control of the company.

Given the firm's investment opportunities and the imperfections in the market, the financial manager should probably apply the residual dividend theory over the long term. In essence, the firm's investment opportunities are projected throughout a multiple-year planning horizon. Given these investment needs, the target debt mix, and the anticipated earnings, then the amount of money available to pay dividends for the planning period may be determined. The dividend payments should then be made so that large and unexpected changes in the dividend per share are avoided.

Stock dividends and stock splits have been used by corporations either in lieu of or to supplement cash dividends. Currently, no empirical evidence identifies a relationship between stock dividends and splits and the market price of the stock. Yet a stock dividend or split could conceivably be used to keep the stock price within an optimal trading range. Also, if investors perceive that the stock dividend contained favorable information about the firm's operations, the price of the stock could increase.

As an alternative to paying a dividend, management can repurchase stock. However, investors may still prefer dividends to a stock repurchase.

STUDY QUESTIONS

13–1.   What is meant by the term *dividend payout ratio?*
13–2.   Explain the tradeoff between retaining internally generated funds and paying cash dividends.

13–3. **a.** What are the assumptions of a perfect market?
b. What effect does dividend policy have on the share price in a perfect market?

13–4. What is the impact of flotation costs on the financing decision?

13-5. **a.** What is the *residual dividend theory?*
b. Why is this theory operational only in the long term?

13–6. Why might investors prefer capital gains to the same amount of dividend income?

13–7. What legal restrictions may limit the amount of dividends to be paid?

13–8. How does a firm's liquidity position affect the payment of dividends?

13–9. How can ownership control constrain the growth of a firm?

13–10. **a.** Why is a stable dollar dividend policy popular from the viewpoint of the corporation?
b. Is it also popular with investors? Why?

13–11. Explain declaration date, date of record, and ex-dividend date.

13–12. What are the advantages of a stock split or dividend over a cash dividend?

13–13. Why would a firm repurchase its own stock?

SELF-TEST PROBLEMS

ST-1. (*Dividend Growth Rate*) Schulz, Inc., maintains a constant dividend payout ratio of 35 percent. Earnings per share last year were $8.20 and are expected to grow indefinitely at a rate of 12 percent. What will be the dividend per share this year? In five years?

ST-2. (*Stock Split*) The debt and equity section of the Robson Corporation balance sheet is shown below. The current market price of the common shares is $20. Reconstruct the financial statement assuming that (a) a 15 percent stock dividend is issued and (b) a two-for-one stock split is declared.

Debt	$1,800,000
Common	
Par ($2; 100,000 shares)	200,000
Paid-in capital	400,000
Retained earnings	900,000
	$3,300,000

STUDY PROBLEMS

13–1. (*Flotation Costs and Issue Size*) Your firm needs to raise $10 million. Assuming that flotation costs are expected to be $15 per share and that the market price of the stock is $120, how many shares would have to be issued? What is the dollar size of the issue?

13–2. (*Flotation Costs and Issue Size*) If flotation costs for a common stock issue are 18 percent, how large must the issue be so that the firm will net $5,800,000? If the stock sells for $85 per share, how many shares must be issued?

13–3. (*Stock Dividend*) RCB has 2 million shares of common stock outstanding. Net income is $550,000, and the P/E ratio for the stock is 10. Management is planning a 20 percent stock dividend. What will be the price of the stock after the stock dividend? If an investor owns 100 shares prior to the stock dividend, does the total value of his or her shares change? Explain.

13–4.   (*Stock Split*) You own 5 percent of Trexco Corporation's common stock, which most recently sold for $98 prior to a planned two-for-one stock split announcement. Before the split there are 25,000 shares of common stock outstanding.

a.   Relative to now, what will be your financial position after the stock split? (Assume the stock price falls proportionately.)

b.   The executive vice-president in charge of finance believes the price will only fall 40 percent after the split because she feels the price is above the optimal price range. If she is correct, what will be your net gain?

13–5.   (*Dividend Policies*) The earnings for Crystal Cargo, Inc., have been predicted for the next five years and are listed below. There are 1 million shares outstanding. Determine the yearly dividend per share to be paid if the following policies are enacted:

a.   Constant dividend payout ratio of 50 percent.

b.   Stable dollar dividend targeted at 50 percent of the earnings over the five-year period.

c.   Small, regular dividend of $.50 per share plus a year-end extra when the profits in any year exceed $1,500,000. The year-end extra dividend will equal 50 percent of profits exceeding $1,500,000.

Year	Profits After Taxes
1	$1,400,000
2	2,000,000
3	1,860,000
4	900,000
5	2,800,000

13–6.   (*Repurchase of Stock*) The Dunn Corporation is planning to pay dividends of $500,000. There are 250,000 shares outstanding, with an earnings per share of $5. The stock should sell for $50 after the ex-dividend date. If instead of paying a dividend, management decides to repurchase stock

a.   What should be the repurchase price?

b.   How many shares should be repurchased?

c.   What if the repurchase price is set below or above your suggested price in part (a)?

d.   If you own 100 shares, would you prefer that the company pay the dividend or repurchase stock?

13–7.   (*Flotation Costs and Issue Size*) D. Butler, Inc., needs to raise $14 million. Assuming that the market price of the firm's stock is $95 and flotation costs are 10 percent of the market price, how many shares would have to be issued? What is the dollar size of the issue?

13–8.   (*Stock Split*) You own 20 percent of Rainy Corp., which recently sold for $86 before a planned two-for-one stock split announcement. Before the split there are 80,000 shares of common stock outstanding.

a.   What is your financial position before the split, and what will it be after the stock split? (Assume the stock falls proportionately.)

b.   Your stockbroker believes the market will react positively to the split and that the price will fall only 45 percent after the split. If she is correct, what will be your net gain?

SELF-TEST SOLUTIONS

SS-1.

Dividend per share = 35% × $8.20
= $2.87

Dividends:
1 year = $2.87 (1 + 0.12)
= $3.21
5 years = $2.87 (1 + 0.12)^5
= $2.87 (1.762)
= $5.06

SS-2.

a. If a 15 percent stock dividend is issued, the financial statement would appear as follows:

Debt	$1,800,000
Common	
Par ($2 par, 115,000 shares)	230,000
Paid-in capital	670,000
Retained earnings	600,000
	$3,300,000

b. A two-for-one split would result in a 100 percent increase in the number of shares. Because the total par value remains at $200,000, the new par value per share is $1 ($200,000/200,000 shares). The new financial statement would be as follows:

Debt	$1,800,000
Common	
Par ($1 par, 200,000 shares)	200,000
Paid-in capital	400,000
Retained earnings	900,000
	$3,300,000

CHAPTER 14
INTRODUCTION TO WORKING-CAPITAL MANAGEMENT

Managing Current Assets and Liabilities • Appropriate Level of Working Capital • Estimation of the Cost of Short-Term Credit • Sources of Short-Term Credit

Traditionally, **working capital** has been defined as the firm's investment in current assets. **Current assets** comprise all assets that the firm expects to convert into cash within the year, including cash, marketable securities, accounts receivable, and inventories. Managing the firm's working capital, however, has come to mean more than simply managing the firm's investment in current assets. In fact, a more descriptive title for this chapter might be "Net Working-Capital Management", where **net working capital** refers to the difference in the firm's current assets and its current liabilities:

$$\text{net working capital} = \text{current assets} - \text{current liabilities} \quad \textbf{(14–1)}$$

Thus, in managing the firm's net working capital, we are concerned with *managing the firm's liquidity*. This entails managing two related aspects of the firm's operations:

1. Investment in current assets
2. Use of short-term or current liabilities

This chapter provides the basic principles underlying the analysis of each of these aspects.

476

In examining investment in current assets and the use of short-term liabilities, two major issues are involved: (1) How much short-term financing should the firm use? and (2) What specific sources of short-term financing should the firm select? We will first use the hedging principle of working-capital management to answer the first of these two questions. We will then answer the second of the questions above: How should the financial manager select sources of short-term credit? In general, three basic factors should be considered in selecting a source of short-term credit: (1) the effective cost of credit, (2) the availability of credit in the amount needed and for the period financing is required, and (3) the influence of the use of a particular credit source on the cost and availability of other sources of financing. We discuss the problem of estimating the cost of short-term credit before introducing the various sources of credit because the same procedure is used for all sources.

The importance of working-capital management cannot be overstated. As we will see, for many firms current assets represent over half of the total assets. Moreover, surveys of financial managers indicate that the majority of their time is taken by the management of the day-to-day operations of the firm. This is largely the management of current assets and liabilities. Finally, for smaller firms, working-capital management takes on even greater importance. For smaller firms, access to capital markets, and the long-term sources of financing they supply, is limited. As such, smaller firms are forced to rely more heavily on short-term sources of financing, such as trade credit, accounts receivable, and inventory loans.

■ MANAGING CURRENT ASSETS AND LIABILITIES

Other things remaining the same, the greater the firm's investment in current assets, the greater its liquidity. As a means of increasing its liquidity, the firm may choose to invest additional funds in cash or marketable securities. Such action involves a tradeoff, however, because such assets earn little or no return. The firm thus finds that it can reduce its risk of illiquidity only by reducing its overall return on invested funds, and vice versa.

Working-Capital Management and the Risk-Return Tradeoff

The **risk-return tradeoff** involved in managing the firm's working capital involves a tradeoff between the firm's liquidity and its profitability. By maintaining a large investment in current assets like cash and inventory the firm reduces the chance of production stoppages and lost sales from inventory shortages and the inability to pay bills on time, which might in turn result in credit rating problems. However, as the firm increases its investment in working capital there is not a corresponding increase in its returns. This means that the firm's return on investment drops because profits are unchanged while the investment in assets increases.

BACK TO THE FUNDAMENTALS

Many of the working-capital decisions made by financial managers involve risk-return tradeoffs between liquidity and profitability. The principles that guide these decisions are the same ones set out in **Axiom 1: The Risk-Return Tradeoff—We Won't Take on Additional Risk Unless We Expect To Be Compensated with Additional Return.** The more current assets held and the more long-term financing used, the less the risk and the less the return.

The firm's use of current versus long-term debt also involves a risk-return tradeoff. *Other things remaining the same, the greater the firm's reliance on short-term debt or current liabilities in financing its asset investments, the greater the risk of illiquidity.* On the other hand, the use of current liabilities offers some very real advantages in that they can be less costly than long-term financing and they provide the firm with a flexible means of financing its fluctuating needs for assets. However, if for some reason the firm has problems raising short-term funds or needs funds for longer than expected, there can be real trouble. Thus, a firm can reduce its risk of illiquidity through the use of long-term debt at the expense of a reduction in its return on invested funds. Once again we see that the risk-return tradeoff involves an increased risk of illiquidity versus increased profitability.

Advantages of Current Liabilities: The Return

Flexibility

Current liabilities offer the firm a flexible source of financing. They can be used to match the timing of a firm's needs for short-term financing. If, for example, a firm needs funds for a three-month period during each year to finance a seasonal expansion in inventories, then a three-month loan can provide substantial cost savings over a long-term loan (even if the interest rate on short-term financing should be higher). The use of long-term debt in this situation involves borrowing for the entire year rather than for the period when the funds are needed, which increases the amount of interest the firm must pay. This brings us to the second advantage generally associated with the use of short-term financing.

Interest Cost

In general, interest rates on short-term debt are lower than on long-term debt for a given borrower. This relationship was introduced in Chapter 2 and is referred to as the **term structure of interest rates.** For a given firm, the term structure might appear as follows:

Loan Maturity	Interest Rate
3 months	4.00%
6 months	4.60
1 year	5.30
3 years	5.90
5 years	6.75
10 years	7.50
30 years	8.25

Note that this term structure reflects the rates of interest applicable to a given borrower at a particular time; it would not, for example, describe the rates of interest available to another borrower or even those applicable to the same borrower at a different time.

Disadvantages of Current Liabilities: The Risk

The use of current liabilities or short-term debt as opposed to long-term debt subjects the firm to a greater risk of illiquidity for two reasons. First, short-term debt, due to its very nature, must be repaid or rolled over more often, and so it increases the possibility that the firm's financial condition might deteriorate to a point where the needed funds might not be available.[1]

A second disadvantage of short-term debt is the uncertainty of interest costs from year to year. For example, a firm borrowing during a six-month period each year to finance a seasonal expansion in current assets might incur a different rate of interest each year. This rate reflects the current rate of interest at the time of the loan, as well as the lender's perception of the firm's riskiness. If fixed rate long-term debt were used, the interest cost would be known for the entire period of the loan agreement.

■ APPROPRIATE LEVEL OF WORKING CAPITAL

Managing the firm's net working capital (its liquidity) has been shown to involve simultaneous and interrelated decisions regarding investment in current assets and use of current liabilities. Fortunately, a guiding principle exists that can be used as a benchmark for the firm's working-capital policies: the **hedging principle,** or **principle of self-liquidating debt.** This principle provides a guide to the maintenance of a level of liquidity sufficient for the firm to meet its maturing obligations on time.[2]

---

[1]The dangers of such a policy are readily apparent in the experiences of firms that have been forced into bankruptcy. Penn Central, for example, had $80 million in short-term debt that it was unable to refinance (roll over) when it became bankrupt.

[2]A value-maximizing approach to the management of the firm's liquidity involves assessing the value of the benefits derived from increasing the firm's investment in liquid assets and weighing them against the added costs to the firm's owners resulting from investing in low-yield current assets. Unfortunately, the benefits derived from increased liquidity relate to the expected costs of bankruptcy to the firm's owners, and these costs are "unmeasurable" by existing technology. Thus, a "valuation" approach to liquidity management exists only in the theoretical realm.

BASIC FINANCIAL MANAGEMENT IN PRACTICE

How Firms Manage Their Working Capital

	Electronic Computers[a]		Book Publishing[b]		Air Trans-portation[c]		Oil and Gas - Exploration[d]		Gasoline Stations[e]		Restau-rants[f]	
Current Assets (%)	72	73	68	70	46	39	48	33	45	48	25	25
Current Liabilities (%)	40	38	43	53	37	43	40	31	38	39	36	38
Long-Term Debt (%)	12	11	17	14	23	26	27	28	27	22	32	33

The above table provides aggregate percent of assets numbers for six different industries and two time periods. The first column of percentages under each industry reflects the average for the corresponding industry for 1990–91, and the second column reflects the 1986–87 average.

Averaged across all industries for both years current assets were 49% of total assets, while current liabilities averaged 40% and long-term debt was only 23%. There is substantial variation in the relative importance of current assets across industries, with electronic computers and book publishing having the highest percent of assets invested in current assets, and restaurants having the lowest. Note also the relationship between current liabilities and long-term debt. With the exception of the restaurant industry, current liabilities are anywhere from two to four times as large as long-term debt.

So what can we conclude? First, current assets are a major component of a firm's investments and can constitute as much as 70 percent of firm assets. Second, most firms maintain current ratios (i.e., current assets/current liabilities) greater than 1, although this relationship varies both across industries and over time. Finally, long-term debt is frequently a less important source of financing (measured in terms of its percent of assets) than are current liabilities. The message is this. Working-capital management is extremely important to the firm's financial well-being and deserves serious consideration!

Interpretation of Statement Studies Figures
RMA cautions that the Studies be regarded only as a general guideline and not as an absolute industry norm. This is due to limited samples within categories, the categorization of companies by their primary Standard Industrial Classification (SIC) number only, and different methods of operations by companies within the same industry. For these reasons, RMA recommends that the figures be used only as general guidelines in addition to other methods of financial analysis.

Reprinted with permission, copyright Robert Morris Associates 1991 (Philadelphia, PA.).

[a]Manufacturers—Electronic Computers SIC #3571.
[b]Manufacturers—Books: Publishing, or Publishing and Printing SIC #2731.
[c]Services—Air Transportation, Scheduled SIC #4512.
[d]Contractors—Oil and Gas Well Drilling SIC #1381.
[e]Retailers—Gasoline Service Stations SIC #5541.
[f]Retailers—Restaurants SIC #5812.

PERSPECTIVE IN FINANCE

In Chapter 12 we discussed the firm's financing decision in terms of the choice between debt and equity sources of financing. There is, however, yet another critical dimension of the firm's financing decision. This relates to the maturity structure of the firm's debt. How should the decision be made as to whether to use short-term or current debt or longer-maturity debt? This is one of the fundamental questions addressed in this chapter and one that is critically important to the financial success of the firm. Basically, the hedging principle is one possible rule of thumb for guiding a firm's debt maturity financing decisions. This principle states that financing maturity should follow the cash-flow-producing characteristics of the asset being financed. For example, an asset that is expected to provide cash flows over an extended period such as five years should, in accordance with the hedging principle, be financed with debt with a pattern of similar cash flow requirements. Note that when the hedging principle is followed, the firm's debt will "self-liquidate" because the assets being financed will generate sufficient cash to retire the debt as it comes due.

Hedging Principle

Very simply, the *hedging principle* involves *matching* the cash-flow-generating characteristics of an asset with the maturity of the source of financing used to finance its acquisition. For example, a seasonal expansion in inventories, according to the hedging principle, should be financed with a short-term loan or current liability. The rationale underlying the rule is straightforward. Funds are needed for a limited period, and when that time has passed, the cash needed to repay the loan will be generated by the sale of the extra inventory items. Obtaining the needed funds from a long-term source (longer than one year) would mean that the firm would still have the funds after the inventories they helped finance had been sold. In this case the firm would have "excess" liquidity, which it either holds in cash or invests in low-yield marketable securities until the seasonal increase in inventories occurs again and the funds are needed. The result of all this would be an overall lowering of firm profits.

Consider an example in which a firm purchases a new conveyor belt system, which is expected to produce cash savings to the firm by eliminating the need for two laborers and, consequently, their salaries. This amounts to an annual savings of $14,000, whereas the conveyor belt costs $150,000 to install and will last 20 years. If the firm chooses to finance this asset with a 1-year note, then it will not be able to repay the loan from the $14,000 cash flow generated by the asset. In accordance with the hedging principle, the firm should finance the asset with a source of financing that more nearly matches the expected life and cash-flow-generating characteristics of the asset. In this case, a 15- to 20-year loan would be more appropriate.

Permanent and Temporary Assets

The notion of *maturity matching* in the hedging principle can be most easily understood when we think in terms of the distinction between **permanent** and **temporary investments in assets** as opposed to the more traditional fixed and current asset categories. A permanent investment in an asset is an investment that the firm expects to hold for a period longer than one year. Note that we are referring to the period the firm plans to hold an investment, not the useful life of the asset. For example, permanent investments are made in the firm's minimum level of current assets, as well as in its fixed assets. Temporary asset investments, on the other hand, are composed of current assets that will be liquidated and *not* replaced within the current year. Thus, some part of the firm's current assets is permanent and the remainder is temporary. For example, a seasonal increase in level of inventories is a temporary investment; the buildup in inventories will be eliminated when it is no longer needed.

Temporary, Permanent and Spontaneous Sources of Financing

Since total assets must always equal the sum of temporary, permanent and spontaneous sources of financing, the hedging approach provides the financial manager with the basis for determining the sources of financing to use at any point.

Now, what constitutes a temporary, permanent, or spontaneous source of financing? Temporary sources of financing consist of current liabilities. Short-term notes payable constitute the most common example of a temporary source of financing. Examples of notes payable include unsecured bank loans, commercial paper, and loans secured by accounts receivable and inventories. Permanent sources of financing include intermediate-term loans, long-term debt, preferred stock, and common equity.

Spontaneous sources of financing consist of trade credit and other accounts payable that arise *spontaneously* in the firm's day-to-day operations. For example, as the firm acquires materials for its inventories, trade credit is often made available spontaneously or on *demand* from the firm's suppliers. Trade credit appears on the firm's balance sheet as accounts payable, and the size of the accounts payable balance varies directly with the firm's purchases of inventory items. In turn, inventory purchases are related to anticipated sales. Thus, part of the financing needed by the firm is spontaneously provided in the form of trade credit.

In addition to trade credit, wages and salaries payable, accrued interest, and accrued taxes also provide valuable sources of spontaneous financing. These expenses accrue throughout the period until they are paid. For example, if a firm has a wage expense of $10,000 a week and pays its employees monthly, then its employees effectively provide financing equal to $10,000 by the end of the first week following a payday, $20,000 by the end of the second week, and so forth. Since these expenses generally arise in direct conjunction with the firm's ongoing operations, they too are referred to as *spontaneous*.

Hedging Principle: Graphic Illustration

The hedging principle can now be stated very succinctly: *Asset needs of the firm not financed by spontaneous sources should be financed in accordance with this rule: Permanent asset investments are financed with permanent sources, and temporary investments are financed with temporary sources.*

The hedging principle is depicted in Figure 14–1. Total assets are broken down into temporary and permanent asset investment categories. The firm's permanent investment in assets is financed by the use of permanent sources of financing (intermediate-and long-term debt, preferred stock, and common equity) or spontaneous sources (trade credit and other accounts payable). For illustration purposes spontaneous sources of financing are treated as if their amount were fixed. In practice, of course, spontaneous sources of financing fluctuate with the firm's purchases and its expenditures for wages, salaries, taxes, and other items that are paid on a delayed basis. Its temporary investment in assets is financed with temporary (short-term) debt.

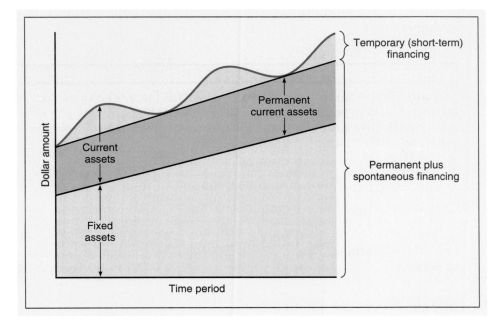

FIGURE 14–1
Hedging Financing
Strategy

▦ ESTIMATION OF COST OF SHORT-TERM CREDIT

Approximate Cost-of-Credit Formula

The procedure for estimating the cost of short-term credit is a very simple one and relies on the basic interest equation:

$$\text{interest} = \text{principal} \times \text{rate} \times \text{time} \qquad \textbf{(14–2)}$$

where *interest* is the dollar amount of interest on a *principal* that is borrowed at some annual *rate* for a fraction of a year (represented by *time*). For example, a six-month loan for $1,000 at 8 percent interest would require an interest payment of $40:

$$\text{interest} = \$1,000 \times .08 \times \frac{1}{2} = \$40$$

We use this basic relationship to solve for the cost of a source of short-term financing or the annual percentage rate (APR) where the interest amount, the principal sum, and the time period for financing are known. Thus, solving the basic interest equation for APR produces[3]

$$\text{APR} = \frac{\text{interest}}{\text{principal} \times \text{time}} \qquad \textbf{(14–3)}$$

or

$$\text{APR} = \frac{\text{interest}}{\text{principal}} \times \frac{1}{\text{time}}$$

---

[3] For ease of computation we will assume a 30 day month and 360 day year in this chapter.

This equation, called the APR calculation, is clarified with the following example.

EXAMPLE

The SKC Corporation plans to borrow $1,000 for a 90-day period. At maturity the firm will repay the $1,000 principal amount plus $30 interest. The effective annual rate of interest for the loan can be estimated using the ARP equation, as follows:

$$\text{APR} = \frac{\$30}{\$1,000} \times \frac{1}{90/360}$$

$$= .03 \times \frac{360}{90} = .12, \text{ or } 12\%$$

The effective annual cost of funds provided by the loan is therefore 12 percent. ■

Annual Percentage Yield Formula

The simple APR calculation does not consider compound interest. To account for the influence of compounding, we can use the following equation:

$$\text{APY} = \left(1 + \frac{i}{m}\right)^m - 1 \qquad \qquad \textbf{(14–4)}$$

where APY is the annual percentage yield, i is the nominal rate of interest per year (12 percent in the above example), and m is the number of compounding periods within a year [$m = 1/\text{TIME} = 1/(90/360) = 4$ in the preceding example]. Thus, the effective rate of interest on the example problem, considering compounding, is

$$\text{APY} = \left(1 + \frac{.12}{4}\right)^4 - 1 = .126, \text{ or } 12.6\%$$

Compounding effectively raises the cost of short-term credit. Because the differences between APR and APY are usually small, we use the simple interest version of APR to compute the cost of short-term credit.

■ SOURCES OF SHORT-TERM CREDIT

Short-term credit sources can be classified into two basic groups: unsecured and secured. **Unsecured** loans include all those sources that have as their security only the lender's faith in the ability of the borrower to repay the funds when due. Major sources of unsecured short-term credit include accrued wages and taxes, trade credit, unsecured bank loans, and commercial paper. **Secured** loans involve the pledge of specific assets as collateral in the event the borrower defaults in payment of principal or interest. Commercial banks, finance companies, and factors are the primary suppliers of secured credit. The principal sources of collateral include accounts receivable and inventories.

Unsecured Sources: Accrued Wages and Taxes

Because most businesses pay their employees only periodically (weekly, biweekly, or monthly), firms accrue a wages payable account that is, in essence, a loan from their employees. For example, if the wage expense for the Appleton Manufacturing Company is $450,000 per week and it pays its employees monthly, then by the end of a four-week month the firm will owe its employees $1.8 million in wages for services they have already performed during the month. Consequently, the employees finance their own efforts through waiting a full month for payment.

Similarly, firms generally make quarterly income tax payments for their estimated quarterly tax liability. This means that the firm has the use of the tax monies it owes based on quarterly profits up through the end of the quarter. In addition, the firm pays sales taxes and withholding (income) taxes for its employees on a deferred basis. The longer the period that the firm holds the tax payments, the greater the amount of financing they provide.

Note that these sources of financing *rise and fall spontaneously* with the level of firm sales. That is, as the firm's sales increase so do its labor expense, sales taxes collected, and income tax. Consequently, these accrued expense items provide the firm with automatic or spontaneous sources of financing.

Unsecured Sources: Trade Credit

Trade credit provides one of the most flexible sources of short-term financing available to the firm. We previously noted that trade credit is a primary source of spontaneous, or on-demand, financing. That is, trade credit arises spontaneously with the firm's purchases. To arrange for credit the firm need only place an order with one of its suppliers. The supplier checks the firm's credit and, if it is good, sends the merchandise. The purchasing firm then pays for the goods in accordance with the supplier's credit terms.

Credit Terms and Cash Discounts

Very often the credit terms offered with trade credit involve a cash discount for early payment. For example, a supplier might offer terms of 2/10, net 30, which means that a 2 percent discount is offered for payment within 10 days or the full amount is due in 30 days. Thus, a 2 percent penalty is involved for not paying within 10 days or for delaying payment from the 10th to the 30th day (that is, for 20 days). The effective annual cost of not taking the cash discount can be quite severe. Using a

TABLE 14–1
Effective Rates of Intereston
Selected Trade Credit Terms

Credit Terms	Effective Rate
2/10, net 60	14.69%
2/10, net 90	9.18
3/20, net 60	27.84
6/10, net 90	28.72

$1 invoice amount, the effective cost of passing up the discount period using the preceding credit terms and our APR equation can be estimated.

$$APR = \frac{\$.02}{\$.98} \times \frac{1}{20/360} \ .3673, \text{ or } 36.73\%$$

Note that the 2 percent cash discount is the *interest* cost of extending the payment period an *additional* 20 days. Note also that the principal amount of the credit is $.98. This amount constitutes the full principal amount as of the 10th day of the credit period, after which time the cash discount is lost. The effective cost of passing up the 2 percent discount for twenty days is quite expensive: 36.73 percent. Furthermore, once the discount period has passed, there is no reason to pay before the final due date (the 30th day). Table 14–1 lists the effective annual cost of a number of alternative credit terms. Note that the cost of trade credit varies directly with the size of the cash discount and inversely with the length of time between the end of the discount period and the final due date.

Stretching of Trade Credit

Some firms that use trade credit engage in a practice called *stretching* of trade accounts. This practice involves delaying payments beyond the prescribed credit period. For example, a firm might purchase materials under credit terms of 3/10, net 60; however, when faced with a shortage of cash, the firm might extend payment to the eightieth day. Continued violation of trade terms can eventually lead to a loss of credit. However, for short periods, and at infrequent intervals, stretching offers the firm an emergency source of short-term credit.

Advantages of Trade Credit

As a source of short-term financing, trade credit has a number of advantages. First, trade credit is conveniently obtained as a normal part of the firm's operations. Second, no formal agreements are generally involved in extending credit. Furthermore, the amount of credit extended expands and contracts with the needs of the firm; this is why it is classified as a spontaneous, or on-demand, source of financing.

Unsecured Sources: Bank Credit

Commercial banks provide unsecured short-term credit in two basic forms: lines of credit and transaction loans (notes payable). Maturities of both types of loans are usually one year or less, with rates of interest depending on the creditworthiness of the borrower and the level of interest rates in the economy as a whole.

Line of Credit

A **line of credit** is generally an informal agreement or understanding between the borrower and the bank as to the maximum amount of credit that the bank will provide the borrower at any one time. Under this type of agreement there is no *legal* commitment on the part of the bank to provide the stated credit. In a **revolving credit agreement,** which is a variant of this form of financing, a legal obligation is involved. The line of credit agreement generally covers a period of one year corresponding to the borrower's *fiscal* year. Thus, if the borrower is on a July 31 fiscal year, its lines of credit will be based on the same annual period.

CREDIT TERMS   Lines of credit generally do not involve fixed rates of interest; instead they state that credit will be extended *at 1/2 percent over prime* or some other spread over the bank's prime rate.[4] Furthermore, the agreement usually does not spell out the specific use that will be made of the funds beyond a general statement, such as *for working-capital purposes.*

Lines of credit usually require that the borrower maintain a minimum balance in the bank throughout the loan period, called a **compensating balance.** This required balance (which can be stated as a percent of the line of credit or the loan amount) increases the effective cost of the loan to the borrower, unless a deposit balance equal to or greater than this balance requirement is ordinarily maintained in the bank.

The effective cost of short-term bank credit can be estimated using the APR equation. Consider the following example:

EXAMPLE

M & M Beverage Company has a $300,000 line of credit that requires a compensating balance equal to 10 percent of the loan amount. The rate paid on the loan is 12 percent per annum, $200,000 is borrowed for a six-month period, and the firm does not currently have a deposit with the lending bank. The dollar cost of the loan includes the interest expense and, in addition, the opportunity cost of maintaining an idle cash balance equal to the 10 percent compensating balance. To accommodate the cost of the compensating balance requirement, assume that the added funds will have to be borrowed and simply left idle in the firm's checking account. Thus, the amount actually borrowed (B) will be larger than the $200,000 needed. In fact, the needed $200,000 will constitute 90 percent of the total borrowed funds because of the 10 percent compensating balance requirement, hence $.90B = \$200,000$, such that $B = \$222,222$. Thus,

---

[4]The *prime rate of interest* is the rate that a bank charges its most creditworthy borrowers.

interest is paid on a $222,222 loan ($222,222 × .12 × 1/2 = $13,333.32), of which only $200,000 is available for use by the firm.[5] The effective annual cost of credit therefore is

$$APR = \frac{\$13,333.32}{\$200,000} \times \frac{1}{180/360} = 13.33\%$$

In the **M & M** Beverage Company example the loan required the payment of principal ($222,222) plus interest ($13,333.32) at the end of the six-month loan period. Frequently, bank loans will be made on a discount basis. That is, the loan interest will be deducted from the loan amount before the funds are transferred to the borrower. Extending the **M & M** Beverage Company example to consider discounted interest involves reducing the loan proceeds ($200,000) in the previous example by the amount of interest for the full six months ($13,333.32). The effective rate of interest on the loan is now:

$$APR = \frac{\$13,333.32}{\$200,000 - \$13,333.32} \times \frac{1}{180/360}$$

$$= .1429, \text{ or } 14.29\%$$

The effect of discounting interest was to raise the cost of the loan from 13.33 percent to 14.29 percent. This results from the fact that the firm pays interest on the same amount of funds as before ($222,222); however, this time it gets the use of $13,333.32 less, or $200,000 − $13,333.32 = $186,666.68.[6] ■

---

[5]The same answer would have been obtained by assuming a total loan of $200,000, of which only 90 percent or $180,000 was available for use by the firm; that is,

$$APR = \frac{\$12,000}{\$180,000} \times \frac{1}{180/360} = 13.33\%$$

Interest is now calculated on the $200,000 loan amount ($12,000 = $200,000 × .12 × 1/2).

[6]If **M&M** needs the use of a full $200,000 then it will have to borrow more than $222,222 to cover both the compensating balance requirement *and* the discounted interest. In fact, the firm will have to borrow some amount B such that

$$B - .10B - (.12 \times 1/2)B = \$200,000$$

$$.84B = \$200,000$$

$$B = \frac{\$200,000}{.84} = \$238,095$$

The cost of credit remains the same at 14.29 percent, as we see below:

$$APR = \frac{\$14,285.70}{\$238,095 - \$23,810 - \$14,285.70} \times \frac{1}{180/360}$$

$$= .1429, \text{ or } 14.29\%$$

Transaction Loans

Still another form of unsecured short-term bank credit can be obtained in the form of **transaction loans.** Here the loan is made for a specific purpose. This is the type of loan that most individuals associate with bank credit and is obtained by signing a promissory note.

Unsecured transaction loans are very similar to a line of credit regarding cost, term to maturity, and compensating balance requirements. In both instances commercial banks often require that the borrower *clean up* its short-term loans for a 30- to 45-day period during the year. This means, very simply, that the borrower must be free of any bank debt for the stated period. The purpose of such a requirement is to ensure that the borrower is not using short-term bank credit to finance a part of its permanent needs for funds.

Unsecured Sources: Commercial Paper

Only the largest and most creditworthy companies are able to use **commercial paper,** which is simply a short-term *promise to pay* that is sold in the market for short-term debt securities.

Credit Terms

The maturity of this credit source is generally six months or less, although some issues carry 270-day maturities. The interest rate on commercial paper is generally slightly lower (.5 percent to 1 percent) than the prime rate on commercial bank loans. Also, interest is usually discounted, although sometimes interest-bearing commercial paper is available.

New issues of commercial paper are either placed directly (sold by the issuing firm directly to the investing public) or dealer placed. Dealer placement involves the use of a commercial paper dealer, who sells the issue for the issuing firm. Many major finance companies, such as General Motors Acceptance Corporation, place their commercial paper directly. The volume of direct versus dealer placements is roughly 4 to 1 in favor of direct placements. Dealers are used primarily by industrial firms that either make only infrequent use of the commercial paper market or, owing to their small size, would have difficulty placing the issue without the help of a dealer.

Commercial Paper as a Source of Short-Term Credit

Several advantages accrue to the user of commercial paper:

1. **Interest rate.** Commercial paper rates are generally lower than rates on bank loans and comparable sources of short-term financing.
2. **Compensating balance requirement.** No minimum balance requirements are associated with commercial paper. However, issuing firms usually find it desirable to maintain lines of credit agreements sufficient to back up their short-term financing needs

in the event that a new issue of commercial paper cannot be sold or an outstanding issue cannot be repaid when due.

3. **Amount of credit.** Commercial paper offers the firm with very large credit needs a single source for all its short-term financing. Because of loan restrictions placed on the banks by the regulatory authorities, obtaining the necessary funds from a commercial bank might require dealing with a number of institutions.[7]

4. **Prestige.** Because it is widely recognized that only the most creditworthy borrowers have access to the commercial paper market, its use signifies a firm's credit status.

Using commercial paper for short-term financing, however, involves a very important *risk*. That is, the commercial paper market is highly impersonal and denies even the most creditworthy borrower any flexibility in terms of repayment. When bank credit is used, the borrower has someone with whom he or she can work out any temporary difficulties that might be encountered in meeting a loan deadline. This flexibility simply does not exist for the user of commercial paper.

Estimation of the Cost of Commercial Paper

The cost of commercial paper can be estimated using the simple effective cost-of-credit equation (APR). The key points to remember are that commercial paper interest is usually discounted and that if a dealer is used to place the issue, a fee is charged. Even if a dealer is not used, the issuing firm will incur costs associated with preparing and placing the issue, and these costs must be included in estimating the cost of credit.

EXAMPLE

The EPG Mfg. Company uses commercial paper regularly to support its needs for short-term financing. The firm plans to sell $100 million in 270-day-maturity paper on which it expects to have to pay discounted interest at a rate of 12 percent per annum ($9,000,000). In addition, EPG expects to incur a cost of approximately $100,000 in dealer placement fees and other expenses of issuing the paper. The effective cost of credit to EPG can be calculated as follows:

$$\text{APR} = \frac{\$9,000,000 + \$100,000}{\$100,000,000 - \$100,000 - \$9,000,000} \times \frac{1}{270/360}$$

$$= .1335, \text{ or } 13.35\%$$

where the interest cost is calculated as $100,000,000 × .12 × [270/360] = $9,000,000 plus the $100,000 dealer placement fee. Thus, the effective cost of credit to EPG is 13.35 percent. ∎

---

[7]Member banks of the Federal Reserve System are limited to 10 percent of their total capital, surplus, and undivided profits when making loans to a single borrower. Thus, when a corporate borrower's needs for financing are very large it may have to deal with a group of participating banks to raise the needed funds.

Secured Sources: Accounts Receivable Loans

Secured sources of short-term credit have certain assets of the firm pledged as collateral to secure the loan. Upon default of the loan agreement, the lender has first claim to the pledged assets in addition to its claim as a general creditor of the firm. Hence, the secured credit agreement offers an added margin of safety to the lender.

Generally, a firm's receivables are among its most liquid assets. For this reason they are considered by many lenders to be prime collateral for a secured loan. Two basic procedures can be used in arranging for financing based on receivables: pledging and factoring.

Pledging Accounts Receivable

Under the **pledging** arrangement the borrower simply pledges accounts receivable as collateral for a loan obtained from either a commercial bank or a finance company. The amount of the loan is stated as a percent of the face value of the receivables pledged. If the firm provides the lender with a *general line* on its receivables, then all of the borrower's accounts are pledged as security for the loan. This method of pledging is simple and inexpensive. However, because the lender has no control over the quality of the receivables being pledged, it will set the maximum loan at a relatively low percent of the total face value of the accounts, generally ranging downward from a maximum of around 75 percent.

Still another approach to pledging involves the borrower's presenting specific invoices to the lender as collateral for a loan. This method is somewhat more expensive in that the lender must assess the creditworthiness of each individual account pledged; however, given this added knowledge the lender will be willing to increase the loan as a percent of the face value of the invoices. In this case the loan might reach as high as 85 percent or 90 percent of the face value of the pledged receivables.

CREDIT TERMS   Accounts receivable loans generally carry an interest rate 2 percent to 5 percent higher than the bank's prime lending rate. Finance companies charge an even higher rate. In addition, the lender will usually charge a handling fee stated as a percent of the face value of the receivables processed, which may be as much as 1 percent to 2 percent of the face value.

EXAMPLE

The A. B. Good Company sells electrical supplies to building contractors on terms of net 60. The firm's average monthly sales are $100,000; thus, given the firm's two-month credit terms, its average receivables balance is $200,000. The firm pledges all its receivables to a local bank, which in turn advances up to 70 percent of the face value of the receivables at 3 percent over prime and with a 1 percent processing charge on *all* receivables pledged. A. B. Good follows a practice of borrowing the maximum amount possible, and the current prime rate is 10 percent.

The APR of using this source of financing for a full year is computed as follows:

$$APR = \frac{\$18,200 + \$12,000}{\$140,000} \times \frac{1}{360/360} = .2157 \text{ or } 21.57\%$$

where the total dollar cost of the loan consists of both the annual interest expense (.13 × .70 × \$200,000 = \$18,200) and the annual processing fee (.01 × \$100,000 × 12 months = \$12,000). The amount of credit extended is .70 × \$200,000 = \$140,000. Note that the processing charge applies to *all* receivables pledged. Thus, the A. B. Good Company pledges \$100,000 each month, or \$1,200,000 during the year, on which a 1 percent fee must be paid, for a total annual charge of \$12,000.

One more point: The lender, in addition to making advances or loans, may be providing certain credit services to the borrower. For example, the lender may provide billing and collection services. The value of these services should be considered in computing the cost of credit. In the preceding example, A. B. Good Company may *save* credit department expenses of \$10,000 per year by pledging all its accounts and letting the lender provide those services. In this case, the cost of short-term credit is only

$$APR = \frac{\$18,200 + \$12,000 - \$10,000}{\$140,000} \times \frac{1}{360/360} = .1443 \text{ or } 14.43\% \quad \blacksquare$$

ADVANTAGES AND DISADVANTAGES OF PLEDGING The primary advantage of pledging as a source of short-term credit is the flexibility it provides the borrower. Financing is available on a continuous basis. The new accounts created through credit sales provide the collateral for the financing of new production. Furthermore, the lender may provide credit services that eliminate or at least reduce the need for similar services within the firm. The primary disadvantage associated with this method of financing is its cost, which can be relatively high compared with other sources of short-term credit, owing to the level of the interest rate charged on loans and the processing fee on pledged accounts.

Factoring Accounts Receivable

Factoring accounts receivable involves the outright sale of a firm's accounts to a financial institution called a *factor*. A **factor** is a firm that acquires the receivables of other firms. The factoring institution may be a commercial finance company that engages solely in the factoring of receivables (known as an *old-line factor*) or it may be a commercial bank. The factor, in turn, bears the risk of collection and, for a fee, services the accounts. The fee is stated as a percent of the face value of all receivables factored (usually from 1 percent to 3 percent).

The factor firm typically does *not* make payment for factored accounts until the accounts have been collected or the credit terms have been met. Should the firm wish to receive immediate payment for its factored accounts, it can borrow from the factor, using the factored accounts as collateral. The maximum loan the firm can obtain is equal to the face value of its factored accounts less the factor's fee (1 percent to 3 percent) less a reserve (6 percent to 10 percent) less the interest on the loan. For example, if $100,000 in receivables is factored, carrying 60-day credit terms, a 2 percent factor's fee, a 6 percent reserve, and interest at 1 percent per month on advances, then the maximum loan or advance the firm can receive is computed as follows:

Face amount of receivables factored	$100,000
Less: Fee (.02 × $100,000)	(2,000)
Reserve (.06 × $100,000)	(6,000)
Interest (.01 × $92,000 × 2 months)	(1,840)
Maximum advance	$ 90,160

Note that interest is discounted and calculated based on a maximum amount of funds available for advance ($92,000 = $100,000 – $2000 – $6000). Thus, the effective cost of credit can be calculated as follows:

$$\text{APR} = \frac{\$1840 + \$2000}{\$90,160} \times \frac{1}{60/360}$$
$$= .2555 \text{ or } 25.55\%$$

Secured Sources: Inventory Loans

Inventory loans provide a second source of security for short-term secured credit. The amount of the loan that can be obtained depends on both the marketability and perishability of the inventory. Some items, such as raw materials (grains, oil, lumber, and chemicals), are excellent sources of collateral, because they can easily be liquidated. Other items, such as work-in-process inventories, provide very poor collateral because of their lack of marketability.

There are several methods by which inventory can be used to secure short-term financing. These include a *floating* or *blanket lien, chattel mortgage, field warehouse receipt,* and *terminal warehouse receipt.*

Under a **floating lien** agreement the borrower gives the lender a lien against all its inventories. This provides the simplest but least secure form of inventory collateral. The borrowing firm maintains full control of the inventories and continues to sell and replace them as it sees fit. Obviously, this lack of control over the collateral greatly dilutes the value of this type of security to the lender.

Under a **chattel mortgage agreement** the inventory is identified (by serial number or otherwise) in the security agreement and the borrower retains title to the inventory but cannot sell the items without the lender's consent.

Under a **field warehouse financing agreement,** inventories used as collateral are physically separated from the firm's other inventories and placed under the control of a third-party field warehousing firm.

The **terminal warehouse agreement** differs from the field warehouse agreement in only one respect. Here the inventories pledged as collateral are transported to a public warehouse that is physically removed from the borrower's premises. The lender has an added degree of safety or security because the inventory is totally removed from the borrower's control. Once again the cost of this type of arrangement is increased because the warehouse firm must be paid by the borrower; in addition, the inventory must be transported to and eventually from the public warehouse.

SUMMARY

Working-capital management involves managing the firm's liquidity, which in turn involves managing (1) the firm's investment in current assets and (2) its use of current liabilities. Each of these problems involves risk—return tradeoffs. Investing in current assets reduces the firm's risk of illiquidity at the expense of lowering its overall rate of return on its investment in assets. Furthermore, the use of long-term sources of financing enhances the firm's liquidity while reducing its rate of return on assets.

The *hedging principle,* or *principle of self-liquidating debt,* is a benchmark for working-capital decisions. Basically, this principle involves matching the cash-flow-generating characteristics of an asset with the cash flow requirements of the source of funds used to finance its acquisition.

Three basic factors provide the key considerations in selecting a source of short-term financing: (1) the effective cost of credit, (2) the availability of financing in the amount and for the time needed, and (3) the effect of the use of credit from a particular source on the cost and availability of other sources of credit.

The various sources of short-term credit can be categorized into two groups: unsecured and secured. Unsecured credit offers no specific assets as security for the loan agreement. The primary sources include trade credit, lines of credit, unsecured transaction loans from commercial banks, and commercial paper. Secured credit is generally provided to business firms by commercial banks, finance companies, and factors. The most popular sources of security involve the use of accounts receivable and inventories. Loans secured by accounts receivable include pledging agreements, in which a firm pledges its receivables as security for a loan, and factoring agreements, in which the firm sells the receivables to a factor. A primary difference in these two arrangements relates to the ability of the lender to seek payment from the borrower in the event the accounts used as collateral become uncollectable. In a pledging arrangement the lender retains the right of recourse in the event of default, whereas in factoring, a lender is generally without recourse.

Loans secured by inventories can be made using one of several types of security arrangements. Among the most widely used are the floating lien, chattel mortgage, field warehouse agreement, and terminal warehouse agreement. The form of agreement used will depend on the type of inventories pledged as collateral and the degree of control the lender wishes to exercise over the loan collateral.

STUDY QUESTIONS

14–1.   Define and contrast the terms *working capital* and *net working capital*.
14–2.   Discuss the risk-return relationship involved in the firm's asset investment decisions as that relationship pertains to working-capital management.
14–3.   What advantages and disadvantages are generally associated with the use of short-term debt? Discuss.
14–4.   Explain what is meant by the statement "The use of current liabilities as opposed to long-term debt subjects the firm to a greater risk of illiquidity."
14–5.   Define the hedging principle. How can this principle be used in the management of working capital?
14–6.   Define the following terms:
   a. Permanent asset investments
   b. Temporary asset investments
   c. Permanent sources of financing
   d. Temporary sources of financing
   e. Spontaneous sources of financing
14–7.   What distinguishes short-term, intermediate-term, and long-term debt?
14–8.   What considerations should be used in selecting a source of short-term credit? Discuss each.
14–9.   How can the formula "interest = principal × rate × time" be used to estimate the effective cost of short-term credit?
14–10. How can we accommodate the effects of compounding in our calculation of the effective cost of short-term credit?
14–11. There are three major sources of unsecured short-term credit other than accured wages and taxes. List and discuss the distinguishing characteristics of each.
14–12. What is meant by the following trade credit terms: 2/10, net 30? 4/20, net 60? 3/15, net 45?
14–13. Define the following:
   a. Line of credit
   b. Commercial paper
   c. Compensating balance
   d. Prime rate
14–14. List and discuss four advantages of the use of commercial paper.
14–15. What risk is involved in the firm's use of commercial paper as a source of short-term credit? Discuss.
14–16. List and discuss the distinguishing features of the principal sources of secured credit based on accounts receivable.

SELF-TEST PROBLEMS

ST-1.   (*Analyzing the Cost of a Commercial Paper Offering*) The Marilyn Sales Company is a wholesale machine tool broker that has gone through a recent expansion of its activities resulting in a doubling of its sales. The company has determined that it needs an additional $200 million in short-term funds to finance peak season sales during roughly six months of the year. Marilyn's treasurer has recommended that the firm use a commercial paper offering to raise the needed funds. Specifically, he has determined that a $200 million offering would require 10 percent interest (paid in advance or discounted) plus a $125,000 placement fee. The paper would carry a six-month (180-day) maturity. What is the effective cost of credit?

ST-2. (*Analyzing the Cost of Short-Term Credit*) The treasurer of the Lights-a-Lot Mfg. Company is faced with three alternative bank loans. The firm wishes to select the one that minimizes its cost of credit on a $200,000 note that it plans to issue in the next 10 days. Relevant information for the three loan configurations is found below:

a. An 18 percent rate of interest with interest paid at year-end and no compensating balance requirement.

b. A 16 percent rate of interest but carrying a 20 percent compensating balance requirement. This loan also calls for interest to be paid at year-end.

c. A 14 percent rate of interest that is discounted plus a 20 percent compensating balance requirement.

Analyze the cost of each of these alternatives. You may assume the firm would not normally maintain any bank balance that might be used to meet the 20 percent compensating balance requirements of alternatives (b) and (c).

STUDY PROBLEMS

14–1. (*Estimating the Cost of Bank Credit*) Paymaster Enterprises has arranged to finance its seasonal working-capital needs with a short-term bank loan. The loan will carry a rate of 12 percent per annum with interest paid in advance (discounted). In addition, Paymaster must maintain a minimum demand deposit with the bank of 10 percent of the loan balance throughout the term of the loan. If Paymaster plans to borrow $100,000 for a period of three months, what is the effective cost of the bank loan?

14–2. (*Estimating the Cost of Commercial Paper*) On February 3, 199X, the Burlington Western Company plans a commercial paper issue of $20 million. The firm has never used commercial paper before but has been assured by the firm placing the issue that it will have no difficulty raising the funds. The commercial paper will carry a 270-day maturity and will require interest based on a rate of 11 percent per annum. In addition, the firm will have to pay fees totaling $200,000 in order to bring the issue to market and place it. What is the effective cost of the commercial paper issue to Burlington Western?

14-3. (*Cost of Trade Credit*) Calculate the effective cost of the following trade credit terms where payment is made on the net due date.

a. 2/10, net 30
b. 3/15, net 30
c. 3/15, net 45
d. 2/15, net 60

14–4. (*Annual Percentage Yield*) Compute the cost of the trade credit terms in problem 14–3 using the compounding formula, or annual percentage yield.

14–5. (*Cost of Short-Term Financing*) The R. Morin Construction Company needs to borrow $100,000 to help finance the cost of a new $150,000 hydraulic crane used in the firm's commercial construction business. The crane will pay for itself in one year and the firm is considering the following alternatives for financing its purchase:

Alternative A —The firm's bank has agreed to lend the $100,000 at a rate of 14 percent. Interest would be discounted, and a 15 percent compensating balance would be required. However, the compensating balance requirement would not be binding on R. Morin because the firm normally maintains a minimum demand deposit (checking account) balance of $25,000 in the bank.

Alternative B —The equipment dealer has agreed to finance the equipment with a one-year loan. The $100,000 loan would require payment of principal and interest totaling $116,300.

a. Which alternative should R. Morin select?

b. If the bank's compensating balance requirement were to necessitate idle demand deposits equal to 15 percent of the loan, what effect would this have on the cost of the bank loan alternative?

14–6. (*Cost of Short-Term Bank Loan*) On July 1, 199X, the Southwest Forging Corporation arranged for a line of credit with the First National Bank of Dallas. The terms of the agreement called for a $100,000 maximum loan with interest set at 1 percent over prime. In addition, the firm has to maintain a 20 percent compensating balance in its demand deposit account throughout the year. The prime rate is currently 12 percent.

a. If Southwest normally maintains a $20,000 to $30,000 balance in its checking account with FNB of Dallas, what is the effective cost of credit through the line-of-credit agreement where the maximum loan amount is used for a full year?

b. Recompute the effective cost of credit to Southwest if the firm will have to borrow the compensating balance and it borrows the maximum possible under the loan agreement. Again, assume the full amount of the loan is outstanding for a whole year.

14–7. (*Cost of Commercial Paper*) Tri-State Enterprises plans to issue commercial paper for the first time in the firm's 35-year history. The firm plans to issue $500,000 in 180-day maturity notes. The paper will carry a 10 1/4 percent rate with discounted interest and will cost Tri-State $12,000 (paid in advance) to issue.

a. What is the effective cost of credit to Tri-State?

b. What other factors should the company consider in analyzing whether to issue the commercial paper?

14–8. (*Cost of Accounts Receivable*) Johnson Enterprises, Inc., is involved in the manufacture and sale of electronic components used in small AM—FM radios. The firm needs $300,000 to finance an anticipated expansion in receivables due to increased sales. Johnson's credit terms are net 60, and its average monthly credit sales are $200,000. In general, the firm's customers pay within the credit period; thus the firm's average accounts receivable balance is $400,000.

Chuck Idol, Johnson's comptroller, approached the firm's bank with a request for a loan for the $300,000 using the firm's accounts receivable as collateral. The bank offered to make the loan at a rate of 2 percent over prime plus a 1 percent processing charge on all receivables pledged ($200,000 per month). Furthermore, the bank agreed to lend up to 75 percent of the face value of the receivables pledged.

a. Estimate the cost of the receivables loan to Johnson where the firm borrows the $300,000. The prime rate is currently 11 percent.

b. Idol also requested a line of credit for $300,000 from the bank. The bank agreed to grant the necessary line of credit at a rate of 3 percent over prime and required a 15 percent compensating balance. Johnson currently maintains an average demand deposit of $80,000. Estimate the cost of the line of credit to Johnson.

c. Which source of credit should Johnson select? Why?

14–9. (*Cost of Factoring*) MDM, Inc., is considering factoring its receivables. The firm has credit sales of $400,000 per month and has an average receivables balance of $800,000 with 60-day credit terms. The factor has offered to extend credit equal to 90 percent of the receivables factored less interest on the loan at a rate of 1 1/2 percent per month. The 10 percent difference in the advance and the face value of all receivables factored consists of a 1 percent factoring fee plus a 9 percent reserve, which the factor maintains. In addition, if MDM, Inc., decides to factor its receivables, it will sell them all, so that it can reduce its credit department costs by $1,500 a month.

a. What is the cost of borrowing the maximum amount of credit available to MDM, Inc., through the factoring agreement?

b. What considerations other than cost should be accounted for by MDM, Inc., in determining whether to enter the factoring agreement?

14–10. (*Cost of Secured Short-Term Credit*) The Sean-Janeow Import Co. needs $500,000 for the three-month period ending September 30, 199X. The firm has explored two possible sources of credit.

1. S-J has arranged with its bank for a $500,000 loan secured by accounts receivable. The bank has agreed to advance S-J 80 percent of the value of its pledged receivables at a rate of 11 percent plus a 1 percent fee based on all receivables pledged. S-J's receivables average a total of $1 million year-round.

2. An insurance company has agreed to lend the $500,000 at a rate of 9 percent per annum, using a loan secured by S-J's inventory of salad oil. A field warehouse agreement would be used, which would cost S-J $2,000 a month.

Which source of credit should S-J select? Explain.

14–11. (*Cost of Short-Term Financing*) You plan to borrow $20,000 from the bank to pay for inventories for a gift shop you have just opened. The bank offers to lend you the money at 10 percent annual interest for the six months the funds will be needed.

a. Calculate the effective rate of interest on the loan.

b. In addition, the bank requires you to maintain a 15 percent compensating balance in the bank. Because you are just opening your business, you do not have a demand deposit account at the bank that can be used to meet the compensating balance requirement. This means that you will have to put 15 percent of the loan amount from your own personal money (which you had planned to use to help finance the business) in a checking account. What is the cost of the loan now?

c. In addition to the compensating balance requirement in (b), you are told that interest will be discounted. What is the effective rate of interest on the loan now?

14–12. (*Cost of Factoring*) A factor has agreed to lend the JVC Corporation working capital on the following terms. JVC's receivables average $100,000 per month and have a 90-day average collection period. (Note that JVC's credit terms call for payment in 90 days and accounts receivable average $300,000 because of the 90-day average collection period.) The factor will charge 12 percent interest on any advance (1 percent per month paid in advance), will charge a 2 percent processing fee on all receivables factored, and will maintain a 20 percent reserve. If JVC undertakes the loan it will reduce its own credit department expenses by $2,000 per month. What is the annual effective rate of interest to JVC on the factoring arrangement? Assume that the maximum advance is taken.

SELF-TEST SOLUTIONS

SS-1. The discounted interest cost of the commercial paper issue is calculated as follows:

Interest expense = $.10 \times \$200,000,000 \times 180/360 = \$10,000,000$

The effective cost of credit can now be calculated as follows:

$$\text{APR} = \frac{\$10,000,000 + \$125,000}{\$200,000,000 - \$125,000 - \$10,000,000} \times \frac{1}{180/360}$$

$$= .1066 \text{ or } 10.66\%$$

SS-2.

a.
$$\text{APR} = \frac{.18 \times \$200,000}{\$200,000} \times \frac{1}{1}$$

$$= .18, \text{ or } 18\%$$

b.
$$\text{APR} = \frac{.16 \times \$200,000}{\$200,000 - (.20 \times \$200,000)} \times \frac{1}{1}$$

$$= .20 \text{ or } 20\%$$

c.
$$\text{APR} = \frac{.14 \times \$200,000}{\$200,000 - (.14 \times \$200,000) - (.2 \times \$200,000)} \times \frac{1}{1}$$

$$= .2121 \text{ or } 21.21\%$$

Alternative (a) offers the lower-cost service of financing, although it carries the highest stated rate of interest. The reason for this is that there is no compensating balance requirement, nor is interest discounted for this alternative.

CHAPTER 15
LIQUID ASSET MANAGEMENT

Why a Company Holds Cash • Cash Management Objectives and Decisions • Collection and Disbursement Procedures • Evaluation of Costs of Cash-Management Services • Composition of Marketable Securities Portfolio • Accounts Receivable Management • Inventory Management • Just-in-Time Inventory Control

Chapter 14 provided an introduction and overview of the concept of working-capital management. In this chapter, we will explore in more depth management of the asset components of the working-capital equation. Accordingly, we will focus on the alternatives available to managers for increasing shareholder wealth with respect to the most important types of current assets: (1) cash, (2) marketable securities, (3) accounts receivable and inventory. These are listed in order of declining liquidity.

Such alternatives will include (1) techniques available to management for favorably influencing cash receipts and disbursements patterns, (2) investments that allow a firm to employ excess cash balances productively, (3) critical decision formulas for determining the appropriate amount of investment in accounts receivable, and (4) methods, such as those pertaining to order quantity and order point issues, for evaluating most suitable levels of inventory.

These issues are important to the financial manager for several reasons. For example, judicious management of cash and near-cash assets allows the firm to hold the minimum amount of cash necessary to meet the firm's obligations in a timely manner. As a result, the firm is able to take advantage of the opportunity to earn a return on its liquid assets and increase its profitability.

501

INTRODUCTION VIDEO CASE 5

The Campeau Bankruptcy: The Sudden Deterioration of Supplier Accounts Receivable
from ABC News, Business World, January 7, 1990

Most small firms are so strapped for cash that they live or die according to the management of their working capital. A few uncollectible credit accounts or some inventory that has to be written off can make the difference between profits and problems. This video case documents how the Campeau retailing empire bankruptcy has created serious problems for many of the small businesses supplying Campeau stores. As the video shows, when one link in the chain of credit sales snaps (or looks like it is about to snap), the effect is felt far down the line. Designers hire contractors to manufacture their designs and factors to collect their receivables. Managing a firm's working capital—its cash, accounts receivable, credit policy, and inventory—is crucial to most firms' financial health. This video case shows how sensitive small firms are to sudden changes in the value of these accounts.

If you were a supplier to Campeau, could you have foreseen the problems? Is this typical in the garment industry? What happens to you if you do not deliver Christmas goods to Campeau?

Wise management of accounts receivable and inventory is important because these two classes of assets generally constitute a large portion of a firm's total assets; taking into consideration all industries in the United States, accounts receivable exceeds 26 percent and inventory approaches 5 percent of the average firm's assets. Any changes in assets of such magnitude to the firm almost certainly will affect its profitability. An increase in accounts receivable, for example, not only results in higher sales through extension of additional trade credit, but also increases the need for financing to support the additional investment. The costs of credit investigation and collection also are increased, as could be bad debt expense. Likewise, a larger investment in inventory, by allowing more efficient production and speedier delivery to customers, leads to increased sales. At the same time, additional financing is required to support the increased level of inventory and the concomitant handling and carrying costs.

With such significance in mind, we begin the study of current asset management by exploring the various aspects of the management of cash and marketable securities. Afterward, we will turn to an analysis of the important issues related to the management of accounts receivable and inventory.

Before proceeding to our discussion of cash management, it will be helpful to distinguish among several terms. **Cash** is the currency and coin the firm has on hand in petty cash drawers, in cash registers, or in checking accounts (i.e., demand deposit accounts) at the various commercial banks. **Marketable securities,** also called near cash or near-cash assets, are security investments that the firm can quickly convert into cash balances. Generally, firms hold marketable securities with very short maturity periods—less than one year. Together, cash and marketable securities constitute the most liquid assets of a firm.

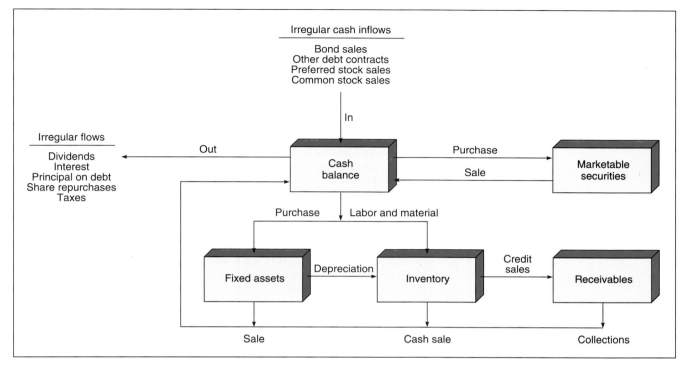

FIGURE 15–1
The Cash Generation and Disposition Process

PERSPECTIVE IN FINANCE

It is useful to think of the firm's cash balance as a reservoir that rises with cash inflows and falls with cash outflows. Any nonfinancial firm (in other words, any company that manufactures products, such as Ford Motor Company) desires to minimize its cash balances consistent with meeting its financial obligations in a timely manner.

Holding too much cash—what analysts tend to call "excess cash"—results in a loss of profitability to the firm. The auto manufacturer, for example, is not in business to build up its cash reservoir. Rather, it wants to manage its cash balance in order to maximize its financial returns because this will enhance shareholder wealth.

■ WHY A COMPANY HOLDS CASH

A thorough understanding of why and how a firm holds cash requires an accurate conception of how cash flows into and through the enterprise. Figure 15–1 depicts the process of cash generation and disposition in a typical manufacturing setting. The arrows designate the direction of the flow—that is, whether the cash balance increases or decreases.

Cash Flow Process

The irregular increases in the firm's cash holdings can come from several external sources. Funds can be obtained in the financial markets from the sale of securities, such as bonds, preferred stock, and common stock, or the firm can enter into nonmarketable debt contracts with lenders such as commercial banks. These irregular cash inflows do not occur on a daily basis. The reason is that external financing contracts or arrangements usually involve huge sums of money stemming from a major need identified by the company's management, and these needs do not occur every day. For example, a new product might be in the launching process, or a plant expansion might be required to provide added productive capacity.

In most organizations the financial officer responsible for cash management also controls the transactions that affect the firm's investment in marketable securities. As excess cash becomes temporarily available, marketable securities are purchased. When cash is in short supply, a portion of the marketable securities portfolio is liquidated.

Whereas the irregular cash inflows are from external sources, the other main sources of cash arise from internal operations and occur on a more regular basis. Over long periods, the largest receipts come from accounts receivable collections and to a lesser extent from direct cash sales of finished goods. Many manufacturing concerns also generate cash on a regular basis through the liquidation of scrap or obsolete inventory. At various times fixed assets may also be sold, thereby generating some cash inflow.

Apart from the investment of excess cash in near-cash assets, the cash balance experiences reductions for three key reasons. First, on an irregular basis, withdrawals are made to (1) pay cash dividends on preferred and common stock shares, (2) meet interest requirements on debt contracts, (3) repay the principal borrowed from creditors, (4) buy the firm's own shares in the financial markets for use in executive compensation plans or as an alternative to paying a cash dividend, and (5) pay tax bills. Again, by an *irregular basis* we mean items *not* occurring on a daily or frequent schedule. Second, the company's capital expenditure program designates that fixed assets be acquired at various intervals. Third, inventories are purchased on a regular basis to ensure a steady flow of finished goods off the production line. Note that the arrow linking the investment in fixed assets with the inventory account is labeled *depreciation*. This indicates that a portion of the cost of fixed assets is charged against the products coming off the assembly line. This cost is subsequently recovered through the sale of the finished goods inventory, since the product selling price will be set by management to cover all the costs of production, including depreciation.

Motives for Holding Cash

The influences described above that affect the firm's cash balance can be classified in terms of the three motives put forth by John Maynard Keynes: (1) the transactions motive, (2) the precautionary motive, and (3) the speculative motive.[1]

[1]John Maynard Keynes, *The General Theory of Employment, Interest, and Money* (New York: Harcourt Brace Jovanovich, 1936).

Transactions Motive

Balances held for transactions purposes allow the firm to meet cash needs that arise in the ordinary course of doing business. In Figure 15–1, transactions balances would be used to meet the irregular outflows as well as the planned acquisition of fixed assets and inventories.

The relative amount of cash needed to satisfy transactions requirements is affected by a number of factors, such as the industry in which the firm operates. It is well known that utilities can forecast cash receipts quite accurately, because of stable demand for their services. Computer software firms, however, have a more difficult time predicting their cash flows. New products are brought to market at a rapid pace, thereby making it difficult to project cash flows and balances precisely.

The Precautionary Motive

Precautionary balances are a buffer stock of liquid assets. This motive for holding cash relates to the maintenance of balances to be used to satisfy possible, but as yet indefinite, needs.

Cash flow predictability also has a material influence on the firm's demand for cash through this precautionary motive. The airline industry provides a typical illustration. Air passenger carriers are plagued with a high degree of cash flow uncertainty. The weather, rising fuel costs, and continual strikes by operating personnel make cash forecasting difficult for any airline. The upshot of this problem is that because of all the things that *might* happen, the minimum cash balances desired by the management of the air carriers tend to be large.

In actual business practice, the precautionary motive is met to a large extent by the holding of a portfolio of *liquid assets,* not just cash. Notice in Figure 15–1 the two-way flow of funds between the company's holdings of cash and marketable securities. In large corporate organizations, funds may flow either into or out of the marketable securities portfolio on a daily basis.

The Speculative Motive

Cash is held for speculative purposes in order to take advantage of potential profit-making situations. Construction firms that build private dwellings will at times accumulate cash in anticipation of a significant drop in lumber costs. If the price of building supplies does drop, the companies that built up their cash balances stand to profit by purchasing materials in large quantities. This will reduce their cost of goods sold and increase their net profit margin. Generally, the speculative motive is the least important component of a firm's preference for liquidity. The transactions and precautionary motives account for most of the reasons why a company holds cash balances.

PERSPECTIVE IN FINANCE

Any company can benefit from a properly designed cash-management system. If you identify what you believe to be a superbly run business organization, the odds are that firm has in place a sound cash-management sys-

tem. Before we explore several cash-management techniques, it is necessary to introduce (1) the risk-return tradeoff, (2) the objectives, and (3) the decisions that comprise the center of the cash-management process. Keep in mind that the billion-dollar company will save millions each year by grasping these concepts, and the small and midsized organization may actually enhance its overall chances of survival.

■ CASH MANAGEMENT OBJECTIVES AND DECISIONS

The Risk-Return Tradeoff

A companywide cash management program must be concerned with minimizing the firm's risk of insolvency. In the context of cash management, the term **insolvency** describes the situation where the firm is unable to meet its maturing liabilities on time. In such a case the company is **technically insolvent** in that it lacks the necessary liquidity to make prompt payment on its current debt obligations. A firm could avoid this problem by carrying large cash balances to pay the bills that come due.

The financial manager must strike an acceptable balance between holding too much cash and too little cash. This is the focal point of the risk-return tradeoff. A large cash investment minimizes the chances of insolvency, but penalizes company profitability. A small cash investment frees excess balances for investment in both marketable securities and longer-lived assets; this enhances company profitability and the value of the firm's common shares, but increases the chances of running out of cash.

BACK TO THE FUNDAMENTALS

The dilemma faced by the financial manager is a clear application of **Axiom 1: The Risk-Return Tradeoff—We Won't Take on Additional Risk Unless We Expect to be Compensated with Additional Return.** To accept the risk of not having sufficient cash on hand, the firm must be compensated with a return on the cash that is invested. Moreover, the greater the risk of the investment in which the cash is placed, the greater the return the firm demands.

The Objectives

The risk-return tradeoff can be reduced to two prime objectives for the firm's cash-management system:

1. Enough cash must be on hand to meet the disbursal needs that arise in the course of doing business.
2. Investment in idle cash balances must be reduced to a minimum.

Evaluation of these operational objectives, and a conscious attempt on the part of management to meet them, gives rise to the need for some typical cash-management decisions.

The Decisions

Two conditions or ideals would allow the firm to operate for extended periods with cash balances near or at a level of zero: (1) a completely accurate forecast of net cash flows over the planning horizon and (2) perfect synchronization of cash receipts and disbursements.

Cash flow forecasting is the initial step in any effective cash-management program. Given that the firm will, as a matter of necessity, invest in some cash balances, certain types of decisions related to the size of those balances dominate the cash-management process. These include decisions that answer the following questions:

1. What can be done to speed up cash collections and slow down or better control cash outflows?
2. What should be the composition of a marketable securities portfolio?

The remainder of this chapter dwells on these two questions.

PERSPECTIVE IN FINANCE

Although the sheer number of cash collection and payment techniques is large, the concepts on which those techniques rest are simple. Controlling *the cash inflow and outflow is a major theme of treasury management. But, within the confines of ethical management, the cash manager is always thinking (1) "How can I speed up the firm's cash receipts?" and (2) "How can I slow down the firm's cash payments and not irritate too many important constituencies, such as suppliers?"*
The critical point is that cash saved *becomes available for investment elsewhere in the company's operations, and at a positive rate of return this will increase total profitability. Grasping the elements of cash management requires that you understand the concept of cash* float. *We address the concept of float and float reduction early in the discussion on collection and disbursement procedures.*

■ COLLECTION AND DISBURSEMENT PROCEDURES

The efficiency of the firm's cash-management program can be enhanced by knowledge and use of various procedures aimed at (1) accelerating cash receipts and (2) improving the methods used to disburse cash. We will see that greater opportunity for corporate profit improvement lies with the cash receipts side of the funds flow process, although it would be unwise to ignore opportunities for favorably affecting cash-disbursement practices.

Managing the Cash Inflow

The reduction of float lies at the center of the many approaches employed to speed up cash receipts. **Float** (or total float) has four elements as follows:

1. **Mail float** is caused by the time lapse from the moment a customer mails a remittance check until the firm begins to process it.
2. **Processing float** is caused by the time required for the firm to process remittance checks before they can be deposited in the bank.
3. **Transit float** is caused by the time necessary for a deposited check to clear through the commercial banking system and become usable funds to the company. Credit is deferred for a maximum of two business days on checks that are cleared through the Federal Reserve System.
4. **Disbursing float** derives from the fact that funds are available in the company's bank account until its payment check has cleared through the banking system.

We will use the term *float* to refer to the total of its four elements just described. Float reduction can yield considerable benefits in terms of usable funds that are released for company use and returns produced on such freed-up balances. As an example, for 1991 IBM reported total revenues of $64.8 billion. The amount of usable funds that would be released if IBM could achieve a one-day reduction in float can be approximated by dividing annual revenues (sales) by the number of days in a year. In this case one day's freed-up balances would be

$$\frac{\text{annual revenues}}{\text{days in year}} = \frac{\$64,800,000,000}{365} = \$177,534,247$$

If these released funds, which represent one day's sales, of approximately $177.5 million could be invested to return 6 percent a year, then the annual value of the one-day float reduction would be

(sales per day) × (assumed yield) = $177,534,247 × .06 = $10,652,055

It is clear that effective cash management can yield impressive opportunities for profit improvement. Let us look now at specific techniques for reducing float.

The Lock-Box Arrangement

The lock-box system is the most widely used commercial banking service for expediting cash gathering. Banks have offered this service since 1946. Such a system speeds up the conversion of receipts into usable funds by reducing both mail and processing float. In addition, it is possible to reduce transit float if lock boxes are located near Federal Reserve Banks and their branches. For large corporations that receive checks from all parts of the country, float reductions of two to four days are not unusual.

Figure 15–2 illustrates an elementary, but typical, cash collection system for a hypothetical firm. It also shows the origin of mail float, processing float, and transit float. In this system the customer places his or her remittance check in the U.S. mail, which is then delivered to the firm's headquarters. This causes the mail float. On the check's arrival at the firm's headquarters (or local collection center), general accounting personnel must go through the bookkeeping procedures needed to prepare them

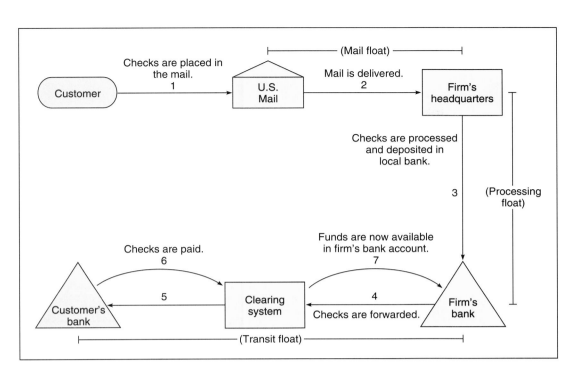

FIGURE 15–2
Ordinary Cash-Gathering System

for local deposit. The checks are then deposited. This causes the processing float. The checks are then forwarded for payment through the commercial bank clearing mechanism. The checks will be charged against the customer's own bank account. At this point the checks are said to be "paid" and become "good" funds available for use by the company that received them. This bank clearing procedure represents transit float and, as we said earlier, can amount to a delay of up to two business days.

The lock-box arrangement shown in Figure 15–3 is based on a simple procedure. The firm's customers are instructed to mail their remittance checks not to company headquarters or regional offices, but to a numbered Post Office box. The bank that is providing the lock-box service is authorized to open the box, collect the mail, process the checks, and deposit the checks directly into the company's account.

Typically a large bank will collect payments from the lock box at one- to two-hour intervals, 365 days of the year. During peak business hours, the bank may pick up mail every 30 minutes.

Once the mail is received at the bank, the checks will be examined, totaled, photocopied, and microfilmed. A deposit form is then prepared by the bank, and each batch of processed checks is forwarded to the collection department for clearance. Funds deposited in this manner are usually available for company use in one business day or less.

The bank can notify the firm via some type of telecommunications system the same day deposits are made as to their amount. At the conclusion

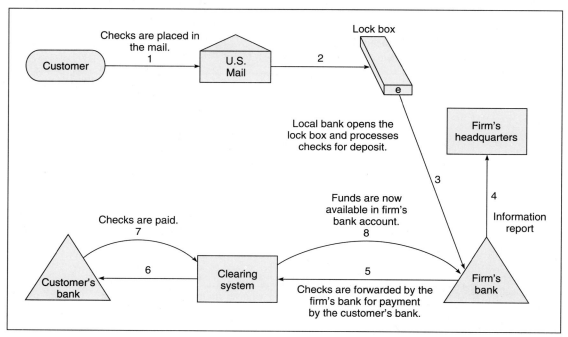

FIGURE 15–3
Simple Lock-Box System

of each day all check photocopies, invoices, deposit slips, and any other documents included with the remittances are mailed to the firm.

Note that the firm that receives checks from all over the country will have to use several lock boxes to take full advantage of a reduction in mail float. The firm's major bank should be able to offer as a service a detailed lock-box study, analyzing the company's receipt patterns to determine the proper number and location of lock-box receiving points.

The two systems described by Figures 15–2 and 15–3 are summarized in Table 15–1. There, the step numbers refer to those shown in Figure 15–2 (the ordinary system). Furthermore, Table 15–1 assumes that the customer and the firm's headquarters or its collection center are located in different cities. This causes the lag of two working days before the firm actually receives the remittance check. We notice at the bottom of Table 15–1 that the installation of the lock-box system can result in funds being credited to the firm's bank account a full *four* working days *faster* than is possible under the ordinary collection system.

Previously in this chapter we calculated the 1991 sales per day for IBM to be $177.5 million and assumed the firm could invest its excess cash in marketable securities to yield 6 percent annually. If IBM could speed up its cash collections by four days, as the hypothetical firm did in Table 15–1, the results would be startling. The gross annual savings to IBM (apart from operating the lock-box system) would amount to $42.6 million, as follows:

Step Numbers	Ordinary System and Time		Advantage of Lock Box
1	Customer writes check and places it in the mail	1 Day	
2	Mail is delivered to firm's headquarters	2 Days	Mail will not have to travel as far. Result: save 1 day
3	Accounting personnel process the checks and deposit them in the firm's local bank	2 Days	Bank personnel prepare checks for deposit. Result: save 2 days
4 and 5	Checks are forwarded for payment through the clearing mechanism	1 Day	As the lock boxes are located near Federal Reserve Banks or branches, transit float can be reduced.
6 and 7	The firm receives notice from its bank that the checks have cleared and the funds are now "good"	1 Day	Result: save 1 day
	Total working days	7	Overall result: Save 4 working days

(sales per day) × (days of float reduction) × (assumed yield)

$$= \$177,534,247 \times (4) \times .06 = \$42,608,219$$

As you might guess, the prospects for generating revenues of this magnitude are important not only to the firms involved, but also to commercial banks that offer lock-box services.

In summary, the benefits of a lock-box arrangement are these:

1. **Increased working cash.** The time required for converting receivables into available funds is reduced. This frees up cash for use elsewhere in the enterprise.
2. **Elimination of clerical functions.** The bank takes over the tasks of receiving, endorsing, totaling, and depositing checks. With less handling of receipts by employees, better audit control is achieved and the chance of documents becoming lost is reduced.

3. **Early knowledge of dishonored checks.** Should a customer's check be uncollectible because of lack of funds, it is returned, usually by special handling, to the firm.

These benefits are not free. Usually, the bank levies a charge for each check processed through the system. The benefits derived from the acceleration of receipts must exceed the incremental costs of the lock-box system, or the firm would be better off without it. Later in this chapter a straightforward method for assessing the desirability of a specific cash-management service, such as the lock-box arrangement, will be illustrated.

Preauthorized Checks (PACs)

Whereas the lock-box arrangement can often reduce total float by two to four days, for some firms the use of PACs can be an even more effective way of converting receipts into working cash. A PAC resembles the ordinary check, but it does not contain nor require the signature of the person on whose account it is being drawn. A PAC is created only with the individual's legal authorization.

The PAC system is advantageous when the firm regularly receives a large volume of payments of a fixed amount from the same customers. This type of cash-management service has proved useful to insurance companies, savings and loan associations, consumer credit firms, leasing enterprises, and charitable and religious organizations. The objective of this system is to reduce both mail and processing float. Notice, in relation to either the typical cash-gathering system (Figure 15–2) or the lock-box system (Figure 15–3), that the customer no longer (1) physically writes his or her own check or (2) deposits such check in the mail.

The operation of a PAC system is illustrated in Figure 15–4. It involves the following sequence of events:

1. The firm's customers authorize it to draw checks on their respective demand deposit accounts.
2. Indemnification agreements are signed by the customers and forwarded to the banks where they maintain their demand deposit accounts. These agreements authorize the banks to honor the PACs when they are presented for payment through the commercial bank clearing system.
3. The firm prepares a magnetic tape that contains all appropriate information about the regular payments.
4. At each processing cycle (monthly, weekly, semimonthly) the corporation retains a hard copy listing of all tape data for control purposes. Usually, the checks that are about to be printed will be deposited in the firm's demand deposit account, so a deposit ticket will also be forwarded to the bank.
5. Upon receipt of the tape the bank will produce the PACs, deposit them to the firm's account, forward them for clearing through the commercial banking system, and return a control report to the firm.

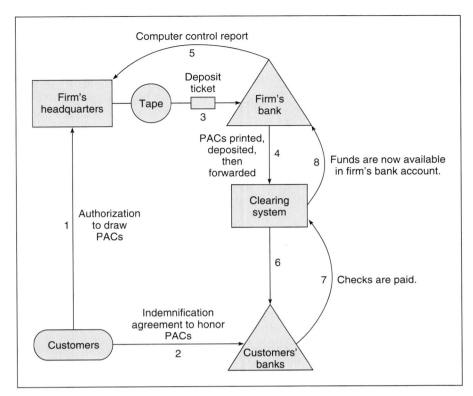

FIGURE 15-4
Preauthorized Check System
(PAC)

For firms that can take advantage of a PAC system, the benefits include the following:

1. **Highly predictable cash flows.**
2. **Reduced expenses.** Billing and postage costs are eliminated, and the clerical processing of customer payments is significantly reduced.
3. **Customer preference.** Many customers prefer not to be bothered with a regular billing. With a PAC system the check is actually written for the customer and the payment made even if he or she is on vacation or otherwise out of town.
4. **Increased working cash.** Mail float and processing float can be dramatically reduced in comparison with other payment processing systems.

Depository Transfer Checks

Both depository transfer checks and wire transfers are used in conjunction with what is known as *concentration banking.* A concentration bank is one where the firm maintains a major disbursing account.

In an effort to accelerate collections, many companies have established multiple collection centers. Regional lock-box networks are one type of approach to strategically located collection points. Even without lock boxes, firms may have numerous sales outlets throughout the country and collect cash over the counter. This requires many local bank accounts to handle daily deposits. Rather than have funds sitting in these multiple bank accounts in different geographic regions of the country, most firms will regularly transfer the surplus balances to one or more concentration banks. Centralizing the firm's pool of cash provides the following benefits:

1. **Lower levels of excess cash.** Desired cash balance target levels are set for each regional bank. These target levels consider both compensating balance requirements and necessary working levels of cash. Cash in excess of the target levels can be transferred regularly to concentration banks for deployment by the firm's top-level management.

2. **Better control.** With more cash held in fewer accounts, stricter control over available cash is achieved. Quite simply, there are fewer problems. The concentration banks can prepare sophisticated reports that detail corporatewide movements of funds into and out of the central cash pool.

3. **More efficient investments in near-cash assets.** The coupling of information from the firm's cash forecast with data on available funds supplied by the concentration banks allows the firm quickly to transfer cash to the marketable securities portfolio.

Depository transfer checks provide a means for moving funds from local bank accounts to concentration accounts. The depository transfer check itself is an unsigned, nonnegotiable instrument. It is payable only to the bank of deposit (the concentration bank) for credit to the firm's specific account. The firm files an authorization form with each bank from which it might withdraw funds. This form instructs the bank to pay the depository transfer checks without any signature. The movement of cash through the use of depository transfer checks can operate with a conventional mail system or an automated system.

When the mail system is used, a company employee deposits the day's receipts in a local bank and fills out a preprinted depository transfer check for the exact amount of the deposit. The company then mails the depository transfer check to the firm's concentration bank. While this document is traveling in the mails, the checks just deposited at the local bank are being cleared. As soon as the concentration bank receives the depository transfer check, the firm's account is credited for the designated amount. The funds credited to the concentration account are not available for the firm's use, of course, until the document has been cleared with the local depository bank for payment.

If the firm's depository banks are geographically dispersed so that the mail will take several days in reaching the concentration bank, then *no* float reduction might be achieved through this system. In an attempt to reduce the mail float associated with conventional depository transfer check systems, some banks have initiated a type of special mail handling of these instruments that can cut as much as one full day off regular mail delivery schedules.

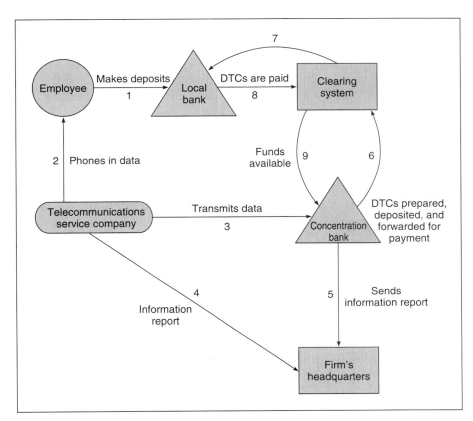

FIGURE 15–5
Automated Depository Transfer
Check System (DTC)

An innovation in speeding cash into concentration accounts is the **automated depository transfer check system.** In this system the mail float involved in moving the transfer document from the local bank to the concentration bank is *eliminated*. Here is how it works.

The local company employee makes the daily deposit as usual. This employee does *not*, however, manually fill out the preprinted depository transfer check; instead, he or she telephones the deposit information to a regional data collection center. Usually, the center is operated for a fee by a firm, such as National Data Corporation. Various data collection centers will accumulate information throughout the day on the firm's regional deposits. Then, at specified cutoff times the deposit information from all local offices is transmitted to the concentration bank.

At this point the concentration bank prepares the depository transfer check and credits it to the company's account. The transfer checks are placed into the commercial bank check-clearing process and presented to the firm's local bank for payment. When paid by the local bank, the funds become available in the concentration account for company use. Major banks claim that funds transferred by use of the automated depository transfer check system can become available for company use in one business day or less. This system is depicted in Figure 15–5.

Wire Transfers

The fastest way to move cash between banks is by use of **wire transfers,** which eliminate transit float. Funds moved in this manner, then, immediately become usable funds or "good funds" to the firm at the receiving bank. The following two major communication facilities are used to accommodate wire transfers:

1. **Bank Wire.** Bank Wire is a private wire service used and supported by approximately 250 banks in the United States for transferring funds, exchanging credit information, or effecting securities transactions.

2. **Federal Reserve Wire System.** The Fed Wire is directly accessible to commercial banks that are members of the Federal Reserve System. A commercial bank that is not on the Bank Wire or is not a member of the Federal Reserve System can use the wire transfer through its correspondent bank.

Wire transfers are often initiated on a standing-order basis. By means of a written authorization from company headquarters, a local depository bank might be instructed to transfer funds regularly to the firm's concentration bank.

As might be expected, wire transfers are a relatively expensive method of marshaling funds through a firm's money management system. Generally, the movement of small amounts does not justify the use of wire transfers.

Management of Cash Outflow

Significant techniques and systems for improving the firm's management of cash disbursements include (1) zero balance accounts, (2) payable-through drafts, and (3) remote disbursing. The first two offer markedly better control over companywide payments, and as a secondary benefit they *may* increase disbursement float. The last technique, remote disbursing, aims solely to increase disbursement float.

Zero Balance Accounts

Large corporations that operate multiple branches, divisions, or subsidiaries often maintain numerous bank accounts (in different banks) for the purpose of making timely operating disbursements. It does make good business sense for payments for purchased parts that go into, say, an automobile transmission to be made by the Transmission and Chassis Division of the auto manufacturer rather than its central office. The Transmission and Chassis Division originates such purchase orders, receives and inspects the shipment when it arrives at the plant, authorizes payment, and writes the appropriate check. To have the central office involved in these matters would be a waste of company time.

What tends to happen, however, is that with several divisions utilizing their own disbursal accounts, excess cash balances build up in outlying banks and rob the firm of earning assets. Zero balance accounts are used to alleviate this problem. The objectives of a zero balance account system are (1) for the firm to achieve better control over its cash payments, (2) to reduce excess cash balances held in regional banks for disbursing purposes, and (3) to increase disbursing float.

Zero balance accounts permit centralized control (at the headquarters level) over cash outflows while maintaining divisional disbursing authority. Under this system the firm's authorized employees, representing their various divisions, continue to write checks on their individual accounts. Note that the numerous individual disbursing accounts are now *all* located in the same concentration bank. Actually, these separate accounts contain no funds at all, thus their appropriate label, "zero balance." These accounts have all the characteristics of regular demand deposit accounts including separate titles, numbers, and statements.

Figure 15–6 presents a schematic of a zero balance account (ZBA) disbursing system. The firm is assumed to have three operating divisions, each with its own ZBA. The system works as follows. The firm's authorized agents write their payment checks as usual against their specific accounts (Step 1). These checks clear through the banking system in the usual way. On a daily basis checks will be presented to the firm's concentration bank (the drawee bank) for payment. As the checks are paid by the bank, negative (debit) balances will build in the proper disbursing accounts (Step 2). At the end of each day the negative balances will be restored to a zero level by means of credits to the zero balance accounts (Step 3); a corresponding reduction in funds is made against the firm's concentration (master) demand deposit account (also Step 3). Each morning a report is electronically forwarded to corporate headquarters reflecting the balance in the master account as well as the previous day's activity in each zero balance account (Step 4). Using the report, the financial officer in charge of near-cash investments is ready to initiate appropriate transactions.

Managing the cash outflow through use of a ZBA system offers the following benefits to the firm with many operating units:

1. Centralized control over disbursements is achieved, even though payment authority continues to rest with operating units.
2. Management time spent on superficial cash-management activities is reduced. Exercises such as observing the balances held in numerous bank accounts, transferring funds to those accounts short of cash, and reconciling the accounts demand less attention.
3. Excess balances held in outlying accounts can be reduced.
4. The costs of cash management can be reduced, as wire transfers to build up funds in outlying disbursement accounts are eliminated.
5. Funds may be made available for company use through an increase in disbursement float. When local bank accounts are used to pay nearby suppliers, the checks clear rapidly. The same checks, if drawn on a ZBA located in a more distant concentration bank, will take more time to clear against the disbursing firm's account.

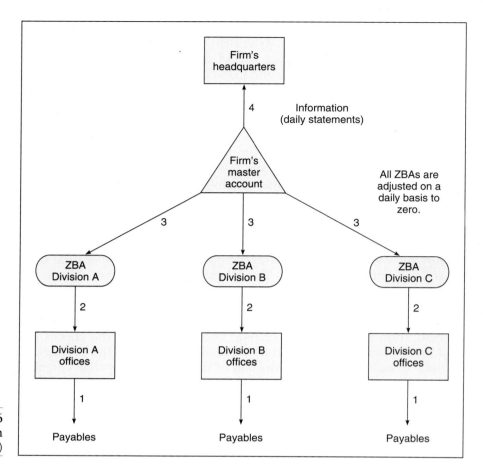

FIGURE 15–6
Zero Balance Account Cash
Disbursement System (ZBA)

Payable-Through Drafts

Payable-through drafts are legal instruments that have the physical appearance of ordinary checks but are *not* drawn on a bank. Instead, payable-through drafts are drawn on and payment is authorized by the issuing firm against its demand deposit account. Like checks, the drafts are cleared through the banking system and are presented to the issuing firm's bank. The bank serves as a collection point and passes the drafts on to the firm. The corporate issuer usually has to return by the following business day all drafts it does not wish to cover (pay). Those documents not returned to the bank are automatically paid. The firm inspects the drafts for validity by checking signatures, amounts, and dates. Stop-payment orders can be initiated by the company on any drafts considered inappropriate.

The main purpose of using a payable-through draft system is *to provide for effective control over field payments*. Central office control over payments begun by regional units is provided as the drafts are reviewed in advance of final payment. Payable-through drafts, for example, are used extensively in the insurance industry. The claims agent does not typically have check-signing authority against a corporate disbursement account. This agent can issue a draft, however, for quick settlement of a claim.

The Federal Reserve System requires transfer of available or "good" funds upon presentation of drafts to the payable-through bank. The payable-through bank will cover drafts but will be reluctant to absorb the float that would occur until the issuing firm authorized payment the next business day. Therefore, the drafts that are presented for payment will usually be charged *in total* against the corporate master demand deposit account. This is for purposes of measuring usable funds available to the firm on that day. Legal payment of the *individual drafts* will still take place after their review and approval by the firm. Figure 15–7 illustrates a payable-through draft system.

Remote Disbursing

A few banks will provide the corporate customer with a cash-management service specifically designed to extend disbursing float. The firm's concentration bank may have a correspondent relationship with a smaller bank located in a distant city. In that remote city the Federal Reserve System is unable to maintain frequent clearings of checks drawn on local banks. For example, a firm that is located in Dallas and maintains its master account there may open an account with a bank situated in, say, Amarillo, Texas. The firm will write the bulk of its payment checks against the account in the Amarillo bank. The checks will probably take at least one business day longer to clear, so the firm can "play the float" to its advantage.

A firm must use this technique of remote disbursing with extreme care. If a key supplier of raw materials located in Dallas has

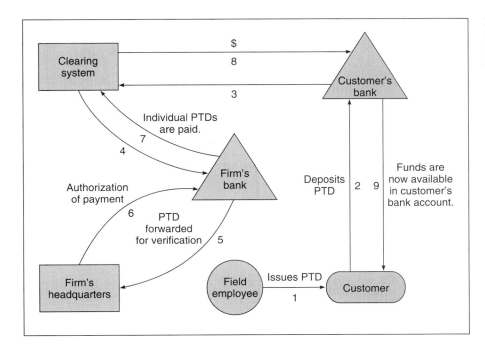

FIGURE 15–7
Payable-Through Draft Cash Disbursement System (PTD)

to wait the extra day for funds drawn on the Amarillo account, the possibility of incurring ill will might outweigh the apparent gain from an increase in the disbursing float. The impact on the firm's reputation of using remote disbursing should be explicitly evaluated. The practice of remote disbursing is discouraged by the Federal Reserve System.

BACK TO THE FUNDAMENTALS

These collection and disbursement procedures are an illustration of **Axiom 2: The Time Value of Money—A Dollar Received Today Is Worth More Than a Dollar Received in the Future.** The faster the firm can take possession of the money to which it is entitled, the sooner the firm can put the money to work generating a return. Similarly, the longer the firm can hold onto the liquid assets in its possession, the greater is the return the firm can receive on such funds.

PERSPECTIVE IN FINANCE

Our previous work in Chapter 12 presented the popular breakeven model used by financial executives, accountants, and economists. The benefit to the firm of a given cash-management service can be assessed in a similar manner. Such a model follows. More complicated methods can be presented (some that involve use of an appropriate company discount rate), but the model below is used by managers and is easily explained to them. The important point is: Cash-management services are not free.

◼ EVALUATION OF COSTS OF CASH-MANAGEMENT SERVICES

A form of breakeven analysis can help the financial officer decide whether a particular collection or disbursement service will provide an economic benefit to the firm. The evaluation process involves a very basic relationship in microeconomics:

$$\text{added costs} = \text{added benefits} \tag{15-1}$$

If equation (15–1) holds exactly, then the firm is no better or worse off for having adopted the given service. We will illustrate this procedure in terms of the desirability of installing an additional lock box. Equation (15–1) can be restated on a per-unit basis as follows:

$$P = (D)(S)(i) \tag{15-2}$$

where P =   increases in per-check processing cost if the new system is adopted

D =   days saved in the collection process (float reduction)

S =   average check size in dollars

i =   the daily, before-tax opportunity cost (rate of return) of carrying cash

Assume now that check processing cost, P, will rise by $.18 a check if the lock box is used. The firm has determined that the average check size, S, that will be mailed to the lock-box location will be $900. If funds are freed by use of the lock box, they will be invested in marketable securities to yield an *annual* before-tax return of 6 percent. With these data it is possible to determine the reduction in check collection time, D, that is required to justify use of the lock box. That level of D is found to be

$$\$.18 = (D) (\$900) \left(\frac{.06}{365} \right)$$

$$1.217 \text{ days} = D$$

Thus, the lock box is justified if the firm can speed up its collections by *more* than 1.217 days. This same style of analysis can be adapted to analyze the other tools of cash management.

Before moving on to a discussion of the firm's marketable securities portfolio, it will be helpful to draw together the preceding material. Table 15–2 summarizes the salient features of the cash-collection and disbursal techniques we have considered here.

◼ COMPOSITION OF MARKETABLE SECURITIES PORTFOLIO

Once the design of the firm's cash receipts and payments system has been determined, the financial manager faces the task of selecting appropriate financial assets for inclusion in the firm's marketable securities portfolio.

General Selection Criteria

Certain criteria can provide the financial manager with a useful framework for selecting a proper marketable securities mix. These considerations include evaluation of the (1) financial risk, (2) interest rate risk, (3) liquidity, (4) taxability, and (5) yields among different financial assets. We will briefly delineate these criteria from the investor's viewpoint.

Financial Risk

Financial risk here refers to the uncertainty of expected returns from a security attributable to possible changes in the financial capacity of the security issuer to make future payments to the security owner. If the chance of default on the terms of the instrument is high (low), then the financial risk is said to be high (low).

In both financial practice and research, when estimates of risk-free returns are desired, the yields available on Treasury securities are consulted and the safety of other financial instruments is weighed against them.

TABLE 15–2
Features of Selected Cash-Collection and Disbursal Techniques: A Summary

Technique	Objective	How Accomplished
Cash-Collection Techniques		
1. Lock-box system	Reduce (1) mail float, (2) processing float, and (3) transit float.	Strategic location of lock boxes to reduce mail float and transit float. Firm's commercial bank has access to lock box to reduce processing float.
2. Preauthorized checks	Reduce (1) mail float and (2) processing float.	The firm writes the checks (the PACs) *for* its customers to be charged against their demand deposit accounts.
3. (Ordinary) Depository transfer checks	Eliminate excess funds in regional banks.	Used in conjunction with concentration banking whereby the firm maintains several collection centers. The transfer check authorizes movement of funds from a local bank to the concentration bank.
4. Automated depository transfer checks	Eliminate the mail float associated with the ordinary transfer check.	Telecommunications company transmits deposit data to the firm's concentration bank.
5. Wire transfers	Move funds immediately between banks. This eliminates transit float in that only "good funds" are transferred.	Use of Bank Wire or the Federal Reserve Wire System.
Cash-Disbursal Techniques		
1. Zero balance accounts	(1) Achieve better control over cash payments, (2) reduce excess cash balances held in regional banks, and (3) possibly increase disbursing float.	Establish zero balance accounts for all of the firm's disbursing units. These accounts are all in the same concentration bank. Checks are drawn against these accounts, with the balance in each account never exceeding $0. Divisional disbursing authority is thereby maintained at the local level of management.
2. Payable-through drafts	Achieve effective central office control over field-authorized payments.	Field office issues drafts rather than checks to settle up payables.
3. Remote disbursing	Extend disbursing float.	Write checks against demand deposit accounts held in distant banks.

Interest Rate Risk

Interest rate risk refers to the uncertainty of expected returns from a financial instrument attributable to changes in interest rates. Of particular concern to the corporate treasurer is the price volatility associated with instruments that have long, as opposed to short, terms to maturity. An illustration can help clarify this point.

Suppose the financial officer is weighing the merits of investing temporarily available corporate cash in a new offering of U.S. Treasury obligations that will mature in either (1) three years or (2) 20 years from the date of issue. The purchase price of the three-year notes or 20-year bonds is at their par value of $1,000 per security.

Item	Three-year Instrument	Twenty-year Instrument
Original price	$1,000.00	$1,000.00
Price after one year	964.84	821.01
Decline in price	$ 35.16	$ 178.99

TABLE 15–3
Market Price Effect of Rise
in Interest Rates

The maturity value of either class of security is equal to par, $1,000, and the coupon rate (stated interest rate) is set at 7 percent, compounded annually.

If after one year from the date of purchase prevailing interest rates rise to 9 percent, the market prices of these currently outstanding Treasury securities will fall to bring their yields to maturity in line with what investors could obtain by buying a new issue of a given instrument. The market prices of *both* the 3-year and 20-year obligations will decline. The price of the 20-year instrument will decline by a greater dollar amount, however, than that of the three-year instrument.

One year from the date of issue the price obtainable in the market-place for the original 20-year instrument, which now has 19 years to go to maturity, can be found by computing P as follows:

$$P = \sum_{t=1}^{19} \frac{\$70}{(1 + .09)^t} + \frac{\$1,000}{(1 + .09)^{19}} = \$821.01$$

In the previous expression (1) T is the year in which the particular return, either interest or principal amount, is received; (2) $70 is the annual interest payment; and (3) $1,000 is the contractual maturity value of the bond. The rise in interest rates has forced the market price of the bond down to $821.01.

Now, what will happen to the price of the note that has two years remaining to maturity? In a similar manner, we can compute its price, P:

$$P = \sum_{t=1}^{2} \frac{\$70}{(1 + .09)^t} + \frac{\$1,000}{(1 + .09)^2} = \$964.84$$

The market price of the shorter-term note will decline to $964.84. Table 15–3 shows that the market value of the shorter-term security was penalized much less by the given rise in the general level of interest rates.

If we extended the illustration, we would see that, in terms of market price, a one-year security would be affected less than a two-year security, a 91-day security less than a 182-day security, and so on. Equity securities would exhibit the largest price changes because of their infinite maturity periods. To hedge against the price volatility caused by interest rate risk, the firm's marketable securities portfolio will tend to be composed of instruments that mature over short periods.

Liquidity

In the present context of managing the marketable securities portfolio, **liquidity** refers to the ability to transform a security into cash. Should an unforeseen event require that a significant amount of cash be immediately available, then a sizable portion of the portfolio might have to be sold. The financial manager will want the cash *quickly* and will not want to accept a large *price concession* in order to convert the securities. Thus, in the formulation of preferences for the inclusion of particular instruments in the portfolio, the manager must consider (1) the period needed to sell the security and (2) the likelihood that the security can be sold at or near its prevailing market price.

Taxability

The tax treatment of the income a firm receives from its security investments does not affect the ultimate mix of the marketable securities portfolio as much as the criteria mentioned earlier. This is because the interest income from most instruments suitable for inclusion in the portfolio is taxable at the federal level. Still, some corporate treasurers seriously evaluate the taxability of interest income and capital gains.

The interest income from only one class of securities escapes the federal income tax. That class of securities is generally referred to as **municipal obligations,** or more simply as **municipals.** Because of the tax-exempt feature of interest income from state and local government securities, municipals sell at lower yields to maturity in the market than do securities that pay taxable interest. The after-tax yield on a municipal obligation, however, could be higher than the yield from a non-tax-exempt security. This would depend mainly on the purchasing firm's tax situation.

Consider Table 15–4. A firm is assumed to be analyzing whether to invest in a one-year tax-free debt issue yielding 6 percent on a $1,000 outlay or a one-year taxable issue that yields 8 percent on a $1,000 outlay. The firm pays federal taxes at the rate of 34 percent. The yields quoted in the financial press and in the prospectuses that describe debt issues are *before-tax* returns. The actual *after-tax* return enjoyed by the investor depends on his or her tax bracket. Notice that the actual after-tax yield received by the firm is only 5.28 percent on the taxable issue versus 6 percent on the tax-exempt obligation. The lower portion of Table 15–4 shows that the fully taxed bond must yield 9.091 percent to make it comparable with the tax-exempt issue.

Yields

The final selection criterion that we mention is a significant one—the yields that are available on the different financial assets suitable for inclusion in the near-cash portfolio. By now it is probably obvious that the factors of (1) financial risk, (2) interest rate risk, (3) liquidity, and (4) taxability all influence the available yields on financial instruments. The yield criterion involves an evaluation of the risks and benefits inherent in all of these factors. If a given risk is assumed, such as lack of liquidity, a higher yield may be expected on the non-liquid instrument.

TABLE 15–4
Comparison of After-Tax Yields

	Tax-exempt Debt Issue (6% Coupon)	Taxable Debt Issue (8% Coupon)
Interest income	$ 60.00	$ 80.00
Income tax (.34)	0.00	27.20
After-tax interest income	$ 60.00	$ 52.80
After-tax yield	$ 60.00 = 6%	$ 52.80 = 5.28%
	$1,000.00	$1,000.00

Derivation of equivalent before-tax yield on a taxable debt issue:

$$r = \frac{r^*}{1-T} = \frac{.06}{1-.34} = 9.901\%$$

where r = equivalent before-tax yield,
  r^* = after-tax yield on tax-exempt security,
  T = firm's marginal income tax rate.

Proof: Interest income [$1,000 x .09091]   = $90.91
      Income tax (.34)   30.91
      After-tax interest income $60.00

Figure 15–8 summarizes our framework for designing the firm's marketable securities portfolio. The four basic considerations are shown to influence the yields available on securities. The financial manager must focus on the risk-return tradeoffs identified through analysis. Coming to grips with these tradeoffs will enable the financial manager to determine the proper marketable securities mix for the company. Let us look now at the marketable securities prominent in firms' near-cash portfolios.

Marketable Security Alternatives

U.S. Treasury Bills

U.S. Treasury bills are the best-known and most popular short-term investment outlet among firms. A Treasury bill is a direct obligation of the United States government sold on a regular basis by the U.S. Treasury. New Treasury bills are issued in denominations of $10,000, $15,000, $50,000, $100,000, $500,000, and $1,000,000. In effect, therefore, one can buy bills in multiples of $5,000 above the smallest purchase price of $10,000 by combining $10,000 bills and $15,000 bills to reach the desired sum.

Considerations	→	Influence	→	Focus Upon	→	Determine
Financial risk		Yields		Risk vs. return		Marketable
Interest rate risk				preferences		securities
Liquidity						mix
Taxability						

FIGURE 15–8
Designing the Marketable Securities Portfolio

Bills currently are regularly offered with maturities of 91, 182, and 365 days. The three-month and six-month bills are auctioned weekly by the Treasury, and the one-year bills are offered every four weeks. Bids (orders to purchase) are accepted by the various Federal Reserve Banks and their branches, which perform the role of agents for the Treasury. Each Monday, bids are received until 1:30 P.M.; after that time they are opened, tabulated, and forwarded to the Treasury for allocation (filling the purchase orders).

Treasury bills are sold on a discount basis; for that reason the investor does not receive an actual interest payment. The return is the difference between the purchase price and the face (par) value of the bill.

The bills are marketed by the Treasury only in *bearer* form. They are purchased, therefore, without the investor's name on them. This attribute makes them easily transferable from one investor to the next. Of prime importance to the corporate treasurer is the fact that a very active secondary market exists for bills. After a bill has been acquired by the firm, should the need arise to turn it into cash, a group of securities dealers stand ready to purchase it. This highly developed secondary market for bills not only makes them extremely liquid, but also allows the firm to buy bills with maturities of a week or even less.

As bills have the full financial backing of the United States government, they are, for all practical purposes, risk free. This negligible financial risk and high degree of liquidity makes the yields lower than those obtainable on other marketable securities. The income from Treasury bills is subject to federal income taxes, but *not* to state and local government income taxes.

Federal Agency Securities

Federal agency securities are debt obligations of corporations and agencies that have been created to effect the various lending programs of the United States government. Five such government-sponsored corporations account for the majority of outstanding agency debt. The "big five" agencies are

1. **The Federal National Mortgage Association (FNMA)**
2. **The Federal Home Loan Banks (FHLB)**
3. **The Federal Land Banks**
4. **The Federal Intermediate Credit Banks**
5. **The Banks for Cooperatives**

It is not true that the "big five" federally sponsored agencies are owned by the United States government and that the securities they issue are fully guaranteed by the government. The "big five" agencies are now entirely owned by their member associations or the general public. In addition, the issuing agency stands behind its promises to pay, not the federal government.

These agencies sell their securities in a variety of denominations. The entry barrier caused by the absolute dollar size of the smallest available Treasury bill—$10,000—is not as severe in the market for agencies.

A wide range of maturities is also available. Obligations can at times be purchased with maturities as short as 30 days or as long as 15 years.

Agency debt usually sells on a coupon basis and pays interest to the owner on a semiannual schedule, although there are exceptions. Some issues have been sold on a discount basis, and some have paid interest only once a year.

The income from agency debt that the investor receives is subject to taxation at the federal level. Of the "big five" agencies, only the income from FNMA issues is taxed at the state and local level.

The yields available on agency obligations will always exceed those of Treasury securities of similar maturity. This yield differential is attributable to lesser marketability and greater default risk. The financial officer might keep in mind, however, that none of these agency issues has ever gone into default.

Bankers' Acceptances

Bankers' acceptances are one of the least understood instruments suitable for inclusion in the firm's marketable securities portfolio. Their part in U.S. commerce today is largely concentrated in the financing of foreign transactions. Generally, an acceptance is a draft (order to pay) drawn on a specific bank by an exporter in order to obtain payment for goods shipped to a customer, who maintains an account with that specific bank.

Because acceptances are used to finance the acquisition of goods by one party, the document is not "issued" in specialized denominations; its dollar size is determined by the cost of the goods being purchased. Usual sizes, however, range from $25,000 to $1 million. The maturities on acceptances run from 30 to 180 days, although longer periods are available from time to time. The most common period is 90 days.

Acceptances, like Treasury bills, are sold on a discount basis and are payable to the bearer of the paper. A secondary market for the acceptances of large banks does exist.

The income generated from investing in acceptances is fully taxable at the federal, state, and local levels. Because of their greater financial risk and lesser liquidity, acceptances provide investors a yield advantage over Treasury bills and agency obligations. In fact, the acceptances of major banks are a very safe investment, making the yield advantage over Treasuries worth looking at from the firm's vantage point.

Negotiable Certificates of Deposit

A **negotiable certificate of deposit, CD,** is a marketable receipt for funds that have been deposited in a bank for a fixed period. The deposited funds earn a fixed rate of interest. These are not to be confused with ordinary passbook savings accounts or nonmarketable time deposits offered by all commercial banks. CDs are offered by major money-center banks. We are talking here about "corporate" CDs—not those offered to individuals.

CDs are offered by key banks in a variety of denominations running from $25,000 to $10,000,000. The popular sizes are $100,000,

$500,000, and $1,000,000. The original maturities on CDs can range from 1 to 18 months.

CDs are offered by banks on a basis differing from Treasury bills; that is, they are not sold at a discount. Rather, when the certificate matures, the owner receives the full amount deposited plus the earned interest.

A secondary market for CDs does exist, the heart of which is found in New York City. Whereas CDs may be issued in registered or bearer form, the latter facilitates transactions in the secondary market and thus is the more common.

Even though the secondary market for CDs of large banks is well organized, it does not operate as smoothly as the aftermarket in Treasuries. CDs are more heterogeneous than Treasury bills. Treasury bills have similar rates, maturity periods, and denominations; more variety is found in CDs. This makes it harder to liquidate large blocks of CDs, because a more specialized investor must be found. The securities dealers who "make" the secondary market in CDs mainly trade in $1 million units. Smaller denominations can be traded but will bring a relatively lower price.

The income received from an investment in CDs is subject to taxation at all government levels. In recent years CD yields have been above those available on bankers' acceptances.

Commercial Paper

Commercial paper refers to short-term, unsecured promissory notes sold by large businesses to raise cash. These are sometimes described in the popular financial press as short-term corporate IOUs. Because they are unsecured, the issuing side of the market is dominated by large corporations, which typically maintain sound credit ratings. The issuing (borrowing) firm can sell the paper to a dealer who will in turn sell it to the investing public; if the firm's reputation is solid, the paper can be sold directly to the ultimate investor.

The denominations in which commercial paper can be bought vary over a wide range. At times paper can be obtained in sizes from $5,000 to $5 million, or even more.

Commercial paper can be purchased with maturities that range from 3 to 270 days. Notes with maturities exceeding 270 days are very rare, because they would have to be registered with the Securities and Exchange Commission—a task firms avoid, when possible, because it is time consuming and costly.

These notes are *generally* sold on a discount basis in bearer form, although sometimes paper that is interest bearing and can be made payable to the order of the investor is available.

The next point is of considerable interest to the financial officer responsible for management of the firm's near-cash portfolio. For practical purposes, there is *no* active trading in a secondary market for commercial paper. This distinguishes commercial paper from all the previously discussed short-term investment vehicles. On occasion, a dealer or finance company (the borrower) will redeem a note prior to its contract maturity date, but this is not a regular procedure. Thus, when the corporation evaluates commercial paper for possible inclusion in its marketable securities portfolio, it should plan to hold it to maturity.

The return on commercial paper is fully taxable to the investor at all levels of government. Because of its lack of marketability, commercial paper in past years consistently provided a yield advantage over other near-cash assets of comparable maturity. The lifting of interest rate ceilings in 1973 by the Federal Reserve Board on certain large CDs, however, allowed commercial banks to make CD rates fully competitive in the attempt to attract funds. Over any time period, then, CD yields *may* be slightly above the rates available on commercial paper.

Repurchase Agreements

Repurchase agreements (repos) are legal contracts that involve the actual sale of securities by a *borrower* to the *lender,* with a commitment on the part of the borrower to *repurchase* the securities at the contract price plus a stated interest charge. The securities sold to the lender are U.S. government issues or other instruments of the money market such as those described above. The borrower is either a major financial institution—most important, a commercial bank—or a dealer in U.S. government securities.

Why might the corporation with excess cash prefer to buy repurchase agreements rather than a given marketable security? There are two major reasons. First, the original maturities of the instruments being sold can, in effect, be adjusted to suit the particular needs of the investing corporation. Funds available for very short periods, such as one or two days, can be productively employed. The second reason is closely related to the first. The firm could, of course, buy a Treasury bill and then resell it in the market in a few days when cash was required. The drawback here would be the risk involved in liquidating the bill at a price equal to its earlier cost to the firm. The purchase of a repo removes this risk. The contract price of the securities that make up the arrangement is *fixed* for the duration of the transaction. The corporation that buys a repurchase agreement, then, is protected against market price fluctuations throughout the contract period. This makes it a sound alternative investment for funds that are freed up for only very short periods.

These agreements are usually executed in sizes of $1 million or more. The maturities may be for a specified time period or may have no fixed maturity date. In the latter case either lender or borrower may terminate the contract without advance notice.

The returns the lender receives on repurchase agreements are taxed at all governmental levels. Because the interest rates are set by direct negotiation between lender and borrower, no regular published series of yields is available for direct comparison with the other short-term investments. The rates available on repurchase agreements, however, are closely related to, but generally *less* than, Treasury bill rates of comparable maturities.

Money Market Mutual Funds

The money market funds sell their shares to raise cash, and by pooling the funds of large numbers of small savers, they can build their liquid-asset portfolios. Many of these funds allow the investor to start an account with as little as $1,000. This small initial investment, coupled with the fact that some liquid-asset funds permit subsequent investments in amounts as small as $100, makes this type of outlet for excess cash suited to the small firm and even the individual. Furthermore, the management of a small enterprise may not be highly versed in the details of short-term investments. By purchasing shares in a liquid-asset fund, the investor is also buying managerial expertise.

Money market funds typically invest in a diversified portfolio of short-term, high-grade debt instruments such as those described above. Some such funds, however, will accept more interest rate risk in their portfolios and acquire some corporate bonds and notes. Money market mutual funds offer the investing firm a high degree of liquidity. By redeeming (selling) shares, the investor can obtain cash quickly. Procedures for liquidation vary among the funds, but shares can usually be redeemed by means of (1) special redemption checks supplied by the fund, (2) telephone instructions, (3) wire instructions, or (4) a letter. When liquidation is ordered by telephone or wire, the mutual fund can remit to the investor by the next business day.

The returns earned from owning shares in a money market fund are taxable at all governmental levels. The yields follow the returns the investor could receive by purchasing the marketable securities directly.

The Yield Structure of Marketable Securities

What type of return can the financial manager expect on a marketable securities portfolio? This is a reasonable question. Some insight can be obtained by looking at the past, although we must realize that future returns are not guided by past experience. It is also useful to have some understanding of how the returns on one type of instrument stack up against another. The behavior of yields on short-term debt instruments over the 1980-1992 period is shown in Table 15-5.

The discussion in this chapter on designing the firm's marketable securities portfolio touched on the essential elements of several near-

| | | | | Commercial | |
Year	T-Bills	Agencies	Acceptances	Paper	CDs
1980	11.51	12.09	12.72	12.66	13.07
1981	14.03	15.28	15.32	15.32	15.91
1982	10.69	11.68	11.89	11.89	12.27
1983	8.61	8.95	8.90	8.88	9.07
1984	9.52	10.13	10.14	10.10	10.37
1985	7.48	8.00	7.92	7.95	8.05
1986	5.98	6.49	6.38	6.49	6.51
1987	5.82	6.47	6.75	6.82	6.87
1988	6.68	7.60	7.56	7.66	7.73
1989	8.12	8.75	8.87	8.99	9.09
1990	7.51	7.99	7.93	8.06	8.15
1991	5.42	5.81	5.70	5.87	5.83
1992	3.45	n.a.	3.62	3.75	3.68

TABLE 15-5
Annual Yields (Percent) on Selected Three-Month Marketable Securities

Source: *Federal Reserve Bulletin*, various issues. Note: n.a. means not available.

TABLE 15-6
Features of Selected Money Market Instruments

Instrument	Denominations	Maturities	Basis	Form	Liquidity	Taxability
U.S. Treasury bills — direct obligations of the U.S. government	$10,000 15,000 50,000 100,000 500,000 1,000,000	91 days 182 days 365 days 9-month not presently issued	Discount	Bearer	Excellent secondary market	Exempt from state and local income
Federal agency securities — obligations of corporations and agencies created to effect the federal government's lending programs	Wide variation; from $1,000 to $1 million	5 days (Farm Credit consolidated systemwide discount notes) to more than 10 years	Discount or coupon; usually on coupon	Bearer or registered	Good for issues of "big five" agencies	Generally exempt at local level; FNMA issues are *not*
Bankers' acceptances — drafts accepted for future payment by commercial banks	No set size; typically range from $25,000 to $1 million	Predominantly from 30 to 180 days	Discount	Bearer	Good for acceptances of large "money market" banks	Taxed at all levels of government
Negotiable certificates of deposit—marketable receipts for funds deposited in a bank for a fixed time period	$25,000 to $10 million	1 to 18 months	Accrued interest	Bearer or registered; bearer is preferable from liquidity standpoint	Fair to good	Taxed at all levels of government
Commercial paper — short-term unsecured promissory notes	$5,000 to $5 million; $1,000 and $5,000 multiples above the initial offering size are sometimes available	3 to 270 days	Discount	Bearer	Poor; no active secondary market in usual sense	Taxed at all levels of government
Repurchase agreements — legal contracts between a borrower (security seller) and lender (security buyer). The borrower will repurchase at the contract price plus an interest charge.	Typical sizes are $500,000 or more	According to terms of contract	Not applicable	Not applicable	Fixed by the agreement; that is, borrower will repurchase	Taxed at all levels of government
Money market mutual funds—holders of diversified portfolios of short-term, high-grade debt instruments	Some require an initial investment as small as $1,000	Your shares can be sold at any time	Net asset value	Registered	Good; provided by the fund itself	Taxed at all levels of government

cash assets. At times it is difficult to sort out the distinguishing features among these short-term investments. To alleviate that problem, Table 15–6 draws together their principal characteristics.

■ ACCOUNTS RECEIVABLE MANAGEMENT

We now turn from the most liquid of the firm's current assets (cash and marketable securities) to those which are less liquid—accounts receivable and inventories. All firms by their very nature are involved in selling either goods or services. Although some of these sales will be for cash, a large portion will involve credit. Whenever a sale is made on credit, it increases the firm's accounts receivable. Thus, the importance of how a firm manages its accounts receivable depends on the degree to which the firm sells on credit.

Accounts receivable typically comprise over 25 percent of a firm's assets. In effect, when we discuss management of accounts receivable, we are discussing the management of one-quarter of the firm's assets. Moreover, because cash flows from a sale cannot be invested until the account is collected, control of receivables takes on added importance; efficient collection determines both profitability and liquidity of the firm.

Size of Investment in Accounts Receivable

The size of the investment in accounts receivable is determined by several factors. First, the percentage of credit sales to total sales affects the level of accounts receivable held. Although this factor certainly plays a major role in determining a firm's investment in accounts receivable, it generally is not within the control of the financial manager. The nature of the business tends to determine the blend between credit sales and cash sales. A large grocery store tends to sell exclusively on a cash basis, whereas most construction-lumber supply firms make their sales primarily with credit.

The level of sales is also a factor in determining the size of the investment in accounts receivable. Very simply, the more sales, the greater accounts receivable. It is not a decision variable for the financial manager, however.

The final determinants of the level of investment in accounts receivable are the credit and collection policies—more specifically, the *terms of sale*, the *quality of customer*, and *collection efforts*. These policies *are* under the control of the financial manager. The terms of sale specify both the time period during which the customer must pay and the terms, such as penalties for late payments or discounts for early payments. The type of customer or credit policy also affects the level of investment in accounts receivable. For example, the acceptance of poorer credit risks and their subsequent delinquent payments may lead to an increase in accounts receivable. The strength and timing of the collection efforts can affect the period for which past-due accounts remain delinquent, which in turn affects the level of accounts receivable. Collection and credit policy decisions may fur-

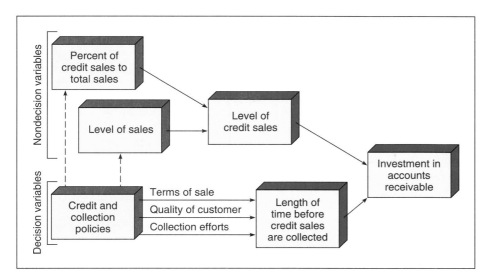

FIGURE 15–9
Determinants of Investment
in Accounts Receivable

ther affect the level of investment in accounts receivable by causing changes in the sales level and the ratio of credit sales to total sales. The factors that determine the level of investment in accounts receivable are displayed in Figure 15–9.

<u>PERSPECTIVE IN FINANCE</u>

As we examine the credit decision, try to remember that our goal is not to minimize losses but to maximize profits. Although we will spend a good deal of time trying to sort out those customers with the highest probability of default, this analysis is only an input into a decision based on shareholder wealth maximization. Essentially a firm with a high profit margin can tolerate a more liberal credit policy than a firm with a low profit margin.

Terms of Sale—Decision Variable

The **terms of sale** identify the possible discount for early payment, the discount period, and the total credit period. They are generally stated in the form a/b net c, indicating that the customer can deduct a percent if the account is paid within b days; otherwise, the account must be paid within c days. Thus, for example, trade credit terms of 2/10, net 30 indicate that a 2 percent discount can be taken if the account is paid within 10 days; otherwise it must be paid within 30 days. Failure to take the discount represents a cost to the customer. For instance, if the terms are 2/10, net 30, the annualized opportunity cost of passing up this 2 percent discount in order to withhold payment for an additional 20 days is 36.73 percent. This is determined as follows:

$$\left(\begin{array}{c} \text{annualized opportunity cost} \\ \text{of forgoing the discount} \end{array} \right) = \frac{a}{1 - a} \times \frac{360}{c - b} \quad \textbf{(15–3)}$$

Substituting the values from the example, we get

$$36.73\% = \frac{.02}{1-.02} \times \frac{360}{30-10} \qquad \textbf{(15–4)}$$

In industry the typical discount ranges anywhere from one-half percent to 10 percent, whereas the discount period is generally 10 days and the total credit period varies from 30 to 90 days. Although the terms of credit vary radically from industry to industry, they tend to remain relatively uniform within any particular industry. Moreover, the terms tend to remain relatively constant over time, and they do not appear to be used frequently as a decision variable.

Type of Customer—Decision Variable

A second decision variable involves determining the *type of customer* who is to qualify for trade credit. Several costs always are associated with extending credit to less credit-worthy customers. First, as the probability of default increases, it becomes more important to identify which of the possible new customers would be a poor risk. When more time is spent investigating the less credit-worthy customer, the costs of credit investigation increase.

Default costs also vary directly with the quality of the customer. As the customer's credit rating declines, the chance that the account will not be paid on time increases. In the extreme case, payment never occurs. Thus, taking on less credit-worthy customers results in increases in default costs.

Collection costs also increase as the quality of the customer declines. More delinquent accounts force the firm to spend more time and money collecting them. Overall, the decline in customer quality results in increased costs of credit investigation, collection, and default.

In determining whether to grant credit to an individual customer, we are primarily interested in the customer's short-run welfare. Thus, liquidity ratios, other obligations, and the overall profitability of the firm become the focal point in this analysis. Credit-rating services, such as Dun & Bradstreet, provide information on the financial status, operations, and payment history for most firms. Other possible sources of information would include credit bureaus, trade associations, Chambers of Commerce, competitors, bank references, public financial statements, and, of course, the firm's past relationship with the customer.

One way in which both individuals and firms are often evaluated as credit risks is through the use of credit scoring. **Credit scoring** involves the numerical evaluation of each applicant. An applicant receives a score based on his or her answers to a simple set of questions. This score is then evaluated according to a predetermined standard, its level relative to the standard determining whether credit should be extended. The major advantage of credit scoring is that it is inexpensive and easy to perform. For example, once the standards are set, a computer or clerical worker without any specialized training could easily evaluate any applicant.

The techniques used for constructing credit-scoring indexes range from the simple approach of adding up default rates associated with the answers given to each question, to sophisticated evaluations using multiple discriminate analysis (MDA). MDA is a statistical technique for calculating the appropriate importance to assign each question used in evaluating the applicant.

Another model that could be used for credit scoring has been provided by Edward Altman, who used multiple discriminant analysis to identify businesses that might go bankrupt. In his landmark study Altman used financial ratios to predict which firms would go bankrupt over the period 1946 to 1965. Using multiple discriminant analysis, Altman came up with the following index:

$$Z = 3.3 \left(\frac{\text{EBIT}}{\text{total assets}} \right) + 1.0 \left(\frac{\text{sales}}{\text{total assets}} \right) + 0.6 \left(\frac{\text{market value of equity}}{\text{book value of debt}} \right)$$

$$+ 1.4 \left(\frac{\text{retained earnings}}{\text{total assets}} \right) + 1.2 \left(\frac{\text{working capital}}{\text{total assets}} \right) \quad \textbf{(15–5)}$$

Altman found that of the firms that went bankrupt over this time period, 94 percent had Z scores of less than 2.7 one year prior to bankruptcy and only 6 percent had scores above 2.7 percent. Conversely, of those firms that did not go bankrupt, only 3 percent had Z scores below 2.7 and 97 percent had scores above 2.7.

PERSPECTIVE IN FINANCE

It is tempting to look at the credit decision as a single yes or no decision based on some simple formula. However, simply to look at the immediate future in making a credit decision would be a mistake. If extending a customer credit means the customer may become a regular customer in the future, it may be appropriate to take a risk that otherwise would not be prudent. Our goal is to ensure that all cash flows affected by the decision at hand are considered, not simply the most immediate cash flows.

Collection Efforts—Decision Variable

The key to maintaining control over collection of accounts receivable is the fact that the probability of default increases with the age of the account. Thus, control of accounts receivable focuses on the control and elimination of past-due receivables. One common way of evaluating the current situation is **ratio analysis.** The financial manager can determine whether accounts receivables are under control by examining the average collection period, the ratio of receivables to assets, the ratio of credit sales to receivables (called the accounts receivable turnover ratio), and the amount of bad debts relative to sales over time. In addition, the manager can perform what is called an aging of accounts receivable to provide a breakdown in both dollars and in percentages of the proportion of receivables that are past due. Comparing the current aging of receivables with past data offers even more control.

Once the delinquent accounts have been identified, the firm's accounts receivable group makes an effort to collect them. For example, a past-due letter, called a *dunning letter,* is sent if payment is not received on time, followed by an additional dunning letter in a more serious tone if the account becomes 3 weeks past due, followed after 6 weeks by a telephone call. Finally, if the account becomes 12 weeks past due, it might be turned over to a collection agency. Again, a direct trade-off exists between collection expenses and lost goodwill on one hand and noncollection of accounts on the other, and this tradeoff is always part of making the decision.

■ INVENTORY MANAGEMENT

Inventory management involves the control of the assets that are produced to be sold in the normal course of the firm's operations. The general categories of inventory include raw materials inventory, work-in-process inventory, and finished goods inventory. The importance of inventory management to the firm depends on the extent of the inventory investment. For an average firm, approximately 4.88 percent of all assets are in the form of inventory. However, the percentage varies widely from industry to industry. Thus the importance of inventory management and control varies from industry to industry also. For example, it is much more important in the automotive dealer and service station trade, where inventories make up 49.72 percent of total assets, than in the hotel business, where the average investment in inventory is only 1.56 percent of total assets.

Purposes and Types of Inventory

The purpose of carrying inventories is to uncouple the operations of the firm—that is, to make each function of the business independent of each other function—so that delays or shutdowns in one area do not affect the production and sale of the final product. Because production shutdowns result in increased costs, and because delays in delivery can lose customers, the management and control of inventory are important duties of the financial manager.

Decision making in investment in inventory involves a basic trade-off between risk and return. The risk is that if the level of inventory is too low, the various functions of business do not operate independently, and delays in production and customer delivery can result. The return results because reduced inventory investment saves money. As the size of inventory increases, storage and handling costs as well as the required return on capital invested in inventory rise. Therefore, as the inventory a firm holds is increased, the risk of running out of inventory is lessened, but inventory expenses rise.

Raw Materials Inventory

Raw materials inventory consists of basic materials purchased from other firms to be used in the firm's production operations. These goods may include steel, lumber, petroleum, or manufactured items such as wire, ball bearings, or tires that the firm does not produce itself.

Regardless of the specific form of the raw materials inventory, all manufacturing firms by definition maintain a raw materials inventory. Its purpose is to uncouple the production function from the purchasing function—that is, to make these two functions independent of each other, so that delays in shipment of raw materials do not cause production delays. In the event of a delay in shipment, the firm can satisfy its need for raw materials by liquidating its inventory.

Work-in-Process Inventory

Work-in-process inventory consists of partially finished goods requiring additional work before they become finished goods. The more complex and lengthy the production process, the larger the investment in work-in-process inventory. The purpose of work-in-process inventory is to uncouple the various operations in the production process so that machine failures and work stoppages in one operation will not affect the other operations. Assume, for example, there are 10 different production operations, each one involving the piece of work produced in the previous operation. If the machine performing the first production operation breaks down, a firm with no work-in-process inventory will have to shut down all 10 production operations. Yet if a firm has such inventory, the remaining 9 operations can continue by drawing the input for the second operation from inventory.

Finished-Goods Inventory

Finished-goods inventory consists of goods on which production has been completed but that are not yet sold. The purpose of a finished-goods inventory is to uncouple the production and sales functions so that it is not necessary to produce the good before a sale can occur—sales can be made directly out of inventory. In the auto industry, for example, people would not buy from a dealer who made them wait weeks or months when another dealer could fill the order immediately.

Stock of Cash

Although we have already discussed cash management at some length, it is worthwhile to mention cash again in the light of inventory management. This is because the *stock of cash* carried by a firm is simply a special type of inventory. In terms of uncoupling the various operations of the firm, the purpose of holding a stock of cash is to make the payment of bills independent of the collection of accounts due. When cash is kept on hand, bills can be paid without prior collection of accounts.

Inventory-Management Techniques

The importance of effective inventory management is directly related to the size of the investment in inventory. Effective management of these assets is essential to the goal of shareholder wealth maximization. To control the investment in inventory, management must solve two problems: the order quantity problem and the order point problem.

Order Quantity Problem

The *order quantity problem* involves determining the optimal order size for an inventory item given its expected usage, carrying costs, and ordering costs.

The economic order quantity (EOQ) model attempts to determine the order size that will minimize total inventory costs. It assumes that

$$\begin{matrix} \text{total} \\ \text{inventory costs} \end{matrix} = \begin{matrix} \text{total} \\ \text{carrying costs} \end{matrix} + \begin{matrix} \text{total} \\ \text{ordering costs} \end{matrix} \quad \textbf{(15–6)}$$

Assuming that inventory is allowed to fall to zero and then is immediately replenished (this assumption will be lifted when we discuss the order point problem), the average inventory becomes Q/2, where Q is inventory order size in units. This can be seen graphically in Figure 15–10.

If the average inventory is Q/2 and the carrying cost per unit is C, then carrying costs become:

$$\begin{matrix} \text{total} \\ \text{carrying costs} \end{matrix} = \left(\begin{matrix} \text{average} \\ \text{inventory} \end{matrix} \right) \left(\begin{matrix} \text{carrying cost} \\ \text{per unit} \end{matrix} \right) \quad \textbf{(15–7)}$$

$$= \left(\frac{Q}{2} \right) C \quad \textbf{(15–8)}$$

where Q = the inventory order size in units
C = carrying costs per unit

The carrying costs on inventory include the required rate of return on investment in inventory, in addition to warehouse or storage costs, wages for those who operate the warehouse, and costs associated with inventory shrinkage. Thus, carrying costs include both real cash flows and opportunity costs associated with having funds tied up in inventory.

FIGURE 15–10
Inventory Level and the
Replenishment Cycle

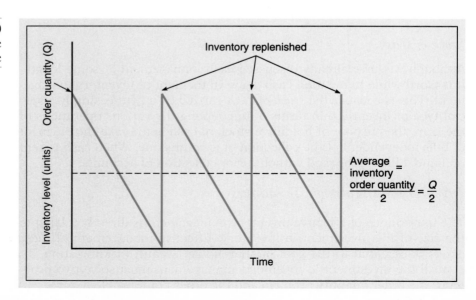

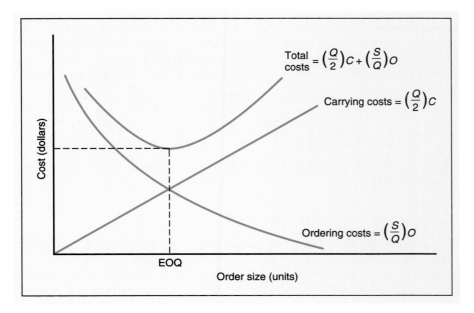

$$\text{Total costs} = \left(\frac{Q}{2}\right)C + \left(\frac{S}{Q}\right)O$$

$$\text{Carrying costs} = \left(\frac{Q}{2}\right)C$$

$$\text{Ordering costs} = \left(\frac{S}{Q}\right)O$$

EOQ

Order size (units)

Cost (dollars)

FIGURE 15–11
Total Cost and EOQ
Determination

The ordering costs incurred are equal to the ordering costs per order times the number of orders. If we assume total demand over the planning period is S and we order in lot sizes of Q, then S/Q represents the number of orders over the planning period. If the ordering cost per order is O, then

$$\begin{array}{ll} \text{total} \\ \text{ordering costs} \end{array} = \left(\begin{array}{l}\text{number}\\\text{of orders}\end{array}\right)\left(\begin{array}{l}\text{ordering cost}\\\text{per order}\end{array}\right) \qquad \textbf{(15–9)}$$

$$= \left(\frac{S}{Q}\right)O \qquad \textbf{(15–10)}$$

where S = total demand in units over the planning period
      O = ordering cost per order

Thus, total costs in equation (15–6) become

$$\text{total costs} = \left(\frac{Q}{2}\right)C + \left(\frac{S}{Q}\right)O \qquad \textbf{(15–11)}$$

Figure 15–11 illustrates this equation graphically.

What we are looking for is the ordering size, Q^*, which provides the minimum total costs. By manipulating equation (15–11), we find that the optimal value of Q—that is, the economic ordering quantity (EOQ)—is

$$Q^* = \sqrt{\frac{2SO}{C}} \qquad \textbf{(15–12)}$$

The use of the EOQ model can best be illustrated through an example.

Suppose a firm expects total demand (*S*) for its product over the planning period to be 5,000 units, whereas the ordering cost per order (*O*) is $200 and the carrying cost per unit (*C*) is $2. Substituting these values into equation (15–12) yields

$$Q^* = \sqrt{\frac{2 \cdot 5000 \cdot 200}{2}} = \sqrt{1,000,000} = 1,000 \text{ units}$$

Thus, if this firm orders in 1,000-unit lot sizes, it will minimize its total inventory costs.

Examination of EOQ Assumptions

Despite the fact that the EOQ model tends to yield quite good results, there are weaknesses in the EOQ model associated with several of its assumptions. When its assumptions have been dramatically violated, the EOQ model can generally be modified to accommodate the situation. The model's assumptions are as follows:

1. **Constant or uniform demand.** Although the EOQ model assumes constant demand, demand may vary from day to day. If demand is stochastic—that is, not known in advance—the model must be modified through the inclusion of a safety stock.
2. **Constant unit price.** The inclusion of variable prices resulting from quantity discounts can be handled quite easily through a modification of the original EOQ model, redefining total costs and solving for the optimum order quantity.
3. **Constant carrying costs.** Unit carrying costs may vary substantially as the size of the inventory rises, perhaps decreasing because of economies of scale or storage efficiency or increasing as storage space runs out and new warehouses have to be rented. This situation can be handled through a modification in the original model similar to the one used for variable unit price.
4. **Constant ordering costs.** Although this assumption is generally valid, its violation can be accommodated by modifying the original EOQ model in a manner similar to the one used for variable unit price.
5. **Instantaneous delivery.** If delivery is not instantaneous, which is generally the case, the original EOQ model must be modified through the inclusion of a safety stock, that is, the inventory held to accommodate any unusually large and unexpected usage during the delivery time.
6. **Independent orders.** If multiple orders result in cost savings by reducing paperwork and transportation cost, the original EOQ model must be further modified. Although this modification is somewhat complicated, special EOQ models have been developed to deal with it.

These assumptions illustrate the limitations of the basic EOQ model and the ways in which it can be modified to compensate for them. An understanding of the limitations and assumptions of the EOQ model provides the financial manager with more of a base for making inventory decisions.

Order Point Problem

The two most limiting assumptions—those of constant or uniform demand and instantaneous delivery—are dealt with through the inclusion of **safety stock,** which is the inventory held to accommodate any unusually large and unexpected usage during delivery time. The decision on how much safety stock to hold is generally referred to as the **order point problem;** that is, how low should inventory be depleted before it is reordered?

Two factors go into the determination of the appropriate order point: (1) the procurement or delivery-time stock and (2) the safety stock desired. Figure 15–12 graphs the process involved in order point determination. We observe that the order point problem can be decomposed into its two components, the **delivery-time stock**—that is, the inventory needed between the order date and the receipt of the inventory ordered—and the safety stock. Thus, the order point is reached when inventory falls to a level equal to the delivery-time stock plus the safety stock.

$$\begin{array}{l} \text{inventory order point} \\ \text{[order new inventory} \\ \text{when the level of inventory} \\ \text{falls to this level]} \end{array} = \left(\begin{array}{c}\text{delivery - time}\\\text{stock}\end{array}\right) + \left(\begin{array}{c}\text{safety}\\\text{stock}\end{array}\right) \quad \textbf{(15–13)}$$

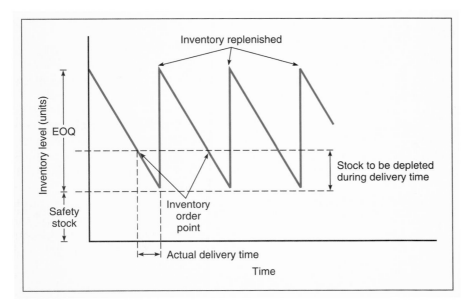

FIGURE 15–12
Order Point Determination

As a result of constantly carrying safety stock, the average level of inventory increases. Whereas before the inclusion of safety stock the average level of inventory was equal to EOQ/2, now it will be

$$\text{average inventory} = \frac{\text{EOQ}}{2} + \text{safety stock} \qquad \textbf{(15–14)}$$

In general, several factors simultaneously determine how much delivery-time stock and safety stock should be held. First, the efficiency of the replenishment system affects how much delivery-time stock is needed. Because the delivery-time stock is the expected inventory usage between ordering and receiving inventory, efficient replenishment of inventory would reduce the need for delivery-time stock.

The uncertainty surrounding both the delivery time and the demand for the product affects the level of safety stock needed. The more certain the patterns of these inflows and outflows from the inventory, the less safety stock required. In effect, if these inflows and outflows are highly predictable, then there is little chance of any stock-out occurring. However, if they are unpredictable, it becomes necessary to carry additional safety stock to prevent unexpected stock-outs.

The safety margin desired also affects the level of safety stock held. If it is a costly experience to run out of inventory, the safety stock held will be larger than it would be otherwise. If running out of inventory and the subsequent delay in supplying customers result in strong customer dissatisfaction and the possibility of lost future sales, then additional safety stock is necessary. A final determinant is the cost of carrying additional inventory, in terms of both the handling and storage costs and the opportunity cost associated with the investment in additional inventory. Very simply, the greater the costs, the smaller the safety stock.

Inflation and EOQ

Inflation affects the EOQ model in two major ways. First, although the EOQ model can be modified to assume constant price increases, often major price increases occur only once or twice a year and are announced ahead of time. If this is the case, the EOQ model may lose its applicability and may be replaced with **anticipatory buying**—that is, buying in anticipation of a price increase to secure the goods at a lower cost. Of course, as with most decisions, there are tradeoffs. The costs are the added carrying costs associated with the inventory. The benefits, of course, come from buying at a lower price. The second way inflation affects the EOQ model is through increased carrying costs. As inflation pushes interest rates up, the cost of carrying inventory increases. In our EOQ model this means that C increases, which results in a decline in Q^*, the optimal economic order quantity:

The Limited: Restocking Inventory Quickly with the Right Stuff

In the fashion industry it is not enough for a store to have inventory on hand; it also must have what is in style. As we all know, fashion trends can change overnight. This is particularly frustrating for fashion retailers because traditionally orders must be placed at least six months in advance. Most fashion retailers have quite a challenge in reacting quickly to new trends and style changes.

The Limited, which has more than 3,000 retail outlets nationwide including Express and Victoria's Secret, has set up an international inventory management system that allows the fashion cycle to be cut to 60 days. It does this by examining daily reports that are taken from point-of-sale computers; information on items sold is fed back to company headquarters. Decisions are then made on what to produce, and those orders are sent by satellite to plants located in Hong Kong. The newly produced goods are then flown back to the United States on chartered flights that arrive four times a week. Once in the United States, the goods are sorted, priced, and shipped out to stores nationwide within 48 hours. As a result the goods go on sale within 60 days of the order.

The Limited's inventory stocking system allows it to be successful by keeping on top of trends. The company's system integrates the firm's global operations in such a way that it has become The Limited's most important competitive weapon.

$$\downarrow Q^* = \sqrt{\frac{2SO}{C \uparrow}} \qquad (15\text{--}15)$$

■ JUST-IN-TIME INVENTORY CONTROL

The **just-in-time inventory control system** is more than just an inventory control system, it is a production and management system. Not only is inventory cut down to a minimum, but the time and physical distance between the various production operations are also reduced. In addition, management is willing to trade off costs to develop close relationships with suppliers and promote speedy replenishment of inventory in return for the ability to hold less safety stock.

The just-in-time inventory control system was originally developed in Japan by Taiichi Okno, a vice-president of Toyota. The idea behind the system is that the firm should keep a minimum level of inventory on hand, relying on suppliers to furnish parts "just in time" for them to be assembled. This is in direct contrast to the traditional inventory philosophy of U.S. firms, which is sometimes referred to as a "just-in-case" system, which keeps healthy levels of safety stocks to ensure that production will not be interrupted. Although large inventories may not be a bad idea when interest rates are low, when interest rates are high they become very costly.

Although the just-in-time inventory system is intuitively appealing, it has not proved easy to implement. Long distances from suppliers and

Making Just-in-Time Inventory Systems Work with Maquiladoras: But Do Maquiladoras Exploit Mexican Workers?

In the late 1970s and early 1980s many U.S. firms moved their manufacturing operations to Asian countries in an effort to reduce production costs. One problem firms have encountered for goods produced abroad is long delivery times. This has been particularly troublesome for firms that have implemented just-in-time inventory systems. To reduce the delivery time firms such as Ford, GM, Chrysler, Dale Electronics, Emerson Electric, Zenith, Honeywell, Hitachi, Sanyo, General Electric, Texas Instruments, and many others have built *maquiladoras*. These are assembly plants operated by non-Mexican companies along the Mexican side of the U.S.-Mexican border. In an effort to help develop both sides of what has historically been an impoverished border region, the first maquiladoras were established in 1966 and given special tariff treatment. By early 1992 there were approximately 1,800 maquiladoras employing approximately one-half million Mexican workers; it has been estimated that by the year 2000 up to 3 million workers could be employed.

In the April 18, 1991, *Wall Street Journal*, Lane Kirkland, president of the AFL-CIO, blasted maquiladoras, stating that they cost hundreds of thousands of Americans their jobs *and* that the Mexicans working at the maquiladoras were "joining the ranks of the most crudely exploited human beings on the planet," citing the low wage rate of $3 to $6 per day. The questions are: Do U.S., Japanese, and European corporations take advantage of Mexican workers by operating plants just south of the U.S. border? Are they exporting U.S. jobs?[1]

On one side are those who argue that maquiladoras exploit the large pool of unskilled Mexicans who have migrated north to these border cities to escape the poverty in inner Mexico. These people are desperate for work and are glad to take jobs at wages that are one-tenth those of employees just over the border. U.S. union officials further charge that maquiladoras took 300,000 U.S. jobs during the 1980s and will increasingly siphon off higher-paid jobs. Additionally, many Mexicans claim that the jobs and money come at too high a social cost; that is, northern Mexico is being Americanized. They are upset by the dilution of Mexican culture created by the spreading use of both English and the U.S. dollar.

The other side of the argument proposes that, far from feeling exploited, Mexican workers often find their clean, air-conditioned work surroundings a relief from their humble homes. Although the pay is low by U.S. standards, these jobs are in high demand and provide an escape from poverty for hundreds of thousands of Mexicans. Moreover, proponents of maquiladoras stress that economics and global competition demand that production seek its lowest cost level. Firms north of the border that fail to transfer operations to gain cost benefits save jobs in the United States only in the short term. In the long term, competition will drive these firms out of business.

Are corporations that build plants south of the border profiting at the expense of exploited Mexican workers and taking jobs away from U.S. workers? What do *you* think?

[1]Based on "The Rise of Gringo Capitalism," *Newsweek*, January 5, 1987, pp. 40-41; "The Magnet of Growth in Mexico's North," *Business Week*, June 6, 1988, pp. 48-50; Cheryl D. Hein, "Maquiladoras: Should U.S. Companies Run for the Border?" *The CPA Journal*, September 1991 (New York Society of CPAs), pp. 14-18; Mariah E. deForest, "Are Maquiladoras a Menace to U.S. Workers?" *Business Horizons*, November 1991 (Indiana University), pp. 82-90.

Adapted by permission from Stephen P. Robbins, *Management*, 3d ed. p. 103. Copyright 1991 by Prentice Hall, Inc.

plants constructed with too much space for storage and not enough access (doors and loading docks) to receive inventory have limited successful implementation. But many firms' relationships with their suppliers have been forced to change. Because firms rely on suppliers to deliver high-quality parts and materials immediately, they must have a close long-term relationship with them. Despite the difficulties of implementation, many U.S. firms are committed to moving toward a just-in-time system. In fact, between 1977 and 1986 the average level of inventory relative to total assets for all American corporations fell by 46.04 percent.

Although the just-in-time system does not at first appear to bear much of a relationship to the EOQ model, it simply alters some of the assumptions of the model with respect to delivery time and ordering costs, and draws out the implications. Actually, it is just a new approach to the EOQ model that tries to produce the lowest average level of inventory possible. If we look at the average level of inventory as defined by the EOQ model, we find it to be

$$\text{average inventory} = \frac{\sqrt{\dfrac{2SO\downarrow}{C}}}{2} + \text{safety stock}\downarrow$$

The just-in-time system attacks this equation in two places. First, by locating inventory supplies in convenient locations, laying out plants in such a way that it is inexpensive and easy to unload new inventory shipments, and computerizing the inventory order system, the cost of ordering new inventory, O, is reduced. Second, by developing a strong relationship with suppliers located in the same geographical area and setting up restocking strategies that cut time, the safety stock is also reduced. The philosophy behind the just-in-time inventory system is that the benefits associated with reducing inventory and delivery time to a bare minimum through adjustment in the EOQ model will more than offset the costs associated with the increased possibility of stock-outs.

SUMMARY

As you recall, several of the axioms that form the foundations of financial management relate to the importance of cash and cash flows. In this chapter, we have developed many of the tools that a financial manager needs to manage the firm's cash and other current assets with the overall objective of ensuring that the firm has an appropriate level of liquidity or net working capital to carry out the goal of maximizing shareholder wealth.

The firm experiences both regular and irregular cash flows. Once cash is obtained, the firm will have three motives for holding cash rather than investing it: to satisfy transactions, precautionary and speculative liquidity needs. To a certain extent, such needs can be satisfied by holding readily marketable securities rather than cash. A significant challenge of cash management, then, is dealing with the tradeoff between the firm's need to have cash on hand to pay liabilities that arise in the course of doing business and the objective of maximizing wealth by reducing to a minimum idle cash balances that earn no return.

Various procedures exist to improve the efficiency of a firm's cash management. Such procedures focus not only (although primarily) on accelerating the firm's cash receipts, but also on improving the methods for disbursing cash. Generally, at the heart of attempts to accelerate cash receipts is a significant effort to reduce the mail, processing and transit elements of the float. Often used in conjunction with concentration banking and a lock-box arrangement are depository transfer checks and wire transfers.

On the cash disbursements side, firms try to prolong the time cash stays in their own accounts by increasing the disbursement float through the use of zero balance accounts, payable-through drafts, and, especially, remote disbursing. The first two of these methods also offer much better central-office control over disbursements. Before any collection or disbursement procedure is introduced, however, a careful analysis should be performed to ensure that expected benefits outweigh the expected costs of such procedures.

Because idle cash earns no return, a financial manager will look for opportunities to invest such cash until it is required in the operations of the company. A variety of different readily marketable securities, which are described in the chapter, are available in the market today. The yields on such securities vary depending on four factors: the (1) financial risk, (2) interest rate risk, (3) liquidity, and (4) taxability of the security. By simultaneously taking into account these factors and the desired rate of return, the financial manager is able to determine the most suitable mix of cash and marketable securities for the firm.

When we consider that accounts receivable constitute approximately 25 percent of total assets for the typical firm, the importance of accounts receivable management becomes even more apparent. The size of a firm's investment in accounts receivable depends on three factors: the percentage of credit sales to total sales, the level of sales, and the credit and collection policies of the firm. The financial manager, however, generally only has control over the terms of sale, the quality of customer, and the collection efforts.

Although the level of investment in inventories by the typical firm is less than the investment in accounts receivable, inventory management and control remains an important function of the financial manager because inventories play a significant role in the operations of the firm. The purpose of holding inventory is to make each function of the business independent of the other functions. The primary issues related to inventory management are: How much inventory should be ordered and when the order should be placed. The EOQ model is used to answer the first of these questions. The order-point model, which depends on the desired levels of delivery-time stock and safety stock, is applied to answer the second question. The relatively new just-in-time approach to inventory control is growing in popularity as an attempt to obtain additional cost savings by reducing the level of inventory a firm needs to have on hand. Instead of depending solely on its own inventories, the firm relies on its vendors to furnish supplies "just-in-time" to satisfy the firm's production requirements.

STUDY QUESTIONS

15–1. What is meant by the cash flow process?
15–2. Identify the principal motives for holding cash and near-cash assets. Explain the purpose of each motive.
15–3. What is concentration banking and how may it be of value to the firm?
15–4. What are the two major objectives of the firm's cash-management system?
15–5. What three decisions dominate the cash-management process?

15–6. Within the context of cash management, what are the key elements of (total) float? Briefly define each element.

15–7. Distinguish between financial risk and interest rate risk as these terms are commonly used in discussions of cash management.

15–8. Your firm invests in only three different classes of marketable securities: commercial paper, Treasury bills, and federal agency securities. Recently, yields on these money market instruments of three months' maturity were quoted at 6.10, 6.25, and 5.90 percent. Match the available yields with the types of instruments your firm purchases.

15–9. What key factors might induce a firm to invest in repurchase agreements rather than a specific security of the money market?

15–10. What factors determine the size of the investment a firm makes in accounts receivable? Which of these factors are under the control of the financial manager?

15–11. If a credit manager experienced no bad debt losses over the past year, would this be an indication of proper credit management? Why or why not?

15–12. What are the risk-return tradeoffs associated with adopting a more liberal trade credit policy?

15–13. What is the purpose of holding inventory? Name several types of inventory and describe their purpose.

15–14. Can cash be considered a special type of inventory? If so, what functions does it attempt to uncouple?

15–15. What are the major assumptions made by the EOQ model?

15–16. How might inflation affect the EOQ model?

SELF-TEST PROBLEMS

ST-1. (*Buying and Selling Marketable Securities*) Mountaineer Outfitters has $2 million in excess cash that it might invest in marketable securities. To buy and sell the securities, however, the firm must pay a transactions fee of $45,000.

    a. Would you recommend purchasing the securities if they yield 12 percent annually and are held for

      1. One month?

      2. Two months?

      3. Three months?

      4. Six months?

      5. One year?

    b. What minimum required yield would the securities have to return for the firm to hold them for three months? (What is the breakeven yield for a three-month holding period?)

ST-2. (*EOQ Calculations*) Consider the following inventory information and relationships for the F. Beamer Corporation:

    1. Orders can be placed only in multiples of 100 units.

    2. Annual unit usage is 300,000. (Assume a 50-week year in your calculations.)

    3. The carrying cost is 30 percent of the purchase price of the goods.

    4. The purchase price is $10 per unit.

    5. The ordering cost is $50 per order.

    6. The desired safety stock is 1,000 units. (This does not include delivery-time stock.)

    7. Delivery time is two weeks.

    Given this information

    a. What is the optimal EOQ level?

    b. How many orders will be placed annually?

    c. At what inventory level should a reorder be made?

STUDY PROBLEMS

15–1. (*Concentration Banking*) Byron Sporting Goods operates in Miami, Florida. The firm produces and distributes a full line of athletic equipment on a nationwide basis. The firm currently uses a centralized billing system. Byron Sporting Goods has annual credit sales of $362 million. Austin National Bank has presented an offer to operate a concentration banking system for the company. Byron already has an established line of credit with Austin. Austin says it will operate the system on a flat-fee basis of $175,000 per year. The analysis done by the bank's cash-management services division suggests that three days in mail float and one day in processing float can be eliminated.

Because Byron borrows almost continuously from Austin National, the value of the float reduction would be applied against the line of credit. The borrowing rate on the line of credit is set at an annual rate of 7 percent. Furthermore, because of the reduction in clerical help, the new system will save the firm $57,500 in processing costs. Byron uses a 365-day year in analyses of this sort. Should Byron accept the bank's offer to install the new system?

15–2. (*Buying and Selling Marketable Securities*) Miami Dice & Card Company has generated $800,000 in excess cash that it could invest in marketable securities. In order to buy and sell the securities, the firm will pay total transactions fees of $20,000.

  a. Would you recommend purchasing the securities if they yield 10.5 percent annually and are held for

    1. One month?

    2. Two months?

    3. Three months?

    4. Six months?

    5. One year?

  b. What minimum required yield would the securities have to return for the firm to hold them for two months? (What is the breakeven yield for a two-month holding period?)

15–3. (*Costs of Services*) Mustang Ski-Wear, Inc., is investigating the possibility of adopting a lock-box system as a cash receipts acceleration device. In a typical year this firm receives remittances totaling $12 million by check. The firm will record and process 6,000 checks over this same period. The Colorado Springs Second National Bank has informed the management of Mustang that it will expedite checks and associated documents through the lock-box system for a unit cost of $.20 per check. Mustang's financial manager has projected that cash freed by adoption of the system can be invested in a portfolio of near-cash assets that will yield an annual before-tax return of 7 percent. Mustang financial analysts use a 365-day year in their procedures.

  a. What reduction in check collection time is necessary for Mustang to be neither better nor worse off for having adopted the proposed system?

  b. How would your solution to (a) be affected if Mustang could invest the freed balances only at an expected annual return of 4.5 percent?

  c. What is the logical explanation for the difference in your answers to (a) and (b)?

15–4. (*Lock-Box System*) Penn Steelworks is a distributor of cold-rolled steel products to the automobile industry. All its sales are on a credit basis, net 30 days. Sales are evenly distributed over its 10 sales regions throughout the United States. Delinquent accounts are no problem. The company has recently undertaken an analysis aimed at improving its cash-management procedures. Penn determined that it takes an average of 3.2 days for customers' payments to reach the head office in Pittsburgh from the time they are mailed. It takes another full day in processing time prior to depositing the checks with a local bank.

Annual sales average $4,800,000 for each regional office. Reasonable investment opportunities can be found yielding 7 percent per year. To alleviate the float problem confronting the firm, the use of a lock-box system in each of the 10 regions is being considered. This would reduce mail float by 1.2 days. One day in processing float would also be eliminated, plus a full day in transit float. The lock-box arrangement would cost each region $250 per month.

a. What is the opportunity cost to Penn Steelworks of the funds tied up in mailing and processing? Use a 365-day year.

b. What would the net cost or savings be from use of the proposed cash-acceleration technique? Should Penn adopt the system?

15–5. (*Cash Receipts Acceleration System*) Peggy Pierce Designs, Inc., is a vertically integrated, national manufacturer and retailer of women's clothing. Currently, the firm has no coordinated cash-management system. A proposal, however, from the First Pennsylvania Bank aimed at speeding up cash collections is being examined by several of Pierce's corporate executives.

The firm currently uses a centralized billing procedure, which requires that all checks be mailed to the Philadelphia head office for processing and eventual deposit. Under this arrangement all the customers' remittance checks take an average of five business days to reach the head office. Once in Philadelphia another two days are required to process the checks for ultimate deposit at the First Pennsylvania Bank.

The firm's daily remittances average $1 million. The average check size is $2,000. Pierce Designs currently earns 6 percent annually on its marketable securities portfolio.

The cash acceleration plan proposed by officers of First Pennsylvania involves both a lock-box system and concentration banking. First Pennsylvania would be the firm's only concentration bank. Lock boxes would be established in (1) San Francisco, (2) Dallas, (3) Chicago, and (4) Philadelphia. This would reduce funds tied up by mail float to three days, and processing float will be eliminated. Funds would then be transferred twice each business day by means of automated depository transfer checks from local banks in San Francisco, Dallas, and Chicago to the First Pennsylvania Bank. Each ADTC costs $15. These transfers will occur all 270 business days of the year. Each check processed through the lock-box system will cost $.18.

a. What amount of cash balances will be freed if Pierce Designs, Inc., adopts the system suggested by First Pennsylvania?

b. What is the opportunity cost of maintaining the current banking setup?

c. What is the projected annual cost of operating the proposed system?

d. Should Pierce adopt the new system? Compute the net annual gain or loss associated with adopting the system.

15–6. (*Marketable Securities Portfolio*) The Alex Daniel Shoe Manufacturing Company currently pays its employees on a weekly basis. The weekly wage bill is $500,000. This means that on the average the firm has accrued wages payable of ($500,000 + $0)/2 = $250,000.

Alex Daniel, Jr., works as the firm's senior financial analyst and reports directly to his father, who owns all of the firm's common stock. Alex Daniel, Jr., wants to move to a monthly wage payment system. Employees would be paid at the end of every fourth week. The younger Daniel is fully aware that the labor union representing the company's workers will not permit the monthly payments system to take effect unless the workers are given some type of fringe benefit compensation. A plan has been worked out whereby the firm will make a contribution to the cost of life insurance coverage for each employee. This will cost the firm $35,000 annually. Alex Daniel, Jr., expects the firm to earn 7 percent annually on its marketable securities portfolio.

a. Based on the projected information, should Daniel Shoe Manufacturing move to the monthly wage payment system?

b. What annual rate of return on the marketable securities portfolio would enable the firm to just break even on this proposal?

15–7. (*Valuing Float Reduction*) The Cowboy Bottling Company will generate $12 million in credit sales next year. Collections of these credit sales will occur evenly over this period. The firm's employees work 270 days a year. Currently, the firm's processing system ties up four days' worth of remittance checks. A recent report from a financial consultant indicated procedures that will enable Cowboy Bottling to reduce processing float by two full days. If Cowboy invests the released funds to earn 6 percent, what will be the annual savings?

15–8. (*Accounts Payable Policy and Cash Management*) Bradford Construction Supply Company is suffering from a prolonged decline in new construction in its sales area. In an attempt to improve its cash position, the firm is considering changes in its accounts payable policy. After careful study it has determined that the only alternative available is to slow disbursements. Purchases for the coming year are expected to be $37.5 million. Sales will be $65 million, which represents about a 20 percent drop from the current year. Currently, Bradford discounts approximately 25 percent of its payments at 3 percent 10 days, net 30, and the balance of accounts are paid in 30 days. If Bradford adopts a policy of payment in 45 days or 60 days, how much can the firm gain if the annual opportunity cost of investment is 12 percent? What will be the result if this action causes Bradford Construction suppliers to increase their prices to the company by 0.5 percent to compensate for the 60-day extended term of payment? In your calculations use a 365-day year and ignore any compounding effects related to expected returns.

15–9. (*Interest Rate Risk*) Two years ago your corporate treasurer purchased for the firm a 20-year bond at its par value of $1,000. The coupon rate on this security is 8 percent. Interest payments are made to bondholders once a year. Currently, bonds of this particular risk class are yielding investors 9 percent. A cash shortage has forced you to instruct your treasurer to liquidate his bond.

a. At what price will your bond be sold? Assume annual compounding.

b. What will be the amount of your gain or loss over the original purchase price?

c. What would be the amount of your gain or loss had the treasurer originally purchased a bond with a four-year rather than a 20-year maturity? (Assume all characteristics of the bonds are identical except their maturity periods.)

d. What do we call this type of risk assumed by your corporate treasurer?

15–10. (*Comparison of After-Tax Yields*) The corporate treasurer of Aggieland Fireworks is considering the purchase of a BBB-rated bond that carries a 9 percent coupon. The BBB-rated security is taxable, and the firm is in the 46 percent marginal tax bracket. The face value of this bond is $1,000. A financial analyst who reports to the corporate treasurer has alerted him to the fact that a municipal obligation is coming to the market with a 5 ½ percent coupon. The par value of this security is also $1,000.

a. Which one of the two securities do you recommend the firm purchase? Why?

b. What must the fully taxed bond yield before tax to make it comparable with the municipal offering?

15–11. (*Trade Credit Discounts*) Determine the effective annualized cost of forgoing the trade credit discount on the following terms:

a. 1/10, net 20

b. 2/10, net 30

c. 3/10, net 30

d. 3/10, net 60

e. 3/10, net 90

f. 5/10, net 60

15–12. (*Altman Model*) The following ratios were supplied by six loan applicants. Given this information and the credit-scoring model developed by Altman (equation [15–5]), which loans have a high probability of defaulting next year?

	EBIT $\overline{\text{Total Assets}}$	Sales $\overline{\text{Total Assets}}$	Market Value of Equity $\overline{\text{Book Value of Debt}}$	Earnings $\overline{\text{Total Assets}}$	Working Capital $\overline{\text{Total Assets}}$
Applicant 1	.2	.2	1.2	.3	.5
Applicant 2	.2	.8	1.0	.3	.8
Applicant 3	.2	.7	.6	.3	.4
Applicant 4	.1	.4	1.2	.4	.4
Applicant 5	.3	.7	.5	.4	.7
Applicant 6	.2	.5	.5	.4	.4

15–13. (*Ratio Analysis*) Assuming a 360-day year, calculate what the average investment in inventory would be for a firm, given the following information in each case:
  a. The firm has sales of $600,000, a gross profit margin of 10 percent, and an inventory turnover ratio of 6.
  b. The firm has a cost of goods sold figure of $480,000 and an average age of inventory of 40 days.
  c. The firm has a cost of goods sold figure of $1,150,000 and an inventory turnover ratio of 5.
  d. The firm has a sales figure of $25 million, a gross profit margin of 14 percent, and an average age of inventory of 45 days.

15–14. (*EOQ Calculations*) A downtown bookstore is trying to determine the optimal order quantity for a popular novel just printed in paperback. The store feels that the book will sell at four times its hardback figures. It would therefore sell approximately 3,000 copies in the next year at a price of $1.50. The store buys the book at a wholesale figure of $1. Costs for carrying the book are estimated at $.10 a copy per year, and it costs $10 to order more books.
  a. Determine the EOQ.
  b. What would be the total costs for ordering the books 1, 4, 5, 10, and 15 times a year?
  c. What questionable assumptions are being made by the EOQ model?

15–15. (*Comprehensive EOQ Calculations*) Knutson Products, Inc., is involved in the production of airplane parts and has the following inventory, carrying, and storage costs:
  1. Orders must be placed in round lots of 100 units.
  2. Annual unit usage is 250,000. (Assume a 50-week year in your calculations.)
  3. The carrying cost is 10 percent of the purchase price.
  4. The purchase price is $10 per unit.
  5. The ordering cost is $100 per order.
  6. The desired safety stock is 5,000 units. (This does not include delivery time stock.)
  7. The delivery time is one week.
  Given the above information:
  a. Determine the optimal EOQ level.
  b. How many orders will be placed annually?
  c. What is the inventory order point? (That is, at what level of inventory should a new order be placed?)

d. What is the average inventory level?
e. What would happen to the EOQ if annual unit sales doubled (all other unit costs and safety stocks remaining constant)? What is the elasticity of EOQ with respect to sales? (That is, what is the percent change in EOQ divided by the percent change in sales?)
f. If carrying costs double, what would happen to the EOQ level? (Assume the original sales level of 250,000 units.) What is the elasticity of EOQ with respect to carrying costs?
g. If the ordering costs double, what would happen to the level of EOQ? (Again assume original levels of sales and carrying costs.) What is the elasticity of EOQ with respect to ordering costs?
h. If the selling price doubles, what would happen to EOQ? What is the elasticity of EOQ with respect to selling price?

SELF-TEST SOLUTIONS

SS-1.

a. Here we must calculate the dollar value of the estimated return for each holding period and compare it with the transactions fee to determine if a gain can be made by investing in the securities. Those calculations and the resultant recommendations follow:

		Recommendation
1. $2,000,000 (.12) (1/12)	= $20,000 < $45,000	No
2. $2,000,000 (.12) (2/12)	= $40,000 < $45,000	No
3. $2,000,000 (.12) (3/12)	= $60,000 > $45,000	Yes
4. $2,000,000 (.12) (6/12)	= $120,000 > $45,000	Yes
5. $2,000,000 (.12) (12/12)	= $240,000 > $45,000	Yes

b. Let (%) be the required yield. With $2 million to invest for three months we have

$2,000,000 (%) (3/12) = $ 45,000
$2,000,000 (%) = $180,000
= $180,000/2,000,000 = 9%

The breakeven yield, therefore, is 9%.

SS-2.

a.
$$EOQ = \sqrt{\frac{2SO}{C}}$$

$$= \sqrt{\frac{2(300,000)(50)}{3}}$$

= 3,162 units, but because orders must be placed in 100 unit lots, the effective EOQ becomes 3,200 units

b.
$$\frac{\text{Total usage}}{\text{EOQ}} = \frac{300,000}{3,200} = 93.75 \text{ orders per year}$$

c. Inventory order point = delivery time + safety stock

$$= \frac{2}{50} \times 300,000 + 1,000$$

$$= 12,000 + 1,000$$

$$= 13,000 \text{ units}$$

The Campeau Bankruptcy: The Sudden Deterioration of Supplier Accounts Receivable
from ABC News, Business World, January 7, 1990

The video case described the problems created by many firms in the garment industry by the Campeau retailing empire bankruptcy. Review the questions we considered when Video Case 5 was introduced on page 502.

Rumors about cash problems at Campeau stores appeared in the business press in early 1989. In April 1989, Campeau was forced to refinance some of its debt, a sign that the firm was having cash flow problems. On November 14, 1989, the *Wall Street Journal* reported that Campeau was in the midst of a working-capital crisis. Other warnings were given directly to Campeau's suppliers by the factoring companies that act as the financing arm of the garment industry. Offsetting the warnings was the fact that the Campeau stores paid their bills on time through the Christmas buying season. The payment history was indicative of financial health. But even if these small firms had been able to determine the severity of Campeau's problems, that may not have been enough to save them.

Because the garment industry sells goods that are dated, it may be particularly prone to sudden changes in the value of receivables and inventory. This "spoilage" effect puts suppliers over a barrel. If the goods don't sell at Christmas they may not have a second chance to sell except at a deep discount. Then, not only would profit margins be squeezed, there would be further delay in receiving the cash (if goods are sold after the Christmas season), which would make the problem worse. This points out why it is important to consider the industry that a firm is in when valuing its inventory and accounts receivable.

The inventories and accounts receivable of suppliers that sold a large portion of their production to the Campeau stores are probably particularly risky. In fact, these firms were probably hurt the most by Campeau's problems. Whenever a single customer makes up a large fraction of a firm's business, that firm is vulnerable. This occurs in more industries than just in the garment industry. Think about automobile suppliers. In the United States they can have only a few customers—GM, Ford, Chrysler, Honda, and so on. Losing one account, or a cutback in purchases by one of those customers, has an immediate and dramatic effect on the supplier's financial health. Firms in that position might think about using their expertise to supply other industries or design contracts that protect them from sudden changes in their major customers' demand.

Discussion questions

1. We discussed how having a single large customer can make a supplier vulnerable. Can you think of ways the customer can exert pressure on the supplier? Does the same degree of bargaining advantage exist if the customer is supplied solely by one supplier as opposed to having several suppliers? What about the capacity of the suppliers?

2. Can you think of other situations in which businesses may be vulnerable to a customer's financial health or even its payment procedures? Examples might be banks and major borrowers or producers with large government contracts. Explain possible problems that might exist in these cases. Do you know of rules that limit such problems?

Suggested reading
Graham, Mary. "Business: Bankrupt and Bullish," *The Atlantic*, March 1992.

LIQUID ASSET
MANAGEMENT

553

CHAPTER 16

INTERNATIONAL BUSINESS FINANCE

Principles of International Trade • Problems in International Financial Management

World trade has grown much faster over the last few decades than world aggregate output (global gross national product [GNP]). For example, global exports and imports were about one-fifth of global aggregate output in 1962. The ratio rose to one-fourth by 1972, one-third by 1982, and it continues to grow. Furthermore, the dollar value of world exports has grown from $129.5 billion in 1962 to $3.3 *trillion* in 1990. This remarkable increase in international trade is reflected in the increased openness of almost all national economies to international influences. For example, the proportion of U.S. GNP accounted for by exports and imports (about one-fifth) is now double what it was two decades ago, and is even higher for manufactured goods (see Figure 16-1). The U.S. Department of Commerce estimates that the United States exports about a fifth of its industrial production and that about 70 percent of all U.S. goods compete directly with foreign goods.

Some industries and states are highly dependent on the international economy. For example, the electronic consumer products and automobile industries are widely considered to be global industries. Futhermore, more than half of all workers in Ohio are employed by firms that depend to some extent on exports.

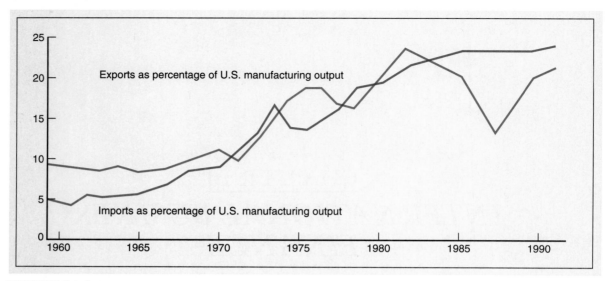

FIGURE 16–1
U. S. Trade as a Share of U. S. Manufacturing Output
Source: U. S. Department of Labor, Bureau of Labor Statistics, 1991;
Organization for Economic Cooperation and Development, 1991

There has also been a rise in the global level of international portfolio and direct investment. **Direct investment** occurs, for example, when a firm builds an off-shore manufacturing facility. **Portfolio investment** involves investment in financial assets or securities with maturities greater than one year, such as the purchase of foreign stocks and bonds. Total foreign investment in the United States now exceeds similar U.S. investment overseas.

A major reason for long-run overseas investments of United States companies is the high rates of return obtainable from these investments. The amount of United States *direct foreign investment (DFI)* abroad is large and growing. Significant amounts of the total assets, sales, and profits of American multinational corporations (MNCs) are attributable to foreign investments and foreign operations. However, direct foreign investment is not limited to American firms. Many European and Japanese firms have operations abroad, too. During the last decade these firms have been increasing their sales and setting up production facilities abroad, especially in the United States.

Capital flows between countries for international financial investment purposes have also been increasing. Many firms, investment companies, and individuals invest in the capital markets in foreign countries. The motivation is twofold: to obtain returns higher than those obtainable in the domestic capital markets and to reduce portfolio risk through international diversification. The result is that financial markets are now more integrated than ever before. In fact, the Eurodollar market is now larger than any other domestic financial market.

Keeping pace with the growth in international trade, foreign exchange markets have also grown rapidly. Weekly trading volume in these globally integrated markets is between $3 trillion and $5 trillion, and exceeds the annual trading volume on the world's securities markets. Even a *purely domestic firm* that buys all its inputs and sells all its output in its home country is not immune to foreign competition, nor can it totally ignore the workings of the international financial markets.

■ PRINCIPLES OF INTERNATIONAL TRADE

In order to fully understand the financial dimensions of international trade we must develop an understanding of the exchange or conversion of one currency for another. In so doing we will consider exchange rate risk, which arises where a firm in one country sells goods or services and in exchange receives payment in the currency of the purchasing nation.

Currency Exchange Rates

Between 1949 and 1970 the exchange rates among the major currencies were fixed. Under this system the U. S. dollar was linked to gold ($35 per ounce), and other currencies were tied to the dollar through a specific *parity rate*. For example, in 1949 the parity rate for the German Deutsche mark (DM) was set at 4.0 DM to $1. The actual exchange rate prevailing on any day was allowed to lie within a narrow band around the parity rate. The DM was allowed to fluctuate between 4.04 and 3.96 per dollar. A country could effect a major adjustment in the exchange rate by changing its parity rate with respect to the dollar. When the currency was made cheaper with respect to the dollar, this adjustment was called a *devaluation*. A *revaluation* resulted when a currency became more expensive with respect to the dollar. Since 1973 a *floating-rate* international currency system has been operating. For most currencies, there are no parity rates and no bands within which the currencies fluctuate.[1] Most major currencies, including the United States dollar, fluctuate freely, depending on their values as perceived by the traders in foreign exchange markets. The country's relative economic strengths, its level of exports and imports, the level of monetary activity, and the deficits or surpluses in its balance of payments (BOP) are all important factors in the determination of exchange rates.[2] Short-term, day-to-day fluctuations in exchange rates are caused by changing supply and demand conditions in the foreign exchange market.

---

[1] The system of floating rates is referred to as the "floating-rate regime."

[2] The balance of payments for the United States reflects the difference between the imports and exports of goods (the trade balance) and services. Capital inflows and outflows are tabulated in the capital account.

The Foreign Exchange Market

The foreign exchange market provides a mechanism for the transfer of purchasing power from one currency to another. This market is not a physical entity like the New York Stock Exchange; it is a network of telephone and cable connections among banks, foreign exchange dealers, and brokers. The market operates simultaneously at three levels. At the first level, customers buy and sell foreign exchange (i.e., foreign currency) through their banks. At the second level, banks buy and sell foreign exchange from other banks in the same commercial center. At the last level, banks buy and sell foreign exchange from banks in commercial centers in other countries. Some important commercial centers for foreign exchange trading are New York, London, Zurich, Frankfurt, Hong Kong, Singapore, and Tokyo.

An example will illustrate this multilevel trading. A trader in Texas may buy foreign exchange (pounds) from a bank in Houston for payment to a British supplier against some purchase made. The Houston bank, in turn, may purchase the foreign currency (pounds) from a New York bank. The New York bank may buy the pounds from another bank in New York or from a bank in London.

Because this market provides transactions in a continuous manner for a very large volume of sales and purchases, the currency markets are **efficient.** In other words, it is difficult to make a profit by shopping around from one bank to another. Minute differences in the quotes from different banks are quickly eliminated. Because of the arbitrage mechanism (discussed later), simultaneous quotes to different buyers in London and New York are likely to be the same.

Two major types of transactions are carried out in the foreign exchange markets: *spot* and *forward transactions.*

Spot Exchange Rates

A typical spot transaction involves an American firm buying foreign currency from its bank and paying for it in dollars. The price of foreign currency in terms of the domestic currency is the *exchange rate.* Another type of spot transaction occurs when an American firm receives foreign currency from abroad. The firm typically would sell the foreign currency to its bank for dollars. These are both **spot transactions** because one currency is exchanged for another currency today. The actual exchange rate quotes are expressed in several different ways, as discussed later. To allow time for the transfer of funds, the *value date* when the currencies are actually exchanged is two days after the spot transaction occurs. Four banks could easily be involved in the transactions: the local banks of the buyer and seller of the foreign exchange, and the money-center banks that handle the purchase and sale in the interbank market. Perhaps the buyer or seller will have to move the funds from one of its local banks to another, bringing even more banks into the transaction.

On the spot exchange market the quoted exchange rate is typically called a direct quote. A *direct quote* indicates the number of units of the home currency required to buy one unit of the foreign currency. That is, in New York the typical exchange-rate quote indicates the number of dollars needed to buy one unit of a foreign currency: dollars per pound, dollars per mark, and so on. The spot rates in columns 2 and 3 of Table 16–1 are the direct exchange quotes taken from the *Wall Street Journal* on January 2, 1992. To buy one pound on December 31, 1991, 1.8695 dollars were needed. To buy one franc and one mark, 19.305 cents and 66.01 cents were needed, respectively. The quotes in the spot market in Paris are given in terms of francs and those in Frankfurt in terms of Deutsche marks.

An *indirect quote* indicates the number of units of foreign currency that can be bought for one unit of the home currency. This reads as pounds per dollar, francs per dollar, and so on. Indirect quotes are given in the last two columns of Table 16–1.

In summary, a direct quote is the dollar/foreign currency rate (\$/FC), and an indirect quote is the foreign currency/dollar rate (FC/\$). Therefore, an indirect quote is the reciprocal of a direct quote and vice versa. The following example illustrates the computation of an indirect quote from a given direct quote.

EXAMPLE

Suppose you want to compute the indirect quotes from the direct quotes of spot rates for pounds, francs, and marks given in column 2 of Table 16–1. The direct quotes are: pound, 1.8695; French franc, .19305; and deutsche mark, .6601. The related indirect quotes are calculated as the *reciprocal* of the direct quote as follows:

$$\text{indirect quote} = \frac{1}{\text{direct quote}}$$

Thus
pounds:

$$\frac{1}{\$1.8695/\pounds} = \pounds.5349/\$$$

francs:

$$\frac{1}{\$.19305/FF} = FF5.1800/\$$$

Deutsche marks:

$$\frac{1}{\$.6601/DM} = DM1.5150/\$ \qquad \blacksquare$$

Notice that the above direct quotes and indirect quotes are identical to those shown in columns 2 and 4 of Table 16–1.

Direct and indirect quotes are useful in conducting international transactions, as the following examples show.

EXAMPLE

An American business must pay 1,000 marks to a German firm on December 31, 1991. How many dollars will be required for this transaction?

$$\$.6601/DM \times DM1000 = \$660.10 \qquad \blacksquare$$

EXAMPLE

An American business must pay \$2,000 to a British resident on December 31, 1991. How many pounds will the British resident receive?

$$\pounds.5349/\$ \times \$2,000 = \pounds1,069.80 \qquad \blacksquare$$

TABLE 16–1
Foreign Exchange Rates
Reported on January 2, 1992

Country	U.S. $ equivalent		Currency[a] per U.S. $	
	Tues.	Mon.	Tues.	Mon.
Australia (Dollar)	.7600	.7600	1.3158	1.3158
Austria (Schilling)	.09363	.09359	10.68	10.69
Belgium (Franc)	.03197	.03196	31.28	31.29
Brazil (Cruzeiro)	.00096	.00095	1040.00	1056.40
Britain (Pound)	1.8695	1.8675	.5349	.5355
30-Day Forward	1.8587	1.8635	.5380	.5366
90-Day Forward	1.8388	1.8368	.5438	.5444
180-Day Forward	1.8098	1.8078	.5525	.5532
Canada (Dollar)	.8654	.8632	1.1555	1.1585
30-Day Forward	.8632	.8613	1.1585	1.1611
90-Day Forward	.8590	.8570	1.1642	1.1699
180-Day Forward	.8538	.8516	1.1713	1.1743
China (Renminbi)	.185185	.183993	5.4000	5.4350
Denmark (Krone)	.1694	.1692	5.9020	5.9100
France (Franc)	.19305	.19292	5.1800	5.1835
30-Day Forward	.19205	.19188	5.2070	5.2115
90-Day Forward	.19015	.19000	5.2590	5.2632
180-Day Forward	.18742	.18721	5.3357	5.3415
Germany (Mark)	.6601	.6590	1.5150	1.5175
30-Day Forward	.6570	.6560	1.5220	1.5245
90-Day Forward	.6511	.6501	1.5358	1.5383
180-Day Forward	.6425	.6414	1.5565	1.5590
Greece (Drachma)	.005714	.005780	175.00	173.00
Hong Kong (Dollar)	.12858	.12853	7.7770	7.7800
India (Rupee)	.03876	.03879	25.80	25.78
Israel (Shekel)	.4464	.4394	2.2400	2.2760
Italy (Lira)	.0008715	.0008697	1147.50	1149.80
Japan (Yen)	.008013	.007962	124.80	125.60
30-Day Forward	.008006	.007955	124.91	125.71
90-Day Forward	.007983	.007932	125.26	126.07
180-Day Forward	.007957	.007907	125.67	126.47
Mexico (Peso)				
Floating rate	.0003237	.0003262	3089.00	3066.01
New Zealand (Dollar)	.5400	.5412	1.8519	1.8477
Philippines (Peso)	.03824	.03839	26.15	26.05
Portugal (Escudo)	.007485	.007413	133.60	134.90
South Korea (Won)	.0013180	.0013148	758.70	760.60
Spain (Peseta)	.010354	.010336	96.58	96.75
Sweden (Krona)	.1807	.1802	5.5355	5.5500
Switzerland (Franc)	.7372	.7377	1.3565	1.3555

[a]Exchange Rates: Tuesday, December 31, 1991. The New York foreign exchange selling rates apply to trading among banks in amounts of $1 million and more, as quoted at 3 p.m. Eastern time by Bankers Trust Co., Telerate Systems, Inc. and other sources. Retail transactions provide fewer units of foreign currency per dollar.

Exchange Rates and Arbitrage

The foreign exchange quotes in two different countries must be in line with each other. The direct quote for U.S. dollars in London is given in pounds/dollar. Because the foreign exchange markets are efficient, the direct quotes for the United States dollar in London, on December 31, 1991, must be very close to the indirect rate of .5349 pounds/dollar prevailing in New York on that date.

If the exchange-rate quotations between the London and New York spot exchange markets were *out of line,* then an enterprising trader could make a profit by buying in the market where the currency was cheaper and selling it in the other. Such a buy-and-sell strategy would involve a zero net investment of funds and no risk bearing, yet it would provide a sure profit. Such a person is called an **arbitrager,** and the process of buying and selling in more than one market to make a risk-less profit is called **arbitrage.** Spot exchange markets are efficient in the sense that arbitrage opportunities do not persist for any length of time. That is, the exchange rates between two different markets are quickly brought *in line,* aided by the arbitrage process. *Simple arbitrage* eliminates exchange rate differentials across the markets for a single currency, as in the preceding example for the New York and London quotes. *Triangular arbitrage* does the same across the markets for all currencies. Covered interest arbitrage eliminates differentials across currency and interest rate markets.

Suppose that London quotes £.5500/$ instead of £.5349/$. If you simultaneously bought a pound in New York for £.5349/$ and sold a pound in London for £.5500/$, you would have (1) taken a zero net investment position since you bought one pound and sold one pound, (2) locked in a sure profit of £.0151/$ *no matter which way* the pound subsequently moves, and (3) set in motion the forces that will eliminate the different quotes in New York and London. As others in the market-place learn of your transaction, they will attempt to make the same transaction. The increased demand to buy pounds in New York will lead to a higher quote there and the increased supply of pounds will lead to a lower quote in London. The workings of the market will produce a new spot rate that lies between £.5349/$ and £.5500/$ and is the same in New York and in London.

Asked and Bid Rates

In the spot exchange market two types of rates are quoted: the asked and the bid rates. The **asked rate** is the rate that the bank or the foreign exchange trader in exchange "asks" the customer to pay in home currency for foreign currency when the bank is selling and the customer is buying. The asked rate is also known as the **selling rate** or the **offer rate.** The **bid rate** is the rate at which the bank buys the foreign currency from the customer by paying in home currency. The bid rate is also known as the **buying rate.** Note that Table 16–1 contains only the selling, offer, or asked rates, and not the buying rate.

The bank sells a unit of foreign currency for more than it pays for it. Therefore, the direct asked quote ($/FC) is greater than the direct bid quote. The difference is known as the **bid-asked spread.** When there is a large volume of transactions and the trading is continuous, the spread is small and can be less than .5 percent (.005) for the major currencies. The spread is much higher for infrequently traded currencies. The spread exists to compensate the banks for holding the risky foreign currency and for providing the service of converting currencies.

Cross Rates

A **cross rate** is the computation of an exchange rate for a currency based on the exchange rates of two other currencies. The following example illustrates how this works.

EXAMPLE

Taking the dollar/pound and the mark/dollar rates from columns 2 and 4 of Table 16–1, we can determine the mark/pound and pound/mark exchange rates.

We see that

$$(\$/£) \times (DM/\$) = (DM/£)$$

$$1.8695 \times 1.5150 = DM2.8323/£$$

Thus, the pound/mark exchange rate is simply the reciprocal of this, or

$$1/2.8323 = £.3531/DM \qquad ■$$

Cross-rate computations make it possible to use quotations in New York to compute the exchange rate between pounds, marks, and francs. Arbitrage conditions hold in cross rates, too. For example, the pound exchange rate in Frankfurt (the direct quote marks/pound) must be 2.8323. The mark exchange rate in London must be .3531 pounds/mark. If the rates prevailing in Frankfurt and London were different from the computed cross rates, then using quotes from New York, a trader could use three different currencies to lock in arbitrage profits through a process called *triangular arbitrage.*

Forward Exchange Rates

A **forward exchange contract** requires delivery, at a specified future date, of one currency for a specified amount of another currency. The exchange rate for the forward transaction is agreed on today; the actual payment of one currency and the receipt of another currency take place at the future date. For example, a 30-day contract on March 1 is for delivery on March 31. Note that the forward rate is not the same as the spot rate that will prevail in the future. The actual spot rate that will prevail is not known today; only the forward rate is known. The actual spot rate will depend on the market conditions at that time; it may be more or less than today's forward rate. **Exchange-rate risk** is the risk that tomorrow's exchange rate will differ from today's rate.

As indicated earlier, it is extremely unlikely that the future spot rate will be exactly the same as the forward rate quoted today. Assume that you are going to receive a payment denominated in pounds from a British customer in 30 days. If you wait the 30 days and then exchange the pounds at the spot rate, you will receive a dollar amount reflecting the exchange rate at that time (30 days hence). As of today, you have no way of knowing the exact dollar value or your future pound receipts. Consequently, you cannot make precise plans about the use of these dollars. If, conversely, you buy a future contract, then you know the exact dollar value of your future receipts, and you can make precise plans concerning their use. The forward contract, therefore, can reduce your uncertainty about the future, and hence the major advantage of the forward market is that of *risk reduction*.

Forward contracts are usually quoted for periods of 30, 90, and 180 days. A contract for any intermediate date can be obtained, usually with the payment of a small premium. Forward contracts for periods longer than 180 days can be obtained by special negotiations with banks. Contracts for periods greater than one year can be costly.

Forward rates, like spot rates, are quoted in both direct and indirect form. The direct quotes for the 30-day and 90-day forward contracts on pounds, francs, and marks are given in column 2 of Table 16–1. The indirect quotes for forward contracts, like spot rates, are reciprocals of the direct quotes. The indirect quotes are indicated in column 4 of Table 16–1. The direct quotes are the dollar/foreign currency rate, and the indirect quotes are the foreign currency/dollar rate similar to the spot exchange quotes.

The 30-day forward quote for pounds is $1.8587 per pound. This means that if one purchases the contract for forward pounds on December 31, 1991, the bank will deliver a pound against the payment of $1.8587 on January 30, 1992. The bank is contractually bound to deliver the pound at this price, and the buyer of the contract is legally obligated to buy it at this price on January 30, 1992. Therefore, this is the price the customer must pay regardless of the actual spot rate prevailing on January 30, 1992. If the spot price of the pound is less than $1.8587, then the customer pays *more* than the spot price. If the spot price is greater than $1.8587, then the customer pays *less* than the spot price.

The forward rate is often quoted at a **premium** to or **discount** from the existing spot rate. For example, the 30-day pound forward rate may be quoted as .0108 discount (1.8587 forward rate—1.8695 spot rate). If the forward contract is selling for more dollars than the spot—that is, a larger direct quote—the pound is said to be selling at a premium. Note that the dollar is expected to strengthen against the pound. The market expects that in the future fewer dollars will be required to buy a pound. Conversely, the pound is expected to be worth fewer dollars in the future. When the forward contract sells for fewer dollars than the spot—a smaller direct quote—the pound is said to be at a discount from the dollar. Notice in column 2 of Table 16–1 that the forward contracts are selling at a discount for pounds, Deutsche marks, and French francs. This premium or discount is also called the *forward-spot differential*.

Notationally, the relationship may be written as

$$F - S = p \text{ (or } d) \qquad \textbf{(16–1)}$$

where

F = the forward rate, direct quote
S = the spot rate, direct quote
p = the premium, if $F > S$
d = the discount, if $S > F$

The premium or discount can also be expressed as an annual percentage rate, computed as follows:

$$\frac{F-S}{S} \times \frac{12}{n} \times 100 = P \ (\text{or } D) \qquad\qquad \textbf{(16–2)}$$

where n = the number of months of the forward contract
         P = the annualized percentage premium, if $F > S$
         D = the annualized percentage discount, if $S > F$

EXAMPLE

Compute the percent-per-annum premium on the 30-day forward pound.

Step 1: Identify F, S, and n.

$$F = 1.8587, \ S = 1.8695, \ n = 1 \text{ month}$$

Step 2: Because S is greater than F, we compute D:

$$D = \frac{1.8587 - 1.8695}{1.8695} \times \frac{12 \text{ months}}{1 \text{ month}} \times 100$$

$$= -6.93\%$$

The percent-per-annum discount on the 30-day pound is –6.93 percent. The percent-per-annum discount on the 30-day and 90-day pound, franc, and mark contracts are computed similarly. The results are shown below:

	30-Day	90-Day
British pound	–6.93%	–6.57%
French franc	–6.22	–6.01
Deutsche mark	–5.64	–5.45

Examples of Exchange-Rate Risk

The concept of exchange-rate risk applies to all types of international businesses. The measurement of these risks, and the type of risk, may differ among businesses. Let us see how exchange risk affects international trade contracts, international portfolio investments, and direct foreign investments.

EXCHANGE-RATE RISK IN INTERNATIONAL TRADE CONTRACTS
The idea of exchange-rate risk in trade contracts is illustrated in the following situations.

CASE I   An American automobile distributor agrees to buy a car from the manufacturer in Detroit. The distributor agrees to pay $6,500 on delivery of the car, which is expected to be 30 days from today. The car is delivered on the 30th day and the distributor pays $6,500. Notice that, from the day this contract was written until the day the car was delivered, the buyer knew the *exact dollar amount* of the liability. There was, in other words, *no uncertainty* about the value of the contract.

CASE II An American automobile distributor enters into a contract with a British supplier to buy a car from the United Kingdom for 3,500 pounds. The amount is payable on the delivery of the car, 30 days from today. From Figure 16–2, we see the range of spot rates that we believe can occur on the date the contract is consummated. On the 30th day, the American importer will pay some amount in the range of $5,843.25 (3,500 × 1.6695) to $7,243.25 (3,500 × 2.0695) for the car. Today, the American firm is not certain what its future dollar outflow will be 30 days hence. That is, the *dollar value of the contract is uncertain.*

These two examples help illustrate the idea of foreign exchange risk in international trade contracts. In the domestic trade contract (Case I), the exact dollar amount of the future dollar payment is known today with certainty. In the case of the international trade contract (Case II), where the *contract is written in the foreign currency,* the exact dollar amount of the contract is not known. The variability of the exchange rate induces variability in the future cash flow.

Exchange-rate risk exists when the contract is written in terms of the foreign currency or *denominated* in foreign currency. There is no direct-exchange risk if the international trade contract is written in terms of the domestic currency. That is, in Case II, if the contract were written in dollars, the American importer would face *no* direct-exchange risk. With the contract written in dollars, the British exporter would bear *all* the exchange risk because the British exporter's future pound

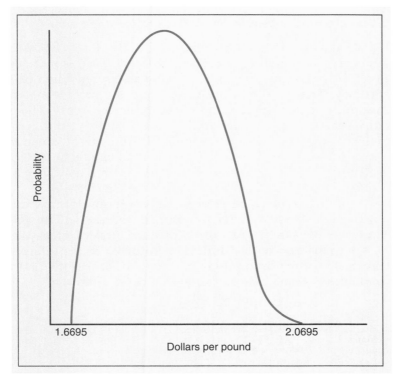

FIGURE 16–2
A Subjective Probability Distribution of the Pound Exchange Rate, 30 Days in the Future

receipts would be uncertain. That is, the British exporter would receive payment in dollars, which would have to be converted into pounds at an unknown (as of today) pound-dollar exchange rate. In international trade contracts of the type discussed here, at least one of the two parties to the contract *always* bears the exchange risk.

Certain types of international trade contracts are denominated in a third currency, different from either the importer's or the exporter's domestic currency. In Case II the contract might have been denominated in, say, the Deutsche mark. With a mark contract, both importer and exporter would be subject to exchange-rate risk.

Exchange risk is not limited to the two-party trade contracts; it exists also in foreign portfolio investments and direct foreign investments.

Exchange Risk in Foreign Portfolio Investments

Let us look at an example of exchange risk in the context of portfolio investments. An American investor buys a German security. The exact return on the investment in the security is unknown. Thus, the security is a risky investment. The investment return in the holding period of, say, three months stated in marks could be anything from –2 to +8 percent. In addition, the mark-dollar exchange rate may depreciate by 4 percent or appreciate by 6 percent in the three-month period during which the investment is held. The return to the American investor, in dollars, will therefore be in the range of –6 to +14 percent.[3] Notice that the return to a German investor, in marks, is in the range of –2 to +8 percent. Clearly, for the American investor, the exchange factor induces a greater variability in the dollar rate of return. Hence, the *exchange rate fluctuations may increase the riskiness* of the investments.

EXCHANGE RISK IN DIRECT FOREIGN INVESTMENT   The exchange risk of a direct foreign investment (DFI) is more complicated. In a DFI the parent company invests in assets denominated in a foreign currency. That is, the balance sheet and the income statement of the subsidiary are written in terms of the foreign currency. The parent company receives the repatriated profit stream in dollars. Thus, the exchange risk concept applies to fluctuations in the dollar value of the *assets* located abroad as well as to the fluctuations in the home-currency-denominated *profit stream*. Exchange risk not only affects immediate profits, it may affect the future profit stream as well.

Although exchange-rate risk can be a serious complication in international business activity, remember **Axiom 1: The Risk-Return Tradeoff: We Won't Take on Additional Risks Unless We Expect to be Compensated with Additional Returns.** In the international markets traders and corporations find numerous reasons that the returns from international transactions outweigh the risks.

---

[3]*Example:* Assume the spot exchange rate is .50 dollars per mark. In three months the exchange rate would be .50 × (1 – .04) = .48 to .50 × (1 + .06) = .53. A $50 investment today is equivalent to a 100-mark investment. The 100-mark investment would return 98 to 108 marks in three months. The return, in the worst case, is 98 marks × .48 = $47.04. The return, in the best case, is 108 marks × .53 = $57.24. The holding-period return on the $50 investment will be between – 6 percent ($47.04 – $50)/$50) and + 14 percent ($57.24 – $50)/$50).

■ PROBLEMS IN INTERNATIONAL FINANCIAL MANAGEMENT

The globalization of world trade poses a variety of problems for the corporate financial manager. We will address these issues in terms of four basic categories: (i) managing the firm's exposure to foreign exchange risk, (ii) managing corporate working capital, (iii) managing the firm's financing decisions and (iv) managing direct foreign investments.

BACK TO THE FUNDAMENTALS

In international transactions, just as in domestic transactions, the key to value is the timing and amounts of cash flow spent and received. However, economic transactions across international borders add an element of risk in that cash flows are denominated in the currency of the country in which business is being transacted. Consequently, the dollar value of the cash flows will depend on the exchange rate that exists at the time cash changes hands. The fact remains, however, that it's cash spent and received that matters. This is the point of **Axiom 3: Cash Is King—Measuring the Timing of Costs and Benefits.**

Exposure to Exchange-Rate Risk

An asset denominated or valued in terms of foreign currency cash flows will lose value if that foreign currency declines in value. It can be said that such an asset is exposed to exchange-rate risk. However, this possible decline in asset value may be offset by the decline in value of any liability that is also denominated or valued in terms of that foreign currency. Thus, a firm would normally be interested in its net exposed position (exposed assets-exposed liabilities) for each period in each currency.

Although expected changes in exchange rates can often be included in the cost-benefit analysis relating to such transactions, in most cases there is an unexpected component in exchange rate changes, and often the cost-benefit analysis for such transactions does not fully capture even the expected change in the exchange rate. For example, price increases for the foreign operations of many MNCs often have to be less than those necessary to offset exchange rate changes fully, owing to the competitive pressures generated by local businesses, as the Japanese car makers found in 1988 for their U.S. sales.

Three measures of foreign exchange exposure are translation exposure, transactions exposure, and economic exposure. Translation exposure arises because the foreign operations of MNCs have accounting statements denominated in the local currency of the country in which the operation is located. For U.S. MNCs, the *reporting currency* for its consolidated financial statements is the dollar, so the assets, liabilities, revenues, and expenses of the foreign operations must be translated into dollars. International transactions often require a payment to be made or received in a foreign currency in the future, so these transactions are exposed to exchange-rate risk. Economic exposure exists over the long term because the value of future cash flows in the reporting currency (i.e., the dollar) from foreign operations is exposed to exchange rate risk. Indeed, the whole stream of future cash flows is exposed. The Japanese automaker situation highlights the effect of economic exposure on a MNC's revenue stream. The three measures of exposure now are examined more closely.

Translation Exposure

Foreign currency assets and liabilities are considered exposed if their foreign currency value for accounting purposes is to be translated into the parent company currency using the current exchange rate—the exchange rate in effect on the balance sheet date. Other assets and liabilities and equity amounts that are translated at the historic exchange rate—the rate in effect when these items were first recognized in the company's accounts—are not considered to be exposed. The rate (current or historic) used to translate various accounts depends on the translation procedure used. For U.S. companies, Financial Accounting Standard Board (FASB) Statement No. 52 specifies the translation procedure to be used.

Transaction exposure can result in exchange rate change-related losses and gains that are realized and have an impact on both reported and taxable income. However, translation exposure results in exchange rate losses and gains that are reflected in the company's accounting books but are unrealized and have little or no impact on taxable income. Thus, if financial markets are efficient and managerial goals are consistent with owner wealth maximization (and if agency and signaling costs are negligible), a firm should not have to waste real resources hedging against possible paper losses caused by translation exposure. However, if there are significant agency or information costs or if markets are not efficient (that is, if translation losses and gains raise information costs for investors, or if they endanger the firm's ability to satisfy debt or other covenants, or if the evaluation of the firm's managers depends on translated accounting data), a firm may indeed find it economical to hedge against translation losses or gains.

Transactions Exposure

Receivables, payables, and fixed-price sales or purchase contracts are examples of foreign currency transactions whose monetary value is fixed at a time different from the time when these transactions are actually completed. **Transactions exposure** is a term that describes the net contracted foreign currency transactions for which the settlement amounts are subject to changing exchange rates. A company normally must set up an additional reporting system to track transactions exposure, because several of these amounts are not recognized in the accounting books of the firm.

Exchange risk may be neutralized or hedged by a change in the asset and liability position in the foreign currency. An exposed asset position (e.g., an account receivable) can be *hedged* or *covered* by creating a liability of the same amount and maturity denominated in the foreign currency (e.g., a forward contract to *sell* the foreign currency). An exposed liability position (e.g., an account payable) can be covered by acquiring assets of the same amount and maturity in the foreign currency (e.g., a forward contract to *buy* the foreign currency). The objective is to have a zero net asset position in the foreign currency. This eliminates exchange risk, since the loss (gain) in the liability (asset) is exactly offset by the gain (loss) in the value of the asset (liability) when the foreign currency appreciates (depreciates). One popular form of hedge is the exchange-market or forward-market hedge. In this hedge the *amount* and the *duration* of the asset (liability) positions are *matched*.

THE FORWARD-MARKET HEDGE   The forward market provides a hedging mechanism. It works as follows: A net asset (liability) position is covered by a liability (asset) in the forward market. Consider again the case of the American firm with a liability of 3,000 pounds that must be paid in 30 days. The firm may take the following steps to cover its liability position:

Step 1: Buy a forward contract today to purchase 3,000 pounds in 30 days. The 30-day forward rate is $1.8587 per pound.
Step 2: On the thirtieth day pay the banker $5,576.10 (3,000 × $1.8587) and collect 3,000 pounds. Pay these pounds to the British supplier.

By the use of the forward contract the American business knows the exact worth of the future payment in dollars ($5,576.10). The exchange risk in pounds is totally eliminated by the net asset position in the forward pounds. In the case of a net asset exposure, the steps open to the American firm are the exact opposite: Sell the pounds forward, and on the future day receive and deliver the pounds to collect the agreed-on dollar amount.

The use of the forward market as a hedge against exchange risk is simple and direct. That is, match the liability or asset position against an offsetting position in the forward market. The forward market hedge is relatively easy to implement. The firm directs its banker that it needs to buy or sell a foreign currency on a future date, and the banker gives a forward quote.

CURRENCY FUTURE AND OPTION CONTRACTS   The forward-market hedge is not adequate for some types of exposure. If the foreign currency asset or liability position occurs on a date for which forward quotes are not available, the forward hedge cannot be accomplished. In addition to the forward-market hedge, a company can also hedge its exposure by buying (or selling) some relatively new instruments—foreign currency futures contracts and foreign currency options. Although futures contracts are similar to forward contracts in that they provide fixed prices for the *required* delivery of foreign currency at maturity, options *permit* but do not require fixed (strike) price foreign currency transactions anytime before maturity. Futures contracts and options differ from forward contracts in that, unlike forward contracts, which are customized regarding amount and maturity date, futures and options are traded in standard amounts with standard maturity dates. In addition, although forward contracts are written by banks, futures and options are traded on organized exchanges, and individual traders deal with the exchange-based clearing organization rather than with each other. In Chapter 17 we will take a more detailed look at these financial instruments.

Economic Exposure

The economic value of a company can vary in response to exchange-rate changes. This change in value may be caused by a rate-change-induced decline in the level of expected cash flows and/or by an increase in the riskiness of these cash flows. **Economic exposure** refers to the overall impact of exchange-rate changes on the value of the firm and includes not only the strategic impact of changes in competitive relationships that arise from exchange-rate changes, but also the economic impact of transactions exposure and, if any, of translation exposure.

Economic exposure to exchange-rate changes depends on the competitive structure of the markets for a firm's inputs and its outputs and how these markets are influenced by changes in exchange rates. This influence, in turn, depends on several economic factors, including price elasticities of the products, the degree of competition from foreign markets and direct (through prices) and indirect (through incomes) impact of exchange-rate changes on these markets. Assessing the economic exposure faced by a particular firm thus depends on the ability to understand and model the structure of the markets for its major inputs (purchases) and outputs (sales).

A company need not engage in any cross-border business activity to be exposed to exchange-rate changes, because product and financial markets in most countries are related and influenced to a large extent by the same global forces. The output of a company engaged in business activity only within one country may be competing with imported products, or it may be competing for its inputs with other domestic and foreign purchasers. For example, a Canadian chemical company that did no cross-border business nevertheless found that its profit margins depended directly on the United States dollar–Japanese yen exchange rate. The company used coal as an input in its production process, and the Canadian price of coal was heavily influenced by the extent to which the Japanese bought United States coal, which in turn depended on the dollar-yen exchange rate.

Although translation exposure need not be managed, it might be useful for a firm to manage its transaction and economic exposures because they affect firm value directly. In most companies, transaction exposure is generally tracked and managed by the office of the corporate treasurer. Economic exposure is difficult to define in operating terms, and very few companies manage it actively. In most companies, economic exposure is generally considered part of the strategic planning process, rather than as a treasurer's or finance function.

Multinational Working-Capital Management

The basic principles of working-capital management for a multinational corporation (MNC) are similar to those for a domestic firm. However, tax and exchange-rate factors are additional considerations for the MNC. For an MNC with subsidiaries in many countries, the optimal decisions in the management of working capital are made by considering the company as a whole. The global or centralized financial decision for an MNC is superior to the set of independent optimal decisions for the subsidiaries. This is the *control* problem of the MNC. If the individual subsidiaries make decisions that are best for them individually, the consolidation of such decisions may not be best for the MNC as a whole. To effect *global* management, sophisticated computerized models—incorporating many variables for each subsidiary—are solved to provide the best overall decision for the MNC.

Before considering the components of working-capital management, we examine two techniques that are useful in the management of a wide variety of working-capital components.

Leading and Lagging: Reducing Exchange Risk

Two important risk-reduction techniques for many working-capital problems are called **leading** and **lagging.** Recall that a net asset (long) position is not desirable in a weak or potentially depreciating currency. If a firm has a net asset position in such a currency, it should expedite the disposal of the asset. The firm should get rid of the asset earlier than it otherwise would have, or *lead,* and convert the funds into assets in a relatively stronger currency. By the same reasoning, the firm should *lag,* or delay the collection against a net asset position in a strong currency. If the firm has a net liability (short) position in the weak currency, then it should delay the payment against the liability, or lag, until the currency depreciates. In the case of an appreciating or strong foreign currency and a net liability position, the firm should lead the payments—that is, reduce the liabilities earlier than it otherwise would have.

These principles are useful in the management of working capital of an MNC. They cannot, however, eliminate the foreign exchange risk. When exchange rates change continuously, it is almost impossible to guess whether or when the currency will depreciate or appreciate. This is why the risk of exchange-rate changes cannot be eliminated. Nevertheless, the reduction of risk, or the increasing of gain from exchange-rate changes, via the lead and lag is useful for cash management, accounts receivable management, and short-term liability management.

Cash Management and Positioning of Funds

Positioning of funds takes on an added importance in the international context. Funds may be transferred from a subsidiary of the MNC in country A to another subsidiary in country B such that the foreign exchange exposure and the tax liability of the MNC as a whole are minimized. It bears repeating that, owing to the *global strategy* of the MNC, the tax liability of the subsidiary in country A may be greater than it would otherwise have been, but the overall tax payment for all units of the MNC is minimized.

The transfer of funds among subsidiaries and the parent company is done by royalties, fees, and transfer pricing. A **transfer price** is the price a subsidiary or a parent company charges other companies that are part of the MNC for its goods or services. A parent that wishes to transfer funds from a subsidiary in a depreciating-currency country may charge a higher price on the goods and services sold to this subsidiary by the parent or by subsidiaries from strong-currency countries.

Centralized cash management of all the affiliates at the global level, achieved with the help of computer models, reduces both the overall cost of holding cash and the foreign exchange exposure of the MNC as a whole with respect to cash. The excess cash balance of one subsidiary is transferred to a cash-deficit subsidiary in the form of a loan. The optimal holdings of cash in different currencies can be evaluated in a manner similar to the optimal portfolio of stocks or bonds.

International Financing and Capital Structure Decisions

An MNC has access to many more financing sources than a domestic firm. It can tap not only the financing sources in its home country that are available to its domestic counterparts, but also sources in the foreign countries in which it operates. Host countries often provide access to low-cost subsidized financing to attract foreign investment. In addition, the MNC may enjoy preferential credit standards because of its size and investor preference for its home currency. An MNC may be able to access third-country capital markets—countries in which it does not operate but which may have large, well-functioning capital markets. Finally, an MNC can also access external currency markets: Eurodollar, Eurocurrency, or Asian dollar markets. These external markets are unregulated, and because of their lower spread, can offer very attractive rates for financing *and* for investments. Because of its ability to tap a larger number of financial markets, the MNC may have a lower cost of capital, and because it may better be able to avoid the problems or limitations of any one financial market, it may have a more continuous access to external finance compared to a domestic company.

Access to national financial markets is regulated by governments. For example, in the United States, access to capital markets is governed by SEC regulations. Access to Japanese capital markets is governed by regulations issued by the Ministry of Finance. Some countries have extensive regulations; other countries have relatively open markets. These regulations may differ depending on the legal residency terms of the company raising funds. A company that cannot use its local subsidiary to raise funds in a given market will be treated as foreign. In order to increase their visibility in a foreign capital market, a number of MNCs are now listing their equities on the stock exchanges of many of these countries.

The external currency markets are predominantly centered in Europe, and about 80 percent of their value is denominated in terms of the U.S. dollar. Thus, most external currency markets can be characterized as Eurodollar markets. Such markets consist of an active short-term money market and an intermediate-term capital market with maturities ranging up to 15 years and averaging about 7 to 9 years. The intermediate-term market consists of the Eurobond and the Syndicated Eurocredit markets. Eurobonds are usually issued as unregistered bearer bonds and generally tend to have higher flotation costs but lower coupon rates compared to similar bonds issued in the United States. A Syndicated Eurocredit loan is simply a large term loan that involves contributions by a number of lending banks. Most large U.S. banks are active in the external currency markets.

In arriving at its capital-structure decisions, an MNC has to consider a number of factors. First, the capital structure of its local affiliates is influenced by local norms regarding capital structure in that industry and in that country. Local norms for companies in the same industry can differ considerably from country to country. Second, the local affiliate capital structure must also reflect corporate attitudes toward exchange rate and political risk in that country, which would normally lead to higher levels of local debt and other local capital. Third, local affiliate capital structure must reflect home country requirements with regard to the company's consolidated capital structure. Finally, the optimal MNC capital structure should reflect its wider access to financial markets, its ability to diversify economic and political risks, and its other advantages over domestic companies.

Direct Foreign Investment (DFI)

An MNC often makes direct foreign investments abroad in the form of plants and equipment. The decision process for this type of investment is very similar to the capital-budgeting decision in the domestic context—with some additional twists. Most real-world capital-budgeting decisions are made with uncertain future outcomes. Recall that a capital-budgeting decision has three major components: the estimation of the future cash flows (including the initial cost of the proposed investment), the estimation of the risk in these cash flows, and the choice of the proper discount rate. We will assume that the NPV criterion is appropriate as we examine (1) the risks associated with direct foreign investment and (2) factors to be considered in making the investment decision that may be unique to the international scene.

BACK TO THE FUNDAMENTALS

Investments across international boundaries give rise to special risks not encountered when investing domestically. Specifically, political risks and exchange-rate risk are unique to international investing. Once again **Axiom 1: The Risk-Return Tradeoff—We Won't Take on Additional Risk Unless We Expect to be Compensated with Additional Return** provides a rationale for evaluating these considerations. Where added risks are present, added rewards are necessary to induce investment.

Risks in Direct Foreign Investments

Risks in domestic capital budgeting arise from two sources: business risk and financial risk. The international capital-budgeting problem incorporates these risks as well as political risk and exchange risk.

BUSINESS RISK AND FINANCIAL RISK   International business risk is due to the response of business to economic conditions in the foreign country. Thus, the U.S. MNC needs to be aware of the business climate in both the United States and the foreign country. Additional business risk is due to competition from other MNCs, local businesses, and imported goods. Financial risk refers to the risks introduced in the profit stream by the firm's financial structure. The financial risks of foreign operations are not very different from those of domestic operations.

POLITICAL RISK   *Political risk* arises because the foreign subsidiary conducts its business in a political system different from that of the home country. Many foreign governments, especially those in the Third World, are less stable than the U.S. government. A change in a country's political setup frequently brings a change in policies with respect to businesses—and especially with respect to foreign businesses. An extreme change in policy might involve nationalization or even outright expropriation of certain businesses. These are the political risks of conducting business abroad. A business with no investment in plants and equipment is less susceptible to these risks. Some examples of political risk are listed below:

1. Expropriation of plants and equipment without compensation
2. Expropriation with minimal compensation that is below actual market value
3. Nonconvertibility of the subsidiary's foreign earnings into the parent's currency—the problem of *blocked funds*
4. Substantial changes in the laws governing taxation
5. Governmental controls in the foreign country regarding the sale price of the products, wages and compensation to personnel, hiring of personnel, making of transfer payments to the parent, and local borrowing
6. Some governments require certain amounts of local equity participation in the business. Some require that the majority of the equity participation belong to their country.

All these controls and governmental actions add risk to the cash flows of the investment from the perspective of the parent company. These risks must be considered before making the foreign investment decision. The MNC may decide against investing in countries with risks of types 1 and 2. Other risks can be borne—provided the returns from the foreign investments are high enough to compensate for them. Insurance against some types of political risks may be purchased from private insurance companies or from the U.S. government Overseas Private Investment Corporation. It should be noted that although an MNC cannot protect itself against all foreign political risks, political risks are also present in domestic business.

EXCHANGE RISK   The exposure of the fixed assets is best measured by the effects of the exchange rate changes on the firm's future earnings stream: that being *economic* exposure rather than *translation* exposure. For instance, changes in the exchange rate may adversely affect sales by making competing imported goods cheaper. Changes in the cost of goods sold may result if some components are imported and their price in the foreign currency changes because of exchange-rate fluctuations. The thrust of these examples is that the effect of exchange-rate changes on income statement items should be properly measured to evaluate exchange risk. Finally, exchange risk affects the dollar-denominated profit stream of the parent company, whether or not it affects the foreign-currency profits.

SUMMARY

The growth of our global economy, the increasing number of multinational corporations, and the increase in foreign trade itself underscore the importance of the study of international finance.

Exchange rate mechanics are discussed in the context of the prevailing floating rates. Under this system, exchange rates between currencies vary in an apparently random fashion in accordance with the supply and demand conditions in the exchange market. Important economic factors affecting the level of exchange rates include the relative economic strengths of the countries involved, the balance-of-payments mechanism, and the countries' monetary policies. Several important exchange-rate terms are introduced. These include the asked and the bid rates, which represent the selling and buying rates of currencies. The direct quote is the units of home currency per unit of foreign currency, and the indirect quote is the reciprocal of the direct quote. Cross-rate computations reflect the exchange rate between two foreign currencies. Finally, simple arbitrage for indirect quote and triangular arbitrage for cross rates are shown to hold. The efficiency of spot exchange markets implies that no arbitrage (riskless) profits can be made by buying and selling currencies in different markets.

The forward-exchange market provides a valuable service by quoting rates for the delivery of foreign currencies in the future. The foreign currency is said to sell at a premium (discount) forward from the spot rate when the forward rate is greater (less) than the spot rate, in direct quotation.

Exchange risk exists because the exact spot rate that prevails on a future date is not known with certainty today. The concept of exchange risk is applicable to a wide variety of businesses, including export - import firms and firms involved in making direct foreign investments or international investments in securities. Exchange exposure is a measure of exchange risk. There are different ways of measuring the foreign exposure, including the net asset (net liability) measurement. Different strategies are open to businesses to counter the exposure to this risk, including the forward market hedge, futures contracts, and options. Each involves different costs.

In discussing working-capital management in an international environment we find leading and lagging techniques useful in minimizing exchange risks and increasing profitability. In addition, funds positioning is a useful tool for reducing exchange risk exposure. The MNC may have a lower cost of capital because it has access to a larger set of financial markets than a domestic company. In addition to the home, host, and third-country financial markets, the MNC can tap the rapidly growing external currency markets. In making capital-structure decisions, the MNC must consider political and exchange risks and host and home county capital-structure norms.

The complexities encountered in the direct foreign investment decision include the usual sources of risk—business and financial—and additional risks associated with fluctuating exchange rates and political factors. Political risk is due to differences in political climates, institutions, and processes between the home country and abroad. Under these conditions the estimation of future cash flows and the choice of the proper discount rates are more complicated than for the domestic investment situation.

STUDY QUESTIONS

16–1. What additional factors are encountered in international as compared with domestic financial management? Discuss each briefly.
16–2. What different types of businesses operate in the international environment? Why are the techniques and strategies available to these firms different?
16–3. What is meant by *arbitrage profits?*
16–4. What are the markets and mechanics involved in generating (a) simple arbitrage profits, (b) triangular arbitrage profits, (c) covered interest arbitrage profits?
16–5. What is meant by (a) exchange risk, (b) political risk?
16–6. How can exchange risk be measured?
16–7. What are the differences between transaction, translation, and economic exposures? Should all of them be ideally reduced to zero?
16–8. What steps can a firm take to reduce exchange risk? Indicate at least two different techniques.
16–9   How are the forward market and the money market hedges affected? What are the major differences between these two types of hedges?
16–10. In the New York exchange market, the forward rate for the Indian currency, the rupee, is not quoted. If you were exposed to exchange risk in rupees, how could you cover your position?
16–11. Compare and contrast the use of forward contracts, futures contracts, and options to reduce foreign exchange exposure. When is each instrument most appropriate?
16–12. Indicate two working-capital management techniques that are useful for international businesses to reduce exchange risk and potentially increase profits.
16–13. How do the financing sources available to an MNC differ from those available to a domestic firm? What do these differences mean for the company's cost of capital?
16–14. What risks are associated with direct foreign investment? How do these risks differ from those encountered in domestic investment?
16–15. How is the direct foreign investment decision made? What are the inputs to this decision process? Are the inputs more complicated than those to the domestic investment problem? If so, why?
16–16. A corporation desires to enter a particular foreign market. The DFI analysis indicates that a direct investment in the plant in the foreign country is not profitable. What other course of action can the company take to enter the foreign market? What are the important considerations?
16–17. What are the reasons for the acceptance of a sales office or licensing arrangement when the DFI itself is not profitable?

SELF-TEST PROBLEMS

The data for Self-Test Problems ST-1 are given in the following table:
Selling Quotes for the German Mark in New York

Country	Contract	$/Foreign Currency
Germany—mark	Spot	.3893
	30-day	.3910
	90-day	.3958

ST-1. You own $10,000. The dollar rate on the German mark is $2.5823/DM. The German mark rate is given in the table above. Are arbitrage profits possible? Set up an arbitrage scheme with your capital. What is the gain (loss) in dollars?

STUDY PROBLEMS

The data for Study Problems 16-1 through 16-7 are given in the following table:

Country	Contract	$/Foreign Currency
Canada—dollar	Spot	.8437
	30-day	.8417
	90-day	.8395
Japan — yen	Spot	.004684
	30-day	.004717
	90-day	.004781
Switzerland — franc	Spot	.5139
	30-day	.5169
	90-day	.5315

16–1. An American business needs to pay (a) 10,000 Canadian dollars, (b) 2 million yen, and (c) 50,000 Swiss francs to businesses abroad. What are the dollar payments to the respective countries?

16–2. An American business pays $10,000, $15,000, and $20,000 to suppliers in Japan, Switzerland, and Canada, respectively. How much, in local currencies, do the suppliers receive?

16–3. Compute the indirect quote for the spot and forward Canadian dollar, yen, and Swiss franc contracts.

16–4. The spreads on the contracts as a percent of the asked rates are 2 percent for yen, 3 percent for Canadian dollars, and 5 percent for Swiss francs. Show, in a table similar to the one above, the bid rates for the different spot and forward rates.

16–5. You own $10,000. The dollar rate in Tokyo is 216.6743. The yen rate in New York is given in the previous table. Are arbitrage profits possible? Set up an arbitrage scheme with your capital. What is the gain (loss) in dollars?

16–6. Compute the Canadian dollar/yen and the yen/Swiss franc spot rate from the data in the table above.

16–7. Compute the simple premium (discount) on the 30-day and 90-day yen, Swiss franc, and Canadian dollar quotes. Tabulate the percent-per-annum deviations as in Table on page 564.

SELF-TEST SOLUTIONS

SS-1.   The German rate is 2.5823 marks/$1, and the (indirect) New York rate is 1/.3893 = 2.5687 marks/$.
Assuming no transaction costs, the rates between German and New York are out of line. Thus, arbitrage profits are possible.

Step 1: Because the mark is cheaper in Germany, buy $10,000 worth of marks in Germany. The number of marks purchased would be:

$$\$10,000 \times 2.5823 = 25,823 \text{ marks}$$

Step 2: Simultaneously sell the marks in New York at the prevailing rate. The amount received on the sale of the marks would be:

$$25,823 \text{ marks} \times \$.3893/\text{mark} = \$10,052.89$$
$$\text{net gain is } \$10,052.89 - \$10,000 = \$52.89$$

CHAPTER 17

CHANGES AND CHALLENGES IN FINANCE

Recent Innovations in Risk Management • Finance in the '90s: The Consequences of Financial Innovation in Corporate Restructuring • Recent Innovations in Raising Capital: Hybrid Securities • The Agency Problem: Changes and Challenges • The CAPM and Market Efficiency: The Challenges from Academia

Over the past 30 years the teaching of finance has evolved from a descriptive presentation of ill-defined decision rules taught through the use of case examples to a science where the logic and decision rules spring from basic economic principles. Today, finance continues to change and develop at an ever increasing speed. Sparked by the changing business environment and developments and discoveries in the academic world, new financing and risk management techniques seem to appear almost daily. As a result, what is being presented in this text may be, unfortunately, outdated by the time the words appear in print.

How do you prepare for a field as dynamic as finance? The answer is to go beyond the answers and understand the logic that drives those answers. This is why the presentation in this text has been crafted around nine underlying axioms. In this chapter we will examine how the practice of finance is evolving and pay special attention to recent developments in the theory of finance, and in particular to challenges to the use of the CAPM, spawned by discoveries in the academic world. In so doing, you will be provided with a sense of the future along with an appreciation of the assumptions and limitations of the theory of finance as we know it today.

This chapter begins with a look at the dynamic nature of finance: how the financial world views problems as opportunities for innovation. Specifically, we focus on the development of the futures and options markets and their use by financial managers to manage risk, and the increased use of hybrid securities by smaller firms to reduce borrowing costs. The changes and challenges brought about by the wave of restructuring that swept corporate America in the 1980's is also examined. We then turn to the myriad of agency problems encountered in the financial world and the changes taking place right now to address them. Specifically, we will look at changes in executive compensation. Many of these changes are being motivated by academic research and the emergence of active institutional investors. Finally, we will examine some unsettling findings from academic circles dealing with market efficiency and the CAPM.

■ RECENT INNOVATIONS IN RISK MANAGEMENT

In response to the volatile interest rates, commodity prices, and exchange rates of the late 1970s and early 1980s financial managers turned to the futures and options markets for relief. During this period the pace of innovation in these markets was staggering. These new financial instruments provided corporations with a low-cost means of hedging away many types of risk associated with possible price fluctuations. For example, futures and options can be used to eliminate risks associated with price fluctuations on raw materials in addition to risks associated with foreign exchange exposure that might be experienced by a corporation exporting goods to another country.

The development of new tools and techniques we see in the field of risk management is just one example of how dynamic and adaptive the field of finance is. The problems facing financial managers, in effect, become the seeds for innovation. The two areas that have seen the most dramatic change over the past 10 years and will continue to foster innovation are futures and options. For this reason we will now present a brief introduction to each of these areas.

A **future,** or **futures contract,** is a contract to buy or sell a stated commodity (such as soybeans or corn) or financial claim (such as U.S. Treasury bonds) at a specified price at some future specified time. It is important to note here that this is a contract that *requires* its holder to buy or sell the asset, regardless of what happens to its value during the interim. The importance of a futures contract is that it can be used by financial managers to lock in the price of a commodity or an interest rate and thereby eliminate one source of risk. For example, if a corporation is planning on issuing debt in the near future and is concerned about a possible rise in interest rates between now and when the debt would be issued, it might sell a U.S. Treasury bond futures contract with the same face value as the proposed debt offering and a delivery date the same as when the debt offering is to occur. Alternatively, with the use of a futures contract, Ralston-Purina or Quaker Oats can lock in the future price of corn or oats whenever they wish. Because a futures contract locks in interest rates or commodity prices, the costs associated with any possible rise in interest rates or commodity prices are completely offset by the profits made by writing the futures interest rate contract. In effect, futures contracts allow the financial manager to lock in future interest and exchange rates or prices for a number of agricultural commodities like corn and oats.

An **option,** or **option contract,** gives its owner the right to buy or sell a fixed number of shares at a specified price over a limited time. Although the market for options seems to have a language of its own, there are only two basic types of options: puts and calls. Everything else involves some variation. A **call option** gives its owner the right to purchase a given number of shares of stock or some other asset at a specified price over a given period. Thus, if the price of the underlying common stock or asset goes up, a call purchaser makes money. This is essentially the same as a "rain check" or guaranteed price. You have the option to buy something, in this case common stock, at a set price. In effect, a call option gives you the right to buy, but it is not a promise to buy. A **put,** on the other hand, gives its owner the right to sell a given number of shares of common stock or some other asset at a specified price over a given period. A put purchaser is betting that the price of the underlying common stock or asset will drop. Just as with the call, a put option gives its holder the right to sell the common stock at a set price, but it is not a promise to sell. Because these are just options to buy or sell stock or some other asset, they do not represent an ownership position in the underlying corporation, as does common stock. In fact, there is no direct relationship between the underlying corporation and the option. An option is merely a contract between two investors.

Recent Innovations in the Options Market

Recently, four additional variations of the traditional option have appeared: the stock index option, the interest rate option, the foreign currency option, and the Treasury bond futures option. Although there will undoubtedly be numerous other innovations in this market before you graduate, these additions to the options markets provide insights to the broad range of problems facing the financial manager that can be addressed with options.

STOCK INDEX OPTIONS   The options on stock indexes were first introduced on the Chicago Board Options Exchange (CBOE) in 1983 and have since proved extremely popular. Although there are a variety of different index options, based on several different broad stock market indexes and also industry indexes such as a computer industry index, the broader stock market indexes have carried the bulk of the popularity of index options. Whereas the industry-based index options have received a somewhat mixed reception, stock index options, in particular the S&P 100 index on the CBOE, have proved to be extremely popular.

In fact, more than 80 percent of all stock index options trading involves the **S&P 100** index. Currently it accounts for over half of the volume of all option trading and has made the CBOE the second largest U.S. securities market, with daily trading occasionally reaching nearly 700,000 contracts. (Remember, each contract involves an option on 100 "shares" of the index.)

The reason for this popularity is simple. These options allow portfolio managers and other investors holding broad portfolios cheaply and effectively to eliminate or adjust the market risk of their portfolio. When we talked about systematic and unsystematic risk, we noted that in a large and well-diversified portfolio, unsystematic risk was effectively diversified away, leaving only systematic risk. Thus, the return on a large and well-diversified portfolio was a result of the portfolio's beta and the movement of the market. As a result, because the movements of the market cannot be controlled, portfolio managers periodically attempt to adjust the beta of the portfolio when they think a change in the market's direction is at hand. Index options allow them to make this change without the massive transaction costs that would otherwise be incurred.

INTEREST RATE OPTIONS   Options on 30-year Treasury bonds are also traded on the CBOE. Although the trading appeal of interest rate options is somewhat limited, they do open some very interesting doors to the financial manager. In terms of the insurance and leverage traits, they allow the financial manager to ensure against the effects of future changes in interest rates. We know that as interest rates rise the market value of outstanding bonds falls; thus, through the purchase of an interest rate put, the market value of a portfolio manager's bonds can be protected. Alternatively, a financial manager who is about to raise new capital through a debt offering and who is worried about a possible rise in interest rates before the offering occurs may purchase an interest rate put. This would have the effect of locking in current interest rates at the maximum level that the firm would have to pay.

FOREIGN CURRENCY OPTIONS   Foreign currency options are the same as the other options we have examined, except the underlying asset is the British pound, the Japanese yen, or some other foreign currency. Although foreign currency options are limited to the Philadelphia Exchange, there is a considerable amount of interest in them largely because of the wide fluctuations foreign currency has had in recent years relative to the dollar. In terms of the insurance traits, these options allow multinational firms to guard against fluctuations in foreign currencies that might adversely affect their operations.

PERSPECTIVE IN FINANCE

An option on a Treasury bond future really holds little advantage over an option on a Treasury bond in terms of ability to reduce interest rate risk. Its advantages stem mainly from the great depth of the Treasury bond futures market.

Using Currency Options to Protect Sales

As firms trade more and more internationally, the need to protect sales against undesirable currency fluctuations becomes more important. For example, Beechcraft might use currency options to protect sales on its Starship aircraft, which are sold in Europe to Swiss customers. Because the Starship is built in the United States and sold abroad, its costs in labor and materials are based on the dollar. However, as the dollar fluctuates relative to the Swiss franc, so must the sales price in Swiss francs for Beechcraft to receive the same amount of dollars on each sale in Switzerland.

Problems surface when the value of the Swiss franc falls relative to that of the dollar. For each sale to bring the same amount of dollars back to Beechcraft, the selling price in Swiss francs would have to be increased.

Unfortunately, increasing prices may lead to lost sales. To guard against this situation Beechcraft may purchase put options on the Swiss franc to cover the anticipated Swiss sales. These puts work just like other puts and would give Beechcraft the option to sell or convert Swiss francs into dollars at a set price. If after the puts are purchased, the Swiss franc falls, Beechcraft could keep its selling prices constant in terms of the Swiss franc and make up for the loss in the currency exchange with the profits on the puts. Conversely, if the value of the Swiss franc rises relative to the value of the dollar, Beechcraft could lower its Swiss price, sell more aircraft, and still bring home the same dollars per sale—all that would be lost is the premium or price paid for the put options.

OPTIONS ON TREASURY BOND FUTURES   Options on Treasury bond futures work the same way as any other option. The only difference between them and other bond options is that they involve the acquisition of a futures position rather than the delivery of actual bonds. To the creative financial manager, they provide a flexible tool to ensure against adverse changes in interest rates while retaining the opportunity to benefit from any favorable interest rate movement that might occur. Although a futures contract establishes an obligation for both parties to buy and sell at a specified price, an option only establishes a right. It is therefore exercised only when it is to the option holder's advantage to do so. A call option on a futures contract does not establish a price obligation, but rather a maximum purchase price. Conversely, a put option on a futures contract is used to establish a minimum selling price. Thus, *the buyer of an option on a futures contract can achieve immunization against any unfavorable price movements, whereas the buyer of a futures contract can achieve immunization against any price movements regardless of whether they are favorable or unfavorable.*

Future Changes and Challenges in the Futures and Options Markets

The growth of the futures and options markets clearly demonstrates that the markets view crises in financial management as opportunities to innovate. The rapid growth of these markets also demonstrates how quickly the tools of the financial manager change. No doubt we will see the same fast-paced innovation in the future; indeed, many of the tools available to you when you enter the workforce have yet to be developed. The financial markets are truly dynamic.

■ FINANCE IN THE '90s: THE CONSEQUENCES OF FINANCIAL INNOVATION IN CORPORATE RESTRUCTURING

Corporate restructuring in the past decade has dramatically affected the perceptions most of us have about business and finance—-not to mention the significant change in the number and structure of firms that existed only a few years ago. In the United States alone, the total value of assets changing hands in the past decade was $1.3 trillion. Of the 500 largest industrial corporations in the U.S. in 1980, 28 percent had been acquired by other firms by 1989. The decade was well known even to the most casual observer as the period of the **hostile takeover,** meaning that managers of the acquired firm resisted being taken over by investors who might be less than friendly to the current management. These years were also characterized by the use of large amounts of leverage in acquiring other companies; this process came to be known as a **leveraged buyout** (LBO). In addition, management buyouts (MBOs), in which managers used large amounts of borrowed funds to buy the firms they managed, occurred with increasing frequency. In short, the business world has taken on a new look as a result of the innovation in financial restructuring of the '80s.

In the 1980s, several large investors such as T. Boone Pickens and Carl Icahn, who came to be known as *corporate raiders,* and several of the major investment banking houses became the brokers of the merger and acquisition activities. The pattern became that of acquiring a conglomerate, breaking it up into its individual business units, and selling off the units to large corporations in the same businesses. Several firms created in this process were temporary organizations intended to last only as long as was required to divest the pieces of the acquired firm to other corporations. Any remaining businesses were then offered to the public, especially when the business unit's value had been enhanced by improvements in the firm's operations.

The *decade of the deal* came to an end in the late 1980s, largely because the huge amounts of debt financing used to fund many of the acquisitions dried up. Also, a recession developed, which resulted in some major firms not being able to meet their debt obligations.

What may we conclude about this era of takeovers, a time when Michael Milken and Carl Icahn became household names? Some believe that it was a time of excesses and greed. Hostile takeovers and management buyouts, particularly, have been blamed for a multitude of problems including massive layoffs. The fear of being taken over by the likes of T. Boone Pickens is thought to have caused managers to reduce significantly their planning horizons. The large debt loads of many of the acquiring and acquired firms have, according to some, increased the instability of the economy and resulted in the general decline of U.S. competitiveness. For these reasons, many states have all but banned hostile takeovers.

Whatever we believe about takeovers during the 1980s, they undoubtedly did include some excesses and greed. After all was said and done, however, the evidence suggests that takeovers during the 1980s represented a return to more specialized and focused firms after years of diversification. Most acquisitions during the latter years involved companies buying other firms in their own lines of business. Most often, firms were taken over, and their various business lines were sold off to different buyers in the same line of business. To a significant extent, hostile takeovers and leveraged buyouts that attracted so much public attention facilitated this process of deconglomeration. Some of the most common objections to takeovers, such as a reduction of competition and cutbacks in employment, investment, and R & D, are not supported by the data.[1]

Although the jury is still out as to the long-term consequences of the 1980s era of acquisitions, the mere fact that the conglomerates failed to deliver as they promised could mean that the performance of many firms as they gain increased focus will improve. We shall see in time.

PERSPECTIVE IN FINANCE

Mergers and acquisitions are usually justified by management on the grounds that merging diversifies the firm, thus reducing risk. However, it may be that the stockholder can diversify personally with more ease and less expense by buying stock in the two companies. There must be other reasons for the merger.

Why Mergers Might Create Wealth

Clearly, for a merger to create wealth it would have to provide shareholders with something they could not get by merely holding the individual shares of the two firms. Such a requirement is the key to the creation of wealth under the capital asset pricing model. Restating the question: What benefits are there to shareholders from holding the stock of a new, single firm that has been created through a merger as opposed to holding stock in the two individual firms prior to their merger? Let's consider some of these benefits.

Tax Benefits

If a merger were to result in a reduction of taxes that is not otherwise possible, then wealth is created by the merger. This can be the case with a firm that has lost money and thus generated tax credits but does not currently have a level of earnings sufficient to use those tax credits. You will recall that losses can be carried back 3 years and forward a total of 15 years. As a result, tax credits that cannot be used and have no value

---

[1]See, for example, Amar Bhide, "The Causes and Consequences of Hostile Takeovers," *Journal of Applied Corporate Finance* (Summer 1989), pp. 36–59.

to one firm can take on value when that firm is acquired by another firm that has earnings sufficient enough to employ the tax credits. In addition, a merger allows for previously depreciated assets to be revalued; thus, wealth is created from the tax benefits arising from the increased depreciation associated with this revaluation of assets.

Reduction of Agency Costs

As we know, the agency problem can occur when the management and ownership of the firm are separate. To compensate for the agency problem, stockholders and bondholders impose a premium on funds supplied to the firm to compensate them for any inefficiency in management. A merger, particularly when it results in a holding company or conglomerate organizational form, may reduce the significance of this problem, because top management is created to monitor the management of the individual companies making up the conglomerate. As a result, management of the individual companies can be effectively monitored without any forced public announcement of proprietary information, such as new product information that might aid competitors. If investors recognize this reduction in the agency problem as material, they may provide funds to the firm at a reduced cost, no longer charging as large an "agency problem premium."

Alternatively, it can be argued that the creation of a conglomerate might result in increased agency costs. Shareholders in conglomerates may think they have less control over the firm's managers as a result of the additional layers of management between them and the decision makers. Moreover, the resultant expenditures necessary to monitor conglomerates, because of their multi-industry nature, may give further rise to agency costs.

Free Cash Flow Problem: A Specific Case of the Agency Problem

The "free cash flow" problem was first identified by Michael Jensen in 1986. Free cash flow refers to the operating cash flow in excess of what is necessary to fund all profitable investments available to the firm; that is, to fund all projects with a positive net present value. As we know from our discussion of shareholder-wealth maximization, this free cash flow should be paid out to shareholders; otherwise it would be invested in projects returning less than the required rate of return, in effect less than shareholders could earn elsewhere.

Unfortunately, managers may not wish to pass these funds to the shareholders because they may think that their power would be reduced. Moreover, if they return these surplus funds, they may be forced to go outside for financing if more profitable investment opportunities are identified at a later date. Certainly, what we are describing here is a form of the agency problem; still, we need to see these actions in the context of the corporate management culture rather than as an attempt by the managers to maintain their own position. That is to say, as economic conditions change, managers who have successfully managed firms over the years of growing markets may have difficulty in adjusting their financial strategies to conditions in which not all cash flows can be invested at the required rate of return. Jensen argues that this was the case in the oil and gas industry in the late 1970s and resulted in much of the merger activity that took place in those markets during that period.[2] A merger can create wealth by allowing the new management to correct this problem by paying this free cash flow to the shareholders by increasing dividends or repurchasing stock, thus reducing free cash flow and allowing the shareholders to earn a higher return on this excess than would have been earned by the firm.

Economies of Scale

Wealth can also be created in a merger through economies of scale. For example, administrative expenses including accounting, data processing, or simply top-management costs, may fall as a percentage of total sales as a result of sharing these resources.

The sharing of resources can also lead to an increase in the firm's productivity. For example, if two firms sharing the same distribution channels merge, distributors carrying one product may now be willing to carry the other, thereby increasing the sales outlets for the products. In effect, wealth would be created by the merger of the two firms and shareholders should benefit.

Unused Debt Potential

Some firms simply do not exhaust their debt capacity. If a firm with unused debt potential is acquired, the new management can then increase debt financing, and reap the tax benefits associated with the increased debt.

Complementarity in Financial Slack

When cash-rich bidders and cash-poor targets are combined, wealth may be created as a result of the positive NPV projects taken by the merged firm that the cash-poor firm would have passed up. Thus, although these cash-poor firms are selling at a fair price, the discounted value of their future cash flow is below their potential price. In effect, a merger allows positive NPV projects to be accepted that would have been rejected if the merger had not occurred.

Removal of Ineffective Management

Any time a merger can result in the replacement of inefficient operations, whether in production or management, wealth should be created. If a firm with ineffective management can be acquired, it may be possible to replace the current management with a more efficient management team, and thereby create wealth. This may be the case with firms that have grown from solely production into production and distribution companies, or R & D firms that have expanded into production and distribution; the managers simply may not know enough about the new aspects of the firm to manage it effectively.

---

[2]Michael C. Jensen, "The Takeover Controversy: Analysis and Evidence," *Midland Corporate Finance Journal* 4 (2) (Summer 1986), pp. 6–32.

Increased Market Power

The merger of two firms can result in an increase in the market or monopoly power of the two firms. Although this can result in increased wealth, it may also be illegal. The Clayton Act, as amended by the Celler-Kefauver Amendment of 1950, makes any merger illegal that results in a monopoly or substantially reduces competition. The Justice Department and the Federal Trade Commission monitor all mergers to ensure that they do not result in a reduction of competition.

Reduction in Bankruptcy Costs

There is no question that firm diversification, when the earnings from the two firms are less than perfectly positively correlated, can reduce the chance of bankruptcy. The question is whether or not there is any wealth created by such an activity. Quite obviously, in the real world there is a cost associated with bankruptcy. First, if a firm fails, its assets in general cannot be sold for their true economic value. Moreover, the amount of money actually available for distribution to stockholders is further reduced by selling costs and legal fees that must be paid. Finally, the opportunity cost associated with the delays related to the legal process further reduces the funds available to the shareholders. Therefore, because costs are associated with bankruptcy, reduction of the chance of bankruptcy has a very real value to it.

The risk of bankruptcy also entails indirect costs associated with changes in the firm's debt capacity and the cost of debt. As the firm's cash flow patterns stabilize, the risk of default will decline, giving the firm an increased debt capacity and possibly reducing the cost of the debt. Because interest payments are tax deductible, whereas dividends are not, debt financing is less expensive than equity financing. Thus, monetary benefits are associated with an increased debt capacity. These indirect costs of bankruptcy also spread out into other areas of the firm, affecting things like production and the quality and efficiency of management. Firms with higher probabilities of bankruptcy may have a more difficult time recruiting and retaining quality managers and employees because jobs with that firm are viewed as less secure. This in turn may result in less productivity for these firms. In addition, firms with higher probabilities of bankruptcy may have a more difficult time marketing their product because of customer concern over future availability of the product. In short, there are real costs to bankruptcy. If a merger reduces this possibility of bankruptcy, it creates some wealth.

Financial Innovation with Efficiency in Mind: Divestitures or "Reverse Mergers"

Although the mergers-and-acquisition phenomenon has been a major influence in restructuring the corporate sector, divestitures, or what we might call "reverse mergers," may have become an equally important factor. In fact, preliminary research to date would suggest that we may be witnessing a "new era" in the making—one where the public corporation has become a more efficient vehicle for increasing and maintaining stockholder wealth.[3] Chew calls it the "new math," when he writes that

> a new kind of arithmetic has come into play. Whereas corporate management once seemed to behave as if 2 + 2 were equal to 5, especially during the conglomerate heyday of the 60's, the wave of reverse mergers seems based on the counter proposition that 5 − 1 is 5. And the market's consistently positive response to such deals seems to be providing broad confirmation of the "new math."[4]

A successful divestiture allows the firm's assets to be used more efficiently and therefore to be assigned a higher value by the market forces. It essentially eliminates a division or subsidiary that does not fit strategically with the rest of the company; that is, it removes an operation that does not contribute to the company's basic purposes.

The different types of divestitures may be summarized as follows:

1. **Selloff.** A selloff is the sale of a subsidiary, division, or product line by one company to another. For example, Radio Corporation of America (RCA) sold its finance company and General Electric sold its metallurgical coal business.

2. **Spinoff.** A spinoff involves the separation of a subsidiary from its parent, with no change in the equity ownership. The management of the parent company gives up operating control of the subsidiary, but the shareholders retain the same percentage ownership in both firms. New shares representing ownership in the diverted assets are issued to the original shareholders on a pro-rata basis.

3. **Liquidation.** A liquidation in this context is not a decision to shut down or abandon an asset. Rather, the assets are sold to another company, and the proceeds are distributed to the stockholders.

4. **Going private.** A company goes private when its stock that has traded publicly is purchased by a small group of investors, and the stock is no longer bought and sold on a public exchange. The ownership of the company is transferred from a diverse group of outside stockholders to a small group of private investors, usually including the firm's management. The leveraged buyout is a special case of going private. As noted earlier in the chapter, the existing shareholders sell their shares to a small group of investors. The purchasers of the stock use the firm's unused debt capacity to borrow the funds to pay for the stock. Thus, the new investors acquire the firm with little, if any, personal investment. However, the firm's debt ratio may increase by as much as tenfold.

In summary, corporate restructuring does not always mean combining firms. It means structuring the firm in the way that makes the

---

[3]See G. Alexander, P. Benson, and J. Kampmeyer, "Investigating the Valuation Effects of Voluntary Corporate Sell-offs," *Journal of Finance* 39 (1984), pp. 503–17; and D. Hearth, "Voluntary Divestitures and Value," *Financial Management* (1984).

[4]Joel M. Stern, and Donald H. Chew, Jr. (eds.), The Revolution in Corporate Finance (New York: Basis Blackwell, 1986), p. 416.

most economic sense. As we have seen here it can mean either putting firms together or taking them apart.

■ RECENT INNOVATIONS IN RAISING CAPITAL: HYBRID SECURITIES

In the late 1980s, partly in response to several large corporate bankruptcies, the spread between interest rates charged to Blue Chip and non-Blue Chip borrowers became quite large. The financial markets attacked the problem through innovation. As a result, in the late 1980s and early 1990s there again was a flurry of innovation in the hybrid debt markets, where conventional debt issues were combined with futures or options. These innovations provided the issuing corporation and the investors purchasing these securities a low-cost method of hedging away interest rate volatility.

To understand many of these innovations it is necessary to understand first what a convertible bond is, as many of these new hybrids are simply variations of the convertible. A brief introduction to convertibles follows. **Convertible debt** is simply a hybrid security that combines debt or preferred stock with an option on the firm's common stock. Today, some of the hybrid securities combine debt with options on interest rates, stock indexes, foreign exchange rates, and commodities like silver, oil, and natural gas.

A **convertible security** is a preferred stock or debt issue that can be exchanged for a specified number of shares of common stock at the will of the owner. It provides the stable income associated with preferred stock or bonds in addition to the possibility of capital gains associated with common stock. This combination of features has led convertibles to be called *hybrid* securities.

When the convertible is initially issued, the firm receives the proceeds from the sale, less flotation costs. This is the only time the firm receives any proceeds from issuing convertibles. The firm then treats this convertible as if it were normal preferred stock or debentures, paying dividends or interest regularly. If the security owner wishes to exchange the convertible for common stock, he or she may do so at any time according to the terms specified at the time of issue. The desire to convert generally follows a rise in the price of the common stock. Once the convertible owner trades the convertibles in for common stock, the owner can never trade the stock back for convertibles. From then on the owner is treated as any other common stockholder and receives only common stock dividends.

Innovative Variations on the Convertible: The New Hybrids

Since 1980 the pace of innovative change through the use of hybrid financing has steadily quickened. While convertibles continue to be popular alternatives for raising funds, the new hybrids of today go well beyond traditional convertibles in terms of creativity. For example, in 1986 Pegasus Gold Corporation, a Canadian gold mining firm, issued

Eurobonds with detachable gold options. For the bondholder this issue provided both a traditional straight bond and gold options. If the price of gold rises, the bondholders benefit along with the firm, and, if not, the bondholders still have a straight bond. Structuring the hybrid in this way significantly reduces the interest rate on the bonds. Other hybrid variations include tying the interest payments to a commodity like copper or silver, or having interest payments vary as the creditworthiness of the issuing firm changes. For example, Magma Copper issued bonds in which the interest payment varied with the prevailing price of copper. Presidio Oil linked the interest payment to the price of natural gas, whereas Manufacturer's Hanover Bank issued bonds that provided for increased interest payments to bondholders if their creditworthiness declined. Again, each of these innovations allowed for funds to be raised at a lower cost than would otherwise have been available.

What has caused this burst of innovation in the debt market? It has been brought about by the competitive nature of the financial markets, where the problems businesses face are viewed by the financial markets as opportunities for innovation. In this case it was the increased spread between the interest rates paid by Blue Chip and less creditworthy corporations that inspired investment bankers to devise the recent wave of hybrids. In short, the less creditworthy firms were looking for a way to make their debt more attractive and therefore reduce its cost, and they found this through the creation of hybrids. In addition, the use of hybrids opened access to the long-term debt markets for some smaller firms that otherwise would not have had access to those markets.

What financial innovations will aid financial managers in raising capital in the future? The answer is that the problems financial managers face, both in an economic and a regulatory sense, will dictate what future financial innovations look like. However, one thing is clear: Very little remains the same in finance for long. Understanding the underlying principles—our nine axioms—and the factors motivating these financial innovations makes the changes much easier to understand. We will now turn to the agency problem and the changes and challenges brewing in that area.

■ THE AGENCY PROBLEM: CHANGES AND CHALLENGES

If the corporation is to truly maximize shareholders' wealth, the interests of the managers and the shareholders must be aligned. In recent years much of the debate on how to resolve the agency problem has centered on how best to structure executive compensation so that managers act in the best interests of shareholders. More recently this debate has erupted into public outrage over large executive salaries. No doubt the controversy over how best to compensate managers and whether managers are overpaid will continue—in fact, it appears the debate is just heating up. After examining this question we will look at a phenomenon generating fewer headlines, but also addressing the agency problem—the emergence of relationship investing and the active investor.

In this section we examine two topics related to the agency problem, which is presented in **Axiom 7: The Agency Problem—Managers Won't Work for the Owners Unless It's in Their Best Interest.** First, we examine the executive compensation package that should be used to align the managers' and the owners' interests. Second, we look at the emergence of relationship investing, which also serves to control the agency problem by making managers more accountable to owners and allowing managers to take a long-term perspective with respect to investments.

 ## INTRODUCTION VIDEO CASE 6

CEO Compensation: Corporate Governance in Inaction?
from ABC News, Nightline, May 20, 1991

The chief executive officers (CEOs) of America's largest corporations earn, on average, 85 times the amount earned by factory workers at those same corporations. In Japan this multiple is 17 and in Germany 23. Possibly more surprising than the magnitude of the salaries is the fact that CEO compensation often does not seem to be linked to the performance of the firm. As the participants in this video segment demonstrate, concern about this inequity is growing. Critics of large compensation packages for corporate CEOs are Professors Bud Crystal and Robert Reich, who are spokesmen from two shareholder rights groups, the Institute of Shareholder Partners and United Shareholders Association. Ben Cohen, CEO of Ben and Jerry's Ice Cream, describes the compensation system in their firm: CEO compensation is limited to about 10 times the salary of the lowest paid employee. Hicks Waldron, a compensation consultant and former CEO of Avon Products, argues that looking at a few extreme cases does not imply that all CEOs are overpaid. He also argues that cultural differences make comparisons between the compensation packages in different countries inappropriate. Are American executives worth these large salaries and bonuses, are CEO salaries out of line, and do stock options solve this problem?

In examining the executive compensation controversy we must keep in mind that our goal is to structure the executive compensation plan in such a way that the agency problem introduced in fundamental **Axiom 7: The Agency Problem — Managers Won't Work for the Owners Unless It's in Their Best Interest** is minimized. This is done by developing a compensation plan that aligns managerial behavior with shareholder objectives.

Executive Compensation: The Debate and the Challenge

The recent outcry over the astronomical level of executive salaries has shifted the debate over executive compensation from the academic to the public arena. Much of the public debate was ignited by the disclosure that the chairman of Time Warner received $78.1 million in compensation in

1990 and was further fueled by reports of what other executives earned. For example, Time Warner made the headlines again in 1992 when it paid its recently ousted co-chief executive officer $15.8 million in severance pay plus $2.9 million in salary, deferred income, and bonuses from 1991. In the spring of 1993 *Business Week* reported that the gains of 10 selected chief executive officers in 1992 from stock options and warrants totaled more than $500 million, an amount that exceeded the sum of all long-term pay for the 363 CEOs included in *Business Week's* 1991 executive pay scoreboard. All of this has sharpened the focus on excessive executive pay and has prompted proposals designed to cap CEO salaries. In fact, the Revenue Reconciliation Act of 1993 denies the deduction for certain compensation in excess of $1 million per year paid by a publicly traded corporation to the CEO and the 4 other most highly compensated officers beginning in 1994. Interestingly, compensation linked to productivity, as well as tax-qualified retirement plan contributions and certain fringe benefits, are excluded from the limit. To fully understand this debate and the changes it will bring in the 1990s we must first understand how an executive compensation package should ideally be designed.

The purpose of an executive compensation plan is to align managerial behavior with shareholder objectives. Without such a plan the managers, regardless of how skilled they are, may simply seek to maximize their own personal wealth and perk consumption. The key to aligning managerial behavior and shareholders' objectives is to tie managerial compensation to changes in shareholder wealth within a plan that is easy to monitor. The plan should curb managers' accumulation of excessive and unnecessary perquisites and incorporate a long term-time horizon that matches that of the shareholders while matching shareholders' and managers' risk.

Perhaps the most common method of linking pay to performance is through stock option plans. With stock option plans the managers are given long-term call options on the company's common stock. As a result, the managers' compensation is tied directly to the returns received by common shareholders. In addition, the incentives provided by options are *long term*. One criticism of such a plan is that stock price movements are not all caused by the managers' decisions, but instead may be caused by some underlying market movement. This has led some executive compensation packages to be based on relative stock performance. Another criticism of using stock options to compensate managers comes from the popular press and is that such packages lead to executive salaries that simply are too high. While citing individuals like Walt Disney's Michael Eisner and Frank Wells, who in late 1992 exercised options worth about $187 million, the press many times overlooks the enormous gains in shareholder wealth that these managers oversaw for their shareholders. Interestingly, although there are abuses in executive compensation, on average executive compensation increases only about $3 for every $1,000 increase in shareholder wealth.[5] Moreover, as the case of Eisner clearly demonstrates, pay for performance does work, and when the executive does an exceptional job the pay will be very high.

[5]For further analysis of the relationship between executive compensation and performance see Michael C. Jensen, "Performance Pay and Top-Management Incentives," *Journal of Political Economy* 98, No. 2 (1990), 225–264.

A high level of compensation can result from a pay-for-performance system in which the executive has performed extremely well, or it can be the result of the agency problem, where the executive is taking advantage of the system. Keep in mind that an executive compensation committee, appointed by the firm's board of directors, generally recommends the CEO's compensation package. Also keep in mind the board of directors, although elected by the shareholders, is generally nominated for election by the CEO and thus may be more sympathetic to the CEO's desires than to the shareholders' best interests. This opens the door for "good old boy" networks to take care of their own and set up a compensation package that rewards, regardless of performance, without attempting to align managers' and shareholders' interests. It is this lack of control and monitoring of the CEO that leads to the agency problem. Still, the debate continues over how best to structure executive compensation packages to eliminate the agency problem. It is important to you as a student of finance to realize the significance of this debate and that it focuses on the elimination of the agency problem. It takes on importance because our goal of maximization of shareholder wealth cannot be realized if managerial behavior is not aligned with shareholder objectives.

Relationship Investing: The Emergence of the Active Investor

Another way in which the agency problem is being addressed is through relationship investing or the emergence of the active investor. Since the 1930s, managerial holding of common stock has declined dramatically, falling from roughly 3 percent to less than .03 percent today. Finally, the pendulum appears to be swinging the other way. Not only have management leveraged buyouts (MBOs) led to increased managerial ownership, but pensions, mutual funds and large investors have increased their monitoring of corporate dealings. Some investors are taking large long-term positions in companies and, in return, are gaining a greater say in what management does and how it operates.

To those staking out large long-term positions in corporations, the advantages are twofold. First, it allows the firm to take on a long-term perspective with regard to investments. For a number of years CEOs have complained about the short-term outlook of investors. However, if the shareholders take on a long-term perspective and a patient attitude with respect to expectations, management may be able to focus on the long term, with the result being an increase in profits, productivity, and competitiveness.

The second advantage gained from relationship investing is increased manager accountability. This results from increased monitoring by large investors who have taken long term ownership positions in the firm. Unfortunately, the board of directors does not do a good job of monitoring the behavior of the managers. Although shareholders vote for the corporate board of directors (generally through proxy voting), who in turn hire and fire management, as mentioned earlier, the system really works the other way around. In reality, management selects both the issues and the board of director nominees. Then management distributes the proxy ballots to the shareholders. Thus, the shareholders are, in effect, offered a slate of nominees selected by management from which to choose. The result is that management effectively selects the directors, who then may have more allegiance to the managers than to the shareholders. This sets up the potential for agency problems in which a divergence of interests between managers and shareholders is allowed to exist, with the board of directors not monitoring the managers on behalf of the shareholders as they should. During the 1992 presidential campaign Ross Perot highlighted this problem in describing his dealings with the General Motors Board of Directors, which he referred to as the CEO's "pet rocks."

Is relationship investing working? It appears that the regular, ongoing monitoring it affords, along with the long-term perspective it allows, does, in fact, work. Examples of relationship investing at work and succeeding include Avon, Sears, and Eastman Kodak. Where will all this lead? In the next decade we will no doubt see an increase in relationship investing. After all, it is a logical way to improve internal corporate control and make the boards more responsive to shareholder objectives rather than managerial objectives, thereby allowing managers to take a long-term perspective on investments. There is no question that the benefits from controlling the agency problem are enormous. Therefore, large shareholders will surely continue their efforts to ensure their voices are heard.

■ THE CAPM AND MARKET EFFICIENCY: THE CHALLENGES FROM ACADEMIA

During the 1970s and 1980s the capital asset pricing model (CAPM) and the concept of market efficiency gained increased acceptance in the corporate world as a result of being relentlessly pushed in college classrooms across America. However, since the stock market crash of 1987, the capital asset pricing model has come under increasing attack from many of those who had championed its use just a few years earlier. Given the widespread use of the CAPM we should become familiar with these criticisms; moreover, we should understand the assumptions and limitations surrounding its use. It does not appear that this problem, and the passionate debate it engenders, will go away soon. It is just one more example of the dynamic nature of financial theory and how important it is to understand its underlying principles.

The CAPM Debate: Beta Is Dead—No It's Not—Is Too!

BACK TO THE FUNDAMENTALS

Much of the debate over the CAPM centers on how best to measure risk in the risk-return tradeoff presented in **Axiom 1: The Risk-Return TradeOff—We Won't Take on Additional Risk Unless We Expect to Be Compensated with Additional Return.** The debate over the validity of the CAPM has taken on the trappings of an academic holy war. Although it may take some time for the field of finance to arrive at a consensus, you should be familiar with the limitations and uncertainties surrounding the CAPM.

In Chapter 8 we introduced the CAPM controversy that erupted in 1992 when Eugene Fama and Kenneth French of the University of Chicago published the findings of an exhaustive study. The study concluded over the past 50 years that beta, which is the CAPM's measure of systematic risk, has not been related to returns. In effect, the risk-return relationship predicted by the CAPM has not held for the past 50 years. To say the least, this is a disturbing finding, in particular to individuals who have for years been supporting the CAPM. It came on the heels of findings that investors may overreact to some announcements, and other studies that indicate the markets may be much more complex than presented by the CAPM. In fact, markets and prices may move based on nonlinear relationships, with bubbles building and eventually bursting. The bottom line is that the process of stock valuation may be much more complex than the CAPM states—in fact, so complex that valuation may be incomprehensible to all but a few. Given the importance of this debate, we will take a closer look at it and its implications.

Where does this leave us? First, the basic risk-return tradeoff presented in Axiom 1 still holds; we just can't be sure that beta is a reasonable way to measure risk. We know that according to the CAPM, systematic risk is the only relevant type of risk. However, as we saw earlier, lifting the assumption of no bankruptcy costs makes unsystematic risk relevant. Thus, although it is important to have a conceptual understanding of the CAPM, this understanding is virtually worthless without an understanding of the assumptions and limitations of the model. Whether the criticisms of the CAPM hold up and whether the CAPM continues to be used or is replaced by a newer alternative only time will tell. In response to the Fama and French allegations, two lines of attack have sprung up. The first involves refinements to the empirical research methods used by Fama and French.[6] Using different empirical techniques and looking at different time periods, these responses find evidence of a risk-return relationship that Fama and French found absent. The second line of attack against the Fama and French allegations involves a theoretical argument offered by Richard Roll and Stephen Ross. They contend that the findings by Fama and French indicate that either the market portfolio used by Fama and French in their testing may not have been efficient, or that a relationship between betas and returns was absent.[7] Unfortunately, we cannot tell which.

So what are we to conclude? Is beta dead? At the very least the latest salvo of criticism has forced the academic community to come to grips with the fundamental shortcomings of the CAPM. The model, like all models that attempt to explain complex real-world phenomena using

---

[6]See Yakov Amihud, Bent Christensen, and Haim Mendelson, "Further Evidence on the Risk-Return Relationship," Working Paper (New York University, 1992); Louis Chan and Josef Lakonishok, "Are the Reports of Beta's Death Premature?" Working Paper, (Champaign - Urbana: University of Illinois, 1992); and S. P. Kothari, J. Shankin, and R. Sloan, "Another Look at the Cross-Section of Expected Stock Returns," Working Paper (University of Rochester, 1992).

[7]See Richard Roll and Stephen A. Ross, "On the Cross-Sectional Relationship Between Expected Returns and Betas, Working Paper (University of California at Los Angeles, July 8, 1992).

simplifying assumptions, is an abstraction and does not "fit the facts" as to the way the world works. Does this mean the model lacks usefulness? We think not. The model points to the need to diversify and identifies the source of the market risk premium as being tied to the risk of the security that cannot be diversified away. Is the model a complete guide to the underlying determinants of the risk-return tradeoff? Probably not. We know that bankruptcy risk is ignored by the CAPM, and this risk is a significant fact of life in the way investors evaluate and value securities. Then, just how useful is the model? We are reminded by the results of Fama and French that the CAPM is, at best, only a crude approximation of the relationship between risk and return. Thus, users are reminded to treat their beta estimates and the corresponding market risk premia estimates with great care. Perhaps we should use only one decimal place rather than six for our CAPM-based cost-of-capital estimates. In summary, because the CAPM provides quantifiable insights into the risk-return tradeoff, it will continue to be used in the absence of a workable alternative understandable to managers, but should only be used mindful of its limitations and underlying assumptions. In the next several years you will see the debate over the CAPM continue to rage—again, an example of the dynamic nature of the discipline of finance.

Market Efficiency and the Crash of 1987

BACK TO THE FUNDAMENTALS

This section relates to **Axiom 6: Efficient Capital Markets—The Markets Are Quick and the Prices Are Right** and presents a challenge to that axiom. It issues a warning that there may be much more going on in the capital markets than we understand now. Because there is no final answer at this time, we should be aware of the complexities and uncertainties involved in valuing assets in the capital markets.

Market efficiency implies that stock price movements respond instantaneously and in an unbiased manner to new information, and that as a result stock prices "fully reflect" all relevant information. However, if stock prices truly reflect the value of the common stock, how could the stock market drop by 23 percent in one day, with a 16.5 percent decline taking place in two hours and forty-five minutes? Certainly the crash of 1987 has caused concern to those financial economists who like to view the stock market as a place of orderly and efficient pricing. Exactly why the market dropped as quickly and dramatically as it did may never be known with certainty. But one theory that has gained considerable backing is that stock prices had deviated from their true value and the crash was a permanent correction, returning prices to their true economic value. This theory asserts that market bubbles exist. That is, prices continue to climb past their economic value—the present value of the future cash flows—with overvaluation supported by the continued rise in prices and the expectation that more price rises will follow. Thus, investors invest in stocks not because of their underlying value but because "stocks are a good investment and they're going to go up in price." As a result, price increases become self-fulfilling. Investors think prices will rise further, so they buy stock, which pushes the stock price even higher. Eventually the market can no longer support these explosive and unjustified stock price increases, and the stock price increases slow down. This, in turn, causes investors to question whether future stock price increases will continue, thus making the future of the bubble more uncertain. Finally, when a news event causes the bubble to burst, prices drop to their economically justified level, or even lower initially, as investors overreact to the drop. Although this scenario seems to describe what happened during October 1987, it is hard to prove scientifically whether a bubble actually existed. Still, early evidence supports the bubble hypothesis.[8] No doubt in the next several years there will be more explanations offered as to what took place and why, but given that there is still no consensus about what caused the crash of 1929, it is not surprising that an explanation has not been found for the crash of 1987.

Other signals indicate there are perhaps pockets of pricing inefficiency in the stock market. For example, researchers have found that small firms, firms with low price-earnings ratios, and firms that attract less analyst attention tend to outperform the market. In addition, researchers have found there are a number of calendar effects. That is, higher returns can be generated by purchasing stocks at particular times. Unfortunately, these pricing inefficiencies are quite interrelated and the problem of disentangling them continues.

In the next decade there will be continued attacks on the concept of market efficiency, with many of these attacks centering on the existence of pricing bubbles, questioning the rationality of investors. What is becoming evident is that there is a lot going on in the stock market. Although we can feel comfortable that security pricing is guided by the present value principles presented in this text, the process of security pricing is far from being completely understood. This makes it even more important that you have an understanding of the principles that guide us and the limitations of what we know about the pricing of assets. Here again is an area of finance where our understanding continues to evolve.

SUMMARY

This chapter examines the dynamic nature of finance: how the financial world views problems as opportunities for innovation. We first examine the development of the futures and options markets and their use by financial managers to manage risk. A **future,** or **futures contract,** is a

---

[8]See Richard Roll, "The International Crash of 1987," in Rishard J. Barro et al. (eds.), *Black Monday and the Future of Financial Markets* (Homewood, IL: Dow Jones-Irwin, 1989).

contract to buy or sell a stated commodity (such as soybeans or corn) or financial claim (such as U.S. Treasury bonds) at a specified price at some future specified time. A futures contract *requires* its holder to buy or sell the asset, regardless of what happens to its value during the interim, and can be used to lock in the price of a commodity or an interest rate and thereby eliminate one source of risk.

A **call option** gives its owner the right to purchase a given number of shares of stock or some other asset at a specified price over a given period. A **put,** on the other hand, gives its owner the right to sell a given number of shares of common stock or some other asset at a specified price over a given period.

The assertion that merger activity creates wealth for the shareholder cannot be maintained with certainty. Only if the merger provides something that the investor cannot do on his or her own can a merger or acquisition be of financial benefit.

A divestiture represents a variety of ways to let go of a portion of the firm's assets. It has become an important vehicle in restructuring the corporation into a more efficient operation.

There have been dramatic innovations in methods of raising capital in recent years, particularly through the use of hybrid securities. To understand many of these innovations it is necessary to understand what a convertible bond is, because many of these new hybrids are variations of the convertible. Convertible debt is a hybrid security that combines debt or preferred stock with an option on the firm's common stock. Today, some hybrid securities combine debt with options on interest rates, stock indexes, foreign exchange rates, and commodities like silver, oil, and natural gas. This surge of innovation in the debt market has been caused by the competitive nature of the financial markets, where the problems businesses face are seen as opportunities for innovation by the financial markets .

In recent years the debate on how to resolve the agency problem has centered on the question of how best to structure executive compensation so that managers act in the best interests of shareholders. The purpose of an executive compensation plan is to align managerial behavior with shareholder objectives. Without such a plan the managers, regardless of how skilled they are, may simply seek to maximize their own personal wealth. A common method of linking pay to performance is through stock option plans. Relationship investing is another way of addressing the agency problem. With relationship investing, investors take large long-term positions in companies and gain a greater say in what management does and how it operates. To those staking out large long-term positions in corporations, the advantages are twofold: It allows the firm to take on a long-term perspective with respect to investments, and it increases manager accountability by allowing close and constant monitoring of them.

During the 1970s and 1980s the capital-asset pricing model and the concept of market efficiency gained increased acceptance in the corporate world. However, since the stock market crash of 1987, the capital asset pricing model, with its beta as its measure of systematic risk, has come under attack from many who had earlier championed its use. These attacks have focused on the CAPM and the concept of market efficiency. Whether the criticisms of the CAPM hold up and whether the CAPM continues to be used or is replaced by a newer alternative remains to be seen. There does not seem to be a workable alternative today that is understandable to managers. Thus, in that the CAPM provides quantifiable insights into the risk-return tradeoff, it will continue to be used, but with awareness of its limitations and assumptions.

Certainly the crash of 1987 has upset those financial economists who see the stock market as orderly and price efficient. Why the market dropped so quickly and dramatically may never be known with certainty. One theory with considerable backing is that stock prices had deviated from their true value and the crash was a permanent correction, returning prices to their true economic value. This theory says market bubbles exist. Moreover, other signals suggest there are pockets of pricing inefficiency in the stock market. Although we can confidently maintain that security pricing is guided by the present value principles presented in this text, the process of security pricing is far from being clearly understood. All this makes it important that you understand the principles and limitation of pricing assets and be prepared for change.

STUDY QUESTIONS

17–1.   What is the difference between a future and an option?
17–2.   Describe a situation in which a financial manager might use a commodity future. Assume that during the period following the transaction the price of that commodity went up. Describe what happened. Then assume that the price of that commodity went down. Now what happened?
17–3.   Describe a situation in which a financial manager might use an interest rate future. Assume that during the period following the transaction the interest rates went up. Describe what happened. Then assume that interest rates went down following the transaction. Now what happened?
17–4.   Define a call option.
17–5.   Define a put option.
17–6.   Why might merger activity create wealth?
17–7.   Explain the different types of divestitures.
17–8.   Convertible bonds generally carry lower coupon interest rates than do nonconvertible bonds. If this is so, does it mean that the cost of capital on convertible bonds is lower than on nonconvertible bonds? Why or why not?
17–9.   What caused the recent flurry of innovation in the debt market?
17–10.   Why is important to pay attention to the way executives are compensated?
17–11.   What advantage can be gained from relationship investing?
17–12.   What does the existence of market bubbles mean for the concept of market efficiency?

CEO Compensation: Corporate Governance in Inaction?
from ABC News, Nightline, May 20, 1991

Although it may be difficult to say whether a CEO deserves a specific level of pay, most people would agree that when a firm performs poorly the CEO should not get a large bonus. The idea that executives should thrive while the firm provides little or no return to its shareholders is unacceptable to most people.

Although pay for performance makes sense, designing an appropriate compensation plan is difficult. Most pay packages include a salary, a bonus, and stock options, with stock options playing an increasingly large role. The prevalence of stock options is due, in part, to their accounting treatment. No costs or expenses are incurred when stock options are granted to executives, so profits are not affected. While the use of stock options can result in enormous returns for executives, they do succeed in making the manager's compensation package closer to that earned by the shareholder. Still, the debate over executive compensation rages on.

Discussion questions
1. Does the enormous difference in pay between executives and employees affect morale?
2. How would you design a CEO pay package? How does your plan create the proper incentives? Would a rational manager accept your pay package?

Suggested readings

COLVIN, GEOFFREY. "How to Pay the CEO Right," *Fortune*, April 6, 1992.

JARRELL, GREGG, "An Overview of the Executive Compensation Debate," *Journal of Applied Corporate Finance*, Winter 1993.

O'BYRNE, STEPHEN, "What Pay for Performance Looks Like: The Case of Michael Eisner," *Journal of Applied Corporate Finance*, Summer 1992.

APPENDIXES

APPENDIX A
Using a Calculator
(a tutorial on the Hewlett-Packard HP 17BII)

As you prepare for a career in business, the ability to use a financial calculator is essential, whether you are in the finance division or the marketing department. For most positions, it will be assumed that you can use a calculator in making computations that at one time were simply not possible without extensive time and effort. The following examples let us see what is possible, but they represent only the beginning of using the calculator in finance.

In demonstrating how calculators may make our work easier, we must first decide which calculator to use. The options are numerous and largely depend on personal preference. We have chosen to demonstrate the Hewlett-Packard HP 17BII.

I. Introductory Comments

In the examples that follow, you are told (1) which keystrokes to use, (2) the resulting appearance of the calculator display, and (3) a supporting explanation.

The keystrokes column tells you which keys to press. The keystrokes shown in an unshaded box tell you to used one of the calculator's dedicated or "hard" keys. For example if $\boxed{+/-}$ is shown in the keystrokes instruction column, press that key on the keyboard of the calculator. To use a function printed in gold lettering above a dedicated key, always press the gold key $\boxed{}$ first, then the function key. For example, keying in 2 and pressing $\boxed{}$ $\boxed{\sqrt{x}}$ calculates the square root of 2.

When the calculator is on, a set of labels appears across the bottom of the display. This is called a *menu*, because it presents you with the choices of what you can do next. Press the key directly beneath the menu label to access that function. Menu keys are represented with a shaded box in the keystrokes column. For example, $\boxed{\text{TIME}}$ displays the current date and time, and the other $\boxed{\text{TIME}}$ menu options.

II. An Important Starting Point

Purpose: Before each new calculation, clear the variables, and if need be, change the number of digits displayed, the number of payments per period, and the beginning or end mode.

Example: You want to display four numbers to the right of the decimal.

Keystrokes	Display	Explanation
$\boxed{\text{DSP}}$	Select display format.	Sets display to show four numbers to the right of the decimal
$\boxed{\text{FIX}}$ 4		
$\boxed{\text{INPUT}}$	0.0000	
$\boxed{\text{CLR}}$	0.0000	Clears display

Example: You can to display two payments per year to be paid at the end of each period.

Keystrokes	Display	Explanation
FIN TVM		Sets number of payments per year at 2 and timing of payment at the end of each period
OTHER		
2 P/YR		
END EXIT	2 P/YR END MODE	

III. Calculating Table Values for:

A. The compound sum of $1 (Appendix B)

Purpose: Compute the table values for Appendix B, the future value of $1.

Method: Solve for the future value of $1: $FVIF_{i,n} = \$1(1 + i)^n$

Example: What is the table value for the compound sum of $1 for 5 years at a 12 percent annual interest rate:

Keystrokes	Display	Explanation
FIN TVM		Displays TVM menu
OTHER		Sets 1 payment per year; END mode
1 P/YR		
END EXIT		
CLEAR DATA	1 P/YR	Clears TVM variables
1 +/− PV	PV = − 1.0000	Stores initial $1 as a negative present value. Otherwise the answer will appear as a negative
5 N	N = 5.0000	Stores number of periods
12 I% YR	I%YR = 12.0000	Stores interest rate
FV	FV = 1.7623	Table value

B. The present value of $1 (Appendix C)

Purpose: Compute the table values for Appendix C, the present value of $1.

Method: Solve for the present value of $1: $PVIF_{i,n} = \dfrac{\$1}{(1 + i)^n}$

Example: What is the table value for the present value of $1 for 8 years at a 10 percent annual interest rate?

Keystrokes	Display	Explanation
FIN TVM CLEAR DATA		Clears TVM variable; verifies the correct number of payments per year and the BEG or END mode
1 +/− FV	FV = − 1.0000	Stores future amount as negative value
8 N	N = 8.0000	Stores number of periods
10 I% YR	I%YR = 10.0000	Stores interest rate
FV	PV = 0.4665	Table value

C. The sum of an annuity of $1 for n periods (Appendix D)

Purpose: Compute the table values for Appendix D, the sum of an annuity of $1.

Method: Solve for the future value of an annuity of $1:

$$FVIFA_{i,n} = \$1 \sum_{t=0}^{n-1} (1 + i)^t$$

which may also be solved as $FVIFA_{i,n} = \dfrac{(1 + i)^n - 1}{i}$

Example: What is the table value for the compound sum of an annuity of $1 for 6 years at a 14 percent annual interest rate?

Keystrokes	Display	Explanation
FIN TVM ▢ CLEAR DATA		Clears TVM variable; verifies the correct number of payments per year and the BEG or END mode
1 +/− PMT	PMT = − 1.0000	Stores annual payment (annuity) as a negative number. Otherwise the answer will appear as a negative
6 N	N = 6.0000	Stores number of periods
14 I% YR	I%YR = 14.0000	Stores interest rate
FV	FV = 8.5355	Table value

D. The present value of an annuity of $1 for n periods (Appendix E)

Purpose: Compute the table values for Appendix E, the present value of an annuity of $1.

Method: Solve for the present value of an annuity of $1:

$$PVIFA_{i,n} = \sum_{i=1}^{n} \frac{\$1}{(1+i)^t}$$

which may also be solved as $PVIFA_{i,n} = \dfrac{1 - [1/(1 + i)^n]}{i}$

Example: What is the table for the present value of an annuity of $1 for 12 years at a 9 percent annual interest rate?

Keystrokes	Display	Explanation
FIN TVM ▢ CLEAR DATA		Clears TVM variable; and verifies the correct number of payments per year and the BEG or END mode
1 +/− PMT	PMT = − 1.0000	Stores annual payment (annuity) as a negative number. Otherwise the answer will appear as a negative
12 N	N = 12.0000	Stores number of periods
9 I% YR	I%YR = 9.0000	Stores interest rate
PV	PV = 7.1607	Table value

APPENDIX B. Compound Sum of $1

n	1%	2%	3%	4%	5%	6%	7%	8%	9%	10%
1	1.010	1.020	1.030	1.040	1.050	1.060	1.070	1.080	1.090	1.100
2	1.020	1.040	1.061	1.082	1.102	1.124	1.145	1.166	1.188	1.210
3	1.030	1.061	1.093	1.125	1.158	1.191	1.225	1.260	1.295	1.331
4	1.041	1.082	1.126	1.170	1.216	1.262	1.311	1.360	1.412	1.464
5	1.051	1.104	1.159	1.217	1.276	1.338	1.403	1.469	1.539	1.611
6	1.062	1.126	1.194	1.265	1.340	1.419	1.501	1.587	1.677	1.772
7	1.072	1.149	1.230	1.316	1.407	1.504	1.606	1.714	1.828	1.949
8	1.083	1.172	1.267	1.369	1.477	1.594	1.718	1.851	1.993	2.144
9	1.094	1.195	1.305	1.423	1.551	1.689	1.838	1.999	2.172	2.358
10	1.105	1.219	1.344	1.480	1.629	1.791	1.967	2.159	2.367	2.594
11	1.116	1.243	1.384	1.539	1.710	1.898	2.105	2.332	2.580	2.853
12	1.127	1.268	1.426	1.601	1.796	2.012	2.252	2.518	2.813	3.138
13	1.138	1.294	1.469	1.665	1.886	2.133	2.410	2.720	3.066	3.452
14	1.149	1.319	1.513	1.732	1.980	2.261	2.579	2.937	3.342	3.797
15	1.161	1.346	1.558	1.801	2.079	2.397	2.759	3.172	3.642	4.177
16	1.173	1.373	1.605	1.873	2.183	2.540	2.952	3.426	3.970	4.595
17	1.184	1.400	1.653	1.948	2.292	2.693	3.159	3.700	4.328	5.054
18	1.196	1.428	1.702	2.026	2.407	2.854	3.380	3.996	4.717	5.560
19	1.208	1.457	1.753	2.107	2.527	3.026	3.616	4.316	5.142	6.116
20	1.220	1.486	1.806	2.191	2.653	3.207	3.870	4.661	5.604	6.727
21	1.232	1.516	1.860	2.279	2.786	3.399	4.140	5.034	6.109	7.400
22	1.245	1.546	1.916	2.370	2.925	3.603	4.430	5.436	6.658	8.140
23	1.257	1.577	1.974	2.465	3.071	3.820	4.740	5.871	7.258	8.954
24	1.270	1.608	2.033	2.563	3.225	4.049	5.072	6.341	7.911	9.850
25	1.282	1.641	2.094	2.666	3.386	4.292	5.427	6.848	8.623	10.834
30	1.348	1.811	2.427	3.243	4.322	5.743	7.612	10.062	13.267	17.449
40	1.489	2.208	3.262	4.801	7.040	10.285	14.974	21.724	31.408	45.258
50	1.645	2.691	4.384	7.106	11.467	18.419	29.456	46.900	74.354	117.386

n	11%	12%	13%	14%	15%	16%	17%	18%	19%	20%
1	1.110	1.120	1.130	1.140	1.150	1.160	1.170	1.180	1.190	1.200
2	1.232	1.254	1.277	1.300	1.322	1.346	1.369	1.392	1.416	1.440
3	1.368	1.405	1.443	1.482	1.521	1.561	1.602	1.643	1.685	1.728
4	1.518	1.574	1.630	1.689	1.749	1.811	1.874	1.939	2.005	2.074
5	1.685	1.762	1.842	1.925	2.011	2.100	2.192	2.288	2.386	2.488
6	1.870	1.974	2.082	2.195	2.313	2.436	2.565	2.700	2.840	2.986
7	2.076	2.211	2.353	2.502	2.660	2.826	3.001	3.185	3.379	3.583
8	2.305	2.476	2.658	2.853	3.059	3.278	3.511	3.759	4.021	4.300
9	2.558	2.773	3.004	3.252	3.518	3.803	4.108	4.435	4.785	5.160
10	2.839	3.106	3.395	3.707	4.046	4.411	4.807	5.234	5.695	6.192
11	3.152	3.479	3.836	4.226	4.652	5.117	5.624	6.176	6.777	7.430
12	3.498	3.896	4.334	4.818	5.350	5.936	6.580	7.288	8.064	8.916
13	3.883	4.363	4.898	5.492	6.153	6.886	7.699	8.599	9.596	10.699
14	4.310	4.887	5.535	6.261	7.076	7.987	9.007	10.147	11.420	12.839
15	4.785	5.474	6.254	7.138	8.137	9.265	10.539	11.974	13.589	15.407
16	5.311	6.130	7.067	8.137	9.358	10.748	12.330	14.129	16.171	18.488
17	5.895	6.866	7.986	9.276	10.761	12.468	14.426	16.672	19.244	22.186
18	6.543	7.690	9.024	10.575	12.375	14.462	16.879	19.673	22.900	26.623
19	7.263	8.613	10.197	12.055	14.232	16.776	19.748	23.214	27.251	31.948
20	8.062	9.646	11.523	13.743	16.366	19.461	23.105	27.393	32.429	38.337
21	8.949	10.804	13.021	15.667	18.821	22.574	27.033	32.323	38.591	46.005
22	9.933	12.100	14.713	17.861	21.644	26.186	31.629	38.141	45.923	55.205
23	11.026	13.552	16.626	20.361	24.891	30.376	37.005	45.007	54.648	66.247
24	12.239	15.178	18.788	23.212	28.625	35.236	43.296	53.108	65.031	79.496
25	13.585	17.000	21.230	26.461	32.918	40.874	50.656	62.667	77.387	95.395
30	22.892	29.960	39.115	50.949	66.210	85.849	111.061	143.367	184.672	237.373
40	64.999	93.049	132.776	188.876	267.856	378.715	533.846	750.353	1051.642	1469.740
50	184.559	288.996	450.711	700.197	1083.619	1670.669	2566.080	3927.189	5988.730	9100.191

n	21%	22%	23%	24%	25%	26%	27%	28%	29%	30%
1	1.210	1.220	1.230	1.240	1.250	1.260	1.270	1.280	1.290	1.300
2	1.464	1.488	1.513	1.538	1.562	1.588	1.613	1.638	1.664	1.690
3	1.772	1.816	1.861	1.907	1.953	2.000	2.048	2.097	2.147	2.197
4	2.144	2.215	2.289	2.364	2.441	2.520	2.601	2.684	2.769	2.856
5	2.594	2.703	2.815	2.932	3.052	3.176	3.304	3.436	3.572	3.713
6	3.138	3.297	3.463	3.635	3.815	4.001	4.196	4.398	4.608	4.827
7	3.797	4.023	4.259	4.508	4.768	5.042	5.329	5.629	5.945	6.275
8	4.595	4.908	5.239	5.589	5.960	6.353	6.767	7.206	7.669	8.157
9	5.560	5.987	6.444	6.931	7.451	8.004	8.595	9.223	9.893	10.604
10	6.727	7.305	7.926	8.594	9.313	10.086	10.915	11.806	12.761	13.786
11	8.140	8.912	9.749	10.657	11.642	12.708	13.862	15.112	16.462	17.921
12	9.850	10.872	11.991	13.215	14.552	16.012	17.605	19.343	21.236	23.298
13	11.918	13.264	14.749	16.386	18.190	20.175	22.359	24.759	27.395	30.287
14	14.421	16.182	18.141	20.319	22.737	25.420	28.395	31.691	35.339	39.373
15	17.449	19.742	22.314	25.195	28.422	32.030	36.062	40.565	45.587	51.185
16	21.113	24.085	27.446	31.242	35.527	40.357	45.799	51.923	58.808	66.541
17	25.547	29.384	33.758	38.740	44.409	50.850	58.165	66.461	75.862	86.503
18	30.912	35.848	41.523	48.038	55.511	64.071	73.869	85.070	97.862	112.454
19	37.404	43.735	51.073	59.567	69.389	80.730	93.813	108.890	126.242	146.190
20	45.258	53.357	62.820	73.863	86.736	101.720	119.143	139.379	162.852	190.047
21	54.762	65.095	77.268	91.591	108.420	128.167	151.312	178.405	210.079	247.061
22	66.262	79.416	95.040	113.572	135.525	161.490	192.165	228.358	271.002	321.178
23	80.178	96.887	116.899	140.829	169.407	203.477	244.050	292.298	349.592	417.531
24	97.015	118.203	143.786	174.628	211.758	256.381	309.943	374.141	450.974	542.791
25	117.388	144.207	176.857	216.539	264.698	323.040	393.628	478.901	581.756	705.627
30	304.471	389.748	497.904	634.810	807.793	1025.904	1300.477	1645.488	2078.208	2619.936
40	2048.309	2846.941	3946.340	5455.797	7523.156	10346.879	14195.051	19426.418	26520.723	36117.754
50	13779.844	20795.680	31278.301	46889.207	70064.812	104354.562	154942.687	229345.875	338440.000	497910.125

n	31%	32%	33%	34%	35%	36%	37%	38%	39%	40%
1	1.310	1.320	1.330	1.340	1.350	1.360	1.370	1.380	1.390	1.400
2	1.716	1.742	1.769	1.796	1.822	1.850	1.877	1.904	1.932	1.960
3	2.248	2.300	2.353	2.406	2.460	2.515	2.571	2.628	2.686	2.744
4	2.945	3.036	3.129	3.224	3.321	3.421	3.523	3.627	3.733	3.842
5	3.858	4.007	4.162	4.320	4.484	4.653	4.826	5.005	5.189	5.378
6	5.054	5.290	5.535	5.789	6.053	6.328	6.612	6.907	7.213	7.530
7	6.621	6.983	7.361	7.758	8.172	8.605	9.058	9.531	10.025	10.541
8	8.673	9.217	9.791	10.395	11.032	11.703	12.410	13.153	13.935	14.758
9	11.362	12.166	13.022	13.930	14.894	15.917	17.001	18.151	19.370	20.661
10	14.884	16.060	17.319	18.666	20.106	21.646	23.292	25.049	26.924	28.925
11	19.498	21.199	23.034	25.012	27.144	29.439	31.910	34.567	37.425	40.495
12	25.542	27.982	30.635	33.516	36.644	40.037	43.716	47.703	52.020	56.694
13	33.460	36.937	40.745	44.912	49.469	54.451	59.892	65.830	72.308	79.371
14	43.832	49.756	54.190	60.181	66.784	74.053	82.051	90.845	100.509	111.19
15	57.420	64.358	72.073	80.643	90.158	100.712	112.410	125.366	139.707	155.567
16	75.220	84.953	95.857	108.061	121.713	136.968	154.002	173.005	194.192	217.793
17	98.539	112.138	127.490	144.802	164.312	186.277	210.983	238.747	269.927	304.911
18	129.086	148.022	169.561	194.035	221.822	253.337	289.046	329.471	375.198	426.875
19	169.102	195.389	225.517	260.006	299.459	344.537	395.993	454.669	521.525	597.625
20	221.523	257.913	299.937	348.408	404.270	468.571	542.511	627.443	724.919	836.674
21	290.196	340.446	398.916	466.867	545.764	637.256	743.240	865.871	1007.637	1171.343
22	380.156	449.388	530.558	625.601	736.781	865.668	1018.238	1194.900	1400.615	1639.878
23	498.004	593.192	705.642	838.305	994.653	1178.668	1394.986	1648.961	1946.854	2295.829
24	652.385	783.013	938.504	1123.328	1342.781	1602.988	1911.129	2275.564	2706.125	3214.158
25	854.623	1033.577	1248.210	1505.258	1812.754	2180.063	2618.245	3140.275	3761.511	4499.816
30	3297.081	4142.008	5194.516	6503.285	8128.426	10142.914	12636.086	15716.703	19517.969	24201.043
40	49072.621	66519.313	89962.188	121388.437	163433.875	219558.625	294317.937	393684.687	525508.312	700022.688

APPENDIX C.   Present Value of $1

n	1%	2%	3%	4%	5%	6%	7%	8%	9%	10%
1	.990	.980	.971	.962	.952	.943	.935	.926	.917	.909
2	.980	.961	.943	.925	.907	.890	.873	.857	.842	.826
3	.971	.942	.915	.889	.864	.840	.816	.794	.772	.751
4	.961	.924	.888	.855	.823	.792	.763	.735	.708	.683
5	.951	.906	.863	.822	.784	.747	.713	.681	.650	.621
6	.942	.888	.837	.790	.746	.705	.666	.630	.596	.564
7	.933	.871	.813	.760	.711	.665	.623	.583	.547	.513
8	.923	.853	.789	.731	.677	.627	.582	.540	.502	.467
9	.914	.837	.766	.703	.645	.592	.544	.500	.460	.424
10	.905	.820	.744	.676	.614	.558	.508	.463	.422	.386
11	.896	.804	.722	.650	.585	.527	.475	.429	.388	.350
12	.887	.789	.701	.625	.557	.497	.444	.397	.356	.319
13	.879	.773	.681	.601	.530	.469	.415	.368	.326	.290
14	.870	.758	.661	.577	.505	.442	.388	.340	.299	.263
15	.861	.743	.642	.555	.481	.417	.362	.315	.275	.239
16	.853	.728	.623	.534	.458	.394	.339	.292	.252	.218
17	.844	.714	.605	.513	.436	.371	.317	.270	.231	.198
18	.836	.700	.587	.494	.416	.350	.296	.250	.212	.180
19	.828	.686	.570	.475	.396	.331	.277	.232	.194	.164
20	.820	.673	.554	.456	.377	.312	.258	.215	.178	.149
21	.811	.660	.538	.439	.359	.294	.242	.199	.164	.135
22	.803	.647	.522	.422	.342	.278	.226	.184	.150	.123
23	.795	.634	.507	.406	.326	.262	.211	.170	.138	.112
24	.788	.622	.492	.390	.310	.247	.197	.158	.126	.102
25	.780	.610	.478	.375	.295	.233	.184	.146	.116	.092
30	.742	.552	.412	.308	.231	.174	.131	.099	.075	.057
40	.672	.453	.307	.208	.142	.097	.067	.046	.032	.022
50	.608	.372	.228	.141	.087	.054	.034	.021	.013	.009

n	11%	12%	13%	14%	15%	16%	17%	18%	19%	20%
1	.901	.893	.885	.877	.870	.862	.855	.847	.840	.833
2	.812	.797	.783	.769	.756	.743	.731	.718	.706	.694
3	.731	.712	.693	.675	.658	.641	.624	.609	.593	.579
4	.659	.636	.613	.592	.572	.552	.534	.516	.499	.482
5	.593	.567	.543	.519	.497	.476	.456	.437	.419	.402
6	.535	.507	.480	.456	.432	.410	.390	.370	.352	.335
7	.482	.452	.425	.400	.376	.354	.333	.314	.296	.279
8	.434	.404	.376	.351	.327	.305	.285	.266	.249	.233
9	.391	.361	.333	.308	.284	.263	.243	.225	.209	.194
10	.352	.322	.295	.270	.247	.227	.208	.191	.176	.162
11	.317	.287	.261	.237	.215	.195	.178	.162	.148	.135
12	.286	.257	.231	.208	.187	.168	.152	.137	.124	.112
13	.258	.229	.204	.182	.163	.145	.130	.116	.104	.093
14	.232	.205	.181	.160	.141	.125	.111	.099	.088	.078
15	.209	.183	.160	.140	.123	.108	.095	.084	.074	.065
16	.188	.163	.141	.123	.107	.093	.081	.071	.062	.054
17	.170	.146	.125	.108	.093	.080	.069	.060	.052	.045
18	.153	.130	.111	.095	.081	.069	.059	.051	.044	.038
19	.138	.116	.098	.083	.070	.060	.051	.043	.037	.031
20	.124	.104	.087	.073	.061	.051	.043	.037	.031	.026
21	.112	.093	.077	.064	.053	.044	.037	.031	.026	.022
22	.101	.083	.068	.056	.046	.038	.032	.026	.022	.018
23	.091	.074	.060	.049	.040	.033	.027	.022	.018	.015
24	.082	.066	.053	.043	.035	.028	.023	.019	.015	.013
25	.074	.059	.047	.038	.030	.024	.020	.016	.013	.010
30	.044	.033	.026	.020	.015	.012	.009	.007	.005	.004
40	.015	.011	.008	.005	.004	.003	.002	.001	.001	.001
50	.005	.003	.002	.001	.001	.001	.000	.000	.000	.000

n	21%	22%	23%	24%	25%	26%	27%	28%	29%	30%
1	.826	.820	.813	.806	.800	.794	.787	.781	.775	.769
2	.683	.672	.661	.650	.640	.630	.620	.610	.601	.592
3	.564	.551	.537	.524	.512	.500	.488	.477	.466	.455
4	.467	.451	.437	.423	.410	.397	.384	.373	.361	.350
5	.386	.370	.355	.341	.328	.315	.303	.291	.280	.269
6	.319	.303	.289	.275	.262	.250	.238	.227	.217	.207
7	.263	.249	.235	.222	.210	.198	.188	.178	.168	.159
8	.218	.204	.191	.179	.168	.157	.148	.139	.130	.123
9	.180	.167	.155	.144	.134	.125	.116	.108	.101	.094
10	.149	.137	.126	.116	.107	.099	.092	.085	.078	.073
11	.123	.112	.103	.094	.086	.079	.072	.066	.061	.056
12	.102	.092	.083	.076	.069	.062	.057	.052	.047	.043
13	.084	.075	.068	.061	.055	.050	.045	.040	.037	.033
14	.069	.062	.055	.049	.044	.039	.035	.032	.028	.025
15	.057	.051	.045	.040	.035	.031	.028	.025	.022	.020
16	.047	.042	.036	.032	.028	.025	.022	.019	.017	.015
17	.039	.034	.030	.026	.023	.020	.017	.015	.013	.012
18	.032	.028	.024	.021	.018	.016	.014	.012	.010	.009
19	.027	.023	.020	.017	.014	.012	.011	.009	.008	.007
20	.022	.019	.016	.014	.012	.010	.008	.007	.006	.005
21	.018	.015	.013	.011	.009	.008	.007	.006	.005	.004
22	.015	.013	.011	.009	.007	.006	.005	.004	.004	.003
23	.012	.010	.009	.007	.006	.005	.004	.003	.003	.002
24	.010	.008	.007	.006	.005	.004	.003	.003	.002	.002
25	.009	.007	.006	.005	.004	.003	.003	.002	.002	.001
30	.003	.003	.002	.002	.001	.001	.001	.001	.000	.000
40	.000	.000	.000	.000	.000	.000	.000	.000	.000	.000
50	.000	.000	.000	.000	.000	.000	.000	.000	.000	.000

n	31%	32%	33%	34%	35%	36%	37%	38%	39%	40%
1	.763	.758	.752	.746	.741	.735	.730	.725	.719	.714
2	.583	.574	.565	.557	.549	.541	.533	.525	.518	.510
3	.445	.435	.425	.416	.406	.398	.389	.381	.372	.364
4	.340	.329	.320	.310	.301	.292	.284	.276	.268	.260
5	.259	.250	.240	.231	.223	.215	.207	.200	.193	.186
6	.198	.189	.181	.173	.165	.158	.151	.145	.139	.133
7	.151	.143	.136	.129	.122	.116	.110	.105	.100	.095
8	.115	.108	.102	.096	.091	.085	.081	.076	.072	.068
9	.088	.082	.077	.072	.067	.063	.059	.055	.052	.048
10	.067	.062	.058	.054	.050	.046	.043	.040	.037	.035
11	.051	.047	.043	.040	.037	.034	.031	.029	.027	.025
12	.039	.036	.033	.030	.027	.025	.023	.021	.019	.018
13	.030	.027	.025	.022	.020	.018	.017	.015	.014	.013
14	.023	.021	.018	.017	.015	.014	.012	.011	.010	.009
15	.017	.016	.014	.012	.011	.010	.009	.008	.007	.006
16	.013	.012	.010	.009	.008	.007	.006	.006	.005	.005
17	.010	.009	.008	.007	.006	.005	.005	.004	.004	.003
18	.008	.007	.006	.005	.005	.004	.003	.003	.003	.002
19	.006	.005	.004	.004	.003	.003	.003	.002	.002	.002
20	.005	.004	.003	.003	.002	.002	.002	.002	.001	.001
21	.003	.003	.003	.002	.002	.002	.001	.001	.001	.001
22	.003	.002	.002	.002	.001	.001	.001	.001	.001	.001
23	.002	.002	.001	.001	.001	.001	.001	.001	.001	.000
24	.002	.001	.001	.001	.001	.001	.001	.001	.000	.000
25	.001	.001	.001	.001	.001	.000	.000	.000	.000	.000
30	.000	.000	.000	.000	.000	.000	.000	.000	.000	.000
40	.000	.000	.000	.000	.000	.000	.000	.000	.000	.000

APPENDIX D. Sum of an Annuity of $1 for *n* Periods

n	1%	2%	3%	4%	5%	6%	7%	8%	9%	10%
1	1.000	1.000	1.000	1.000	1.000	1.000	1.000	1.000	1.000	1.000
2	2.010	2.020	2.030	2.040	2.050	2.060	2.070	2.080	2.090	2.100
3	3.030	3.060	3.091	3.122	3.152	3.184	3.215	3.246	3.278	3.310
4	4.060	4.122	4.184	4.246	4.310	4.375	4.440	4.506	4.573	4.641
5	5.101	5.204	5.309	5.416	5.526	5.637	5.751	5.867	5.985	6.105
6	6.152	6.308	6.468	6.633	6.802	6.975	7.153	7.336	7.523	7.716
7	7.214	7.434	7.662	7.898	8.142	8.394	8.654	8.923	9.200	9.487
8	8.286	8.583	8.892	9.214	9.549	9.897	10.260	10.637	11.028	11.436
9	9.368	9.755	10.159	10.583	11.027	11.491	11.978	12.488	13.021	13.579
10	10.462	10.950	11.464	12.006	12.578	13.181	13.816	14.487	15.193	15.937
11	11.567	12.169	12.808	13.486	14.207	14.972	15.784	16.645	17.560	18.531
12	12.682	13.412	14.192	15.026	15.917	16.870	17.888	18.977	20.141	21.384
13	13.809	14.680	15.618	16.627	17.713	18.882	20.141	21.495	22.953	24.523
14	14.947	15.974	17.086	18.292	19.598	21.015	22.550	24.215	26.019	27.975
15	16.097	17.293	18.599	20.023	21.578	23.276	25.129	27.152	29.361	31.772
16	17.258	18.639	20.157	21.824	23.657	25.672	27.888	30.324	33.003	35.949
17	18.430	20.012	21.761	23.697	25.840	28.213	30.840	33.750	36.973	40.544
18	19.614	21.412	23.414	25.645	28.132	30.905	33.999	37.450	41.301	45.599
19	20.811	22.840	25.117	27.671	30.539	33.760	37.379	41.446	46.018	51.158
20	22.019	24.297	26.870	29.778	33.066	36.785	40.995	45.762	51.159	57.274
21	23.239	25.783	28.676	31.969	35.719	39.992	44.865	50.422	56.764	64.002
22	24.471	27.299	30.536	34.248	38.505	43.392	49.005	55.456	62.872	71.402
23	25.716	28.845	32.452	36.618	41.430	46.995	53.435	60.893	69.531	79.542
24	26.973	30.421	34.426	39.082	44.501	50.815	58.176	66.764	76.789	88.496
25	28.243	32.030	36.459	41.645	47.726	54.864	63.248	73.105	84.699	98.346
30	34.784	40.567	47.575	56.084	66.438	79.057	94.459	113.282	136.305	164.491
40	48.885	60.401	75.400	95.024	120.797	154.758	199.630	295.052	337.872	442.580
50	64.461	84.577	112.794	152.664	209.341	290.325	406.516	573.756	815.051	1163.865

n	11%	12%	13%	14%	15%	16%	17%	18%	19%	20%
1	1.000	1.000	1.000	1.000	1.000	1.000	1.000	1.000	1.000	1.000
2	2.110	2.120	2.130	2.140	2.150	2.160	2.170	2.180	2.190	2.200
3	3.342	3.374	3.407	3.440	3.472	3.506	3.539	3.572	3.606	3.640
4	4.710	4.779	4.850	4.921	4.993	5.066	5.141	5.215	5.291	5.368
5	6.228	6.353	6.480	6.610	6.742	6.877	7.014	7.154	7.297	7.442
6	7.913	8.115	8.323	8.535	8.754	8.977	9.207	9.442	9.683	9.930
7	9.783	10.089	10.405	10.730	11.067	11.414	11.772	12.141	12.523	12.916
8	11.859	12.300	12.757	13.233	13.727	14.240	14.773	15.327	15.902	16.499
9	14.164	14.776	15.416	16.085	16.786	17.518	18.285	19.086	19.923	20.799
10	16.722	17.549	18.420	19.337	20.304	21.321	22.393	23.521	24.709	25.959
11	19.561	20.655	21.814	23.044	24.349	25.733	27.200	28.755	30.403	32.150
12	22.713	24.133	25.650	27.271	29.001	30.850	32.824	34.931	37.180	39.580
13	26.211	28.029	29.984	32.088	34.352	36.786	39.404	42.218	45.244	48.496
14	30.095	32.392	34.882	37.581	40.504	43.672	47.102	50.818	54.841	59.196
15	34.405	37.280	40.417	43.842	47.580	51.659	56.109	60.965	66.260	72.035
16	39.190	42.753	46.671	50.980	55.717	60.925	66.648	72.938	79.850	87.442
17	44.500	48.883	53.738	59.117	65.075	71.673	78.978	87.067	96.021	105.930
18	50.396	55.749	61.724	68.393	75.836	84.140	93.404	103.739	115.265	128.116
19	56.939	63.439	70.748	78.968	88.211	98.603	110.283	123.412	138.165	154.739
20	64.202	72.052	80.946	91.024	102.443	115.379	130.031	146.626	165.417	186.687
21	72.264	81.698	92.468	104.767	118.809	134.840	153.136	174.019	197.846	225.024
22	81.213	92.502	105.489	120.434	137.630	157.414	180.169	206.342	236.436	271.028
23	91.147	104.602	120.203	138.295	159.274	183.600	211.798	244.483	282.359	326.234
24	102.173	118.154	136.829	158.656	184.166	213.976	248.803	289.490	337.007	392.480
25	114.412	133.333	155.616	181.867	212.790	249.212	292.099	342.598	402.038	471.976
30	199.018	241.330	293.192	356.778	434.738	530.306	647.423	790.932	966.698	1181.865
40	581.812	767.080	1013.667	1341.979	1779.048	2360.724	3134.412	4163.094	5529.711	7343.715
50	1668.723	2399.975	3459.344	4994.301	7217.488	10435.449	15088.805	21812.273	31514.492	45496.094

APPENDIX D. Sum of an Annuity of $1 for *n* Periods *(continued)*

n	21%	22%	23%	24%	25%	26%	27%	28%	29%	30%
1	1.000	1.000	1.000	1.000	1.000	1.000	1.000	1.000	1.000	1.000
2	2.210	2.220	2.230	2.240	2.250	2.260	2.270	2.280	2.290	2.300
3	3.674	3.708	3.743	3.778	3.813	3.848	3.883	3.918	3.954	3.990
4	5.446	5.524	5.604	5.684	5.766	5.848	5.931	6.016	6.101	6.187
5	7.589	7.740	7.893	8.048	8.207	8.368	8.533	8.700	8.870	9.043
6	10.183	10.442	10.708	10.980	11.259	11.544	11.837	12.136	12.442	12.756
7	13.321	13.740	14.171	14.615	15.073	15.546	16.032	16.534	17.051	17.583
8	17.119	17.762	18.430	19.123	19.842	20.588	21.361	22.163	22.995	23.858
9	21.714	22.670	23.669	24.712	25.802	26.940	28.129	29.369	30.664	32.015
10	27.274	28.657	20.113	31.643	33.253	34.945	36.723	38.592	40.556	42.619
11	34.001	35.962	38.039	40.238	42.566	45.030	47.639	50.398	53.318	56.405
12	42.141	44.873	47.787	50.895	54.208	57.738	61.501	65.510	69.780	74.326
13	51.991	55.745	59.778	64.109	68.760	73.750	79.106	84.853	91.016	97.624
14	63.909	69.009	74.528	80.496	86.949	93.925	101.465	109.611	118.411	127.912
15	78.330	85.191	92.669	100.815	109.687	119.346	129.860	141.302	153.750	167.285
16	95.779	104.933	114.983	126.010	138.109	151.375	165.922	181.867	199.337	218.470
17	116.892	129.019	142.428	157.252	173.636	191.733	211.721	233.790	258.145	285.011
18	142.439	158.403	176.187	195.993	218.045	242.583	269.885	300.250	334.006	371.514
19	173.351	194.251	217.710	244.031	273.556	306.654	343.754	385.321	431.868	483.968
20	210.755	237.986	268.783	303.598	342.945	387.384	437.568	494.210	558.110	630.157
21	256.013	291.343	331.603	377.461	429.681	489.104	556.710	633.589	720.962	820.204
22	310.775	356.438	408.871	469.052	538.101	617.270	708.022	811.993	931.040	1067.265
23	377.038	435.854	503.911	582.624	673.626	778.760	990.187	1040.351	1202.042	1388.443
24	457.215	532.741	620.810	723.453	843.032	982.237	1144.237	1332.649	1551.634	1805.975
25	554.230	650.944	764.596	898.082	1054.791	1238.617	1454.180	1706.790	2002.608	2348.765
30	1445.111	1767.044	2160.459	2640.881	3227.172	3941.953	4812.891	5873.172	7162.785	8729.805
40	9749.141	12936.141	17153.691	22728.367	30088.621	39791.957	52570.707	69376.562	91447.375	120389.375

n	31%	32%	33%	34%	35%	36%	37%	38%	39%	40%
1	1.000	1.000	1.000	1.000	1.000	1.000	1.000	1.000	1.000	1.000
2	2.310	2.320	2.330	2.340	2.350	2.360	2.370	2.380	2.390	2.400
3	4.026	4.062	4.099	4.136	4.172	4.210	4.247	4.284	4.322	4.360
4	6.274	6.362	6.452	6.542	6.633	6.725	6.818	6.912	7.008	7.104
5	9.219	9.398	9.581	9.766	9.954	10.146	10.341	10.539	10.741	10.946
6	13.077	13.406	13.742	14.086	14.438	14.799	15.167	15.544	15.930	16.324
7	18.131	18.696	19.277	19.876	20.492	21.126	21.779	22.451	23.142	23.853
8	24.752	25.678	26.638	27.633	28.664	29.732	30.837	31.982	33.167	34.395
9	33.425	34.895	36.429	38.028	39.696	41.435	43.247	45.135	47.103	49.152
10	44.786	47.062	49.451	51.958	54.590	57.351	60.248	63.287	66.473	69.813
11	59.670	63.121	66.769	70.624	74.696	78.998	83.540	88.335	93.397	98.739
12	79.167	84.320	89.803	95.636	101.840	108.437	115.450	122.903	130.822	139.234
13	104.709	112.302	120.438	129.152	138.484	148.474	159.166	170.606	182.842	195.928
14	138.169	149.239	161.183	174.063	187.953	202.925	219.058	236.435	255.151	275.299
15	182.001	197.996	215.373	234.245	254.737	276.978	301.109	327.281	355.659	386.418
16	239.421	262.354	287.446	314.888	344.895	377.690	413.520	452.647	495.366	541.985
17	314.642	347.307	383.303	422.949	466.608	514.658	567.521	625.652	689.558	759.778
18	413.180	459.445	510.792	567.751	630.920	700.935	778.504	864.399	959.485	1064.689
19	542.266	607.467	680.354	761.786	852.741	954.271	1067.551	1193.870	1334.683	1491.563
20	711.368	802.856	905.870	1021.792	1152.200	1298.809	1463.544	1648.539	1856.208	2089.188
21	932.891	1060.769	1205.807	1370.201	1556.470	1767.380	2006.055	2275.982	2581.128	2925.862
22	1223.087	1401.215	1604.724	1837.068	2102.234	2404.636	2749.294	3141.852	3588.765	4097.203
23	1603.243	1850.603	2135.282	2462.669	2839.014	3271.304	3767.532	4336.750	4989.379	5737.078
24	2101.247	2443.795	2840.924	3300.974	3833.667	4449.969	5162.516	5985.711	6936.230	8032.906
25	2753.631	3226.808	3779.428	4424.301	5176.445	6052.957	7073.645	8261.273	9642.352	11247.062
30	10632.543	12940.672	15737.945	19124.434	23221.258	28172.016	34148.906	41357.227	50043.625	60500.207

APPENDIX E. Present Value of an Annuity of $1 for *n* Periods

n	1%	2%	3%	4%	5%	6%	7%	8%	9%	10%
1	.990	.980	.971	.962	.952	.943	.935	.926	.917	.909
2	1.970	1.942	1.913	1.886	1.859	1.833	1.808	1.3783	1.759	1.736
3	2.941	2.884	2.829	2.775	2.723	2.673	2.624	2.577	2.531	2.487
4	3.902	3.808	3.717	3.630	3.546	3.465	3.387	3.312	3.240	3.170
5	4.853	4.713	4.580	4.452	4.329	4.212	4.100	3.993	3.890	3.791
6	5.795	5.601	5.417	5.242	5.076	4.917	4.767	4.623	4.486	4.355
7	6.728	6.472	6.230	6.002	5.786	5.582	5.389	5.206	5.033	4.868
8	7.652	7.326	7.020	6.733	6.463	6.210	5.971	5.747	5.535	5.335
9	8.566	8.162	7.786	7.435	7.108	6.802	6.515	6.247	5.995	5.759
10	9.471	8.983	8.530	8.111	7.722	7.360	7.024	6.710	6.418	6.145
11	10.368	9.787	9.253	8.760	8.306	7.887	7.499	7.139	6.805	6.495
12	11.255	10.575	9.954	9.385	8.863	8.384	7.943	7.536	7.161	6.814
13	12.134	11.348	10.635	9.986	9.394	8.853	8.358	7.904	7.487	7.103
14	13.004	12.106	11.296	10.563	9.899	9.295	8.746	8.244	7.786	7.367
15	13.865	12.849	11.938	11.118	10.380	9.712	9.108	8.560	8.061	7.606
16	14.718	13.578	12.561	11.652	10.838	10.106	9.447	8.851	8.313	7.824
17	15.562	14.292	13.166	12.166	11.274	10.477	9.763	9.122	8.544	8.022
18	16.398	14.992	13.754	12.659	11.690	10.828	10.059	9.372	8.756	8.201
19	17.226	15.679	14.324	13.134	12.085	11.158	10.336	9.604	8.950	8.365
20	18.046	16.352	14.878	13.590	12.462	11.470	10.594	9.818	9.129	8.514
21	18.857	17.011	15.415	14.029	12.821	11.764	10.836	10.017	9.292	8.649
22	19.661	17.658	15.937	14.451	13.163	12.042	11.061	10.201	9.442	8.772
23	20.456	18.292	16.444	14.857	13.489	12.303	11.272	10.371	9.580	8.883
24	21.244	18.914	16.936	15.247	13.799	12.550	11.469	10.529	9.707	8.985
25	22.023	19.524	17.413	15.622	14.094	12.783	11.654	10.675	9.823	9.077
30	25.808	22.397	19.601	17.292	15.373	13.765	12.409	11.258	10.274	9.427
40	32.835	27.356	23.115	19.793	17.159	15.046	13.332	11.925	10.757	9.779
50	39.197	31.424	25.730	21.482	18.256	15.762	13.801	12.234	10.962	9.915

n	11%	12%	13%	14%	15%	16%	17%	18%	19%	20%
1	.901	.893	.885	.877	.870	.862	.855	.847	.840	.833
2	1.713	1.690	1.668	1.647	1.626	1.605	1.585	1.566	1.547	1.528
3	2.444	2.402	2.361	2.322	2.283	2.246	2.210	2.174	2.140	2.106
4	3.102	3.037	2.974	2.914	2.855	2.798	2.743	2.690	2.639	2.589
5	3.696	3.605	3.517	3.433	3.352	3.274	3.199	3.127	3.058	2.991
6	4.231	4.111	3.998	3.889	3.784	3.685	3.589	3.498	3.410	3.326
7	4.712	4.564	4.423	4.288	4.160	4.039	3.922	3.812	3.706	3.605
8	5.146	4.968	4.799	4.639	4.487	4.344	4.207	4.078	3.954	3.837
9	5.537	5.328	5.132	4.946	4.772	4.607	4.451	4.303	4.163	4.031
10	5.889	5.650	5.246	5.216	5.019	4.833	4.659	4.494	4.339	4.192
11	6.207	5.938	5.687	5.453	5.234	5.029	4.836	4.656	4.487	4.327
12	6.492	6.194	5.918	5.660	5.421	5.197	4.988	4.793	4.611	4.439
13	6.750	6.424	6.122	5.842	5.583	5.342	5.118	4.910	4.715	4.533
14	6.982	6.628	6.303	6.002	5.724	5.468	5.229	5.008	4.802	4.611
15	7.191	6.811	6.462	6.142	5.847	5.575	5.324	5.092	4.876	4.675
16	7.379	6.974	6.604	6.265	5.954	5.669	5.405	5.162	4.938	4.730
17	7.549	7.120	6.729	6.373	6.047	5.749	5.475	5.222	4.990	4.775
18	7.702	7.250	6.840	6.467	6.128	5.818	5.534	5.273	5.033	4.812
19	7.839	7.366	6.938	6.550	6.198	5.877	5.585	5.316	5.070	4.843
20	7.963	7.469	7.025	6.623	6.259	5.929	5.628	5.353	5.101	4.870
21	8.075	7.562	7.102	6.687	6.312	5.973	5.665	5.384	5.127	4.891
22	8.176	7.645	7.170	6.743	6.359	6.011	5.696	5.410	5.149	4.909
23	8.266	7.718	7.230	6.792	6.399	6.044	5.723	5.432	5.167	4.925
24	8.348	7.784	7.283	6.835	6.434	6.073	5.747	5.451	5.182	4.937
25	8.422	7.843	7.330	6.873	6.464	6.097	5.766	5.467	5.195	4.948
30	8.694	8.055	7.496	7.003	6.566	6.177	5.829	5.517	5.235	4.979
40	8.951	8.244	7.634	7.105	6.642	6.233	5.871	5.548	5.258	4.997
50	9.042	8.305	7.675	7.133	6.661	6.246	5.880	5.554	5.262	4.999

APPENDIX E. Present Value of an Annuity of $1 for *n* Periods (*continued*)

n	21%	22%	23%	24%	25%	26%	27%	28%	29%	30%
1	.826	.820	.813	.806	.800	.794	.787	.781	.775	.769
2	1.509	1.492	1.474	1.457	1.440	1.424	1.407	1.392	1.376	1.361
3	2.074	2.042	2.011	1.981	1.952	1.923	1.896	1.868	1.842	1.816
4	2.540	2.494	2.448	2.404	2.362	2.320	2.280	2.241	2.203	2.166
5	2.926	2.864	2.803	2.745	2.689	2.635	2.583	2.532	2.483	2.436
6	3.245	3.167	3.092	3.020	2.951	2.885	2.821	2.759	2.700	2.643
7	3.508	3.416	3.327	3.242	3.161	3.083	3.009	2.937	2.868	2.802
8	3.726	3.619	3.518	3.421	3.329	3.241	3.156	3.076	2.999	2.925
9	3.905	3.786	3.673	3.566	3.463	3.366	3.273	3.184	3.100	3.019
10	4.054	3.923	3.799	3.682	3.570	3.465	3.364	3.269	3.178	3.092
11	4.177	4.035	3.902	3.776	3.656	3.544	3.437	3.335	3.329	3.147
12	4.278	4.127	3.985	3.851	3.725	3.606	3.493	3.387	3.286	3.190
13	4.362	4.203	4.053	3.912	3.780	3.656	3.538	3.427	3.322	3.223
14	4.432	4.265	4.108	3.962	3.824	3.695	3.573	3.459	3.351	3.249
15	4.489	4.315	4.153	4.001	3.859	3.726	3.601	3.483	3.373	3.268
16	4.536	4.357	4.189	4.003	3.887	3.751	3.623	3.503	3.390	3.283
17	4.576	4.391	4.219	4.059	3.910	3.771	3.640	3.518	3.403	3.295
18	4.608	4.419	4.243	4.080	3.928	3.786	3.654	3.529	3.413	3.304
19	4.635	4.442	4.263	4.097	3.942	3.799	3.664	3.539	3.421	3.311
20	4.657	4.460	4.279	4.110	3.954	3.808	3.673	3.546	3.427	3.316
21	4.675	4.476	4.292	4.121	3.963	3.816	3.679	3.551	3.432	3.320
22	4.690	4.488	4.302	4.130	3.970	3.822	3.684	3.556	3.436	3.323
23	4.703	4.499	4.311	4.137	3.976	3.827	3.689	3.559	3.438	3.325
24	4.713	4.507	4.318	4.143	3.981	3.831	3.692	3.562	3.441	3.327
25	4.721	4.514	4.323	4.147	3.985	3.834	3.694	3.564	3.442	3.329
30	4.746	4.534	4.339	4.160	3.995	3.842	3.701	3.569	3.447	3.332
40	4.760	4.544	4.347	4.166	3.999	3.846	3.703	3.571	3.448	3.333
50	4.762	4.545	4.348	4.167	4.000	3.846	3.704	3.571	3.448	3.333

n	31%	32%	33%	34%	35%	36%	37%	38%	39%	40%
1	.763	.758	.752	.746	.741	.735	.730	.725	.719	.714
2	1.346	1.331	1.317	1.303	1.289	1.276	1.263	1.250	1.237	1.224
3	1.791	1.766	1.742	1.719	1.696	1.673	1.652	1.630	1.609	1.589
4	2.130	2.096	2.062	2.029	1.997	1.966	1.935	1.906	1.877	1.849
5	2.390	2.345	2.302	2.260	2.220	2.181	2.143	2.106	2.070	2.035
6	2.588	2.534	2.483	2.433	2.385	2.339	2.294	2.251	2.209	2.168
7	2.739	2.677	2.619	2.562	2.508	2.455	2.404	2.355	2.308	2.263
8	2.854	2.786	2.721	2.658	2.598	2.540	2.485	2.432	2.380	2.331
9	2.942	2.868	2.798	2.730	2.665	2.603	2.544	2.487	2.432	2.379
10	3.009	2.930	2.855	2.784	2.715	2.649	2.587	2.527	2.469	2.414
11	3.060	2.978	2.899	2.824	2.752	2.683	2.618	2.555	2.496	2.438
12	3.100	3.013	2.931	2.853	2.779	2.708	2.641	2.576	2.515	2.456
13	3.129	3.040	2.956	2.876	2.799	2.727	2.658	2.592	2.529	2.469
14	3.152	3.061	2.974	2.892	2.814	2.740	2.670	2.603	2.539	2.477
15	3.170	3.076	2.988	2.905	2.825	2.750	2.679	2.611	2.546	2.484
16	3.183	3.088	2.999	2.914	2.834	2.757	2.685	2.616	2.551	2.489
17	3.193	3.097	3.007	2.921	2.840	2.763	2.690	2.621	2.555	2.492
18	3.201	3.104	3.012	2.926	2.844	2.767	2.693	2.624	2.557	2.494
19	3.207	3.109	3.017	2.930	2.848	2.770	2.696	2.626	2.559	2.496
20	3.211	3.113	3.020	2.933	2.850	2.772	2.698	2.627	2.561	2.497
21	3.215	3.116	3.023	2.935	2.852	2.773	2.699	2.629	2.562	2.498
22	3.217	3.118	3.025	2.936	2.853	2.775	2.700	2.629	2.562	2.498
23	3.219	3.120	3.026	2.938	2.854	2.775	2.701	2.630	2.563	2.499
24	3.221	3.121	3.027	2.939	2.855	2.776	2.701	2.630	2.563	2.499
25	3.222	3.122	3.028	2.939	2.856	2.776	2.702	2.631	2.563	2.499
30	3.225	2.124	3.030	2.941	2.857	2.777	2.702	2.631	2.564	2.500
40	3.226	2.125	3.030	2.941	2.857	2.778	2.703	2.632	2.564	2.500
50	3.226	2.125	3.030	2.941	2.857	2.778	2.703	2.632	2.564	2.500

APPENDIX F
Check Figures for Selected End-of-Chapter Problems

CHAPTER 1

1-1. Taxable income = $526,800
Tax liability = $179,112

1-3. Taxable income = $365,000
Tax liability = $124,100

1-5. Taxable income = ($38,000)
Tax liability = $0

1-7. Taxable income = $153,600
Tax liability = $43,154

1-9. Taxable income = $370,000
Tax liability = $125,800

1-11. Taxable income = $1,813,000
Tax liability = $616,420

1-13.

1987 $ 6,000 pay	1991 $10,000 pay
1988 $ 6,000 refund	1992 $19,450 refund
1989 $ 1,500 pay	1993 $ 7,500 pay
1990 $ 15,450 pay	1994 $ 11,250 refund

CHAPTER 2

2-1. 11.28%

2-3. 12.35%

2-4. a. The logic here is based on the expectations theory of the term structure of interest rates.

CHAPTER 3

3-1. $500,000

3-3. a. Total Assets Turnover = 2.
b. Sales = $17.5m; Percentage increase = 75%.
c. For last year, OIROI = 20%. Projected OIROI = 35%.

3-5.

RATIO	1994
Current Ratio	4.0x
Acid-test (Quick) Ratio	1.92x
Average Collection Period	107 days
Inventory Turnover	1.36x
Operating Income Return on Investment	13.8%
Operating Profit Margin	24.8%
Total Asset Turnover	.56x

Inventory Turnover	1.36x
Fixed Asset Turnover	1.04x
Debt Ratio	34.6%
Times Interest Earned	5.63x
Return on common equity	10.5%.

3-7. a.

Cash inflows from customers	$199,500
Cash paid to suppliers	$85,500
Other operating cash outflows and interest payments	$24,500
Cash tax payments	$2,500
Total cash flows from operations	$87,000
Purchase of fixed assets	($142,500)
Issue of preferred stock	$231,000
Mortgages payable reduced	($150,000)
Payment of dividend	($18,000)
Net change in cash	$7,500

Adjustments to Reconcile Net Income

Depreciation	$34,500
Amortization of patents	$9,000
Decrease in accounts receivable	$12,000
Decrease in inventory	$3,000
Increase in prepaid expenses	($1,500)
Decrease in accounts payable	($12,000)
Increase in taxes payable	$7,500

3-9. a.

Total Asset Turnover	= 2.25
Operating Profit Margin	= 11.11%
Operating Income Return on Investment	= 25%

b.

Operating Income Return on Investment	= 19.5%

c. Return on common equity

Post-renovation analysis:	= 14.5%
Pre-renovation analysis:	= 20%

3-11. a.

Current Ratio	= 1.84
Acid-Test Ratio	= .72
Debt Ratio	= .55
Times Interest Earned	= 8
Inventory Turnover	= 5.48
Fixed Asset Turnover	= 2.22
Return on equity	= 23.4%

c. Net Cash from Operating
Activities $57,000
Net Cash from Investing
Activities   ($14,200)
Net Cash from Financing
Activities   ($43,800)
Net Decrease in Cash $1,000

CHAPTER 4

4-1. Total Assets = $1.8 million
4-3. Total Assets = $2 million
Fixed Assets = $800,000
Inventories = $1 million
4-5. Cash   NO
Marketable Securities   NO
Accounts Payable   YES
Notes Payable   NO
Plant and Equipment   NO
Inventories   YES
4-7. **a.** Notes Payable $1.11 million
b. Current Ratio (before) = 2 times
Current Ratio (after) = 1.12 times
4-9.
Cumulative Borrowing

Jan	Feb	March	April	May	June	July
0	0	$52,100	$96,721	$52,688	0	0

CHAPTER 5

5-1. **a.** $12,970
c. $3,019.40
5-2. **a.** n = 15 years
5-3. **b.** 5%
c. 9%
5-4. **b.** PV = $235.20
5-5. **a.** $6,289
c. $302.89
5-6. **c.** $1,562.96
5-7. **a.** FV_1 = $10,600
FV_5 = $13,380
FV_{15} = $23,970
5-9. **a.** $6,690
b. Semiannual: $6,720
Bimonthly: $6,740
5-11. Year 1: 18,000 books
Year 2: 21,600 books
Year 3: 25,920 books
5-13. $6,108.11
5-15. 8%
5-17. $658,197.85

5-21. **b.** $8,333.33
5-22. $824.36
5-26. $6,509
5-28. 22%
5-29. $6,934.81
5-32. **a.** $1,989.73
5-35. $15,912
5-37. 36.47%

CHAPTER 6

6-1. $752.52
6-3. 4.8%
6-5. 5.29%
6-7. **a.** $863.78
b. Market Value $707.63 when required
rate of return is 15%
Market Value $1,171.19 when required
rate of return is 8%

CHAPTER 7

7-1. $116.67
7-3. **a.** 8.5%
b. $42.50
7-5. **a.** 18.9%
b. $28.57
7-7. 7.2%
7-9. $39.96
7-11. **a.** 10.91%
b. $36
7-13. **a.** Bond: $938.46
Preferred Stock: $86.67
Common Stock: Growth Rate (g) = 7%;
Value = $16.46

CHAPTER 8

8-1. $\bar{k}$ = 9.1% σ^2 = 9.39% σ = 3.06%
8-3. A: $\bar{k}$ = 16.7%; σ^2 = 102.5%; σ = 10.12%
B: $\bar{k}$ = 9.2%; σ^2 = 12.76%; σ = 3.57%
8-5. The beta is approximately 0.5.
8-7. 10.56%
8-9. Asman: For time = 2, 20%; Salinas: for
time = 3, 14.29%
8-11. **a.** 15.8%
b. 0.95

CHAPTER 9

9-1. **a.** IRR=7%
b. IRR=17%
9-3. **a.** IRR=approximately 19%

9-5. a. payback period = 4 years
discounted payback period = 5.37 years

9-7. a. Project A:
payback period = 2.5 years
discounted payback period = 3.84 years

9-11. a. $NPV_A = \$136.30$
$NPV_B = \$455.$
b. $PI_A = 1.2726$
$PI_B = 1.09$
c. $IRR_A = 40\%$
$IRR_B = 20\%$

9-13. a. Payback A = 1.589 years
Payback B = 3.019 years
b. $NPV_A = \$8,743$
$NPV_B = \$11,615$
c. $IRR_A = 40\%$
$IRR_B = 30\%$

CHAPTER 10

10-1. a. $6,800
b. $3,400
c. No taxes
d. $1,020

10-3. a. 2.75 years
b. $10,628.16

10-5. a. $560,000
b. Cash flow after tax: $116,170

10-7. a. $40,100
e. 2.37 years

10-10. NPV = –$330

CHAPTER 11

11-1. a. $k_d(1-t) = 6.53\%$
b. $k_{nc} = 14.37\%$
c. $k_c = 15.14\%$
d. $k_p = 8.77\%$
e. $k_d(1-t) = 7.92\%$

11-3. a. $k_d(1-t) = 5.28\%$
b. $k_{nc} = 9.85\%$
c. $k_d(1-t) = 7.63\%$
d. $k_p = 8.24\%$
e. $k_c = 11.90\%$

11-5. $k_d(1-t) = 7.23\%$
11-7. $k_d(1-t) = 8.48\%$

11-9. $k_c = 18.74\%$

11-11. a. $V_b = \$1,320.52$
b. $NP_0 = \$1,181.87$
c. 423 bonds
d. $k_d(1-t) = 7.21\%$

11-13. $k_o = 15.07\%$

11-17. *Breaks in Weighted Marginal Cost Curve*
Debt $750,000
Preferred $625,000; $1,250,000
Common $1,000,000
Weighted Cost of Capital
$0 - $625,000   10.88%
$625,001 - $750,000   10.96%
$750,001 - $1,000,000   11.56%

11-19. Cost of debt 5.28%; 5.94%; 6.93%
Cost of preferred 10.625%; 11.333%
Cost of common 13.16%; 13.90%; 14.20%
Weighted Cost of Capital
$0 – $250,000   10.543%
$250,001 – $500,000   10.987%
$500,001 – $625,000   11.185%

CHAPTER 12

12-1. a. 1.67 times
b. 1.11 times
c. 1.85 times
d. $18,326,693.23
e. (25%) (1.85) = 46.25%

12-3. a. F = $780,000
b. $S_B = \$1,560,000$

12-5. a. P = $6.875 (selling price per unit)

12-6. a. 1,200 units
b. $600,000
c. 1.316 times
d. 26.32%

12-9. a. EBIT = $2,000,000
b. EPS will be $1.00 for each plan
d. Plan B

CHAPTER 13

13-1. 95,238 shares; $11,428,560
13-3. Value before and after dividend $275.00.
13-5. a. Year Dividend
1    $0.70
3    $0.93
b. Target dividend $0.90
13-7. 163,743 shares; $15,555,556

CHAPTER 14

14-1. Rate = 13.79%

14-3. **a.** Rate = 36.73%

    b. Rate = 74.23%

14-7. **a.** Rate = 16.27%

14-10. Pledging: Rate = 16%

    Inventory loan: Rate = 13.8%

14-12. Rate = 12.37%

CHAPTER 15

15-1. Yes; the company will save $160,199 annually.

15-3. **a.** Need to speed up collections by more than 0.5214 day.

    b. Cash collections would have to be accelerated by more than 0.8110 day.

15-5. **a.** $4,000,000

    b. $240,000

    c. $48,600

    d. Yes; net annual gain = $191,400

15-7. **a.** $5,333

15-9. **a.** $912.44

    b. The loss will be $87.56.

    c. The capital loss here would be only $17.59.

    d. Interest rate risk. This leads to the maturity premium discussed in Chapter 2.

15-11. **a.** 36.36%

    b. 36.73%

    c. 55.67%

15-13. **a.** Average inventory = $90,000.

    b. $53,333

15-15. **a.** EOQ = 7,071 units or rounded to 7,100.

    b. 35.2 orders per year.

CHAPTER 16

16-1. **b.** $9,368

    c. $25,695

16-3. Canada: 1.1853; 1.1881; 1.1912
Japan: 213.4927; 211.9992; 209.1613
Switzerland: 1.9459; 1.9346; 1.8815

16-5. Net gain = $149.02

16-7. Canada: (2.85%); (1.99%)
Japan: 8.45%; 8.28%
Switzerland: 7%; 13.7%

16-9. $.0046945/yen

GLOSSARY

Accelerated Depreciation Techniques. Techniques that allow the owner of the asset to take greater amounts of depreciation during the early years of its life, thereby deferring some of the taxes until later years.

Accrual Method. A method of accounting whereby income is recorded when earned, whether or not the money has been received at that time, and expenses are recorded when incurred, whether or not any money has actually been paid out.

Acid Test Ratio. (Current assets – inventories) ÷ current liabilities. This ratio is a more stringent measure of liquidity than the current ratio in that it subtracts inventories (the least liquid current asset) from current assets.

Acquisition. A combination of two or more businesses into a single operational entity.

Agency Costs. The costs, such as a reduced stock price, associated with potential conflict between managers and investors when these two groups are not the same.

Amortized Loans. Loans that are paid off in equal periodic payments.

Annuity. A series of equal dollar payments for a specified number of years.

Arbitrage-Pricing Model. A theory that relates stock returns and risk. The theory maintains that security returns vary from their expected amounts when there are unanticipated changes in basic economic forces. Such forces would include unexpected changes in industrial production, inflation rates, term structure of interest rates, and the difference between interest rates of high-and-low risk bonds.

Arbitrageur. A person involved in the process of buying and selling in more than one market to make a riskless profit.

Arrearage. An overdue payment, generally referring to omitted preferred stock dividends.

Automated Depository Transfer System. A system that moves funds from local bank accounts to concentration accounts electronically. This eliminates the mail float from the local banks to the concentration banks.

Average Collection Period. Accounts receivable/(annual credit sales/365). A ratio that expresses how rapidly the firm is collecting its credit accounts.

Balance Sheet. A basic accounting statement that represents the financial position of a firm on a given date.

Balance Sheet Leverage Ratios. Financial ratios used to measure the extent of a firm's use of borrowed funds calculated using information found in the firm's balance sheet.

Bankers' Acceptances. A draft (order to pay) drawn on a specific bank by a seller of goods in order to obtain payment for goods that have been shipped (sold) to a customer. The customer maintains an account with that specific bank.

Bank Wire. A private wire service used and supported by approximately 250 banks in the United States for transferring funds, exchanging credit information, or effecting securities transactions.

Beta. The relationship between an investment's returns and the market returns. This is a measure of the investment's nondiversifiable risk.

Bond. A long-term (ten-year or more) promissory note issued by the borrower, promising to pay the owner of the security a predetermined and fixed amount of interest each year.

Bond Par Value. The face value appearing on the bond, which is to be returned to the bondholder at maturity.

Book Value. The depreciated value of a company's assets (original cost less accumulated depreciation) less the outstanding liabilities.

Book-Value Weights. The percentage of financing provided by different capital sources as measured by their book values from the company's balance sheet.

Break-Even Analysis. An analytical technique used to determine the quantity of output or sales that results in a zero level of earnings before interest and taxes (EBIT). Relationships among the firm's cost structure, volume of output, and EBIT are studied.

Business Risk. The relative dispersion or variability in the firm's expected earnings before interest and taxes (EBIT). The nature of the firm's operations causes its business risk. This type of risk is affected by the firm's cost structure, product demand characteristics, and intra-industry competitive position. In capital-structure theory, business risk is distinguished from financial risk. See **Financial Risk.**

Call Option. A call option gives its owner the right to purchase a given number of shares of stock or some other asset at a specified price over a given time period.

Call Premium. The difference between the call price and the security's par value.

Call Provision. A provision that entitles the corporation to repurchase its bonds or preferred stock from their holders at stated prices over specified periods.

Capital Asset. All property used in conducting a business other than assets held primarily for sale in the ordinary course of business or depreciable and real property used in conducting a business.

Capital Asset Pricing Model. An equation stating that the expected rate of return on a project is a function of (1) the risk-free rate, (2) the investment's systematic risk, and (3) the expected risk premium in the market.

Capital Budgeting. The decision-making process with respect to investment in fixed assets. Specifically it involves measuring the incremental cash flows associated with investment proposals and evaluating those proposed investments.

Capital Gain or Loss. As defined by the revenue code, a gain or loss resulting from the sale or exchange of a capital asset.

Capital Market. All institutions and procedures that facilitate transactions in long-term financial instruments.

Capital Rationing. The placing of a limit by the firm on the dollar size of the capital budget.

Capital Structure. The mix of long-term sources of funds used by the firm. This is also called the firm's capitalization. The relative total (percentage) of each type of fund is emphasized.

Cash Breakdown Analysis. Another version of breakeven analysis that includes only the cash costs of production within the cost components. This means noncash expenses, like depreciation, are omitted in the analysis.

Cash Budget. A detailed plan of future cash flows. This budget is composed of four elements: cash receipts, cash disbursements, net change in cash for the period, and new financing needed.

Cash Flow Process. The process of cash generation and disposition in a typical business setting.

Cash Flow Statement. An accounting statement that computes the firm's cash inflows and outflows for a given time period.

Certainty Equivalents. The amount of cash a person would require with certainty to make him/her indifferent between this certain sum and a particular risky or uncertain sum.

Characteristic Line. The line of "best fit" through a series of returns for a firm's stock relative to the market returns. The slope of the line, frequently called beta, represents the average movement of the firm's stock returns in response to a movement in the market's returns.

Chattel Mortgage Agreement. A loan agreement in which the lender can increase his/her security interest by having specific items of inventory identified in the loan agreement. The borrower retains title to the inventory but cannot sell the items without the lender's consent.

Clientele Effect. The belief that individuals and institutions that need current income will invest in companies that have high dividend payouts. Other investors prefer to avoid taxes by holding securities that offer only small dividend income but large capital gains. Thus, we have a "clientele" of investors.

Commercial Paper. Short-term unsecured promissory notes sold by large businesses in order to raise cash. Unlike most other money market instruments, commercial paper has no developed secondary market.

Compensating Balance. A balance of a given amount that the firm maintains in its demand deposit account. It may be required by either a formal or informal agreement with the firm's commercial bank. Such balances are usually required by the bank (1) on the unused portion of a loan commitment, (2) on the unpaid portion of an outstanding loan, or (3) in exchange for certain services provided by the bank, such as check-clearing or credit information. These balances raise the effective rate of interest paid on borrowed funds.

Compounding. The process of determining the future value of a payment or series of payments when applying the concept of compound interest.

Compound Interest. The situation in which interest paid on the investment during the first period is added to the principal and, during the second period, interest is earned on the original principal plus the interest earned during the first period.

Concentration Bank. A bank where the firm maintains a major disbursing account.

Constant Dividend Payout Ratio. A dividend payment policy in which the percentage of earnings paid out in dividends is held constant. The dollar amount fluctuates from year to year as profits vary.

Contractual Interest Rate. The interest rate to be paid on a bond expressed as a percent of par value.

Contribution Margin. The difference between a product's selling price and its unit variable costs. It is usually measured on a per unit basis.

Convertibles. Preferred stock or debentures that can be exchanged for a specified number of shares of common stock at the will of the owner.

Corporate Bylaws. Regulations that govern the internal affairs of the corporation, designating such items as the time and place of the shareholders' meetings, voting rights, the election process for selecting members of the board of directors, the procedures for issuing and transferring stock certificates, and the policies relating to the corporate records.

Corporation. An entity that *legally* functions separate and apart from it owners.

Cost of Capital. The rate that must be earned in order to satisfy the required rate of return of the firm's investors. It may also be defined as the rate of return on investments at which the price of the firm's common stock will remain unchanged. The cost of capital is based on the opportunity cost of funds as determined in the capital markets.

Cost of Common Stock. The rate of return the firm must earn in order for the common stockholders to receive their required rate of return. The rate is based on the opportunity cost of funds for the common stockholders in the capital markets.

Cost of Debt. The rate that has to be received from an investment in order to achieve the required rate of return for the creditors. The cost is based on the debtholders' opportunity cost of debt in the capital markets.

Cost of Preferred Stock. The rate of return that must be earned on the preferred stockholders' investment to satisfy their required rate of return. The cost is based on the preferred stockholders' opportunity cost of preferred stock in the capital markets.

Cost-Volume-Profit Analysis. Another way of referring to ordinary break-even analysis.

Coupon Interest Rate. The interest to be paid annually on a bond as a percent of par value, which is specified in the contractual agreement.

Coverage Ratios. A group of ratios that measure a firm's ability to meet its recurring fixed charge obligations, such as interest on long-term debt, lease payments, and/or preferred stock dividends.

Credit Scoring. The numerical evaluation of credit applicants where the score is evaluated relative to a predetermined standard.

Cross Rates. The indirect computation of the exchange rate of one currency from the exchange rates of two other currencies.

Cumulative Feature. A requirement that all past unpaid preferred stock dividends can be paid before any common stock dividends are declared.

Current Ratio. Current assets/current liabilities. A ratio that indicates a firm's degree of liquidity by comparing its current assets to its current liabilities.

Date of Record. Date at which the stock transfer books are to be closed for determining the investor to receive the next dividend payment. See **Ex-Dividend Date.**

Debenture. Any unsecured long-term debt.

Debt Capacity. The maximum proportion of debt that the firm can include in its capital structure and still maintain its lowest composite cost of capital.

Debt Ratio. Total liabilities/total assets. A ratio that measures the extent to which a firm has been financed with debt.

Declaration Date. The date upon which a dividend is formally declared by the board of directors.

Default Risk. The uncertainty of expected returns from a security attributable to possible changes in the financial capacity of the security issuer to make future payments to the security owner. Treasury securities are considered to be default-free. Default risk is also referred to as "financial risk" in the context of marketable securities management.

Degree of Combined Leverage. The percentage change in earnings per share caused by a percentage change in sales. It is the product of the degree of operating leverage and the degree of financial leverage.

Depository Transfer Checks. A means for moving funds from local bank accounts to concentration accounts. The depository transfer check itself is an unsigned, nonnegotiable instrument. It is payable only to the bank deposit for credit to the firm's specific account.

Depreciation. The means by which an asset's value is expensed over its useful life for federal income tax purposes.

Direct Quotes. The exchange rate that indicates the number of units of the home currency required to buy one unit of foreign currency.

Disbursing Float. Funds available in the company's bank account until its payment check has cleared through the banking system.

Discount Bond. A bond that sells at a discount below par value.

Discounting. The inverse of compounding. This process is used to determine the present value of a cash flow.

Discount Rate. The interest rate used in the discounting process.

Diversifiable Risk. See **Unsystematic Risk.**

Dividend Payout Ratio. The amount of dividends relative to the company's net income or earnings per share.

Dividend Yield. The dividend per share divided by the price of the security.

Dunning Letters. Past-due letters sent out to delinquent accounts.

EBIT. Common financial notation for earnings before interest and taxes.

EBIT-EPS Indifference Point. The level of earnings before interest and taxes (EBIT) that will equate earnings per share (EPS) between two different financing plans.

Economic Failure. Situation in which the company's costs exceed its revenues. Stated differently, the internal rates of return on investments are less than the firm's cost of capital.

Efficient Market. A market in which the values of all assets and securities at any instant in time fully reflect all available information.

EPS. Typical financial notation for earnings per (common) share.

Equivalent Annual Annuity (EAA). An annuity cash flow that yields the same present value as the project's NPV. It is calculated by dividing the projects' NPV by the appropriate $PVIFA_{1\%, n \, yr}$.

Eurodollar Market. This is a banking market in U.S. dollars outside the U.S. Large sums of U.S. dollars can be borrowed or invested in this unregulated financial market. Similar external markets exist in Europe and Asia and for other major currencies.

Exchange Risk. The variability in future cash flows caused by variations in the exchange rates.

Ex-Dividend Date. The date upon which stock brokerage companies have uniformly decided to terminate the right of ownership to the dividend, which is four days prior to the record date.

Expected Rate of Return. The arithmetic mean or average of all possible outcomes where those outcomes are weighted by the probability that each will occur.

Ex-Rights Date. The date on or after which the stock sells without rights.

External Common Equity. A new issue of common stock.

Factor. A firm that acquires the receivables of other firms. A commercial finance company that engages solely in the factoring of receivables is known as an old-line factor.

Factoring of Accounts Receivable. The outright sale of a firm's accounts to another party (the factor) without recourse. The factor, in turn, bears the risk of collection.

Fair Value. The present value of an asset's expected future cash flows.

Federal Agency Securities. Debt obligations of corporations and agencies created to carry out the lending programs of the U.S. government.

Federal Reserve System. The U.S. central banking system.

Field Warehouse Financing Agreement. A security agreement in which inventories are used as collateral, physically separated from the firm's other inventories, and placed under the control of a third-party field warehousing firm.

Financial Analysis. The assessment of a firm's financial condition or well being. Its objectives are to determine the firm's financial strengths and to identify its weaknesses. The primary tool of financial analysis is the financial ratio.

Financial Assets. Claims for future payment by one economic unit upon another.

Financial Intermediaries. Major financial institutions, such as commercial banks, savings and loan associations, credit unions, life insurance companies, and mutual funds, that assist the transfer of savings from economic units with excess savings to those with a shortage of savings.

Financial Leverage. The use of securities bearing a fixed (limited) rate of return to finance a portion of the firm's assets. Financial leverage can arise from the use of either debt or preferred stock financing. The use of financial leverage exposes the firm to financial risk.

Financial Markets. Institutions and procedures that facilitate transactions in all types of financial claims (securities).

Financial Risk. The added variability in earnings available to the firm's common shareholders, and the added chance of insolvency caused by the use of securities bearing a limited rate of return in the firm's financial structure. The use of financial leverage gives rise to financial risk.

Financial Structure Design. The activity of seeking the proper mixture of a firm's short-term, long-term, and permanent financing components to minimize the cost of raising a given amount of funds.

Financial Structure. The mix of *all* funds sources that appear on the right-hand side of the balance sheet.

Fixed Asset Turnover. Sales/fixed assets. A ratio indicating how effectively a firm is using its fixed assets to generate sales.

Fixed Costs. Charges that do not vary in total amount as sales volume or the quantity of output changes over some relevant range of output.

Flotation Costs. The underwriter's spread and issuing costs associated with the issuance and marketing of new securities.

Foreign Direct Investment. Physical assets, such as plant and equipment, acquired outside a corporation's home country but operated and controlled by that corporation.

Formal Control. Control vested in the stockholders having the majority of the voting common shares.

Futures Contract. A futures contract is a contract to buy or sell a stated commodity (such as soybeans or corn) or financial claim (such as U.S. Treasury bonds) at a specified price at some future, specified time.

General Partnership. A partnership in which all partners are fully liable for the indebtedness incurred by the partnership.

Gross Income. The firm's dollar sales from its product or services less the cost of producing or acquiring the product or service.

Gross Profit Margin. Gross profit/net sales. A ratio denoting the gross profit of the firm as a percentage of net sales.

Hedge. A means to neutralize exchange risk on an exposed asset position, whereby a liability of the same amount and maturity is created in a foreign currency.

Hedging Principle. A working capital management policy which states that the cash flow generating characteristics of a firm's investments should be matched with the cash flow requirements of the firm's sources of financing. Very simply, short-lived assets should be financed with short-term sources of financing while long-lived assets should be financed with long-term sources of financing.

Holding-Period Return. The return an investor would receive from holding a security for a designated period of time. For example, a monthly holding-period return would be the return for holding a security during a particular month.

Hostile Takeover. A merger or acquisition in which management resists the group initiating the transaction.

Hurdle Rate. The required rate of return used in capital budgeting.

Income Statement. A basic accounting statement that measures the results of a firm's operations over a specified period, commonly one year. Also known as the profit and loss statement. The bottom line of the income statement shows the firm's profit or loss for the period.

Incremental Cash Flows. The cash flows that result from the acceptance of a capital-budgeting project.

Indenture. The legal agreement between the firm issuing the bonds and the bond trustee who represents the bond-holders, providing the specific terms of the loan agreement.

Indirect Quote. The exchange rate that expresses the required number of units of foreign currency to buy one unit of home currency.

Information Asymmetry. The difference in accessibility to information between managers and investors, which may result in a lower stock price than would be true if we had conditions of certainty.

Insolvency. The inability to meet interest payments or to repay debt at maturity.

Interest-Rate Parity Theory. States that (except for the effect of small transaction costs) the forward premium or discount should be equal and opposite in size to the difference in the national interest rates for securities of the same maturity.

Interest-Rate Risk. The uncertainty that envelops the expected returns from a security caused by changes in interest rates. Price changes induced by interest-rate changes are greater for long-term than for short-term financial instruments.

Internal Common Equity. Profits retained within the business for investment purposes.

Internal Growth. A firm's growth rate in earnings resulting from reinvesting company profits rather than distributing the earnings in the form of dividends. The growth rate is a function of the amount retained and the return earned on the retained funds.

Internal Rate of Return (IRR). A capital-budgeting technique that reflects the rate of return a project earns. Mathematically it is the discount rate that equates the present value of the inflows with the present value of the outflows.

Intrinsic Value. The present value of the investment's expected future cash flows, discounted at the investor's required rate of return.

Inventory Loans. Loans secured by inventories. Examples include floating or blanket lien agreements, chattel mortgage agreements, field warehouse receipt loans, and terminal warehouse receipt loans.

Inventory Turnover Ratio. Cost of goods sold/inventory. A ratio that measures the number of times a firm's inventories are sold and replaced during the year. This ratio reflects the relative liquidity of inventories.

Investment Banker. A financial specialist who underwrites and distributes new securities and advises corporate clients about raising new funds.

Investor's Required Rate of Return. The minimum rate of return necessary to attract an investor to purchase or hold a security.

Junk Bonds. Any bond rated BB or below.

Just-in-Time Inventory Control. A production and management system in which inventory is cut down to a minimum through adjustments to the time and physical distance between the various production operations. Under this system the firm keeps a minimum level of inventory on hand, relying upon suppliers to furnish parts "just-in-time" for them to be assembled.

Lead and Lag Strategies. Techniques used to reduce exchange risk where the firm maximizes its asset position in the stronger currency and its liability position in the weaker currency.

Least-Square Regression. A procedure for "fitting" a line through a scatter of observed data points in a way that minimizes the sum of the squared deviations of the points from the fitted line.

Leveraged Buyout. A corporate restructuring where the existing shareholders sell their shares to a small group of investors. The purchasers of the stock use the firm's unused debt capacity to borrow the funds to pay for the stock.

Limited Partnership. A partnership in which one or more of the partners has limited liability, restricted to the amount of capital he/she invests in the partnership.

Line of Credit. Generally an informal agreement or understanding between the borrower and the bank as to the maximum amount of credit the bank will provide the borrower at any one time. Under this type of agreement there is no "legal" commitment on the part of the bank to provide the stated credit. See Revolving Credit Agreement.

Liquidation Value. The dollar sum that could be realized if an asset were sold independently of the going concern.

Liquidity. A firm's ability to pay its bills on time. Liquidity is related to the ease and quickness with which a firm can convert its noncash assets into cash, as well as the size of the firm's investment in noncash assets vis-à-vis its short-term liabilities.

Liquidity Preference Theory. The shape of the term structure of interest rates is determined by an investor's additional required interest rate in compensation of additional risks.

Liquidity Ratios. Financial ratios used to assess the ability of a firm to pay its bills on time. Examples of liquidity ratios include the current ratio and the acid test ratio.

Loan Amortization Schedule. A breakdown of the interest and principle payments on an amortized loan.

Long-Term Residual Dividend Policy. A dividend plan by which the residual capital is distributed smoothly to the investors over the planning period.

Mail Float. Funds tied up during the time that elapses from the moment a customer mails his/her remittance check until the firm begins to process it.

Marginal Cost of Capital. The cost of capital that represents the weighted cost of each additional dollar of financing from all sources, debt, preferred stock, and common stock.

Marginal Tax Rate. The tax rate that would be applied to the next dollar of income.

Market Equilibrium. The situation in which expected returns equal required returns.

Market Risk. See **Systematic Risk**

Market Segmentation Theory. The shape of the term structure of interest rates implies that the rate of interest for a particular maturity is determined solely by demand and supply for a given maturity. This demand is independent of the demand and supply for securities having different maturities.

Market Value. The value observed in the market place, where buyers and sellers negotiate a mutually acceptable price for the asset.

Market-Value Weights. The percentage of financing provided by different capital sources, measured by the current market prices of the firm's bonds and preferred and common stock.

Marketable Securities. Security investments that the firm can quickly convert into cash balances.

Maturity Date. The date upon which a borrower is to repay a loan.

Merger. A combination of two or more businesses into a single operational entity.

Money Market. All institutions and procedures that facilitate transactions in short-term instruments issued by borrowers with very high credit ratings.

Money Market Mutual Funds. Investment companies that purchase a diversified array of short-term, high-grade (money market) debt instruments.

Monitoring Costs. A form of agency costs. Typically these costs arise when bond investors take steps to ensure that protective covenants in the bond indenture are adhered to by management.

Mortgage Bonds. Bonds secured by a lien on real property.

Multinational Corporation. A corporation with holdings and/or operations in more than one country.

Mutually Exclusive Projects. A set of projects that perform essentially the same task, so that acceptance of one will necessarily mean rejection of the others.

Negotiable Certificates of Deposit. Marketable receipts for funds deposited in a bank for a fixed period. The deposited funds earn a fixed rate of interest. More commonly, these are called CDs.

Net Income. A figure representing the firm's profit or loss for the period. It also represents the earnings available to the firm's common *and* preferred stockholders.

Net Income Available to Common Equity (Also Net Common Stock Earnings). Net income after interest, taxes and preferred dividends.

Net Operating Loss Carryback and Carryforward. A tax provision that permits the taxpayer first to apply the loss against the profits in the three prior years (carryback). If the loss has not been completely absorbed by the profits in these three years, it may be applied to taxable profits in each of the seven following years (carryforward).

Net Present Value (NPV). A capital-budgeting concept defined as the present value of the project's annual net cash flows after tax less the project's initial outlay.

Net Profit Margin. Net income/sales. A ratio that measures the net income of the firm as a percent of sales.

Net Working Capital. The difference between the firm's current assets and its current liabilities.

Non-Diversifiable Risk. See **Systematic Risk.**

Nominal Interest Rate. The interest rate paid on debt securities without an adjustment for any loss in purchasing power.

Normal Probability Distribution. A special class of bell-shaped distributions with symmetrically decreasing density, where the curve approaches but never reaches the X axis.

Operating Income Return on Investment. The ratio of net operating income divided by total assets.

Operating Leverage. The responsiveness to sales changes of the firm's earnings before interest and taxes. This responsiveness arises from the firm's use of fixed operating costs.

Operating Profit Margin. Net operating income/sales. A firm's earnings before interest and taxes. This ratio serves as an overall measure of operating effectiveness.

Opportunity Cost of Funds. The next best rate of return available to the investor for a given level of risk.

Optimal Capital Structure. The capital structure that minimizes the firm's composite cost of capital (maximizes the common stock price) for raising a given amount of funds.

Optimal Range of Financial Leverage. The range of various capital structure combinations that yield the lowest overall cost of capital for the firm.

Option Contract. An option contract gives its owner the right to buy or sell a fixed number of shares at a specified price over a limited time period.

Organized Security Exchanges. Formal organizations involved in the trading of securities. Such exchanges are tangible entities that conduct auction markets in listed securities.

Over-the-Counter Markets. All security markets except the organized exchanges. The money market is an over-the-counter market. Most corporate bonds also are traded in this market.

Partnership. An association of two or more individuals joining together as co-owners to operate a business for profit.

Par Value. On the face of a bond, the stated amount that the firm is to repay upon the maturity date.

Payable-Through Draft. A legal instrument that has the physical appearance of an ordinary check but is not drawn on a bank. A payable-through draft is drawn on and paid by the issuing firm. The bank serves as a collection point and passes the draft on to the firm.

Payback Period. A capital-budgeting criterion defined as the number of years required to recover the initial cash investment.

Payment Date. The date on which the company mails a dividend check to each investor of record.

Percent of Sales Method. A method of financial forecasting that involves estimating the level of an expense, asset, or liability for a future period as a percent of the sales forecast.

Perfect Markets. Hypothetical markets under the assumptions that (1) information is readily available to all investors at no cost, (2) there are no transaction costs, (3) investment opportunities are readily accessible to all prospective investors, and (4) financial distress and bankruptcy costs are nonexistent.

Permanent Investment. An investment that the firm expects to hold longer than one year. The firm makes permanent investments in fixed and current assets. Contrast with **Temporary Investments.**

Perpetuity. An annuity with an infinite life.

Pledging Accounts Receivable. A loan the firm obtains from a commercial bank or a finance company using its accounts receivable as collateral.

Portfolio Beta. The relationship between a portfolio's returns and the market returns. It is a measure of the portfolio's nondiversifiable risk.

Portfolio Diversification Effect. The fact that variations of the returns from a portfolio or combination of assets may be less than the sum of the variation of the individual assets making up the portfolio.

Preauthorized Checks (PACs). A check that resembles the ordinary check but does not contain or require the signature of the person on whose account it is being drawn. A PAC is created only with the individual's legal authorization. The PAC system is advantageous when the firm regularly receives a large volume of payments of a fixed amount from the same customer over a long period.

Preemptive Right. The right entitling the common shareholder to maintain his/her proportionate share of ownership in the firm.

Present Value. The value in today's dollars of a future payment discounted back to present at the required rate of return.

Price/Earnings Ratio (P/E). The price the market places on $1 of a firm's earnings. For example, if a firm has an earnings per share of $2, and a stock price of $30, its price/earnings ratio is 15 ($30 ÷ $2).

Processing Float. Funds tied up during the time required for the firm to process remittance checks before they can be deposited in the bank.

Profit Budget. A budget of forecasted profits based on information gleaned from the cost and sales budgets.

Profit Margins. Financial ratios (sometimes simply referred to as margins) that reflect the level of firm profits relative to sales. Examples include the gross profit margin (gross profit divided by sales), operating profit margin (operating earnings divided by sales), and the net profit margin (net profit divided by sales).

Profitability Index (PI). A capital budgeting criterion defined as the ratio of the present value of the future net cash flows to the initial outlay.

Pro Forma Income Statement. A statement of planned profit or loss for a future period.

Prospectus. A condensed version of the full registration statement filed with the Securities and Exchange Commission that describes a new security issue.

Proxy. A means of voting in which a designated party is provided with the temporary power of attorney to vote for the signee at the corporation's annual meeting.

Purchasing Power Parity. In the long run, exchange rates adjust so that the purchasing power of each currency tends to remain the same and, thus, exchange rate changes tend to reflect international differences in inflation rates. Countries with high rates of inflation tend to experience declines in the value of their currency.

Put Option. A put option gives its owners the right to sell a given number of shares of common stock or some other asset at a specified price over a given time period.

Real Assets. Tangible assets like houses, equipment, and inventories; real assets are distinguished from financial assets.

Real Interest Rate. The nominal rate of interest less any loss in purchasing power of the dollar during the time of the investment.

Remote Disbursing. A cash management service specifically designed to extend disbursing float.

Repurchase Agreements. Legal contracts that involve the sale of short-term securities by a borrower to a lender of funds. The borrower commits to repurchase the securities at a later date at the contract price plus a stated interest charge.

Required Rate of Return. The minimum rate of return necessary to attract an investor to purchase or hold a security. It is also the discount rate that equates the present value of the cash flows with the value of the security.

Residual Dividend Theory. A theory asserting that the dividends to be paid should equal the equity capital left over after the financing of profitable investments.

Restrictive Covenants. Provisions in the loan agreement that place restrictions on the borrower and make the loan immediately payable and due when violated. These restrictive covenants are designed to maintain the borrower's financial condition on a par with that which existed at the time the loan was made.

Return on Common Equity. Net income available to the common stockholders/common equity. A ratio relating earned income to the common stockholder's investment.

Return on Total Assets. Net income/total assets. This ratio determines the yield on the firm's assets by relating net income to total assets.

Return-Risk Line. A specification of the appropriate required rates of return for investments having different amounts of risk.

Revolving Credit Agreement. An understanding between the borrower and the bank as to the amount of credit the bank will be legally obligated to provide the borrower. See **Line of Credit**.

Right. A certificate issued to common stockholders giving them an option to purchase a stated number of new shares at a specified price during a two- to ten-week period.

Risk. The possible variation associated with the expected return measured by the standard deviation or coefficient of variation.

Risk-Adjusted Discount Rate. A method for incorporating the project's level of risk into the capital budgeting process, in which the discount rate is adjusted upward to compensate for higher-than-normal risk or downward to compensate for lower-than-normal risk.

Riskless Rate of Return. The rate of return on risk-free investments, such as the interest rate on short-term U.S. government securities.

Risk Premium. The additional return expected for assuming risk.

Salvage Value. The value of an asset or investment project at the end of its usable life.

Scenario Analysis. Simulation analysis that focuses on an examination of the range of possible outcomes.

Secondary Market. Transactions in currently outstanding securities. This is distinguished from the new issues or primary market.

Secured Credit. Sources of credit that require security in the form of pledged assets. In the event the borrower defaults in payment of principal or interest, the lender can seize the pledged assets and sell than to settle the debt.

Securities and Exchange Commission (SEC). The federal agency created by the Securities Exchange Act of 1934 to enforce federal securities laws.

Securities Exchange Act of 1933. A regulation that requires registration of certain new issues of public securities with the Securities and Exchange Commission (SEC). The registration statement should disclose all facts relevant to the new issue that will permit an investor to make an informed decision.

Securities Exchange Act of 1934. This act enables the SEC to enforce federal securities laws. The major aspects of the 1934 act include: 1. Major securities exchanges are required to register with the SEC; 2. insider-trading is regulated; 3. stock price manipulation by investors is prohibited; 4. the SEC has control over proxy procedures; 5. the Board of Governors of the Federal Reserve System is given the responsibility of setting margin requirements.

Security Market Line. The return line that reflects the attitudes of investors regarding the minimal acceptable return for a given level of systematic risk.

Selling Group. A collection of securities dealers that participates in the distribution of new issues to final investors. A selling group agreement links these dealers to the underwriting syndicate.

Semivariable Costs. Charges that behave as variable costs over certain ranges of output and as fixed costs over other ranges of output.

Simulation. The process of imitating the performance of an investment project through repeated evaluations, usually using a computer. In the general case, experimentation upon a mathematical model that has been designed to capture the critical realities of the decision-making situation.

Sinking Fund. A required annual payment that allows for the periodic retirement of debt.

Sole Proprietorship. A business owned by a single individual.

Spin-Off. The separation of a subsidiary from its parent, with no change in the equity ownership. The management of the parent company gives up operating control over the subsidiary, but the shareholders maintain their same percentage ownership in both firms. New shares representing ownership in the averted company are issued to the original shareholders on a pro-rate basis.

Spontaneous Financing. The trade credit and other accounts payable that arise "spontaneously" in the firm's day-to-day operations.

Spot Transaction. A transaction made immediately in the market place at the market price.

Stable Dollar Dividend per Share. A dividend policy that maintains a relatively stable dollar dividend per share over time.

Standard Deviation. A statistical measure of the spread of a probability distribution calculated by squaring the difference between each outcome and its expected value, weighting each value by its probability, summing over all possible outcomes, and taking the square root of this sum.

Stock Dividend. A distribution of shares of up to 25 percent of the number of shares currently outstanding, issued on a pro-rata basis to the current stockholders.

Stock Market Value. (See **Market Value.**)

Stock Split. A stock dividend exceeding 25 percent of the number of shares currently outstanding.

Stock Repurchases. The repurchase of common stock by the issuing firm for any of a variety of reasons, resulting in a reduction of shares outstanding.

Straight-Line Depreciation. A method for computing depreciation expenses in which the cost of the asset is divided by the asset's useful life.

Stretching on Trade Credit. Failing to pay within the prescribed credit period. For example, under credit terms of 2/10, net 30, a firm would be stretching its trade credit if it failed to pay by the 30th day and paid on the 60th day.

Subchapter S Corporation. A corporation that, because of specific qualifications, is taxed as though it were a partnership.

Subscription Price. The price for which the security may be purchased in a rights offering.

Systematic Risk (Nondiversifiable Risk or Market Related Risk). The portion of variations in investment returns that cannot be eliminated through investor diversification. These variations result from factors that affect all stocks.

Target Debt Ratio. A desired proportion of long-term debt in the firm's capital structure. Alternatively, it may be the desired proportion of total debt in the firm's financial structure.

Taxable Income. Gross income from all sources, except for allowable exclusions, less any tax deductible expenses.

Tax Liability. The amount owed the federal, state, or local taxing authorities.

Temporary Financing. Financing (other that spontaneous sources) that will be repaid within a period of one year or less. Included among these sources of short-term debt are secured and unsecured bank loans, commercial paper, loans secured by accounts receivable, and loans secured by inventories.

Temporary Investments. These investments are comprised of the firm's investment in current assets that will be liquidated and not replaced within a period of one year or less. Examples include seasonal expansions in inventories and accounts receivable.

Terminal Warehouse Agreement. A security agreement in which the inventories pledged as collateral are transported to a public warehouse that is physically removed from the borrower's premises. This is the safest (and a costly) form of financing secured by inventory.

Term Loans. Loans that have maturities of one to ten years and are repaid in periodic installments over the life of the loan. Term loans are usually secured by a chattel mortgage on equipment or a mortgage on real property.

Term Structure of Interest Rates. The relationship between interest rates and the term to maturity, where the risk of default is held constant.

Times Interest Earned Ratio. Earnings before interest and taxes (EBIT)/interest expense. A ratio that measures the firm's ability to meet its interest payments from its annual operating earnings.

Total Asset Turnover. Sales/total tangible assets. An overall measure of the relation between the firm's tangible assets and the sales they generate.

Trade Credit. Credit made available by a firm's suppliers in conjunction with the acquisition of materials. Trade credit appears on the balance sheet as accounts payable.

Transaction Loan. A loan where the proceeds are designation for a specific purpose—for example, a bank loan used to finance the acquisition of a piece of equipment.

Transit Float. Funds tied up during the time necessary for a deposited check to clear through the commercial banking system and become usable funds to the company.

Treasury Bills. Direct debt obligations of the U.S. government sold on a regular basis by the U.S. Treasury.

Trend Analysis. An analysis of a firm's financial ratios over time.

Unbiased Expectations Theory. The shape of the term structure of interest rates is determined by an investor's expectations about future interest rates.

Underwriting. The purchase and subsequent resale of a new security issue. The risk of selling the new issue at a satisfactory (profitable) price is assumed by the investment banker.

Underwriting Syndicate. A temporary association of investment bankers formed to purchase a new security issue and quickly resell it at a profit. Formation of the syndicate spreads the risk of loss among several investment bankers, thereby minimizing the risk exposure of any single underwriter.

Undiversifiable Risk. The portion of the variation in investment returns that cannot be eliminated through investor diversification.

Unique Risk. See **Unsystematic Risk.**

Unsecured Credit. All sources of credit that have as their security only the lender's faith in the borrower's ability to repay the funds when due.

Unsystematic Risk (Firm-Specific Risk or Unique Risk). The portion of the variation in investment returns that can be eliminated through investor diversification. These variations result from factors that are unique to the particular firm.

Value of a Bond. The present value of the interest payments, I_1 in period t, plus the present value of the redemption or par value of the indebtedness, M, at the maturity date.

Value of a Security. The present value of all future cash inflows expected to be received by the investor owning the security.

Variable Costs. Charges that vary in total as output changes. Variable costs are fixed per unit of output.

Weighted Cost of Capital. A composite of the individual costs of financing incurred by each capital source. A firm's weighted cost of capital is a function of (1) the individual costs of capital, (2) the capital structure mix, and (3) the level of financing necessary to make the investment.

Weighted Marginal Cost of Capital. The composite cost for each additional dollar of financing. The marginal cost of capital represents the appropriate criterion for making investment decisions.

Working Capital. A concept traditionally defined as a firm's investment in current assets. Net working capital refers to the difference between current assets and current liabilities.

Yield to Maturity. The rate of return the investor will earn if the bond is held to maturity.

Zero Balance Accounts. A cash management tool that permits centralized control over cash outflow while maintaining divisional disbursing authority. Objectives include: 1. Achieve better control over cash payments; 2. reduce excess cash balances held in regional banks for disbursing purposes; and 3. increase disbursing float.

INDEX

Subject

Corporate Name

Table B. Compound Sum of $1: $(1 + i)^n$

Period	1%	2%	3%	4%	5%	6%	7%	8%	9%	10%	12%	14%	15%	16%	18%	20%	24%	28%	32%	36%
1	1.0100	1.0200	1.0300	1.0400	1.0500	1.0600	1.0700	1.0800	1.0900	1.1000	1.1200	1.1400	1.1500	1.1600	1.1800	1.2000	1.2400	1.2800	1.3200	1.3600
2	1.0201	1.0404	1.0609	1.0816	1.1025	1.1236	1.1449	1.1664	1.1881	1.2100	1.2544	1.2996	1.3225	1.3456	1.3924	1.4400	1.5376	1.6384	1.7424	1.8496
3	1.0303	1.0612	1.0927	1.1249	1.1576	1.1910	1.2250	1.2597	1.2950	1.3310	1.4049	1.4815	1.5209	1.5609	1.6430	1.7280	1.9066	2.0972	2.3000	2.5155
4	1.0406	1.0824	1.1255	1.1699	1.2155	1.2625	1.3108	1.3605	1.4116	1.4641	1.5735	1.6890	1.7490	1.8106	1.9388	2.0736	2.3642	2.6844	3.0360	3.4210
5	1.0510	1.1041	1.1593	1.2167	1.2763	1.3382	1.4026	1.4693	1.5386	1.6105	1.7623	1.9254	2.0114	2.1003	2.2878	2.4883	2.9316	3.4360	4.0075	4.6526
6	1.0615	1.1262	1.1941	1.2653	1.3401	1.4185	1.5007	1.5869	1.6771	1.7716	1.9738	2.1950	2.3131	2.4364	2.6996	2.9860	3.6352	4.3980	5.2899	6.3275
7	1.0721	1.1487	1.2299	1.3159	1.4071	1.5036	1.6058	1.7138	1.8280	1.9487	2.2107	2.5023	2.6600	2.8262	3.1855	3.5832	4.5077	5.6295	6.9826	8.6054
8	1.0829	1.1717	1.2668	1.3686	1.4775	1.5938	1.7182	1.8509	1.9926	2.1436	2.4760	2.8526	3.0590	3.2784	3.7589	4.2998	5.5895	7.2058	9.2170	11.703
9	1.0937	1.1951	1.3048	1.4233	1.5513	1.6895	1.8385	1.9990	2.1719	2.3579	2.7731	3.2519	3.5179	3.8030	4.4355	5.1598	6.9310	9.2234	12.166	15.916
10	1.1046	1.2190	1.3439	1.4802	1.6289	1.7908	1.9672	2.1589	2.3674	2.5937	3.1058	3.7072	4.0456	4.4114	5.2338	6.1917	8.5944	11.805	16.059	21.646
11	1.1157	1.2434	1.3842	1.5395	1.7103	1.8983	2.1049	2.3316	2.5804	2.8531	3.4785	4.2262	4.6524	5.1173	6.1759	7.4301	10.657	15.111	21.198	29.439
12	1.1268	1.2682	1.4258	1.6010	1.7959	2.0122	2.2522	2.5182	2.8127	3.1384	3.8960	4.8179	5.3502	5.9360	7.2876	8.9161	13.214	19.342	27.982	*40.037
13	1.1381	1.2936	1.4685	1.6651	1.8856	2.1329	2.4098	2.7196	3.0658	3.4523	4.3635	5.4924	6.1528	6.8858	8.5994	10.699	16.386	24.758	36.937	54.451
14	1.1495	1.3195	1.5126	1.7317	1.9799	2.2609	2.5785	2.9372	3.3417	3.7975	4.8871	6.2613	7.0757	7.9875	10.147	12.839	20.319	31.691	48.756	74.053
15	1.1610	1.3459	1.5580	1.8009	2.0789	2.3966	2.7590	3.1722	3.6425	4.1772	5.4736	7.1379	8.1371	9.2655	11.973	15.407	25.195	40.564	64.358	100.71
16	1.1726	1.3728	1.6047	1.8730	2.1829	2.5404	2.9522	3.4259	3.9703	4.5950	6.1304	8.1372	9.3576	10.748	14.129	18.488	31.242	51.923	84.953	136.96
17	1.1843	1.4002	1.6528	1.9479	2.2920	2.6928	3.1588	3.7000	4.3276	5.0545	6.8660	9.2765	10.761	12.467	16.672	22.186	38.740	66.461	112.13	186.27
18	1.1961	1.4282	1.7024	2.0258	2.4066	2.8543	3.3799	3.9960	4.7171	5.5599	7.6900	10.575	12.375	14.462	19.673	26.623	48.038	85.070	148.02	253.33
19	1.2081	1.4568	1.7535	2.1068	2.5270	3.0256	3.6165	4.3157	5.1417	6.1159	8.6128	12.055	14.231	16.776	23.214	31.948	59.567	108.89	195.39	344.53
20	1.2202	1.4859	1.8061	2.1911	2.6533	3.2071	3.8697	4.6610	5.6044	6.7275	9.6463	13.743	16.366	19.460	27.393	38.337	73.864	139.37	257.91	468.57
21	1.2324	1.5157	1.8603	2.2788	2.7860	3.3996	4.1406	5.0338	6.1088	7.4002	10.803	15.667	18.821	22.574	32.323	46.005	91.591	178.40	340.44	637.26
22	1.2447	1.5460	1.9161	2.3699	2.9253	3.6035	4.4304	5.4365	6.6586	8.1403	12.100	17.861	21.644	26.186	38.142	55.206	113.57	228.35	449.39	866.67
23	1.2572	1.5769	1.9736	2.4647	3.0715	3.8197	4.7405	5.8715	7.2579	8.9543	13.552	20.361	24.891	30.376	45.007	66.247	140.83	292.30	593.19	1178.6
24	1.2697	1.6084	2.0328	2.5633	3.2251	4.0489	5.0724	6.3412	7.9111	9.8497	15.178	23.212	28.625	35.236	53.108	79.496	174.63	374.14	783.02	1602.9
25	1.2824	1.6406	2.0938	2.6658	3.3864	4.2919	5.4274	6.8485	8.6231	10.834	17.000	26.461	32.918	40.874	62.668	95.396	216.54	478.90	1033.5	2180.0
26	1.2953	1.6734	2.1566	2.7725	3.5557	4.5494	5.8074	7.3964	9.3992	11.918	19.040	30.166	37.856	47.414	73.948	114.47	268.51	612.99	1364.3	2964.9
27	1.3082	1.7069	2.2213	2.8834	3.7335	4.8223	6.2139	7.9881	10.245	13.110	21.324	34.389	43.535	55.000	87.259	137.37	332.95	784.63	1800.9	4032.2
28	1.3213	1.7410	2.2879	2.9987	3.9201	5.1117	6.6488	8.6271	11.167	14.421	23.883	39.204	50.065	63.800	102.96	164.84	412.86	1004.3	2377.2	5483.8
29	1.3345	1.7758	2.3566	3.1187	4.1161	5.4184	7.1143	9.3173	12.172	15.863	26.749	44.693	57.575	74.008	121.50	197.81	511.95	1285.5	3137.9	7458.0
30	1.3478	1.8114	2.4273	3.2434	4.3219	5.7435	7.6123	10.062	13.267	17.449	29.959	50.950	66.211	85.849	143.37	237.37	634.81	1645.5	4142.0	10143.
40	1.4889	2.2080	3.2620	4.8010	7.0400	10.285	14.974	21.724	31.409	45.259	93.050	188.88	267.86	378.72	750.37	1469.7	5455.9	19426.	66520.	*
50	1.6446	2.6916	4.3839	7.1067	11.467	18.420	29.457	46.901	74.357	117.39	289.00	700.23	1083.6	1670.7	3927.3	9100.4	46890.	*	*	*
60	1.8167	3.2810	5.8916	10.519	18.679	32.987	57.946	101.25	176.03	304.48	897.59	2595.9	4383.9	7370.1	20555.	56347.	*	*	*	*

*FVIF > 99,999.

Table C. Present Value of $1: $\dfrac{\$1}{(1 + i)_n}$

Period	1%	3%	5%	6%	7%	8%	9%	10%	11%	12%	13%	14%	15%	16%	17%	18%	19%	20%	24%	28%
1	.9901	.9709	.9524	.9434	.9346	.9259	.9174	.9091	.9009	.8929	.8850	.8772	.8696	.8621	.8547	.8475	.8403	.8333	.8065	.7813
2	.9803	.9426	.9070	.8900	.8734	.8573	.8417	.8264	.8116	.7972	.7831	.7695	.7561	.7432	.7305	.7182	.7062	.6944	.6504	.6104
3	.9706	.9151	.8638	.8396	.8163	.7938	.7722	.7513	.7312	.7118	.6930	.6750	.6575	.6407	.6244	.6086	.5934	.5787	.5245	.4768
4	.9610	.8885	.8227	.7921	.7629	.7350	.7084	.6830	.6587	.6355	.6133	.5921	.5718	.5523	.5336	.5158	.4987	.4823	.4230	.3725
5	.9515	.8626	.7835	.7473	.7130	.6806	.6499	.6209	.5934	.5674	.5428	.5194	.4972	.4761	.4561	.4371	.4190	.4019	.3411	.2910
6	.9420	.8375	.7462	.7050	.6663	.6302	.5963	.5645	.5346	.5066	.4803	.4556	.4323	.4104	.3898	.3704	.3521	.3349	.2751	.2274
7	.9327	.8131	.7107	.6651	.6227	.5835	.5470	.5132	.4817	.4523	.4251	.3996	.3759	.3538	.3332	.3139	.2959	.2791	.2218	.1776
8	.9235	.7894	.6768	.6274	.5820	.5403	.5019	.4665	.4339	.4039	.3762	.3506	.3269	.3050	.2848	.2660	.2487	.2326	.1789	.1388
9	.9143	.7664	.6446	.5919	.5439	.5002	.4604	.4241	.3909	.3606	.3329	.3075	.2843	.2630	.2434	.2255	.2090	.1938	.1443	.1084
10	.9053	.7441	.6139	.5584	.5083	.4632	.4224	.3855	.3522	.3220	.2946	.2697	.2472	.2267	.2080	.1911	.1756	.1615	.1164	.0847
11	.8963	.7224	.5847	.5268	.4751	.4289	.3875	.3505	.3173	.2875	.2607	.2366	.2149	.1954	.1778	.1619	.1476	.1346	.0938	.0662
12	.8874	.7014	.5568	.4970	.4440	.3971	.3555	.3186	.2858	.2567	.2307	.2076	.1869	.1685	.1520	.1372	.1240	.1122	.0757	.0517
13	.8787	.6810	.5303	.4688	.4150	.3677	.3262	.2897	.2575	.2292	.2042	.1821	.1625	.1452	.1299	.1163	.1042	.0935	.0610	.0404
14	.8700	.6611	.5051	.4423	.3878	.3405	.2992	.2633	.2320	.2046	.1807	.1597	.1413	.1252	.1110	.0985	.0876	.0779	.0492	.0316
15	.8613	.6419	.4810	.4173	.3624	.3152	.2745	.2394	.2090	.1827	.1599	.1401	.1229	.1079	.0949	.0835	.0736	.0649	.0397	.0247
16	.8528	.6232	.4581	.3936	.3387	.2919	.2519	.2176	.1883	.1631	.1415	.1229	.1069	.0930	.0811	.0708	.0618	.0541	.0320	.0193
17	.8444	.6050	.4363	.3714	.3166	.2703	.2311	.1978	.1696	.1456	.1252	.1078	.0929	.0802	.0693	.0600	.0520	.0451	.0258	.0150
18	.8360	.5874	.4155	.3503	.2959	.2502	.2120	.1799	.1528	.1300	.1108	.0946	.0808	.0691	.0592	.0508	.0437	.0376	.0208	.0118
19	.8277	.5703	.3957	.3305	.2765	.2317	.1945	.1635	.1377	.1161	.0981	.0829	.0703	.0596	.0506	.0431	.0367	.0313	.0168	.0092
20	.8195	.5537	.3769	.3118	.2584	.2145	.1784	.1486	.1240	.1037	.0868	.0728	.0611	.0514	.0433	.0365	.0308	.0261	.0135	.0072
25	.7798	.4776	.2953	.2330	.1842	.1460	.1160	.0923	.0736	.0588	.0471	.0378	.0304	.0245	.0197	.0160	.0129	.0105	.0046	.0021
30	.7419	.4120	.2314	.1741	.1314	.0994	.0754	.0573	.0437	.0334	.0256	.0196	.0151	.0116	.0090	.0070	.0054	.0042	.0016	.0006
40	.6717	.3066	.1420	.0972	.0668	.0460	.0318	.0221	.0154	.0107	.0075	.0053	.0037	.0026	.0019	.0013	.0010	.0007	.0002	.0001
50	.6080	.2281	.0872	.0543	.0339	.0213	.0134	.0085	.0054	.0035	.0022	.0014	.0009	.0006	.0004	.0003	.0002	.0002	.0001	*
60	.5504	.1697	.0535	.0303	.0173	.0099	.0057	.0033	.0019	.0011	.0007	.0004	.0002	.0001	.0001	*	.0000	*	*	*

*The factor is zero to four decimal places.